The Papers of
Thomas Jefferson

VOLUME 10 continues the story of Jefferson's services as minister to France and as a leading spokesman in Europe for American principles and culture. During the latter half of 1786 the thirteen states, bound together by Articles of Confederation, were engaged in slow but important negotiations regarding piracy in the Mediterranean, Americans held captive by Algiers, debts to European bankers and former officers in Washington's armies, a treaty with Prussia, navigation of the Mississippi River, and trade with France.

Marauding Barbary pirates and clamoring European creditors pressed hard on American prestige and solvency and imposed great demands on the patience and resourcefulness of Jefferson and his colleague in London, John Adams. The efforts of these two future Presidents form an interesting chapter in American diplomatic history. They continually urged Congress to meet the obligations incurred during the Revolution, and even as complex negotiations were carried on for the release of captured Americans, Jefferson attempted to organize the Atlantic community in a concerted move against the depredations of the Barbary States.

Along with his official duties Jefferson took a friendly interest in the welfare of Americans in Europe and Europeans in America, and neglected no opportunity to culti-

...pect and affection for the ...States. He was particularly ...nsure accuracy (and favor- ...tment) in French writings ...ica, and he wrote extensive ...for Démeunier's articles in ...*clopédie Méthodique*. ...on's untiring intellectual ...was stimulated by the ...ortunities of Paris. A con- ...of wines and books, an ...naturalist, a patriotic his- ...efferson also wrote to his ...respondents about harpsi- ...haps, prosody, air currents, ..., prize money, and kings. ...the charming Maria Cos- ...his right wrist dislocated, ...h his left hand a remark- ...r explaining to her how ...rebuked his Heart for ...ntly engaging [its] affec- ...r circumstances that must ...great deal of pain."

...UT THE SERIES

...pers of Thomas Jefferson ...2-volume series including ...he 18,000 letters written ...n but also, in full or in ...the more than 25,000 let- ...n to him. A group of ...olumes will form a chron- ...ies of the correspondence; ...be followed by approxi- ...volumes of special writ- ...ticular subjects.

...ehensive 2-volume index ...ded; in the meantime, ...indexes covering about ...es will be issued. An ...olumes 1-6 is available. ...nt of 10 per cent is given ...ers to the series.

THE PAPERS OF
Thomas Jefferson

Volume 10
22 June to 31 December 1786

JULIAN P. BOYD, EDITOR

MINA R. BRYAN AND FREDRICK AANDAHL
ASSOCIATE EDITORS

PRINCETON, NEW JERSEY
PRINCETON UNIVERSITY PRESS
1954

Copyright, 1954, by Princeton University Press
London: Geoffrey Cumberlege, Oxford University Press
L.C.CARD 50-7486

Printed in the United States of America by
Princeton University Press, Princeton, New Jersey

DEDICATED TO THE MEMORY OF
ADOLPH S. OCHS
PUBLISHER OF THE NEW YORK TIMES
1896-1935
WHO BY THE EXAMPLE OF A RESPONSIBLE
PRESS ENLARGED AND FORTIFIED
THE JEFFERSONIAN CONCEPT
OF A FREE PRESS

ADVISORY COMMITTEE

FISKE KIMBALL, *CHAIRMAN*
FRANCIS L. BERKELEY, JR.
SOLON J. BUCK
L. H. BUTTERFIELD
GILBERT CHINARD
HENRY STEELE COMMAGER
HAROLD W. DODDS
LUTHER H. EVANS
A. WHITNEY GRISWOLD
BRECKINRIDGE LONG
ARCHIBALD MAC LEISH
DUMAS MALONE
BERNARD MAYO
RICARDO A. MESTRES
SAMUEL E. MORISON
HOWARD W. SMITH
DATUS C. SMITH, JR.
IPHIGENE OCHS SULZBERGER
WILLIAM J. VAN SCHREEVEN
LAWRENCE C. WROTH
JOHN C. WYLLIE

CONSULTANTS AND STAFF

PROFESSOR ARCHIBALD T. MAC ALLISTER, *Consultant in Italian*
PROFESSOR RAYMOND S. WILLIS, *Consultant in Spanish*
FRANCE C. RICE, *Consultant in French*
HOWARD C. RICE, JR., *Consultant*, Princeton University Library
DOROTHY S. EATON, *Consultant*, The Library of Congress
LAURA B. STEVENS, *Proof Editor*

GUIDE TO EDITORIAL APPARATUS

1. TEXTUAL DEVICES

The following devices are employed throughout the work to clarify the presentation of the text.

[. . .], [. . . .]   One or two words missing and not conjecturable.
[. . .][1], [. . . .][1]   More than two words missing and not conjecturable; subjoined footnote estimates number of words missing.
[ ]   Number or part of a number missing or illegible.
[roman]   Conjectural reading for missing or illegible matter. A question mark follows when the reading is doubtful.
[*italic*]   Editorial comment inserted in the text.
⟨*italic*⟩   Matter deleted in the MS but restored in our text.
⟦ ⟧   Record entry for letters not found.

2. DESCRIPTIVE SYMBOLS

The following symbols are employed throughout the work to describe the various kinds of manuscript originals. When a series of versions is recorded, *the first to be recorded is the version used for the printed text.*

Dft   draft (usually a composition or rough draft; later drafts, when identifiable as such, are designated "2d Dft," &c.)
Dupl   duplicate
MS   manuscript (arbitrarily applied to most documents other than letters)
N   note, notes (memoranda, fragments, &c.)
PoC   polygraph copy
PrC   press copy
RC   recipient's copy
SC   stylograph copy
Tripl   triplicate

All manuscripts of the above types are assumed to be in the hand of the author of the document to which the descriptive symbol pertains. If not, that fact is stated. On the other hand, the follow-

GUIDE TO EDITORIAL APPARATUS

ing types of manuscripts are assumed *not* to be in the hand of the author, and exceptions will be noted:

FC   file copy (applied to all forms of retained copies, such as letter-book copies, clerks' copies, &c.)

Tr   transcript (applied to both contemporary and later copies; period of transcription, unless clear by implication, will be given when known)

3. LOCATION SYMBOLS

The locations of documents printed in this edition from originals in private hands, from originals held by institutions outside the United States, and from printed sources are recorded in self-explanatory form in the descriptive note following each document. The locations of documents printed from originals held by public institutions in the United States are recorded by means of the symbols used in the National Union Catalog in the Library of Congress; an explanation of how these symbols are formed is given above, Vol. 1: xl. The list of symbols appearing in each volume is limited to the institutions represented by documents printed or referred to in that and previous volumes.

CLU   William Andrews Clark Memorial Library, University of California at Los Angeles
CSmH   Henry E. Huntington Library, San Marino, California
Ct   Connecticut State Library, Hartford, Connecticut
CtY   Yale University Library
DLC   Library of Congress
DNA   The National Archives
ICHi   Chicago Historical Society, Chicago
IHi   Illinois State Historical Library, Springfield
MB   Boston Public Library, Boston
MH   Harvard University Library
MHi   Massachusetts Historical Society, Boston
MHi: AMT   Adams Family Papers, deposited by the Adams Manuscript Trust in Massachusetts Historical Society
MdAA   Maryland Hall of Records, Annapolis
MdAN   U.S. Naval Academy Library
MeHi   Maine Historical Society, Portland

GUIDE TO EDITORIAL APPARATUS

MiU-C   William L. Clements Library, University of Michigan
MoSHi   Missouri Historical Society, St. Louis
MWA   American Antiquarian Society, Worcester
NBu   Buffalo Public Library, Buffalo, New York
NcU   University of North Carolina Library
NHi   New-York Historical Society, New York City
NK-Iselin   Letters to and from John Jay bearing this symbol are used by permission of the Estate of Eleanor Jay Iselin.
NN   New York Public Library, New York City
NNC   Columbia University Libraries
NNP   Pierpont Morgan Library, New York City
NNS   New York Society Library, New York City
NcD   Duke University Library
NjP   Princeton University Library
PBL   Lehigh University Library
PHC   Haverford College Library
PHi   Historical Society of Pennsylvania, Philadelphia
PPAP   American Philosophical Society, Philadelphia
PPL-R   Library Company of Philadelphia, Ridgway Branch
PU   University of Pennsylvania Library
RPA   Rhode Island Department of State, Providence
RPB   Brown University Library
Vi   Virginia State Library, Richmond
ViHi   Virginia Historical Society, Richmond
ViU   University of Virginia Library
ViW   College of William and Mary Library
ViWC   Colonial Williamsburg, Inc.
WHi   State Historical Society of Wisconsin, Madison

4. OTHER ABBREVIATIONS

The following abbreviations are commonly employed in the annotation throughout the work.

Second Series   The topical series to be published at the end of this edition, comprising those materials which are best suited to a classified rather than a chronological arrangement (see Vol. 1: xv-xvi).
TJ   Thomas Jefferson

[ix]

GUIDE TO EDITORIAL APPARATUS

TJ Editorial Files   Photoduplicates and other editorial materials in the office of *The Papers of Thomas Jefferson*, Princeton University Library

TJ Papers   Jefferson Papers (Applied to a collection of manuscripts when the precise location of a given document must be furnished, and always preceded by the symbol for the institutional repository; thus "DLC: TJ Papers, 4:628-9" represents a document in the Library of Congress, Jefferson Papers, volume 4, pages 628 and 629.)

PCC   Papers of the Continental Congress, in the National Archives

RG   Record Group (Used in designating the location of documents in the National Archives.)

SJL   Jefferson's "Summary Journal of letters" written and received (in DLC: TJ Papers)

SJPL   "Summary Journal of Public Letters," an incomplete list of letters written by TJ from 16 Apr. 1784 to 31 Dec. 1793, with brief summaries, in an amanuensis' hand (in DLC: TJ Papers, at end of SJL).

5. SHORT TITLES

The following list includes only those short titles of works cited with great frequency, and therefore in very abbreviated form, throughout this edition. Their expanded forms are given here only in the degree of fullness needed for unmistakable identification. Since it is impossible to anticipate all the works to be cited in such very abbreviated form, the list is appropriately revised from volume to volume.

Atlas of Amer. Hist., Scribner, 1943   James Truslow Adams and R. V. Coleman, *Atlas of American History*, N.Y., 1943

Biog. Dir. Cong.   *Biographical Directory of Congress, 1774-1927*

B.M. Cat.   British Museum, *General Catalogue of Printed Books*, London, 1931—. Also, *The British Museum Catalogue of Printed Books 1881-1900*, Ann Arbor, 1946

B.N. Cat.   *Catalogue général des livres imprimés de la Bibliothèque Nationale. Auteurs.*

Burnett, *Letters of Members*   Edmund C. Burnett, ed., *Letters of Members of the Continental Congress*

Cal. Franklin Papers   *Calendar of the Papers of Benjamin Franklin in the Library of the American Philosophical Society*, ed. I. Minis Hays

GUIDE TO EDITORIAL APPARATUS

CVSP *Calendar of Virginia State Papers . . . Preserved in the Capitol at Richmond*

DAB *Dictionary of American Biography*

DAE *Dictionary of American English*

DAH *Dictionary of American History*

DNB *Dictionary of National Biography*

Dipl. Corr., 1783-89 *The Diplomatic Correspondence of the United States of America, from the Signing of the Definitive Treaty of Peace . . . to the Adoption of the Constitution*, Washington, Blair & Rives, 1837, 3 vol.

Evans Charles Evans, *American Bibliography*

Ford Paul Leicester Ford, ed., *The Writings of Thomas Jefferson*, "Letterpress Edition," N.Y., 1892-1899.

Fry-Jefferson Map *The Fry & Jefferson Map of Virginia and Maryland: A Facsimile of the First Edition*, Princeton, 1950

Gottschalk, *Lafayette, 1783-89* Louis Gottschalk, *Lafayette between the American Revolution and the French Revolution (1783-1789)*, Chicago, 1950

Gournay *Tableau général du commerce, des marchands, négocians, armateurs, &c., . . . années 1789 & 1790*, Paris, n.d.

HAW Henry A. Washington, ed., *The Writings of Thomas Jefferson*, Washington, 1853-1854

Hening William W. Hening, *The Statutes at Large; Being a Collection of All the Laws of Virginia*

Henry, *Henry* William Wirt Henry, *Patrick Henry, Life, Correspondence and Speeches*

JCC *Journals of the Continental Congress, 1774-1789*, ed. W. C. Ford and others, Washington, 1904-1937

JHD *Journal of the House of Delegates of the Commonwealth of Virginia* (cited by session and date of publication)

Jefferson Correspondence, Bixby *Thomas Jefferson Correspondence Printed from the Originals in the Collections of William K. Bixby*, ed. W. C. Ford, Boston, 1916

Johnston, "Jefferson Bibliography" Richard H. Johnston, "A Contribution to a Bibliography of Thomas Jefferson," *Writings of Thomas Jefferson*, ed. Lipscomb and Bergh, xx, separately paged following the Index.

L & B Andrew A. Lipscomb and Albert E. Bergh, eds., *The Writings of Thomas Jefferson*, "Memorial Edition," Washington, 1903-1904

GUIDE TO EDITORIAL APPARATUS

L.C. Cat.   *A Catalogue of Books Represented by Library of Congress Printed Cards*, Ann Arbor, 1942-1946; also *Supplement*, 1948.

Library Catalogue, 1783   Jefferson's MS list of books owned and wanted in 1783 (original in Massachusetts Historical Society)

Library Catalogue, 1815   *Catalogue of the Library of the United States*, Washington, 1815

Library Catalogue, 1829   *Catalogue. President Jefferson's Library*, Washington, 1829

MVHR   *Mississippi Valley Historical Review*

OED   *A New English Dictionary on Historical Principles*, Oxford, 1888-1933

PMHB   *The Pennsylvania Magazine of History and Biography*

Randall, *Life*   Henry S. Randall, *The Life of Thomas Jefferson*

Randolph, *Domestic Life*   Sarah N. Randolph, *The Domestic Life of Thomas Jefferson*

Sabin   Joseph Sabin and others, *Bibliotheca Americana. A Dictionary of Books Relating to America*

Sowerby   *Catalogue of the Library of Thomas Jefferson*, compiled with annotations by E. Millicent Sowerby, Washington, 1952-53

Swem, *Index*   E. G. Swem, *Virginia Historical Index*

Swem, "Va. Bibliog."   Earl G. Swem, "A Bibliography of Virginia," Virginia State Library, *Bulletin*, VIII, X, XII (1915-1919)

TJR   Thomas Jefferson Randolph, ed., *Memoir, Correspondence, and Miscellanies, from the Papers of Thomas Jefferson*, Charlottesville, 1829

Tucker, *Life*   George Tucker, *The Life of Thomas Jefferson*, Philadelphia, 1837

Tyler, *Va. Biog.*   Lyon G. Tyler, *Encyclopedia of Virginia Biography*

Tyler's Quart.   *Tyler's Quarterly Historical and Genealogical Magazine*

VMHB   *Virginia Magazine of History and Biography*

Wharton, *Dipl. Corr. Am. Rev.*   *The Revolutionary Diplomatic Correspondence of the United States*, ed. Francis Wharton

WMQ   *William and Mary Quarterly*

CONTENTS

Guide to Editorial Apparatus vii
Jefferson Chronology 2

1786 continued

The Article on the United States in the *Encyclopédie Méthodique* 3
    I. Answers to Démeunier's First Queries, 24 *January* 11
    II. Additional Queries, with Jefferson's Answers
        [ca. *January-February*] 20
    III. From Jean Nicolas Démeunier [*February?*] 30
    IV. Jefferson's Observations on Démeunier's Manuscript,
        22 *June* 30
    V. To Jean Nicolas Démeunier [26 *June*] 61
    VI. From Jean Nicolas Démeunier [26 *June*] 64
To John Adams, 23 *June* 65
From Madame d'Houdetot, 23 *June* 66
From John Bondfield, 24 *June* 66
From John Adams, 25 *June* 68
From Lucy Ludwell Paradise, 25 *June* 69
To Rayneval, 25 *June* 70
From John Adams, 26 *June* 70
From Thomas Barclay to the American Commissioners, 26 *June* 71
To Thomas Elder, 26 *June* 72
From David Rittenhouse, 26 *June* 73
To Du Portail and Others, 27 *June* 73
To John Paul Jones, 27 *June* 74
From John Paradise, with Enclosure, 27 *June* 75
From Taher Fennish to the American Commissioners [28 *June*] 76
From Francis Hopkinson, 28 *June* 77
From John Adams, 29 *June* 79
From Robert Murdoch, 29 *June* 79
From Pierre Castaing, 30 *June* 81
From St. Victour & Bettinger, 30 *June* 81
From Samuel Chase, *June* 82
From Ralph Izard, 1 *July* 83
From Lefévre, Roussac & Cie., 1 *July* 85
From Du Portail, 2 *July* 85

CONTENTS

From John Adams, *3 July*	86
From Henry Champion, *3 July*	87
Court of Naples to De Pio, *4 July*	88
From John Paul Jones, *4 July*	88
From Maupin, *4 July*	89
From Madame de Doradour, *5 July*	90
To Ebenezer Gearey, Jr., *5 July*	91
To John Paul Jones, *5 July*	91
From William Stephens Smith, *5 July*	92
From Duperré Delisle and St. John de Crèvecoeur, *7 July*	92
From John Paul Jones, with Enclosure, *7 July*	93
To John Lamb, *7 July*	95
American Commissioners to John Lamb, *29 June*	96
From John Ledyard, *7 July*	97
From Abbé Gibelin, *8 July*	98
To John Jay, *8 July*	99
To William H. Sargeant, *8 July*	101
From Charles Thomson, *8 July*	102
To John Adams, *9 July*	105
From James Currie, *9 July*	107
To James Monroe, *9 July*	111
From Thomas Smith, *9 July*	115
To William Stephens Smith, *9 July*	115
To Charles Burney, *10 July*	117
To Abbé Gibelin, *10 July*	119
To John Paul Jones, *10 July*	119
From John Paul Jones, *10 July*	120
[To John Ledyard, *10 July*]	120
[To Maupin, *10 July*]	120
To John Paradise, *10 July*	120
To Lucy Ludwell Paradise, *10 July*	121
To David Ramsay, *10 July*	122
[To Rayneval, *10 July*]	122
To John Adams, *11 July*	123
From Lewis Alexander, *11 July*	125
To Mary Barclay, *11 July*	126
To St. John de Crèvecoeur, *11 July*	127
To Ferdinand Grand, *11 July*	128
To John Paul Jones, *11 July*	129
From Lefévre, Roussac & Cie., *11 July*	129
From De Pinto, *11 July*	129

CONTENTS

From Ferdinand Grand, *12 July*	130
From Lewis Littlepage, *12 July*	130
From Richard O'Bryen, *12 July*	131
From Edmund Randolph, *12 July*	133
From John Banister, Jr., *14 July*	134
From John Jay, *14 July*	134
From John Bondfield, *15 July*	136
From William Carmichael, *15 July*	137
From John Lamb, *15 July*	139
From John Adams, *16 July*	140
Thomas Barclay to the American Commissioners, *16 July*	141
From Cambray, *16 July*	142
From James Monroe, *16 July*	142
To Lafayette, with Enclosure, *17 July*	145
From John Banister, *18 July*	148
From William Carmichael, *18 July*	149
From John Lamb, *18 July*	151
From William Stephens Smith, *18 July*	152
From Giovanni Fabbroni, *20 July*	155
From Maupin, *20 July*	156
From Madame de Tessé, *20 July*	157
From Madame de Tott, *20 July*	160
From James Bowdoin, *22 July*	160
To Francis Eppes, *22 July*	160
To the Governor of Virginia, *22 July*	161
From Abigail Adams, *23 July*	161
To John Banister, Jr., *24 July*	162
From Boyetet, *24 July*	163
To André Limozin, *24 July*	164
From Dumoulin de Seille & Son, *24 July*	164
To John Stockdale, *24 July*	165
From Eliza House Trist, *24 July*	166
[From John Banister, Jr., *27 July*]	170
To John Ledyard, *27 July*	170
From St. Lambert, *27 July*	171
[To John Stockdale, *27 July*]	172
To Boyetet, *28 July*	172
From Stephen Cathalan, Jr., *28 July*	173
From John Paradise, *28 July*	174
From Charles Thomson, *30 July*	175
From John Adams, *31 July*	176

CONTENTS

From William Carmichael, *31 July*	178
Thomas Barclay to the American Commissioners, *July*	181
From Cavelier, Fils, *1 August*	181
From Abbé Morellet *[1 August]*	181
To Jean-Armand Tronchin, with Enclosures, *1 August*	182
From George Washington, *1 August*	186
〚From Madame d'Anterroches, *2 August*〛	188
From Lafayette, *2 August*	188
From André Limozin, *2 August*	188
From Jean-Armand Tronchin, *2 August*	189
From G. K. van Hogendorp, *2 August*	190
From Létombe, *3 August*	191
From John Bondfield, *5 August*	191
From Schweighauser & Dobrée, *5 August*	192
〚From John Banister, Jr., *6 August*〛	193
To Achard Frères, *7 August*	193
To Anthony Garvey, *7 August*	193
From Ferdinand Grand, *7 August*	194
From William Macarty, *7 August*	195
To John Adams, *8 August*	195
To John Bondfield, *8 August*	196
To Stephen Cathalan, Jr., *8 August*	197
To André Limozin, *8 August*	197
To John Paradise, *8 August*	198
To Lefévre, Roussac & Cie., *8 August*	199
To St. Lambert, *8 August*	200
To Dumoulin de Seille & Son, *8 August*	200
From John Stockdale, *8 August*	201
To Abigail Adams, *9 August*	202
From Paul Bentalou, *9 August*	204
To Jean Jacques Bérard & Cie., *9 August*	205
To Pierre Dessin, *9 August*	206
To the Governor of Virginia, *9 August*	206
From John Paul Jones, *9 August*	208
To Francis Lewis, *9 August*	210
To William Stephens Smith, *9 [i.e., 10] August*	211
Jefferson's Suggestions for Republishing the Cruz Cano Map of South America *[ca. August]*	216
From Ferdinand Grand, *10 August*	217
John Lamb to the American Commissioners, *10 August*	218
From Abbé Morellet *[10 August]*	219

CONTENTS

Thomas Barclay to the American Commissioners, *11 August*	220
To John Jay, *11 August*	220
From André Limozin [*11 August*]	223
To James Monroe, *11 August*	223
To Abbé Morellet, *11 August*	225
To Richard Cary, *12 August*	226
To the Governor of Virginia, *12 August*	228
From James Madison, *12 August*	229
From Abbé Morellet [*12 August*]	236
To the Commissioners of the Treasury, *12 August*	237
To John Adams, *13 August*	238
From Madame de Grégoire, *13 August*	239
To Benjamin Hawkins, *13 August*	240
To John Jay, *13 August*	241
〚To John Stockdale, *13 August*〛	242
To George Wythe, *13 August*	243
To John Banister, with a Note to Anne Blair Banister, *14 August*	246
To Benjamin Franklin, *14 August*	247
From Plowden W. Garvey, *14 August*	248
To Francis Hopkinson, *14 August*	248
To David Humphreys, *14 August*	250
From John Paul Jones, *14 August*	253
From André Limozin, *14 August*	253
From Zachariah Loreilhe, *14 August*	254
From Champagne, *15 August*	255
From Lucy Ludwell Paradise, *15 August*	255
To John Banister, Jr., *16 August*	256
From André Caron, *16 August*	257
From John Paul Jones, *16 August*	258
To John Ledyard, *16 August*	258
From John Ledyard, *16 August*	258
From Thomas Mann Randolph, Jr., *16 August*	260
To Vergennes, *16 August*	261
To Brissot de Warville, *16 August*	261
To Samuel Adams and John Lowell, *17 August*	264
From William Carmichael, *17 August*	265
To Dangirard & De Vernon, *17 August*	267
〚To R. & A. Garvey, *17 August*〛	269
〚To André Limozin, *17 August*〛	269
Deposition of Richard Riddy, *17 August*	269

CONTENTS

From Hugon de Bassville, *18 August*	269
To De Blome, *18 August*	270
From John Jay, *18 August*	271
To Schweighauser & Dobrée, *18 August*	272
From the Abbés Arnoux and Chalut, *19 August*	273
To André Limozin, *19 August*	273
To William Macarty, *19 August*	274
From James Monroe, *19 August*	274
From Dangirard & De Vernon [*ca. 20 August*]	279
To Edward Bridgen, *21 August*	280
From the Georgia Delegates in Congress, *21 August*	280
From John Paul Jones, *21 August*	281
To John Paul Jones, *21 August*	282
To Dorcas Montgomery, *21 August*	282
To Mirabeau [*21 August*]	283
From Robert Robertson, *21 August*	283
To William Carmichael, *22 August*	284
From John Richard, *22 August*	289
From Sarsfield, *22 August*	289
From Jean Jacques Bérard & Cie., *23 August*	290
From Zachariah Loreilhe, *23 August*	290
From William Stephens Smith, *23 August*	291
From St. Victour & Bettinger, *24 August*	292
To Pierre Dessin, *24 August*	292
To Lafayette, *24 August*	293
To Robert Robertson, *24 August*	294
〚From Valade, *24 August*〛	295
From Hugon de Bassville [*25 August*]	295
To Hugon de Bassville, *25 August*	295
To Paul Bentalou, *25 August*	296
To C. W. F. Dumas, *25 August*	297
To G. K. van Hogendorp, *25 August*	297
To De Vernon, *25 August*	300
To St. John de Crèvecoeur, *26 August*	300
From V. & P. French & Nephew, *26 August*	301
To John Adams, *27 August*	302
From John Banister, Jr., *27 August*	303
To Zachariah Loreilhe, *27 August*	304
To Lucy Ludwell Paradise, *27 August*	304
To Thomas Mann Randolph, Jr., *27 August*	305
From Madame de Lafayette, *28* [*August*]	309

[xviii]

CONTENTS

To Zachariah Loreilhe, *28 August*	309
〚From Achard Frères, *29 August*〛	310
From Lafayette, *30 August*	310
To Thomas Barclay, *31 August*	313
From William Stephens Smith, *1 September*	315
To Ezra Stiles, *1 September*	316
Polytype and Other Methods of Printing *[1786]*	318
I. Invitation to David Harris	325
II. Estimate for Printing *Notes on Virginia* by Polytype	325
III. Notes on Abbé Rochon's Method	325
From Paul Bentalou, *2 September*	326
From André Limozin, *2 September*	327
From John Paul Jones, *3 September*	329
From William Carmichael, *4 September*	329
From Zachariah Loreilhe, *4 September*	331
〚From Badon, *before 5 September*〛	331
To John Banister, Jr., *7 September*	332
From ——— to Madame d'Enville, *8 September*	332
From Pierre Dessin, *9 September*	333
From Abbé Morellet *[9 September?]*	333
Thomas Barclay to the American Commissioners, with Enclosure, *10 September*	334
From John Adams, *11 September*	348
From Abbé Morellet *[11 September?]*	350
From Benjamin Putnam *[before 11 September]*	351
From François Soulés, *11 September*	352
From Biron, *12 September*	353
From C. W. F. Dumas, *12 September*	354
From Lefévre, Roussac & Cie., *12 September*	356
From Lewis Littlepage, *12 September*	357
Thomas Barclay to the American Commissioners, *13 September*	357
To William Stephens Smith, *13 September*	362
To François Soulés, *13 September*	363
Jefferson's Comments on François Soulés' *Histoire* *[July-September]*	364
I. Comments on Soulés' *Histoire*	368
II. Answers to Soulés' Queries	377
To John Stockdale, *13 September*	384
〚To Mary Barclay, *14 September*〛	384
〚To Biron, *14 September*〛	384
From Etienne Clavière, *14 September*	384

CONTENTS

From Ezra Stiles, *14 September*	385
From John Banister, Jr., *16 September*	387
From James Maury, *17 September*	387
Thomas Barclay to the American Commissioners, *18 September*	389
From William Stephens Smith, *18 September*	393
From Maria Cosway *[20 September]*	393
From Fantin Latour, *20 September*	394
To Charles Thomson, *20 September*	395
[From Nathaniel Tracy, *before 20 September*]	396
To Thomas Barclay, *22 September*	396
To William Carmichael, *22 September*	396
To C. W. F. Dumas, *22 September*	397
From William Stephens Smith, *22 September*	398
From John Bondfield, *23 September*	399
To William Stephens Smith, *23 September*	400
From La Rouerie, *25 September*	400
From James Smith *[25 September]*	401
To John Adams, *26 September*	402
From Thomas Barclay, *26 September*	403
From C. W. F. Dumas, *26 September*	404
To John Jay, *26 September*	405
American Commissioners to John Lamb *[26 September]*	407
To the Prévôt des Marchands et Echevins de Paris, with Enclosure, *27 September*	407
From Jean Baptiste Le Roy, *28 September*	410
From William Carmichael, *29 September*	411
From Madame de Tessé, *29 September*	413
To Rayneval, with Enclosure, *30 September*	414
From Richard Peters, *1 October*	416
From William Stephens Smith, *1 October*	417
Thomas Barclay to the American Commissioners, *2 October*	418
Treaty with Morocco	419
From José da Maia, *2 October*	427
From William Carmichael, *3 October*	427
From John Jay, *3 October*	430
From William Stephens Smith, *4 October*	431
To Maria Cosway *[5 October]*	431
From Maria Cosway *[5 October]*	433
From C. W. F. Dumas, *6 October*	434
From Thevenard, *6 October*	435
From Abbé André, *7 October*	436

[xx]

CONTENTS

To William Macarty, 7 October	436
From Benjamin Franklin, 8 October	437
From John Trumbull, with a Note from Maria Cosway, 9 October	438
From John Lamb, 10 October	441
To Lewis Littlepage, 10 October	442
From Jean Chas, 11 October	442
[From De Langeac, 11 October]	443
To Maria Cosway, 12 October	443
From John Jay, 12 October	455
To De Langeac, 12 October	455
From James Monroe, 12 October	456
To Maria Cosway, 13 October	458
From Madame de Marmontel [13 October]	459
To John Trumbull, 13 October	460
From John Bondfield, 14 October	461
From the Rhode Island Delegates in Congress, 14 October	461
From Edward Rutledge, 14 October	463
To Achard Frères, 15 October	465
From Louis Guillaume Otto, 15 October	465
To Vergennes, with Enclosure, 15 October	467
From Circello, 17 October	468
From C. W. F. Dumas, 17 October	468
From Charles Boromée LeBrun, 17 October	469
From C. W. F. Dumas, 19 October	470
To De Corny, 20 October	470
From Plowden W. Garvey, 20 October	471
From Zachariah Loreilhe, 20 October	472
To Stael de Holstein, 20 October	472
To Vergennes, 20 October	472
From Achard Frères, 21 October	473
From Calonne, 22 October	474
To William Stephens Smith, 22 October	478
To John Adams, 23 October	479
From C. W. F. Dumas, with Enclosures, 23 October	480
From Francis Eppes, 23 October	483
To John Jay, 23 October	484
From Lafayette [23 October]	486
To John Adams, 27 October	487
To John Jay, 27 October	487
From John Jay, 27 October	488
To David Ramsay, 27 October	490

CONTENTS

From John Bondfield, *28 October*	492
Circular Letter to United States Consular Agents, *29 October*	493
From Maria Cosway *[30 October]*	494
To Charles Boromée LeBrun, *30 October*	496
To Zachariah Loreilhe, *30 October*	497
From William Macarty, *30 October*	497
From Vergennes, *31 October*	497
To Chastellux *[October]*	498
To Martha Jefferson *[October]*	499
From Jean Durival, with Enclosure, *1 November*	499
From Antoine-Félix Wuibert, *1 November*	501
From John Banister, Jr., *2 November*	503
To John Bondfield, *2 November*	503
To Calonne, *2 November*	504
To André Limozin, *2 November*	504
From C. W. F. Dumas, *3 November*	504
To Lafayette, *3 November*	505
From John Trumbull, *3 November*	506
[From Cavalier, Fils, *4 November*]	507
To Martha Jefferson, *4 November*	507
From Vergennes, *4 November*	507
To John Bondfield, *6 November*	508
To St. John de Crèvecoeur, *6 November*	509
Thomas Barclay to the American Commissioners, *7 November*	509
To Jean Durival, *7 November*	511
From Francis Hopkinson, *8 November*	511
From David Ramsay, *8 November*	513
From Brissot de Warville, *10 November*	514
From William Jones, *10 November*	515
From John Paradise, *10 November*	516
[From John Bondfield, *11 November*]	516
To Famin, *11 November*	517
To Anthony Garvey, *11 November*	517
From William Stephens Smith, *11 November*	518
To John Banister, *12 November*	519
To John Jay, with Enclosure, *12 November*	519
From Zachariah Loreilhe, *12 November*	523
From James Smith, *12 November*	524
To Jean Baptiste Le Roy, *13 November*	524
From [Madame de La Rochefoucauld?] *13 November*	530
[From Vergennes, *ca. 14 November*]	531

[xxii]

CONTENTS

To George Washington, *14 November*	531
Thomas Barclay to the American Commissioners, *15 November*	535
From William Carmichael, *15 November*	536
From Maria Cosway *[17 November]*	538
From C. W. F. Dumas, *17 November*	540
To Ralph Izard, *18 November*	540
From Presolle, *18 November*	542
To Maria Cosway, *19 November*	542
To Zachariah Loreilhe, *19 November*	543
To Dorcas Montgomery, *19 November*	543
To Martin Oster, *19 November*	544
To ——— Wernecke, *19 November*	545
From John Stockdale, *20 November*	545
To John Trumbull, *20 November*	546
From José da Maia, *21 November*	546
To Achard Frères, *22 November*	547
[From Stephen Cathalan, Jr., *22 November*]	547
To Colonia, *22 November*	547
[From Tarbé, *23 November*]	548
[From Brissot de Warville, *23 November*]	548
From John Ledyard, *25 November*	548
From James Madison, *25 November*	549
From Chenier de St. André, *26 November*	550
From Vergennes, *26 November*	551
From Abraham Walton, *26 November*	551
[From Henry Champion, for Zachariah Loreilhe, *27 November*]	552
From Maria Cosway *[27 November]*	552
From Duler, *27 November*	552
From William Stephens Smith, *28 November*	553
To Madame de Tott, *28 November*	553
From Madame de Tott, *28 November*	554
To John Bondfield, *29 November*	554
To Maria Cosway, *29 November*	555
[From Guiraud & Portas, *29 November*]	555
From John Trumbull, *29 November*	556
From John Adams, *30 November*	556
To Abigail Adams *[November]*	557
From C. W. F. Dumas, *1 December*	558
From John Jay, *1 December*	559
[To the Ambassadors of Portugal and Russia, *1 December*]	559

[xxiii]

CONTENTS

Jefferson's Proposed Concert of Powers against the Barbary States [July-December]	560
I. Proposed Convention against the Barbary States	566
II. Proposed Confederation against the Barbary States	569
To Philippe-Denis Pierre, *1 December*	570
From Jean Chas, *2 December*	571
〚From C. W. F. Dumas, *2 December*〛	571
From Abigail Adams Smith, *2 December*	572
From Thomas Barclay, *4 December*	573
From Madame de Doradour, *4 December*	573
From James Madison, *4 December*	574
From William Macarty, *5 December*	578
From William Stephens Smith, *5 December*	578
From Wilt, Delmestre & Co., *6 December*	579
To Jean Chas, *7 December*	580
To Gelhais, *7 December*	580
To Abraham Walton, *7 December*	581
From Hilliard d'Auberteuil, with Enclosure, *8 December*	582
From Michel Capitaine, *8 December*	583
To St. John de Crèvecoeur, *8 December*	583
To Duler, *8 December*	583
From Ezra Stiles, *8 December*	584
To John Stockdale, *8 December*	586
〚From Lewis Alexander, *9 December*〛	587
From Francis Hopkinson, *9 December*	587
From James Maury, *10 December*	588
To R. & A. Garvey, *11 December*	588
To Wilt, Delmestre & Co., *11 December*	589
From John Bondfield, *12 December*	589
From St. John de Crèvecoeur *[13 December]*	591
From John Jay, *13 December*	592
From André Limozin, *13 December*	592
From George Wythe, *13 December*	592
From John Bartram, *14 December*	593
To Elizabeth Wayles Eppes, *14 December*	594
To Francis Eppes, *14 December*	594
From John Jay, *14 December*	596
To Eliza House Trist, *15 December*	599
From St. John de Crèvecoeur, *16 December*	601
To André Limozin, *16 December*	601
To James Madison, *16 December*	602

[xxiv]

CONTENTS

From William Carmichael, *17 December*	606
To Charles Thomson, *17 December*	608
To John Trumbull, *17 December*	610
To James Monroe, *18 December*	611
To Nicholas Lewis, *19 December*	614
From André Limozin *[19 December]*	616
From John Stockdale, *19 December*	617
To John Adams, *20 December*	618
To Colonia, *20 December*	619
To William Stephens Smith, *20 December*	620
To Abigail Adams, *21 December*	621
From S. J. Neele, *21 December*	621
From Abraham Walton, *21 December*	622
From De Blome, *22 December*	622
From George Wythe, *22 December*	622
To Brissot de Warville, *23 December*	623
To Benjamin Franklin, *23 December*	624
To Francis Hopkinson, *23 December*	625
[From Francis Coffyn, *24 December*]	627
To Maria Cosway, *24 December*	627
To James Maury, *24 December*	628
To Ezra Stiles, *24 December*	629
[From John Banister, *25 December*]	630
From Nathaniel Barrett, *25 December*	630
From Brissot de Warville, *25 December*	630
To C. W. F. Dumas, *25 December*	630
To James Buchanan and William Hay, *26 December*	632
To William Carmichael, *26 December*	632
To Richard Cary, *26 December*	635
To Fantin Latour, *26 December*	636
To José da Maia, *26 December*	636
From Brissot de Warville *[26 December]*	637
To Thomas Barclay, *27 December*	637
From Brissot de Warville, *27 December*	638
From Ducrest, *27 December*	639
To the Georgia Delegates in Congress, *27 December*	640
To Mézières, *27 December*	640
To Ferdinand Grand, *28 December*	641
From Jan Ingenhousz, *28 December*	641
From the Rev. James Madison, *28 December*	642
From C. W. F. Dumas, *29 December*	644

CONTENTS

To Benjamin Vaughan, *29 December*	646
From Peter Carr, *30 December*	648
To John Jay, *31 December*	649
To La Valette, *31 December*	651
From David S. Franks, *December*	651
From David S. Franks *[December]*	651
From Madame de Tott *[December?]*	652
From La Rochefoucauld	652
Petition of an Impostor, with Jefferson's Comments	653

ILLUSTRATIONS

FACING PAGE

MADAME DE TOTT PAINTING THE PORTRAIT   178
OF MADAME DE TESSÉ

This miniature on ivory by an unidentified artist brings together in appropriate relationship two of Jefferson's French friends and correspondents: the Comtesse de Tessé (Adrienne-Catherine de Noailles, 1741-1814) and her protégée, Sophie-Ernestine de Tott (ca. 1759-ca. 1840?). The Comtesse de Tessé encouraged her protégée's talent for "pallet and pencil," as did Jefferson (see TJ to Madame de Tott, 5 Apr. 1787). The miniature reproduced here was painted in the 1780's, when Jefferson was a frequent visitor at the Hôtel de Tessé; it was perhaps painted by the Baron de Tott, who was himself an amateur artist of some ability. On the relationship of the two women, see Madame de Tessé to TJ, 20 July 1786, note. (Courtesy of the Comte de Pusy Lafayette, Château de Vollore, Puy-de-Dôme, through Howard C. Rice, Jr.)

"LES PLAISIRS DE CHAVILLE"   178

Watercolor, executed ca. 1785 by the Baron de Tott, who has included himself at the extreme left. This intimate glimpse of the salon at Chaville, the country residence of the De Tessés near Versailles, shows Madame de Tessé seated before a lectern, at the right. Facing her, engrossed in knitting, is Madame de Tott. The drowsy gentleman at Madame de Tessé's right is her husband, René-Mans, Sire de Froulay, Comte de Tessé, Grand d'Espagne, Premier Ecuyer de la Reine, &c. &c. (1736-1814). Next to him is M. Sénac de Meilhan (1736-1803), a habitué of Madame de Tessé's salon, a writer of some note in his day, now remembered chiefly for his novel *L'Emigré*. The other gentleman is possibly the Marquis de Mun, another faithful follower. (Courtesy of Madame Michel de Larminat, née Hennocque de Lafayette, Paris and Château de Beaumont, Le Chartre-sur-le-Loir, Sarthe, through Howard C. Rice, Jr.)

JOHN TRUMBULL'S SKETCH FOR "THE   179
DECLARATION OF INDEPENDENCE," WITH JEFFERSON'S
FLOOR PLAN OF INDEPENDENCE HALL

These sketches, both on the same sheet of paper, were made while Trumbull was staying with Jefferson in Paris in September 1786. On 28 Dec. 1817, when Trumbull was working on the life-size replica of his famous painting for the rotunda of the Capitol at Washington, he wrote Jefferson: "I have made considerable progress in the large picture of the Declaration of Independence, for the Capitol. . . . You recollect the Composition which you kindly assisted me to sketch at Chaillot; the Committee who drew up the Declaration form the principal Group, by which means I place yourself and some other of the most eminent Characters conspicuously—the figures large as Life." See TJ to David Humphreys, 14 Aug. 1786; *The Auto-*

[xxvii]

ILLUSTRATIONS

FACING PAGE

biography of Colonel John Trumbull, ed. Theodore Sizer, p. 146-7 (note 268), 311; John Trumbull to TJ, 3 Mch. and 28 Dec. 1817. (Courtesy of The Yale Gallery of Fine Arts.)

SPECIMEN PAGES OF POLYTYPE PRINTING 210

These two specimens, probably presented to Jefferson by Hoffman himself, contain portions of Abbé Rochon's report on Hoffman's invention as read before the Académie des Sciences on 8 Feb. 1786 and illustrate one of the features claimed for the invention—that is, that the printer required only enough type to compose a page or even a few lines, which could then be printed, the type distributed, another page or part of a page be composed and printed, and so on. These two examples were clearly printed from polytype plates made from the same type. The full page is on a thin, buff colored, laid paper without water-mark; the outlines of the plate are clearly discernible because of ink smudge, but there is no plate-impression in the paper. The page of nine lines, evidently printed first, has similar characteristics save that the paper has a greenish tint. For a description of Hoffman's method, see the Editorial Note to the series of documents entitled "Polytype and Other Methods of Printing," p. 318-24, especially p. 322-3. In DLC: TJ Papers, 19:3263 (immediately following the two pages illustrated here) there is another sheet of paper endorsed by Jefferson "Printing"; it also contains a partial description of the Hoffman method, but it is on a larger sheet of paper than the two here illustrated and there is a well-defined plate-impression such as that produced by ordinary intaglio engraving. (Courtesy of The Library of Congress.)

PARIS IN 1787, SHOWING EARLIER CITY WALLS AND 211
THE NEW WALL OF THE FARMERS-GENERAL

Map engraved by P. F. Tardieu. The new "wall of circumvallation," as Jefferson called it—designated here as "Clôture sous Louis XVI"—was not a fortification like several of the earlier city ramparts shown, or like the later wall built by Thiers in the 1840's, but a tax barrier designed to make the collection of municipal customs duties more effective. It served to increase public criticism of the farmers-general, provoking a storm of pamphlets, satirical verse, puns and witticisms. The wall, which considerably extended the city limits, was authorized in 1782; in January 1785 the plans drawn up by the architect Claude-Nicolas Ledoux were approved and work continued thenceforward for several years. Ledoux's plan included neo-classic toll-houses (bureaux), flanking each of the forty-seven gates (barrières). General hostility to the wall made it difficult for people to view objectively Ledoux's imaginative gateways, which were nicknamed "*Calonnades*" in derision of the Minister of Finance, and which even Jefferson ironically referred to as the "palaces by which we are to be let out and in" (see TJ to David Humphreys, 14 Aug. 1787). The so-called "boulevards extérieurs" of the present day mark the line of the wall of the farmers-general. (Courtesy of the Bibliothèque Nationale, through Howard C. Rice, Jr.)

[xxviii]

ILLUSTRATIONS

FACING PAGE

THE HALLE AUX BLEDS, PARIS, BY MARECHAL, 1786   434

These two pen and wash drawings of the Grain Market ("Meal Market" or "Corn Market") were executed by the French artist Maréchal the same year that Jefferson went to study its construction—a utilitarian object that took on a romantic aspect when Jefferson met Maria Cosway there. The market, a circular edifice around an open court, was completed by the architect Le Camus de Mézières in 1767; some ten years later the work of covering this courtyard with a rotunda was entrusted to Legrand and Molinos, who revived a method of construction described by the Renaissance architect Philibert Delorme in his *Nouvelles inventions pour bien bâtir et à petits frais* (first edition, 1561). Jefferson, who first studied this dome with a public market for Richmond in mind, later recalled it when discussing the rotunda of the Capitol in Washington with Benjamin Latrobe, and also when devising a plan for a dock in Washington. The market as Jefferson knew it was demolished in the 1880's to make way for another structure, built on the same circular site, the present Bourse du Commerce. The curious column visible in Maréchal's drawing, however, is still extant; it was built in 1572 by the architect Jean Bullant for Catherine de Medici who, according to tradition, used to wind her way up its inside staircase to read the stars with her astrologer. Thus this column still marks the spot where Jefferson met Maria Cosway on a summer day in August 1786. See TJ to Maria Cosway, 12 Oct. 1786; Benjamin Latrobe to TJ, 18 Feb. 1804; TJ to Latrobe, 8 Sep 1805; TJ to Lewis Wiss, 27 Nov. 1825. (Courtesy of the Cabinet des Estampes, Collection Destailleur, Bibliothèque Nationale, through Howard C. Rice, Jr.)

JEFFERSON'S FIRST LETTER TO MARIA COSWAY   435
WRITTEN WITH HIS LEFT HAND

The earliest extant letter written by Jefferson with his left hand after an accident which dislocated his right wrist. See this letter and note under 5 Oct. 1786. (Courtesy of Charles Geigy-Hagenbach, Basel, Switzerland.)

TRUMBULL'S MINIATURES OF JEFFERSON PAINTED FOR   466
MARIA COSWAY AND ANGELICA SCHUYLER CHURCH

These miniatures, both replicas of the portrait of Jefferson executed by John Trumbull in Paris in 1787 in the original small painting of "The Declaration of Independence," were presented in 1788 to Mrs. Cosway and Mrs. Church by Trumbull. On 21 July 1788 Mrs. Church wrote Jefferson: "accept the good wishes of Maria and Angelica. Mr. Trumbull has given us each a picture of you. Mrs. Cosways is a better likeness than mine, but then I have a better elsewhere and so I console myself." On 19 Aug. 1788 Mrs. Cosway wrote Jefferson: "Wish me joy, for I possess your Picture. Trumbull has procured me this happiness which I shall ever be gratfull for."—The miniature painted for Maria Cosway was discovered in 1952 by Miss Elizabeth Cometti at the Collegio di Maria SS. Bambina, at

[xxix]

ILLUSTRATIONS

FACING PAGE

Lodi, Italy, the college established by Mrs. Cosway in 1812. See Elizabeth Cometti, "Maria Cosway's Rediscovered Miniature of Jefferson," WMQ, 3d ser., IX (1952), 152-5. (Courtesy of Collegio di Maria SS. Bambina, and of Miss Cometti.)—The miniature painted for Angelica Schuyler Church was bequeathed to the Metropolitan Museum of Art in 1924 by Cornelia Cruger, a descendant of Mrs. Church. See Fiske Kimball, "The Life Portraits of Jefferson," American Philosophical Soc., *Proceedings*, LXXXVIII (1944), 504-5. (Courtesy of The Metropolitan Museum of Art.)

RICHARD COSWAY'S MINIATURE OF MARIA COSWAY 467

Miniature on ivory, painted by Maria Cosway's husband, whose miniatures on ivory were notable for the exquisite transparent effect achieved on that medium, his distinctive treatment of the hair, and the clear brightness of the eyes. George C. Williamson (*Richard Cosway R.A.*, London, 1905) describes Cosway's miniatures as "so lightly laid upon the ivory as to appear almost as though . . . blown into position, . . . an aerial thing of graceful lightness, that, like a bit of gossamer, had rested upon the ivory and had become fixed there." (Courtesy of The Henry E. Huntington Library and Art Gallery.)

JOHN TRUMBULL'S PORTRAIT OF ANGELICA 467
SCHUYLER CHURCH

Group portrait of Mrs. Church, her son Philip, and servant, painted in London in 1784. Trumbull had met John Barker Church in America in 1777. Soon afterward Church met and married Angelica Schuyler, eldest daughter of Gen. Philip Schuyler, and their acquaintance with Trumbull continued in Boston in 1778 and 1779 where they lived and Trumbull was studying. The friendship was renewed in London in 1784. Church not only remained on friendly terms with Trumbull but assisted him financially while the latter was in England (*The Autobiography of Colonel John Trumbull*, ed. Theodore Sizer, p. 90, 93-5). Mrs. Church visited Paris in the winter of 1787-1788 and was doubtless introduced to Jefferson by Trumbull, who was staying with Jefferson at the time. The correspondence between Jefferson and Mrs. Church, which began early in 1788 and continued until 1802, equals that with Maria Cosway, Abigail Adams, and Mme. de Tessé in sprightliness, mutual understanding, and affection. (Courtesy of Peter B. Olney, Old Saybrook, Conn.)

VOLUME 10

22 June to 31 December 1786

JEFFERSON CHRONOLOGY

1743 · 1826

1743.	Born at Shadwell.
1772.	Married Martha Wayles Skelton.
1775-76.	In Continental Congress.
1776-79.	In Virginia House of Delegates.
1779-81.	Governor of Virginia.
1782.	His wife died.
1783-84.	In Continental Congress.
1784-89.	In France as commissioner and minister.
1790-93.	U.S. Secretary of State.
1797-1801.	Vice President of the United States.
1801-09.	President of the United States.
1826.	Died at Monticello.

VOLUME 10

22 June to 31 December 1786

22 June. Completed observations on Démeunier's article on the United States.

28 June. Treaty between Morocco and the United States delivered to Thomas Barclay.

ca. 2 Aug. John Trumbull arrived in Paris.

[ca. 1-15 Aug.?] Met Maria Cosway.

3 Aug.-13 Sep. Conferred with François Soulés concerning his *Histoire des troubles de l'Amérique Anglaise.*

13 Sep. Awarded honorary degree of Doctor of Laws by Yale University.

18 Sep. Dislocated his right wrist.

28 Sep. Houdon's bust of Lafayette presented to the City of Paris on behalf of the State of Virginia.

22 Oct. Regulations on American trade with France formally stated in a letter from Calonne to Jefferson.

1 Dec. Proposals for concerted action against the Barbary States submitted to some members of the diplomatic corps.

THE PAPERS OF THOMAS JEFFERSON

The Article on the United States in the *Encyclopédie Méthodique*

I. ANSWERS TO DeMEUNIER'S FIRST QUERIES, 24 JAN. 1786
II. ADDITIONAL QUERIES, WITH JEFFERSON'S ANSWERS [ca. JAN.-FEB. 1786]
III. DeMEUNIER TO JEFFERSON [FEB.? 1786]
IV. JEFFERSON'S OBSERVATIONS ON DeMEUNIER'S MANUSCRIPT, 22 JUNE 1786
V. JEFFERSON TO DeMEUNIER [26 JUNE 1786]
VI. DeMEUNIER TO JEFFERSON [26 JUNE 1786]

EDITORIAL NOTE

On 25 Oct. 1786 William Short wrote to William Nelson: "You speak of the Encyclopedia. It will be a valuable work Sir in as much as all human science will be there brought together and arranged in a methodical manner. The different parts of the work are allotted to different persons to execute, and as it is impossible to find a sufficient number of learned men fit for and willing to engage in such a work, some of the parts must necessarily be illy executed. That which relates to the different States of America had been committed to a M. de Meunier who is a young man really of talents. He treats the political subjects in general of that work. What he had said under the head of the Etats Unis was as erroneous and as false as might be expected from a man who had made the Abbe Raynal his model, and his own lively imagination his guide. Fortunately he has candor, and after putting this article under Mr. Jefferson's inspection, he readily struck out and altered the most flagrant errors. It remains at present as different from what he had written it, as to matters of fact, as virtue from vice, and as to reflexions it is changed from censure to eulogy. Still however this article is very imperfect, and frequently contains circumstances very improper for an article of the kind; this is however my opinion and may not be yours when you read it: but is it not a melancholy reflexion my dear Nelson, that writings of this sort, that books that we are taught to worship from our infancy, should be merely the works of hazard and uncertainty?" (PrC in DLC: Short Papers).

THE ENCYCLOPEDIE METHODIQUE 1786

This, in brief and in words that reflected substantially the opinion of Jefferson, is the story of Jefferson's effort to rectify errors and correct impressions in the article on the United States prepared by Jean Nicolas Démeunier for the second volume of the section called *Economie Politique et Diplomatique* of the *Encyclopédie Méthodique*. (For Jefferson's comments and other relevant information on the six-months' exchange between him and young Démeunier, see TJ to Van Hogendorp, 25 Aug. 1786; to Adams, 27 Aug. 1786; to Ezra Stiles, 1 Sep. 1786; to Washington, 14 Nov. 1786; to Girardin, 28 Aug. 1814; see also La Rochefoucauld to TJ, 4 Jan. 1786; Démeunier to TJ, 6 and 21 Jan. and 9 Apr. 1786; Sowerby, No. 2950; Howard C. Rice, Jr., *Le Cultivateur Américain*, p. 32; Julia Post Mitchell, *St. Jean de Crèvecoeur*, p. 263-4; Malone, *Jefferson*, II, 107-8.)

Jean Nicolas Démeunier, "Secrétaire particulier de *Monsieur*" (brother of Louis XVI), was thirty-five when La Rochefoucauld introduced him to the American minister. He had already published (1784) the first of the four volumes of his section of the *Encyclopédie*. Jefferson had wasted little time with such an author as Hilliard d'Auberteuil and others whose work he did not esteem, but Démeunier commanded his earnest attention not merely because of his connection with the Court and because La Rochefoucauld had recommended him, but also because his articles would be included in the *Encyclopédie*, a work which Jefferson had endeavored to acquire when it was first announced and which he had promoted among his friends in America. Nothing could be done about the articles on some of the separate states that had already appeared in Démeunier's first volume—the Carolinas, Connecticut, New England, and America—but Jefferson labored assiduously to improve the article on the United States and the remaining articles on some of the separate states, especially that on Virginia.

Some of the amplifications and corrections made by Démeunier as a result of Jefferson's criticisms are indicated in the notes to the present group of documents. Not all of the traces of this effective collaboration can be discerned, however, for no copy of any stage of Démeunier's manuscript has been found and it is also evident that many of the suggestions and criticisms offered were made orally rather than in writing. For example, with respect to Jefferson's remarks on the Virginia Revisal of the Laws (Document I, paragraph 1), Démeunier translated and incorporated almost all of these remarks and then added: "En 1776, l'assemblée générale chargea cinq commissaires de la revision des anciennes loix et de la rédaction des loix nouvelles; l'un de ces commissaires mourut bientôt après, un second refusa cet emploi, et l'âge d'un troisieme ne lui permit pas de se livrer à des méditations si pénibles. Les deux autres, M. Jefferson . . . et M. Whythe ont fait eux seuls cet immense travail. Ils l'ont présenté à l'assemblée de Virginie en 1779" (*Encyclopédie Méthodique*, section *Economie Politique et Diplomatique*, II, article Etats-Unis, 400; hereafter in this group of documents cited as *Economie*, II, 400). At this time Jefferson had just received a copy of the *Report of the Committee of Revisors* of 1784 containing the letter of Wythe and Jefferson of 18 June 1779 which set forth the fact that the work had officially been completed by the three remaining members

[4]

EDITORIAL NOTE

of the committee; an editorial note in the pamphlet also made the same statement (Vol. 2: 302, 312). He may or may not have shown the *Report* to Démeunier, but the latter's remark about "l'âge d'un troisieme" could have come only from Jefferson himself and it evidently came orally since there is nothing corresponding to such information in Jefferson's various notes and observations on Démeunier's manuscript. Also, two years later Démeunier wrote gratefully: "Les excellentes notes que J'ai recueillies dans nos Conversations ont été souvent La réponse Verbale à Mille questions que vous m'avés permis de vous Faire" (Démeunier to TJ, 11 Feb. 1788).

There existed at least two stages of Démeunier's manuscript before Jefferson wrote his Observations (Document IV) upon his return from London, and there may have been more. At the first interview, which Démeunier asked to be "un peu Long" since he had "beaucoup de choses à soumettre à votre examen," he possibly had a rough draft of the article on the United States and he may have had similar drafts for one or more of the articles on the separate states. It is very likely, for example, that he would have had the article on Kentucky at this first meeting, for that article was based largely on Filson's *Histoire de Kentucke* which had been translated at Crèvecoeur's suggestion and a copy of which Crèvecoeur sent to La Rochefoucauld on 14 Nov. 1785 (Rice, *Le Cultivateur Americain*, p. 32).

The article on the United States at this stage may have consisted of the earlier sections, which were either documentary in character (e.g., texts of the Declaration of Independence and the Articles of Confederation) or were drawn largely from the writings of Abbé Raynal. But another interview and two sets of written queries after Jan. 21 (Documents I and II) produced Démeunier's promise to correct and expand the article on the United States, to transcribe the result, and to submit it to Jefferson (Document III). On 9 Apr., while Jefferson was in London, Démeunier fulfilled this promise by forwarding the manuscript. In his comments on the fifth volume of John Marshall's *Life of Washington*, Jefferson stated that Démeunier "called on me with the article . . . 'Etats Unis' which he had prepared ready for the press, and begged I would revise it, and make any notes on it which I should think necessary towards rendering it correct" (DLC: TJ Papers, 233: 41765). This has led to the assumption that what Démeunier submitted to Jefferson was a proof of the article on the United States and not a manuscript (Malone, *Jefferson*, II, 107-8). But here, of course, Jefferson was writing almost thirty years after the event and was addressing himself to another point. The pagination and other circumstances show that what Jefferson examined and returned to Démeunier on 22 June 1786 was a manuscript and not a set of proofs.

Indeed, Jefferson's examination of the second stage of the article was so thoroughgoing that it is not unreasonable to suppose that a third manuscript emerged before the article was set in type. However, it is more probable that Démeunier merely altered the text when necessary and occasionally inserted in it such passages as Jefferson's comments on the Society of the Cincinnati and on finance, even at times retaining his own matter when it was in conflict with Jefferson's. There were at least 323 pages in Démeunier's manuscript when Jefferson last examined it. Since the separately-printed article embraced only 89 pages (though in double-column quarto) *after* Jefferson's extensive interpolations had been added, it may be assumed that in preparing this manuscript for Jefferson's inspection Démeunier had followed the customary practice of leaving half of each page blank for the recording of comments and corrections. This would have made it easier to send the corrected manuscript to the printer. Yet, if this is what actually happened, Démeunier himself must have set down the corrections, for Jefferson's Observations were written as a separate manuscript, of which he retained a press copy.

The manuscript of Jefferson's Observations also went through several stages. Some of the matter repeated what he had given Démeunier earlier in response to the two sets of queries, and all of it was evidently written first in a rough draft and a fair copy of the major part of it then prepared for Démeunier. This manuscript has never been printed in full; it was finished and sent to Démeunier on Thursday, 22 June. The following Sunday the two men had a further consultation about the article, and on 26 June Jefferson forwarded additional materials to Démeunier (Document v). The fulsome compliments in Démeunier's reply (Document vi) could scarcely have embarrassed Jefferson as much as the actual statements in the published article. In speaking of the Virginia constitution in Section IV, Démeunier named Jefferson as one of the citizens of Virginia "les plus respectables par ses emplois, par son patriotisme, par ses lumières, et par son zèle"; again, in the article on Virginia, he described him as "l'un des citoyens les plus éclairés de la république de *Virginie*" (*Economie*, II, 367; III, 636). "He has paid me for my trouble, in the true coin of his country," Jefferson wrote to Adams, "most unmerciful compliment."

But what disturbed him much more was the fact that Démeunier, contrary to Jefferson's expectations, had dispatched the manuscript to the printer without giving Jefferson an opportunity to see it again "after he had corrected it." For this reason, wrote Jefferson in acute disappointment, "He has still left in a great deal of the Abbé Raynal, that is to say a great deal of falsehood, and he has stated other things on bad information" (TJ to Adams, 27 Aug. 1786). Démeunier may have felt, with some justice, that the American minister's embarrassing thoroughness was in danger of turning the official author's name into a mere pseudonym for one who had been asked only to advise and criticize but who threatened to become the real author.

If so, Jefferson labored with characteristic zeal rather to promote his country's name than his own authorship. Nothing could emphasize this more precisely—or more ironically—than the most important aspect of Jefferson's collaboration, that part of his Observations pertaining to the Society of the Cincinnati. Although he was, as he candidly explained to Démeunier, "one who was an enemy to the institution from the first moment of it's conception," Jefferson nevertheless set forth for the *Encyclopédie* what is probably the best apology for the origins of the Society of the Cincinnati ever written. An unwilling champion of that institution, he was obliged in the course of his apology to depart from

EDITORIAL NOTE

strict historical accuracy and to attribute to the founders motives that he believed were nonexistent or at most secondary among the causes leading to the establishment of the Society. This document is one of the most striking examples to be found in the entire mass of Jefferson's papers of his ability to argue and defend a position in which he did not believe. His motive in doing so may be found in Démeunier's original comment on the Cincinnati, which, Jefferson later declared, "was an unjust and incorrect Philippic against General Washington and the American officers in general. I wrote a substitute for it, which he adopted, but still retaining considerable of his own matter and interspersing it in various parts" (notes on Vol. v, Marshall's *Life of Washington*; DLC: TJ Papers, 233: 41764-5).

The article on American public finance was also a valuable part of Jefferson's contribution. "De Meunier had prepared a poor article on that head," he explained to Girardin, "and sent it to me for correction before it was printed. I found it necessary to write the Article entire. He retained his own, but added mine. You will readily distinguish the ideas of a stranger from those of one who had had a part in the transactions. I wrote it when everything was fresh in my mind and when I was fully master of the subject" (TJ to Girardin, 28 Aug. 1814). The fact that Jefferson remembered this so clearly almost three decades after the event is evidence enough of his disappointment that Démeunier had retained so much of "the ideas of a stranger."

In his notes on the fifth volume of Marshall's *Life of Washington*, Jefferson wrote that he had furnished Démeunier with "most of the matter of his 5th. 6th. 8th. 9th. and 10th sections of the article 'Etats Unis.'" In a more contemporaneous letter he went even further and specifically disavowed responsibility "for the whole of the article"; he then added: "The two first sections are taken chiefly from the Abbé Raynal, and they are therefore wrong exactly in the same proportion. The other sections are generally right. Even in them however there is here and there an error" (TJ to Van Hogendorp, 25 Aug. 1786). Insofar as Jefferson's statements imply that he had nothing to do with the earlier sections, they are misleading. In both the first section (political history of the colonies up to the Revolution) and the second (causes of the Revolution), Démeunier drew heavily upon Abbé Raynal's *Histoire Philosophique et Politique des Deux Indes*, and these were the parts to which Jefferson objected most. Nevertheless, as is evident from Jefferson's Observations, he commented upon the entire manuscript, his first note having reference to page 8 and the last to page 323. The manner in which Démeunier employed Jefferson's comments on these earlier sections may not have been wholly pleasing, but the fact remains that Jefferson made observations upon them and Démeunier incorporated these observations in his text. An example of how this was done occurs in reference to Jefferson's first comment (see Document iv, note 1). Referring to Raynal as "un écrivain célèbre," Démeunier quoted him as follows on the elements of population forming the British colonies in America:

"L'Amerique angloise . . . se remplissoit de trois sortes d'habitans. Les hommes libres formoient la première classe, et c'étoit la plus nombreuse. Une seconde classe des colons fut autrefois composée de malfaiteurs, que la métropole condamnoit à être transportés en Amérique, et qui devoient un service forcé de sept ou de quatorze ans aux planteurs qui les achetoient des tribunaux de justice. On se dégoûta un peu tard, il est vrai, de ces hommes corrumpus et toujours prêts à commettre de nouveaux crimes." At this point Démeunier broke into Raynal's observations and inserted, in indirect quotation, a literal and complete translation of Jefferson's entire comment on the malefactors that had been sent to America. He then resumed the quotation from Raynal and gave at length Raynal's account of the system of indentured servants. In this account, Raynal referred to "cette espèce d'esclavage" and, after a general description, concluded with these observations: "L'Amérique forme des recrues pour la culture, comme les princes pour la guerre, avec les mêmes artifices, mais un but moins honnête et peut-être plus inhumain: car qui sait le rapport de ceux qui meurent et de ceux qui survivent à leurs espérances?" This and other strictures, commented Démeunier, were regarded by enlightened and humane citizens of America only as exaggerations and ill-founded reproaches. He then introduced an accurate translation of the whole of Jefferson's commentary on the system of indentured servants, including some inaccuracies that were probably as glaring as Raynal's—for example, the statement that it was only in Europe that "these people are deceived by those who carry them over" and that "it is only in Europe that this deception is heard of."

This example may serve to show the manner in which Démeunier employed Jefferson's observations. He used all but a minute fraction of the extensive matter that Jefferson supplied; his translations were exact and literal so far as possible; and he interspersed this matter at various points in the article on the United States and occasionally in those on the separate states. He usually retained the quotations and other materials from Raynal, Crèvecoeur, Mably, Turgot, Richard Price, and others. Even Jefferson's minor corrections of phraseology were utilized by Démeunier, as when he altered "plongés dans la mer" to "plongés dans l'eau." He employed Jefferson's materials fully and translated them faithfully even when an occasional championing of republicanism involved criticism of absolutism. Thus Démeunier rendered Jefferson's eloquent passage about the energy of republican government—a passage prophetic of another observation in the First Inaugural: "On a dit que le gouvernement fédéral des *Etats-Unis* et le gouvernement particulier des diverses provinces manquent d'énergie, qu'il leur est difficile de contenir les individus et les *états*: le fait est vrai, et c'est un inconvénient. Mais l'énergie des gouvernemens absolus vient d'une force armée, et de la bayonette toujours placée sur la poitrine de chaque citoyen. La tranquillité qui en résulte, ressemble beaucoup à la tranquillité du tombeau, et il faut avouer qu'une pareille énergie a aussi ses inconvéniens. Les *Etats-Unis* pèsent les inconvéniens des deux côtés, et ils aiment mieux se soumettre à ceux du premier. Si on compare les délits que les citoyens d'Amérique peuvent commettre impunément, avec les délits que commet le souverain dans les autres pays, on trouvera que ceux-ci sont en plus grand nombre, plus facheux et plus accablans pour la dignité de l'homme . . ." (*Economie*, II, 376).

EDITORIAL NOTE

There is no doubt that Démeunier valued Jefferson's expert assistance. But he was himself a scholar of some accomplishment, he was particularly versed in political theory, and he had prepared himself for this article by consulting the standard works on America as well as other individuals (Crèvecoeur, for example). At their consultation on Sunday, 25 June, Démeunier may very well have led Jefferson to believe that he would again revise the manuscript and once more submit the result to Jefferson's scrutiny. But it is quite understandable why he did not do so. First, Jefferson objected to some of Démeunier's own views, particularly those on finance. Second, the *Encyclopédie* was a learned work, not a vehicle for propaganda—and Jefferson's comments on indentured servitude, on finance, on the Society of the Cincinnati, and on other American affairs proved conclusively that he wished to put the most favorable aspect on every subject treated, even to the point of urging the elimination of observations by Démeunier that might "alarm the states and damp their dispositions to strengthen the hands of Congress." It was Jefferson's duty as minister, as it was his consistent belief and effort, to uphold the dignity of America and to strengthen the union; but it was also Démeunier's duty as one of the responsible editors of the principal work of learning then in progress to see that his materials were comprehensive, reliable, and free from undue bias. He paid Jefferson's materials the compliment of utilizing them almost wholly and of presenting them largely in indirect quotation—a fact which led to later unpleasantness because of Mazzei's remarks (see Démeunier to TJ, 11 Feb. 1788; TJ to Démeunier, 15 Feb. 1788)—but with each revision of his manuscript the materials offered had grown in volume. This suggests a final reason why Démeunier sent his manuscript directly to press without submitting it again to Jefferson: there must have been limitations of space, time, and proportion that had to be observed. What Démeunier had already included from the American minister had caused the article on the United States to go to disproportionate length. For example, in the printed volumes under Démeunier's editorship, the article on France ran to only forty pages, nine of which were occupied with the text of the 1786 commercial treaty with England; the article on England embraced fifty pages; that on Spain, twenty-eight; that on Russia, forty-six; and that on Prussia, twenty. The United States, youngest of the powers and smallest in population and military resources, received by contrast a total of eighty-nine pages. This, of course, was in addition to the separate articles on each of the thirteen states. Of the latter, by far the longest was that on Virginia, the materials of which were drawn almost wholly from *Notes on Virginia* and from conversations with Jefferson; its length was greater than that accorded France and equal to that given Russia—or forty-six pages.

Some of this disproportionate emphasis may have been a result of the widespread public interest existing in Europe in everything pertaining to America, but there is no room for doubt that the length of the contributions made by Jefferson—considering only those that can be identified and measured—was a chief cause of the expansion. It is evident, too, that Jefferson had persuaded Démeunier to expand the article on the United States beyond what he had originally planned (see Document III).

These facts, though helping to explain why Démeunier did not again submit his manuscript to Jefferson, did not lessen the latter's disappointment. Mazzei was at this time at work on his *Recherches sur les Etats Unis* and Jefferson may have communicated to him, as he did to others, something of his feeling of regret that Démeunier had not eliminated all traces of Raynal from his article. It is certain that he lent to Mazzei the press copy of the matter that he had sent to Démeunier, for Mazzei numbered the pages of the press copies of Documents I, II, IV, and V in a single sequence extending from 1 to 72 (see notes to these documents; possibly other materials such as calculations and notes were included in Mazzei's sequence of numbered pages: see note 30, Document IV). This is not the place to consider Mazzei's use of this material, but his numbered sequence of pages is of significance in relation to a possible major alteration that Démeunier may have made at Jefferson's suggestion. In DLC: TJ Papers, 22: 3737-48 there is a press copy of a series of twelve unnumbered pages beginning at the point indicated in note 3 and concluding at the point indicated in note 23 of Document IV; these pages are an integral part of Jefferson's Observations, but have in the course of time become misplaced—they should occupy pages 3121-32 in TJ Papers—and have not been published in any previous edition (see Ford, IV, 160-1, where the omission occurs). They pertain to pages 49 to 90 of Démeunier's manuscript and they embrace Jefferson's criticisms of statements that were drawn, for the most part, from Abbé Raynal and Hilliard d'Auberteuil. The fact that these pages contained no new materials, but consisted primarily of corrections of statements by these two authors, is sufficient to explain why they were not submitted to Mazzei and were not, therefore, included in Mazzei's sequence of numbering. But it is to be noted also that these twelve unnumbered pages pertain entirely to comments on individual states from New Hampshire to Georgia—including some (the Carolinas, Connecticut, New England) that had been treated in Démeunier's first volume published in 1784. There is in Démeunier's published article, at the end of the first section, the following: "Nous indiquons à l'article particulier de chacun des *Etats-Unis* la position dans laquelle se trouvoient les colonies de l'Amérique septentrionale, au moment où la plupart d'entr'elles ont déclaré leur indépendance. Nous nous contenterons de dire ici que toutes les colonies de l'Amérique angloise n'avoient pas la même forme de gouvernement . . ." (*Economie*, II, 349; the particular paragraphs following this quotation were in the manuscript originally, for Jefferson offered correction of one or two words in the first of them (at the places indicated by note 2, Document IV—"Pa. 18 . . . P. 19.").

An obvious inference to be drawn from these facts is that this section originally contained a general view of the thirteen separate states in respect to commerce, population, boundaries, and other customary topics as well as governments. If so—and it would be difficult if not impossible to explain Jefferson's comments on pages 49 to 90 of Démeunier's manuscript on any other ground—then it is apparent that, for some reason, Démeunier restricted this section merely to a summary com-

I. ANSWERS TO FIRST QUERIES

ment of the diversity of government among the thirteen states, and separated the remaining matter in it from the article on the United States, perhaps to reintroduce it under the separate headings of the individual states (see Document IV, notes 10, 12, and 14 for examples of Jefferson's corrections of this section of Démeunier's manuscript which are to be found in the published volumes under separate states and not in the article on the United States). It is easy to conjecture how such a decision could have been reached. The materials that Jefferson had recently received on Virginia alone would have indicated the desirability of such a course. Jefferson himself may have suggested it. The extended account of Virginia, which is in large measure a summary of *Notes on Virginia*, is one indication that he may have been responsible. That state received almost as much space in *Economie* as Massachusetts, New York, and Pennsylvania combined. (It is to be noted that a good part of Jefferson's Virginia materials was included in the article on the United States; these materials embraced the account of the Revisal of the Laws and also the full text of the Act for Establishing Religious Freedom, which Démeunier inserted there as an example of "la tolérance la plus illimitée qu'on ait vu dans aucune contrée de la terre," *Economie*, IV, 641).

While the conclusion is conjectural, it nevertheless seems highly probable that such a major alteration did take place in the manuscript; that it may have been agreed upon during the discussions on 25 June; and that Jefferson himself may have suggested it. If so, this single act made him responsible for one of the greatest of all the increases in space that he stimulated in the articles pertaining to America in the *Encyclopédie*. It would also go further in explaining why, after that date, Démeunier did not resubmit his manuscript for inspection.

After this meeting and the exchange on Monday, 26 June, Jefferson and Démeunier evidently did not communicate again until, in mid-August, the separately-printed *Essai sur les États-Unis Par M. Démeunier, Secrétaire ordinaire de Monsieur, frère du Roi, & censeur royal* came from the press (Sowerby, No. 2950).

I. Answers to Démeunier's First Queries

Jan. 24. 1786.

1. On the original establishment of the several states, the civil code of England, from whence they had emigrated, was adopted. This of course could extend only to general laws, and not to those which were particular to certain places in England only. The circumstances of the new states obliged them to add some new laws which their special situation required, and even to change some of the general laws of England in cases which did not suit their circumstances or ways of thinking. The law of descents for instance was changed in several states.   On the late revolution, the

THE ENCYCLOPEDIE METHODIQUE 1786

changes which their new form of government rendered necessary were easily made. It was only necessary to say that the powers of legislation, the judiciary and the executive powers, heretofore exercised by persons of such and such descriptions, shall henceforth be exercised by persons to be appointed in such and such manners. This was what their constitutions did.   Virginia thought it might be necessary to examine the whole code of law, to reform such parts of it as had been calculated to produce[1] a devotion to monarchy, and to reduce into smaller volume such useful parts as had become too diffuse. A Committee was appointed to execute this work; they did it; and the assembly began in Octob. 1785. the examination of it, in order to change such parts of the report as might not meet their approbation and to establish what they should approve. We may expect to hear the result of their deliberations about the last of February next. I have heard that Connecticut undertook a like work: but I am not sure of this, nor do I know whether any other of the states have or have not done the same.

2. The Constitution of New-Hampshire established in 1776. having been expressly made to continue only during the contest with Great Britain, they proceeded, after the close of that to form and establish a permanent one, which they did. The Convention of Virginia which organised their new government had been chosen before a separation from Gr. Britain had been thought of in their state. They had therefore none but the ordinary powers of legislation. This leaves their act for organising the government subject to be altered by every legislative assembly and tho no general change in it has been made, yet it's effect has been contracted in several special cases. It is therefore thought that that state will appoint a Convention for the special purpose of forming a stable constitution. I think no change has been made in any other of the states.

3. The following is a rough estimate of the particular debts of some of the states as they existed in the year of 1784.

	Dollars		
New Hampshire	500,000	United States principal of	
Rhode Island	430,000	Foreign debt nearly	7,000,000
Massachusets	5,000,000	The principal of the do-	
Connecticut	3,439,086⅔	mestic debt is some-	
Virginia	2,500,000	where between 27½ million and 35½ million—call it therefore	31,500,000
			38,500,000

I. ANSWERS TO FIRST QUERIES

The other states not named here are probably indebted in the same proportion to their abilities. If so, and we estimate their abilities by the rule of quotaing them, those 8 states will owe about 14 millions, and consequently the particular debts of all the states will amount to 25 or 26 millions of dollars.

5.[2] A particular answer to this question would lead to very minute details. One general idea however may be applied to all the states. Each having their separate debt, and a determinate proportion of the federal debt, they endeavour to lay taxes sufficient to pay the interest of both of these, and to support their own and the federal government. These taxes are generally about one or one and a half percent on the value of[3] property, and from $2\frac{1}{2}$ to 5 percent on foreign merchandise imported. But the paiment of this interest regularly is not accomplished in many of the states. The people are as yet not recovered from the depredations of the war. When that ended, their houses were in ruin, their farms waste, themselves distressed for clothing and necessaries for their household. They cannot as yet therefore bear heavy taxes.   For the paiment of the principal no final measures are yet taken. Some states will have lands for sale, the produce of which may pay the principal debt. Some will endeavor to have an exceeding of their taxes to be applied as a sinking fund. And all of them look forward to the increase of population, and of course an increase of productiveness in their present taxes to enable them to be sinking their debt. This is a general view. Some of the states have not yet made even just efforts for satisfying either the principal or interest of their public debt.

6. By the close of the year 1785, there had probably passed over about 50,000 emigrants. Most of these were Irish. The greatest number of the residue were Germans. Philadelphia receives most of them, and next to that, Baltimore and New York.

7. Nothing is decided as to Vermont. The four Northernmost states wish it to be received into the Union. The middle and Southern states are rather opposed to it. But the great difficulty arises with New-York which claims that territory. In the beginning every individual of that state revolted at the idea of giving them up. Congress therefore only interfered from time to time to prevent the two parties from coming to an open rupture. In the mean while the minds of the New Yorkers have been familiarizing to the idea of a separation and I think it will not be long before they will consent to it. In that case the Southern and Middle states will doubtless acquiesce, and Vermont will be received into the Union.

THE ENCYCLOPEDIE METHODIQUE 1786

Le Maine, a part of the government of Massachusets, but detached from it (the state of N. Hampshire lying between) begins to desire to be separated. They are very weak in numbers as yet; but whenever they shall attain a certain degree of population, there are circumstances which render it highly probable they will be allowed to become a separate member of the union.

8. It is believed that the state of Virginia has by this time made a second cession of lands to Congress, comprehending all those between the meridian of the mouth of the Great Kanhaway, the Ohio, Mississippi and Carolina boundary. Within this lies Kentuckey. I beleive that their numbers are sufficient already to entitle them to come into Congress, and that their reception there will only incur the delay necessary for taking the consent of the several assemblies. There is no other new state as yet approaching the time of it's reception.

10. The number of Royalists which left New York, South Carolina and Georgia, when they were evacuated by the British army, was considerable, but I am absolutely unable to conjecture their numbers. From all the other states I suppose perhaps two thousand[4] may have gone.

11. The Confederation is a wonderfully perfect instrument, considering the circumstances under which it was formed. There are however some alterations which experience proves to be wanting. These are principally three. 1. To establish a general rule for the admission of new states into the Union. By the Confederation no new state, except Canada, can be permitted to have a vote in Congress without first obtaining the consent of all the thirteen legislatures. It becomes necessary to agree what districts may be established into separate states, and at what period of their population they may come into Congress. The act of Congress of April 23. 1784. has pointed out what ought to be agreed on. To say also what number of votes must concur when the number of voters shall be thus enlarged. 2. The Confederation, in it's eighth article, decides that the quota of money to be contributed by the several states shall be proportioned to the value of the landed property in the state. Experience has shewn it impracticable to come at this value. Congress have therefore recommended to the states to agree that their quotas shall be in proportion to the number of their inhabitants, counting 5. slaves however but as equal to 3. free inhabitants. I believe all the states have agreed to this alteration except Rhode-island. 3. The Confederation forbids the states individually to enter into treaties of commerce, or of any other nature, with foreign na-

I. ANSWERS TO FIRST QUERIES

tions; and it authorizes Congress to establish such treaties, with two reservations however, viz., that they shall agree to no treaty which would 1. restrain the legislatures from imposing such duties on foreigners, as natives are subjected to; or 2. from prohibiting the exportation or importation of any species of commodities. Congress may therefore be said to have a power to regulate commerce, so far as it can be effected by conventions with other nations, and by conventions which do not infringe the two fundamental reservations beforementioned. But this is too imperfect, because till a convention be made with any particular nation, the commerce of any one of our states with that nation may be regulated by the state itself. And even when a convention is made, the regulation of the commerce is taken out of the hands of the several states only so far as it is covered or provided for by that convention or treaty. But treaties are made in such general terms, that the greater part of the regulations would still result to the legislatures. Let us illustrate these observations by observing how far the commerce of France and of England can be affected by the state legislatures. As to England, any one of the legislatures may impose on her goods double the duties which are paid by other nations; may prohibit their goods altogether; may refuse them the usual facilities for the recovering their debts or withdrawing their property, may refuse to receive their Consuls or to give those Consuls any jurisdiction. But with respect to France, whose commerce is protected by a treaty, no state can give any molestation to that commerce which is defended by the treaty. Thus, tho' a state may exclude the importation of all wines (because one of the reservations aforesaid is that they may prohibit the importation of any species of commodities) yet they cannot prohibit the importation of *French* wines particularly, while they allow wines to be brought from other countries. They cannot impose heavier duties on French commodities than on those of other nations. They cannot throw peculiar obstacles in the way of their recovery of debts due to them &c. &c. because these things are provided for by treaty. Treaties however are very imperfect machines for regulating commerce in the detail. The principal objects in the regulation of our commerce would be 1. to lay such duties, restrictions, or prohibitions on the goods of any particular nation as might oblige that nation to concur in just and equal arrangements of commerce, 2. to lay such uniform duties on the articles of commerce throughout all the states as may avail them of that fund for assisting to bear the burthen of public expences. Now this cannot be done by the states separately;

because they will not separately pursue the same plan. New-Hampshire cannot lay a given duty on a particular article, unless Massachusets will do the same; because it will turn the importation of that article from her ports into those of Massachusets, from whence they will be smuggled into New Hampshire by land. But tho Massachusets were willing to concur with N. Hampshire in laying the same duty, yet she cannot do it, for the same reason, unless Rhode-island will also. Nor can Rhode island without Connecticut, nor Connecticut without N. York, nor N. York without N. Jersey, and so on quite to Georgia. It is visible therefore that the commerce of the states cannot be regulated to the best advantage but by a single body, and no body so proper as Congress. Many of the states have agreed to add an article to the Confederation for allowing to Congress the regulation of their commerce, only providing that the revenues to be raised on it, shall belong to the state in which they are levied. Yet it is beleived that Rhode island will prevent this also. An everlasting recurrence to this same obstacle will occasion a question to be asked: How happens it that Rhode island is opposed to every useful proposition? Her geography accounts for it, with the aid of one or two observations. The cultivators of the earth are the most virtuous citizens and possess most of the amor patriae. Merchants are the least virtuous, and possess the least of the amor patriae. The latter reside principally in the sea-port towns; the former in the interior country. Now it happened that of the territory constituting Rhode island and Connecticut, the part containing the sea-ports was erected into a state by itself and called Rhode-island, and that containing the interior country was erected into another state called Connecticut for tho it has a little seacoast, there are no good ports in it. Hence it happens that there is scarcely one merchant in the whole state of Connecticut, while there is not a single man in Rhode island who is not a merchant of some sort. Their whole territory is but a thousand square miles, and what of that is in use is laid out in grass farms almost entirely. Hence they have scarcely any body[5] employed in agriculture. All exercise some species of commerce. This circumstance has decided the characters of these two states. The remedies to this evil are hazardous. One would be to consolidate the two states into one. Another would be to banish Rhode island from the union. A third to compel her submission to the will of the other twelve. A fourth for the other twelve to govern themselves according to the new propositions and to let Rhode island go on by herself according to the antient articles. But the dangers and difficulties attending all these remedies are obvious.

I. ANSWERS TO FIRST QUERIES

These are the only alterations proposed to the confederation, and the best of them is the only additional power which Congress is thought to need.

12. Congress have not yet ultimately decided at what rates they will redeem the paper money in the hands of the holders. But a resolution of   1784. has established the principle, so that there can be little doubt but that the holders of paper money will receive as much real money as the paper was actually worth at the time they received it, and an interest of 5. percent from the time they received it. It's worth will be found in the depreciation table of the state wherein it was received, these depreciation tables having been formed according to the market prices of the paper money at different epochs.

13. Those who talk of the bankruptcy of the U.S. are of two descriptions. 1. Strangers who do not understand the nature and history of our paper money. 2. Holders of that paper-money who do not wish that the world should understand it. Thus when, in March 1780. the paper money being so far depreciated that 40. dollars of it would purchase only 1. silver dollar, Congress endeavored to arrest the progress of that depretiation by declaring they would emit no more, and would redeem what was in circulation at the rate of one dollar of silver for 40 of paper; this was called by the brokers in paper-money, a bankruptcy. Yet these very people had only given one dollar's worth of provisions, of manufactures, or perhaps of silver for their forty dollars, and were displeased that they could not in a moment multiply their silver into 40. If it were decided that the U.S. should pay a silver dollar for every paper dollar they emitted, I am of opinion (conjecturing from loose data of my memory only as to the amount and true worth of the sums emitted by Congress and by the several states) that a debt, which in it's just amount is not more perhaps than 6 millions of dollars, would mount up to 400 millions, and instead of assessing every inhabitant with a debt of about 2. dollars, would fix on him thirty guineas which is considerably more than the national debt of England affixes on each of it's inhabitants, and would make a bankruptcy where there is none. The real just debts of the U.S. which were stated under the 3d. query, will be easily paid by the sale of their lands, which were ceded to them on the fundamental condition of being applied as a sinking fund for this purpose.

14. *La Canne à sucre* est un erreur du traducteur de M. Filson. Le mot Anglois 'cane' veut dire 'arundo' en latin, et 'roseau' ou

'Canne' en Français. Le traducteur en a fait le 'canne à sucre,' probablement que le 'Caffier' est une erreur semblable.

15. The whole army of the United States was disbanded at the close of the war. A few guards only were engaged for their magazines. Lately they have enlisted some two or three regiments to garrison the posts along the Northern boundary of the U.S.

16. 17. The U.S. do not own at present a single vessel of war; nor has Congress entered into any resolution on that subject.

18. I conjecture there are 650,000 negroes in the five Southernmost states and not 50,000 in the rest. In most of these latter, effectual measures have been taken for their future emancipation. In the former nothing is done towards that. The disposition to emancipate them is strongest in Virginia. Those who desire it, form as yet the minority of the whole state, but it bears a respectable proportion to the whole in numbers and weight of character, and it is continually recruiting by the addition of nearly the whole of the young men as fast as they come into public life. I flatter myself it will take place there at some period of time not very distant. In Maryland and N. Carolina, a very few are disposed[6] to emancipate. In S. Carolina and Georgia not the smallest symptom of it, but, on the contrary, these two states and N. Carolina continue importations of negroes. These have been long prohibited in all the other states.

19. In Virginia, where a great proportion of the legislature consider the constitution but as other acts of legislation, laws have been frequently passed which controuled it's effect. I have not heard that in the other states they have ever infringed their constitutions; and I suppose they have not done it; as the judges would consider any law as void, which was contrary to the constitution. Pennsylvania is divided into two parties, very nearly equal, the one desiring to change the constitution, the other opposing a change. In Virginia there is a part of the state which considers the act for organising their government as a constitution and are content to let it remain. There is another part which considers it only as an ordinary act of the legislature, who therefore wish to form a real constitution, amending some defects which have been observed in the act now in force. Most of the young people as they come into office arrange themselves on this side, and I think they will prevail ere long. But there are no heats on this account. I do not know that any of the other states propose to change their constitutions.

20. I have heard of no malversations in office which have been of any consequence: unless we consider as such some factious transactions in the Pennsylvania assembly; or some acts of the

I. ANSWERS TO FIRST QUERIES

Virginia assembly which have been contrary to their constitution. The causes of these were explained in the preceding article.

21. Broils among the states may happen in the following ways. 1. A state may be embroiled with the other twelve by not complying with the lawful requisitions of Congress. 2. Two states may differ about their boundaries. But the method of settling these is fixed by the Confederation, and most of the states which have any differences of this kind are submitting them to this mode of determination; and there is no danger of opposition to the decree by any state. The individuals interested may complain, but this can produce no difficulty. 3. Other contestations may arise between two states, such as pecuniary demands, affrays among their citizens, and whatever else may arise between any two nations. With respect to these there are two opinions. One that they are to be decided according to the 9th. article of the Confederation, which says that 'Congress shall be the last resort in all differences between two or more states, concerning boundary, jurisdiction, *or any other cause whatever,*' and prescribes the mode of decision, and the weight of reason is undoubtedly in favor of this opinion. Yet there are some who question it.

It has been often said that the decisions of Congress are impotent, because the Confederation provides no compulsory power. But when two or more nations enter into a compact, it is not usual for them to say what shall be done to the party who infringes it. Decency forbids this. And it is as unnecessary as indecent, because the right of compulsion naturally results to the party injured by the breach. When any one state in the American Union refuses obedience to the Confederation by which they have bound themselves, the rest have a natural right to compel them to obedience. Congress would probably exercise long patience before they would recur to force; but if the case ultimately required it, they would use that recurrence. Should this case ever arise, they will probably coerce by a naval force, as being more easy, less dangerous to liberty, and less likely to produce much bloodshed.

It has been said too that our governments both federal and particular want energy; that it is difficult to restrain both individuals and states from committing wrongs. This is true, and it is an inconvenience. On the other hand that energy which absolute governments derive from an armed force, which is the effect of the bayonet constantly held at the breast of every citizen, and which resembles very much the stillness of the grave, must be admitted also to have it's inconveniences. We weigh the two together, and like best to submit to the former. Compare the number of wrongs committed with impunity by citizens among us, with those committed by the sovereigns in other countries, and the last will be found most numerous, most oppressive on the mind, and most degrading of the dignity of man.[7]

22. The states differed very much in their proceedings as to British property; and I am unable to give the details. In Virginia, the sums sequestered in the treasury remain precisely as they did at the conclusion of the peace. The British having refused to make satisfaction for the slaves they carried away, contrary to the treaty of peace, and to deliver up the posts within our limits, the execution of that treaty is in some degree suspended. Individuals however are paying off their debts to British subjects, and the laws even permit the latter to recover them judicially. But as the amount of these debts are 20 or 30 times the amount of all the money in circulation in that state, the same laws permit the debtor to pay his debt in seven equal and annual paiments.

PrC (DLC); pages 1-14 of the sequence of pages numbered by Mazzei; entirely in TJ's hand, with a number of deletions and interlineations, some of which have been indicated in the notes below; at foot of first page of MS: "Monsieur de Meusnier, author of that part of the Encyclopedie [Méth]odique which is entitled Economie politique et diplomatique." These answers must have been copied by TJ from a previous draft, but such a draft has not been found.

[1] This word is interlined in substitution for "support," deleted.

[2] There is no number "4" in the sequence of numbered answers; such a number would have occurred, as answer number 5 does, at the beginning of a new page. The pages of the MS are numbered in the hand of Philip Mazzei and no page in his sequence of numbers is missing; if a page of the PrC dropped out, as is possible, this was done before Mazzei received the MS.

[3] The words "land, slaves" were deleted at this point.

[4] As originally phrased this passage read: "I suppose between two and three thousand."

[5] The words "no person" were deleted at this point.

[6] Preceding five words interlined in substitution for the following deleted passage: "There is a feeble disposition."

[7] The following is deleted at this point: "22. This was answered under the first Article."

II. Additional Queries, with Jefferson's Answers

[ca. Jan.-Feb. 1786]

Additional questions of M. de Meusnier, and answers

1. What has led Congress to determine that the concurrence of seven votes is requisite in questions which by the Confederation

II. ADDITIONAL QUERIES

are submitted to the decision of a Majority of the U.S. in Congress Assembled?

The IXth. article of Confederation, §. 6. evidently establishes three orders of questions in Congress. 1. The greater ones, which relate to making peace or war, alliances, coinage, requisitions for money, raising military force, or appointing it's commander in chief. 2. The lesser ones, which comprehend all other matters submitted by the Confederation to the federal head. 3. The single question of adjourning from day to day. This gradation of questions is distinctly characterised by the article.

In proportion to the magnitude of these questions, a greater concurrence of the voices composing the Union was thought necessary. Three degrees of concurrence, well distinguished by substantial circumstances, offered themselves to notice. 1. A concurrence of a *majority of the people* of the Union. It was thought that this would be ensured by requiring the voices of nine states; because according to the loose estimates which had then been made of the inhabitants, and the proportion of them which were free, it was believed that even the nine smallest would include a majority of the free citizens of the Union. The voices therefore of nine states were required in the greater questions. 2. A concurrence of the *majority of the states*. Seven constitute that majority. This number therefore was required in the lesser questions. 3. A concurrence of the *Majority of Congress*, that is to say, of the states actually present in it. As there is no Congress when there are not seven states present, this concurrence could never be of less than four states. But these might happen to be the four smallest, which would not include one ninth part of the free citizens of the Union. This kind of majority therefore was entrusted with nothing but the power of adjourning themselves from day to day.

Here then are three kinds of majorities: 1. Of the people. 2. Of the states. 3. Of the Congress; each of which is entrusted to a certain length.

Tho the paragraph in question be clumsily expressed, yet it strictly enounces it's own intentions. It defines with precision the *greater* questions for which nine votes shall be requisite. To the *lesser* questions it then requires a *majority of the U.S. in congress assembled*: a term indeed which will apply either to the number seven, as being a *majority of the states*, or to the number four, as being *a majority of Congress*. Which of the two kinds of majority was meant? Clearly that which would leave a still smaller kind for the decision of the question of adjournment. The contrary would be absurd.

This paragraph therefore should be understood as if it had been expressed in the following terms. 'The United States in Congress assembled shall never engage in war &c. but with the consent of nine states; nor determine any other question but with the consent of a majority of the whole states; except the question of adjournment from day to day, which may be determined by a majority of the states actually present in Congress.'

2. *How far is it permitted to bring on the reconsideration of a question which Congress has once determined?*

The first Congress which met being composed mostly of persons who had been members of the legislatures of their respective states, it was natural for them to adopt those rules in their proceedings to which they had been accustomed in their legislative houses; and the more so as these happened to be nearly the same, as having been copied from the same original, the British parliament. One of those rules of proceeding was, that 'a question once determined cannot be proposed a second time in the same session.' Congress, during their first session, in the autumn of 1774, observed this rule strictly. But before their meeting in the spring of the following year, the war had broke out. They found themselves at the head of that war in an Executive as well as Legislative capacity. They found that a rule, wise and necessary, for a Legislative body, did not suit an Executive one, which being governed by events must change their purposes, as those change. Besides, their session was likely then to become of equal duration with the war; and a rule which should render their legislation immutable during all that period could not be submitted to. They therefore renounced it in practice, and have ever since continued to reconsider their questions freely. The only restraint as yet provided against the abuse of this permission to reconsider, is that when a question has been decided, it cannot be proposed for reconsideration but by some one who voted in favor of the former decision, and declares that he has since changed his opinion. I do not recollect accurately enough whether it be necessary that his vote should have decided that of his state, and the vote of his state have decided that of Congress.

Perhaps it might have been better when they were forming the federal constitution, to have assimilated it as much as possible to the particular constitutions of the states. All of these have distributed the Legislative, executive and judiciary powers into dif-

II. ADDITIONAL QUERIES

ferent departments. In the federal constitution the judiciary powers are separated from the others; but the legislative and executive are both exercised by Congress. A means of amending this defect has been thought of. Congress having a power to establish what committees of their own body they please, and to arrange among them the distribution of their business, they might on the first day of their annual meeting appoint an executive committee, consisting of a member from each state, and refer to them all executive business which should occur during their session; confining themselves to what is of a legislative nature, that is to say to the heads described in the 9th. article as of the competence of 9 states only, and to such other questions as should lead to the establishment of general rules. The journal of this committee of the preceding day might be read the next morning in Congress, and considered as approved, unless a vote was demanded on a particular article, and that article changed. The sessions of Congress would then be short, and when they separated, the Confederation authorizes the appointment of a committee of the states, which would naturally succeed to the business of the Executive committee. The legislative business would be better done, because the attention of the members would not be interrupted by the details of execution; and the executive business would be better done, because business of this nature is better adapted to small than great bodies. A monarchical head should confide the execution of it's will to departments consisting each of a plurality of hands, who would warp that will as much as possible towards wisdom and moderation, the two qualities it generally wants. But a republican head founding it's decree originally in these two qualities should commit them to a single hand for execution, giving them thereby a promptitude which republican proceedings generally want. Congress could not indeed confide their executive business to a smaller number than a committee consisting of a member from each state. This is necessary to ensure the confidence of the Union. But it would be gaining a great deal to reduce the executive head to thirteen, and to debarrass themselves of those details. This however has as yet been the subject of private conversations only.

3. Calculating the federal debts by the interest they pay, their principal would be much more than is stated under the 3d. of the former queries. The reason for this is that there is a part of the money put into the loan office which was borrowed under a special contract that whatever depreciation might take place on the prin-

cipal, the interest should be paid in hard money on the nominal amount, Congress only reserving to itself the right, whenever they should pay off the principal, to pay it according to it's true value, without regard to it's nominal one. The amount of this part of the debt is 3,459,200 dollars. From the best documents in my possession I estimate the capital of the federal debt as follows.

Foreign debt.		Dollars
Spanish loan		174,000
Farmers general of France	345,710ᵗᵗ.5	156,798
Individuals in France		250,000
Crown of France, in it's own right	24,000,000ᵗᵗ	4,444,444
To Holland, guaranteed by France	10,000,000	1,851,851
Dutch loan of 5 million of florins		2,020,202
Dutch loan of 2 million of florins		808,080
		9,705,375
Domestic debt as stated in Apr. 1783, since which there is no better state.		
Loan office debt		11,463,802
Credits in the treasury books		638,042
Army debt		5,635,618
Unliquidated debt estimated at		8,000,000
Commutation to the army		5,000,000
Bounty due to Privates		500,000
Deficiencies of this estimate supposed		2,000,000
		33,237,462
Whole debt foreign and domestic		42,942,837

The result as to the foreign debt is considerably more than in the estimate I made before. That was taken on the state of the Dutch loans as known to Congress in 1784. The new estimate of 1785 however (lately come to hand) shews those loans to be completed up to 7. millions of florins, which is much more than their amount in the preceding statements. The domestic debt too is made somewhat higher than in the preceding answer to the 3d query. I had in that taken the statement of 1783. for my basis, and had endeavored to correct that by the subsequent liquidations of 1784. and 1785. On considering more maturely those means of correction, I apprehend they will be more likely to lead to error; and that, upon the whole, the statement of 1783. is the surest we can have recourse to. I have therefore adopted it literally.

II. ADDITIONAL QUERIES

4. A succinct account of Paper money.

Previous to the late revolution, most of the states were in the habit, whenever they had occasion for more money than could be raised immediately by taxes, to issue paper notes or bills, in the name of the state, wherein they promised to pay to the bearer the sum named in the note or bill. In some of the states no time of paiment was fixed, nor tax laid to enable paiment. In these the bills depreciated, but others of the states named in the bill the day when it should be paid, laid taxes to bring in money enough for that purpose, and paid the bills punctually on or before the day named. In these states, paper money was in as high estimation as gold and silver. On the commencement of the late revolution, Congress had no money. The external commerce of the states being suppressed, the farmer could not sell his produce, and of course could not pay a tax. Congress had no resource then but in paper money. Not being able to lay a tax for it's redemption they could only promise that taxes should be laid for that purpose so as to redeem the bills by a certain day. They did not foresee the long continuance of the war, the almost total suppression of their exports, and other events which rendered the performance of their engagement impossible. The paper money continued for a twelvemonth equal to gold and silver. But the quantities which they were obliged to emit for the purposes of the war exceeded what had been the usual quantity of the circulating medium. It began therefore to become cheaper, or as we expressed it, it depreciated as gold and silver would have done, had they been thrown into circulation in equal quantities. But not having, like them, an intrinsic value, it's depreciation was more rapid and greater than could ever have happened with them. In two years it had fallen to two dollars of paper for one of silver. In three years to 4. for 1., in 9. months more it fell to 10. for 1. and in the six months following, that is to say, by Sep. 1779. it had fallen to 20. for 1. Congress, alarmed at the consequences which were to be apprehended should they lose this resource altogether, thought it necessary to make a vigorous effort to stop it's further depreciation. They therefore determined in the first place that their emissions should not exceed 200. millions of dollars, to which term they were then nearly arrived, and tho' they knew that 20 dollars of what they were then issuing would buy no more for their army than one silver dollar would buy, yet they thought it would be worth while to submit to the sacrifice of 19. out of 20. dollars, if they could thereby stop further depreciation. They therefore published an address to their constituents in which they renewed their original declarations that this paper money should be redeemed at dollar for dollar, they proved the ability of the states to do this, and that their liberty would be cheaply bought at that price. The declaration was ineffectual. No man received the money at a better rate; on the contrary in six months more, that is by March 1780, it was fallen to 40. for 1. Congress then tried an experiment of a different kind. Considering their former offers to redeem this money at par, as relinquished by the general refusal to take it but in progressive depreciation, they required the whole to be brought in, declared it should be redeemed at it's present value of 40 for 1. and that they would give to the holders new bills reduced in their denomination to the sum of gold or silver which was actually to be paid for them. This would reduce the nominal sum of the mass in circulation to the present worth of that mass, which was 5 millions, a sum not too great for the circulation of the states, and which they therefore hoped would not depreciate further, as they continued firm in their purpose of emitting no more. This effort was as unavailing as the former. Very little of the money was brought in. It continued to circulate and to depreciate till the end of 1780., when it had fallen to 75. for one, and the money circulated from the French army being by that time sensible in all the states North of the Potowmac, the paper ceased it's circulation altogether, in those states. In Virginia and N. Carolina it continued a year longer, within which time it fell to 1000 for 1. and then expired, as it had done in the other states, without a single groan. Not a murmur was heard on this occasion among the people. On the contrary universal congratulations took place on their seeing this gigantic mass, whose dissolution had threatened convulsions which should shake their infant confederacy to it's center, quietly interred in it's grave. Foreigners indeed who do not, like the natives, feel indulgence for it's memory, as of a being which has vindicated their liberties and fallen in the moment of victory, have been loud and still are loud. A few of them have reason. But the most noisy are not the best of them. They are persons who have become bankrupt by unskilful attempts at commerce with America. That they may have some pretext to offer to their creditors, they have bought up great masses of this dead money in America, where it is to be had at 5000 for 1. and they shew the certificates of their paper possessions as if it had all died in their hands, and had been the cause of their bankruptcy. Justice will be done to all, by paying to all persons what this money actually cost them, with an interest of 6. per cent from the time they received it. If difficulties present themselves in the ascertaining

II. ADDITIONAL QUERIES

the epoch of the receipt, it has been thought better that the state should lose by admitting easy proofs, than that individuals and especially foreigners should, by being held to such as would be difficult, perhaps impossible.[1]

5. Virginia certainly owed two millions sterling to Great Britain at the conclusion of the war. Some have conjectured the debt as high as three millions. I think that state owed near as much as all the rest put together. This is to be ascribed to peculiarities in the tobacco trade. The advantages made by the British merchants on the tobaccoes consigned to them were so enormous that they spared no means of increasing those consignments. A powerful engine for this purpose was the giving good prices and credit to the planter, till they got him more immersed in debt than he could pay without selling his lands or slaves. They then reduced the prices given for his tobacco so that let his shipments be ever so great, and his demand of necessaries ever so œconomical, they never permitted him to clear off his debt. These debts had become hereditary from father to son for many generations, so that the planters were a species of property annexed to certain mercantile houses in London.

6. The members of Congress are differently paid by different states. Some are on fixed allowances, from 4. to 8. dollars a day. Others have their expences paid and a surplus for their time. This surplus is of two, three, or four dollars a day.

7. I do not believe there has ever been a moment when a single whig in any one state would not have shuddered at the very idea of a separation of their state from the Confederacy. The tories would at all times have been glad to see the Confederacy dissolved even by particles at a time, in hopes of their attaching themselves again to Great Britain.

8. The 11th. article of Confederation admits Canada to accede to the Confederation at it's own will; but adds that 'no other colony shall be admitted to the same, unless such admission be agreed to by nine states.' When the plan of April 1784 for establishing new states was on the carpet, the committee who framed the report of that plan, had inserted this clause 'provided new states agree to such admission, according to the reservation of the 11th of the articles of Confederation.' It was objected 1. that the words of the confederation 'no other colony' could refer only to the residuary possessions of Gr. Britain, as the two Floridas, Nova Scotia &c. not being already parts of the Union; that the law for 'admitting' a new member into the Union could not be applied to a territory which was already in the union, by making part of a state which was a

member of it. 2. that it would be improper to allow 'nine' states to receive a new member, because the same reason which rendered that number proper now would render a greater one proper when the number composing the Union should be increased. They therefore struck out this paragraph, and inserted a proviso that 'the consent of so many states in Congress shall be first obtained as may at the time be competent,' thus leaving the question whether the 11th. article applies to the admission of new states to be decided when that admission shall be asked. See the Journ. of Congress of Apr. 20. 1784. Another doubt was started in this debate, viz. whether the agreement of the nine states required by the Confederation was to be made by their legislatures or by their delegates in Congress? The expression adopted viz. 'so many states in Congress is first obtained' shew what was their sense of this matter. If it be agreed that the 11th. article of the Confederation is not to be applied to the admission of these new states, then it is contended that their admission comes within the 13th. article, which forbids 'any alteration unless agreed to in a Congress of the U.S. and afterwards confirmed by the legislatures of every state.' The independance of the new states of Kentucké and Frankland will soon bring on the ultimate decision of all these questions.

9. Particular instances whereby the General assembly of Virginia have shewn that they consider the ordinance called their Constitution as every other ordinance or act of the legislature, subject to be altered by the legislature for the time being. The Convention which formed that Constitution declared themselves to be the house of delegates during the term for which they were originally elected, and, in the autumn of the year, met the Senate elected under the new constitution, and did legislative business with them. At this time there were malefactors in the public jail and there was as yet no court established for their trial. They passed a law appointing certain members by name, who were then members of the Executive council to be a court for the trial of these malefactors, tho' the constitution had said, in it's first clause, that 'no person should exercise the powers of more than one of the three departments, legislative, executive and judiciary, at the same time.' This proves that the very men who had made that constitution understood that it would be alterable by the General assembly. This court was only for that occasion. When the next general assembly met after the election of the ensuing year, there was a new set of malefactors in the jail, and no court to try them. This assembly passed a similar law to the former, appointing certain members

II. ADDITIONAL QUERIES

of the Executive council to be an occasional court for this particular case. Not having the journals of assembly by me, I am unable to say whether this measure was repeated afterwards. However they are instances of *executive and judiciary* powers exercised by the same persons under the authority of a law made in contradiction to the Constitution. 2. There was a process depending in the ordinary courts of justice between two individuals of the name of Robinson and Fauntleroy, who were relations, of different descriptions, to one Robinson a British subject lately dead. Each party claimed a right to inherit the lands of the decedent according to the laws. Their right would by the constitution have been decided by the judiciary courts; and it was actually depending before them. One of the parties petitioned the assembly (I think it was in the year 1782) who passed a law deciding the right in his favor. In the following year, a Frenchman, master of a vessel, entered into port without complying with the laws established in such cases, whereby he incurred the forfeitures of the law to any person who would sue for them. An individual instituted a legal process to recover these forfeitures, according to the law of the land. The Frenchman petitioned the assembly, who passed a law deciding the question of forfeiture in his favor. These acts are occasional repeals of that part of the constitution which forbids the same persons to exercise legislative and judiciary powers at the same time. 3. The assembly is in the habitual exercise of directing during their sessions the Executive what to do. There are few pages of their journals which do not furnish proofs of this, and consequently instances of the *legislative and executive* powers exercised by the same persons at the same time. These things prove that it has been the uninterrupted opinion of every assembly, from that which passed the ordinance called the Constitution, down to the present day, that their acts may controul that Ordinance, and of course that the state of Virginia has no fixed Constitution at all.

PrC (DLC); entirely in TJ's hand, with several deletions and corrections; pages 14-24, 26-28 of the sequence of pages numbered by Mazzei; see note 1. THE NEW ESTIMATES THAT HAVE LATELY COME TO HAND: TJ received on 18 Jan. 1786 R. H. Lee's letter of 29 Oct. 1785 on the new estimates; he also received two days afterward additional information from the Commissioners of the Treasury (see TJ to Commissioners, 26 Jan. 1786; Commissioners to TJ, 6 Dec. 1785). Hence it is possible that he may have prepared the answers to Démeunier's additional queries very soon after having answered the first set.

[1] Page 24 of Mazzei's numbered sequence of pages ends at this point, and its text does not extend to the normal limit of a page of text in this PrC. There is no page 25 in Mazzei's sequence but, since this appears to be the conclusion of the discussion of paper money and since there is no gap in the numbers of the queries, it is evident that none of the text is missing and that Mazzei made an error in numbering.

III. From Jean Nicolas Démeunier

Vendredi [Feb. ? 1786]
rue de La Sourdiere No. 15.

M. Démeunier est penetré de reconnoissance de tout ce que Monsieur Jefferson a La bonté de faire pour Lui. Il est si agreable et si heureux, d'avoir L'honneur de Causer avec un homme si parfaitement instruit, si Zelé pour Les choses interessantes, et si interessant Lui même à tous égards, que M. Démeunier prendra peutêtre La Liberté de Lui demander encore quelques momens.

Il va Corriger et etendre Le Morceau sur Les etats-unis, d'après Les renseignemens de Monsieur Jefferson; il Le Fera Transcrire ensuite, et il aura L'honneur de Le Lui envoyer. Il ose esperer que cette Lecture ne deplaira pas au Ministre des etats unis. Il Le prie d'agréer sa reconnoissance et ses respects.

RC (DLC); undated, but since Démeunier was usually prompt in responding to TJ's aids, it is reasonable to assume that the "Vendredi" on which this letter was written was the Friday following the Tuesday (24 Jan. 1786) on which TJ wrote the answers to the first set of queries.

IV. Jefferson's Observations on Démeunier's Manuscript

Observations on the article Etats-unis prepared for the Encyclopedie

Pa. 8.[1] The Malefactors sent to America were not in sufficient number to merit enumeration as one class out of three which peopled America. It was at a late period of their history that this practice began. I have no book by me which enables me to point out the date of it's commencement. But I do not think the whole number sent would amount to 2000, and being principally men, eaten up with disease, they married seldom and propagated little. I do not suppose that themselves and their descendants are at present 4000, which is little more than one thousandth part of the whole inhabitants.

Indented servants formed a considerable supply. These were poor Europeans who went to America to settle themselves. If they could pay their passage it was well. If not, they must find means of paying it. They were at liberty therefore to make an agreement with any person they chose, to serve him such a length of time as they agreed on, on condition that he would repay to the master

IV. JEFFERSON'S OBSERVATIONS

of the vessel the expences of their passage. If being foreigners unable to speak the language, they did not know how to make a bargain for themselves the captain of the vessel contracted for them with such person as he could. This contract was by deed indented, which occasioned them to be called indented servants. Sometimes they were called Redemptioners, because by their agreement with the master of the vessel they could *redeem* themselves from his power by paying their passage, which they frequently effected by hiring themselves on their arrival as is before mentioned. In some states I know that these people had a right of marrying themselves without their master's leave, and I did suppose they had that right every where. I did not know that in any of the states they demanded so much as a week for every day's absence without leave. I suspect this must have been at a very early period while the governments were in the hands of the first emigrants, who being mostly labourers, were narrow minded and severe. I know that in Virginia the laws allowed their servitude to be protracted only two days for every one they were absent without leave.   So mild was this kind of servitude, that it was very frequent for foreigners who carried to America money enough, not only to pay their passage, but to buy themselves a farm, it was common I say for them to indent themselves to a master for three years, for a certain sum of money, with a view to learn the husbandry of the country.—I will here make a general observation. So desirous are the poor of Europe to get to America, where they may better their conditions that, being unable to pay their passage, they will agree to serve two or three years, on their arrival there, rather than not go. During the time of that service they are better fed, better clothed, and have lighter labour than while in Europe. Continuing to work for hire a few years longer, they buy a farm, marry, and enjoy the sweets of a domestic society of their own. The American [go]vernments are censured for permitting the species of ser[vitude] which lays the foundation of the happiness of these people. But what should these governments do? Pay the passage of all those who chuse to go into their country? They are not able; nor, were they able, do they think the purchase worth the price. Should they exclude these people from their shores? Those who know their situations in Europe and America, would not say that this is the alternative which humanity dictates. But it is said these people are deceived by those who carry them over. But this is done in Europe. How can the American governments prevent it? Should they punish the deceiver? It seems more incumbent on the European government, where the act is done, and where a public injury is sustained from it. However it is only in Europe that this deception is heard of. The individuals are generally satisfied in America with their adventure, and very few of them wish not to have made it. I must add that the Congress have nothing to do with this matter. It belongs to the legislatures of the several states.

Pa. 18. line 4. '[. . .] province de la N. Angleterre.' lisez 'de deux provinces [. . . .]'[2]

[I]b. l. 3 from the bottom. Lisez 'la Maryland, la Pennsylvanie et la Delaware.'

P. 19. l. 13. Lisez '[. . . .]'[2]

P. 26. 'Une puissance, en effet, devoit statuer, en dernier ressort, sur les relations que pouvoient nuire ou servir au bien general' &c. The account of the settlement of the colonies, which precedes this paragraph, shews that that settlement was not made by public authority, or at the public expence, of England; but by the exertions and at the expence of individuals. Hence it happened that their constitutions were not formed systematically but according to the circumstances which happened to exist in each. Hence too, the principles of the political connection between the old and new countries were never settled. That it would have been advantageous to have settled them is certain: and particularly to have provided a body which should decide in the last resort all cases wherein both parties were interested. But it is not certain that that right would have been given, or ought to have been given to the parliament; much less that it resulted to the parliament without having been given to it expressly. Why was it necessary there should have been a body to decide in the last resort? Because it would have been for the good of both parties. But this reason shews it ought not to have been the parliament, because that would have exercised it for the good of one party only.

⟨Pa. 49. *'Le continent se divise en dix grandes parties, savoir &c.' No such division exists. The term 'New England' does indeed comprehend New Hampshire, Massachusets, Rhode island and Connecticut, because these were originally but one state, and was then called New England. But Virginia and Carolina are not general divisions including several states. They are particular states only. Of course this division of the author has no term in it which includes N. York, N. Jersey, Pennsylvania, Delaware, Maryland and Georgia.*⟩[3]

Pa. 59. 'La nouvelle Angleterre n'a pas moins de trois cens milles sur les bords de la mer, et s'etend à plus de 50 milles dans

IV. JEFFERSON'S OBSERVATIONS

les terres.'[4] New England, comprehending N. Hampshire Massachusets, Rhode island and Connecticut, which were originally one state called New England, extends from the mouth of Byram river to the mouth of St. Croix crossing the neck of Cape cod without counting it's circuit 550 miles of that country which are of 826 toises each. It extended into the country, that is to say due West by it's charter to the South sea and by the treaty of Paris to the Missisipi. But the deed of Massachusets to Congress dated Apr. 19. 1785. cedes all their lands Westward of New York. Now from Boston due West to the New York boundary, is 120 miles. This is the narrowest part of Massachusets.

Pa. 60 'Ils (i.e: les Colons de la nouvelle Angleterre) font une commerce tres lucratif de café, de coton, et de cacao.'[5] Neither coffee nor cacao grow in any part of the U.S. nor cotton north of Maryland. If the author means that the New Englanders exercise a lucrative commerce in these articles between the countries of their growth and any other part of the world, I can assure him they do not. No more passes through their hands than they consume themselves.

Pa. 60. The author states the number of fishermen from N. England as follows:

	sailors
Cod-fishery	4000
Mackerel and herring	6000
Whale	7500
	17,500

But when these fisheries were in their highest perfection which was at the commencement of the late war, the numbers employed were as follows:

Cod-fishery	2700
Mackerel and herring	600
Whale	2000
	5300

Pa. 61. 'Les autres provinces (i.e. N. Hampsh. Rh. isld. and Connecticut) intimidées se soumirent au Monarque et tous les emplois militaires y furent desormais à la nomination royale.'][6] Rhode island and Connecticut retained their charters to the last, and were nearly as independant of England as they are now. The crown could appoint no officer in either of those states except those of the customs, nor had it any negative on their laws.

THE ENCYCLOPEDIE METHODIQUE 1786

Pa. 62.[7] 'La Nouvelle Hampshire s'eten depuis la baie de Massachuset jusque au fleuve St. Laurent.'][6] The colony of Canada lies between N. Hampshire and the river St. Lawrence.

Ib. 'La population de Massachuset est de 900,000 habitans.'][6] It is only of 350,000. I must here be indulged with a note of some length, because it will be the basis for correcting all the author's mistakes as to the number [of] inhabitants in the several states. On the 22. June 1775. Congress first resolved to emit paper money. The sum resolved on was 2. millions of dollars. They declared then 'that the 12 confederated colonies (for Georgia had not yet joined them) should be pledged for the redemption of these bills.' To ascertain in what proportion each should stand bound, the members from each state were desired to declare, from their seats, the number of inhabitants in their respective states. They were very much unprepared for such a declaration, because no circumstance in the previous administration of the colony affairs had required a knowlege of the number of inhabitants. They guessed however as well as they could. The following are the numbers of inhabitants then conjectured, and the proportions of the 2 millions of dollars with which each state stands charged in the treasury books.

	inhabitants	dollars
N. Hampshire	100,000	82,713
Massachusets	350,000	289,496
Rhode isld.	58,000	47,973
Connecticut	200,000	165,426
N. York	200,000	165,426
N. Jersey	130,000	107,527
Pennsylvania	300,000	248,139
Delaware	30,000	24,813
Maryland	250,000	206,783
Virginia	400,000	330,852
North Carolina	200,000	165,426
South Carolina	200,000	165,426
	2,418,000	2,000,000

On the 29th. of July following it became necessary to emit 3. millions of dollars more, and they then made their first requisition on the states to provide funds for sinking their proportions at fixed periods, ascertaining these proportions by the same scale, only adding to it the numbers for Georgia. They continued to use the same scale during the continuation of hostilities. As a proof of

IV. JEFFERSON'S OBSERVATIONS

this I will observe that having on the 2d. of Nov. 1781. voted and apportioned 8. millions of dollars, the state of N. Hampshire complained that it was over-rated, as they had found in fact that their numbers were 82,200 only. Congress in their answer Apr. 1. 1782 (see their journals) say 'that as no actual numeration of the inhabitants of each state hath yet been obtained by Congress, the computed number which formed the basis of the first requisition made on the states the 29th. of July 1775. was adhered to.' However on the 18th. of April 1783. being to call on the states for the annual sum of a million and a half of dollars for 25 years to pay the interest of their public debt, they proceeded to make a new estimate. The following numbers and apportionment were the result.

	inhabitants	Dollars
N. Hampshire	82,200	52,708
Massachusets	350,000	224,427
Rhode island	50,400	32,318
Connecticut	206,000	132,091
New York	200,000	128,243
New Jersey	130,000	83,358
Pennsylvania	320,000	205,189
Delaware	35,000	22,443
Maryland	220,700	141,517
Virginia	400,000	256,487
North Carolina	170,000	109,006
South Carolina	150,000	96,183
Georgia	25,000	16,030
	2,339,300	1,500,000

The numbers here imputed to the five Southern states are considerably below what were given in by their members. But a considerable proportion of the inhabitants composing them being slaves, and slaves being of less value in a state than freemen, Congress made abatements. I will observe further that tho the apportionments of money (except in the instance of June 22. 1775) are always entered in the journals of Congress, the numbers of inhabitants, by which they were regulated, were never entered. The secretary of Congress wrote them on a separate paper as they were given in in the first instance, and in that of April 1783. the Committee charged with the subject stated them on paper. The members of Congress separately took copies of these, communicated them freely without doors, and they were printed in the public papers.

THE ENCYCLOPEDIE METHODIQUE 1786

Pa. 62. La longueur de Massachuset est de 112 miles et sa largeur de 28.][6] The breadth is the double of what is here stated, of that part of Massachusets which lies on the South side of N. Hampshire, and the detached part called Le Maine, which lies on the East side of N. Hampshire is five times as large. So that the whole of Massachusets is 12 times as large as the author states it, if he had the whole in view; and if he had the Southern division only in view, that alone is still twice as large. Besides it is leading readers into error to speak of the extent of a small district of a country in terms which induce them to beleive that the whole is spoken of.

Pa. 63. Boston est la capitale de la nouvelle Angleterre, et peut etre de toute l'Amerique Septentrionale.][6] It would give ideas more precise and more conformable to truth to say that Boston is the capital of Massachusets and among the largest cities of N. America.

Pa. 64. Il n'est point de ville en Amerique qui se rapproche plus de Londres [que Boston][8] tant pour la magnificence des edifices et l'elegance des meubles et des vetemens, que pour l'urbanité des moeurs &c.][9] In urbanity and hospitality Boston is equal to any part of America, but [in] buildings and furniture Philadelphia takes the lead, without doubt.

65. L'etendue de cette isle charmante [Rhode island][8] ne suffit qu'a 60,000 habitans.][6] The state of Rhodeisland comprehends the island of that name, with several others, and a territory on the main called Providence. It has been seen that the whole state contains only 50,400 inhabitants. But the author is here speaking of the island of Rhodes alone, in contra distinction to Providence. That island is about one fifteenth part of the state in extent and contains between eight and ten thousand inhabitants the greatest part of which live in the town of Newport.

66. Rhode-island est situee au Nord de Boston, à une distance de 60. milles tout au plus.][6] The distance is right, but there is a small error of North instead of South, as to the course, Rhode island lying very nearly due South of Boston.

67. Ses principales villes sont Brentford et Newhaven. Cette derniere est le rendezvous de toute la colonie.][6] Brentford in inconsiderable compared with Hartford, Newhaven, New London, Middletown. There is no such thing as a place of rendezvous for the whole colony. Their legislature meets at New-haven and Hartford.

Ib.[10] La Nouvelle York n'occupe sur le bord de la mer qu'un espace de 20. milles.][6] Long-island is a part of the state of New

IV. JEFFERSON'S OBSERVATIONS

York and is upwards of 100 miles long on the seacoast. It covers the continent of New York altogether from the sea.

69. Longue-island produit du tabac, qui le dispute à celui de Maryland.][6] The reader will be deceived if he infers from hence that tobacco is one of the articles of the produce of Long island which enters into commerce. Some individual there may have a few plants for curiosity or his own use, but nothing more. Maryland and the states South of that are the only ones which make tobacco for market. This plant is too tender for the more Northern climates of that continent; and if raised at all in well sheltered situations, it is too small in quantity and too indifferent in quality to be found at market.

70.[11] La Nouvelle York compte 250,000 habitants.][6] It's numbers, as have been already shewn, are 200,000 only.

71.[12] Le Nouveau Jersey située entre l'Ocean et les terres inconnues qui la bornent au Nord.][6] The Northern boundary of New-Jersey begins on the Hudson's river about 20 miles above the city of New-York, and runs in a direct course nearly W.N.W. to the nearest part of the Delaware, about 45 miles distant. It will not be supposed that this is a terra incognita. In fact, N. Jersey is bounded on the East, North, and West by the best settled parts of New York and Pennsylvania.

73. Ils (c'est à dire la Pennsylvanie et la Delaware) n'ont été separés qu'au moment de la revolution.][6] Pennsylvania and Delaware were always as independant of each other as England and Hanover. They had always the same governor, but the states were absolutely distinct, having each it's own legislature, judicatures, and other offices. The governor resided at Philadelphia, but went whenever necessary to Newcastle the seat of his other government.

75.[13] Jamais le sang humain n'avoit souillé cette terre [Pennsylvanie][8] avant le regne de Georges III.][6] It had hung as many criminals before that reign as any of the other states, and had been the theatre of much bloodshed in war.

76. Suivant le calcul du Congrés general, (la Pennsylvanie) portoit sa population, en 1774, à 350,000 habitans.][6] The estimate of 1774. had made them only 300,000. That of 1783 raised them to 320,000.

77. La profondeur de la Pennsylvanie n'a d'autres limites que celles de sa population et de sa culture.][6] The boundaries of Pennsylvania are fixed by it's charter, by lines of latitude on the North and South; by the river Delaware on the East, and a parallel to that, five degrees of longitude distant, on the West.

78. Philadelphie située au confluent du Schuylkill et de la Delaware.][14] It is about seven miles above that confluence.

79. Une superbe bibliotheque devenue publique en 1732 par les soins de l'illustre Franklin.][15] This deservedly illustrious man has too many claims of his own to the esteem of mankind to wish to rob others of their little pittance. The library here spoken of was the property of a Mr. Logan, was by his will left for public use; but some equivocal expressions produced a contestation which has to this moment kept it's doors shut both to the public and to individuals.

Ib. On comptoit a Philadelphie 20,000 habitans.][6] They were reckoned at that time between fifty and sixty thousand.

80. En 1773. on à commencé á fortifier l'entree du fleuve Delaware.][6] No attempt was ever made to fortify it's entrance. The fortifications which were erected were about 150 miles above the entrance of the bay of Delaware, and 40 miles above where it begins to be called the river of Delaware.

Ib. On la fait monter (i.e. la Marylande) á 320,000 habitans.][16] The estimate of 1783. was of 220,700.

Ib. La baie de Chesapeak s'enfonce d'environ 250 milles dans les terres.][6] About 190 miles.

81.[17] Les habitans de Maryland fournissent en echange pour le rum de Barbades et le vin de Madere des etoffes de soie et de laine, des toiles de cotton, des armes à feu, et toutes les especes de quincailleries, qu'ils savent fabriquer.][6] I think Maryland never fabricated a single yard of silk, woollen or cotton stuff, or a fire arm for exportation. She exports bar and pig-iron, but very little if any wrought iron. Her exports are tobacco, flour, maize, pork, bar and pigiron, not one of which does this author enumerate as of her produce, but ascribes to her precisely those articles which she does not export.

Pa. 82. S'il n'y a point d'exageration dans les calculs de Congrés on n'y compte pas (c'est à dire dans la Virginie) moins de 650,000 habitans, y compris les esclaves dont le nombre est evalué á 150,000.][6] Congress never stated them at more than 400,000, and it is as untrue as it is indecent to charge on them the author's own exaggeration. They fixed the numbers of this state below reality for the reason before assigned. Their true numbers, according to an estimate since made in the state itself, are 567,614: of which I am sorry to say there are 270,762 slaves instead of 150,000 as stated by the author.

84. Les pouvoirs trop etendus du gouverneur ne laissoient aux

IV. JEFFERSON'S OBSERVATIONS

deputés des comtés aucune influence dans le gouvernement.][6] They made all the laws however, requiring only the governor's assent to them; and they alone could furnish supplies of money. These are the offices of the parliament in Gr. Britain, and will any body say that parliament has no influence in the government?

Pa. 84. Les retributions arbitraires des pasteurs Anglicans.][6] Their salaries were fixed by law, and were moderate enough being worth about 100 guineas a year.

Ib. Les appels au Conseil Britannique, et definitivement à la cour d'Angleterre.][6] The appeal from the supreme judicature in the colony was to the king and council in England. There could be no further appeal.

Ib. Ils n'ont d'autres villes que James town et Williamsburgh, et cette Capitale est moins une ville qu'un superbe village, ou l'on compte environ 2000 hommes.][6] Jamestown has but one family living in it. Williamsburg, to have 2000 men, should have from eight to ten thousand inhabitants; but it never had more than 1800 of every age, sex and condition.

86. La Caroline septentrionale a pour bornes immediates la Virginie, la Georgie, l'Ocean, et les Apalaches.][6] North Carolina is bounded by Virginia, South Carolina, the Ocean and the Missisipi.

87. The author makes the exports from N. Carolina amount to no more than a million and a half of livres tournois. I am not accurately enough informed to say what this sum should be; but combining the best estimates I have seen with my own knolege of the country I beleive they must have been at the beginning of the war two millions and a half.

88. Le Congrès en fait monter la population à 300,000 hommes.][6] Their estimate of 1774 was 200,000 inhabitants; that of 1783 was of 170,000.

Pa. 89.[18] On commence à fabriquer dans la Caroline du Sud des etoffes melées de laine et de soie; elle en fait des envois aux colonies voisines.][6] Neither sends to the other states, nor makes stuffs of this or any other kind.[19] Her inhabitants are occupied in making rice and Indigo.[20]

Ib. Sa population est d'environ 250,000 habitans.][6] The estimate of 1774. was 200,000, that of 1783 was 150,000.[21]

Ib. Les deux Carolines reunies occupent un espace de 200 milles dans les terres.][6] They extended by the treaty of Paris to the Missisipi which is about 700 miles from their sea-coast.

90.[22] La Georgie a pour bornes la riviere de Savannah du coté du nord, et celle d'Alatamaha du coté du midi.][6] The river Alatamahé is about the center of the state.[23]

Page 105. As to the change of the 8th. article of Confederation for quotaing requisitions of money on the states.

By a report of the Secretary of Congress dated Jan. 4. 1786. eight states had then acceded to the proposition, to wit, Massachus. Connect. N. York, N. Jersey, Pennsylva., Maryland, Virginia, and N. Carolina.

Congress on the 18th. of Apr. 1783. recommended to the states to invest them with a power for 25. years to levy an impost of 5. per cent. on all articles imported from abroad. N. Hamp. Mass. Conn. N. Jer. Pensva., Delaware, Virga., N. Cara., S. Cara., had complied with this before the 4th. of Jan. 1786. Maryland had passed an act for the same purpose; but by a mistake in referring to the date of the recommendation of Congress, the act failed of it's effect. This was therefore to be rectified. Since the 4th. of January, the public papers tell us that Rhode island has complied fully with this recommendation. It remains still for N. York and Georgia to do it. The exportations of America, which are tolerably well known, are the best measure for estimating the importations. These are probably worth about 20 millions of dollars annually. Of course this impost will pay the interest of a debt to that amount. If confined to the foreign debt, it will pay the whole interest of that, and sink half a million of the capital annually. The expences of collecting this impost will probably be 6. per cent on it's amount, this being the usual expence of collection in the U.S. this will be 60,000 dollars.

On the 30th. of April 1784. Congress recommended to the states to invest them with a power for 15 years to exclude from their ports the vessels of all nations not having a treaty of commerce with them; and to pass as to all nations an act on the principles of the British navigation act. Not that they were disposed to carry these powers into execution with such as would meet them in fair and equal arrangements of commerce; but that they might be able to do it against those who should not. On the 4th. of Jan. 1786. N. Hamp. Mass. Rho. isld. Connect. N. York. Pensva., Maryld. Virga., and N. Carola. had done it. It remained for N. Jers. Delaware, S. Carola., and Georgia to do the same.

In the mean time the general idea has advanced before the demands of Congress, and several states have passed acts for vesting Congress with the whole regulation of their commerce, reserving the revenue arising from these regulations to the disposal of

IV. JEFFERSON'S OBSERVATIONS

the state in which it is levied. The states which, according to the public papers have passed such acts, are N. Hamp. Mass. Rho. isld. N. Jers. Del. and Virga.: but, the assembly of Virga., apprehensive that this disjointed method of proceeding may fail in it's effect, or be much retarded, passed a resolution on the 21. of Jan. 1786. appointing commissioners to meet others from the other states whom they invite into the same measure, to digest the form of an act for investing Congress with such powers over their commerce as shall be thought expedient, which act is to be reported to their several assemblies for their adoption. This was the state of the several propositions relative to the impost, and regulation of commerce at the date of our latest advices from America.[24]

Pa. 125. The General assembly of Virginia, at their session in 1785, have passed an act declaring that the District called Kentuckey shall be a separate and independent state, on these conditions. 1. That the people of that district shall consent to it. 2. That Congress shall consent to it and shall receive them into the federal union. 3. That they shall take on themselves a proportionable part of the public debt of Virginia. 4. That they shall confirm all titles to lands within their district made by the state of Virginia before their separation.[25]

Page 131. 'Et sur six assemblées à peine trouve-t-on.' &c., jusques à, 'elles feront un meilleur choix,' page 132. I think it will be better to omit the whole of this passage for reasons which shall be explained in conversation.

Page 139. It was in 1783 and not in 1781. that Congress quitted Philadelphia.

Page 140. 'Le Congrés qui se trouvoit à la portée des rebelles fut effrayé.' I was not present on the occasion but I have had relations of the transaction from several who were. The conduct of Congress was marked with indignation and firmness. They received no propositions from the mutineers. They came to the resolutions which may be seen in the journals of June 21. 1783. They adjourned regularly and went through the body of the mutineers to their respective lodgings. The measures taken by Mr. Dickinson, the president of Pennsylvania, for punishing this insult, not being satisfactory to Congress, they assembled 9. days after at Princetown in Jersey. The people of Pennsylvania sent petitions declaring their indignation at what had past, their devotion to the federal head, and their dispositions to protect it, and praying them to return; the legislature, as soon as assembled, did the same thing; the Executive whose irresolution had been so exceptionable made

THE ENCYCLOPEDIE METHODIQUE 1786

apologies. But Congress were now removed; and to the opinion that this example was proper, other causes were now added sufficient to prevent their return to Philadelphia.

Pa. 153. l. 8. '400,000 millions,' should be '400, millions.'

Pa. 154. l. 3. from the bottom. Omettez 'plus de,' and l. 2. 'c'est a dire plus d'un milliard.'

Pa. 155. l. 2. Omit 'la dette actuelle' &c. And also, 'Les details de cette espece' &c. to the end of the paragraph 'celle des etats-unis' pa. 156. The reason is that these passages seem to suppose that the several sums emitted by Congress at different times, amounting nominally to 200 Millions of dollars, had been actually worth that at the time of emission, and of course that the souldiers and others had received that sum from Congress. But nothing is further from the truth. The souldier, victualler or other person who received 40 dollars for a service at the close of the year 1779, received in fact no more than he who received one dollar for the same service in the year 1775 or 1776 because in those years the paper money was at par with silver; whereas by the close of 1779. forty paper dollars were worth but one of silver, and would buy no more of the necessaries of life. To know what the monies emitted by Congress were worth to the people at the time they received them, we will state the date and amount of every several emission, the depreciation of paper money at the time, and the real worth of the emission in silver or gold.

Emission		Sum emitted	Depreciation	Worth of the sum emitted in silver dollars	
1775.	June 23.	2,000,000		2,000,000	
	Nov. 29.	3,000,000.		3,000,000	5,000,000.
1776.	Feb. 17.	1,000,000		4,000,000	
	Aug. 13.	5,000,000		5,000,000	9,000,000.
1777.	May. 20.	5,000,000	$2\frac{2}{3}$	1,877,273	
	Aug. 15.	1,000,000.	3.	$333,333\frac{1}{3}$	
	Nov. 7.	1,000,000	4.	250,000	
	Dec. 3.	1,000,000	4.	250,000	$2,710,606\frac{1}{3}$
1778.	Jan. 8.	1,000,000	4.	250,000	
	22.	2,000,000	4.	500,000	
	Feb. 16.	2,000,000	5	400,000	
	Mar. 5.	2,000,000	5	400,000	
	Apr. 4.	1,000,000	6.	$166,666\frac{2}{3}$	
	11.	5,000,000.	6.	$833,333\frac{1}{3}$	

IV. JEFFERSON'S OBSERVATIONS

[Apr.] 18.	500,000.	6.	83,333⅓	
May 22	5,000,000	5.	1,000,000	
June 20.	5,000,000	4.	1,250,000	
July 30.	5,000,000	4½	1,111,111.	
Sep. 5.	5,000,000	5.	1,000,000	
26.	10,000,100.	5.	2,000,020.	
Nov. 4.	10,000,100.	6.	1,666,683⅓	
Dec. 14.	10,000,100.	6.	1,666,683⅓	12,327,831
1779. Jan. 14.	24,447,620*	8.	3,055,952½	
Feb. 3.	5,000,163.	10.	500,016.	
12.	5,000,160.	10.	500,016.	
Apr. 2.	5,000,160	17	294,127	
May 5.	10,000,100.	24.	416,670⅚	
June 4.	10,000,100	20.	500,005	
July 17.	15,000,280.	20.	750,014	
Sep. 17.	15,000,260.	24.	625,010⅚	
Oct. 14.	5,000,180.	30.	166,672⅔	
Nov. 17.	10,050,540.	38½	261,053	
29.	10,000,140.	38½	259,743	7,329,282½
	200,000,000.		36,367,719⅚	

* The sum actually voted was 50,000,400. but part of it was for exchange of old bills, without saying how much. It is presumed that these exchanges absorbed 25,552,780. because the remainder 24,447,620 with all the other emissions preceding Sep. 2. 1779 will amount to 159,948,880. the sum which Congress declares to be then in circulation.

Thus it appears that the 200 millions of Dollars emitted by Congress were worth to those who received them but about 36. millions of silver dollars. If we estimate at the same value the like sum of 200 millions supposed to have been emitted by the states, and state the Federal debt, foreign and domestic, at about 43. Millions, and the state debts at about 25 millions, it will form an amount of 140. millions of Dollars, or 735 millions of livres Tournois, the total sum which the war has cost the inhabitants of the U.S. It continued 8. years from the battle of Lexington to the cessation of hostilities in America. The annual expence then was about 17,500,000 Dollars, while that of our enemies was a greater number of guineas.

It will be asked How will the two masses of Continental and of State money have cost the people of the U.S. 72. millions of dollars, when they are to be redeemed now with about six millions? I answer that the difference, being 66. millions has been lost on the paper bills separately by the successive holders of them. Every one thro whose hands a bill passed, lost on that bill what it lost in value, during the time it was in his hands. This was a real tax on him;

THE ENCYCLOPEDIE METHODIQUE 1786

and in this way the people of the united states actually contributed those 66. millions of dollars during the war, and by a mode of taxation the most oppressive of all, because the most unequal of all.

Pa. 157. l. 2. from bottom. 'cinquantieme' this should be 'dixieme.'

Pa. 158. l. 8. 'Elles ont fait des reductions.' They have not reduced the debt, but instead of expressing it in paper money, as formerly, they express it by the equivalent sum in silver or gold, being the true sum it has cost the present creditor, and what therefore they are bound in justice to pay him. For the same reason strike out the words 'ainsi reduites' second line from the bottom.

Pa. 161. l. 8. 'point de remboursements en 1784.' Except the interest.

Pa. 166. bottom line. 'Et c'est une autre economie' &c. The reason of this is that in 1784. purchases of lands were to be made of the Indians which were accordingly made. But in 1785. they did not propose to make any purchase. The money desired in 1785, 5000 dollars, was probably to pay agents residing among the Indians, or balances of the purchase of 1784. These purchases will not be made every year, but only at distant intervals as our settlements are extended; and it may be taken for a certainty that not a foot of land will ever be taken from the Indians without their own consent. The sacredness of their right is felt by all thinking persons in America as much as in Europe.

Pa. 170. Virginia is quotaed the highest of any state in the Union. But during the war, several states appear to have pai[d m]ore, because they were free from the enemy, whilst Virginia was cruelly ravaged. The requisition of 1784. was so quotaed on the several states as to bring up their arrearages so that when they should have paid the sums then demanded all would be on an equal footing. It is necessary to give a further explanation of this requisition. The requisitions of 1,200,000. Dol. of 8. millions and 2. millions had been made during the war, as an experiment to see whether in that situation, the states could furnish the necessary supplies. It was found they could not. The money was thereupon obtained by loans in Europe; and Congress meant by their requisition of 1784. to abandon the requisitions of 1,200,000 and of 2. millions, and also one half of the 8 millions. But as all the states almost had made some paiments in part of that requisition, they were obliged to retain such a proportion of it as would enable them [to] call for equal contributions from all the others.

Pa. 171. I cannot say how it has happened that the debt of

IV. JEFFERSON'S OBSERVATIONS

Connecticut is greater than that of Virginia. The latter is the richest in her productions, and perhaps made greater exertions to pay for her supplies in the course of the war.

172. 'Les Americains si vantés, aprés une banqueroute' &c. The objections made to the U.S. being here condensed together in a short compass, perhaps it would not be improper to condense the answers in as small a compass, in some such form as follows. That is, after the words 'aucun espoir' add, 'but to these charges it may be justly answered that those are no bankrupts who acknolege the sacredness of their debts in their just and real amount, who are able within a reasonable time to pay them, and who are actually proceeding in that paiment; that they furnish actually the supplies necessary for the support of their government; that their officers and souldiers are satisfied, as the interest of their debt is paid regularly, and the principals are in a course of paiment; that the question whether they fought ill, should be asked of those who met them at Bunker's hill, Bennington, Still-water, King's mountain, the Cowpens, Guilford and the Eutaws; and that the charges of ingratitude, madness, infidelity and corruption are easily made by those[26] to whom falsehoods cost nothing; but that no instances in support of them have been produced or can be produced.'

Pa. 187. 'Les officiers et les soldats ont eté payés' &c. The balances due to the officers and souldiers have been ascertained, and a certificate of the sum given to each; on these the interest is regularly paid; and every occasion is seised of paying the principals by receiving these certificates as money, whenever public property is sold, till a more regular and effectual method can be taken for paying the whole.

Pa. 191. 'Quoique la loi dont nous parlons, ne s'observe plus en Angleterre.' Blackstone B.1.c.10. pa. 372. 'An alien born may purchase lands or other estates: but not for his own use; for the king is thereupon entitled to them.'—'Yet an alien may acquire a property in goods, money and other personal estate, or may hire a house for his habitation, for this is necessary for the advancement of trade.'—'Also an alien may bring an action concerning personal property, and may make a will and dispose of his personal estate.'—'When I mention these rights of an alien, I must be understood of alien *friends* only, or such whose countries are in peace with ours; for alien *enemies* have no rights, no privileges, unless by the king's special favour, during the time of war.'—'An Alien *friend* may have personal actions, but not real; an alien *enemy* shall have neither real, personal, nor mixt actions. The reason why an alien *friend*

THE ENCYCLOPEDIE METHODIQUE 1786

is allowed to maintain a personal action is, because he would otherwise be incapacitated to merchandise, which may be as much to our prejudice as his.' Cuningham's law dict. voce Aliens. The above is the clear law of England, practised from the earliest ages to this day, and never denied. The passage quoted by M. de Meusnier from 2. Blackstone ch. 26. is from his chapter 'of title to things *personal by occupancy*.' The word *'personal'* shews that nothing in this chapter relates to lands, which are *real* estate, and therefore this passage does not contradict the one before quoted from the same author B.1.c.10. which sais that the lands of an alien belong to the king. The words 'of title by *occupancy*' shew that it does not relate to *debts*, which being a moral existence only, cannot be the subject of *occupancy*. Blackstone in this passage B.2.c.26. speaks only of personal goods of an alien which another may find and seize as prime occupant.

Pa. 193. 'Le remboursement presentera des difficultés.' Des sommes considerables' &c.[27] There is no difficulty nor doubt on this subject. Every one is sensible how this is to be ultimately settled. Neither the British creditor, nor the state will be permitted to lose by these paiments. The debtor will be credited for what he paid according to what it was really worth at the time he paid it, and he must pay the balance. Nor does he lose by this. For if a man, who owed 1000 dollars to a British merchant, paid 800 paper dollars into the treasury when the depreciation was at 8. for 1. it is clear he paid but 100. real dollars, and must now pay 900. It is probable he received those 800. dollars for 100. bushels of wheat, which were never worth more than 100 silver dollars. He is credited therefore the full worth of his wheat. The equivoque is in the use of the word 'dollar.'

Pa. 223. l. 6. 'Le comité charge de cette revision a publie son travail' rather say 'the committee charged with this work reported it in the year 1779 to the assembly, who ordered it to be printed for consideration in the year 1781 and who in their session of 1785. 6. passed between 30 and 40. of the bills, meaning to resume it at their successive sessions till they shall have gone thro' the whole.'

Pa. 225. 'Mais elle y a eté inserée depuis.' Rather say 'But they prepared an amendment with an intention of having it proposed at the time the bill should be under discussion before the assembly. Selon cette amendment les enfans des esclaves demeureroient &c.'

Pa. 226. l. 11. "Qu'on abolisse les privileges du clergé." This privilege originally allowed to the clergy, is now extended to every man, and even to women. It is a right of exemption from capital

IV. JEFFERSON'S OBSERVATIONS

punishment for the first offence in most cases. It is then a pardon by the law. In other cases the Executive gives the pardon. But when laws are made as mild as they should be, both those pardons are absurd. The principle of Beccaria is sound. Let the legislators be merciful but the executors of the law inexorable. As the term 'privileges du clergé' may be misunderstood by foreigners, perhaps it will be better to strike it out here, and to substitute the word 'pardon.'

Pa. 238. 'Plongés dans la mer.' The English word 'ducked' means 'to plunge the party into water' no matter whether of the sea, a river, or pond.

Pa. 239. 'Les commissaires veulent' &c. Manslaughter is the killing a man with design, but in a sudden gust of passion, and where the killer has not had time to cool. The first offence is not punished capitally, but the second is. This is the law of England and of all the American states; and is not a new proposition. Those laws have supposed that a man whose passions have so much dominion over him as to lead him to repeated acts of murder, is unsafe to society: that it is better he should be put to death by the law, than others more innocent than himself on the movements of his impetuous passions.

Ib. l. 12. 'Mal-aisé d'indiquer la nuance precise &c.' In forming a scale of crimes and punishments, two considerations have principal weight. 1. The atrocity of the crime. 2. The peculiar circumstances of a country which furnish greater temptations to commit it, or greater facilities for escaping detection. The punishment must be heavier to counterbalance this. Was the first the only consideration, all nations would form the same scale, but as the circumstances of a country have influence on the punishment, and no two countries exist precisely under the same circumstances, no two countries will form the same scale of crimes and punishments. For example, in America, the inhabitants let their horses go at large in the uninclosed lands which are so extensive as to maintain them altogether. It is easy therefore to steal them and easy to escape. Therefore the laws are obliged to oppose these temptations with a heavier degree of punishment. For this reason the stealing of a horse in America is punished more severely than stealing the same value in any other form. In Europe where horses are confined so securely that it is impossible to steal them, that species of theft need not be punished more severely than any other. In some countries of Europe, stealing fruit from trees is punished capitally. The reason is that it being impossible to lock fruit trees up in coffers, as we do our money, it is impossible to oppose physical bars to this species of theft. Moral ones are therefore opposed by the laws. This to an unreflecting American appears the most enormous of all the abuses of power; because he has been used to see fruits hanging in such quantities that if not taken by men they would rot: he has been used to consider it therefore as of no value, as not furnished materials for the commission of a crime. This must serve as an apology for the arrangement of crimes and punishments in the scale under our consideration. A different one would be formed here; and still different ones in Italy, Turkey, China &c.

Pa. 240. 'Les officiers Americains' &c., to pa. 264. 'qui le meritoient.' I would propose to new-model this Section in the following manner. 1. Give a succinct history of the origin and establishment of the Cincinnati. 2. Examine whether in it's present form it threatens any dangers to the state. 3. Propose the most practicable method of preventing them. Having been in America during the period in which this institution was formed, and being then in a situation which gave me opportunities of seeing it in all it's stages, I may venture to give M. de Meusnier materials for the 1st. branch of the preceding distribution of the subject. The 2d. and 3d. he will best execute himself. I should write it's history in the following form.

When on the close of that war which established the independance of America, it's army was about to be disbanded, the officers, who during the course of it had gone thro the most trying scenes together, who by mutual aids and good offices had become dear to one another, felt with great oppression of mind the approach of that moment which was to separate them never perhaps to meet again. They were from different states and from distant parts of the same state. Hazard alone could therefore give them but rare and partial occasions of seeing each other. They were of course to abandon altogether the hope of ever meeting again, or to devise some occasion which might bring them together. And why not come together on purpose at stated times? Would not the trouble of such a journey be greatly overpaid by the pleasure of seeing each other again, by the sweetest of all consolations, the talking over the scenes of difficulty and of endearment they had gone through? This too would enable them to know who of them should succeed in the world, who should be unsuccessful, and to open the purses of all to every labouring brother. This idea was too soothing not to be cherished in conversation. It was improved into that of a regular association, with an organised administration, with periodical

IV. JEFFERSON'S OBSERVATIONS

meetings general and particular, fixed contributions for those who should be in distress, and a badge by which not only those who had not had occasion to become personally known should be able to recognise one another, but which should be worne by their descendants to perpetuate among them the friendships which had bound their ancestors together. Genl. Washington was at that moment oppressed with the operation of disbanding an army which was not paid, and the difficulty of this operation was increased by some two or three of the states having expressed sentiments which did not indicate a sufficient attention to their paiment. He was sometimes present when his officers were fashioning in their conversations their newly proposed society. He saw the innocence of it's origin, and foresaw no effects less innocent. He was at that time writing his valedictory letter to the states, which has been so deservedly applauded by the world. Far from thinking it a moment to multiply the causes of irritation, by thwarting a proposition which had absolutely no other basis but of benevolence and friendship, he was rather satisfied to find himself aided in his difficulties by this new incident, which occupied, and at the same time soothed the minds of the officers. He thought too that this institution would be one instrument the more for strengthening the federal band, and for promoting federal ideas. The institution was formed. They incorporated into it the officers of the French army and navy by whose sides they had fought, and with whose aid they had finally prevailed extending it to such grades as they were told might be permitted to enter into it. They sent an officer to France to make the proposition to them, and to procure the badges which they had devised for their order. The moment of disbanding the army having come on before they could have a full meeting to appoint their president, the General was prayed to act in that office till their first general meeting, which was to be held at Philadelphia in the month of May following. The laws of the society were published. Men who read them in their closets, unwarmed by those sentiments of friendship which had produced them, inattentive to those pains which an approaching separation had excited in the minds of the institutors, Politicians, who see in every thing only the dangers with which it threatens civil society, in fine, the labouring people, who, shielded by equal laws, had never seen any difference between man and man, but had read of terrible oppressions which people of their description experience in other countries from those who are distinguished by titles and badges, began to be alarmed at this new institution. A remarkeable silence however was observed. Their sollicitudes were long confined within the circles of private conversation. At length however a Mr. Burke, chief justice of South Carolina, broke that silence. He wrote against the new institution; foreboding it's dangers. Very imperfectly indeed, because he had nothing but his imagination to aid him. An American could do no more: for to detail the real evils of aristocracy they must be seen in Europe. Burke's fears were thought exaggerations in America; while in Europe it is known that even Mirabeau has but faintly sketched the curses of hereditary aristocracy as they are experienced here, and as they would have followed in America had this institution remained. The epigraph of Burke's pamphlet was 'Blow ye the trumpet in Zion.' It's effect corresponded with it's epigraph. This institution became first the subject of general conversation. Next it was made the subject of deliberation in the legislative assemblies of some of the states. The governor of South Carolina censured it in an address to his assembly. The assemblies of Massachusets, Rhode island and Pennsylvania condemned it's principles. No circumstance indeed brought the consideration of it expressly before Congress, yet it had sunk deep into their minds. An offer having been made to them on the part of the Polish order of divine providence to receive some of their distinguished citizens into that order, they made that an occasion to declare that these distinctions were contrary to the principles of their confederation.   The uneasiness excited by this institution had very early caught the notice of General Washington. Still recollecting all the purity of the motives which gave it birth, he became sensible that it might produce political evils which the warmth of these motives had masked. Add to this that it was disapproved by the mass of the citizens of the Union. This alone was reason strong enough in a country where the will of the majority is the law, and ought to be the law. He saw that the objects of the institution were too light to be opposed to considerations as serious as these; and that it was become necessary to annihilate it absolutely. On this therefore he was decided. The first annual meeting at Philadelphia was now at hand. He went to that, determined to exert all his influence for it's suppression. He proposed it to his fellow officers, and urged it with all his powers. It met an opposition which was observed to cloud his face with an anxiety that the most distressful scenes of the war had scarcely ever produced. It was canvassed for several days, and at length it was no more a doubt what would be it's ultimate fate. The order was on the point of receiving it's annihilation by the vote of a very great

IV. JEFFERSON'S OBSERVATIONS

majority of it's members. In this moment their envoy arrived from France, charged with letters from the French officers accepting with cordiality the proposed badges of union, with sollicitations from others to be received into the order, and with notice that their respectable sovereign had been pleased to recognise it, and to permit his officers to wear it's badge. The prospect was now changed. The question assumed a new form. After the offer made by them, and accepted by their friends, in what words could they clothe a proposition to retract it which would not cover themselves with the reproaches of levity and ingratitude? Which would not appear an insult to those whom they loved? Federal principles, popular discontent, were considerations whose weight was known and felt by themselves. But would foreigners know and feel them equally? Would they so far acknolege their cogency as to permit without any indignation the eagle and ribbon to be torn from their breasts by the very hands which had placed them there? The idea revolted the whole society. They found it necessary then to preserve so much of their institution as might continue to support this foreign branch, while they should prune off every other which could give offence to their fellow citizens; thus sacrificing on each hand to their friends and to their country. The society was to retain it's existence, it's name, it's meetings, and it's charitable funds; but these last were to be deposited with their respective legislatures; the order was to be no longer hereditary, a reformation which had been even pressed from this side the Atlantic; it was to be communicated to no new members; the general meetings instead of annual were to be triennial only. The eagle and ribbon indeed were retained; because they were worn, and they wished them to be worn, by their friends who were in a country where they would not be objects of offence; but themselves never wore them. They laid them up in their bureaus with the medals of American independance, with those of the trophies they had taken and the battles they had won. But through all the United states no officer is seen to offend the public eye with the display of this badge. These changes have tranquilised the American states. Their citizens do justice to the circumstance which prevented a total annihilation of the order. They feel too much interest in the reputation of their officers, and value too much whatever may serve to recall to the memory of their allies the moments wherein they formed but one people. Tho they are obliged by a prudent foresight to keep out every thing from among themselves which might pretend to divide them into orders, and to degrade one description of men below another, yet they hear with pleasure that their allies whom circumstances have already placed under these distinctions, are willing to consider it as one to have aided them in the establishment of their liberties, and to wear a badge which may recall them to their remembrance; and it would be an extreme affliction to them if the domestic reformation which has been found necessary, if the censures of individual writers, or if any other circumstances should discourage the wearing their badge, or lessen it's reputation.[28]

This short but true history of the order of the Cincinnati, taken from the mouths of persons on the spot who were privy to it's origin, and progress, and who know it's present state, is the best apology which can be made for an institution which appeared to be, and was really, so heterogeneous to the governments in which it was erected. It should be further considered that, in America, no other distinction between man and man had ever been known, but that of persons in office exercising powers by authority of the laws, and private individuals. Among these last the poorest labourer stood on equal ground with the wealthiest Millionary, and generally on a more favoured one whenever their rights seemed to jar. It has been seen that a shoemaker, or other artisan, removed by the voice of his country from his work bench into a chair of office, has instantly commanded all the respect and obedience which the laws ascribe to his office. But of distinctions by birth or badge they had no more idea than they had of the mode of existence in the moon or planets. They had heard only that there were such, and knew that they must be wrong. A due horror of the evils which flow from these distinctions could be excited in Europe only, where the dignity of man is lost in arbitrary distinctions, where the human species is classed into several stages of degradation, where the many are crouched under the weight of the few, and where the order established can present to the contemplation of a thinking being no other picture than that of God almighty and his angels trampling under foot the hosts of the damned. No wonder then that the institution of the Cincinnati could be innocently conceived by one order of American citizens, could raise in the other orders only a slow, temperate, and rational opposition, and could be viewed in Europe as a detestable parricide.

The 2d. and 3d. branches of this subject, nobody can better execute than M. de Meusnier. Perhaps it may be curious to him to see how they strike an American mind at present. He shall

IV. JEFFERSON'S OBSERVATIONS

therefore have the ideas of one who was an enemy to the institution from the first moment of it's conception, but who was always sensible that the officers neither foresaw, nor intended the injury they were doing to their country.

As to the question then, Whether any evil can proceed from the institution as it stands at present, I am of opinion there may. 1. From the meetings. These will keep the officers formed into a body; will continue a distinction between civil and military which it would be for the good of the whole to obliterate as soon as possible; and military assemblies will not only keep alive the jealousies and the fears of the civil government, but give ground for these fears and jealousies. For when men meet together, they will make business if they have none; they will collate their grievances, some real, some imaginary, all highly painted; they will communicate to each other the sparks of discontent; and these may engender a flame which will consume their particular, as well as the general, happiness. 2. The charitable part of the institution is still more likely to do mischief, as it perpetuates the dangers apprehended in the preceding clause. For here is a fund provided of permanent existence. To whom will it belong? To the descendants of American officers of a certain description. These descendants then will form a body, having a sufficient interest to keep up an attention to their description, to continue meetings, and perhaps, in some moment, when the political eye shall be slumbering, or the firmness of their fellow-citizens relaxed, to replace the insignia of the order, and revive all it's pretentions. What good can the officers propose which may weigh against these possible evils? The securing their descendants against want? Why afraid to trust them to the same fertile soil, and the same genial climate which will secure from want the descendants of their other fellow-citizens? Are they afraid they will be reduced to labour the earth for their sustenance? They will be rendered thereby both honester and happier. An industrious farmer occupies a more dignified place in the scale of beings, whether moral or political, than a lazy lounger, valuing himself on his family, too proud to work, and drawing out a miserable existence by eating on that surplus of other mens' labour which is the sacred fund of the helpless poor. A pitiful annuity will only prevent them from exerting that industry and those talents which would soon lead them to better fortune.

How are these evils to be prevented? 1. At their first general meeting let them distribute the funds on hand to the existing objects of their destination, and discontinue all further contribu-

THE ENCYCLOPEDIE METHODIQUE 1786

tions. 2. Let them declare at the same time that their meetings general and particular shall thenceforth cease. And 3. let them melt up their eagles and add the mass to the distributable fund that their descendants may have no temptation to hang them in their button holes.

These reflections are not proposed as worthy the notice of M. de Meusnier. He will be so good as to treat the subject in his own way, and no body has a better. I will only pray him to avail us of his forcible manner to evince that there is evil to be apprehended even from the ashes of this institution, and to exhort the society in America to make their reformation complete; bearing in mind that we must keep the passions of men on our side even when we are persuading them to do what they ought to do.

Pa. 268. 'Et en effet la population &c.—270. Plus de confiance.'

'To this we answer that no such census of the numbers was ever given out by Congress nor even presented to them: and further that Congress never has at any time declared by their vote the number of inhabitants in the respective states. On the 22d. of June 1775 they first resolved to emit paper money. The sum resolved on was 2. millions of dollars. They declared then that the 12 confederated colonies (for Georgia had not yet joined them) should be pledged for the redemption of these bills.' To ascertain in what proportion each state should be bound, the members from each were desired to say as nearly as they could what was the number of the inhabitants of their respective states. They were very much unprepared for such a declaration. They guessed however as well as they could. The following are the numbers, as they conjectured them, and the consequent apportionment of the 2. millions of dollars.

	inhabitants	
New Hampshire	100,000	82,713
Massachusets	350,000	289,496
Rhode island	58,000	47,973
Connecticut	200,000	165,426
New York	200,000	165,426
New Jersey	130,000	107,527
Pennsylvania	300,000	248,139
Delaware	30,000	24,813
Maryland	250,000	206,783
Virginia	400,000	330,852
North Carolina	200,000	165,426
South Carolina	200,000	165,426
	2,418,000	2,000,000

IV. JEFFERSON'S OBSERVATIONS

Georgia having not yet acceded to the measures of the other states, was not quotaed: but their numbers were generally estimated at about 30,000 and so would have made the whole 2,448,000 persons of every condition. But it is to be observed that tho' Congress made this census the basis of their apportionment, yet they did not even give it a place in their journals; much less publish it to the world with their sanction. The way it got abroad was this. As the members declared from their seats the number of inhabitants which they conjectured to be in their state, the secretary of Congress wrote them on a peice of paper, calculated the portion of 2 million of dollars accordingly, and entered the sum only in the journals. The members however for their own satisfaction and the information of their states, took copies of this numeration and sent them to their states. From thence they got into the public papers: and when the English news-writers found it answer their purpose to compare this with the numeration of 1783, as their principle is 'to lie boldly, that they may not be suspected of lying' they made it amount to 3,137,809. and ascribed it's publication to Congress itself.

In April 1785. Congress being to call on the states to raise a million and a half of dollars annually for 25 years it was necessary to apportion this among them. The states had never furnished them with their exact numbers. It was agreed too that in this apportionment 5. slaves should be counted as 3 freemen only. The preparation of this business was in the hands of a Committee. They applied to the members for the best information they could give them of the numbers of their states. Some of the states had taken pains to discover their numbers. Others had done nothing in that way, and of course were now where they were in 1775 when their members were first called on to declare their numbers. Under these circumstances, and on the principle of counting three fifths only of the slaves, the Committee apportioned the money among the states and reported their work to Congress. In this they had assessed S. Carolina as having 170,000 inhabitants. The delegates for that state however prevailed on Congress to assess them on the footing of 150,000 only, in consideration of the state of total devastation in which the enemy had left their country. The difference was then laid on the other states, and the following was the result.

THE ENCYCLOPEDIE METHODIQUE 1786

	inhabitants	Dollars
New Hampshire	82,200	52,708
Massachusets	350,000	224,427
Rhodeisland	50,400	32,318
Connecticut	206,000	132,091
New York	200,000	128,243
New Jersey	130,000	83,358
Pennsylvania	320,000	205,189
Delaware	35,000	22,443
Maryland	220,700	141,517
Virginia	400,000	256,487
N. Carolina	170,000	109,006
S. Carolina	150,000	96,183
Georgia	25,000	16,030
	2,339,300	1,500,000

Still however Congress refused to give this numeration the sanction of a place in their journals, because it was not formed on such evidence as a strict attention to accuracy and truth required. They used it from necessity, because they could get no better rule, and they entered on their journals only the apportionment of money. The members however, as before, took copies of the numeration which was the ground work of the apportionment, sent them to their states, and thus this second numeration got into the public papers, and was by the English ascribed to Congress, as their declaration of their present numbers. To get at the real numbers which this numeration supposed we must add 20,000 to the number on which S. Carolina was quotaed; we must consider that 700,000 slaves are counted but as 420,000 persons, and add on that account 280,000. This will give us a total of 2,639,300 inhabitants of every condition in the 13 states, being 221,300 more than the numeration of 1775. instead of 798,509 less which the English papers asserted to be the diminution of numbers in the United states according to the confession of Congress itself.'[29]

Pa. 272. 'Comportera peut-etre une population de 30. millions.'
The territories of the United states contain about a million of square miles, English. There is in them a greater proportion of fertile lands than in the British dominions in Europe. Suppose the territory of the U.S. then to attain an equal degree of population with the British European dominions; they will have an hundred millions of inhabitants.   Let us extend our views to what may be the population of the two continents of North and South

[56]

IV. JEFFERSON'S OBSERVATIONS

America, supposing them divided at the narrowest part of the isthmus of Panama. Between this line and that of 50°. of North latitude the Northern continent contains about 5. millions of square miles, and South of this line of division the Southern continent contains about 7. millions of square miles. I do not pass the 50th. degree of Northern latitude in my reckoning, because we must draw a line somewhere, and considering the soil and climate beyond that, I would only avail my calculation of it, as a make weight, to make good what the colder regions within that line may be supposed to fall short in their future population. Here are 12. millions of square miles then, which at the rate of population before assumed, will nourish 1200 millions of inhabitants, a number greater than the present population of the whole globe is supposed to amount to. If those who propose medals for the resolution of questions, about which nobody makes any question, those who have invited discussions on the pretended problem whether the discovery of America was for the good of mankind? Let them,[30] I say, would have viewed it only as doubling the numbers of mankind, and of course the quantum of existence and happiness, they might have saved their money and the reputation which their proposition has cost them. The present population of the inhabited parts of the U.S. is of about 10. to the square mile; and experience has shewn us that wherever we reach that the inhabitants become uneasy, as too much compressed, and go off in great numbers to search for vacant country. Within 40 years their whole territory will be peopled at that rate. We may fix that then as the term beyond which the people of those states will not be restrained within their present limits; we may fix it too as the term of population which they will not exceed till the whole of those [two conti]nents are filled up to that mark, that is to say, till they shall contain 120 millions of inhabitants. The soil of the country on the Western side of the Missisipi, it's climate, and it's vicinity to the U.S. point it out as the first which will receive population from that nest. The present occupiers will just have force enough to repress and restrain the emigrations to a certain degree of consistence. We have seen lately a single person go and decide on a settlement at Kentucky, many hundred miles from any white inhabitants, remove thither with his family and a few neighbors, and though perpetually harrassed by the Indians, that settlement in the course of 10. years has acquired 30,000 inhabitants, it's numbers are increasing while we are writing, and the state of which it formerly made a part has offered it independance.

THE ENCYCLOPEDIE METHODIQUE 1786

⟨Pa. 280. *'Et il est à desirer'* &c. *On the 16th. of March 1785. it was moved in Congress that the proposition for preventing slavery in the new states should be referred to a committee, and it was accordingly referred by the vote of 8. states against 3 but I have not seen that any thing further has been done in it. I hope the friends of the natural rights of man will continue our efforts till they succeed.*⟩[31]

Pa. 280, line 5. 'Huit des onze etats' &c. Say 'there were 10. states present. 6. voted unanimously for it, 3. against it, and one was divided: and seven votes being requisite to decide the proposition affirmatively, it was lost. The voice of a single individual of the state which was divided, or of one of those which were of the negative, would have prevented this abominable crime from spreading itself over the new country. Thus we see the fate of millions unborn hanging on the tongue of one man, and heaven was silent in that awful moment! But it is to be hoped it will not always be silent and that the friends to the rights of human nature will in the end prevail. On the 16th. of March 1785. it was moved in Congress that the same proposition should be referred to a Committee, and it was referred by the votes of 8. states against 3. We do not hear that any thing further is yet done on it.'

Pa. 280. Note (a). I would wish this note to be omitted.

Pa. 281. 'L'acte federatif lui donne le droit de prononcer sur tout ce qui a rapport au bien general de l'union' and line 6. the word 'ainsi.' It is better to omit these words. The passage stands right without them, and they would give a false idea not only of the principle on which Congress proceeded, but of their general powers.

Pa. 283. line 4. from bottom. '8. per cent, excepté en Virginie ou il etoit de 6. per cent' say '5. per cent in most, if not in all the states, and still continues the same.'

Pa. 286. 'L'autorité du Congrés etoit necessaire.' The substance of the passage alluded to in the Journ. of Congr. May 26. 1784. is 'that the authority of Congress to make requisitions of troops during peace is questioned, that such an authority would be dangerous, combined with the acknoleged one of emitting or of borrowing money, and that a few troops only being wanting to guard magazines, and garrison the frontier posts, it would be more proper at present to *recommend* than to require.'

Pa. 287. 'Nous n'osons nous permettre &c.—ce n'est pas tout' in the 4th. line of the next page. I think all this passage had bet-

[58]

IV. JEFFERSON'S OBSERVATIONS

ter be left out. It will alarm the states and damp their dispositions to strengthen the hands of Congress.[32]

Pa. 291. l. 8. from the bottom. 'Tous les terreins qui se trouvent en deça.' Say 'toute la territoire de Kentucky qui est en deça.'

Pa. 291. l. 6. from bottom. After 'appartenoient' add 'au de la des montagnes Alleghanie.'

Pa. 296. 'Consentement *unanime*.' The words in the original are the '*joint* consent of Congress and of the particular state.' On the part of Congress the vote need not be *unanimous*. Seven states will suffice. This observation shews that the passage 'on sera peutetre surpris' to 'dont nous parlons' should be omitted.

Pa. 301. 'Environ.' The word 'probablement' might be better, because it is probable that the cessions of Georgia will be such as will make up the number of new states 16.

Pa. 301. 'Il s'ecoulera peut-etre un demi siecle' &c. See what has been said on population pa. 272.

Pa. 301. l. 3. from bottom. 'Huit ou dix ans.' It would be safer to say 'peu d'années.'

Pa. 302. '40,000' should not this be '30,000'? Also pa. 304.

Pa. 304. 'Canne à sucre' is a mistaken translation of the English word 'cane' which means a reed i.e. canne, ou, roseau. It is the Arundo phragmitis of the botanists. By 'Coffee tree' the author must mean some tree bearing berries which are used as coffee. There can certainly be no coffee tree in that latitude.

Pa. 307. Omit the note (a). It has been before observed that Virginia has consented to the independance of Kentucky, but the consent of Kentucky itself and of Congress are still wanting.

Pa. 334. '150,000.' I am of opinion that the proportion of persons to warriors among the Indians may be generally estimated at about 10. to 3. Consequently we must not reckon that nations of Indians containing 25,000 warriors have more than about 80,000 persons.

Pa. 334. line 2. from bottom. '11. degrees' say '12 or 15 degrees.'

Pa. 323. between line 7. and 8. I can make a communication to M. de Meusnier which I dare say he will be glad to give an account of at this place.[33]

Finished June 22. 1786.

PrC (DLC); pages 29-64 of the sequence of pages numbered by Mazzei. The original of this PrC (missing) must have been an enclosure in a letter from TJ to Démeunier, for an entry in SJL under 22 June reads: "Demeusnier. s[ee] c[opy]." But such a covering letter has not been found.

[1] This refers to page 8 of Démeunier's MS, wherein there was a quotation from Raynal, *Histoire Philosophique et Poli-*

THE ENCYCLOPEDIE METHODIQUE 1786

tique des Deux Indes, Neuchâtel, 1783-84, VIII, 230, concerning malefactors and indentured servants among colonists of British America. Démeunier incorporated all of TJ's comment on this subject (*Economie*, II, 346-7).

[2] One or two words missing.

[3] This paragraph deleted in MS. It occurs at the top of the first of the twelve unnumbered pages referred to above in the Editorial Note and in note 23, below.

[4] The quotation is from Raynal, *Histoire*, VIII, 104. Démeunier retained Raynal's quotation but did not employ Jefferson's comment in his article on Massachusetts (*Economie*, III, 289).

[5] This and the quotation from "Pa. 61" of Démeunier's MS have not been identified.

[6] Closing bracket in MS; here and elsewhere TJ employed a closing bracket (but no opening bracket) to separate the quotation from his own comment.

[7] TJ also included in his comment on "Pa. 268" of the MS the list of inhabitants and proportions of requisitions, and Démeunier inserted the list in his text at that point. The quotation drawn from "Pa. 62" ("La population de Massachuset est de 900,000 habitans") is from Raynal, *Histoire*, VIII, 104.

[8] Brackets in MS.

[9] Quotation from Raynal, *Histoire*, VIII, 110.

[10] Quotation from Raynal, *Histoire*, VIII, 110. Démeunier amended the description in accordance with TJ's comment in the article on New York (*Economie*, IV, 708).

[11] Quotation from Raynal, *Histoire*, VIII, 119.

[12] Quotation from Hilliard d'Auberteuil, *Essais Historiques et Politiques sur les Anglo-Americains*, I, 30. Démeunier used TJ's description of the boundaries of New Jersey in his article on that state (*Economie*, IV, 734).

[13] Quotation from Hilliard d'Auberteuil, *Essais Historiques*, I, 35.

[14] Quotation from Raynal, *Histoire*, VIII, 148. Démeunier used TJ's correction in his article on Pennsylvania (*Economie*, III, 582).

[15] Quotation is from Raynal, *Histoire*, VIII, 149. "Une superbe bibliotheque" could more appropriately be applied to the Loganian Library, which was willed to the City of Philadelphia in 1752, but TJ erred in implying that Franklin did not found a library in 1732: in that year there was formed, under Franklin's leadership, the Library Company of Philadelphia.

[16] Quotation from Raynal, *Histoire*, VIII, 156.

[17] Quotation from Raynal, *Histoire*, VIII, 262.

[18] Quotation from D'Auberteuil, *Essais Historiques*, I, 50-1.

[19] Following this point, TJ first wrote, then deleted: "It is the least peopled of any of the states, and the thinner the population, the less disposition to manufactures."

[20] At this point TJ wrote, then deleted: "It is thought they will begin to make some tobacco."

[21] As first written, this passage read: "The estimate of 1783 was 250,000. At the beginning of the war it was estimated higher. I am not certain at what precisely, but I am sure it was at more than 50,000 inhabitants." He then altered the phraseology to read as above.

[22] Quotation from Raynal, *Histoire*, VIII, 191.

[23] The sequence of unnumbered pages referred to in Editorial Note, and also in note 3 above, ends here. From this point on, Démeunier's use of TJ's Observations is traceable in the article on the United States.

[24] Preceding three paragraphs translated and inserted in Démeunier's text (*Economie*, II, 374), following which Démeunier commented: "On enverra ensuite cet acte aux diverses assemblées législatives, et il est clair que des mesures si bien prises doivent avoir un heureux succès."

[25] This passage concerning Kentucky may have been in Démeunier's text in Section V (*Economie*, II, 377), where there is an appended note reading: "Il est vraisemblable qu'elles le sont aujourd'hui: car nous dirons plus bas que Kentuke est sur le point d'être admis à l'union américaine" (this was a note to the final sentence of the 8th answer provided by TJ to Démeunier's additional queries; Document II, above). If so, Démeunier removed it for discussion in Section XXII (*Economie*, II, 421).

[26] Following this TJ wrote, then deleted: "by whom truth and falsehood is spoken with equal indifference."

[27] This sentence was deleted by Démeunier (*Economie*, II, 393).

[28] Démeunier incorporated all of TJ's proposed history of the Cincinnati in *Economie*, II, 406-8, embracing TJ's text to this point beginning with the words "When on the close of that war...." The remainder of TJ's com-

ment from this point on was intended merely for Démeunier's guidance, not for inclusion in his text, and it was not included.

[29] There is no beginning quotation mark in MS.

[30] TJ deleted the words "if they" and substituted "Let them," but did not correct the remainder of the sentence. He probably intended it to read: "Let them, I say, view it only. . . ." In DLC: TJ Papers, 18:3145 there is a page of calculations in TJ's hand (not a PrC) on which he based his comparison of areas in square miles of North and South America. This page bears the number "79" in Mazzei's hand in the upper right-hand corner.

[31] This paragraph deleted in PrC.

[32] It would be interesting to know what passage TJ thought would alarm the states. Evidently it had to do with the power of Congress to raise troops. Démeunier must have altered the text at this point in accordance with TJ's wishes. The whole of the passage as published in the article reads as follows: "En 1784, le congrès se décida à lever un petit nombre de troupes pour la garde des frontières du N. O. et pour protéger les commissaires chargés des négociations avec les sauvages; il fut résolu dans une de ses assemblées, qu'on feroit aux différens états la *requisition* de ces soldats; mais un membre observa avec raison que l'autorité du congrès étoit incertaine; qu'il seroit obligé d'emprunter de l'argent dans les Etats-Unis ou chez l'Etranger pour la solde de ces troupes; que les troupes réglées en temps de paix sont fort dangereuses dans les gouvernemens démocratiques; que sur une affaire aussi importante, il falloit que les députés prissent l'avis de leurs provinces, et il vint à bout de faire changer le mot de *réquisition* en celui de *recommandation*. Pour que le gouvernement des Etats-Unis ait la force du moment, nécessaire en bien des occasions, il faut que le corps législatif de l'union puisse dans un besoin urgent lever des troupes, et c'est encore un article sur lequel il convient d'augmenter ses pouvoirs. Il s'agit seulement de restraindre son autorité, et peut-être de la borner à six mois ou à un an."

[33] The communication that TJ suggested for insertion here was that contained in his communication of 26 June 1786 (see Document v in the present series).

V. To Jean Nicolas Démeunier

[26 June 1786]

Mr. Jefferson presents his compliments to M. de Meusnier and sends him copies of the 13th. 23d. and 24th. articles of the treaty between the K. of Prussia and the United States. In the negociation with the minister of Portugal at London, the latter objected to the 13th. article. The observations which were made in answer to his objections, Mr. Jefferson incloses. They are a commentary on the 13th. article. Mr. de Meusnier will be so good as to return the sheet on which these observations are, as Mr. Jefferson does not retain a copy of it.

If M. de Meusnier proposes to mention the facts of cruelty of which he and Mr. Jefferson spoke yesterday, the 24th. article will introduce them properly, because they produced a sense of the necessity of that article. These facts are 1. the death of upwards of 11,000 American prisoners in one prison ship (the Jersey) and in the space of 3. years. 2. General Howe's permitting our prisoners taken at the battle of Germantown and placed under a guard in the

THE ENCYCLOPEDIE METHODIQUE 1786

yard of the Statehouse of Philadelphia to be so long without any food furnished them that many perished with hunger. Where the bodies laid, it was seen that they had eaten all the grass round them within their reach, after they had lost the power of rising or moving from their place. 3. The 2d. fact was the act of a commanding officer: the 1st. of several commanding officers and for so long a time as must suppose the approbation of government. But the following was the act of government itself. During the periods that our affairs seemed unfavourable and theirs succesful, that is to say after the evacuation of New York, and again after the taking of Charlestown in South Carolina, they regularly sent our prisoners taken on the seas and carried to England to the E. Indies. This is so certain, that in the month of Novemb. or Decemb. 1785. Mr. Adams having officially demanded a delivery of the American prisoners sent to the East Indies, Ld. Carmarthaen answered officially 'that orders were immediately issued for their discharge.' M. de Meusnier is at liberty to quote this fact. 4. A fact not only of the Government but of the parliament, who passed an act for that purpose in the beginning of the war, was the obliging our prisoners taken at sea to join them and fight against their countrymen. This they effected by starving and whipping them. The insult on Capt. Stanhope, which happened at Boston last year, was a consequence of this. Two persons, Dunbar and Lorthrope, whom Stanhope had treated in this manner (having particularly inflicted 24 lashes on Dunbar) meeting him at Boston, attempted to beat him. But the people interposed and saved him. The fact is referred to in that paragraph of the declaration of independance which sais 'he has constrained our fellow citizens taken captive on the high seas, to bear arms against their country, to become the executioners of their friends and brethren, or to fall themselves by their hands.' This was the most afflicting to our prisoners of all the cruelties exercised on them. The others affected the body only, but this the mind. They were haunted by the horror of having perhaps themselves shot the ball by which a father or a brother fell. Some of them had constancy enough to hold out against half allowance of food and repeated whippings. These were generally sent to England and from thence to the East Indies. One of these escaped from the East Indies and got back to Paris, where he gave an account of his sufferings to Mr. Adams who happened to be then at Paris.

M. de Meusnier, where he mentions that the slave-law has been passed in Virginia, without the clause of emancipation, is pleased

V. TO DEMEUNIER

to mention that neither Mr. Wythe nor Mr. Jefferson were present to make the proposition they had meditated; from which people, who do not give themselves the trouble to reflect or enquire, might conclude hastily that their absence was the cause why the proposition was not made; and of course that there were not in the assembly persons of virtue and firmness enough to propose the clause for emancipation. This supposition would not be true. There were persons there who wanted neither the virtue to propose, nor talents to enforce the proposition had they seen that the disposition of the legislature was ripe for it. These worthy characters would feel themselves wounded, degraded, and discouraged by this idea. Mr. Jefferson would therefore be obliged to M. de Meusnier to mention it in some such manner as this. 'Of the two commissioners who had concerted the amendatory clause for the gradual emancipation of slaves Mr. Wythe could not be present as being a member of the judiciary department, and Mr. Jefferson was absent on the legation to France. But there wanted not in that assembly men of virtue enough to propose, and talents to vindicate this clause. But they saw that the moment of doing it with success was not yet arrived, and that an unsuccesful effort, as too often happens, would only rivet still closer the chains of bondage, and retard the moment of delivery to this oppressed description of men. What a stupendous, what an incomprehensible machine is man! Who can endure toil, famine, stripes, imprisonment or death itself in vindication of his own liberty, and the next moment be deaf to all those motives whose power supported him thro' his trial, and inflict on his fellow men a bondage, one hour of which is fraught with more misery than ages of that which he rose in rebellion to oppose. But we must await with patience the workings of an overruling providence, and hope that that is preparing the deliverance of these our suffering brethren. When the measure of their tears shall be full, when their groans shall have involved heaven itself in darkness, doubtless a god of justice will awaken to their distress, and by diffusing light and liberality among their oppressors, or at length by his exterminating thunder, manifest his attention to the things of this world, and that they are not left to the guidance of a blind fatality.

PrC (DLC: TJ Papers, 18: 3155-62); without date and not recorded in SJL, but written on the same day as Démeunier's reply (Document VI of the present series); this text occupies p. 65-72 in the sequence of pages numbered by Mazzei. Not recorded in SJL. Enclosure: This, evidently, was the draft of the Commissioners' observations respecting contraband that TJ wrote, as described in Vol. 9: 431 (DLC: TJ Papers, 17:2971-4). The three articles that TJ transmitted were not strictly speaking an enclosure, for they preceded his letter; that this was their original form, as it is now in TJ Papers, 18:3155-62, is proved by Mazzei's numbering and also by Démeunier's use. Démeunier incorporated the whole of the three articles in his text (*Economie*, II, 427), following which he quoted briefly from the second paragraph of TJ's letter.

M. DE MEUSNIER, WHERE HE MENTIONS . . . THE SLAVE-LAW: Démeunier evidently did not alter his original statement, but merely inserted parts of this paragraph with additions of his own, as follows: "7o. Le comité veut affranchir tous les esclaves qui naîtront après les nouvelles loix. Le Bill tel que l'avoient rédigé les commissaires chargés de la revision, ne contenoit pas cette clause, mais M. Jefferson et M. Whythe vouloient proposer, lorsqu'on le discuteroit, que les enfans des esclaves demeurassent avec leur pere jusqu'à un certain âge; qu'on les instruisît ensuite aux frais de l'état des détails de l'agriculture; qu'on leur apprît les arts et les sciences selon leur disposition, jusqu'à ce que les femmes eussent 18 ans, et les mâles 21; qu'à cette époque on les établît dans quelques cantons, avec des armes, des meubles, des instrumens, des outils, des semences et quelques animaux domestiques, que certe petite colonie fût déclarée libre et indépendante, et qu'elle fût sous l'alliance et la protection de l'état de Virginie, jusqu'à ce qu'elle eût acquis de la force, et qu'on envoyât en d'autres parties du monde, des navires qui rapporteroient un égal nombre de blancs. Malheureusement M. Jefferson s'est trouvé à Paris, et M. Whythe, en sa qualité de juge, n'a pu assister à l'assemblée générale, lorsque le bill a passé; la nouvelle loi de Virginie déclare seulement, qu'il n'y aura plus d'esclaves dans cette république, que ceux qui s'y sont trouvés le premier jour de la session de 1785, 86, et les descendans des femmes esclaves. On a très-bien fait de défendre l'importation des esclaves; mais la nouvelle loi ne statue rien sur l'affranchissement général: et sans en importer de nouveaux le nombre de ceux qui s'y trouvent, augmentera tous les jours par leur réproduction seule. Si la population des blancs double tous les vingt ans, celle des noirs augmente dans une proportion plus grande encore. Il ne faut pas croire que l'absence de M. Jefferson et M. Whythe, ait seule empêché qu'on ne proposât l'émancipation. Il se trouvoit à l'assemblée générale des hommes assez courageux et assez honnêtes pour la demander, et assez éclairés pour appuyer la proposition de toute l'éloquence dont elle est susceptible, (nous en citerons un seul, M. Maddisson qui à 30 ans étonne les nouvelles républiques par son éloquence, sa sagesse et son génie); mais ils ont vu que la pluralité des membres du corps législatif, n'étoit pas encore disposée à une si belle révolution. Ils ont craint qu'un effort inutile ne resserrât les chaînes de l'esclavage, et ne reculât l'époque où on affranchiroit les nègres. L'homme est un être bien étonnant et bien incompréhensible! pour défendre sa liberté, il souffre la fatigue, la faim, les coups de fouet, la prison et la mort, et le moment d'après les nobles sentimens qui l'ont soutenu dans de cruelles épreuves, ne font plus d'impression sur lui, et il impose à d'autres hommes une servitude qui, dans la durée d'une heure, produit plus de peines et de douleur, que l'assujettissement contre lequel il a pris les armes, n'en eût produit dans des siecles. Il faut donc attendre que le progrès des lumières et des sentimens de la justice naturelle, amène la réforme: et lorsqu'on examine la force de raison et l'humanité des hommes d'état, qui, par leur influence personnelle et par leurs écrits, dirigent les conseils des nouvelles républiques, on ne doute point, que leur ame généreuse ne triomphe de la cupidité de leurs concitoyens. On regrette seulement, que l'émancipation des esclaves n'ait pas lieu dans la ferveur de leur nouvel état: on eût tranché d'une manière plus nette les difficultés du détail que présentera l'exécution de la réforme" (*Economie*, II, 401-2). The tribute to Madison must have come from TJ in discussion with Démeunier.

VI. From Jean Nicolas Démeunier

Lundi. [26 June 1786]

Je Venois d'ecrire Les traits de Cruauté dont Monsieur Jef-

[64]

ferson m'a fait L'honneur de me parler hier. Lorsque j'ai reçu son billet, Je L'ai placé à L'endroit où je Felicite Les americains des devastations, des incendies, et des forfaits que se sont permis Les Anglois, et je dirai en parlant du traité avec Le roi de prusse quel heureux effet ont produit ces abominables violences.

J'avois ajouté aussi ce qui regarde L'*amendement* du Bill sur les esclaves, et Je me sais bon gré d'avoir deviné qu'il convenoit de parler de L'Assemblée generale de Virginie à peu près dans Les mêmes Termes que Monsieur Jefferson.

J'Aurai L'honneur de Lui renvoyer Les Feuilles, dont il n'a pas gardé Copie. Je Les joindrai à La traduction de La Loi sur La Tolérance.

Je Voudrois avoir L'honneur d'etre connu davantage de Monsieur Jefferson; il Verroit combien Je suis penetré de ses bontés; avec quel plaisir Je L'Entends; et combien J'admire Son esprit Superieur, Ses Connoissances Si exactes et Si profondes, Sa grandeur d'ame et Sa Vertu qu'on peut egaler, mais qu'il est impossible de Surpasser. Lorsque Je regarde tout ce qu'il S'est donné la peine d'ecrire pour moi, Lorsque Je Songe à la vivacité de Son Zele, Je Felicite L'Amerique d'avoir un pareil Citoyen, et Je Compte pour des momens de plaisir et de bonheur, Ceux où il m'est permis de L'ecouter.

Je Le Supplie d'agréer mes hommages, mes respects et mes remerciemens bien sinceres.

RC (DLC); endorsed; assigned to the present date because the first Monday after TJ finished his Observations and transmitted them with Démeunier's MS was 26 June 1786. Enclosure: "Les Feuilles" which TJ had asked to be returned in his of this date (see note there).

To John Adams

Dear Sir Paris June 23. 1786.

I hear of a conveyance which allows me but a moment to write to you. I inclose a copy of a letter from Mr. Lamb. I have written both to him and Mr. Randall agreeable to what we had jointly thought best. The Courier de l'Europe gives us strange news of armies marching from the U.S. to take the posts from the English. I have received no public letters and not above one or two private ones from America since I had the pleasure of seeing you, so I am in the dark as to all these matters. I have only time left to address heaven with my good wishes for Mrs. Adams and Miss Adams, and to assure you of the sincere esteem with which I

have the honour to be Dear Sir your most obedt. & most humble servt,
TH: JEFFERSON

RC (MHi: AMT); endorsed in part: "ansd. 3. July. 1786." PrC (DLC). Enclosure: Copy of John Lamb to TJ, 5 June 1786.

The fact that TJ had last received a letter from America on 24 May no doubt caused him to overstate the case: actually he had received at least seven American letters since his return from London—those from William Temple Franklin, 18 Jan.; John Banister, Sr., 19 Jan.; Nathaniel Tracy, 22 Mch.; George Wythe, 10 Jan. and 10 Feb.; Francis Hopkinson, 28 Mch.; and Benjamin Franklin, 20 Mch. 1786. On the same day that the present letter was written, TJ received a substantial amount of mail from America containing letters from Madison, 22 Jan. and 18 Mch.; Walker, 4 Feb.; Sullivan, 4 Mch.; Hopkinson, 8 Mch. and 1 May; Thomson, 6 Apr.; Otto, 10 May; Monroe, 11 May; Lewis, 9 and 11 May; Duer, 11 May; and John Jay, 5 May (one public and one private). An entry in SJL under 23 June 1786 shows that the CONVEYANCE was Thomas Elder.

From Madame d'Houdetot

Sannois Le 23. juin 1786.

J'ay L'honneur de Remercier avec Bien de La Sensibilité Monsieur De Jefferson des nouvelles qu'il a Bien voulû me donner du Venerable Docteur Franklin. J'ay apris avec une Extrême joye que ses Voeux, auxquels je joins tous les Miens pour la prosperité de sa patrie, ont une heureuse perspective. Je suis attachée intimement à cette prosperité si interessante pour l'humanité, et ma Veneration est profonde pour Ceux qui y Contribuent. Je prie Monsieur Jefferson de Vouloir Bien assurer Le Cher et Venerable Docteur de ces Sentimens et de Vouloir Bien Recevoir pour Luy même Ceux que ma sincere et tendre Estime Luy a voués. Je ne serés plus à Sannois passé Le Vingt huit de Ce Mois, et j'iray diner Dehors le Vingt Sept. Si le Mercredy vingt huit Monsieur Jefferson Etait Libre, ce serait le dernier jour où je pourrais le voir D'icy à l'Automne, parceque je Vais Voyager ailleurs. S'il pouvait Venir dimanche prochain Vingt Cinq, il me ferait un Extrême plaisir, Et trouverait Encore toute la Societé.

LA CTESSE D'HOUDETOT

RC (DLC). Neither the present letter, nor that which TJ presumably wrote transmitting NOUVELLES . . . DU VENERABLE DOCTEUR FRANKLIN is recorded in SJL. TJ must have written soon after 24 May, the date on which he received Franklin's letter of 20 Mch. 1786, q.v.

From John Bondfield

SIR   Bordeaux 24 June 1786

Since mine of the 10th Instant I have received the 17th Inst.

24 JUNE 1786

33 Cases and the 20th Inst. 17 Cases, together fifty Cases, No. 1 à 50 containing 30 fusils each as particularised by two Certificates received with the said Cases signed Dubois d'Escordal Captain of the Royal Artillery Inspecteur of the fire Arms of the Manufactory of Tulle residing at Tulle for the service of the Navy and Colonies.

The Cases are in good order, agreable to the instructions contain'd in Monsr. St. Victoires Letter that you transmitted me. The[y] shall be cased with an Oild Cloth to prevent the moist Air and damp of the Ship to penetrate and over that a case of straw and canvas wraper. They will be shipt on board the Comte d'Artois, Cap. Gregory, for Portsmouth who will sail the begining of July and I shall follow the Letter of your instructions in every particular.

These fusils are subject to two Duties say Droits d'Entré of 3½℔% on the valuation which with the Sol ℔ livré amounts to Six ℔ Cent, also le Droit de sortie. These two Dutys are to your prejudice which I apprehend you were not appriz'd of. It is also of National prejudice to france which I apprehend Le Marquis de la Fayet will take measures to endeavour to remove. All Commercial Nations who export to foreigners their manufactories in lieu of loading them with extra charges Grant Bountys to obtain, encrease and continue the foreign demand by supplying them at a lower rate than other nations. Where the entire substance of the Article thus exported is the growth, Produce and workmanship of the nation, whatever of that article is consumed by foreign Nations is entire gain to the Kingdom that supply them. Should you be able to obtain on this Article indulgence for the Duties, a Letter from the Minister must be sent me to recover the Drawback of the Duties I am paying.

I have forwarded by the publick Roullier who will arrive in Paris 13 or 14 July, Twelve Doz. Claret and twelve Doz. Vin de grave in eight Cases of three Doz. bottles each which I hope will get safe to your hand.

The Articles for Mr. Eppes are all packt up and shall be shipt on board the Comte d'Artois.

I received last post a Letter under my Cover for Mess. Buchanan and Hay, Richmond which by the address appears to be your writing and seal. It shall go by the said ship.

With respect I have the honor to be Sir Your most Obedient Humble Servant,   JOHN BONDFIELD

RC (DLC); addressed and endorsed. Noted in SJL as received 28 June 1786.

From John Adams

DEAR SIR   London June 25. 1786

Last night I received yours of the 16. Mr. Lamb has not written to me. Mr. Randal I have expected every day, for a long time, but have nothing from him, but what you transmitted me. My opinion of what is best to be done, which you desire to know is, that Mr. Lamb be desired to embark immediately for New York, and make his Report to Congress and render his account, and that Mr. Randal be desired to come to you first and then to me, unless you think it better for him to embark with Lamb. It would be imprudent in us, as it appears to me to incurr any further Expence, by sending to Constantinople, or to Algiers, Tunis or Tripoli. It will be only so much Cash thrown away, and worse, because it will only increase our Embarrassment, make us and our Country ridiculous, and irritate the Appetite of these Barbarians already too greedy.—I have no News of the Clementine Captain Palmer.

The Sweedish Minister here, has never asked me any Question concerning the Island of St. Bartholomew. I suspect there are not many confidential Communications made to him, from his Court; he has been here 20 or 30 years and has married an English Lady, and is a Fellow of the Royal Society. From these Circumstances he may be thought to be *too well* with the English. This is merely conjecture. Your Advice was the best that could be given.

The Kings Visit to Cherbourg will have a great Effect upon a Nation whose Ruling Passion is a Love of their Sovereign, and the Harbour may and will be of Importance. But the Expectation of an Invasion will do more than a Real one.

Mrs. Adams and *Mrs. Smith* have taken a Tour to Portsmouth. We took Paines Hill in our Way out, and Windsor, in our Return; but the Country in general disappointed us. From Guilford to Portsmouth is an immense Heath. We wished for your Company, which would have added greatly to the Pleasure of the Journey. Pray have you visited the Gardens in France? How do you find them? Equal to the English?

With great Regard I am dear Sir your Friend & humble Sert,
                                                JOHN ADAMS

RC (DLC). FC (MHi: AMT); in Smith's hand. Noted in SJL as received 1 July 1786.

From Lucy Ludwell Paradise

Sir   June 25. 1786.

I return your Excellency a thousand thanks for your kind and friendly letter. I wish it was in my power to acquaint you that the time was fixed, and that we had taken our passage for our return to dear Virginia. Since you left us I thought proper (seeing the affairs of Mr. Paradise grow worse, and worse every day, as my truly good friend Dr. Bancroft will acquaint you) to write a letter to Dr. Price to beg he would use his influence with him, to go, and take my daughter and myself with him. Mr. Paradise promised Dr. Price, and Dr. Bancroft that he would go by the 15th. of July, and if he could not support his family in his absence, he would take them likewise. He has a debt of above Two thousand pounds and as yet no Ship is arrived, and I fear his Creditors begin to be a little uneasy about their money. Mr. Seward a friend of Mr. Paradises offered to pay the Sum of Two hundred pound and above to one of his Creditors if he would go directly, and take his family with him. He has refused him, and seems determined to stay in England at all events. I have ever since I was married been begging Mr. Paradise to carry me home, and he from time to time have put me off. Was he a man that had Ten Thousand a Year, he ought to have granted my request, as it was neither unreasonable nor unjust. But in the Situation he is at present, without a farthing in this part of the world to support him, or his family, I think, I have a right to demand that if he will not go himself and take his family with him, he ought to let me go, and to have the whole management of my property. I wish your Excellency would give me your opinion upon this Subject. I forgot to tell you, that he had only his life Interest in the Estate, as likewise, the Interes of the money in the Funds of England. I must beg of your Excellency to write to me by the first opportunity. I am in great affliction as Dr. Bancroft will tell you. He has received the letters for which act of friendship, I return your Excellency my most sincere thanks. Adieu Dear Sir And believe me to be your Excellencys most obliged humble Servant and friend,   L. Paradise

P.S. He sees it is the wish of my heart to go home and therefore he will keep me here as long as he can. Be my *friend and Support*.

RC (DLC); endorsed. Noted in SJL as received 5 July 1786, "by Dr. Bancroft."

To Rayneval

Sir Paris June 25[.] 1786.

I have received letters from two citizens of the United States of the names of Geary and Arnold, informing me that having for some time past exercised commerce in London and having failed, they were obliged to leave that country; that they came over to Dunkirk and from thence to Brest, where, one of them having changed his name the more effectually to elude the search of his creditors, they were both imprisoned by order of the Commandant. They are uninformed whether it is at the suit of their creditors, or because one of them had changed his name. But they are told that the Commandant has sent information of his proceedings to your office. I have some reason to suppose their creditors are endeavoring to obtain leave to remove them to England, where their imprisonment would be perpetual. Unable to procure information elsewhere, I take the liberty of asking you whether you know the cause of their imprisonment, and of solliciting your attention to them so far as that nothing may take place against them by surprize, and out of the ordinary course of the law. I have the honour to be with sentiments of the most perfect esteem and respect Sir Your most obedient & most humble servant, Th: Jefferson

PrC (DLC). RC (Arch. Aff. Etr., Paris, Corr. Pol, E.-U., xxxi; Tr in DLC).

From John Adams

Dear Sir Grosvenor Square June 26. 1786

Sometime Since I received from Gov. Bowdoin some Papers relating to Alexander Gross, with an earnest desire that I would communicate them to the French Ambassador here. I did so and his Excellency was so good as to transmit them to the Comte De Vergennes. Mr. Bartholomy however advised me to write to you upon the Subject, that you might prevent it from being forgotten.

Inclosed is a Letter, which I received yesterday from Griffin Green at Rotterdam, with a Paper inclosed dated Dunkirk 15. June. 1786. relating to this unhappy Man. What can be done for his Relief I know not. Neither the Ransom Money nor the other Charges I Suppose can ever be paid, for Government never is expected to redeem such Hostages and his Relations are not able. If this is the Truth as I suppose it is, it would be better for the

[70]

French Government and for the Persons interested, to set him at Liberty, than to keep him a Prisoner at Expence.

Let me pray you to minute this affair among your Memorandums to talk of, with the Comte De Vergennes and Mr. Rayneval, when you are at Versailles. They will shew you the Papers, which have been transmitted them through the Comte D'Adhemar.

I wrote you on the 23d. of May ulto. and on the 6th. inst. which Letters I hope you have received. Yours, JOHN ADAMS

RC (DLC). FC (MHi: AMT); in Smith's hand. Noted in SJL as received 1 July 1786. Enclosures (DLC): Griffin Greene to John Adams, 18 June 1786, recommending to his attention the case of Alexander Gross, together with Gross' affidavit dated Dunkirk, 15 June 1786. Gross' statement of the case is essentially the same as that outlined in Robert Murdoch to TJ, 29 June 1786. See TJ to Montmorin, 6 Dec. 1787.

From Thomas Barclay to the American Commissioners

GENTLEMEN   Morocco 26th. June 1786

This day Week we arrived here, Since which I have had two audiences from His Majesty, the first a public one, and the second a private one of yesterday. It is but a few minutes since I heard that a Courrier will depart this Evening for Daralbeyda, and I have not time to enter into particulars. It will be agreable however for you to know that the last draught of the treaty is made, and will probably be signed in a few days, and that our stay here will not exceed that of a week from this time. I believe you will be satisfied on the whole, as there is only one Article more I could wish to see inserted and that I really think in all human probability will never prove of the least Consequence.

I shall proceed to Tangiers, and take an early opportunity of sending you a more detailed Account of my proceedings. In the mean time I recommend your transmitting as soon as possible, through Mr. Carmichael, the Powers to treat with Tunis and Tripoli and (if Mr. Lamb has declined all further concern) for Algiers.

If you had a Treaty with the Porte I flatter myself the rest would follow and at all Events Tunis and Tripoli should be invited to our friendship.

There is a young man now under my Care who has been a Slave, some time with the Arabs in the Desert. His name is James Mercier born at the Town of Suffolk, Nansemond County, Virginia. The

26 JUNE 1786

King sent him after the first Audience, and I shall take him to Spain. I have not time to add but that I am Gentlemen, Your most obedient, humble servant, THOS. BARCLAY

RC (DLC); in Franks' hand, signed by Barclay; addressed to TJ at Paris; endorsed. Another RC (MHi: AMT); in Franks' hand, signed by Barclay; addressed to Adams at London; endorsed by W. S. Smith: "Recd and a Copy sent to Mr Jay 23d August 1786." Tr (DNA: PCC, No. 87, I); in Short's hand. Tr (MHi); in Smith's hand; at foot of text: "true Copy London 23d August 1786. W. S. Smith." Tr (DNA: PCC, No. 107). Noted in SJL as received "about the 11th"; it is evident, however, that it was received on 13 Aug. (see TJ to Adams, 13 Aug. 1786). On 17 Aug. TJ also recorded in SJL: "T. Barclay, dupl of June 26."

MOROCCO, the capital city named in the dateline of this letter, is now called Marrakesh; and DARALBEYDA is one of the older forms of the name of the modern city of Casablanca.

To Thomas Elder

SIR Paris June 26. 1786.

In the short time which I had the pleasure of being with you here, I forgot to ask the favor of you to take charge of some books for my nephew Peter Carr who is at Williamsburg. They are some which I desired Mr. Stockdale in Piccadilly opposite Burlington house to send to him the last year; but when I was in London he had not yet done it. I write the catalogue of them below and the dates of the orders. Mr. Stockdale will be so good as to pay all charges of package, portage and freight &c. in London. If you pass up James river, you can put them ashore at Burwell's ferry or Jamestown by means of the ferry boat, writing a line to my nephew who is at Mr. Maury's grammar school in Wmsburg; or if you cannot put them ashore, Dr. Currie will receive them at Richmond, and reimburse any expences they may occasion. Your favour herein will much oblige Sir your most obedt. humble servt, TH: JEFFERSON

1785. July 28. Herodotus Gr. Lat. 9. vols. 12 mo. } the editions of Foulis in Glasgow.
Thucydides Gr. Lat. 8 vols. 12 mo.
Xenoph. Hellenica. Gr. Lat. 4 v. 12 mo.
Cyri. expeditio Gr. Lat. 4. v. 12 mo.
Memorab. Socrates, Gr. 12 mo.
Ciceronis opera. 20. vols. in 16s.
Martin's Philosophical grammar. 8 vo.
Martin's Philosophia Britannica. 3. vols. 8 vo.
Sep. 26. Baretti's Spanish & English dictionary

PrC (MHi).

[72]

From David Rittenhouse

Dear Sir   Philadelphia June 26th. 1786

Your favour of Jan. 25th. I received some time ago, and likewise all the Nautical Almanacs you mention, except that for 1790. As a small return for all your favours, I beg you will accept a Copy of the second Volume of the Transactions of our Philosophical Society, which I have sent to Mr. Adams at London requesting him to transmit it to you. Shou'd you be furnished with the publication before this arrives it will serve to oblige some friend.—I wou'd willingly have sent you my observations on the Western Country, but have not had time to Copy it. I am at present engaged in preparing for a Tour to the Northern Boundary of this State which will require my Attention for the remainder of this Season. Indeed I have for some years past been such a Slave to public Business that I have had very few leisure hours more than must necessarily be indulged to a crazy Constitution, and on this principle I account for the little figure I make in the Transactions. I have nevertheless laboured with all my might in the few intervals I cou'd snatch for the purpose to Improve Astronomical Timekeepers, and hope ere long to give you a good account of my success.

The threatned War between the Emperor and the Dutch appears to be happily blown over. Does not this affair, and several others of a similar kind which have happened within a few years past, afford some grounds to hope that Mankind are grown wiser, and that Wars in future will be unknown. I most devoutly wish for the Honour of Human Nature, nay for that of divine Providence, this happy Period may soon arrive. Give my best respects to Miss Patty. I hope She will improve in every thing Amiable, and do honour to the countries which have given her Birth and Education.

I am, Dr. Sir, with the most affectionate regard your very Humble Servant,   DAVD. RITTENHOUSE

RC (DLC). Noted in SJL as received 21 Aug. 1786.

To Du Portail and Others

Sir   Paris June 27. 1786.

I had the honor of informing you some time ago that I had written to the Board of treasury on the subject of the arrearages of interest due to the foreign officers, and urging the necessity of paying them. I now inclose the extract of a letter which I have just received from them, and by which you will perceive that their funds were not in a condition for making that paiment in the moment of receiving my letter, but that they would be attentive to make it in the first moment it should be in their power. There is still a second letter of mine on the way to them, on the same subject, which will again press for exertions in this business, which however I am satisfied they will not fail to do their utmost in. It will give me real pleasure to inform you of effectual provision for this purpose in the first moment possible being with sentiments of esteem and respect Sir Your most obedient & most humble servant, TH: JEFFERSON

PrC (DLC); at foot of text: "Du Portail M. de la Rouerie Comte de Cambrai Colo. Gouvion." These names are also listed in SJL under this date with the following notation: "same form." Enclosure: Extract from letter of Commissioners of the Treasury to TJ, 9 May 1786.

I HAD THE HONOR OF INFORMING YOU SOME TIME AGO: See TJ to Cambray, 20 Jan. 1786 and TJ to La Rouerie, 26 Jan. 1786.

To John Paul Jones

SIR Paris June 27. 1786.

Since I had the honour of seeing you the other evening a letter from the board of treasury is come to hand,[1] instructing me to receive the monies which you have collected here for the prizes, with an order justifying your paiment of them to me. There is a paragraph in the letter which looks as if they meant I should settle with you your proportion of these monies. It is not quite explicit, and moreover I feel myself so incompetent to it that I shall refer it back to them. I will therefore beg the favour of you to say what you would think a reasonable allowance for your trouble in this business, which I will represent to the Commissioners, and that you will consider the order I have received as operating on the balance only which I shall desire Mr. Grand to receive; I have the honor to be with very sincere esteem and respect, Sir, your most obedient and most humble servant, TH: JEFFERSON

PrC (DLC). [1] TJ inadvertently wrote "hands."

From John Paradise, with Enclosure

Dear Sir   June 27th. 1786

I am so ill that I am obliged to have recourse to the assistance of my Daughter to thank you for your very obliging letter, and to inform you that the plan concerted between your excellency, Dr. Bancroft, and myself about my going to Virginia, is totally altered. I am to go, but not till next Spring, and then it will be with my wife and children. How this alteration came to pass you will learn from Dr. Bancroft, who is thoroughly acquainted with every circumstance concerning this affair, and whose kindness to me and mine must ever be remembered by us with the deepest sense of gratitude. I have executed your commission with regard to the harpsicord, and I hope soon to be able to give you some account of the modern greek language. In the mean while I have the honour to be with the greatest respect Your excellency's most obliged humble servant,
                                                        John Paradise

ENCLOSURE
Charles Burney to John Paradise

Dear Sir   June 19th. 1786.

I beg you will acquaint Mr. Jefferson that he flatters me very much by his remembrance, and that I shall have great pleasure in executing the commission with Kirkman. I went to him immediately on receiving your Note, and have bespoke a double Harpsichord of him, which is to fulfill, as nearly as possible, every Idea and wish contained in Mr. Jefferson's Letter. The Machine for the Swell, resembling a Venetian-blind, will be applied; the Stops and machinery for moving them and the Swell will be perfectly simple and unembarrassing to the Tuner; the Lid of the Case will be of *solid* Mahogany; but the sides cannot, if the wood is beautiful, as the knots and irregularities in the grain, by expanding and contracting different ways, will prevent the Instrument from ever remaining long in tune; but Kirkman will answer for securing the side from all effects of weather and climate, by making them of well-seasoned Oak, and veneering them with thick, fine, long Mahogany, in one Pannel. By this means he has sent Harpsichords to every part of the Globe where the English have any commerce, and never has heard of the wood-work giving way. The Front will be solid, and of the most beautiful wood in his possession. The Instrument will be ready to deliver in about 6 weeks; and the price, without Walker's machine, and exclusive of packing-case and Leather-cover, will be 66 Guineas. The Cover and packing-case will amount to about 2 Gs. and ½. A Desk to put up in the Harpsichord will not be charged separately, but be reckoned a part of the Instrument.

With respect to Walker's Celestine stop, I find that Kirkman is a

28 JUNE 1786

great enemy to it. He says that the Resin, used on the silk thread that produces the tone, not only clogs the wheels and occasions it to be frequently out of order; but in a short time, adheres so much to the strings as to destroy the tone of the instrument. This may be partly true and partly rival's prejudice. I am not sufficiently acquainted with this stop to determine these points; but I will talk with Walker on the subject, and try to discover whether he admits the difficulties or can explain them off; and whether he has found out any such method of giving motion to his *Bow-string* as that suggested by Mr. Jefferson.

Ma Lettre tire en longueur; but being unfortunately out of the reach of a conversation with your very intelligent correspondent, *vivâ voce*, I was ambitious to let him know that I entered heartily into the business in question, and give him all the information in my power on each particular article of his commission.

I am, dear Sir, with very sincere regard, & most respectful Compliments to Mr. Jefferson, your obedt. and most humble Servant,

CHAS. BURNEY

RC (DLC); in the hand of Lucy, the eldest daughter, and signed by Paradise; endorsed. Noted in SJL as received 5 July 1786, "by Dr. Bancroft."

Though Burney's letter (DLC) was not mentioned as an enclosure, it was evidently transmitted by Bancroft (see TJ to Burney and also to Paradise, both dated 10 July 1786). MR. WALKER: Adam Walker, who patented the "celestina" in 1772 (see *Grove's Dictionary of Music and Musicians* under "Sostinente Pianoforte"; see also Walker to TJ, 20 Aug. 1787).

From Taher Fennish to the American Commissioners

[28 June 1786]

Grace to God who is the Sole unity Whose Kingdom is the only Existing one.

To their Excellencies John Adams and Thomas Jefferson Esqrs. This is to Acquaint you that I am ordered by the Emperor my Master (whom God preserve) to Acknowledge the receipt of your Letter, Signed London and Paris on the first and Eleventh of October 1785, which has been delivered into his own hands by the Honble. Thomas Barclay Esqr. who Came to this Court, in order to negotiate an Amicable Peace between My Master (whom God preserve) And all his Dominions, and those of the united States of America. This Matter has been happily concluded to the satisfaction of all Parties, The Contents of this Treaty, you will learn from your Envoy the Said Thomas Barclay to whom His Imperial [Majesty][1] has delivered it, together with a Letter for the United States.

I have likewise His Imperial Majesty's order to assure you of his

28 JUNE 1786

entire Aprobation of the Conduct of your Envoy, who has behaved himself with integrity and honor Since his arrival in our Country Appearing to be a Person of good understanding, And therefore His Imperial Majesty has been Graciously pleased to give him two honorable favourable and unparalleled audiences, Signifying his Majesty's perfect Satisfaction at his conduct.

As I am Charged with the affairs of your Country at this Court, I Can assure you that I will do all That lies in my power to promote the friendly intercourse that is So happily begun, And of the Assistance I have already given in your affairs, your Envoy will Acquaint you, and Concluding I do Sincerely remain, Morocco the first day of the blessed Month of Ramadan 1200. Sign'd the Servt of the King my Master Whom God Preserve,

TAHER BEN ABDELHACK FENNISH

RC (MHi: AMT); translation in clerk's hand, with signatory line, the name of Taher Fennish, and the attestation signed by Nuñez in the latter's hand; at head of text: "Translation of the letter from his Excellency Sidi Hadg Taher Ben Abdelhack Fennish to their Excellencies John Adams & Thomas Jefferson Esqrs."; at foot of text: "I do hereby certify that the above is a true Translation from the Arabic Language of the Annexed Letter, Morocco the 16th. July 1786. Isaac Cardoza Nunez." Tr (DNA: PCC, No. 91, I); in Short's hand; with caption and attestation as in the foregoing, together with "(Copy) No. 6." (see Barclay to Commissioners, 2 Oct. 1786). PrC of foregoing (DLC). RC (MHi: AMT); in Arabic; the editors are indebted to Prof. T. Cuyler Young, Department of Oriental Languages and Literatures, Princeton University, for identifying this as the RC.

[1] The clerk omitted "Majesty"; Short's Tr, which was copied from this translation, makes the same omission.

From Francis Hopkinson

MY DEAR SIR   Philada. June 28th. 1786

I would fain deserve the good Character you were pleased to give me in one of your late Letters—that of a punctual Correspondent. Our Volume of Philosophical Transactions made it's first Appearance in public yesterday and to Day I shall put one on the way at last to your Hand.

I have lately been in New Jersey and saw a Bird which a Country man had shot, and is I think a Curiosity. This Bird is of the Heron Species, and is certainly a Stranger amongst us. It has three long and very white Feathers growing out of the Top of it's Head but these are so formed as to look more like pieces Bobbin, or silk Cord, than Feathers, and very beautiful. But what I thought most remarkable, is, that to the middle Claw of each

[77]

foot he had annexed a perfect *small-tooth'd Comb*, with which I suppose he comb'd his elegant Plumage. I have got one of the Feet, and two of the Feathers of the Crest, which, when a better Opportunity offers, I will send to you for Monsr. Buffon, with such a description of the Bird, as I can give. After all, it is more than probable that this may be no Curiosity to so great a natural Historian as Mr. Buffon. I have not yet got Mr. Colden's Pamphlet on Gravitation but, as I told you before, am sure you can get his work more at large at Mr. Dodsley's Shop Pal-mal London who published it in the year 1752 or 54, I have forgot which.

I have been this week past closely engaged in Church Business. We are making some Reform in our Discipline and Worship, for which, the Revolution has afforded a very favourable Opportunity. Clerical and Lay Deputies from New York, New Jersey, Pennsylvania, Delaware, Maryland, Virginia and South Carolina attended for this Purpose. This is the Second Convention that has assembled on this Business A new Book of Common Prayer has been published for Consideration. I will send you one together with our Journals when a better Opportunity offers than the present. Our Organization will be complete when we shall have obtained the *divine Succession* in Consecration from the Bishops of England, who seem well disposed to communicate it as we have a Letter to that Purpose signed by 19 Bishops of England. The Convention made me their Secretary, so that I have had Business enough on hand.

I sent you a Description of my *Spring-Block* for assisting a Vessel in sailing, but have not yet made the Experiment. My spare Time and Attention is at present much engaged in a Project to make the Harmonica or musical Glasses to be played with Kees, like an Organ. I am now far forward in this Scheme and have little Doubt of Success. It has in vain been attempted in France and England. It may therefore seem too adventurous in me to undertake it, but the Door of Experiment is open; in Case of Disappointment the Projector is the only Sufferer. Adieu! & believe me ever Your affectionate Friend & humble Servant,

FRAS. HOPKINSON

RC (DLC). PrC (Edward Hopkinson, Jr., Philadelphia, 1947). Noted in SJL as received 23 Aug. 1786.

Hopkinson was at least correct in thinking that the mysterious bird was OF THE HERON SPECIES; it was the Night Heron (*Nyctiardea*) and like other herons possessed a pectinate middle claw; see Hopkinson to TJ, 8 Nov. 1786.

From John Adams

Dear Sir London June 29. 1786

Inclosed is a Letter to Mr. Lamb and another to Mr. Randall: if you approve them please to Sign them and send them on. Why those Gentlemen have lingered in Spain I know not. I have long expected to hear of their Arrival in Paris. Possibly they wait for orders. If so, the inclosed will answer the End.

The Chev. De Pinto told me on Wednesday that he had orders from his Court to inform me, that the Queen had sent a Squadron to cruise in the Mouth of the Streights, and had given them orders to protect all Vessels belonging to the United States of America, against the Algerines equally with Vessels of her own Subjects. With much Affection yours, John Adams

RC (DLC). FC (MHi: AMT); in Smith's hand. Noted in SJL as received 5 July 1786, "by Dr. Bancroft." Enclosures: (1) Letter to P. R. Randall (DLC); in the hand of John Adams, signed and dated by Adams 29 June 1786, authorizing Randall to go directly to America with Lamb if he prefers, but adding: "our Desire is rather that you should come first to Paris and London that we may avail ourselves of an opportunity of conversing with you more particularly upon the affairs of the United States with those of Affrica." This letter was not sent by TJ because Randall arrived in Paris on 2 July (see TJ to Adams, 9 July 1786). (2) Letter to John Lamb, q.v. under 7 July 1786, the date TJ signed and sent it on to Lamb.

The gesture of the Queen of Portugal in offering protection to vessels flying the American flag was reported to Congress by Adams in a letter of 27 June. When this was read in Congress, the Rhode Island delegates reported to the governor of their state that it was "An instance of Magnanimity . . . worthy of imitation, and demands our grateful acknowledgm'ts, as we have nothing better to offer her in payment" (Adams to Congress, 27 June 1786, DNA: PCC, No. 84, VI; Rhode Island Delegates to John Collins, 28 Sep. 1786, Burnett, *Letters of Members*, VIII, No. 506.

From Robert Murdoch

Sir Dunkerque 29 June 1786

The following narrative of a distressd Subject of the United States of America, was lately communicated to me by Jonathan Jackson Esqr. of Boston, at whose instance I take the Liberty to lay the matter before your Excellency, after having visited the Unhappy Person and heard a repetition of the circumstances from his own mouth.

Alexander Grosse, born at Cape-Cod in the Bay of Boston, and bred a seaman, embarkd at Cowhasset in 1777 on board a Vessell bound to Iza-Cape, under the Command of his cousin Captain Samuel Grosse, was captured by the Brittish and carried into

29 JUNE 1786

Liverpool, where he was pressd and put on board a Tender, conveyd to Plymouth and orderd on board the Duke, man of war of 90 Guns, where he remaind four years, 'till at last he got an Oppertunity to Escape, deserting that Service and his Pay for the above period. He fled to Southampton and there got on board the Sloop Charlotte bound to Corke, where he hoped to procure a passage out to America; but this Sloop chanced to be taken on the voyage, by the Comptesse d'Avaux privateer, Captain Cary of Boulogne sur Mer, who ransomd said Sloop for Two hundred Guineas the 29th february 1782 and took poor Grosse as Hostage, who made no objections thereto, thinking it a favourable circumstance and not doubting but he wou'd soon be set at Liberty, when instead of returning to England, his intention was to embrace the first oppertunity of proceeding direct to America from Some French-port. The prospect was flattering but alas! the Event proved the Source of his greater missfortune. He was landed here by Captn. Cary and lodged in our Prison, where unfortunately he has remaind ever since, destitute of Friends or Money, and without any other hopes of relief but through your [Excellencys clemency and powerfull][1] interference, for the proprietor of the Sloop Charlotte a Mr. Lockyer of Southampton, unable to do honour to his affairs or discharge the Ransom-bill, has fled from his Creditors and his Country and all their researches to find him out hitherto have proved in vain. Consequently the wretched Prisoner has no prospect of relief from that quarter, and his own familly I understand are not in a Situation to advance him a Shilling. The Captors allow him for Subsistance Twenty four sols per day, but its to be feard their benevolence may grow cool, on observeing themselves the dupe of Lockyer, and induce them to confine their bounty to the Prison allowance, Shoud he remain much longer a burthen to them.

[I shall not trouble your Excellency with any further comment on this Subject. Your Publick as well as private Character is so amiable that I am persuaded it is enough on my part, to lay the perticulars of his hapless Situation before you, to induce your Excellency to interfere in his behalf.][1] I have the honour to subscribe myself with the most profound respect your Excellency's most obedient verry Humble Servant,   Robt. Murdoch

RC (DLC). Noted in SJL as received 2 July 1786. See Adams to TJ, 26 June 1786.

[1] Brackets in MS: probably inserted by TJ to indicate omissions to be made in copying the letter for transmittal to the French authorities.

[80]

From Pierre Castaing

A l'hotel d angleterre pres Jacobins

Monsieur A Bordeaux ce 30 Juin 1786.

Lorsque Je partis de L'amerique, Il y a pres de deux ans, Monsieur le general Gates M'honnora d'une lettre pour votre Excellence, laquelle J'ai differé de vous faire parvenir par le desir que J'avois d'avoir l'honneur de vous la presenter Moy-Même; Mes esperances Sont vaines, et Je suis a present sur mon depart pour Saint Domingue.

Monsieur Du Portail, et Monsieur le Chr. de la Luzerne, M'honnorent de leur recommandations pour ce pays la; Puis-je me flatter que votre Excellence voudra bien m'honnorer de la Sienne; Les faveurs que J'ai reçue de Messieurs les ameriquains lorsque J'avois l'honneur de les Servir Me Soumettent deja a de grandes Obligations, et Je M'estime heureux d'avoir de mon Mieux donné des preuves de Mon Zel dans une révolution aussi mémorable que Celle de l'independence de L'Amerique.

Je ne Cesse de faire des Voeux pour leur prosperité et de desirer les Occasions de leur prouver ma reconnoissance.

J'ay l'honneur d'etre avec le plus profond Respect Monsieur Votre Tres humble et Tres obeissant Serviteur,   Castaing

RC (DLC); endorsed. Noted in SJL as received 8 July 1786. Enclosure: Horatio Gates to TJ, 16 Aug. 1784, q.v., second letter under that date.

From St. Victour & Bettinger

Monsieur   rue des Blancs manteaux No. 44. Paris le 30 Juin 1786.

Nous avons l'honneur de vous remettre cyjoint copie des deux certificats expediés par le Capitaine d'artillerie en residence a la Manufacture de Tulle, le premier en datte du 29 may dernier, pour 33 caisses contenant 990. fusils a 27^{tt} 10s piece, prix du Roy, compris les frais d'emballages et de

transport, montant a	27225.^{tt}
le Second en datte du 13 de ce mois pour	
17 caisses contenant 510 fusils au même prix	14025.
Ensemble	41250.^{tt}

Nous y joignons copie de la lettre de M. John Bondfield de Bordeaux, en datte du 20 de ce mois par laquelle conformement aux Instructions que vous avez bien voulu lui adresser, nous accuse la reception de l'expédition de 33 caisses contenant 990 fusils

JUNE 1786

mentionnés dans le certificat en datte du 29 may et Nous accuse par postcriptum la reception de la lettre de Voiture et du certificat en datte du 13 Juin pour 17 caisses contenant 510 fusils.

Nous avons enfin l'honneur de Vous remettre copie des deux conventions double faittes avec M. Thos. Barclay les 5. et 14 Janvier dernier.

Nous vous prions, Monsieur, de vouloir bien Nous indiquer a qui nous devons nous adresser pour le payement de ces deux livraisons. Nous remettrons a la personne qui en sera chargée, Si vous l'approuvés ainsi, avec la quittance de M. Bettinger autorisé a cet effet, les originaux des deux certificats qui prouvent l'expedition et des lettres de M. John Bonfield qui constatent la reception.

Nous avons l'honneur d'etre très respectueusement Monsieur Vos très humbles et très obeissans serviteurs, ST. VICTOUR
BETTINGER

RC (Vi); endorsed by TJ: "Arms Bettinger & St. Victor 41,250ᵗᵗ." Enclosures (Vi): Certificates of inspection of arms, signed by Dubois d'Escordal, dated 29 May and 13 June 1786, and endorsed by TJ; letter of John Bondfield to Bettinger, 20 June 1786, acknowledging the receipt of cases 1 to 33, containing arms for Virginia, with a postscript acknowledging the receipt of cases 34 to 50. Copies of the two agreements made by Thomas Barclay on behalf of the state of Virginia with St. Victour & Bettinger were transmitted by Barclay to Patrick Henry on 16 Jan. 1786 and are to be found in Vi.

From Samuel Chase

Annapolis, June [1786]. Introduces Richard Ridgely, of Baltimore, who wishes to procure a loan of £7,000 sterling in France; TJ may be questioned about Ridgely in connection with the negotiation; Ridgely has real estate in Baltimore worth five times the amount of the loan he is seeking; the funds are to be used in improving that property, thus increasing its value. "To secure the payment and to give Recovery of Money lent by foreigners to Citizens of this State on Mortgage-lands, it is provided by law that on the actual loan of Money, on Interest not exceeding Six per Cent, any Mortgage made for the Security of payment is valid in law, and if the Money borrowed is not paid, agreeably to Contract, the Court of Chancery is directed to foreclose the Mortgage of his Equity of Redemption, and to order a Sale to discharge the Mortgage, and if any Deficiency the same later paid by the Mortgagor."

RC (DLC); MS mutilated, part of the date being torn away. Not recorded in SJL but endorsed by TJ with his left hand and, therefore, probably received in the latter part of October or early in November 1786 (see TJ to Maria Cosway, 5 Oct. 1786).

[82]

From Ralph Izard

Dear Sir   Charleston 1st. July 1786.

I received a few Weeks ago, in the Country, your favour of so old a date as 26th. Septr., and am glad to find that the Commercial Papers which I sent you, had at last got to your hands. England is not disposed to enter into a Treaty with us upon principles of equity, and is determined to exclude us from the West India Trade as much as possible. This is a very troublesome piece of business, and the Adventurers, particularly those from the Northern States, have sustained, and will continue to sustain considerable losses. The conduct of France with regard to her Islands, unfortunately encourages the British Government to persist. This appears to me impolitic in many points, but particularly so in one. There are many well wishers to Great Britain in every State on this Continent, at all times ready to trump up imaginary causes of dissatisfaction, and to draw invidious comparisons between the past, and present times. The present state of the Commerce of America with the West Indies, certainly can not be added to the Catalogue of advantages which she has derived from the Revolution, and I should imagine that France would find her account in not letting America feel even that disadvantage. I have considered attentively, and I think impartially what has been said on the propriety of the Mother Country's enjoying the monopoly of the Commerce of her Colonies, as a compensation to protection, and I think the arguments plausible, but by no means conclusive. If France were to remove all restraints on this subject, G. Britain would unquestionably be compelled to follow her example.—Our Western Posts are not to be delivered up, and the reason given is, because in some of the States the Legislatures have thrown obstructions in the way of the recovery of Debts. I am sorry that such a pretext has been given; but before the passing of the Laws complain'd of, G. Britain did not shew any disposition to give up the Posts. Certain it is that if the Courts of Law were to be open'd for the recovery of Debts generally, and without restriction and property made liable to be seized, and sold by the Sheriff for Cash, many persons would be ruined, who have property to four times the value of their Debts. The British Merchants and the Tories, who lost little, or nothing by the War, are in possession of the greatest part of the Specie in the Country and would enrich themselves at the expence of the real Friends of America, who risked everything for her defence. This would doubtless be an evil of considerable magnitude; but in my opinion it would be better that the Treaty should be fulfilled, and the Law take it's course, than that a reproach should be cast on so many States in the Union. It is to be lamented that at the negociation of the general Treaty of Peace it had not been provided that no *greater* obstruction should be thrown in the way of the recovery of British Debts *than those of the Citizens of America*, instead of the words which now stand in the Treaty. The reasonableness of such a Proposition must have been obvious to the British Negociators, and could not have been opposed. I have great doubts with regard to the utility of the Posts in question. If the Spaniards had had the Country ceded to them, which those Posts are intended to command, I believe it would be no disadvantage to the United States. But I am sorry that the British should keep possession of them, and that we should be in so weak a condition as to be unable to compel them to do us justice. Mr. Barclay, I am told, has been sent by Congress to Algiers. I shall be glad to hear of the success of his Mission. It is really shocking that the Powers of Europe, who have the means in their hands of crushing those Miscreants, should suffer them to lay the whole maritime World under contribution. I have given directions to the Printer of the Columbian Herald to send you his Paper by every opportunity, to the care of Mr. Jay, as you desire. M. de Chateaufort the French Consul for this Department, who goes to France by way of England, will take charge of this Packet, and forward it with his Ambassador's Dispatches to Versailles. Whenever our Laws are printed they shall be forwarded to you. As I have been writing to a Politician, I have touched upon Politics; but I find myself more satisfactorily employed when engaged in anything that relates to Agriculture. It is greatly to be lamented that in our Climate the Country should be unhealthy at this Season, and that we should be obliged to come to Town, and continue there the greatest part of the Summer, and Autumn. I procured last Spring a few Lentils from a French Vessel, and I think they will answer very well, not only here, but in Virginia, and will be a valuable assistant in every respect to Indian Corn. The French call it Nentille: I do not know why for they spell it Lentille. My second Daughter Charlotte is lately married to Mr. Smith, a very sensible, and worthy young Gentleman of this place and my eldest a few days ago made me a Grandfather, by bringing a little Girl into the World. Mrs. Izard joins me in offering our Compliments to Miss Jefferson, and I have the honour to be with great regard Dr. Sr. Your most obt. Servant, RA. IZARD.

RC (DLC). Noted in SJL as received 3 Oct. 1786.

From Lefévre, Roussac & Cie.

MONSIEUR						Lisbonne ce 1r. Juillet 1786

Le Sr. Jn. Bapte. Pecquet qui se trouve un peu indisposé vient de nous remettre la lettre dont vous l'avés honoré le 5. May qui a rapport à une commission de vin dont vous le chargeâtes pendant son Séjour à Paris; il attendoit vos nouveaux ordres pour sçavoir la quantité que vous en désiriés de chaque qualité. Afin de ne pas en retarder d'avantage l'expedition, nous allons vous en envoyer un essay de chaque Sorte par un bâtiment françois qui partira incessamment pour Roüen où nous l'adresserons à Mrs. Achard freres et Compe. avec ordre de vous le faire parvenir; et ils en prendront comme nous le remboursement de leurs débours sur vous même, Monsieur, comme il est d'usage.

Le Sr. Pecquet croyant s'appercevoir que la lettre qu'il eut l'honneur de vous écrire le 9. Xbre. dernier ne vous étoit pas parvenue, vous en trouverés ci-inclus la copie ainsi que celle qui y etoit jointe pour M. Francklin. Ce brave homme qui est penetré de gratitude des bontés que le Congrés a bien voulu avoir pour lui à vôtre recommandation, espere qu'il sera encore assés heureux d'être utile à vos nationaux.

Nous sommes charmés, Monsieur, que cette occasion nous procure celle de vous être de quelqu'utilité. Comme notre maison ne vous est pas connue, vous pouvés, si vous le jugés à propos, en prendre information des principales maisons de Banque de Paris notamment de celle de M. Grand.

Nous avons L'honneur d'être avec des Sentimens distingués, Monsieur, Vos très humbles et très obéissans Serviteurs,

LE FÉVRE, ROUSSAC & CE.

RC (MHi); endorsed. Noted in SJL as received 20 July 1786. Enclosures (DLC): Dupl of Pecquet to TJ, 9 Dec. 1785, q.v.; Dupl of Pecquet to Benjamin Franklin, 9 Dec. 1785. See also TJ to Pecquet, 5 May 1786.

From Du Portail

Paris, 2 July 1786. Acknowledges TJ's letter of 27 June and its enclosure. He feels that the Commissioners of the Treasury have not paid sufficient attention to the fact that his own representations revolve principally on a failure to receive the arrearages of 1784; however, he will await with patience the time when the state of her finances will permit the United States to meet her engagements. He hopes this will be soon, less from personal interest than from the "plaisir infini que me fera tout Ce qui annoncera la prosperite d'un pays que j'aimeray toute ma vie et Ce qui Contribuera a luy donner en europe la Consideration dont il doit jouir."

RC (MoSHi). Noted in SJL as received 4 July 1786.

From John Adams

DEAR SIR   London July 3. 1786.

Yours of the 23 of June is come to hand, with a Copy of Mr. Lambs of 6 June[1] from Aranjuez.

There is no Intelligence from America of Armies marching to take the Posts from the English. The News was made as I Suppose against the opening of the Three Per Cents, and it had the intended Effect to beat down the Stocks a little.

Altho the Posts are important, the war with the Turks is more So. I lay down a few Simple Propositions.

1. We may at this Time, have a Peace with them, in Spight of all the Intrigues of the English or others to prevent it, for a Sum of Money.

2. We never Shall have Peace, though France, Spain, England and Holland Should use all their Influence in our favour without a Sum of Money.

3. That neither the Benevolence of France nor the Malevolence of England will be ever able materially to diminish or Increase the Sum.

4. The longer the Negotiation is delayed, the larger will be the Demand.

From these Premisses I conclude it to be wisest for Us to negotiate and pay the necessary Sum, without Loss of Time. Now I desire you and our noble Friend the Marquis to give me your opinion of these four Propositions. Which of them do you deny? or doubt? If you admit them all do you admit the Conclusion? Perhaps you will Say, fight them, though it Should cost Us a great Sum to carry on the war, and although at the End of it we should have more Money to pay as presents. If this is your Sentiment, and you can persuade the Southern States into it, I dare answer for it that all from Pensylvania inclusively northward, would not object. It would be a good occasion to begin a Navy.

At present we are Sacrificing a Million annually to Save one Gift of two hundred Thousand Pounds. This is not good Œconomy. We might at this hour have two hundred ships in the Mediterranean, whose Freight alone would be worth two hundred Thousand Pounds, besides its Influence upon the Price of our Produce. Our Farmers and Planters will find the Price of their Articles Sink very low indeed, if this Peace is not made. The Policy of Christendom has made Cowards of all their Sailors before the Standard of Mahomet. It would be heroical and glorious in Us, to restore Courage to ours. I doubt not we could accomplish it, if we should set about it in earnest. But the Difficulty of bringing our People to agree upon it, has ever discouraged me.

You have Seen Mr. Randall before this no doubt, if he is not fallen Sick on the Road.

This Letter is intended to go by Mr. Fox. The Chev. De Pinto's Courier unfortunately missed a Packet, which delayed him and consequently the Treaty a Month. The Queen his Mistress, as I wrote you a few Days Since, has given orders to her Squadron cruising in the Streights to protect all Vessels belonging to the United States. This is noble and Deserves Thanks.

Accept the Sincerest Assurances of Esteem and Affection from dear Sir your most obedient   JOHN ADAMS

Mrs. Adams having read this letter finds it deficient in not having added her best respects to Mr. Jefferson and sincere thanks for his petitions.[2]

RC (DLC); addressed in hand of W. S. Smith: "His Excellency Thos. Jefferson"; endorsed. Noted in SJL as received 10 July 1786 "by Mr. Fox." FC (MHi: AMT); in Smith's hand.

[1] Lamb's letter was actually dated 5 June 1786.
[2] Postscript is in Abigail Adams' hand.

From Henry Champion

SIR   L'Orient 3rd July 1786

The post before last I had the honor to receive a Letter from your Excellency address'd to Mr. Loreilhe. That Gentleman is now in Bordeaux, and being encharg'd with his and Mr. Barclay's affairs, I have done the needfull with the half dozen Copies you inclos'd. I have had it translated and each American here shall have one. I also translated the new agreement made the 4th. May and forwarded many Copies to America, as well made it public here. I have the honor to be Your Excellency's Most obedient Most humble Servt.,   HENRY CHAMPION

RC (MHi); endorsed by TJ: "L'Oreilhe." Noted in SJL as received 7 July 1786. TJ's LETTER ... TO MR. LOREILHE was the circular of 31 May 1786.

Court of Naples to De Pio

Napoli 4 Luglio 1786

Non vi è dubbio che il progetto di Mr. Jefferson sarebbe l'unico per mettere gli Algerini alla ragione, ma per eseguirlo vi si richiederebbe il concorso e il consenso di altre Potenze. Il Re Nostro Signore non sarebbe lontano dal far causa comune, quando vi fossero degli altri. Per ora però non può entrare in veruno impegno, giacchè trovasi di avere spedito un negoziatore per trattare la Pace con quella Reggenza.

RC (MoSHi); without signature or name of addressee; endorsed in TJ's hand: "letter to Monsr. del Pio from his court."
Translation: There is no doubt that Mr. Jefferson's project would be the only one to bring the Algerians to terms, but in order to put it into effect there would be required the cooperation and consent of other Powers. Our Lord the King would not be far from joining in the common cause, provided there were others. For the present, however, he cannot assume any obligation since he happens to have sent a negotiator to discuss Peace with that Regency. For IL PROGETTO DI MR. JEFFERSON—his proposals for concerted operations among European powers at war with the Barbary states—see under 1 Dec. 1786. No letter from TJ transmitting the proposals to Del Pio has been found, and none from Del Pio to TJ enclosing the present communication; these preliminary negotiations, therefore, must have been carried on informally and in person.

From John Paul Jones

Sir   Paris, July 4th, 1786.

I have the honor to enclose for your examination the documents of my proceedings with those of this government, in the settlement I have obtained of the prize-money belonging to the officers and crews of the squadron I commanded in the late war in Europe, at the expense of His Most Christian Majesty, but under the flag of the United States. By these documents I presume you will be convinced that, from a want of sufficient knowledge of circumstances, it would have been very difficult, if not impossible, for any other man, (except Dr. Franklin, who never would act in it,) to have gone through this business. Mr. Barclay made no progress in it, though he was charged with it by Congress two years and a half before I undertook it. I could not obtain an allowance in favor of the captors for the service of their prizes as prison-ships in the Texel, nor for the damage done to the Serapis at L'Orient, previous to her sale; but I have taken care of the honor of the American flag. The American captors pay nothing towards the support of the Royal Hospital of Invalids; and His Majesty has generously renounced, in favor of the captors, the proportion of the sale of the merchant prizes, which, by the laws of the flag of America, he might have retained. I ask the favor of you to return me those papers, with your observations.

I enclose, also, a note of my expenses since I arrived in Europe on this business. When I am honored with your sentiments on this subject, I will prepare copies of the within papers, and, I flatter myself, comply to your satisfaction with the order you have received from the Board of Treasury. I have the honor, &c.

MS not found. Text printed from Sherburne, *John Paul Jones*, p. 276-7. The enclosed papers, which were returned to Jones in TJ's letter of 5 July, cannot be precisely identified, but see Jones to TJ, 7 July 1786 and enclosure.

From Maupin

Monsieur

rue du pont aux choux, petit hotel de poitou a paris le 4 juillet 1786.

Il s'en faut bien que les hommes les plus renommés pour leur Science et leur Sagesse, soient toujours Sages: il me seroit facile de vous en citer de grands exemples, mais je me borne a faire part a Votre Excellence, et dans sa personne, aux Etats unis, de mes découvertes sur la vigne, les vins et les terres, c'est a dire sur les objets qui importent le plus a l'aisance des peuples et des nations.

J'aurois pu, Monsieur, ajouter mes principaux ecrits aux deux demi feuilles que j'ai l'honneur de vous adresser, mais j'ai pensé que je devois attendre que Votre Excellence m'eut fait l'honneur de me marquer Ses Sentimens, aux offres que je lui fais de lui donner sur toutes les parties que j'ai publiées, tous les eclaircissemens qu'elle croira necessaires, et qui dépendront de moi.

Tout ce que je demande a Votre Excellence, c'est qu'elle veuille bien lire les deux écrits que j'ai l'honneur de lui communiquer, et qu'au lieu de Se borner a ne voir que par les yeux des autres, elle veuille bien voir aussi par les Siens et examiner par elle même.

Cette pratique, Monsieur, pour etre la plus equitable, la plus judicieuse, et la plus prudente, peut bien n'etre pas la plus commune, mais elle est la seule par la quelle on puisse éviter d'etre trompé, et Votre Excellence est surement trop Sage pour la dédaigner dans une affaire ou il s'agit des interets les plus chers et les plus precieux des peuples et des Etats unis de l'Amerique.

J'ai l'honneur d'etre avec un profond respect Monsieur Votre tres humble et tres obeissant Serviteur, Maupin

RC (DLC); endorsed. Noted in SJL as received 4 July 1786. Enclosures not identified, but evidently three of Maupin's pamphlets on viticulture and viniculture were sent with this letter (see Maupin to TJ, 20 July 1786); these probably included *Nouvelle méthode non encore publiée pour planter et cultiver la vigne à beaucoup moins de frais . . . joints à la Théorie ou leçon sur le temps le plus convenable de couper la vendange* (Paris, 1782); *L'Art de la vigne, contenant une nouvelle méthode économique de cultiver la vigne, avec les expériences qui en ont été faites* (Paris, 1779); and *Supplément nécessaire à la science des académies . . . ou nouvelle demonstration . . . de mes principales découvertes concernant la vigne, les vins, les cidres, les terres, les grains, les bois* (Paris, 1784; see Sowerby, Nos. 785, 818, and 1216). Inquiries of the Bibliothèque Nationale and of particular authorities on viniculture have not elicited any facts concerning Maupin's full name or dates of birth and death.

From Madame de Doradour

ce 5 juillet [1786?]

Vous devés être bien etonné, Monsieur, d'avoir été sy longtems sans avoir de mes nouvelles, mais il y a douzes jours que la fievre ne me quite pas; elle est un peu moins forte depuis deux. Je suis d'une foiblesse ettonante, je prend des bains, cela ne fortifie pas. Je n'ai pas pus me rendre encore ches moi; je suis malade ches une de mes parentes. J'espere cependant être en etat d'aller m'etablir dans mon chateau à la fin de cette semaine. Vous aurrés, Monsieur, la bonté d'y adresser votre premire lettre (par issoir en auvergnne, au chateau de sarlant). J'ai reçu celle que vous m'avés fait l'honneur de m'ecrire. Je ne peut pas vous en adresser une pour mon mari ainsi que vous avés bien voullue le permettre, etant trop foible pour ecrire longtems. Milles empressés compliments à Melle. votre fille, que je vous suplie, Monsieur, d'embrasser de ma part, et de daignner agreer l'assurance de l'attachement avec lequel j'ai l'honneur d'être, Monsieur, Votre tres humble et tres obeissante servante, DUBOURG DORADOUR

Permettes que tout vos Messieurs trouvent ici mes tres humble compliments.

RC (DLC); endorsed. The year has been conjectured from internal evidence—Mme. de Doradour was re-established at the address here given when she wrote TJ on 4 Dec. 1786, q.v.

CELLE QUE VOUS . . . M'ECRIRE: No letters to Mme. de Doradour have been found and there are none recorded in SJL for this period, except that of 11 Feb. 1787; the letters acknowledged here and elsewhere were probably brief covering notes transmitting letters from her husband, who was in Virginia at this time, and therefore no copies were kept or records made of them.

To Ebenezer Gearey, Jr.

SIR Paris July 5. 1786

I wrote you on the 13th. of June acknoleging the receipt of your letters previous to that. I made application to the Minister to prevent any measures being carried into effect against yourself or Mr. Arnold by surprise, and to obtain your liberty if your confinement was in the line of the police only. Orders were immediately given for your discharge, which I hope have come to hand before now and had their effect. Yesterday being the first day on which audiences could be obtained at Versailles since the King's departure for Cherbourg, it was the first opportunity I had of knowing that your discharge had been obtained, and that the orders were issued. I am Sir your very humble servt., TH: JEFFERSON

PrC (DLC).

To John Paul Jones

SIR Paris July 5. 1786.

I have now the honour to return you the papers you inclosed for my perusal. I am thoroughly satisfied that no person could so well have settled those matters as yourself. Your particular knowlege of all circumstances relative to them gave you the advantages which no other person possessed. With respect to the allowance to be made you for your trouble, I took the liberty of mentioning to you that I thought it could not be settled but by the board of treasury and that even they perhaps may be obliged to recur to Congress for instructions. I have therefore only to repeat what I before had the honor of proposing to you, that, retaining the sum which you think should be allowed you, you will be so good as to consider the order of the Treasury as operating on the balance only, which whenever you shall be so good as to name to me, I will take measures for it's being deposited to answer the intentions of the treasury. I have the honor to be with much respect and esteem Sir Your most obedt. humble servt., TH: JEFFERSON

PrC (DLC). The papers enclosed in Jones to TJ, 4 July 1786, and returned with the present letter have not been identified; see Jones to TJ, 7 July 1786.

From William Stephens Smith

Dear Sir   London July 5th. 1786 No. 16. Wimpole street

I have received yours of the 16th. Ulto. When I sent the press I gave the Gentleman who carried it a Letter for you of the 21st. of May which you do not acknowledge the receipt of, or at least but one of that date. It contained the ammount of what I gave for the press, which was 5 Guineas and 5/ for the Box = £5.10. The press shall be sent agreable to your request. I am called off, and have only time to assure you of my most Perfect respect and to enclose a Letter or rather a press Copy of one received last night from Mr. Barcklay. Yours sincerely,   W. S. Smith

RC (MHi); endorsed. Noted in SJL as received 10 July 1786 "by Mr. Fox." Enclosure: Tr of Thomas Barclay to the American Commissioners, 10 June 1786.

From Duperré Delisle and St. John de Crèvecoeur

Monsieur   Caën ce 7 juillet 1786

Permetez-moi, sous les auspices de Mr. St. Jean de Crevecoeur Consul pour le Roi à Neuyork, d'implorer vos bons offices auprès du Congrès pour faire rendre justice à de malheureux cultivateurs des environs de Caën qui sont propriétaires d'un grand nombre d'éffets de papier-monnoie des differens états unis. Ils s'apellent Pelcerf, et ces éffets leur sont échus de la succession de francois Pelcerf mort en 1779 à Accomak en Virginie où il éxercoit la profession de chirurgien. Tout ce qu'il avoit, ayant été vendu, a produit, frais deduits, cinq mille trois cent quatre vingt quatorze dollars en papier monnoie dont le Capitaine Barboutin, chargé de l'éxécution testamentaire du défunt, s'est saisi et qu'il a remis aux héritiers Pelcerf à son retour en france. Cet objet est absolument nul pour eux, si vous ne daignez pas vous interesser à Leur sort: Les papiers publics annoncent que les Etats unis ont pris des mesures pour satisfaire aux engagemens qu'ils ont contractés envers les differentes nations en y repandant leur papier. Mais ces mesures ne sont presque pas connües dans la Capitale du Royaume et sont absolument ignorées dans le fond de nos Provinces. J'ai espéré que par esprit de justice autant que par honneteté vous vous porteriez à me donner des réenseignemens à ce sujet, afin que je puisse les communiquer aux malheureux qui m'ont réclamé et aux quels je dois aide et protection, comme étant mes justiciables. Mr. de

Crevecoeur connoit leur triste scituation et comme mon compatriote, mon parent et mon ami, il veut bien joindre ses instances aux miennes. Je vous prie d'être bien persuadé de ma reconnoisance ainsi que des sentimens respectueux avec les quels j'ai l'honneur d'être Monsieur Votre très humble et Obeisst. serviteur,

DUPERRÉ DELISLE
Lt. gl. au bailliage de Caën

I Shou'd Take it as a Singular Favor, if your Excellency wou'd Take Mr. de Lisle's request into particular Consideration; it has not been in my power to give him any Satisfactory answer to the many questions he has ask'd me; not being Just Now Sufficiently acquainted with the State of things in America. This Gentelman is a Kinsman of mine Much respected by and well known to the Comte and the Comtesse d'houdetot. I gladly Embrace This opportunity of recalling myself to, and presenting your Excellency with the assurances of the unfeigned Respect and Esteem wherewith I have the Honor of Subscribing myself, Your Excellency's Most Obedient Humble Servant,

ST. JOHN DE CREVECŒUR

RC (DLC); the note from Crèvecoeur is written on verso of second leaf. Noted in SJL as received 10 July 1786. See TJ to Crèvecoeur, 11 July 1786. In ViWC there is a "Translation of Part of Mr. Delisle's Letter"; this is in Crèvecoeur's hand and evidently was addressed to him by Delisle on or shortly before 7 July 1786. It reads in part: "I beg you'd confer with Mr. Jefferson on the means to ascertain the Value of the Continental Money now in the hands of the Pelcerf's heirs"; this extract is endorsed "De Lisle" by TJ in his left hand, a fact which suggests that Crèvecoeur must have given it to TJ in the autumn of 1786.

From John Paul Jones, with Enclosure

SIR *Paris, July 7th*, 1786.

I have the honor to enclose and submit to your consideration the account I have stated of the prize money in my hands, with sundry papers that regard the charges. I cannot bring myself to lessen the dividend of the American captors by making any charge either for my time or trouble. I lament that it has not yet been in my power to procure for them advantages as solid and extensive as the merit of their services. I would not have undertaken this business from any views of private emolument that could possibly have resulted from it to myself, even supposing I had recovered or should recover a sum more considerable than the penalty of my

[93]

7 JULY 1786

bond. But I was anxious to force some ill-natured persons to acknowledge that, if they did not tell a wilful falsehood, they were mistaken when they asserted "that I had commanded a squadron of privateers!" And, the war being over, I made it my first care to shew the brave instruments of my success that their rights are as dear to me as my own.

It will, I believe, be proper for me to make oath before you to the amount charged for my ordinary expenses. I flatter myself that you will find no objection to the account as I have stated it, and that you are of opinion, that after this settlement has been made between us, my bond ought to stand cancelled, as far as regards my transactions with the Court of France. Should any part of the prize money remain in the treasury, without being claimed, after sufficient time shall be elapsed, I beg leave to submit to you—to the treasury—and to Congress, whether I have not merited by my conduct since I returned to Europe that such remainder should be disposed of in my favor? I have the honor to be with great esteem, &c.

ENCLOSURE

Amount of Prize-Money belonging to the American Part of the Crew of the Bon-[Homme]-Richard (and to some few Foreigners, whose Names and qualities are inserted in the [roll], with the] Amount also of the Prize-Money belonging to the Crew of the Alliance; [received at] L'Orient, by order of the Marechal de Castries, in Bills on Paris £181,039-1s-10d

From which deduct Vizt.

[Nett] amount of my ordinary expences since I arrived in Europe to [settle] the Prize-Money belonging to the Citizens and Subjects of America, who served on board the Squadron I commanded, under the Flag of the United-States at the expence of his most Christian Majesty [stated] to his Excellency Thos. Jefferson Esqr. the 4th. of this Month	£47,972-11s-0d
[Paid] the draft of Mr. le Jeune for the amount of Prize-Money due to Jacque Tual, Pilot of the Alliance	670-13-6
Amount of Prize-Money Paid Mr. de Blondel, Lieutenant of Marines of the Pallas, as stated on the Roll of the Bon-Homme-Richard	283-0-0

[94]

Advances made to sundry Persons, which stand at my Credit on [the roll] of the Bon-Homme-Richard	264-9-6
[Advances] made to sundry Persons belonging to the Bon-Homme-Richard; [these] advances do not stand at my Credit in the Roll settled at L'Orient by Mr. le Jeune, because the Commissrs. had neglected to send him [the origin]al Roll from the Bureau at Versailles; but that Commis[sary has] rectified that ommission by his Certificates dated Septr. 5th. and Feb. 22d. 1786	6,385-0-0
[My share] by the Roll, as Captain of the Bon-Homme-Richard	13,201-5-6
	68,866-19-6[1]
	£112,172- 2-4

Paris July 7th. 1786 (Signed) JPAUL JONES

MS not located. Text printed from Sherburne, *John Paul Jones*, p. 277-8. Enclosure (missing); printed from a slightly mutilated Tr (DLC: John Paul Jones Papers); in Jones' hand; at head of text: "No. 13"; at foot of text: "[. . .] the Kingdom of France to wit, The within named John Paul Jones made Oath before me on the holy Evangelists that his ordinary expences since his Arrival in Europe for the purpose of receiving the Prize-Money within stated have amounted to forty seven thousand nine hundred and seventy two livres eleven sous tournois. Given under my Hand this fifth day of August 1786. Th: Jefferson." The accompanying "sundry papers" have not been identified.

[1] The itemized figures actually total 68,776-19-6 livres tournois.

To John Lamb

SIR Paris July 7. 1786.

Since writing my letter of the 20th instant,[1] in which I mentioned to you the joint desire of Mr. Adams and myself that you should repair to Congress for the purpose of giving them what information you could, the inclosed letter came to me from Mr. Adams. As it was drawn by him to be signed by us both and forwarded to you, I have signed it and inclose it herewith. I should have thought this unnecessary, but that my first letter did not leave you as much at liberty as this will to go directly to New York by sea or to come by the way of Marseilles and Paris. If the latter should not occasion more delay than I suppose it will, it would be preferable, because

[95]

it is probable the information you can give us may be applied usefully by us in the execution of the commands of Congress. But if this route should occasion a considerable delay it would be better to take such other as shall lose least time. I am Sir Your very humble servant, TH: JEFFERSON

PrC (DLC). Enclosure: Commissioners to Lamb, following. The entries in SJL for this and the joint letter to Lamb are bracketed and "Mr. Grand" written after the bracket.

[1] An error for "ultimo."

American Commissioners to John Lamb

SIR

The Importance of Peace with the Algerines, and the other Inhabitants of the Coast of Barbary, to the United States, renders it necessary that every information which can be obtained, should be laid before Congress.

And as the demands for the Redemption of Captives, as well as the amount of Customary Presents, are so much more considerable, than seem to have been expected in America, it appears to us necessary that you should return, without loss of Time to New York, there to give an account to Congress of all the particulars which have come to your knowledge as well as of your own proceedings, and of the Monies which have been paid on account of the United States, in consequence of your draughts upon their minister in London.

From Congress when you arrive there you will receive orders for your future Government and in the meantime we have no further occasion for your Services in Europe.

If you know of a Certain Passage immediately from any port in Spain, we advise you to avail yourself of it; if not, we think it most adviseable for you to come to Paris, and from thence, after having consulted with Mr. Jefferson, to repair to L'Orient, and embark for New York, in the first Packett. As the Instructions we send to Mr. Randal, are to come on to Paris in his way to America, unless he should choose to accompany you from some port in Spain, we desire you to furnish him with money for his Expences to Paris, and London out of the Cash already in your Hands, and we recommend to him as well as to you all reasonable Attention to Economy.

We are Sir your most Obedn. Humble Servts.,
London June 29. 1786   JOHN ADAMS
Paris July 7. 1786.   TH: JEFFERSON

RC (MdAN); in the hand of W. S. Smith, signed and dated by John Adams, 29 June 1786 and by TJ, 7 July 1786; endorsed in an unidentified hand: "Ministrs. Orders for Mr Lambs return." Tr (DLC); in the hand of William Short, including Adams' name and his date of signing; signed and dated by TJ. This letter, sent to TJ in Adams' letter of 29 June, was forwarded to Lamb in TJ's letter of 7 July.

From John Ledyard

SIR   St Germain en Laye July 7th 86

It is with great defference that I write you a letter of this kind; and yet was you a king or the minister of a king I should not have wrote it had the access been the same.

Attraction appears to be the first natural cause of motion in all bodies. I suppose the whole system of modern natural philosophy rests upon it whenever it respects *motion*. This being the case that particular motion which respects magnetism becomes a part of this universal cause. As motion is as universal as existance so it is as various as universal. To assign reasons therefore for the motion of a part and not the whole is partial.

If the Sun is the center of attractive motion why is it not also the center of that motion we observe in the magnetic needle. If it is, it immediately follows that as the central cause, it is the greatest cause. If it is the greatest cause in what manner as such does it operate on the magnetic needle to produce that motion which we call the *variation* of the needle.

If the Sun has an effect upon the motion of the magnetic needle, those motions can be made a matter of calculation and reduceable to rule.

I only offer one reason why I can suppose the Sun to operate on the motion of the magnetic needle, which is that the greatest variation of the needle seems to be when at the greatest distance from the Sun and that variation an inclination to the Sun.

This Idea of the sun having the particular influence just mentioned struck me as new, rational and worthy communicating to you. If it should appear so to you I shall be exceedingly honoured.

The letter left for me at your address was from a Gentleman at

8 JULY 1786

Edinburgh concerning my affair with the Marquis of Buckingham from whom I expect some intelligence in about a week.

In returning from Paris as I was walking on the skirt of a wood by the side of the high road about ten o clock I heard a horse stumble and fall and a Person give one groan. I sprang into the road to see what was the matter and found a Man down under his horse and both so entangled together that neither could rise. In making a suden strong effort to disengage the Man I so much strained my loins that I have been ever since Confined to my room—but am better. The Man was much hurt.

I have the honor to be Sr. Your much obliged most respectfull & most humble servt., J Ledyard

RC (DLC); endorsed. Noted in SJL as received 7 July 1786.

From Abbé Gibelin

Chez M. L'Evêque duc de Laon
grand aumonier de la Reine
rüe du fauxbourg St. honoré
Paris 8e juillet 1786.

Etant chargé, Monsieur, de la procuration de M. le Cher. de Fleury, colonel du regiment de Pondichery, mon ami, qui a servi longtems en amerique, j'ai envoyé plusieurs fois depuis six mois chés M. Grand, banquier, pour toucher les arérages de deux Contracts constitués au profit de cet officier par Les états-unis. Mais on m'a répondu constamment qu'on n'avait encore reçu aucun ordre de la tresorerie pour payer Ces arérages. Je suis d'autant plus surpris de ce retard que l'an passé je touchai la même somme presque à L'échéance.

Permettés moi, Monsieur, de m'adresser à vous pour apprendre les raisons de Ces longueurs qui me mettent dans le plus grand embarras par rapport aux engagemens que M. de fleury a pris en partant pour L'Inde dans la Confiance qu'il etait que les arérages de ses contracts seraient payés exactement.

J'ose me flatter que vous voudrés bien me donner quelques éclaircissemens sur Cet objet et je vous prie d'agréer l'assurance des Sentimens respectueux avec lesquels j'ai L'honneur d'être Monsieur Votre très humble et très obéissant Serviteur,

L'Abbé Gibelin

RC (DLC); endorsed. Noted in SJL as received 8 July 1786.

[98]

To John Jay

Sir Paris July 8. 1786.

My letters to you by the last French packet were dated May 12. 22, 23. 27. and I sent by the way of London one dated May 31. Since this I have been honoured with yours of May 5. The letter therein inclosed for Mr. Dumas has been duly forwarded; and the report on the subject of the Consular convention I delivered to the Count de Vergennes the first levee day after the return of the king, who was gone to Cherburg at the time of my receiving it. Mr. Randall being so far on his return, and meaning to go by the way of London, where his stay will be short, he will be the bearer of this letter, with which I have an opportunity of inclosing the last letters I have received from Mr. Barclay and Mr. Lamb. Mr. Barclay left Cadiz soon after the date of his letter. I wrote to Mr. Lambe on the 20th. of June, with the concurrence of Mr. Adams, to repair to Congress with all possible dispatch, recommending but not enjoining his coming by the way of Marseilles and Paris, supposing it possible that the information he might communicate, might be usefully applied by Mr. Adams and myself in the execution of the commands of Congress. I afterwards wrote him another letter desiring expressly that if this route was likely to retard much his attendance on Congress, he would take such other as should be shortest.

At the desire of Monsieur Houdon I have the honour to inclose to you his propositions for making the equestrian statue of General Washington.

In the Autumn of the last year I received letters from an American master of a ship of the name of Asquith informing me that he had had a most disastrous passage across the Atlantic, that they had put into Brest when in such distress that they were obliged to make the first port possible, that they had been immediately seised by the officers of the Farmers general, their vessel and her lading seised, and that themselves were then in jail suffering from every want. Letters by every post gave me to beleive their distress was very real. As all their cash was soon exhausted, and the winter setting in very severely, I desired a merchant in Brest to furnish them a livre a day a peice. It was some time before I could be ascertained of the nature of the proceedings against them. It proved at length to be a prosecution for endeavoring to introduce tobacco in contraband. I was induced to order this allowance from evidence that the men, six in number, must inevitably perish if left to the pittance allowed by the Farmers general to their prisoners, and from a hope that the matter would soon be decided. I was led on by this delusive hope from week to week and month to month, and it proved to be ten months before they were discharged. I applied early to Count de Vergennes, and was informed by him that the matter being in a regular course of law, there could be no interference, and that if the sentence should be against them, I might expect a remission of so much of it as should depend on the king. They were condemned to forfeit their vessel and cargo, to a fine, and to the gallies. The fine and condemnation to the gallies were remitted immediately by the king, but the forfeiture of vessel and cargo being for the benefit of the farmers he could not remit that. They were also to pay the expenses of their prosecution and to remain in jail till they did it. So that upon the whole I was obliged to advance for them 2620^{tt} 2s being somewhat upward of 100 guineas; for which I informed Asquith from the beginning he must consider himself as answerable to the United States. I accordingly inclose the account shewing the purposes for which the money was paid, and his own original acknowlegement that it was for his use. I own I am incertain whether I have done right in this; but I am persuaded some of them would have perished without this advance. I therefore thought it one of those cases where citizens being under unexpected calamity have a right to call for the patronage of the public servants. All the disinterested testimony I have ever been able to get has been in favor of the innocence of these men. Count de Vergennes however believed them guilty; and I was assured the depositions regularly taken were much against them. I inclose herewith the state of their case as it appeared to me in the beginning, and as I communicated it by letter to the minister.

Having been lately desired by the Swedish Ambassador here to state to him what I thought the best measure for rendering the island of Saint Bartholomew useful to the commerce of Sweden and the United States, I did it in a letter of which I inclose a copy. My view in doing it is that if any further or better measure should occur to Congress, on it's being communicated to me, I can still suggest it to the Ambassador, probably before any final decision.

It being material that the reduction of the duties on Whale oil, which would expire with the close of this year, should be revived in time for the whale men to take measures in consequence, we have applied for a continuance of the reduction, and even for an abolition of all duties. The Committee, of the creation of which

8 JULY 1786

I informed you in my letter of May 27, and of which the M. de la fayette is a member, were in favor of the abolition. But there is little prospect, perhaps none at all, of obtaining a confirmation of their sentence. I have no doubt of a continuance of the abatement of the duties on the footing stated in that letter. The term of three years will probably be adopted. The gazettes of Leyden and of France from the former to the present date, accompany this. I have the honour to be with sentiments of the most perfect esteem & respect Sir, your most obedient humble servant,

TH: JEFFERSON

RC (DNA: PCC, No. 98, 1). PrC (DLC). Tr (DNA: PCC, No. 107). Enclosures: (1) Barclay to Commissioners, 23 May 1786. (2) Lamb to TJ, 20 May 1786. (3) Houdon's proposals for making a bronze equestrian statue of George Washington (Tr, in hand of Short, of the French text, DNA: PCC, No. 87, 1; PrC of Short's Tr is in DLC: TJ Papers, 22: 3768-72; translation by John Pintard is in DNA: PCC, No. 87, 1; clerk's copy of both English and French texts is in DNA: PCC, No. 107); Chinard, *Houdon in America*, p. 15-20, prints both Houdon's proposals and an accompanying memorandum giving prices and artists' names of a number of bronze statues executed in Europe; these are printed from the originals in Houdon's hand, of which a French and English text exists in DLC: TJ Papers, 53: 8987-8990, 8992, but Chinard does not discuss the relationship of the proposals transmitted to Jay in the present letter and another set of proposals existing in Houdon's hand in an English text only and found in DLC: TJ Papers, 53: 8991. In this second set of proposals, printed at the end of July 1789, Houdon offers to make the bronze equestrian statue for 1,000,000 livres, the work to be completed in eight years, whereas the proposals enclosed by TJ to Jay submitted terms of 600,000 livres and ten years; see notes to the "second proposition" for other variations in phraseology; also Hart and Biddle, *Houdon*, p. 195-6. (4) John Mehegen to TJ, 7 Oct. 1785. (5) Extract of Borgnis Desbordes, Frères to TJ, 4 Nov. 1785. (6) TJ to Vergennes, 14 Nov. 1785, and enclosures. (7) Account of disbursements of Diot & Co., enclosed in Borgnis Desbordes, Frères to TJ, 12 June 1786. (8) TJ to Stael de Holstein, 12 June 1786.

To William H. Sargeant

SIR   Paris July 8. 1786.

I have been honoured with your favor of June 15. inclosing a letter to young Mr. Bannister, which I have forwarded to him at Bourdeaux where he is at present. My last letter from him is dated June 5. He said his health was then incertain, sometimes tolerably well, at others less so. I wrote his father on the 6th. of May last, and shall take care to inform him as often as I can of the state of his son's health.—I inclose you a copy of Mr. Morris's agreement with the farmer's general on the subject of tobacco; being that to which the order of the king and council refers. It could not be printed in time to send out with the copies of the order, whence

[101]

8 JULY 1786

it may not have happened to come to your hands. I thank you kindly for your offer of bearing my letters to my friends in Virginia. I am unfortunately so engaged at this moment as to be unable to avail myself of it. Indeed it is not long since I have written to many of them. To such as enquire for me I will thank you to present my affectionate regard, which be pleased to accept of yourself also from Sir Your most obedient humble servt.,   TH: JEFFERSON

PrC (DLC). At foot of text TJ wrote "Constable," and so endorsed PrC on verso. But the first was written in his left hand and therefore not before Oct. (see TJ to Maria Cosway, 5 Oct. 1786, note). Entry in SJL under this date contains no record of a letter to Constable, but there is one for a letter to Sargeant, sent "by Mr. Randall," who was going to London. Enclosure: Printed copy of Robert Morris' contract with the farmers-general (see enclosure to TJ to Jay, 27 May 1786).

From Charles Thomson

DEAR SIR   New York July 8. 1786

I have just received by the way of Baltimore your letter of the 22 April with the new invented lamp, for which I return you my most hearty thanks. I conclude you were disappointed in sending the one you mentioned in a former letter by Col. Senf, as he never called on me. The one you have now sent is an elegant piece of furniture, if it were not otherwise valuable on account of its usefulness. I am informed this kind of lamps is coming into use in Philadelphia and made there. I wish I could send you any thing from this country worth your acceptance. But arts here are yet in their infancy; and though Philadelphia begins to imitate yet has she not arrived to the perfection of inventing. I have heard much of those mills near London, which are worked by steam, but cannot learn whether the steam is applied as an immediate agent for turning the wheels or raising water for that purpose. I am informed that there is a man in South-Carolina who has invented a machine to raise an immense quantity of water in a short space of time, by which it is said he can flood rice grounds, or draw off the water from drowned lands with great ease and little expence. I have not met with any person who could give me an Account of the principles on which it is constructed, how it is worked or what may be the probable expence. The inventor of the steam boat, which is to go against the stream has applied to several legislatures, which have passed laws giving him for a number of years the exclusive privilege of constructing those boats, but I have not heard that any are yet built and in use.

[102]

8 JULY 1786

During the course of last week we have had here for several evenings a display of Northern lights. The wind had blown for some days from south west and the weather was warm and dry. As my house nearly fronts the S.S.W. and has a large opening back, I had a full and beautiful view of the lights from the windows of my back parlour, which is raised one story from the ground, the opposite houses only intercepting about four or five degrees from the horizon. As I viewed them on friday evening the 30 June there appeared just over the tops of the houses a white luminous cloud extending in a horizontal position from NE to N.W. From this cloud, at different places darted up successive streams of light tapering to points, some of them to the heighth of 50 degrees. The stars were bright and the north pole clearly discernable among the streamers, so that by it I could judge of their heighth. Some times the white cloud appeared in places a little darkened before the stream ascended, in which cases I observed the ascending stream was tinged with red and continued to have a redish hue. Having a lofty steeple in view to guide my eye and direct my judgment I observed two or three of the streamers which rose in the North east and were of this hue, moving with a slow but regular progressive motion towards the North, still continuing perpendicular and very high. From one of them I thought I saw a flash of lightening; but not seeing it repeated I concluded I was mistaken. The light was so great as to cast a shadow from my body and from my hand against a wall. On the following evening viz. Saturday July 1. we had nearly the same appearance but not in so great a degree. These you will observe are only common phenomena, which philosophers have endeavoured to account for on various principles and about which I should not have troubled you but for a phenomenon which appeared on Saturday night. This was a luminous Belt, or stream of light forming a great and regular bow from east to west. At what time it made its first appearance or how it was first formed, whether instantaneously or by degrees, I cannot say as I did not see its first formation. My attention was called to it about half after 10 o clock. It was then quite compleat, and seemed to form an Arch passing through the zenith from horizon to horizon. As I viewed it to the west, it seemed to rise from behind the opposite houses like a stream of pale white light about a yard broad, spreading as it advanced to the zenith to two or three times that breadth. Viewed to the East, it had the same appearance down to the horizon where its breadth appeared the same as just over the tops of the houses to the west. I watched it for half an hour during which time it continued invariably the same. At length to the east I saw it drawing to a point at the horizon and gradually abating in light for four or five degrees upwards. After it seemed to have vanished to that heighth or rather more, it darted down at short intervals from the luminous part a pointed quivering stream. Soon after the light began to abate through the whole circle. I did not continue to watch it till it wholly disappeared as I was indisposed and afraid of catching cold; but I am told it lasted till about half past eleven. I have conversed with a person who saw it at a place about 30 miles north from this City. There it had the same appearance and seemed to pass through the zenith. I have written to Philadelphia to know whether it was seen there, but have not yet receivd an answer. The day following was very hot. Monday morning was overcast, but sultry. About 9 o clock the Sun broke out and it seemed as if we should have a very hot day; but about noon there arose a dark smoky vapour which covered the whole heavens, sometimes so thick as quite to hide the sun sometimes only obscuring it so as to make it appear like a great ball of fire or a dark red full moon. This smoky vapour last the whole day and in the evening there was a smell very much like that from burning green brush wood. Next day the Vapour continued but in a much less degree. Since that we have had two thunder gusts which have cleared the air and the northern lights have disappeared. I mention the circumstances before and after the phenomenon only to point out to you the state of the atmosphere.

I have sometimes had it in contemplation to hazard some thoughts on the general Deluge and endeavour by an hypothesis somewhat different from any I have seen to prove not only the possibility but the probability, I had almost said the certainty of the waters covering the whole Earth. But having lately had a cursory reading of an ingenious piece written on the subject by a Mr. Whitehurst, which I dare say you have seen, I should be glad first to know your Opinion of his hypothesis and reasoning. And while your thoughts are turned to the subject I wish you to consider what would be the probable effects of a sudden change of the position of the earth, say for instance by an alteration of the poles, an inclination of the axis 23½ degrees, or a change in the Annual Orbit. I do not mean by this to divert your attention from political subjects in which I find you have been usefully employed. I have read with much pleasure the two papers containing observations on the transportation of flour, and on Contraband. I am glad they were written and delivered. For though at present the object is not obtained, yet I am confident if the proper moment is watched and improved, the arguments there stated will on some future Occasion have due weight and influence. Mrs. T. desires to be remembered to you and to your Daughter. I am with unfeigned affection & esteem Dear Sir Your obedient humble Servt, CHAS THOMSON

RC (DLC: TJ Papers). FC (DLC: Thomson Papers); varies slightly in spelling and punctuation. Noted in SJL as received 22 Aug. 1786.

For TJ's opinion on MR. WHITEHURST . . . HIS HYPOTHESIS AND REASONING, see TJ to Thomson, 17 Dec.

1786. The TWO PAPERS CONTAINING OBSERVATIONS . . . ON FLOUR, AND ON CONTRABAND were those drawn by TJ and presented to the Portuguese minister, De Pinto, during the negotiations in London in Mch.-Apr. 1786; see under 25 Apr. 1786.

To John Adams

DEAR SIR Paris July 9. 1786.

I wrote you last on the 23d. of May.[1] Your favor of that date did not come to hand till the 19th. of June. In consequence of it I wrote the next day letters to Mr. Lamb and Mr. Randall, copies of which I have now the honour to inclose you. In these you will perceive I had desired Mr. Randall, who was supposed to be at Madrid, to return immediately to Paris and London, and to Mr. Lambe, supposed at Alicant, I recommended the route of Marseilles and Paris, expecting that no direct passage could be had from Alicant to America, and meaning on his arrival here to advise him to proceed by the way of London, that you also might have an opportunity of deriving from him all the information he could give. On the 2d. of July Mr. Randall arrived here and delivered me a letter from Mr. Lambe dated May 20. of which I inclose you a copy, as well as of another of June 5. which had come to hand some time before. Copies of these I have also sent to Mr. Jay. Yours of the 29th. of June by Dr. Bancroft and inclosing a draught of a joint letter to Mr. Lambe, came to hand on the 5th. inst. I immediately signed and forwarded it, as it left him more at liberty as to his route than mine had done. Mr. Randall will deliver you the present and supply the informations heretofore received. I think with you that Congress must begin by getting money. When they have this, it is a matter of calculation whether they will buy a peace, or force one, or do nothing.

I am also to acknolege the receipt of your favors of June 6. 25. and 26. The case of Grosse shall be attended to. I am not certain however whether my appearing in it may not do him harm by giving the captors a hope that our government will redeem their citizen. I have therefore taken measures to find them out and sound them. If nothing can be done privately I will endeavour to interest this government.

Have you no news yet of the treaty with Portugal? Does it hang with that court? My letters from N. York of the 11th. of May inform me that there were then 11. states present and that they should ratify the Prussian treaty immediately. As the time for exchange of ratifications is drawing to a close, tell me what is to be done, and how this exchange is to be made. We may as well have this settled between us before the arrival of the ratification, that no time may be lost after that. I learn through the Marechal de Castries that he has information of New York's having ceded the impost in the form desired by Congress, so as to close this business. Corrections in the acts of Maryland, Pennsylvania, &c. will come of course. We have taken up again the affair of whale oil, that they may know in time in America what is to be done in it. I fear we shall not obtain any further abatement of duties; but the last abatement will be continued for three years. The whole duties paiable here are nearly 102 livres on the English ton, which is an atom more than four guineas according to the present exchange.

The monopoly of the purchase of tobacco for this country which had been obtained by Robert Morris had thrown the commerce of that article into agonies. He had been able to reduce the price in America from 40/ to 22/6 lawful the hundred weight, and all other merchants being deprived of that medium of remittance the commerce between America and this country, so far as it depended on that article, which was very capitally too, was absolutely ceasing. An order has been obtained obliging the farmers general to purchase from such other merchants as shall offer, 15,000 hogsheads of tobacco at 34, 36, and 38 livres the hundred according to the quality, and to grant to the sellers in other respects the same terms as they had granted to Robert Morris. As this agreement with Morris is the basis of this order I send you some copies of it which I will thank you to give to any American (not British) merchants in London who may be in that line. During the year this contract has subsisted, Virginia and Maryland have lost 400,000£ by the reduction of the price of their tobacco.

I am meditating what step to take to provoke a letter from Mrs. Adams, from whom my files inform me I have not received one these hundred years. In the mean time present my affectionate respects to her and be assured of the friendship and esteem with which I have the honour to be Dear Sir Your most obedient and most humble servt., TH: JEFFERSON

RC (MHi: AMT); endorsed, in part: "16 July Ansd." PrC (DLC). Enclosures: (1-2) Tr of TJ to Lamb, and to Randall, both 20 June 1786; (3) Lamb to Commissioners, 20 May 1786; (4) Lamb to TJ, 5 June 1786; (5) printed copies of Morris' contract with the farmers-general (see enclosure to TJ to Jay, 27 May 1786).

[1] TJ's last letter to Adams is dated 23 June; Adams' letter to which he refers is dated 23 May.

From James Currie

DEAR SIR   Richmond July 9th. 1786.

I sit down in the midst of bustle and confusion to acknowledge the honors I have receeived from you by your letters wrote me since the receipt of mine by L. L. Page. [Littlepage] I knew nothing of Mr. Jays affair and his at the time I wrote by him or perhaps my letter would have been couched in a different Style. I think with you entirely on that Subject, and wish LP. prudence and gratitude had predominated over, what I imagine he conceived a proper return for the injury sustained by Mr. Jay's treatment at N. York on his way to France. I thank you for Scheele, &c., &c. Books sent me, tho I have had little time as yet to peruse them; I thank you Sir likewise for your attention to procure me the Encyclopedia on the best terms.

Yours of the 27 Sepr. 85. Jany. 28th. 86 from Paris and that of the 24 March 86 by Dr. Lyons are before me, and permit me if you please to apologise for my not being so pointed in Writing as I could wish, and the honor of your correspondence absolutely demands; and withal my own inclination prompts me to it, as one of the things most desireable of all others to me. In future I'll certainly be more regular if agreeable to you. I have ever remembred you respectfully to the families of Ampthill and Tuckahoe, to whom it gives much pleasure, as well as your other enquiring friends, to hear of your wellfare. Pray how does Miss Jefferson. I hope very well. Several enquiries have been made of me by different people. Miss Juddy Randolph very particularly inquisitive. I expect every thing from her under your Auspices. I wish when she comes here if ever that period arrives she may like us as well as when she left us. I'll be pleased, if you'll tender her my best wishes and most respectfull regards, if you ple[ase.] Dr. Lyons arrived here some time ago. I find him agreeable and well informed, for the time he spent in Europe. Your letter alone would induce me

9 JULY 1786

to show him every attention in my power, tho he has real merit. He advised with me whether he should settle here. Inclination leads him, and he says he wishes not for an immediate run of business, but to settle where he can have new society and ultimately secure business. Therefore he has had my Voice for it, the more the merrier but the fewer the better cheer; his own mer[it,] the Fathers influence, his own connexions and our faundness of novelty will be different sources from which he'll draw business, and debts and per adventure the Primum Mobile (to a young man without fortune) in the End—I mean Money—enough of this. I received A. Stuarts letter and gave it to him. Pray how comes it by the bye they make me pay for all your letters tho franked. If A. Stuart procures the things mentioned my care will not be wanting to forward them, as soon as possible.

As several ships are about sailing for France I believe chartered by Mr. Alexander or others, I sent a Box (from Coll. N. Lewis sent to my care to be forwarded you, containing Nutts leaves Seeds &c. &c. the produce of this country) down the River to Gosport to my friend there Mr. Nickolls, the partner of R. Morris of Philadelphia and B. Harrison Jr. here to wait for this letter to be forwarded you immediately and of which I have no doubt he will do without loss of time. Your Book by Dr. Lyons to me, I regard as a particular favor. I observe London and its people and the whole Empire you respect as rather unfriendly to us. I am perfectly satisfied your observation is a just one. Policy or Interest or something else it is to be hoped, may make them ultimately our firm friends if not for our sakes for their own. I shall say nothing of Congress or their affairs as they are all much better known to you than I am able to inform.—We have at present gloomy prospects for the ensuing year. The greatest fresh in this and other Rivers ever known but in May 1772 has laid waste Crops of all kinds from the Pt of Fork to Ampthill inclusive. D. Ross and Coll. T. M. R., your friends are among the principal sufferers. Corn here now sells at 1 guinea and 30/ ℔ Barrell. There will not be half a Crop of wheat made, even in the high lands with the Rust &c. &c. in it. Tobacco at 1 Pistole ℔ C., our taxes high, Extravagance rather upon the increase.

Mr. Henry is still Governor. His and all the Other officers of Governments Salaries were curtailed Under the Auspices of Thos. Underwood of Goochland and other reformers. Harrison got the Chair last Session after a violent struggle about residence and non residence; last Election the Surry men have left him out, and

9 JULY 1786

the high Sheriff of C City died before the time of Election and Otway Byrd, his Successor being out of the way at the time to enter upon his new Office there was no Election. Of course the assembly must meet before the writ can be Issued which will prevent Col. H. having the Chair should he be sent a delegate, at least I suppose so, tho I know very little of those matters.— Tyler of C. City is made one of the Judges of the admiralty in place of Benjn. Waller deceased. Coll. R. R. [Richard Randolph] of Curles after a tedious Gouty and Bilious disorder yielded to the fate that awaits us all sooner or later (last month). He was very unhappy towards the latter End of his life; his affairs being much embarassed I believe kept his mind constantly anxious and unhappy. Coll. Cary continues to live. I believe unless he kills himself he'll become almost boney throughout before his dissolution. He seems chiefly sinew at present. He is reelected Senator and grows deafer. Maddison is reelected for his County after considerable opposition; at the Instance of Genl. Washington, I have been told, old Geo. Mason comes in and several new Members from whom considerable things are expected in our critical situation. The two Nicholas's, Geo. and Jack are to represent Albemarle next session. Fry was in the last, now left out, as is likewise Col. E. Carter, and Wilson N did not offer, wishing to pay attention to his wife and the culture of Tobacco &c. &c. of a Domestick nature.—I have some reason to think Mr. Henry will not continue to act another year as Governor however this is only surmise. The Canal from W. Ham goes on apace and they have marked out 3 different traces for its coming after passing Belvidere into a Bason which last will probably be marked out in the ground bounded by the lower End of my stable lot Eastward and to the W. by the hill terminating the flat ground lotts near the river on this side, as I write, from my own house and well over a considerable number of low lying lotts, upwards, towards the main street as it is continued, and next the river itself by a Wall built across the Ravine or Gulley above where the Tobacco warehouses stand, very near where Mr. Andw. Ronald lives if you remember it.—This is not certain at present but thought probable by the directors Messrs. E. Rand[olph,] Ross and Harvie. It will depend upon the proprietors of the lotts liberality. As I own some on both sides, this way and next the River, I offer to give up a part as the other will be more valuable; but if they overflow, the whole to be paid its proper value. I hope others will do the same and matters will go on smoothly. It is certainly a great Object with this

9 JULY 1786

Country. Would to God it was Effected speedily. You have a number of shares in the Canal, I forget how many.—Your plan of the Capitol came here some time after the receipt of Your letter to me mentioning it. They seem to think, some of them, it is upon a small scale for the purpose intended, but it is adopted and the larger scale on which we were proceeding laid aside, part of the foundation lifted and yours going on. I wish it may be in forwardness enough before next Session to prevent their putting a Stop to it altogether, at least for the present. Tho it will suit our finances better than the other, being less expensive, yet the great Opposition last session by Innis, Prentis and their adherents below and above to any Capital at all at present, I am afraid will now go down unless it be in such forwardness as to impose Silence on their tongues, Eloquent to a Prodigy on a Theme so interesting, as they say, to their Constituents and the Country at large in its present distressed almost irremediable situation.—We have had another religious Convention here and have chose a Bishop (The Revd. Mr. Griffiths). There is to be this month a general Convention of the Clergy of the U. States in Philadelphia for religious purposes and a Commercial Committee from the United States in Alexandria to propose something proper for Congress to be invested with for the benefit of the Trade in General. The Indians have been troublesome of late on our frontiers. Coll. Wm. Christian about 2 Mos. ago was killed by them. He was in pursuit at the head of a small party. The Indian who killed him lay himself on the ground mortally wounded and had just cunning and strength enough left to draw the trigger of his Gun unperceived by Ch:, then asking him some questions. The Indian did not survive 3 minutes and C[hristian] never reached home. An officer then with him shared the same fate almost at the same instant from another Indian in a similar situation, exactly. There were no other Indians there or near them at the time, known of at least. They are now likewise very troublesome in the Back parts of Georgia which state had some Gunns &c. &c. sent from here tother day for their assistance. The Spaniards tis supposed Connive or indeed abett them in this matter. We Celebrated Independence here tother day by eating an Excellent dinner at Anderson's Tavern and drinking a number of proper toasts. We had the Band of Music, the discharge of Cannon, colors flying, &c. &c., manifesting our joy. Same day superseded Jno. Harvie Esqr. late Mayor, his time being out, of course, and elected for the ensuing Year Wm. Pennock Esqr. an Industrious and flourishing Merchant here. They are all well at Eppington at present. Miss Polly wont leave Mrs. Eppes. All your other friends and relations as far as I recollect are well. I dare say you are tired of my Nonsense. McLurg continues Indolent tho respectable and an agreeable Companion. The Consequences of the late fresh in the beginning of last month has hurt the Air in the Neighbourhood of the River. A good number of Children in and about Town have yielded their liv[es] to its banefull influence. I beg you'll Excuse this miscellaneous Hotch Potch. Yourself are to blame as you encouraged me in it before. Begging and hoping youll do me the honor to write me Often, and every thing you think will be agreeable or usefull to me communicate if you please, and allow me with great sincerity and much truth to subscribe myself Yr Excellency's most Obedient & respectfull H Servt, JAMES CURRIE

RC (DLC); on page three Currie wrote at least one line in the left margin, but only remnants of letters may now be discerned; endorsed. Noted in SJL as received 6 Dec. 1786. Currie's sentences have been punctuated in two or three places for the sake of clarity.

TJ's letter of 24 MARCH 86 BY DR. LYONS has not been found and is not recorded in SJL. He did, however, send letters by Lyons to Randolph and Cary on 7 Feb. 1786. These were letters of introduction, and doubtless the missing one to Currie of 24 Mch. was also. It was probably sent to Lyons in response to the latter's letter of 27 Feb. 1786. Short had already given Lyons a letter of introduction to Currie, dated 1 Feb. 1786, which the latter acknowledged on 9 July, saying of Lyons: "He seems to be an agreeable young man and has been studious while in Philadelphia and in Europe. . . . I shall surely pay him every proper attention in my power in sympathy to Mr. J. and your letters as well as on his own Account." Currie also added: "Mr. Jefferson to whose Excellency I do myself the honor by this Opportunity to write . . . will inform you of any little Domestic Anecdotes worth your knowing that have occurred to me during my writing and to which I refer you. It gives me much pleasure and does me honor, seriously I write it, to receive Mr. Jefferson's letters or you[rs]" (Currie to Short, 9 July 1786; DLC: Short Papers). YOUR BOOK BY DR. LYONS: This presentation copy of *Notes on Virginia* has not been found (Coolie Verner, "Mr. Jefferson Distributes his *Notes*," *Bull., N.Y.P.L.*, Vol. 56 [1952], p. 171).

To James Monroe

DEAR SIR   Paris July 9. 1786.

I wrote you last on the 10th. of May, since which your favor of May 11. has come to hand. The political world enjoys great quiet here. The King of Prussia is still living, but like the snuff of a candle which sometimes seems out, and then blazes up again. Some think that his death will not produce any immediate effect in Europe. His kingdom, like a machine will go for some time with the winding up he has given it. The King's visit to Cherbourg has made a great sensation in England and here. It proves to the world

9 JULY 1786

that it is a serious object to this country, and that the King commits himself for the accomplishment of it. Indeed so many cones have been sunk that no doubt remains of the practicability of it. It will contain, as is said, 80 ships of the line, be one of the best harbours in the world, and by means of two entrances on different sides will admit vessels to come in and go out with every wind. The effect of this in another war with England defies calculation.— Having no news to communicate I will recur to the subjects of your letter of May 11.

With respect to the new states were the question to stand simply in this form, How may the ultramontane territory be disposed of so as to produce the greatest and most immediate benefit to the inhabitants of the maritime states of the union? the plan would be more plausible of laying it off into two or three states only. Even on this view however there would still be something to be said against it which might render it at least doubtful. But it is a question which good faith forbids us to receive into discussion. This requires us to state the question in it's just form, How may the territories of the Union be disposed of so as to produce the greatest degree of happiness to their inhabitants? With respect to the Maritime states nothing, or little remains to be done. With respect then to the Ultramontane states, will their inhabitants be happiest divided into states of 30,000 square miles, not quite as large as Pennsylvania, or into states of 160,000 square miles each, that is to say three times as large as Virginia within the Alleghaney? They will not only be happier in states of a moderate size, but it is the only way in which they can exist as a regular society. Considering the American character in general, that of those people particularly, and the inergetic nature of our governments, a state of such extent as 160,000 square miles would soon crumble into little ones. These are the circumstances which reduce the Indians to such small societies. They would produce an effect on our people similar to this. They would not be broken into such small peices because they are more habituated to subordination, and value more a government of regular law. But you would surely reverse the nature of things in making small states on the ocean and large ones beyond the mountains. If we could in our consciences say that great states beyond the mountains will make the people happiest, we must still ask whether they will be contented to be laid off into large states? They certainly will not; and if they decide to divide themselves we are not able to restrain them. They will end by separating from our confederacy and becoming it's enemies. We had better then look forward and see what will be the probable course of things. This will surely be a division of that country into states of a small, or at most of a moderate size. If we lay them off into such, they will acquiesce, and we shall have the advantage of arranging them so as to produce the best combinations of interest. What Congress has already done in this matter is an argument the more in favour of the revolt of those states against a different arrangement, and of their acquiescence under a continuance of that. Upon this plan we treat them as fellow citizens. They will have a just share in their own government, they will love us, and pride themselves in an union with us. Upon the other we treat them as subjects, we govern them, and not they themselves; they will abhor us as masters, and break off from us in defiance. I confess to you that I can see no other turn that these two plans would take, but I respect your opinion, and your knowlege of the country too much, to be over confident in my own.

I thank you sincerely for your communication that my not having sooner given notice of the arrets relative to fish gave discontent to some persons. These are the most friendly offices you can do me, because they enable me to justify myself if I am right, or correct myself if wrong. If those who thought I might have been remiss would have written to me on the subject, I should have loved them for their candour and thanked them for it; for I have no jealousies nor resentments at things of this kind where I have no reason to beleive they have been excited by a hostile spirit, and I suspect no such spirit in a single member of Congress. You know there were two arrets, the first of Aug. 30. 1784. the 2d. of the 18th. and 25th. of September 1785. As to the first it would have been a sufficient justification of myself to say that it was in the time of my predecessor, nine months before I came into office, and that there was no more reason for my giving information of it when I did come into office than of all the other transactions which preceded that period. But this would seem to lay a blame on Dr. Franklin for not communicating it which I am conscious he did not deserve. This government affects a secrecy in all it's transactions, whatsoever, tho they be of a nature not to admit a perfect secrecy. Their arrets respecting the islands go to those islands and are unpublished and unknown in France except in the bureau where they are formed. That of Aug. 1784. would probably be communicated to the merchants of the seaport towns also. But Paris having no commercial connections with them, if any thing makes

9 JULY 1786

it's way from a seaport town to Paris, it must be by accident. We have indeed agents in these seaports; but they value their offices so little that they do not trouble themselves to inform us of what is passing there. As a proof that these things do not transpire here, nor are easily got at, recollect that Mr. Adams, Doctr. Franklin and myself were all here on the spot together from Aug. 1784. to June 1785., that is to say 10. months, and yet not one of us knew of the Arret of Aug. 1784. On Sep. 18 and 25 1785. the second was passed[1] and here alone I became responsible. I think it was about 6. weeks before I got notice of it, that is in November. On the 20th. of that month writing to Count de Vergennes on another subject I took occasion to remonstrate to him on that. But from early in November when the Fitzhughs went to America, I had never a confidential opportunity of writing to Mr. Jay from hence directly for several months. In a letter of Dec. 14.[2] to Mr. Jay I mentioned to him the want of opportunity to write to him confidentially, which obliged me at that moment to write by post viâ London and on such things only as both post offices were welcome to see. On the 2d. January Mr. Bingham setting out for London, I wrote to Mr. Jay, sending him a copy of my letter to Ct. de Vergennes, and stating something which had passed in conversation on the same subject. I prayed Mr. Bingham to take charge of the letter, and either to send it by a safe hand or carry it himself as circumstances should render most adviseable. I beleive he kept it to carry himself. He did not sail from London till about the 12th. of March, nor arrive in America till the middle of May. Thus you see what causes had prevented a letter which I had written on the 20th. of November from getting to America till the month of May. No wonder then if notice of this arret came first to you by the way of the W. Indies; and in general I am confident that you will receive notice of the regulations of this country respecting their islands by the way of those islands before you will from hence. Nor can this be remedied but by a system of bribery which would end in the corruption of your own ministers, and produce no good adequate to the expence. Be so good as to communicate these circumstances to the persons who you think may have supposed me guilty of remissness on this occasion.

 I will turn to a subject more pleasing to both, and give you my sincere congratulations on your marriage. Your own dispositions and the inherent comforts of that state will ensure you a great addition of happiness. Long may you live to enjoy it, and enjoy it in full measure. The interest I feel in every one connected with you

[114]

will justify my presenting my earliest respects to the lady, and of tendering her the homage of my friendship. I shall be happy at all times to be useful to either of you and to receive your commands. I inclose you the bill of lading of your Encyclopedie. With respect to the remittance for it, of which you make mention, I beg you not to think of it. I know by experience that proceeding to make a settlement in life, a man has need of all his resources; and I should be unhappy were you to lessen them by an attention to this trifle. Let it lie till you have nothing else to do with your money. Adieu my dear Sir and be assured of the esteem with which I am your friend & servt., TH: JEFFERSON

RC (NN). PrC (DLC). Noted in SJL as sent "by Mr. Randall." Enclosure not found.

1 As originally written, this passage read: "In Sep. 1785. the second was published"; TJ then altered this by deletion and interlineation to read as above.
2 An error for Dec. 24.

From Thomas Smith

SIR   Tours July 9th. 86

After having kept your letter for so long a while, I am almost ashamed to send it you; but remaining only a few days in Paris, I had not time to pay my respects to you, as it was my intention to do. I did not send it by the post, as I was in doubt whether or not it was a letter of introduction to your Excellency.

My delay, I trust, has not been a matter of importance. I have the honour to be your very humble Servt., THOMAS SMITH

RC (MHi); endorsed. Noted in SJL as received 14 July 1786. Enclosure: Adams to TJ, 16 May 1786. The author of the present letter is not to be confused with an impostor who employed the same name in appealing to TJ (see his undated petition printed at the end of 1786).

To William Stephens Smith

DEAR SIR   Paris July 9. 1786.

I wrote you last on the 16th. of June. Since that your favors of May 21. 21. and June 12. have come to hand. The accounts of the K. of Prussia are such that we may expect his exit soon. He is like the snuff of a candle; sometimes seeming to be out; then blazing up again for a moment. It is thought that his death will not be followed by any immediate disturbance of the public tranquillity; that his kingdom may be considered as a machine which will go

[115]

of itself a considerable time with the winding up he has given it. Besides this he has for some time employed his successor in his councils, who is endeavoring to possess himself of and to pursue his uncle's plan of policy. The connection which has long subsisted between the Van Staphorsts, the Grands, and this court is known to you. I think it probable that private sollicitations first suggested the late appointment and might be the real efficient cause of it. The ostensible one, and which has some reality too, is the accomodation of the lenders in Holland. It will doubtless facilitate the borrowing money there for this country, and multiply the partisans of the new alliance. The policy of this country is indeed wise. What would have been said a dozen years ago had any one pretended to foretell that in that short space of time France would get Holland, America and even England under her wing?

We have had here some strong altercations between the court and the parliament of Bourdeaux. The latter used a language which a British parliament would not have dared to use. The court was in the wrong and will have the wisdom and moderation to recede. The question is whether lands called Alluvions, on the river Garonne belong to the king or to the proprietors to whose soil they have been added.

I have received by Dr. Bancroft the portable copying press. It is perfectly well made. Be so good as to present my compliments and thanks to Mr. Cavallo for his attention to it. To yourself I suppose you would rather I should present the money. This I will do the moment you will inform me of the sum. In your letter of May 21. you mention that you had paid the maker £5-10. But a former letter gave me reason to believe you had to pay something to another person for a board or the box or something else. I will beg the favor of you at the same time to inform me what a pair of chariot harness will cost in London, plated, not foppish but genteel, and I will add the price, or not add it to the bill I shall send you, according as I shall find it when compared with prices here. Cannot you invent some commissions for me here, by way of reprisal for the vexations I give you? Silk stockings, gillets, &c. for yourself, gewgaws and contrivances for Madame? à propos, All hail, Madame! May your nights and days be many and full of joy! May their fruits be such as to make you feel the sweet union of parent and lover, but not so many as that you may feel their weight! May they be handsome and good as their mother, wise and honest as their father, but more milky!—For your old age I will compose a prayer thirty years hence.

10 JULY 1786

To return to business (for I am never tempted to pray but when a warm feeling for my friends comes athwart my heart) they tell me that they are about altering Dr. Ramsay's book in London in order to accomodate it to the English palate and pride. I hope this will not be done without the consent of the author, and I do not believe that will be obtained. If the booksellers of London are afraid to sell it I think it can be sold here. Even the English themselves will apply for it here. It is very much esteemed by those who have read it. The French translation will be out in a short time. There is no gutting in that. All Europe will read the English transactions in America, as they really happened. To what purpose then hoodwink themselves? Like the foolish Ostrich who when it has hid it's head, thinks it's body cannot be seen. I will beg the favor of you to prevail on Mr. Dilly to send me 50. copies by the Diligence. We shall see by the sale of these what further number we may call for. I will undertake to justify this to the author. They must come unbound. It will be necessary at the same time to put into some of the English papers the following advertisement. 'The bookseller, to whom Dr. Ramsay's history of the revolution of S. Carolina was addressed for sale, having been advised that the executing that commission would expose him to the actions of certain persons whose conduct in America, as therein represented, is not in their favor, the public are hereby notified that they may be furnished with the said work either in the original English, or well translated into French, by writing to Froullé, libraire au quai des Augustins à Paris, and franking their letters. An opportunity of sending it to London occurs every week by the Diligence.' Send me a paper or two with this advertisement in it.

To put an end to your trouble I will wish you a good night. I beg your pardon, I had forgot that you would have it without my wishes: I bid you therefore a simple Adieu, with assurances of my friendship & esteem, TH: JEFFERSON

RC (MHi: Washburn Collection); endorsed, in part: "ansr. 18th." PrC (DLC). Noted in SJL as sent "by Mr. Randall."

To Charles Burney

SIR   Paris July 10. 1786.

I took the liberty, through Mr. Paradise, of asking your advice in the purchase of a harpsichord. He has transmitted me a letter you were pleased to write him on that subject. The readiness with

10 JULY 1786

which you have been so good as to act in this matter excites my warmest gratitude, and I beg you to accept of my thanks for it. The objection made by Kirkman to the resin of Walker's bowstring has some weight but I think by wiping the strings from time to time with a spunge moistened in water or in some other fluid, which will dissolve the resin without attacking the metal of the string, the evil may be relieved. It would remain to use Walker's stop sparingly; but in the movements to which it is adapted I think it's effect too great not to overweigh every objection. That it should be worked however either by a weight or a spring is very desireable. The constant motion of the foot on a treadle diverts the attention and dissipates the delirium both of the player and hearer. Whenever either yourself or Mr. Paradise will be so good as to notify me that the instrument is ready, with information of the cost of that, it's appendages, packages and delivery at the waterside, I will send by return of the post a banker's bill for the money with directions to whom to deliver it. Are organs better made here or in London? I find that tho' it is admitted the London workmen make the best harpsichords and piano-fortes, it is said the best organs are made here. I omitted in London to visit the shop of any organ-maker, but you are so much the better judge, that your decision would be more satisfactory. Indeed if it would not be too great a liberty I would ask the favor of your description of a proper organ for a chamber 24 feet square and 18. feet high, with the name of the best workman in that way in London. I feel all the impropriety of the freedom I am taking, and I throw myself on your goodness to pardon it. The reading your account of the state of music in Europe had prepared me to expect a great deal of pleasure from your acquaintance; and the few moments I was so happy as to pass with you, were a proof that my expectations would have been fully gratified, had not the shortness of time which obliged me to hurry from object to object, deprived me of opportunities of cultivating your acquaintance. I must be contented therefore with offering you my hommage by letter, and assuring you of the esteem and respect with which I have the honour to be Sir Your most obedient & most humble servant,

TH: JEFFERSON

PrC (DLC). Noted in SJL as sent "by Mr. Randall."
HE HAS TRANSMITTED ME A LETTER: See Paradise to TJ, 27 June 1786.

To Abbé Gibelin

Sir   Paris July 10. 1786.

On receiving information from the foreign officers that paiment was not made of their interest for the year 1785. I wrote to the board of treasury at New York. I have the honour to inclose you an extract of a letter I have just received from them, by which you will perceive that their funds were not in a condition for making that paiment in the moment of receiving my letter, but that they would be attentive to make it as soon as it should be in their power. Their orders will come to Mr. Grand, who will take care to give notice to all the persons interested to apply for their monies as soon as he shall be enabled to pay it. I have the honour to be Sir your most obedient & most humble servt.,
                                                  Th: Jefferson

PrC (DLC); at foot of text: "M. l'Abbé Gibelin for M. le Chevr. Fleury." Enclosure: Extract (last paragraph) of Commissioners of the Treasury to TJ, 9 May 1786.

To John Paul Jones

Sir   Paris July 10. 1786.

An opportunity having occurred of writing to America and to England by a person leaving Paris to-day, I have been unable sooner to answer the letter with which you honoured me two days ago. On recurring to the letter of the Board of treasury it becomes more evident to me that it does not empower me to settle the sum to which you are entitled; and that their meaning as to the arrangement they desire me to take with you respected only the sum which they naturally supposed your expences had obliged you to apply out of the whole mass of 181,039^{tt}-1-10 for which their order was. So that the want of power to make any settlement which shall be final, as well as my incompetence to it forbid my doing any thing more than receive the balance to which your own claims do not extend. This seems, by the account which you have been so obliging as to send me, to be 112,172^{tt}-2-4 which I will desire Mr. Grand to recieve whenever you shall be so good as to notify to me your wish to pay it. I have the honour to be with very sincere esteem and respect Sir your most obedient & most humble servant,
                                                  Th: Jefferson

PrC (DLC). The person leaving paris to-day was Randall.

From John Paul Jones

Sir Paris, July 10th, 1786.

After what you mentioned to me before your favor of this date, respecting the imperfect powers you have received from the Board of Treasury, I did not expect you to make a settlement with me that should be final for the prize money I have recovered. But as I have produced, and still offer you proofs to support the charges I have made, I naturally flattered myself and I still hope you will do me the favor to receive and transmit them to Congress with your sentiments. This becomes the more necessary to me at present, because from what Dr. Bancroft tells me of the application to the Court of Denmark, it will be necessary for me to continue in Europe for some time longer, and to take your advice on some farther steps to obtain an answer from that government.

With respect to the balance of the prize money I have recovered, you may if you please give an immediate order on me for the amount, or I will pay it into your own hands. I have the honor, &c.

MS not found. Text printed from Sherburne, *John Paul Jones*, p. 278-9. Noted in SJL as received 11 July 1786.

To John Ledyard

[*Paris, 10 July 1786.* An entry in SJL under this date reads: "Ledyard. Sun the cause of magnetic attraction." Not found. See Ledyard to TJ, 7 July 1786.]

To Maupin

[*Paris, 10 July 1786.* An entry in SJL under this date reads: "Maupin. To buy his works." Not found. See Maupin to TJ, 4 and 20 July 1786.]

To John Paradise

Dr Sir Paris July 10. 1786.

I am honoured with your letter by Dr. Bancroft inclosing one from Dr. Burney for which I return you my thanks, and now trouble you with one to that gentleman. I have had with Dr. Bancroft much conversation on your subject. We concur in pro-

[120]

posing to you a short trip to Paris, and in thinking it will relieve your health, and place you in a situation to decide on your plans more according to the dictates of your own judgment. He is lodged at the Place Louis XV. We could find for you lodgings in the same quarter, and there would only be the fine walk of the Champs Elysées between us. I should certainly spare nothing to make your time agreeable, and perhaps the Doctor and myself could aid you in your determination. The necessary expence of the journey would be small, as would be the residence of a single person here without a family. Mr. Trumbull is setting out for this place and would be an agreeable companion. You are the best and only judge however of it's expediency. I shall be happy in every occasion of serving you, and of testifying the sincerity of the esteem with which I have the honour to be Dear Sir your most obedient & most humble servt., TH: JEFFERSON

PrC (DLC). Noted in SJL as sent "by Mr. Randall." Enclosure: TJ to Charles Burney, 10 July 1786.

To Lucy Ludwell Paradise

DEAR MADAM   Paris July 10. 1786.

I have duly received the favour of your letter by Doctr. Bancroft and am sensible of the honour of the confidence you are pleased to repose in me. I wish it were in my power, more than it is, to promote those measures which the interests of your family seem to require. I have taken the liberty of writing to Mr. Paradise on the subject, a liberty greater than perhaps could be justified. Were my right to interfere to be measured by my good wishes, it would indeed be boundless. Dr. Bancroft and myself think that would Mr. Paradise take a flying trip to this place we could aid him in his determinations as to what is best to be done. It is not too late for the present season; the expence of the journey to him, coming as a single person, would be small, and perhaps might be compensated by your care at home. I submit this proposition to your better judgment. If you approve it, you will of course give it the weight of your influence. I pray you to present my respect to Miss Paradise and to be assured of the esteem with which I have the honor to be Dear Madam your most obedient and most humble servant,   TH: JEFFERSON

PrC (DLC). Noted in SJL as sent "by Mr. Randall."

To David Ramsay

Sir   Paris July 10. 1786.

I am honoured with your letter of May 3. and obliged by your kind notice of what I had written on the subject of my own state. If I have any merit from it, it is in being fully sensible of it's imperfections.—It is time you should hear something of a much more important work, that written by yourself. The translation and printing go on slowly. I do not think they are half finished. The Marquis de Chastellux thinks it well translated. The circumstance which renders the delay more interesting to you is that the twelvemonth's credit which the bookseller has for the money to be paid you, counts from the time of publication. I had no idea that the interval between the commencement and completion of the work would have been so long. Dilly being afraid to sell your book in London, and Dr. Bancroft informing me he was about to gut it in order to accomodate it to the English pride and palate, I have written to Colo. Smith to endeavor to prevent it's being done till your consent can be obtained. It has been read in the original, in it's present state, by many here and is highly esteemed. I am of opinion we can sell it here, even to the English themselves, as the Diligence furnishes a weekly conveyance from here to London which will not add above 6d. to the price. I have therefore desired Colo. Smith to send 50. copies here, and to advertize in the London papers the address of the Bookseller here who will furnish them, and the conveyance by which they may be obtained. We shall see by the sale of these whether we may hope to sell the rest of the impression here. I should be sorry that any circumstances should occasion the disguising those truths which it equally concerns our honour and the just infamy of our enemies to have handed down to posterity in their true light. I thank you for your undertaking as to the plants I wrote for, and venture to repeat my sollicitations of your attention to them. I have the honour to be with the most perfect respect, Sir, your most obedient & most humble servant,

Th: Jefferson

PrC (DLC). Noted in SJL as sent "by Mr. Randall."

To Rayneval

[*Paris, 10 July 1786.* An entry in SJL under this date reads: "M. de Reyneval. Passport for 24 doz. and a pipe of wine." Not found.]

To John Adams

Dear Sir Paris July 11. 1786.

Our instructions relative to the Barbary states having required us to proceed by way of negotiation to obtain their peace, it became our duty to do this to the best of our power. Whatever might be our private opinions, they were to be suppressed, and the line marked out to us, was to be followed. It has been so honestly, and zealously. It was therefore never material for us to consult together on the best plan of conduct towards these states. I acknolege I very early thought it would be best to effect a peace thro' the medium of war. Tho' it is a question with which we have nothing to do, yet as you propose some discussion of it I shall trouble you with my reasons. Of the 4. positions laid down in your letter of the 3d. instant, I agree to the three first, which are in substance that the good offices of our friends cannot procure us a peace without paying it's price, that they cannot materially lessen that price, and that paying it, we can have the peace in spight[1] of the intrigues of our enemies. As to the 4th. that the longer the negotiation is delayed the larger will be the demand, this will depend on the intermediate captures: if they are many and rich the price may be raised; if few and poor it will be lessened. However if it is decided that we shall buy a peace, I know no reason for delaying the operation, but should rather think it ought to be hastened. But I should prefer the obtaining it by war. 1. Justice is in favor of this opinion. 2. Honor favors it. 3. It will procure us respect in Europe, and respect is a safe-guard to interest. 4. It will arm the federal head with the safest of all the instruments of coercion over their delinquent members and prevent them from using what would be less safe. I think that so far you go with me. But in the next steps we shall differ. 5. I think it least expensive. 6. Equally effectual. I ask a fleet of 150. guns, the one half of which shall be in constant cruise. This fleet built, manned and victualled for 6. months will cost 450,000£ sterling. It's annual expence is 300£ sterl. a gun, including every thing: this will be 45,000£ sterl. a year. I take British experience for the basis of my calculations, tho' we know, from our own experience, that we can do, in this way, for pounds lawful, what costs them pounds sterling. Were we to charge all this to the Algerine war it would amount to little more than we must pay if we buy peace. But as it is proper and necessary that we should establish a small marine force (even were we to buy a peace from the Algerines,) and as that force laid up in our dockyards would cost us

[123]

11 JULY 1786

half as much annually as if kept in order for service, we have a right to say that only 22,500£ sterl. per ann. should be charged to the Algerine war. 6. It will be as effectual. To all the mismanagements of Spain and Portugal urged to shew that war against those people is ineffectual, I urge a single fact to prove the contrary where there is any management. About 40. year ago, the Algerines having broke their treaty with France, this court sent Monsr. de Massac with one large and two small frigates, he blockaded the harbour of Algiers three months, and they subscribed to the terms he dictated. If it be admitted however that war, on the fairest prospects, is still exposed to incertainties, I weigh against this the greater incertainty of the duration of a peace bought with money, from such a people, from a Dey 80. years old, and by a nation who, on the hypothesis of buying peace, is to have no power on the sea to enforce an observance of it.

So far I have gone on the supposition that the whole weight of this war would rest on us. But 1. Naples will join us. The character of their naval minister (Acton), his known sentiments with respect to the peace Spain is officiously trying to make for them, and his dispositions against the Algerines give the greatest reason to believe it. 2. Every principle of reason tells us Portugal will join us. I state this as taking for granted, what all seem to believe, that they will not be at peace with Algiers. I suppose then that a Convention might be formed between Portugal, Naples and the U.S. by which the burthen of the war might be quotaed on them according to their respective wealth, and the term of it should be when Algiers should subscribe to a peace with all three on equal terms. This might be left open for other nations to accede to, and many, if not most of the powers of Europe (except France, England, Holland and Spain if her peace be made) would sooner or later enter into the confederacy, for the sake of having their peace with the Pyratical states guarantied by the whole. I suppose that in this case our proportion of force would not be the half of what I first calculated on.

These are the reasons which have influenced my judgment on this question. I give them to you to shew you that I am imposed on by a semblance of reason at least, and not with an expectation of their changing your opinion. You have viewed the subject, I am sure in all it's bearings. You have weighed both questions with all their circumstances. You make the result different from what I do. The same facts impress us differently. This is enough to make me suspect an error in my process of reasoning tho' I am not able to detect it. It is of no consequence; as I have nothing to say in the decision, and am ready to proceed heartily on any other plan which may be adopted, if my agency should be thought useful. With respect to the dispositions of the states I am utterly uninformed. I cannot help thinking however that on a view of all circumstances, they might be united in either of the plans.

Having written this on the receipt of your letter, without knowing of any opportunity of sending it, I know not when it will go; I add nothing therefore on any other subject but assurances of the sincere esteem and respect with which I am Dear Sir your friend & servant,

TH: JEFFERSON

RC (MHi: AMT). PrC (DLC).
1 TJ's adoption of Adams' spelling in this case (see Adams to TJ, 3 July 1786) was probably deliberate; nowhere else does he use this form.

From Lewis Alexander

GENTLEMAN   Bayonne 11th: July 1786

I am honour'd with Your Esteem'd favour dated 22d: and the treaty imprinted bettween Mr. Morris, and the farmer General, the prejudice of this treaty for American trade is evident, the price for their Tobacco would otherwise Continue on the rate of 40 and 42^{tt} p. Cwt. to the farmers, even after a Choice made of part of their Cargoes Suitable for our Merchants that they generally would pay at 45 and 50.^{tt} p. Cwt. In this Consideration my father Mr. D alexandre reclaim'd in June last Year from Mr. De Callone to prohibit the farmer General making any other regulated treaty Concerning furnishment of Tobacco. He, at Same time addressed You Copy there of, and I had the honour of repeating it You in my late letter dated 9th. late. This prohibition is granted, but with the Condition of an allowance on the price to Supply for the transport of Tobacco to their Manufactorys which is oposite to the advantage on the freedom of three ports his majesty granted for encouragement of united States Commerce. On the Contrary the farmer General ought to be oblig'd to give a preference to the Cargos imported in our free ports, without any deduction that will in Some manner oblig'd the american merchants to Consign their Expeditions to the ports of havre, and morlaise, where their Cargos Composed of only Tobacco will injoy the priviledge of paying no duty. They will nevertheless be obliged to Come to one of our free ports, to take in there load in Brandy for returns which is very

11 JULY 1786

inconvinient, and I hope You will interceed in Court to have this Condition reformed the prejudice resulting for united States merchants and its very equal for the farmer General to provision their Tobaccos in our free ports, where they have no other incovinient, but the transport to their manufactorys, *there might be one easily established here.* I hope You have Aproved and Sollicited Sir, the particular of my father's demand in the above mentioned letter to Mr. Callone and obtain in Case of necessity, that all marchandize imported at our Port, for the account of united States Subjects, may be exposed at publick Sale without paying the regulated Duty of 4d. ℔ liver for the Controle. This duty amounts upwards of those formerly payd to the Custom house before the freedom of our Port. If You Could obtain this liberty great advantage would result for American traders. It would furnish us the best means to Expedit at ready money, the remainders of their Cargos, that may tarry long without, in our Stores, Expeditions in Sale and returns being the very Soul of trade. I hope Sir, You will Contribute in this point of it, with Your demand, that will favour and Strengthen mine.

I have not the least doubt You have precautiously opposed Your representation to our Minister that the demand of Some of our Smallest merchants of this port, and St. Jean de Lus for a duty at 2.^{lt} ℔ quintl. to be laid on the Strange fish imported here, may not be admitted. This demand is Considered ridiculous, and unreasonable by our best merchants. They refused Signing this reclamation as Contrary to the freedom of the port. You will permitt me Sir, to notice You every particular that may tend to the advantage of united States, that there trade may prosper as I much desire. I am with profound Respect Gentleman Your very Hum: & obt Servt, LEWIS ALEXANDER

RC (DLC). Noted in SJL as received 20 July 1786.
MY LATE LETTER: Alexander's letter is dated 10, not 9 June 1786.

To Mary Barclay

July 11, 1786

Mr. Jefferson has the honour of presenting his respects to Mrs. Barclay and of informing her that by a letter from Mr. Barclay dated the 10th. of June, he learns he was then arrived in good health at Mogadore in Marocco, that he was received with distinguished attention and honour, by orders from the emperor, that the Governor of Marocco with a guard of 30 men had been sent to escort him to the city of Marocco, to which place he was immediately to set out, and there he would see the emperor.

There had long been some little matters of account whereon Mr. Jefferson was indebted to Mr. Barclay. He repeatedly desired to know them but Mr. Barclay's occupations would not permit him to examine them; on the last application Mr. Barclay said he would leave the account with Mrs. Barclay. Mr. Jefferson has been long intending to do himself the honour of seeing Mrs. Barclay at St. Germain's, but has hitherto been unable. He still proposes that pleasure. But without awaiting that he would be obliged to Mrs. Barclay to let him know the sum he is indebted to Mr. Barclay, which he will take care to remit to her. He wishes her much health and happiness.

RC (Mrs. Darrell T. Lane, Washington, D.C.). PrC (MHi). Not recorded in SJL.

To St. John de Crèvecoeur

SIR   Paris July 11. 1786.

I have been honored with a letter from M. Delisle Lt. Gl. au bailliage de Caën, to which is annexed a postscript from yourself. Being unable to write in French so as to be sure of conveying my true meaning, or perhaps any meaning at all, I will beg of you to interpret what I have now the honour to write.

It is true that the United states, generally, and most of the separate states in particular, are endeavoring to establish means to pay the interest of their public debt regularly, and to sink it's principal by degrees. But as yet their efforts have been confined to that part of their debts which is evidenced by *certificates*. I do not think that any state has yet taken measures for paying their *paper money* debt. The principle on which it shall be paid I take to be settled, tho' not directly yet virtually, by the resolution of Congress of June 3. 1784., that is that they will pay the holder or his representatives what the money was worth at the time he received it, with an interest from that time of 6. per centum per annum. It is not said in the letter whether the money received by Barboutin was Continental money, or Virginia money; nor is it said at what time it was received. But that M. Delisle may be enabled to judge what the 5398 dollars were worth in hard money when Barboutin received them, I will state to you what was the worth of one hard dollar both in Continental and Virginia money through the whole

11 JULY 1786

of the years 1779. and 1780. within some part of which it was probably received.

Continental money			Virginia money		
1779. Jan.	9	$7\frac{72}{100}$	1779 Jan. 8	1780 Jan. 42
	24	$8\frac{30}{100}$	Feb. 10	Feb. 48
Feb.	11	$9\frac{13}{100}$	Mar. 10	Mar. 50
Mar.	2	10	Apr. 16	Apr. 60
Apr.	3	$11\frac{12}{100}$	May 20	May 60
May	10	$12\frac{81}{100}$	June 20	June 65
June	23	$14\frac{3}{10}$	July 22	July 65
Aug.	8	$16\frac{60}{100}$	Aug. 22	Aug. 70
Sep.	28	20	Sep. 24	Sep. 72
Nov.	22	$25\frac{6}{100}$	Oct. 28	Oct. 73
1780. Feb.	2	$33\frac{44}{100}$	Nov. 36	Nov. 74
Mar.	18	40.	Dec. 40	Dec. 75

Thus you see that in Jan. 1779. 7 dollars and 72 hundredths of a dollar of Continental paper were worth one dollar of silver, and at the same time 8. dollars of Virginia paper were worth one dollar of silver: &c. After Mar. 18. 1780. Continental paper received in Virginia will be estimated by the table of Virginia paper.—I advise all the foreign holders of paper money to lodge it in the office of their Consul for the state where it was received, that he may dispose of it for their benefit the first moment that paiment shall be provided by the state or Continent.—I had lately the pleasure of seeing the Coun[tess] d'Houditot well at Sanois, and have now that of assuring you of the perfect esteem and respect with which I have the honor to be Dear Sir your most obedient humble servt.,

TH: JEFFERSON

PrC (DLC).

To Ferdinand Grand

SIR   Paris July 11. 1786.

In consequence of the within order, Commodore Jones is ready to pay the sum of 112,172^{tt}-2s-4d, which be pleased to receive from him for the use of the United states, giving him a receipt for the specific sum on the back of the order. I shall hereafter have the honor of explaining to you the purposes to which the board of treasury have appropriated this sum. I have the honor to be with

[128]

great esteem and respect Sir your most obedient & most humble servant,
TH: JEFFERSON

PrC (DLC). Enclosure missing; see Jones to TJ, 7 July 1786.

To John Paul Jones

Dear Sir   Paris July 11. 1786.

I am perfectly ready to transmit to America any accounts or proofs you may think proper. No body can wish more that justice may be done you, nor is more ready to be instrumental in doing whatever may ensure it. It is only necessary for me to avoid the presumption of appearing to decide where I have no authority to do it. I will this evening lodge in the hands of Mr. Grand the original order of the board of treasury, with instructions to receive from you the balance you propose to pay, for which he will give you a receipt on the back of the order. I will confer with you when you please on the affair of Denmark, & am with very great esteem Dr. Sir Your most obedient & most humble servt.,
TH: JEFFERSON

RC (Brit. Mus., Add. MSS 21506). PrC (DLC).

From Lefévre, Roussac & Cie.

Lisbon, 11 July 1786. Enclose an invoice for 140 bottles of wine of different sorts, shipped five days ago, on the ship *François l'Union,* Capt. Jn. Vollet, and consigned to Achard Frères, Rouen, for TJ's account. Their charge of 68,400 reis is calculated at 432 reis for 3 livres; have drawn 60-day sight draft, for 450 livres, on TJ to the order of De Brissac & Paulet. They have exercised the utmost care in selecting these wines; trust TJ will be satisfied; and that he will feel confident in using their services in the future.

RC (MHi); 1 p.; in French. Recorded in SJL as received 29 July 1786. Enclosure missing.

From De Pinto

Monsieur   à Londres Ce 11me. Juillet 1786

Une digrétion de quelques jours à La Campagne m'a Empeché d'avoir L'honneur de vous remercier plus tôt, Monsieur, du present estimable que Le Collonel Smith m'a remis de vôtre part. Permetez

12 JULY 1786

Monsieur, que je vous temoigne toute mà reconnoissance, et que je vous assure en même tems, que je conserverois toujour vôtre Livre comme une marque pretieuse de vôtre amitié, et de vôtre soubvenir à mon Egard.

J'ait L'honeur d'etre avec autant de Consideration que de respect Monsieur Vôtre tres heumble et tres obeissant Serviteur,

LE CHR. DE PINTO

RC (MHi); endorsed. Noted in SJL as received 20 July 1786.

The presentation copy of *Notes on Virginia* which De Pinto here acknowledges has not previously been recorded and is not listed in the census compiled by Coolie Verner ("Mr. Jefferson Distributes his *Notes*," *Bull. N.Y.P.L.*, Vol. 56 [1952], p. 171).

From Ferdinand Grand

SIR Paris 12th. July 1786.

I have the honour to inform you that in consequence of your desire, Commodore Paul Jones has paid me, one hundred twelve thousand, one hundred Seventy two Livers, two Sols, four deniers, where with I Shall follow your order. I Specifyed the above Sum on the back of the bill drawn by the Treasury, mentioning it to be the ballance of the Sum mentioned there in, according to Commodore Jones's accounts to be Submitted to congress. I am very respectfully Sir Your most obedient humble Servant,

GRAND

RC (DLC).

From Lewis Littlepage

SIR Warsaw. 12th. July. 1786.

Having recieved no intelligence from Virginia respecting the affair which Governor Henry entrusted to me, the result of which I had the honor to communicate to your Excellency in Paris, I cannot conceal my uneasiness upon that point, and must entreat you to inform me whether it has as yet been settled to your satisfaction. I at the same time repeat my former offers upon that subject and will with pleasure submit to any inconvenience rather than expose you to even a delay which may be embarrassing.

Permit me at the same time to assure you of the high sense of gratitude which I entertain for your generous and friendly conduct upon this occasion, added to the respect and veneration with which

12 JULY 1786

I have the honor to be your Excellency's most obedient and most humble Servant, LEWIS LITTLEPAGE

RC (DLC); endorsed. Noted in SJL as received 3 Sep. 1786.

From Richard O'Bryen

SIR Algiers July 12th. 1786

Since the arrival of Mr. Lamb at Algiers I wrote you several letters informing you of some particulars which came within my observation. Mr. Lamb has actually agreed with the Dey of Algiers for the redemption of us unfortunate captives. It is near three months since Mr. Lamb left Algiers and was to get the money in four months. I hope for our sakes, and the honor of his country, that he will not deviate from his word with the Dey of Algiers. We recieved a few lines from Mr. Lamb by the Spanish Brig. Mr. Lamb says he had stated our situation to you some months ago and that he had not recieved any answer from you or from Mr. Adams and therefore can not tell what will be determined on in our behalf.

He mentions in his letter that it was not in his power to redeem us as his orders were not to go higher than 200 dollars per man. I never blamed him for not redeeming us as there was so small a sum appropriated for that use, as he repeatedly told me and others. It is near one year since we are in the fetters of slavery without having any account from the Continent, and lately within the time that Mr. Lamb arrived here without any assurances from our Country or Countrymen, and Mr. Lamb's letter has struck us with the most poignant grief so that our gloomy unfortunate situation affects us beyond our expression or your Imagination. We try to administer consolation to our unfortunate crews; but poor fellows endure the severities of slavery. I am confident our Country must have resolved on something respecting us before this time. Certainly Liberty that is the basis of America will never let twenty one unfortunate citizens remain slaves to the Turkish yoke.

The other day when I was in the Dey's palace to see the boys, that belonged to my vessel, the next man to the Dey asked me when I had heard from Mr. Lamb, and asked me if I did not expect to go clear soon. I said I did not know, and he said that the American Ambassador had agreed with the Dey to give 50,000 dollars and to get the money in four months time which he often tells the boys.

12 JULY 1786

The Algerines have taken several prizes this cruise. They went out the 27th. of May and to day the last of them returned into port.

A Russian ship of 700 ton loaded with wine   15 Men
A Leghorn ship of 20 Guns and   44 men
Two Genoa barks of the Coast.
One Neapolitan, but is returned being taken in a Spanish bay.
One Spaniard taken but the vessel returned.
A Brig under Imperial colours—all Genoese on board. A hard task to clear her but is given up, those people being much afraid of the Emperor. Four Portuguee fishing boats taken off Cape St. Vincent —15 Portuguese fishermen.

One of the Algerines went out of the coast of Portugal where they took the Fishermen off Cape St. Vincents.

We should be happy in hearing from you respecting our redemption or if it is our hard lot here to remain we must make the best of it.

I remain your most obedient & very unfortunate

RICHD O BRYEN

Tr (DNA: RG 59, Consular Dispatches); in Short's hand; endorsed, in a clerk's hand: "Algiers July 12, 1786. O Brien Richd."; without indication of addressee. PrC (MHi: AMT). Recorded in SJL as received by TJ on 3 Aug. 1786.

On the day before this letter was written, O'Bryen wrote Carmichael giving essentially the same information and stating: "The Brig Lamb arrived at Algiers the 10th. We recieved a few lines from Mr. Lamb, dated at Alicant, wherein he informs us that he had stated our situation to Mr. Jefferson and Mr. Adams but that he had recieved no answer to any of his letters. Therefore he cannot tell what they will conclude on.—It is three months since Mr. Lamb wrote to Mr. Jefferson informing him of the Dey's demands for us very unfortunate Americans, and as we have not recieved any letter from any Person in America or yet we have not had any assurances from any the Ministers in Europe, since they have known of the enormous sum that is asked for our freedom, it has struck us with the most poignant grief, and we are more disheartened at present than any period since our captivity, so that I assure you Sir that Life is a burthen to me whilst under the present gloomy situation. . . . Mr. Lamb says . . . that he had orders to go no higher than 200 Dollars a man. Is it possible that Ministers who should know what Captives were generally redeemed at should send Mr. Lamb to Algiers and only allow him to go so high as 200 Doll: p man. But as Mr. Lamb has told us so many different stories respecting his orders that we cannot believe them all to be true. . . . I hope never to see him in Algiers on any business for the United States except to chuse mules and Barbary horses and Borickers" (O'Bryen to Carmichael, 11 July 1786; Tr in Short's hand in DNA: RG 59, Consular Dispatches; PrC of same in MHi: AMT; the former was enclosed in TJ to Jay, 11 Aug. and the latter in TJ to Adams, 8 Aug. 1786). O'Bryen also wrote Adams on 25 July 1786 that he was "Shure Congress could not have gotten a more unfit man" than Lamb; he added that the risks of mail would not permit him to "write . . . of some particulars, but I have wrote by a safe Oppertunity to Mr. Jefferson" (MHi: AMT).

From Edmund Randolph

Dear Sir   Richmond July 12. 1786.

Many unforeseen accidents, and particularly a long indisposition have occasioned the delay, which has occurred in the acknowledgment of your friendly attention in the present of books.

Since the receipt of them, your favor concerning the capitol came to hand; after the most painful anxiety at the tardy movement of the plan to Virginia. We are at length relieved by its arrival. A council of directors was immediately called, and with some difficulty the plan was carried thro! But I am exceedingly afraid that we have committed some blunder even now. I directed Mr. Dobie, our superintendant, and an adept in draughtmanship, to furnish me with a narrative of our proceedings in technical language. When completed, it shall be forwarded. At present, however, I will give you some imperfect idea of it.—The plan sent to you was a mere assay; that adopted by us was very different. When your plan was examined, it was conceived, that without adhering to precisely the same front, it would be enough to follow the same proportions. By this doctrine we were rescued from a great embarrassment, for the lowland interest and a strong party of the upland, in the assembly, are labouring to stop the progress of the building. To pull up all that had been done, would have been to strengthen the opposition. We have therefore resolved to pursue your plan in every respect, except the extension of front. By this means we have been obliged to remove only one side wall and a few partition walls.

The apparent scarcity of cash has excited a great clamour for paper money: an expedient very acceptable to those who are in debt, or are unwilling to purchase the precious metals by labour. But the firmness of Madison and Mason will, I trust, defeat the attempt to emit it. Mr. Henry intends to resign the government, and wishes to be a member at the next session. His politics are not known, but are supposed not to run vehemently against paper money.

The James river canal goes on rapidly and promises full success. But the subscribers are so delinquent in the necessary advances, that, I fear, our work may be stagnated.

I am on the point of departing from this unwholesome place to breathe the mountain air; without which I could not survive the summer.

14 JULY 1786

Believe me to be my dear sir with the greatest sincerity yr. friend & serv:, EDM: RANDOLPH

RC (DLC); endorsed. Noted in SJL as received 6 Dec. 1786.

From John Banister, Jr.

DEAR SIR Libourne July 14th. 1786

From the information given you by Mr. Randal respecting me you must suppose I am on the eve of arriving at Paris. It was not possible for me to set out so early as I intended, but left Bordeaux only five days ago. Having stoped here for nine days to look at the country around which is very beautuful, I am taken so unwell as to be wholly unable to proceed on my journey. I am much in suspence respecting the steps I should at present take, and must beg you for your advice. My health is so precarious that it is impossible for me to employ my time to any great utility. I am in the disagreeable situation of being far distant from any friends whose attentions might in some degree remove the inconveniences under which I labor. The expences I am obliged to incur exceed the sum limited by my Father, and I find little benefit from European climates. Weighing these reasons I am induced to turn my eyes on my native country, though I do not determine on going except on the concurrence of your opinion with mine. You knowing my Fathers thoughts respecting me, will be better able to judge of the propriety of this step; and I must request the favor of you to do it without reserve. In your last you asked me if I had seen the Canal of Languedoc. I not only saw it but traced every foot of it entering it at the Mediterranean and leaving it on its junction with the Garonne. It is a work of great curiosity, and utility, and must have been the effect of much labor. With every wish for your prosperity I am yours respectfully, JNO BANISTER JUNR

RC (MHi); endorsed: "Banister Jno Junr. chez Bertrand. Libourne." Noted in SJL as received 22 July 1786.

From John Jay

DR SIR New York 14th. July 1786

Since my last to you of 16 Ult: I have been honored with your Letters of 23d. and a joint one from you and Mr. Adams of 25th. April.

[134]

14 JULY 1786

Considering the Importance of our Commerce with Portugal, it gives me Pleasure to learn that a Treaty with that Kingdom was nearly concluded. Until our Affairs shall be more perfectly arranged we shall treat under Disadvantages, and therefore I am not surprised that our Negociations with Britain and Barbary are unpromising. To be respectable abroad it is necessary to be so at Home, and that will not be the Case until our public Faith acquires more Confidence, and our Government more Strength.

When or how these great Objects will be attained can scarcely be conjectured. An Uneasiness prevails through the Country and may produce eventually the desired Reformations, and it may also produce untoward Events. Time alone can decide this and many other Doubts, for Nations like Individuals are more frequently guided by Circumstances, than Circumstances by them.

I am not charged to communicate to you any Instructions, though I have Reason to think that some will be ready by the Time the next Packet will sail. Nor have I any very interesting Intelligence to transmit. The british Government at New Brunswick have lately given Uneasiness to Massachusetts by extending their Jurisdiction farther than the Treaty will warrant; and from the present State of our Indian Affairs, there is Reason to apprehend Trouble with them. They appear dissatisfied with their late Cessions to us, and it is not improbable that they will give Interruption to our Surveyors. How far these People may be instigated by our Neighbours is not decided; but the Asperity observable in the british Nation towards us, creates Suspicions that they wish to see our Difficulties of every kind encrease and accumulate. Indeed I fear that other European Nations do not regard us entirely without Jealousy. There are some little Circumstances which look as if the Dutch regret our having found the Way to China, and that will doubtless be more or less the Case with every Nation with whose commercial Views we may interfere. I am happy in reflecting that there can be but little Clashing of Interests between us and France, and therefore that she will probably continue disposed to wish us well and do us good, especially if we honestly fulfil our pecuniary Engagements with her. These Engagements however give me much Concern. Every Principle and Consideration of Honor, Justice and Interest call upon us for good Faith and Punctuality, and yet we are unhappily so circumstanced that the Monies necessary for the Purpose are not provided, nor in such a Way of being provided as they ought to be. This is owing not to any Thing wrong in Congress, but to their not possessing that Power of Coercion without which

15 JULY 1786

no Government can possibly attain the most salutary and constitutional Objects. Excuses and Palliations, and Applications for more Time make bad Remittances; and will afford no Inducements to our Allies or others to afford us similar Aids on future Occasions.

I herewith send a Packet for you from Mr. Hopkinson, and the public Papers. The latter will inform you of the Death of Genl. Greene. This is a serious Loss to his Country as well as his Family, and is universally and justly lamented.

With great Esteem & Regard I have the honor to be &c.,

JOHN JAY

FC (DNA: PCC, No. 121). Noted in SJL as received 22 Aug. 1786. Dft (NK–Iselin). The packet FROM MR. HOPKINSON was probably the second volume of the *Transactions* of the American Philosophical Society (see Hopkinson to TJ, 28 June 1786).

From John Bondfield

Bordeaux, 15 July 1786. Has shipped on board the *Comte d'Artois*, Capt. Stephen Gregory, 50 cases of arms, numbered 1 to 50, from the manufactory at Tulle, addressed to the governor of Virginia for the account of that state; lists papers enclosed. The governor must return an "especially authenticated" certificate to cancel Bondfield's bond for the safe delivery of the arms. Has drawn draft in favor of M. Ladurantic, payable 29 July, for his expenditures. "I have given uncommon attention to have the Cases most securely packt that should they be exposed by unforeseen Events to wet or Damps I am perswaided the Coats I have put on them will preserve them against all Accidents. I met with difficulty to obtain permission to ship them. Arms and all warlike Stores are prohibited to be sent out of the Kingdom and cannot be shipt without a special permission from the Governor or Intendant of the Province. Both being absent the Subdelegate was apprehendsive." Suggests that TJ procure a general order for future shipments. Has shipped sundry articles for Francis Eppes to the care of Charles Carter of Shirley, on James River; encloses an account for this shipment, amounting to 119 l. 18s. 9d. together with one for wine forwarded to TJ on 24 June, amounting to 498 l. for which he will draw on TJ in accordance with TJ's instructions. Inquires whether, in case of failure of direct conveyance to Virginia, future arms could be sent to Philadelphia. Has communicated the resolutions of the committee held at Berni to "the Trade of this City, Rochfort, Rochelle and Bayonne."

RC (DLC); 4 p.; endorsed. Noted in SJL as received 20 July 1786. Enclosures: (1) Bill of lading (Vi), dated 12 July, signed by Stephen Gregory. (2 and 3) bills of entry (Vi), the first dated 10 July, showing duties paid in the amount of 243₶-5-11, and the second, dated 11 July, showing duties in the amount of 472₶-5-6. (4) account of Bondfield's expenditures for the state of Virginia (Vi), signed and dated 15 July, endorsed, in TJ's hand: "Virga. arms. 2043₶-12-1." (5) Invoice for articles shipped to Francis Eppes in

[136]

accordance with TJ's instructions in his letter to Bondfield, 24 Jan. 1786 and for 8 cases of wine sent to TJ in Paris (DLC; see Bondfield to TJ, 24 June 1786).

From William Carmichael

Dear Sir Madrid 15 July 1786

I received a few days ago the Letter which your Excellency did me the honor to write me the 20th Ulto. inclosing Letters for Messrs. Lamb and Randall. To the Former I have transmitted your Letters. The Latter I suppose you will have seen long before this can reach you and from him you will have learnt more than I wished or chose to put on paper. I am happy to find that two of my bills have been paid. I take the Liberty of inclosing to your Excellency a protest of one twice protested and which I renewed in consequence of your advice on that particular Affair. It is incomprehensible to me that my bills should be protested for want of advice. Such Letters take not three minutes, but I see that I am to be distressed, If it is possible to distress me in my pecuniary arrangements. It is not possible in this Country. I dare say my conduct has inspired confidence and tomorrow If I asked 50 thousand dollars or a larger Sum I could obtain it without hesitation or difficulty. Mr. Grand is possibly in advance for the United States and doth not chuse to make further Advances. If this is the Case I ought to be advised; and in that case I should draw no more on him or any other in Europe, but wait patiently for remittances and in the mean time rely on my own personal credit here. Your Intelligence from America and from Doctor Franklin operates as a Cordial on my spirit and I firmly beleive has retarded the attacks of the bile which generally Torment me at this Season of the year here.

I am sorry to learn that our Treaty with Portugal encounters more difficulties than I thought it would, after your communication to me on that Subject.

[This Country has signed its peace with Algiers, but there are still arrangements to be made that require Time patience and Address. I send you a letter which I received from thence this Moment, as I have not time to copy it you will please to return it to me. I wish not to derogate from the merit or services of any one, But justice to myself and still more to the interests and honor of our Country oblige me to say, that our peace with the Barbary States could have been negotiated here with much less Expence, with much less Noise and with a greater probability of success than in the mode adopted by Congress. A Negotiation with Algiers is not yet to be regarded as desperate. It is a question of calculation. Whenever *our Republic* will act and think for themselves, They will do what they please, until that period, we shall be the partridge and its young ones. We shall never be respected until we respect ourselves. As you may not possibly have heard from Mr. Barclay since his arrival in Africa I inclose you copies of a Letter which I received from his Excellency the Ct. de Florida Blanca with extracts from those received from the Agent of Spain in Morrocco and from a Minister of the Emperor which I intreat you to forward to Congress by the first occasion. As few opportunities from hence offer for the transmission of my dispatches I make no comment on the Nature of these Letters as I am persuaded you will at once see the good faith and candour with which this Ministry acts on our behalf. This Court will observe the same Conduct with respect to the Barbary powers in General, The moment it can efficaciously interfere.][1] I mention nothing of the Foreign or even Interior politics of this court, because I have remarked that in your answers to my letters, you appeared not disposed to enter into any observations on such Subjects. Mr. Randall whom I beg leave to recommend to your Notice will have given you a map which I obtained with much difficulty here. I am happy to hear that Mr. Barclay has forwarded some of the books you wished to have and which I have sought for in Villadolid Sarogassa and Valencia in vain. I have several in hand that I have procured by accident and which I mean to send by the first safe conveyance directly to Paris. I have promised a letter to Mr. Galves who goes Minister to Berlin and I beg you for political as well as personal reasons to shew that Gentleman every mark of Attention and civility. Altho' I have not the honor to be personally known to you, I flatter myself that you will not hesitate to attend to my introduction of any one to your acquaintance Coming from hence, because I do assure you that I will never take that Liberty, without a view of obtaining Friends or shewing civilities to those who have been friends to our Country here.

I have the honor to be With the greatest respect Your Excys Most Obedt. & Humble Sevt,   WM. CARMICHAEL

RC (DLC). Tr of an extract (DNA: PCC, No. 87, I; see note 1, below); in the hand of Short. Tr of extract (DNA: PCC, No. 107). Noted in SJL as received 26 July 1786. Enclosures: (1) Protest of draft by Carmichael; (2) O'Bryen to Carmichael, 11 July 1786 (see note to O'Bryen to TJ, 12 July 1786); (3) Floridablanca to Carmichael, 13 July 1786, transmitting an extract of a letter from Juan Manuel Salmon, Spanish consul general in Morocco, to Floridablanca, 27 June 1786, reporting that Barclay had been well received, and an extract of a letter from Lasby Effendy, Minister of Morocco, to Salmon, without date, assuring Salmon that all possible consideration will be given to Barclay because he came under the sponsorship of the King of Spain (Tr of Floridablanca's letter and its enclosures, in the hand of Short, together with a translation, in an unidentified hand, in DNA: PCC, No. 87, I; PrC of Short's Tr in DLC; another Tr in DNA: PCC, No. 107).

[1] The text in brackets is so marked in RC, indicating the passage to be copied for the extract to be sent to Jay; see TJ to Jay, 11 Aug. 1786.

From John Lamb

Alicant July 15th. 1786

I received Your Excellency's letters of the 20th. ultimo and finde by them that Mr. Randall had not then come to Paris. By Mr. Randall I Stated the exact Situation of our affaires at Algiers and Sent forward a Duplicate of the Same to Congress; the Demands at Algiers no Doubt will be Great. My health by no means will admit of undertakeing the Journey Your Excellency points out. I Daresay my indisposition will be a Suffitient excuse. If it is not, in Duty to my Self of necessity have no further pretentions to this bussiness and begg that my Reasonable accounts may be Settled. It will Take Sum time to collect my accounts. I am under bonds at Barcelona for the money I extracted for the purposes of Algiers. I left the Vessel in the Spanish Servis, when I Left Algiers, as I wrote, and She now is here under Quarenteen and cannot Yeot be come at, not Doubting but I Should have gone back to Algiers left maney things there, but as soon as may be will collect all, and my accounts. When that is Done I hope I Shall be Settled with in Europe as that was promised before I left America. My letter of Credite will be returned to Your Excellencys Orders. I have Drawn as I have Advised. I have letters Daited Algiers the 11th. July 1786 then no more of our Vessels were Taken. It is highly necessary that Sum Orders Should be Given on Account of our unfortunate people in Algiers. I have presumed to Supply them with upwards of Eight hundred heard Dollars for their passed Expences and Cloathing.

With Due Respect Your Excellencys most Obedient Hmbl Servt.,

JOHN LAMB

RC (DLC). Dupl (DNA: PCC, No. 91, II); varies slightly in phraseology but not in substance. Tr (DNA: PCC, No. 87, I); in Short's hand. PrC (MHi: AMT). Tr (DNA: PCC, No. 107). Noted in SJL as received 26 July 1786. Enclosed in TJ to Jay, 11 Aug. 1786.

From John Adams

DEAR SIR   London July 16. 1786

Last night Mr. Randal arrived with yours of the 9th. If the Prussian Treaty arrives to you, I think you will do well to Send Mr. Short with it to the Hague and Exchange it with Thulemeier, and get it printed in a Pamphlet Sending a Sufficient Number to you and to me. If it comes to me and you approve, I will Send Some one[1] or go myself.

The Chevr. De Pinto's Courier unfortunately missed a Packet by one Day, which obliged him to wait a month at Falmouth for another. The Chevalier was greatly chagrined at the Delay. He is much obliged for your Notes, and I Should be more so for another Copy, having Sent mine to my Brother Cranch, who writes me that your Argument in favour of American Genius, would have been much Strengthened, if a Jefferson had been Added to a Washington, a Franklin and a Rittenhouse. I wrote you lately that the Queen of Portugal had ordered her Fleet cruising in the Streights to protect all Vessells belonging to American Citizens equally with those of her own Subjects against the Algerines.

Boylstons Vessell Arrived in Boston, with Sugars, and he expects another Vessell hourly, with which he will go again to France. He desires me, to express his obligations to you and the Marquis, for your former Assistance. Coffin Jones has Sent a Vessel to L'Orient, with another Cargo of oil. The French Government would do well to encourage that Trade. If they do not, it will go elsewhere. It is in vain for French or English to think, that Sperma Cæti oil cannot find a Market but in their Territories. It may find a Market in every City that has dark nights, if any one will do as Boylston did, go and shew the People its qualities by Samples and Experiments. The Trade of America in oil and in any Thing else will labour no longer, than public Paper is to be sold under Par. While a Bit of Paper can be bought for five shillings that is worth twenty, all Capitals will be employed in that Trade, for it is certain there is no other that will yeild four hundred Per Cent Profit, clear of Charges and Risques.

As soon as this lucrative Commerce shall cease We shall see American Capitals employed in sending all where it will find a Market, that is all over Europe if France does not wisely monopolise it as she may, if she will. Inclosed is an oration of Dr. Rush.

I am my dear Sir, your most obedient   JOHN ADAMS

RC (DLC); addressed by Smith; endorsed. FC (MHi: AMT); in Smith's hand. Noted in SJL as received 2 Aug. 1786. Enclosure: Benjamin Rush, *An Oration delivered before the American Philosophical Society, Held in Philadelphia on the 27th of February, 1786: Containing an Enquiry into the Influence of Physical Causes upon the Moral Faculty.* 2d ed., London, C. Dilly, 1786 (Sabin 74236).

There were others who agreed with Cranch that TJ's argument would have been strengthened IF A JEFFERSON HAD BEEN ADDED to the following sentence in *Notes on Virginia*: "We produce a Washington, a Franklin, a Rittenhouse." In the margin of the second copy that TJ gave to David Rittenhouse there is written opposite this sentence: "and a Jefferson" (handwriting unidentified; Coolie Verner, "Mr. Jefferson Distributes His *Notes*," *Bull. N.Y.P.L.,* Vol. 56 [1952], p. 171, identifies but does not locate a second Rittenhouse copy; this second copy is in the possession of Miss Elizabeth Sergeant Abbot of Philadelphia, a descendant of Rittenhouse; "The Rittenhouse Orrery," *Princeton University Library Chronicle,* XV [1954], 201).

[1] Adams first wrote "Smith," then substituted "Some one"; FC reads as above.

Thomas Barclay to the American Commissioners

GENTLEMEN   Morocco 16th. July 1786

I wrote you the 26th. of last Month and expected to have followed my Letter in a week, but several unforeseen Matters have hitherto detained us; however I expect we shall set out tomorrow or the day following. The 13th. Instt. the Treaty was sent to me by the Effendi, since which some important Alterations have been made, which the Villainy and carelessness of the Talbe Houdrani (to whom the drawing was committed) made necessary; and yesterday it was again delivered from Tahar Fennish to whose hands the King committed the arrangement of the Matter. It still wants an additional Article, or rather a Declaration which His Majesty has permitted to be made in his Name but which he desired might not make a Part of the treaty. When this is done, it will stand as I described it in my last Letter, Vizt. "there is only one Article more I wish to see inserted and that I think will never prove of any Consequence."

When I send you the Treaty it will be necessary to accompany it with some Remarks with which I will not now trouble you and the only one I shall make is, that the King throughout the whole has acted in a Manner the most gracious and condescending, and I really believe the Americans possess as much of his Respect and Regard as does any Christian Nation whatever. If you should think my services at Algiers, Tunis and Tripoli necessary, I hope your commands will meet me in the South of Spain, for after return-

16 JULY 1786

ing to Paris it will be utterly impossible for me to engage further in the Business. A Peace with the Barbary Powers is absolutely essential to the Commerce of our Country, and I think a general one might be made notwithstanding the impediments that appear. The Emperor has ordered five Frigates on a Cruize in the Atlantic Ocean. He is now at Peace with all the World except Russia, Malta, Hamburg and Dantzick. A treaty with the first of these Powers was concluded on, and the Articles drawn, but it was afterwards broke off. The Emperor complains much of the treatment he receives from England, and Mr. Duff who came here some time ago as Pro-Consul returned the day before we arrived, highly offended at his reception, the Emperor having refused to receive the Letter which Lord Sydney wrote, saying he would read no Letters from England but such as were written by the King. I had a Letter yesterday from Mr. Carmichael and was in great hopes it would have covered one from you, but I am hitherto without the pleasure of hearing from you.

I am allways, Gentlemen, Your most obt. humble servant,

Thos. Barclay

RC (DLC); in Franks' hand, signed by Barclay. Dupl (DLC); not signed. Another Dupl (MHi: AMT); in Franks' hand, signed by Barclay; endorsed in part: "Rec'd 1st. Septr. Copies forwarded to America & France of the same date" and "Rece'd & forwarded 31st August 1786 for Forrest & Stoddart Wm. Pratt." Tr (DNA: PCC, No. 87, I); in Short's hand. Tr (DLC); in hand of William Stephens Smith. Tr (DNA: PCC, No. 107). Noted in SJL as received 24 Aug. 1786.

From Cambray

Château de Villers aux Erables, 16 July 1786. Has just returned from a journey and received TJ's letter enclosing the extract of a letter from the commissioners of the treasury; has never doubted the good faith of the United States in regard to their obligation to the foreign officers; attributed the delay in meeting them to an "impossibilité momentanée, telle qu'on en voit des exemples dans tous les Governemens"; is sorry TJ was absent when he called on him in the spring.

RC (DLC); 2 p.; endorsed. Noted in SJL as received 21 July 1786. See TJ to Du Portail and others, 27 June 1786.

From James Monroe

Dear Sir   New York July 16th. 1786

I have not heard from you for several months past, the last being dated sometime previous to your removal to London. Not knowing

[142]

16 JULY 1786

you would have staid so long I have wrote you by every packet to France. We have now present 12. States and hope this will be the case for some time. Soon after my arrival here in the winter I suggested to you my apprehensions that the condition of the act of cession from Virga. which respected the extent of the States to be erected over the ceded territory was an impolitick one and that it might be proper to recommend it to the State to alter it. A proposition of this effect was submitted to Congress which ultimately pass'd advising that it be vested in Congress to divide the said territory into not less than 3. nor more than 5. States. But the investigation of this subject has open'd the eyes of a part of the union so as to enable them to view the subject in a different light from what they have heretofore done. They have therefore manifested a desire to rescind every thing they have heretofore done in it, particularly to increase the number of Inhabitants which should entitle such States to admission into [the] confederacy, and to make it depend on their having on[e] 13th. part of the free inhabitants of the U.S. This wit[h] some other restrictions they wish to impose on them evinces plainly the policy of these men to be to keep them out of the confederacy altogether. I consider this as a dangerous and very mischievous kind of *policy*[1] and *calculated to throw them into the hands of Britain*. I know not with certainty whether they will be able to carry this point but if it is press'd and a probability of being carried we shall object to the power of the U.S. to determine the numbers without the consent of the State. It having been left open in the act, does by no means put it in the power of the U.S. to make such restrictions on this head as to defeat the condition altogether. If they do not therefore agree with the delegation to leave it upon the ground of April 23d. 1784. we shall propose a subsequent convention between the parties as to that point, and deny the right of the U.S. to act otherwise in it. In my last I advis'd you of an *intrigue* on foot under the *management of Jay to occlude the Missisipi supported by the delegation* of *Massachusets*. Since my last no further measures have been openly taken in the business, yet it is not relinquish'd. As yet there hath not been a fair tryal of the sense of Congress on the subject. I have a conviction in my own mind that *Jay* has manag'd *this negociation dishonestly*. On the other hand I am persuaded that *the minister here* has no *power* on the subject, yet I am firmly persuaded that he has conducted himself in such manner in this business as to give him and *his court hopes* which *the sen[se]* of *Congress* nor *his instruct[ion]s authorise*. Having been on all for-

[143]

16 JULY 1786

eign business laterly, indeed since you left us, I have had an opportunity of knowing *him* well, and this communication is founded in circumstances this opportunity hath given me. The *Massachusets delegates* except *the president* whose talents and merits have been greatly overated (tho preferable greatly in the latter instance to his brethern) are without exception *the most illiberal* I have ever seen from *that state.* Two of these *men* whose names are *Dane*[2] *and King* are elected for the next year which is my motive for making known to you this circumstance. It may possibly be of some service to you, as I shall leave Congress, to possess information, of this kind. The former is I believe *honest*[3] but *the principles* of the latter I doubt.—It has been propos'd and supported by our State to have a Colonial government establish'd over the western districts and to cease at the time they shall be admitted into the confederacy; we are fully persuaded it will be beneficial to the setlers and to the U.S. and especially those to whose frontiers such establishment form'd an immediate barrier. This hath not been decided on, and hath only been postpon'd in consequence of the inordinate schemes of some men above alluded to as to the whole policy of the affairs of that country. I am not aware of any thing else that I can give you new. In October I shall leave this for Virga. and shall settle in Fredricksburg for the purpose of commencing the practice of the law. I hope by this you have reachd Paris again and at home, that you have been well pleasd with your trip. Mr. Madison writes me today [he] is at Phila. and intends in a few days a visit here. I am Dear Sir yr. affectionate friend & servant,
JAS. MONROE

RC (DLC); several passages are written in code and were decoded by TJ interlineally. Noted in SJL as received 22 Aug. 1786.

THE PRESIDENT: Nathaniel Gorham; on 15 May 1786 Gorham succeeded David Ramsay as chairman of Congress in the absence of John Hancock, who had been elected president on 23 Nov. 1785 but who had not attended. Hancock's resignation was laid before Congress on 5 June 1786 and Gorham was elected president the next day.

[1] This and the following words in italics are written in code and have been decoded by the editors, employing Code No. 9.

[2] TJ decoded this word as "Dana," doubtless having in mind Francis Dana; Monroe wrote the numerals for, and intended, "Dane," i.e., Nathan Dane who served in Congress in 1785 and 1786 and was elected on 27 June 1786 to serve for a year from that date.

[3] Monroe erroneously wrote "333" for "336," the code numeral for "honest"; TJ decoded it as "honest."

To Lafayette, with Enclosure

Dear Sir   Paris July 17. 1786.

I have now the honour of inclosing to you an estimate of the Exports and Imports of the United states. Calculations of this kind cannot pretend to accuracy, where inattention and fraud combine to suppress their objects. Approximation is all they can aim at. Neither care nor candour have been wanting on my part to bring them as near the truth as my skill and materials would enable me to do. I have availed myself of the best documents from the customhouses which have been given to the public; and have been able to rectify these in many instances by information collected by myself on the spot in many of the states. Still remember however that I call them but approximations and that they must present some errors as considerable as they were unavoidable.

Our commerce divides itself into European and West Indian. I have conformed my statement to this division.

On running over the catalogue of American imports, France will naturally mark out those articles with which she could supply us to advantage; and she may safely calculate that after a little time shall have enabled us to get rid of our present incumbrances and of some remains of attachment to the particular forms of manufacture to which we have been habituated, we shall take those articles which she can furnish on as good terms as other nations, to whatever extent she will enable us to pay for them. It is her interest therefore, as well as ours, to multiply the means of paiment. These must be found in the catalogue of our Exports, and among these will be seen neither gold nor silver. We have no mines of either of these metals. Produce therefore is all we can offer. Some articles of our produce will be found very convenient to this country for her own consumption. Others will be convenient as being more commerciable in her hands than those she will give in exchange for them. If there be any which she can neither consume, nor dispose of by exchange, she will not buy them of us, and of course we shall not bring them to her.—If American produce can be drawn into the ports of France, the articles of exchange for it will be taken in those ports, and the only means of drawing it hither is to let the merchant see that he can dispose of it on better terms here than any where else. If the market price of this country does not in itself offer this superiority, it may be worthy of consideration whether it should be obtained by such abatements of duties, and even by such other encouragements as

17 JULY 1786

the importance of the article may justify. Should some loss attend this in the beginning, it can be discontinued when the trade shall be well established in this channel.

With respect to the West India commerce, I must apprise you that this estimate does not present it's present face. No materials have enabled us to say how it stands since the war. We can only shew what it was before that period. New regulations have changed our situation there much for the worse. This is most sensibly felt in the Exports of fish and flour. The surplus of the former, which these regulations throw back on us, is forced to Europe, where, by increasing the quantity, it lessens the price; the surplus of the latter is sunk; and to what other objects this portion of industry is turned, or turning, I am not able to discover. The Imports too of Sugar and Coffee are thrown under great difficulties. These increase the price; and being articles of food for the poorer class (as you may be sensible on observing the quantities consumed) a small increase of price places them above the reach of this class, which being very numerous, must occasion a great diminution of consumption. It remains to see whether the American will endeavour to baffle these new restrictions in order to indulge his habits; or will adapt his habits to other objects which may furnish emploiment to the surplus of industry formerly occupied in raising that bread which no longer finds a vent in the West Indian market. If instead of either of these measures, he should resolve to come to Europe for coffee and sugar, he must lessen equivalently his consumption of some other European articles in order to pay for his coffee and sugar, the bread with which he formerly paid for them in the West Indies not being demanded in the European market. In fact the catalogue of Imports offers several articles more dispensible than coffee and sugar. Of all these subjects, the Committee and yourself are the most competent judges. To you therefore I trust them with every wish for their improvement, and with sentiments of that perfect esteem and respect with which I have the honour to be, Dear Sir, your most obedient and most humble servant, TH: JEFFERSON

ENCLOSURE

ESTIMATE OF THE EXPORTS OF THE
UNITED STATES OF AMERICA.

	To Europe	To West Indies	Total
	Louis	Louis	Louis
Fish	107,000	50,000	157,000
Fish-oil	181,688	9,562	191,250

17 JULY 1786

Fish-bones	8,400		8,400
Salted meats		131,500	131,500
Live-stock		99,000	99,000
Butter, cheese		18,000	18,000
Flour, Bread, 660,000 barrels	330,000	330,000	660,000
Wheat, 2,210,000 bushels	331,000		331,000
Indian corn, Pulse	30,000	61,000	91,000
Rice, 130,000 barrels	189,350	70,650	260,000
Indigo	51,700		51,700
Tobacco, 87,000 hogsheads	1,305,000		1,305,000
Potash, 20,000 barrels	49,000		49,000
Peltry	184,900		184,900
Flax-seed	79,500		79,500
Hemp	21,000		21,000
Iron, Copper	84,000	6,000	90,000
Turpentine &c. 60,000 barrels	29,410	1,840	31,250
Timber, Lumber	82,000	164,000	246,000
Ships 300	216,500		216,500
Miscellanies	22,000		22,000
	3,302,448	941,552	4,244,000

ESTIMATE OF THE IMPORTS OF THE
UNITED STATES OF AMERICA.

From Europe and Africa.

Woollen cloths of every description.
Linens of every description.
Hosiery. Hats.
Gloves. Shoes. Boots. Sadlery, and other
  things of leather.
Silks. Gold and Silver lace Jewellery.
  Millinery. Toys.
East India goods.
Porcelaine. Glass. Earthen ware.
Silver. Copper. Brass. Tin. Pewter. Lead.
  Steel. Iron, in every form.
Upholstery. Cabinet work. Painter's colours.
Cheese. Pickles. Confitures. Chocolate.
Wine. 2000. tons @ 100 Louis. 200,000
  Louis. Brandy. Beer.
Medicinal drugs. Snuff. Bees-wax.
Books. Stationary.
Mill-stones. Grindstones. Marble.
Sail cloth. Cordage. Ship chandlery.
  Fishing-tackle.
Ivory. Ebony. Baywood. Dyewood.
Slaves.

          Louis   livres sous
          3,039,000   0   0

         Louis   livres
Salt. 521,225. bushels
  @ 24. sous.   26,061   6

18 JULY 1786

From the West Indies.

Salt. 500,484. bushels					
@ 24. sous.	25,024	4	16		
Fruits	2,239	12			
Cocoa 576,589 ℔.					
@ 12 sous.	25,798	12			
Coffee 408,494. ℔.					
@ 16. sous.	15,249	14	8		
Sugar. 10,232,432. ℔.	168,007				
Molasses. 3,645,464.					
gallons @ 24. sous.	186,281	19	4		
Rum. 3,888.370 gallons				Louis	livres sous
@ 2ᵗᵗ 14s	437,441	15		927,438	8 8
Ginger Pimenta.	1,395	1	4		
Cotton. 356,591. ℔.					
@ 24. sous.	17,829	13	4		
Skins	7,870	6			
Indigo 4,352 ℔. @ 5ᵗᵗ 8s	979	4	16		
Ivory. Turtle shell.	247	4	16		
Lignum vitae. Sarsaparilla.					
Fustic. Annettas.	5,170				
Logwood.	13,624	21			
Mahogany.	20,280¹				

                                                    3,966,438   8   8

PrC (DLC). Tr (DNA: PCC, No. 87, I); in Short's hand. Tr (DNA: PCC, No. 107). Enclosure: PrC (DLC). Tr (DLC); in an unidentified hand of estimate of imports, only. Tr (DNA: PCC, No. 87, I); in Short's hand, with minor variations in spelling and punctuation, and one error (see note 1, below). Tr (DNA: PCC, No. 107); with the same error as the preceding Tr.

For the immediate background and circumstances surrounding this letter, see Gottschalk, *Lafayette, 1783-89*, p. 240 ff.

¹ Short copied this figure as "23,280."

From John Banister

DEAR SIR   July 18th. 1786

I wrote you last Month by the Portsmouth, enclosing authentick Papers in explanation of Mr. Mark's agency for your Friends in paris. I have this Moment applied to Mr. Black on this Subject and I think his explanations will all be made out against an opportunity again occurs of paying my respects to you by letter. I think Mr. Mark means well and will do in the end what is incumbent on him as a Trustee, should any contrary indications turn up, I shall immediately give you notice. I have not heard of Jack for a long time. I wish he may be well in Body, and improv-

[148]

ing in Mind. I wish to hear from you when business permits. I am with the most perfect esteem Dr. Sir, your Friend & Servant,

J Banister

RC (MHi); endorsed. Noted in SJL as received 6 Sep. 1786.
I WROTE YOU LAST MONTH: An error for Banister's letter of 12 May 1786.

From William Carmichael

Dear Sir   Madrid 18 July 1786

I have just received the inclosed Letters from Mr. Lamb which I forward by the same Courier to whom I intrusted my last for Your Excellency. Mr. Lamb writes me that his health not permitting him to journey by land he has resigned his commission and means immediately to close his public accompts. The Ct. D'Expilly and Another Agent of Spain employed at Algiers and at Tunis are now here. The first is much attached to me and the Other I shall cultivate and thro' their means be enabled to obtain intelligence with respect to the situation of Affairs on the Barbary Coast and make such Insinuations as yourself and Mr. Adams may judge proper for the Public interest. Whatever may be the decision of Congress I think it necessary to induce the Algerines to beleive that the United States are more disposed to be at peace than at war with them. Their Minister of Marine desires peace with us, and appears apprehensive of seeing American Cruisers in the Mediterranean. I have ways of cultivating his Friendly disposition and exciting his apprehensions. The Ct. Expilly informed me of a circumstance that marks Strongly the Rancor of the British in all parts of the world to us. I omitted mentioning it to you, because I wished to have previously an exact detail of the Transaction in writing from the Ct. himself. He tells me that after Mr. Lambs departure from Algiers, the British Consul at Barcelona Mr. Gregory advised Mr. Logie Consul at Algiers, that the Spanish papers procured by Mr. Lamb for his Vessel were not regular, that Mr. Lamb had taken with him 80000 Ps. &c. and that the Dey might seize the vessel as American property. Mr. Logie immediately communicated this information to the Dey; The Vessel having been sent at the Ct. D'Expillys desire to Tunis on public business. The Dey replied that he had permitted the American Officers to Land, that they were gone away and as he supposed, had taken their money with them, That the vessel was now under his protection and Concluded by telling the Consul to mind his

18 JULY 1786

own business and not intermeddle in future with what did not concern him. This Conduct of the British Consuls must arise from the Court, for their private Characters are good and they are men of Liberal and humane principles. As soon as the Treaty is published I will send you a copy of it. D'Expilly will return in a few weeks to Algiers to terminate the ransom of the Slaves and to aid the Neapolitan and Portuguese envoys in their Negotiation, The Success of which is doubtful. These Pirates will have Russia and the Emperor on their hands, as in the last cruise They have taken a Russian vessel worth 80000 Ps. and a Tuscan ship with forty Prisoners. The Russian Minister at this court, to whom I gave the first information of this capture, tells me that he will write to the Dey as a Pacha of the Turkish Empire and inclose him a copy of the Article of their Treaty with the Port, demanding an immediate restitution of the Vessel and People with damages. He added that he is sure of the approbation of his Sovereign, who will be pleased to see one of her Ministers writing in a haughty State to a Power that all Europe courts at present. When shall we be in a situation to do this? [The Chevalier de Bourgoyng Secretary to the French Embassy at this Court is now at Paris. He will probably wait upon you in my name, to take your Commands for me. I should be sorry that you should not have the pleasure of his acquaintance. I believe there is no foreigner better informed of the Situation of this Country in all respects than he is. He is the most intimate friend I have had in this Country and will take a pleasure in giving you every information that he can do with propriety and I know you will not ask more.][1] I have this moment received a Letter for Mr. Lamb which I suppose to be from you and shall forward it this night to Alicant.

I have the honor to be, with Great respect, Your Excys. Most Obedt. Hble. Servt., WM. CARMICHAEL

P.S. I have just remarked your card of the 7th July which escaped my attention when I wrote the Above. The Letter inclosed is from Mrs. Lamb advising me that by her husbands direction she had drawn upon me for 500 Stg. I forward the Letter for his advice, he has left Money in my Bankers hands here But of which I never chose to have the disposition.[2] You will please to excuse this manner of adding to my Letter.

RC (DLC); endorsed. Tr of extracts (DNA: PCC, No. 87, I); in Short's hand. PrC of foregoing (MHi: AMT). Tr of extracts (DNA: PCC, No. 107). Enclosures: (1) Lamb to TJ, 15 July 1786 and its Dupl. (2) Mrs. Lamb to Carmichael (missing). YOUR CARD OF THE 7TH JULY: On

[150]

this date TJ wrote Lamb and also sent him the joint letter from Adams and himself, both of which were bracketed in SJL as being carried by (or perhaps sent for forwarding to) "Mr. Grand." Possibly TJ also sent with these letters a visiting card with a memo for Carmichael. If so, it was not recorded in SJL and has not been found.

[1] The text in brackets (supplied) is marked in RC for omission in Tr, and is not included in Short's Tr.
[2] Short's Tr ends at this point.

From John Lamb

Alicant. July 18th. 1786

July 15th. I forwarded to Your Excellency a letter of which this is realy a duplicate as my first may not come to hand. I find Your Excellency had not received my letters I wrote by Mr. Randall. In them I Gave an Exact Account of Algiers as I could collect whilst I Stayed in that place. And likewise how we were Situated their, and Sent Duplicates of the Same to Congress, and by safe opertunityes, one Via Cales[1] under cover to Mr. Gardoqui, Directly to new york, and Mr. Randall writes me of the 20th. June Bourdeaux that he hath forwarded the other Imediately to Philidelphia, So that thier is not the least Doubt of Congress haveing a full account of all my Proceedings as I were present my Self, for I can add nothing to the account I have Given to Your Excellencys neither to Congress were I present. I have forwarded a Coppy of all my letters to Congress, since I have been on this business, at the time I wrote to Excellencys. My Indisposition will not permitt me to undertake the Journey that Your Excellencys have pointed out. Therefore I am under the necessity to begg a Settlement of my Reasonable Accounts Since I have been on this Journey, and Returne the letter of Credite to Your Excellencys Orders. I had Commensed an acquaintance with one of the princaple officers at Algiers, and from him I had Greate Expectations of a Settlement with that Regency by next Season; Or at least to have the last price for Our Unfortunate people, and what they would have for a peace, and to Strive for hostile proceedings to sease for one Year so that Congress might have more time to prepare, and supposed that in case I brought to pass the above which I had every Incouragment of, it would at least be worth the Expences we have allread been at. These were my reasons and these my Prospect and in consequence of the same thought best to Porsevear, and Exibeted as Soon as I possible Could, to ministers and Likewise to Congress, as I well knowed, how far Short the Apropiation was for the peace and that none Could be Added to

18 JULY 1786

it by Gentelmen abroad. It is my Opinion that it is out of the Power of the united States to force those people to a compliance of a peace; and to have them Going on in the maner they Do it is not so well. To buy a peace will no Doubt cost a considerable Sum, but however notions of a Strong navy hath Given the preference to a purchase &c.

I am Sencable that Your Excellencys have received maney letters from Gentelmen on my mission, and I think they wrote without consideration as in fact when they wrote they knowed nothing of the matter. A coppy hath been Sent to Your Excellency from algiers or rather forwarded from Madrid. The Gentelman whome wrote that letter knowd nothing of my business in Algiers and of Course Could not write the Truth. I find Some of the Sentances in his letter, speaking of my Business, is intirely false; it is necessary to have Sum order given on account of our people in Algiers. They were Stripped of their cloathing and had maney necessary Debts against them when I came to Algiers. Out of humanity, I paid for their Cloath and the rest of their obligation I paid, looking on them but Reasonable, and they amounted with what money I left to Upwards of Eight hundred heard Dollars, leaving Sum money with them; now they write me it is Allmost out and verey Soon they will be in a verey miserable Condition indeed.

I am with Due Respect Your Excellency Most obedient Hmbl. Servt., JOHN LAMB

RC (DLC); endorsed. Tr (DNA: PCC, No. 87, 1); in the hand of Short, who corrected Lamb's spelling and grammar, with the result that this letter and others of Lamb's as published in *Dipl. Corr.*, I, 802-04, and elsewhere, cause the author to appear more literate than he actually was. PrC of foregoing (MHi: AMT). Tr (DNA: PCC, No. 107). Recorded in SJL as received 4 Aug. 1786.

[1] Thus in RC, but Short altered his reading in Tr so that it is difficult to tell whether he intended it for "Cadiz" or "Calais." The former is more probable; the text in *Dipl. Corr.*, I, 802-04, reads "Cadiz."

From William Stephens Smith

DEAR SIR London July 18th. 1786.

Agreable to your request I have been to Woodmason's as I informed you in my last. He was to have sent the press to Mr. Garvey at Rouen, and in addition to the mode of obtaining payment suggested by you I have told him if it would be more convenient I would pay his Bill immediately after you had acknowledged the receipt of the press. This seemed to suit him best. The Letters which you requested Mr. Appleton to leave with me are all forwarded to America, agreable to your wish which was expressed in a note accompanying them, and some are probably there by this time. I called at No. 20 Charles street and delivered the Letters seperately agreable to their address. The Gentleman has put off every Idea of his voyage untill the Spring. What will be the consequence I cannot pretend to say. I fear the worst. But I can see no end to be answered by advising him for he will ultimately follow his own opinions. The same thing which prevents him from going to America I suppose will keep him from visiting Paris, viz. want of confidence in the prudence of his family, during his absence. This is what no arguments will remove, it is rivited on his mind and sway's his Conduct.

I find you can be furnish'd with a sett of harness such as you discribe neat and simple for 15 Guineas, one ornamented with studds from 18 Guineas to 20 pounds and so on to 40. If either of the extremes or any grade between them should suit you a line will accomplish what you wish. I have visited Mr. Dilly. His foreman promises to send the 50 Copies as you wish, after which the paragraph shall enter the paper. To publish first would frighten him, and he would not send the Books. I am much obliged for your observations on the appointment lately made in Holland, and for the intelligence you give relative to the King of Prussia. His conduct relative to his successor merits applause, and considering the distance at which he has always kept him, and the suspicions respecting him, which appear'd in a strict attention to his movements &c. it appears as one of those great lines of Character which has marked his reign—that at this period of his Life conscious of an approaching dissolution, he can calmly call into his council a person to whom in a short time he must according to the course of nature surrender his Empire and who hitherto he has kept at the most awfull distance. It is the first instance I have ever heard of, of a Tyrant at the close of Life, moving with seeming composure down the stream, and in his last stage making arrangements for the happiness (at least of what remains) of his people and by instructing personally his successor, endeavour to furnish him with the ability of preserving the peace and tranquility of his Kingdoms. It may and I do not doubt, it will operate as you expect, as it relates to internal tranquility, but how will it affect his Neighbours. The Candidate for the Crown is not respected, he is considered a weak Prince, involved in Debauchery and has never displayed the least mark of a great Character. Under these lines, may it not be expected, that some exertions will be made for the

18 JULY 1786

recovery of fame and territory which the enterprizing Spirit of Frederick in the course of his reign has deprived them of. Will not the Emperor endeavour to elivate himself in his tomb? But I will cease to plague you with questions.

I have the pleasure to inform you that by advices from New York, I am informed they have had another election and Colonel's Hamilton and Varrick are of the assembly. This look's well, it indicates a change of measures in that state, which must prove benificial, for they are men of understanding, of liberal minds, have the honour of their Country in view, and are friends to federal measures. They hold the articles of a National Treaty paramount to the particular Laws of a State, and are disposed to press a complyance with national obligations as necessary to justice, and the establishment of a respectability of Character.

Your prayers and good wishes have added to my obligations, and as you are never tempted to pray but when a warm feeling for your friends comes athwart your heart, your prayer on this occasion comes with such an additional weight, that I know not how to answer them, but by connecting them with the circumstance which gave rise to them. I devoutly say, *for what we have received may the Lord make us truly thankfull. Amen.*

Mrs. Smith desires her respectfull Compliments and begs me to inclose a small list of articles which she would be obliged if you would permit Petit to purchase for her.

I enclose a small peice taken from a New York paper descriptive of an animal found on the Ohio; it is novel and will give a subject of speculation. It is singular that he should have remained so long unknown.

Colo. Humphreys's arrival is also anounced in another, and as I have tormented Mr. Mazzia with a very long Letter on the Abbé Reynald and an account of the Battle of Long Island, I take the liberty of enclosing for him an account of that action taken from the British Annual register, which is pretty good.

With Compliments to the Marquis and his Lady and Madme. De Tasse and if I may, to the fair Grecian, I am Dr. Sir, your obliged Humble Servt., W. S. SMITH

RC (MHi). Noted in SJL as received 2 Aug. 1786. Enclosures: The papers and the account of the Battle of Long Island have not been found. The list of articles desired by Abigail Adams Smith is as follows:

"12 ells of black lace, at 6 Livres an ell to be bought Au Grand Mogol, rue d vis-à-vis l'ancienne Comedie Française. 6 ells of Cambrick at 15 Livres an ell, to be bought of Mr. Groff. Rue des deux Portes St. Sauveur. A pair of Corsets to be made by Mademoiselle Sanson, price 24 livres" (MS in Mrs. Smith's hand, undated, MHi. Mrs. Smith evidently forgot the name of the

[154]

street where the black lace was to be obtained; it was Rue des Fossés St. Germain).

The LETTERS YOU REQUESTED MR. APPLETON TO LEAVE WITH ME were those of 31 May 1786 to the Governors of Virginia and Maryland and to John Jay, which, according to the entry in SJL, were sent "viâ London, by Appleton." But the NOTE ACCOMPANYING THEM from TJ to Smith has not been found and is not recorded in SJL. The letters that Smith DELIVERED . . . SEPERATELY were those to THE GENTLEMAN, John Paradise, 25 May 1786, and to his wife, Lucy Ludwell Paradise, 29 May 1786; the former enclosing TJ's letters of introduction to various Virginians (see TJ to Cary and Others, 29 May 1786). THE FAIR GRECIAN: Madame de Tott.

From Giovanni Fabbroni

MONSIEUR   Florence ce 20 Juillet 1786

Avant que de repondre à votre obligeante lettre, j'ai voulu me mettre en état de repondre à la question dont vous m'avez honoré.

J'ai trouvé deux familles de Tagliaferri, l'une qui existe à Marradi, et l'autre à Lozzole dans une partie de la Toscane qui s'appelle Mugello, et toutes les deux réconnoissent une même souche qu'on croit être partie de Tagliaferro, Village qui porte leur nom. J'ai vu les deux chefs de ces deux familles. L'un qui s'appelle Francesco di Guiseppe Tagliaferri, et c'est de celle de Marradi. L'autre, plus agé, s'appelle Giovanni Tagliaferri. Ces sont des honnêtes gens de campagne, et le premier m'a paru être plus à son aise. Ils m'ont dit avoir conservé le souvenir qu'une année d'une famine memorable il y eût un de leur famille qui s'en alla de chez eux, mais il ne sçurent pas où. Il eût en Toscane une grande famine en 1709, ou dans le siecle passé. Je leur ai demandé si c'était à cette epoque qu'eut lieu l'emigration; ils m'ont repondu de ne pas le scavoir. Ils ont chez eux leurs coats of arms et je vous en envoye ici l'esquisse. Ces bons gens seroient fort contents d'avoir quelques renseignements sur la famille transplantée en Amérique, et qui a fait faire ces recherches. Si vous avez de quoi les satisfaire, vous m'obligerez beaucoup.

Mon frere vient de publier ici avec l'agrément du Gouvernement un ouvrage elementaire en forme de catechisme sur l'agriculture. Je tâcherai de trouver une occasion pour avoir l'honneur de vous en remettre un exemplaire. Peut-être pourra-t-il servir pour reveiller l'idée de mieux l'executer dans vos Pays où l'agriculture doit avoir fait des progrès aussi grands que rapides. Que je serois flaté de pouvoir vous le présenter de moi-même et avoir l'honneur d'etre connu personellement d'un homme tel que vous, dont j'admire depuis longtemps le caractere moral et les talens. Mes circon-

20 JULY 1786

stances s'y opposent, il faut donc que je me borne à me confirmer avec le plus profond respect Monsieur &c

Jean Fabbroni

P.S. Ces Taliaferri m'ont avoué qu'ils ne sont gueres à leur aise, quoiqu'ils ayent un peu de terrein, et qu'ils suivent le commerce des chapeaux de paille.

Tr (DLC); in Short's hand. Noted in SJL as received 11 Aug. 1786. Enclosure (DLC): Tr of a memorandum concerning the Tagliaferro family in Tuscany, summarizing the information in Fabbroni's letter and giving the number of members in the families, their names and occupations; together with a crude pen sketch of the family coat of arms. Translations of the letter and memorandum are printed in WMQ, 2d ser., IV (1924), 192-4, 199.

MON FRERE VIENT DE PUBLIER . . . UN OUVRAGE: This was Adamo Fabbroni's *Istruzzioni elementari di Agricoltura*, Perugia [1786]; see Sowerby, No. 770.

From Maupin

Monsieur a paris ce 20 juillet 1786.

Je ne voudrois pas moins que faire le bien de toutes les nations, et quelque grande que soit cette entreprise, je n'en desespere point a l'egard des Etats unis de l'Amerique, si, après la lecture de mes differens ouvrages, Votre Excellence juge a propos de les faire passer a sa nation.

J'ai deja eu l'honneur d'offrir a Votre Excellence tous les éclaircissemens qui dépendoient de moi, et je lui reitere les mêmes offres, non seulement par zele, mais encore par reconnoissance de la marque d'estime qu'elle a bien voulu m'accorder, en faisant prendre les trois ouvrages que je lui avois annoncés. J'y en ai ajouté un quatrieme, qui me paroit necessaire a tous les pays, mais qui l'est encore bien plus particulierement a un pays nouveau, ou toutes les plantations de la vigne, a quelques unes près peut etre, sont encore a faire.

Tous les procedés ou moyens, que j'ai proposés dans ces ouvrages, sont faits, j'ose le dire, Monsieur, pour produire partout les plus grands biens, mais pour cela, je ne le sais que trop, il est necessaire qu'ils soient distingués, et que mes différens projets obtiennent, dans tous les Gouvernemens, toute l'attention et la faveur qu'ils peuvent meriter.

C'est dans cette vue et cette esperance seule, Monsieur, que je me suis determiné a notifier mes decouvertes a tous les Ministres etrangers, et en particulier a Votre Excellence par la premiere lettre que j'ai eu l'honneur de lui adresser avec les deux écrits qui y etoient joints.

J'ai temoigné dans cette lettre, Monsieur, que je desirois surtout que le Gouvernement d'Amerique, en s'aidant s'il le juge a propos, des lumieres des autres, voulut bien aussi s'aider principalement des siennes. J'en ai donné plusieurs raisons; mais comme j'attache a cette particularité ou précaution, une si grande importance que, sans elle, je regarde comme generalement impossibles les differens genres de biens que je voudrois procurer a tous les pays, j'ai cru devoir en faire connoitre la necessité a Votre Excellence par le memoire imprimé que j'ai l'honneur de lui adresser, et que je la suplie de faire passer sous les yeux de son Gouvernement.

Cet ecrit, quoique polémique, ou plutot parce qu'il est polémique, contient sur mes differentes découvertes, des analyses et des details qui, a mon avis, peuvent en etre regardés comme la demonstration.

J'ai l'honneur d'etre avec un profond respect Monsieur Votre tres humble et tres obeissant serviteur,   MAUPIN

RC (DLC); endorsed. Noted in SJL as received 20 July 1786. The fourth pamphlet enclosed in the present letter has not been identified; but for the titles of others sent to TJ, see Maupin's letter of 4 July 1786.

From Madame de Tessé

a Chaville ce 20 juillet. [1786]

Me. de Tessé presente à Monsieur jefferson l'hommage de son admiration et de sa Reconnoissance pour ce qu'il a daigné lui adresser hier. Si les opprimés de chaque contrée de l'europe pouvoient se faire entendre ils Reclameroient surement la publication d'un acte qui deploie les privileges de l'homme avec tant de noblesse et de simplicité. Le catalogue des plantes de la virginie ne quittera point Me. de Tessé, ce sera son encyclopedie. Elle desire bien que quelques affaires conduisent Monsieur jefferson à versailles, dans l'espoir que Châville en profiteroit.

RC (DLC); endorsed: "Tessé Mme. de." The year in the date has been supplied from internal evidence. Not recorded in SJL.

This and the following are the first extant letters in the correspondence between TJ and Madame de Tessé and TJ and Madame de Tott; it is likely that both letters were in response to others by TJ, accompanied by the gifts here acknowledged, but no such letters from him have been found. The correspondence with Madame de Tessé extended, at intervals, until the death of the countess in 1814, but that with Madame de Tott, limited to the few letters written while TJ was in Paris, gives only a glimpse of this young woman. In TJ's correspondence the names of the two women are coupled, as they are in the miniature of Madame de Tott painting the portrait of Madame de Tessé (see illustration in this volume). The relationship between the two women becomes clearer if it is realized at once that "Madame de Tott" was actually *Mademoiselle* de Tott; the "Madame" was only a courtesy title, probably assumed by her after her mother's death, as the oldest woman in the family—a

20 JULY 1786

practice common among the nobility (for this reason, and because TJ himself referred to her by this assumed title, the form "Madame de Tott" will be used by the Editors).

Madame de Tessé (Adrienne-Catherine de Noailles) was but two years older than TJ; she not only shared his interests in horticulture, literature, and the arts, but was sympathetic with the liberal philosophy of the age. The editor of the memoirs of the Marquise de Montagu, sister of Madame de Lafayette and niece of Madame de Tessé, revealed both her appearance and some of these interests in his characterization: "Madame de Tessé was in every respect a remarkable person: small, piercing eyes, a pretty face marred at the age of twenty by small pox, which, it is said, was no worry to her thanks to her precocious mind; a fine mouth, but slightly misshapen by nervous tic which made her grimace when talking, and, in spite of all that, an imposing air, grace and dignity in all her movements, and above all, infinitely witty. She was one of those ladies of the Old Regime, captivated by the philosophical ideas of the century, and intoxicated by the seductive innovations which were to bring about, in their eyes, the regeneration and happiness of our country. In a word, she was a liberal and a philosopher. In philosophy, Voltaire, with whom she was closely connected, was her master; in politics, M. de La Fayette, her nephew, was her hero" (*Anne-Paule Dominique de Noailles, Marquise de Montagu*, Paris, 1889, p. 108-9). The reminiscences of the Marquise de Montagu also give a delightful and affectionate picture of Madame de Tessé during the Emigration. A good manager, the countess had succeeded in transferring some capital abroad, and thus was able to help others who had been less foresighted. She bought a farm at Lowemberg in the canton of Fribourg in Switzerland and later acquired the estate of Wittmold on Lake Ploen in Holstein, which became havens not only for herself and her husband, but for many others. Here, always surrounded by a sizable household and such old friends as the Marquis de Mun and his son, Madame de Tessé, a brilliant and tireless conversationalist, held court in the manner of her salon at Chaville in the days of the Ancien Régime. There were interminable readings at these evening sessions—*Clarissa Harlow* (which lasted a whole month), then *Tristram Shandy*, followed by Plutarch's *Lives*, and occasionally an *Oraison Funèbre* of Bossuet. After the return from exile and installation in still another country place, at Aulnay, near Paris, the indomitable countess was again the center of a great circle of nieces, nephews, grandnieces and grandnephews. Here she and her husband (who seems to have been a silent participant in her salon) celebrated their golden wedding anniversary at a memorable family gathering in 1805. The Count de Tessé died at Aulnay on 21 Jan. 1814, and Madame de Tessé's death followed a week later (same, 288 ff., 328-9; a less flattering portrait of Madame de Tessé is that contained in the *Souvenirs de la Marquise de Créquy de 1710 à 1803*, Paris, Garnier, n.d., VI, 80-3, ed. Maurice Cousin; the Marquise de Créquy was aunt to the Count de Tessé).

The beginning of the relationship between Madame de Tessé and Madame de Tott occurred some years before TJ's arrival in Europe and stemmed from another person, Charles de Pougens (1755-1833), a man of letters and of art, a "philosopher," and at one time a bookseller and publisher. His reminiscences, published in 1834 when Madame de Tott was still living, and the letters exchanged in varying combinations of writer-recipient relationships among himself, Madame de Tott, Madame de Tessé, and the Count de Fortia, his friend and confidant, present all of the elements of a novel of sensibility by Samuel Richardson or Jean-Jacques Rousseau (*Mémoires et Souvenirs de Charles de Pougens, commencés par lui et continués par Mme Louise B. de Saint-Léon*, Paris, 1834). About 1777 Pougens, possessing talent for both literature and art, journeyed to Italy to pursue the study of painting in Rome. He visited the ruins of Herculaneum, wandered in the Coliseum by moonlight, and won admission at the age of twenty-two to the Academy of Painting, Sculpture and Architecture of Rome for his picture, "Le Marchand d'Esclaves." The Count and Countess de Tessé, who had no children, were then journeying in Rome and met Pougens. Presently, as a result of serious illness, Pougens became partially blind, and Madame de Tessé forthwith adopted him as her protégé and bestowed upon him the same maternal affection that she manifested toward her nieces and nephews, including Lafayette, who was the hus-

[158]

band of her niece and namesake, Adrienne de Noailles. Returning from Rome, Pougens stopped for a time at Lyons, where he underwent treatment for his eyes by a doctor who evidently only aggravated the malady and produced total blindness. At Lyons the unfortunate young man met a family just returned from the Near East—the Baron de Tott, his wife, and their three daughters, the eldest of whom was Sophie-Ernestine (Madame de Tott). The baron, a soldier and amateur musician and painter, was born in France in 1733 but had spent some twenty-three years in the Near East before his return to France about 1779. His reminiscences, which appeared in 1784, contain grounds for supposing that the Baroness de Tott may have been of Greek origin, a fact that would explain TJ's bantering references to the daughter, Madame de Tott, as a Greek (*Mémoires du Baron de Tott sur les Turcs et les Tartares*, Paris, 1785 edn., p. 44; see TJ to Madame de Tessé, 20 Mch. 1787). The De Tott family befriended the afflicted Pougens in Lyons. Soon after their return to Paris, the Baroness de Tott died, and, because of the connection with Pougens, Madame de Tessé not only offered hospitality to Baron de Tott, but also took the daughters under her care. Sophie-Ernestine was of marriageable age, but her family was "sans fortune" and the plans for a match proposed by her father were not suited to her inclination. She remained for a time in a convent, but made frequent visits to Madame de Tessé, who permitted her to call her "Maman." Soon, perhaps early in 1781, a crisis arose which revealed the real reason for Sophie-Ernestine's lack of enthusiasm for the various marriages proposed—she and Charles de Pougens were deeply in love. From Madame de Tessé's viewpoint, this was impossible: neither of the young people possessed means, and, too, Pougens' blindness posed an insuperable obstacle. Madame de Tessé reasoned with her protégé, and, at her insistence, he left Paris for a sojourn in Geneva; at the same time she exacted from the lovers a promise that they would not communicate during the separation. In an extraordinary and revealing letter to Pougens from Chaville, 27 Apr. 1781, and occupying some twenty-seven pages in Pougens' *Mémoires* (p. 305-32), Madame de Tessé, in "gentleness mixed with much bitterness," poured out to her "dear son" all the reasons and sentiments that rent her mind and heart, for she had discovered that the promise had been violated and that the lovers had been corresponding secretly. "Never," she wrote in one of the several revealing passages, "until I came to love you and love Sophie, did my life have any meaning to me; I was useless until both of you made me necessary.... All my thoughts are devoted to serving you; you will some day realize to what extent." Pougens eventually returned to Paris from exile, but in 1783 Madame de Tessé informed him that "Ernestine no longer loves you." For a time he continued his visits to the Hôtel de Tessé; then, when he had assurances from Madame de Tessé that she would provide for Madame de Tott's future, he ceased his visits entirely. Thus, ultimately, Madame de Tessé gained her point by losing her adopted son, although Sophie-Ernestine remained with her. But by then Lafayette had returned from America and she extended her protective influence to him (see Madame de Tessé to TJ, 30 Mch. 1787). In his *Mémoires*, written late in life, Pougens concludes his own account of the love affair with Madame de Tott with these cryptic sentences: "Ernestine, if you are still alive and if this account falls into your hands, you may judge whether or not I have exaggerated the virtues of him who was once so dear to you. You were ungrateful to him, but were you not also ungrateful to your adopted mother? Search your soul, consult your memories, and if they do not bring remorse, then I pity you from the depths of my heart" (*Mémoires*, p. 113-14). From this and other hints, it is evident that Madame de Tessé and Madame de Tott parted at some time during the 1790's and that this resulted from another love affair. There is no mention of Madame de Tott in the correspondence of TJ and Madame de Tessé after 1800.

The ACTE QUI DEPLOIE LES PRIVILEGES DE L'HOMME may have been the French text of the Act for Establishing Religious Freedom, which Démeunier translated and forwarded to TJ in his letter of 26 June 1786 and which TJ put into print in order to make the text available to various persons in Europe (see St. Lambert to TJ, 27 July 1786; TJ to St. Lambert, 8 Aug. 1786; Malone, *Jefferson*, II, 103-4). If so, this is the earliest reference to the separate printing of the text; it is natural to suppose that Madame de Tessé would have been among the first to whom TJ would have addressed a copy. His letter of transmittal—one must have accompanied it—has not been found and is not recorded in SJL. If only the Act was sent to Madame de Tessé, this would suggest that he had already presented to her a copy of *Notes on Virginia*. This was almost certainly the case, though there seems to be no documentary evidence of such a presentation.

From Madame de Tott

A Châville ce 20 Juillet. [1786]

Mad. de Tott a Reçu avec bien de La Reconnoissance Le Charmant petit Livre que Monsieur Jefferson a eu La bonté de lui envoyer; elle n'est pas encore en état de L'entendre, mais elle va Redoubler de zèle pour Répondre aux soins Obligeants de Monsieur Jefferson. Elle Le Supplie d'agréer mille Compliments et ses Remerciments Les plus Sincères.

RC (MoSHi); endorsed; the year in the date has been supplied from internal evidence. Not recorded in SJL.

LE CHARMANT PETIT LIVRE may have been a copy of *Notes on Virginia* but it may also have been some classical work.

From James Bowdoin

SIR   Boston July 22d. 1786.

I had the pleasure of your Letter of the 8th. February, and thank your Excellency for the information contained in it.

The young Gentleman, who will do himself the honour of waiting upon you with this Letter, is Mr. Appleton, a Son of the Intendent of the United States loan office in this Town. He is in the mercantile line, and has conducted with reputation.

The Father, a very worthy character, expressing a desire that his Son might be introduced to you, I have the honour of writing by him for that purpose; and am with great esteem, Sir, Your Excellency's Most Obedient Humble Servant,

JAMES BOWDOIN

RC (DLC); in a clerk's hand, signed by Bowdoin; endorsed. TJ noted in SJL under 20 Sep. 1786, receipt of a letter from Bowdoin without indicating the date of the letter; this doubtless is the letter referred to.

To Francis Eppes

Paris, 22 July 1786. "Your letters of April 11th, and Mr. Lewis's of March 14th, come to hand the 29th of June. I perceive they were to

[160]

have come by Colonel Le Maire, but I hear nothing of his arrival. I had fondly flattered myself to receive my dear Polly with him, an idea which I cannot relinquish whatever be the difficulties."

MS not found. Text quoted above has been taken from Randall, *Life,* I, 476, where this extract is printed from a letter then in the possession of TJ's grandchildren.

To the Governor of Virginia

SIR   Paris July 22. 1786

An opportunity offering at a moment's warning only to London, I have only time to inform your Excellency that we have shipped from Bourdeaux fifteen hundred stand of arms for the state of Virginia of which I now inclose the bill of lading. A somewhat larger number of cartouch boxes have been prepared here, are now packing, and will go to Havre immediately to be shipped thence. As soon as these are forwarded I will do myself the honour of sending you a state of the expenditures for these and other objects. The residue of the arms and accoutrements are in a good course of preparation. I have the honour to be with sentiments of the highest respect Your Excellency's most obedient and most humble servant,   TH: JEFFERSON

RC (Vi); endorsed, in part: "Enclosing Bill of Lading for Arms for Va. &c."; at foot of text: "Govr of Virginia." PrC (DLC). For the enclosed bill of lading, see Bondfield to TJ, 15 July 1786.

From Abigail Adams

DEAR SIR   London july 23. 1786

Mr. Trumble will have the honour of delivering this to you. The knowledge you have of him, and his own merit will ensure him a favourable reception. He has requested a Letter from me, and I would not refuse him, as it gives me an opportunity of paying my respects to a Gentleman for whom I entertain the highest esteem, and whose portrait dignifies a part of our room, tho it is but a poor substitute for those pleasures which we enjoy'd some months past.

We console ourselves however by the reflection which tends to mollify our grief for our [depar]ted Friends; that they are gone to a better Country, an[d to a] Society more congenial to the benevolence of their minds.

[161]

I Supposed Sir that Col. Smith was your constant correspondent, and that his attention, left me nothing to inform you of. This Country produced nothing agreeable and our own appears to be takeing a Nap, as several vessels have lately arrived without a scrip, from any creature. By one of the papers we learn that Col. Humphries was safely arrived.

Perhaps neither of the Gentlemen may think to acquaint you, that the Lords of the admiralty have orderd home Captain Stanhopes Ship, and calld upon him for a justification of his conduct to Govenour Bowdoin, that having received what he offerd as such, they voted it not only unsatisfactory, but his conduct highly reprehensible. As such they have represented it to his Majesty, and Captain Stanhope will not be permitted to return to that Station again. Thus far we must give them credit.

I suppose you must have heard the report respecting Col. Smith —that he has taken my daughter from me, a contrivance between him and the Bishop of St. Asaph. It is true he tenderd me a son as an equivilent and it was no bad offer. But I had three Sons before, and but one daughter. Now I have been thinking of an exchange with you Sir. Suppose you give me Miss Jefferson, and in some [fu]ture day take a Son in lieu of her. I am for Strengthening [the] federal union.

Will you be so good as to let petite apply to my shoe maker for 4 pr. of silke shoes for me. I would have them made with straps, 3 pr. of summer silke and one pr. blew sattin. Col. Trumble will deliver you a guiney for them. Whenever I can be of service to you here, pray do not hessitate to commission me. Be assured you confer a favour upon your Humble Servant,   A ADAMS

RC (DLC); a few words or parts of words missing where seal was broken. Noted in SJL as received 1 Aug. 1786. A GENTLEMAN . . . WHOSE PORTRAIT DIGNIFIES A PART OF OUR ROOM: An allusion to the portrait of TJ by Mather Brown, painted in Mch.-Apr. 1786; see Vol. 1: lvii, 3.

To John Banister, Jr.

SIR   Paris July 24. 1786.

I received yesterday your favor of the 16th. inst. I had expected you here every day for some time, which was the reason why I had not forwarded to you the inclosed letters which have been some days in my hands. I am sorry you are stopped on the road by ill health. With respect to the expediency of your return to America, no person can be so good a judge as yourself. Your object in coming to Europe was the reestablishment of your health. You best know in what degree this has taken place. Judging from your letters I am afraid it is not mended in any great degree. If it be merely as it was, you will judge of the preponderance of the other arguments for and against your remaining in Europe. I think you were better while in England. Perhaps the climate of that country was friendly to your health, or, which is more probable, perhaps the physicians of that country, the best in the world, could be of service to you. Might it be better therefore for you to pass some time there before you return ultimately to your own country? In the mean while you could take the advice of your father on the subject. On these things it would be presumption in me to offer advice. No body can judge so well as yourself, to whom all the circumstances are known on which a decision depends. If I can be useful in any plan which you may adopt, command me with freedom, being with much sincerity Dear Sir your friend & servt.,

Th: Jefferson

PrC (DLC); endorsed. Noted in SJL as directed "chez Bertrand. Libourne." The enclosed letters have not been identified.

From Boyetet

Rue nre Dame des Victoires N. 12.
Monsieur A Paris Le 24 Juillet 1786.

Je ne Puis Refuser aux Sollicitations d'une maison honnete de St. Quentin, les démarches nécéssaires pour lui faire obtenir Justice, et Je les dirige avec d'autant plus de confiance vers vous Monsieur, que Je Suis persuadé que vous Sentirés qu'un des premiers moyens d'etablir entre les deux nations les liaisons de commerce dont leurs intérêts Respectifs les rendent Susceptibles, comme on S'en occupe, c'est d'assurer la plus grande éxactitude et ponctualité dans les engagemens Reciproques.

J'ai L'honneur de vous remettre cy Joint, Monsieur, La note que cette maison m'a fourni. Mr. Le duc de la Vauguyon, par égard et consideration pour le Congrés, a fait Suspendre les démarches qu'elle avoit fait faire a Madrid, pour obliger Mr. Barclai, Son débiteur a payer, mais ce n'a eté que dans la Confiance que la lettre de Change qu'elle tireroit sur Mr. Champion, correspondant de Mr. Barclai a L'orient, Seroit payée comme il l'avoit offert. Cette Traite a eté protestée et la promesse est Restée sans éffet. Il est facheux qu'un homme, qui a la Confiance du Congrés, donne lieu a des plaintes de Cette nature, mais il le Seroit encore plus pour Cette maison, que l'employ dont il est Revetu put le Soustraire au payement de ses engagemens, ou au moins lui fournir les moyens de l'eluder.

Cest de Rechef avec la plus grande confiance que J'ai L'honneur de Vous adresser les representations de cette maison, et que Je me Flate que Vous Voudrés bien lui procurer la Justice qu'elle demande.

Je Suis avec Respect Monsieur Votre trés humble et trés obeissant Serviteur,   BOYETET
               Commissre. genl. du Commerce

RC (DLC); endorsed. Noted in SJL as received 24 July 1786. Enclosure (DLC: TJ Papers, 12: 1953): clerk's copy of state of the case of Veuve Samuel Joly l'aîné et fils, of St. Quentin in Picardie, involving Thomas Barclay's purchase from that firm on 24 Jan. 1785 of goods valued at 7504tt for which he promised to pay in nine months; the statement declared that on 13 Nov. 1785 and again on 28 Jan. 1786 the firm had endeavored to collect the amount due, but without success; that they had drawn on Barclay on 3 Mch. 1786 and, instead of payment, received word of his departure for Madrid; that they had instituted proceedings against him there; that their representative had obtained from Floridablanca, governor of Madrid, an order confining Barclay to that city until he had discharged his indebtedness; that, after he had promised to pay, Barclay's detention was waived; but that his draft drawn on Henry Champion of L'Orient had been protested and returned. See TJ to Boyetet, 28 July 1786.

To André Limozin

SIR   Paris July 24. 1786.

I have taken the liberty to desire the Sieur de Presolle to send to your address some packages of cartouch boxes for the state of Virginia. I will beg the favor of you to receive and forward them by some vessel going into James river. Your draft on me for charges shall be paid on sight. I have the honor to be with much respect Sir your most obedient & most humble servt.,

                                        TH: JEFFERSON

PrC (MHi); endorsed.

From Dumoulin de Seille & Son

SIR   at Royan in the Saintonge 24. July 1786.

We have the honour to present you our most humble Respects, and Beseech you to take in Consideration that we take the Liberty to Inform you.

24 JULY 1786

Being Corespondents of the Consuls of different foreign nations which trade in the harbours of Bordeaux, Rochefort, and other Neighbouring Places Exporting of it the Provisions and Marchandises fit for their Maintenance, and our advantageous Situation to the Intrance of the garonne Ablening us to give our Cares and helps to foreign and National vessels, as also to their Captains which Dwell there, we should think to fail to the Respect owing to the united states which you represent, if we Did not request the honour to offer you our services for the Same Subject, and understanding that there are not any traders in these provinces who are Instituted By your Power, to Interest themselves in the Behalf of the People of your Nation in the Circumstances which Concern trade to the Difficultys to which one might be Exposed, and particularly those of Shipwrecke and running a ground.

To these Causes, we ask you to grant us the post of vice Agent or Consul in this Place if you find us worthy of it, which we shall fulfil with all the Zeal and Exactitude that your trust Can require, if our offers don't appear Indiscreet to you, and Agree to the Welfare which may Insue for the Nation, we Beseech you to honour us with a satisfactory Answer.

We have the honour to be with the ustmost respect Sir your Excellency's most humble and Respectful Servants,

DUMOULIN DE SEILLE
father and son
Vice Consul of the Denmark
Norwege and Islande

RC (ViWC); endorsed. Noted in SJL as received 4 Aug. 1786.

To John Stockdale

SIR   Paris July 24. 1786.

I must beg the favor of you to send me the books underwritten. There is a stage coach established between London and Paris, which comes once a week. I do not know from what house in London it comes, but you will readily learn on enquiry. They not only bring passengers but take in small packages also. This I think will be the best means of conveyance. I pray you therefore to avail me of it, and am Sir your very humble servt.,   TH: JEFFERSON

Homeri Ilias. Greek. 2. vols. folio. The edition of Foulis, Glasgow.
Homeri Odyssea, Greek. 2. vols. folio. The edition of Foulis, Glasgow

Schrevelii lexicon. A new edition in large octavo, containing besides the Greek and latin part, a part in Latin and Greek, and another with the Greek roots.

Mc.Intosh and Capper's voiages. The smallest edition.

Andrews' history of the late war. The numbers after 24. I have 24 nos. complete.

Andrews' history of the war. Another copy complete.

Soule's histoire des troubles de l'Amerique. I have the two first volumes; if any more be come out, I shall be glad to receive them; or whenever they do come out.

Bell's Shakespeare. The nos. since 25. I have 25. numbers. On fine paper.

Monthly and Critical reviews since those I have received.

Jeffery's historical chart.

Priestly's biographical chart, with 2. of the pamphlets, the one I received with mine wanting several leaves.

Evans's map of the middle colonies.

Send the above books unbound, all of them.

PrC (DLC). The following note appears in SJL after the entry for this letter: "2d copy Mc.Intosh's travels for M. fayette."

From Eliza House Trist

Philadelphia July 24th 1786

I cannot review the time that has elapsed since the receipt of your obliging and kind favor by Messrs. Fitzhughs without feeling a mortification at the negligence and ingratitude which the delay seems to accuse me. Shortly after it came to hand I was prevailed on by my friend Mrs. Simms of Alexandria to accompany her return from a visit to her friends in this quarter. This trip with my indisposition which of late has had few intermissions and being ignorant of private oppertunities which I wou'd have preferd to writing by post are the pleas by which I must defend my self. If the real sentiment of my heart cou'd be disclosed I shou'd not fear an acquittal. It has never accused me of insensibility to the favors and friendship which I have experienced and if I had less of this Virtue I cou'd not be particularly impress'd with the marks of kind attention which your goodness has condescended to bestow on me. Surrounded by multitudes and immersed in business, the favor has a peculiar title to my gratitude. "The ways of Heaven are dark and intricate puzzled in mazes and perplex'd with errors."[1] I fancy your situation will verify [terrestially?] the poets observation. I wish for your own sake as well as that of your friends that you had compleated your embassy. I fear we shall be too long deprived of your society. My inclination is good if I dared to take the liberty to advise you to make your stay in that country as short as possible. There is a great difference betwixt a servant and a Slave, tho the public dont seem to be allways sensible of the distinction. I am happy to find your sentiments of your own country unchanged. We have great reason to be satisfied with what nature has done for us, and if we knew the value of the blessings we have within our reach, we shou'd be a happy people. We hourly experience the bad effects of refinement, which a connection with foreign countries has been the means of introducing among us. We have accumulated our wants and lessen'd the means of satisfying them, in fact we are very poor and very proud. But thank God the industrious will allways find a support by seeking it in the bosom of the earth which offers its treasures to every hand that will dig for them. I have but lately return'd from my trip to Alexandria. I had not the satisfaction of seeing any of my Virginia friends except Mr. Mercer. I wish'd very much to have seen your little daughter but the distance was so great I cou'd not make it practacable to get there. I am told she has a great aversion to going to france, which I suppose will prevent her friends from gratifying your desire with respect to a reunion with her in Europe. My health was much benefited by my jaunt as well as my spirits which have been more depress'd since my return to my native country owing in a great measure to want of active employment. It is well for us that our necessities oblige us to exert our selves. I have found occupation to be a most salutary restoritive to a diseased mind but I have too little resolution to force my mind to do what my inclination is repugnant to. I very sensibly feel my obligation to you for your kind attention to the interest of my son more particularly as you must be so much engaged in matters which wou'd exclude such objects from less generous and benevolent minds and I speak the literal truth when I say this very unexpected mark of your friendship has seldom been in my thoughts without tears of gratitude being at the same time in my eyes. I fear Browses relations live at too great a distance from London for you to have executed your kind intention towards us, but as chance may perhaps some time or other afford you an opportunity of being serviceable to us, I will mention to you that Hore Browse Trist, Uncle to my Son and whom he was named after, resides

24 JULY 1786

at his Seat about a mile from Totnes Devonshire. Almost all of his other relations live in that country. There is a distant relation, Richd. Trist, in London. My Husband while in that city made his house his home. He then lived in Arundel street Strand. If you shou'd ever visit England again and cou'd meet with Richd. Trist he wou'd be able to inform you more particularly of Browses relations. I have heard Mr. Trist mention an Uncle he had by the name of Earl who lived about twenty miles out of London. His Estate is in St. Kitts. I have little expectation of ever receiveing any favors of the family. The death of my Husband they probably may think has dissolved the connection with me but my Son has a better claim to their notis. I flatter my self he never will discredit his family. I have received several letters from Mr. Trists Sister Mrs. Champernowne, both before and since his death which are as friendly and affectionate as I cou'd expect. She tells me that what she writes is the sentiments of the whole family. I can not expect them to feel as much interested in my welfare as if I had been personally acquainted with them. They very likely never heard my name mention'd except by their Brother. The part of the country they live in has very little intercourse with this place and few or none of my friends have ever been in their company. From Mrs. Champernowne I learn that the Mother of Mr. Trist who died in the year 84 left by will £1000 in trust, the interest during his life to be drawn by him for the education of his children and the whole after his death to be divided among his children. I have not yet had a copy of the gift and am at a loss as to the most proper steps to be taken by me as Guardian of my Son for obtaining it and applying it to his benefit. Indeed the information I have received of the matter is very imperfect. Shou'd it happen in your way to learn any thing concerning it so that you cou'd advise me on the occasion I need not repeat how gratefull I shou'd be for the favor. As Mr. Trists Brothers are without male children it is possible Browse may take of further donations as they happen to die, if not succeed as heir. Hore Browse Trist is the Eldest of them. He is at present in possession of an estate of 3000 pr. An. As far as I can learn 1000 of that income came by the Mother but a certain sum of it to be apropriated to the portioning the younger children. I can not tell wether it is intail'd but the estate by the Father is intail'd on the Male heir. The present possessor H.B.T. never was married, is pretty far advanced in years and exceedingly emaciated with chronic deseases. The second son Browse Trist is a Clergyman, has been married several years and has three

24 JULY 1786

daughters. Nicholas Trist my late Husband is the next. James who was the youngest died in 82 by a fall from his Horse after having been Rector of Torbryan 2 Weeks, a living supposed to be worth 1500 pr. An. in the Gift of the elder Brother. He inherits it from an Uncle by the name of Nicholas Trist who died in 82 intestate after the death of James Browse who was Rector of Woodleigh, was presented by his Brother to the living of Torbryan. There are 3 sisters. Mrs. Champernowne is a Widdow with one child, a daughter. Maud is married to a Gentleman of the law by the name of Taylor, the other to a Mr. Hilby. All I believe live in Totnes. There is an old Lady widdow to a counsellor by the name of Taylor. She is a sister to old Mr. Trist, is very rich, and the family have great expectations from her. I am quite at a loss about any matter in that country. Mr. Trist in his Will does not make any mention of property in England but desires all he possesses may be divided between his Wife and child. But the commandant who is a frenchman agreeable to the laws of that country seems to have confined his will to the property on the Mississippi annexing an inventory, so that with respect to his property in England if he had any he died intestate. I fear I have trespassed on your patience by the repetition of what can not amuse you. I wish I had it in my power to afford you entertainment but I am quite out of the way of hearing or knowing any thing worthy to be noted. Deaths and marriages are frequent enough but not among the Great. Mr. Willson the lawyer lost his Lady about 3 months ago in a consumtion, a loss indeed for she was an amiable Woman and has left a family of small children. I hear Mr. Randolph the Attorney has lately lost a child God son to our friend Madison who is now with us. He intends shortly for N. York. He no doubt will write you from there and will be better able to inform you what the *great ones* are doing than I can. Every now and then we hear of an Honble. Gentleman geting a wife or else we shou'd not know there existed such a Body as Congress. I suppose you have had official accounts of the marriages that have taken place among the members of that August Body. My Brother Sam has lately bowed at the altar of Hyman with a young lady by the name of *Conroe*. Their marriage was rather or quite Clandestine for it was not known by any of the family for 2 Weeks. I dont know their motives for keeping it a secret. Her family had no objection to the connection and ours cou'd have none. I think it wou'd have been more prudent to have postponed the matter a little longer. Business at this time is very dull. My Mother has been in the country some

27 JULY 1786

time. Browse is well and improves in his learning equal to my most sanguine wishes. If his Masters dont flatter at present he is reading Ovid and Ceasar. I put him the last Winter to learn french at nights but it was more than he cou'd attend to. I was afraid to crowd his memory with more than it can bear; at the same time I am anxious that he shou'd not lose any time. I am ignorant what wou'd be the best plan for me to persue and those who I advise with differ so much in opinion that I am quite embarras'd for fear of doing too much. I perhaps err on the opisite side.—I had thrown my pen aside with an intent to have copied and of course curtail'd this tedious epistle. But Mr. Madison has just inform'd me that he sets out for N. York to morrow Morning. As I dont wish to lose the oppertunity as he has promised to forward it I send it defective as it is accompanied with the best wishes of our whole family for your health and happiness. And believe me to be with unfeigned regard & respect Your much Obliged friend,   ELIZA TRIST

I forgot to mention the Death of General Green in the state of Georgia. His Death was sudden, occasioned by a Stroke of the Sun.

RC (MHi). Noted in SJL as received 22 Sep. 1786.
[1] Except for punctuation and spelling, Mrs. Trist's quotation was accurate; the lines are from Addison's *Cato*, Act I, Sc.i.

From John Banister, Jr.

[*Bordeaux, 27 July 1786.* Recorded in SJL as received 30 July 1786. Not found; see French & Nephew to TJ, 26 Aug. 1786, in which this letter was enclosed.]

To John Ledyard

SIR   Paris July 27. 1786.

The Baron de Grimm spoke to me on Sunday last on the subject of your affairs. He said you had desired him to transact with you thro' me, to which he should have had no objection, but that he had informed the Empress from the beginning that it was with the M. de la fayette he was negotiating the matter and that therefore he should not be justified in treating it with any other person. On the receipt of your letter this morning, knowing that the Marquis

[170]

would leave town tomorrow for two months, I instantly wrote to him to let him know nothing would be done with any other person during his absence, and prayed him to see Baron Grimm before he left town as well to get for you a present supply as to know explicitly whether you are to look for a continuance of it. As soon as I receive his reply I will send it to you. I am sorry it is not in my power to send you your book. Very soon after I received it from you I lent it to Madame de la fayette, who has been obliged to lend it from hand to hand and has never returned it. I am Sir your very humble servt.,   TH: JEFFERSON

PrC (DLC). Not recorded in SJL but entered in SJPL.

There is no record in SJL of a letter received from Ledyard on this date nor is a letter from TJ to Lafayette recorded; neither has been found. See Lafayette to TJ, 2 Aug. 1786. For an account of Ledyard and the BARON DE GRIMM, see Gottschalk, *Lafayette, 1783-89*, p. 266-9. YOUR BOOK: Evidently a copy of Ledyard's recollections, *A Journal of Captain Cook's Last Voyage to the Pacific Ocean*, 1783.

From St. Lambert

eaubonne 27 juillet [1786]

Un petit voiage que j'ai fait, monsieur, a retardé Le plaisir que j'ai eu de recevoir Votre Lettre et ma réponse. Je crois que Votre république vient de rendre un des plus grands services qu'on puisse rendre à L'humanité; c'est aux peuples qui commencent à etablir La raison; elle trouve trop de prejugés établis chés Les peuples anciens, ce n'est que le Tems, Le progrès Des lumieres, et L'exemple qui peuvent y ramener peu à peu Le regne de Cette malheureuse raison; Vos republiques nous instruisent, monsieur, et Vos institutions feront peutêtre un jour chés nous ce que Les philosophes anglois et Les notres n'ont fait que nous faire esperer.

Il seroit trés utile que L'acte de Votre assemblée fut imprimé en europe Dans toutes Les langues, ce seroit aux papiers publics à le répandre, mais il ne faut pas Le confier aux nôtres, ils Le tronqueroient, ils L'altereroient, ou ne L'imprimeroient pas. Le courier de L'europe et la gazette de Leide, celle des deux ponts pourroient rendre ce service.

Deux choses surtout m'ont plu beaucoup dans cet acte, 1º Le mot de *Liberté religieuse* au Lieu de le mot de *Tolérance* qui me deplait infiniment, car pour avoir Le droit de *Tolerer* il faut avoir celui d'*empecher*. 2º C'est de dispenser tous Les citoiens de donner de L'argent au ministre choisi par d'autres. Ce moien est excellent

27 JULY 1786

pour empecher à jamais Le clergé d'etre un corps et un corps redoutable, il aura peu de tete et peu d'argent.

Mde. d'houdetot est trés sensible à Votre souvenir, recevés mes remerciemens et L'assurance de La veneration que Vous m'inspirés.

RC (MHi); unsigned; endorsed by TJ: "St. Lambert"; the year has been supplied in the date from internal evidence and TJ's letter to St. Lambert, 8 Aug. 1786, q.v. Pencilled drawing of floor plans on verso.

VOTRE LETTRE: TJ's letter, probably enclosing a printed copy of the English text of the Act for Establishing Religious Freedom, has not been found and is not recorded in SJL. CELLE DES DEUX PONTS: the *Gazette des Deux-Ponts*, published at Mannheim.

To John Stockdale

[*Paris, 27 July 1786*. An entry in SJL under this date reads: "Stockdale. 2d copy Mc.Intosh's travels for M. fayette." Not found. See TJ to Stockdale 24 July 1786.]

To Boyetet

SIR   Paris July 28. 1786.

I have been honored with your letter of the 24th. inst. asking my interference on behalf of the house of les Srs. Veuve Samuel Joly l'ainé et fils of St. Quentin, on account of a bill of exchange drawn in their favor by Mr. Barclay the American consul for France on M. Champion. The desire of doing what would be agreeable to you, as well as what would be just would have engaged me to have concurred in lessening the disappointment of that house, had it been in my power. But I must observe to you that Mr. Barclay, as Consul general of the United states, is in no wise dependant on me, nor subject to my controul in any thing relative to his office, and moreover that this transaction is not relative to his office, but is altogether of a private nature. I cannot presume to conjecture what may be the cause of this disappointment; whether Mr. Barclay has objections to the bill, whether the application for it was at a time and place when he could not pay it, or whether his correspondent has wrongfully refused to answer his draught. But from the worth of Mr. Barclay, with which I am well acquainted, and which has recommended him to the very high esteem of Congress, I am persuaded that there is no need to apply to any person but himself to obtain the paiment, if it be just, and a compensation for any delay which may have been injurious. I shall be happy to find an occasion wherein I may more effectually execute your wishes and testify the

PrC (DLC); lacks complimentary close and signature which in RC was carried over to another page.

From Stephen Cathalan, Jr.

Sir   Marseilles the 28th. July 1786

I have received in due time the two Letters you favoured me with, the 31th. May and 22 June Past, inclosing a Copy of the resolution made by the Farmers General on the Subject of Tobacco and a copy of the treaty between them and Mr. Morris for a large quantity of that commodity.

I have communicated those Pieces to the Marchants interested in the American trade and to the Person appointed here by the Farmers for the Purchase of Tobacco, who had no advice of that late regulation, which is now public being printed in our *Journal de Provence*; I have observed to that Gentleman that this regulation being made on account of the treaty with M. Morris which is only for the Northern Ports of France, is not for Marseilles or Cette [Sète], where is a Large Manufacture, and that those Ports being placed high up in the Mediterranean, the American Vessels cannot venture in that Sea without running the risk of being taken by Barbarian Pirates, and in Sending here tobacco in French or neutral vessels, the Freight and charges are dearer a third more than shipping that article for the northern Ports of France, the voyage being great dill longer.

I have also advised my american Friend and having Advice of a Parcel of 200 Blls. of Flour and only 20 hogsh. Duty of Tobacco for experiment which I daily expect to my adress, I have resolved to writte by this Post to the Farmers general a Letter on that Subject, of which you will find here inclosed a Copy, and if you approve it's contents, I will be much obliged to you to protect it with your credit.

You will see that I go in with you for the benefit of that article, and in all occasions, when it has been in my Power, I have acted as much as I could, and have wished for the wellfare and prosperity of the united states of america.

I have the honor to be with respect Sir Your most obedt. humble Servant, Per Procuration of my Father,
                             Stephen Cathalan Junr.

This Letter will be deliver'd to you by Sir John Lambert, as your direction at Paris is not in your Letters.

RC (DLC); at foot of first page: "Honble. Th. Ielferson Esqr. at Paris"; but more correctly addressed on cover in Cathalan's hand, with "Gr. Chaillot" added by another; endorsed. Noted in SJL as received 4 Aug. 1786. Enclosure (DLC): Copy of a letter from Cathalan to the farmers-general, 28 July 1786, stating that several American business firms are willing to trade with Marseilles, bringing wheat and tobacco to be exchanged for manufactured goods; that the dangers and costs of carrying produce to that port are greater than to L'Orient or Bordeaux; that the prices quoted in the agreement of Berni are only for Bordeaux and other Atlantic ports, Marseilles and Sète are not mentioned; that there is an important factory of the farmers-general at Sète; and that Marseilles can also be a storage point for tobacco to be exchanged for the manufactures from Piedmont and Italy. Cathalan also asked what price the farmers-general would pay for tobacco at Sète, what length of time these prices would hold, and what quantity the farmers-general would take per year.

From John Paradise

Dear Sir   London July 28. 1786.

Your very obliging letter gave me inexpressible satisfaction; as it afforded me convincing proofs of my holding that rank in your friendship, which it has ever been my ardent wish to enjoy. I entirely concur with your Excellency and with the inestimable Doctor Bancroft in opinion, that a trip to Paris would be productive of many good consequences. I thought so when the Doctor was in England, and mentioned it to Mrs. Paradise, more than once. But alas! my dear Sir, this trip, trifling as the expence may be with which it will be attended, I am at present totally unable to take, being, to speak the plain truth of the matter, literally ἀνάργυρος.[1] There are indeed friends, and not few, who would willingly and cheerfully assist me; but a very worthy Gentleman, with whom I have lived in habits of the strictest intimacy for these twenty years and upwards, has some time ago in a manner forced upon me the loan of one hundred and fifty pounds, which it has not yet been in my power to reimburse; and the thoughts of my being dependant upon him, though he has never given me the slightest cause to feel the dependance, are so exquisitely tormenting to me, that for the future I am determined (and Heaven and Earth will bear me witness, that what I am going to say comes from my very heart) sooner to starve and become an ἑλώριον Κύνοις Οἰωνοῖσί τε Πᾶσι,[2] than apply to a friend, be he ever so dear to me, for pecuniary assistance. I have, however, at last received two letters from my Steward, one dated the 22d. of April, the other the 26th. of the same month, in both of which he informs me that he has shipped on board a Vessel called the George and commanded by Captain Walter Wallace, forty four hogsheads of tobacco; that he would be able to send fifteen or twenty hogsheads more by the first good ship that should sail after the George; and that the George was to sail the 1st. of June. As soon then as this blessed George arrives, and no words can express with what anxiety we expect it, I shall be able to raise some supplies from my merchant, and then will set off for Paris without delay; for I really long to have one more interview with your Excellency before I leave Europe, as it is on you and you alone that all my hopes depend. Doctor Burney, who was with me a few days ago, desired me to acquaint you, that in consequence of the letter with which he has been honoured by you he went to Kirkman's to enquire what state the double harpsicord was in, which he had bespoken for you; and though he found it on the stocks, he was informed that it would be near a fortnight before it could be played on in the way of trial. This being the case the Doctor will postpone his answer to your Excellency's letter till it is finished, and ready for Mr. Walker's Machinery, with whom he will have a conference previous to the instruments being placed in his hands; the result of which shall be communicated to you, as well as the Doctor's opinion of the comparative excellence of French and English organs. He went out of Town the day after I had the pleasure of seeing him, for about a fortnight, and begged that these particulars may be communicated to you as a preface to the letter which he shall write at his return. My Wife and daughters join with me in every good wish to you and your amiable family. I beg to be remembered with the sincerest affection to Doctor Bancroft, and have the honour to be with the greatest respect Dear Sir your most obliged humble Servt.,   JOHN PARADISE

RC (DLC). There is the following entry in SJL under 2 Aug. 1786: "J. Paradise. London. July 20. & dupl. of July 28." No copy of a letter dated 20 July has been found, and since the present is clearly an answer to TJ's of 10 July, it follows that it is not a duplicate of another of 28 July but of the missing letter of 20 July.

1 Without silver.
2 A prey to dogs and vultures.

From Charles Thomson

DEAR SIR   New york July 30. 1786.

I have received your letter of the 10 of May and am happy in the opportunity of being serviceable to you or any of your friends. I shall with pleasure honor the draughts of Mr. Watson or Mr.

31 JULY 1786

Eveleigh and take care of and forward the seeds and plants as you desire. While on this subject I shall beg leave to mention a circumstance I have heard touching the introducing the native plants of one country into another. The late Duke of Argyle being fond of gardening and desirous of having some of the indigenous plants of America engaged a captain of a vessel on whom he had conferred some favours, to go, on his arrival in America, into the woods and after raking off the leaves to scrape or pare off about a quarter of an inch deep of the surface of the earth, put it into hogsheads and bring it to him. When it arrived he had a bed prepared in his garden and spread the American earth over it to the same depth it was pared off from the native soil. The consequence was, as I have been informed, that there came up next year a number of plants, many of which were quite new in that country, and undescribed by any botannical writer.

On the 8th. of this Month I acknowledged the receipt of your favour of the 22d. of April and troubled you with an account of a singular phenomenon that appeared in our sky on the night of the 1st. at the same time with a Northern light. I wrote also to you on the 6th. of April and acknowledged the receipt of yours of the 8 Oct. I hope my letters have got safe to hand. With the greatest esteem and affection I am Dr. Sir your sincere Friend & Servt., CHAS. THOMSON

RC (DLC: TJ Papers); endorsed. FC (DLC: Thomson Papers). Noted in SJL as received 22 Sep. 1786.

From John Adams

DEAR SIR   London July 31. 1786

I have received the Ratification of the Prussian Treaty, and next Thursday Shall Sett off for the Hague in order to exchange it with the Baron De Thulemeyer.

Your favour of the 11th. instant I have received. There are great and weighty Considerations urged in it in favour of arming against the Algerines, and I confess, if our States could be brought to agree in the Measure, I Should be very willing to resolve upon eternal War with them. But in Such a Case We ought to conduct the War with Vigour, and protect our Trade and People. The Resolution to fight them would raise the Spirits and Courage of our Countrymen immediately, and we might obtain the Glory of finally breaking up these nests of Banditti. But Congress will never, or at least not for years, take any such Resolution, and in the mean time our Trade and Honour suffers beyond Calculation. We ought not to fight them at all, unless we determine to fight them forever.

This thought is I fear, too rugged for our People to bear. To fight them at the Expence of Millions, and make Peace after all by giving more Money and larger Presents than would now procure perpetual Peace Seems not be be œconomical.—Did Monsieur De Massac carry his Point without making the Presents? Did Louis 14. obtain his Point without making the Presents? Has not France made Presents ever Since? Did any Nation ever make Peace with any one Barbary State, without making the Presents? Is there one Example of it? I believe not, and fancy you will find that even Massac himself made the Presents.

I agree in opinion of the Wisdom and Necessity of a Navy for other Uses, but am apprehensive it will only make bad worse with the Algerines. I will go all Lengths with you in promoting a Navy, whether to be applied to the Algerines or not. But I think at the Same time We should treat. Your Letter however has made me easier upon this Point.—Nevertheless I think you have rather undercalculated the Force necessary to humble the Algerines. They have now fifty Gun Boats, which being Small objects in Smooth Water, against great Ships in rough Water are very formidable. None of these existed in the time of Monsieur Massac. The Harbour of Algiers too is fortified all round, which it was not in Mr. Massac's time, which renders it more difficult and dangerous to attempt a Blockade.

I know not what dependence is to be had upon Portugal and Naples, in Case of a War with the Barbarians. Perhaps they might assist us in some degree.

Blocking Algiers would not obtain Peace with Morocco Tunis or Tripoli, so that our Commerce would still be exposed.

After all, tho I am glad We have exchanged a Letter on the subject, I percieve that neither Force nor Money will be applied. Our States are so backward that they will do nothing for some years. If they get Money enough to discharge the Demands upon them in Europe, already incurred, I shall be agreably disappointed. A Disposition Seems rather to prevail among our Citizens to give up all Ideas of Navigation and naval Power, and lay themselves consequently at the Mercy of Foreigners, even for the Price of their Produce. It is their Concern, and We must submit, for your Plan of fighting will no more be adopted than mine of negotiating.

31 JULY 1786

This is more humiliating to me, than giving the Presents would be. I have a Letter from Mr. Jay of 7. July, by Packet, containing nothing but an Acknowledgement of the Receipt our Letter of 25. of April.

N. Hampshire and R. Island have suspended their Navigation Acts and Massachusetts now left alone will suspend theirs, so that all will be left to the Convention, whose system, if they form one, will not be compleated, adopted and begin to operate under Several Years.

Congress have received the Answer which you saw, to my Memorial of 30 Nov. and Mr. Ramsay writes me, he is not distressed at it, because it will produce a repeal of all the Laws, against recovering private Debts. With every Sentiment of Friendship I am yours, JOHN ADAMS

RC (DLC). FC (MHi: AMT); in Smith's hand, with a number of minor omissions and errors, evidently caused by haste in copying from RC, since Smith was ordinarily very accurate. Noted in SJL as received 21 Aug. 1786.

From William Carmichael

DEAR SIR Madrid 31 July 1786

Since I had the honor of conveying to you the communications made to me by the Ct. de Florida Blanca respecting the Mission of Mr. Barclay in Morrocco I have received the inclosed Letter for your Excellency from that Gentleman, the contents of which are known to me. I do not know what Congress may decide with regard to the other Barbary states, But I am persuaded that in our actual circumstances negotiation will cost us less than Armaments, altho' I desire to see the commencement of a Military marine. I have hinted that it might be possible to draw in the Italian Powers in case that hostile measures should be adopted by the States, to contribute in some measure to defray the immense expence that these Armaments must occasion. I beg leave to recommend to your Excellencys Consideration this circumstance. I flatter myself that I have acquired the Confidence of the Corps Diplomatic from Italy to this Court and I think, or I should not mention to you, that I may be of some use to inspire sentiments and to sketch the outlines of projects advantageous to our Interests, should Congress decide to arm instead of negotiating, or should that Body conclude it best to negociate fortiter in re sauviter in modo. The Court of Spain has conducted itself so generously in

[173]

Madame de Tott painting the portrait of Madame de Tessé. (See p. xxvii.)

"Les plaisirs de Chaville." (See p. xxvii.)

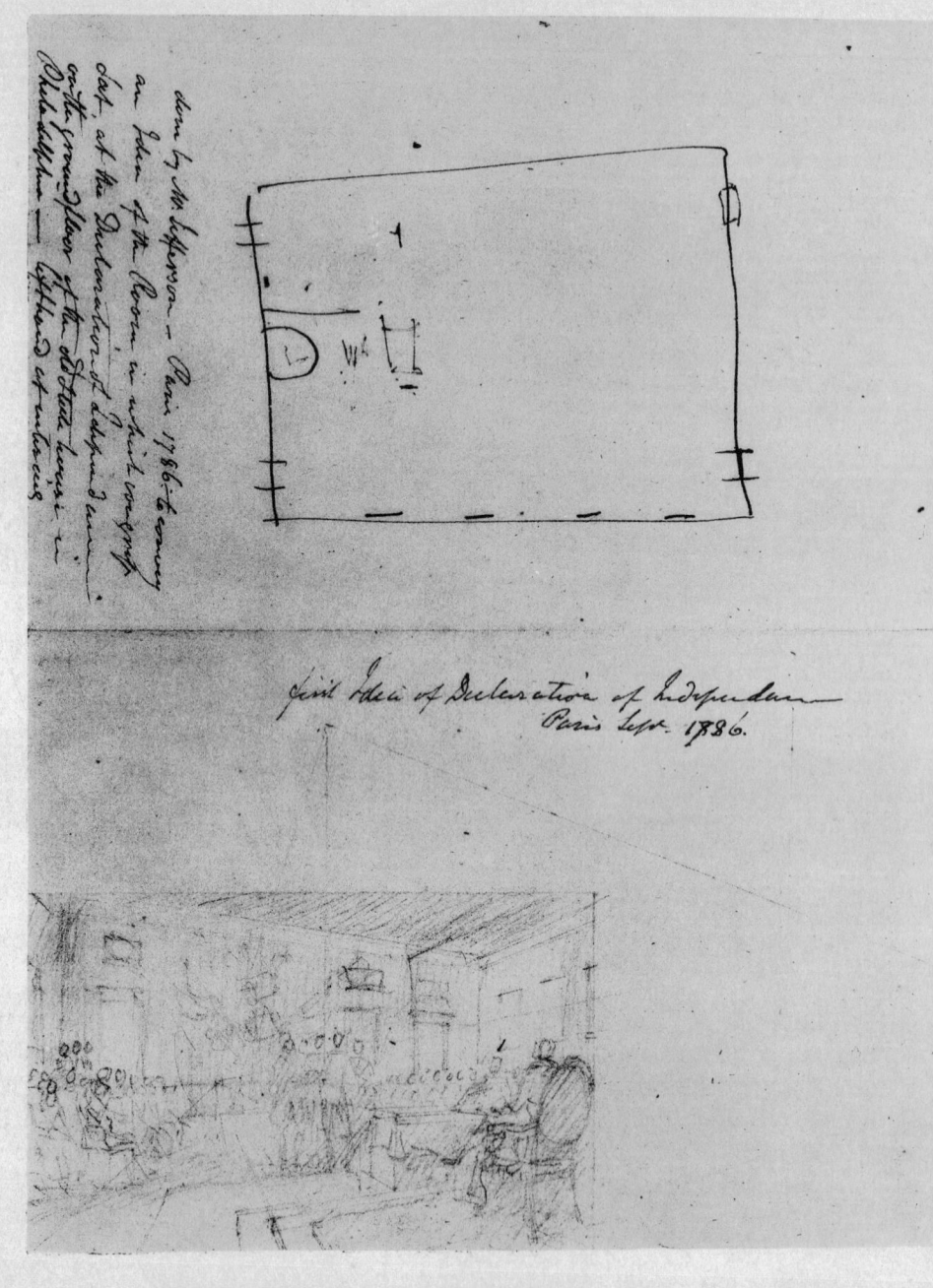

John Trumbull's sketch for "The Declaration of Independence," with Jefferson's floor plan of Independence Hall. (See p. xxvii.)

31 JULY 1786

our Affair with the Emperor of Morrocco, I have so many reasons to be assured of the King and Minister's desire to serve us in promoting our accommodation with the other Barbary powers, That If my advice could have the Least weight, I should counsel our Ministers to sollicit the good offices of his C. M. to further the views of the States on this head. I will stake my reputation on the best endeavours of Spain and forfeit all confidence if the Ct. de Florida Blanca doth not act as effecaciously as circumstances will permit him to effect what he hath already promised me. You Sir ought to know our present Situation, particularly with G.B. I have just learned *positively* what I suspected long ago that the British Ministry would accomodate their Disputes with respect to the Mosquito shore with Spain. This has been done to the Satisfaction of this Court. Campo at London has the merit of this sort of convention, Tho' the Minister of G.B. here has had the whole trouble. I have not seen the articles of this arrangement, but I know that the British are to evacuate the Mosquito shore and that they think themselves recompensed by cessions more extensive in another quarter. [I had almost determined not to write you on foreign politics. But when I reflect that you represent my country and that all *positive* information that you may receive with respect to what occupies the Attention of a great part of Europe cannot be displeasing to you but the Contrary, I cannot refrain from observing that][1] the Accommodation between this Court and that of Naples as proposed by France, will not be accepted. At the same time permit me to ask you in what State our Treaty is with Naples. I have a sure channel to convey such Insinuations as may be thought proper to the Persons who have the influence most important there. Mr. Lamb's bad State of health, it seems, doth not permit his speedy return to America. There is little appearance that either Naples or Portugal will make their peace with the Regency. Our Treaty meets with Obstacles much greater than you apprehended with Portugal. Permit me to tell you that there is a great probability that the Ambassador of that Nation here will be appointed first Minister, that the Chevalier Pinto is of another party, [that This Ambassador has offered in case Congress sent a Minister to Portugal, to engage the Queen to insinuate that it would please her to have me nominated and this he constantly repeats to me. For which I can give you no other reason than that I am on the best footing with a Lady who has the care of the Infanta Carlotta daughter of the Prince of Asturias now established in portugal.][1] The Ct. de F. B. has been indisposed for some time. This is a

31 JULY 1786

public Misfortune but still more to me personally. Mr. Barclay mentions to me that the English are in disgrace in Morrocco. If your powers from Congress are so extensive as to admit Mr. Barclays negotiating in Barbary, If even you can conjointly with Mr. Adams take upon you what certainly I would do [unknown and unprotected as I am][1] to consult the Public Interest without orders, You will Allow that gentleman to make overtures, in order to prevent hostilities and at least to give time to Congress to adopt such measures as they may Juddge proper. Be assured that all that I can do to second the operations of a man proper to be employed as he is, I shall do chearfully. [I have no late news from America and shall be Obliged to you for all information that you may have received from thence. Altho I have not the honor to be personally known to you, I beg your Excellency to be perswaded that I have no other Ambition than to be esteemed by those whom the Suffrages of their Country and their own merit have entitled to universal esteem. My only cause of discontent is that I have preferred the respectability of my representation and what I thought the honor of my country in a crisis, where that representation was necessary, to my personal interests. But I have more than enough to leave this country without exposing myself either personally or in a public character. Of this I wish Messrs. Grand to be persuaded. They are the first persons who ever protested a bill of Exchange drawn by me a public Servant of Congress, and they ought to remember that perhaps I was the first Person that was the means of procuring them commissions which raised their house from its former Obscurity. Mr. George Grand also ought to remember that in Consideration of my Attachment to his family and from respect to the Advice of a friend whom I venerate I did not expose him for having dared to break the Seal of Letters addressed to me from a chargè des affairs of America. I have all the proofs that I could wish on this Subject. Hitherto I have treated with lenity a person to whom I never gave any provocation Because I respected his friends and connections. I am sorry to trouble you with similar details, but I feel and I speak too often after my feelings and never more than when I have the honor to Assure you of the great regard and Esteem of Dr. Sir Your Excellencys Obliged & Humble Servt.,   WM. CARMICHAEL][1]

RC (DLC). Tr of extracts (DNA: PCC, No. 87, I); in Short's hand, with numerous corrections in spelling and punctuation. Tr of extracts (DNA: PCC, No. 107). Noted in SJL as received "about" 11 Aug., but doubtless received 13 Aug. (see TJ to Adams and to Jay, both dated 13 Aug. 1786). Enclosure: Barclay to Commissioners, 26 June 1786.

[180]

¹ The text in brackets (supplied) is marked in RC for exclusion, and is not, therefore, in the Tr which TJ forwarded to Jay.

Thomas Barclay to the American Commissioners

GENTLEMEN   Mogadore July 1786

I wrote you from Morocco under date of the 16th. As I do not know when that Letter is likely to reach you, I trouble you now with a Copy of it, and as I shall set out in a few days for Tangiers, I defer until my arrival in Europe being particular. I am Gentlemen, Your most obedt. humble servt.,   THOS BARCLAY

RC (DLC); in Franks' hand, signed and addressed to TJ at Paris in Barclay's hand. Tr (DNA: PCC, No. 87, I); in Short's hand; enclosed, along with Barclay's enclosure in the present letter, in TJ to Jay, 26 Sep. 1786. Tr (DNA: PCC, No. 107). Noted in SJL as received 3 Sep. 1786. Enclosure: Dupl of Barclay to Commissioners, 16 July 1786.

This letter was probably written about 25 July 1786. In his letter of 16 July Barclay told the Commissioners that he expected to "set out tomorrow or the day following" from the capital of Morocco; and in a letter to John Adams of 31 July, dated at Mogadore, he said: "Tomorrow, I am to sett out on my way to Tangers" (MHi: AMT, enclosing copy of Barclay's letter to Jay of 30 July 1786 which informed him of the conclusion of the treaty and of his intention to send it "by express from the first Port I can reach in Europe to Mr. Jefferson and from him and Mr. Adams you will have the particulars"; Tr of both in DLC: TJ Papers, 23: 3922-3).

From Cavelier, Fils

Dieppe, 1 Aug. 1786. Has informed the local merchants of the regulations of Berni. Capt. Joseph Atkins, of the ship *l'Esperance,* arrived at that port with a cargo of tobacco from Alexandria; has offered his services to Atkins who intends to proceed to L'Orient to sell his ship then go to Lisbon; Atkins has no letters for TJ; if TJ has commissions for Atkins, Cavelier will transmit them. Barclay asked him to write to him but he does not have the address.

RC (DLC); 4 p.; in French; endorsed. Noted in SJL as received 3 Aug. 1786.

From Abbé Morellet

mardi. [1 Aug. 1786]

Mr. Mazzei m'a demandé de renvoyer à Monsieur jefferson une correction qu'il a faite dans certains calculs de son ouvrage. Voicy les feuilles que j'ai reçües et dont j'ai profité pour corriger la traduction.

[181]

1 AUGUST 1786

J'espere que monsieur jefferson veut bien s'occupper de finir la carte. Je prens la liberté de lui faire observer qu'il est essentiel que le graveur ait fini sa besogne au moins vers le commencement ou le milieu d'octobre afin qu'on ait le tems d'envoyer la planche à paris et d'en tirer le nombre d'exemplaires necessaires pour accompagner le livre c'est à dire 1500. On ne peut pas mettre l'ouvrage en vente plus tard que la fin de novembre. Il n'est pas possible que le livre se passe de la carte. D'après cela je prie Monsieur jefferson de faire son arrangement avec le graveur de maniere qu'on lui renvoye la planche aussi tôt qu'elle sera gravée. Il n'est pas moins important d'empecher qu'on ne tire des epreuves de la carte en angletterre car si l'on renvoyoit la planche usée les cartes ni le livre ne se vendroient plus icy que très difficilement. Je salüe très respectueusement Monsieur jefferson en le remerciant de la jolie carte enluminée qu'il m'a envoyée.

L' A. MORELLET

RC (DLC); endorsed; undated, but written on a Tuesday before 10 Aug. 1786, which would have been either 1 or 8 Aug.; the former seems more probable. See TJ to Smith, 9 Aug. 1786; Morellet to TJ, 10 and 12 Aug. 1786; TJ to Morellet, 11 Aug. 1786. Enclosure: Some unidentified "feuilles" from the MS of *Notes on Virginia*, perhaps containing some of the corrected calculations which TJ had made as a result of his collaboration with Jean Nicolas Démeunier, the PrC of which he had lent to Mazzei (see Editorial Note to Démeunier's article on the United States, under 22 June 1786).

To Jean-Armand Tronchin, with Enclosures

SIR   Paris Aug. 1. 1786.

According to your desire I wrote two letters to America to enquire after the fate of Mr. Gallatin. One was to Mr. Savary, from whom I have as yet received no answer. The second was to Mr. Jay Secretary for foreign affairs to the United States. He put the paragraph of my letter into the public papers, desiring those who knew any thing of Mr. Gallatin to communicate what they knew. He soon after received several letters on that subject which have this moment come to my hands from him, and which I now do myself the honour to inclose to you. I hope they will not only quiet the fears of his family for his life and health, but as to his fortune also. I have the honour to be with sentiments of the highest esteem and respect Sir your most obedient & most humble servt.,

TH: JEFFERSON

1 AUGUST 1786

ENCLOSURE I

Savary to Jay

Philadelphia 10th June 1786.

The Printers of Newspapers continuing to publish the Advertisement sent to them by Mr. Jay, at the request of Mr. Jefferson, about the pretended Murder of Mr. Albert Gallatin, of Geneva, several Friends and Acquaintances of that Gentleman having written to Mr. Jay, to contradict this false Intelligence, the Subscriber now in this City and whose Name is mentioned in the Advertisement, thinks it his Duty to inform the Public, that this Anecdote about the Murder of Mr. Gallatin; and Mr. Senator Duval, which was published last Year in the Virginia Newspapers (altho' related with so many Particulars) has always been without any Foundation or Probability, as during five months which the Subscriber has spent with Mr. Gallatin, Mr. Duval and their Surveyors &c. on the River Ohio, and on the Rivers and Creeks that run into it, they have not seen one single Indian in that part of the Country. SAVARY DE VALCOULAN

ENCLOSURE II

Banks to Jay

SIR Philadelphia 7th. June 1786

I am a Virginian and perfectly acquainted with Mr. Albert Gallatin, a Genevan, who is supposed by his Friends to be dead. The paragraph in the Virginia Paper which gave such Information is perfectly untrue. Mr. Gallatin has been fortunate in his Acquisitions of Land in Company with Mr. Savary. The former is now living about 50 Miles from Pitsburgh and very much respected by those who know him.

An Advertisement which appeared in this Day's Paper has occasioned this Letter. The Honorable Colonel Munroe will tell you how far it may be confided in. I am yr. humble Servant, HENY. BANKS

ENCLOSURE III

Dunscomb to Jay

SIR Richmond June 1st. 1786

I receive a degree of Pleasure in informing you that Mr. Gallatin was not killed by the Indians. It is not long since he was in this City, and by this Day is expected to be in Philadelphia. This Information I would have given some time ago, but expected it would have been communicated from a Store in which he was intimately acquainted in this Place, nor was I other ways advised until half an Hour ago. I am with Respect & Regard Sr. your most obedt. hble. Servt.,
AW. DUNSCOMB

ENCLOSURE IV

Charton to Jay

SIR Philadelphia May 14th. 1786.

In consequence of Mr. Jefferson's Letter to you, that was inserted

[183]

in the Newspaper by your Desire, I take the Liberty to address you respecting the Subject it was wrote for.

I am perfectly well acquainted with Mr. Albert Galatin who was reported some time ago to have met with so terrible a Fate, and I have the Satisfaction to assure that he is still living; what gave rise to such a Report I don't know, but I was lately at Richmond with Mr. Savary de Valsoulon who was all the Time with Mr. Galatin in the back parts of Virginia, and who has told me, that none of their Party had received or likely to receive the least Alarm from the Indians.

Mr. Galatin only went back to George-Creek, the Place of his Settlement, in March last, and I have no Doubt has written to his Family, to contradict the News that had given them so much Pain.

It is with very great Reason that my Authority has been given by Mr. Dubey, and I feel happy that it has been the means of Mr. Galatin's Friend's having Hopes that he was not dead. I like to think that they are by this Time entirely recovered from their Anxiety, but I dare to say they will be extremely pleased with the Information, that will be sent to them, through your good and kind Offices. I have the Honor to be &c.   Hy Ss. Charton

ENCLOSURE V

Terrasson to Jay

Monsieur   Philadelphie 12 May 1786

Mes liaisons intimes avec M. A. Gallatin m'engagent de satisfaire a l'avertissement que vous avez fait inserer dans les papiers publiques a son Sujet.

Les bruits de sa mort ont été d'autant plus prematures qu'il est venu lui même en trez bonne santé au commencement de fevrier dernier dans cette Ville d'ou il est reparti au commencement de Mars pour sa plantation sur le Monongahela en Pensilvanie absolument à l'abry des sauvages, dont il m'a assuré n'avoir même recontré aucun pendant les longues excursions qu'il a fait sur les Bords de la Riviere Ohio.

Pendant son sejour ici, il a reçu diverses lettres de Geneve, ou on lui annoncoit un heritage et il ya a repondu par differentes voyes en envoyant sa procuration à ce Sujet, ce qui doit à cette heure avoir parfaitement tranquillise sa Famille.

J'ai l'honneur d'etre avec une parfaite consideration, Monsieur, Votre tres humble & tres obéissant Serviteur,

Amy. Terrason
1er. Deputé de la Nation françois en cette Ville

ENCLOSURE VI

Du Ponceau to Jay

Sir   Philadelphia 14th. May 1786

Having seen the Advertisement you have caused to be put in the

1 AUGUST 1786

public Papers respecting Mr. Gallatin, I think it my Duty to inform you that on the 20th. February last, the same Person was at my Office, and executed a Letter of Attorney to Messieurs Colladon and Hentoch of Geneva to transact his business for him in that Commonwealth. He called himself Abraham Alphonse Albert Gallatin, Citizen of Geneva, and told me he was the same Man who had been killed by the Savages in the Fredericksburg Gazette. I believe he is now returned to the back Counties of Virginia, tho' I cannot well assert it. I shall be happy if this Information proves any ways satisfactory to the Family of that young Gentleman, tho' I believe it probable that they have by this Time received more direct Intelligence respecting him. I have the Honor to be &c.,

       PETER S. DU PONCEAU
       Attorney at Law & Noty. Public.
       Philadelphia

E N C L O S U R E   VII

Morris to Jay

DEAR SIR   Philadelphia May 13. 1786

I have this moment read in one of our Newspapers a paragraph relative to Mr. Albert Gallatin of Geneva, with a request to any Person acquainted to give you Information respecting him, and it gives me Pleasure to be able to assure you that Mr. Gallatin is living; he escaped the Fate meditated for him by the Indians; he dined with me in February last; I bought a Bill of Exchange of him for £100 Stlg. dated the 27th. February 1786, drawn upon Messrs. Peter and Charles van Notten & Co. London, and forwarded by the Last french Packet, a pacquet of Letters for his Friends in Geneva, which he left at my Office for that Purpose. He is gone back to his Lands and thinks very highly of them.

I am Dr. Sir your obt. hble: Servt.,   ROBERT MORRIS

RC (Archives d'Etat, Geneva, Switzerland). Tr (same); French translation. Enclosures (Tr in English and French; same).

The letter that TJ asserted he wrote TO MR. SAVARY has not been found and is not recorded in SJL; but see Tronchin to TJ, 22 Jan. 1786; TJ to Jay, 27 Jan. 1786; and Jay to TJ, 16 June 1786. When TJ first was asked by Tronchin for information about the man who was to become his close colleague and friend, he promised to take particular pains in making inquiries, but said that he was afraid Gallatin was no longer living since he had received certain information that his companion Duval had been killed (Tronchin to Puérari, Secretary of State of the Republic of Geneva, 26 Jan. 1786; Archives d'Etat, Geneva). On 2 Aug. 1786 Tronchin wrote to Puérari: "Mr. de Jefferson . . . m'an-nonçea hier à Versailles qu'il venoit d'apprendre que M. Gallatin n'étoit point mort, et qu'il attendoit à chaque instant des dépêches d'Amérique qui lui porteroient les détails les plus satisfaisans à ce sujet. Effectivement le soir même j'en reçois les 7 numéros cy joint avec une lettre qui me les transmettoit. J'ai répondu à Mr. de Jefferson une lettre de remerciement et de reconnoissance de ses bons offices: Si dans votre première dépêche, Monsieur, vous voulez bien confirmer ce que je lui ai dit de la part de Messeigneurs; cette attention le flattera et me fera plaisir parce que je suis très attaché à Mr. de Jefferson, homme d'un très grand mérite et fort considéré" (same). For other information on this episode, see Henry Adams, *Life of Albert Gallatin* (Philadelphia, 1880), p. 45-66. TJ's cordial relations with Tronchin continued, and late in 1786

[185]

he presented to the minister copies of the Act for Establishing Religious Freedom, one of which Tronchin forwarded to Puérari under cover of the following letter: "J'ai l'honneur, Monsieur, de vous envoier ci joint l'acte de la République de Virginie qui établit la liberté de Religion, que Mr. de Jefferson m'a envoié en Anglois en Italien et en françois; cette pièce est si curieuse que je pense qu'elle vous fera plaisir; il en résulte qu'on peut être Magistrat même Député au Congrès, que l'on [soit] Turc, Brame ou Chrétien: il me semble que c'est pousser la tolérance au delà des bornes d'une constitution raisonnable où l'unité des opinions doit être amenée par les moyens les plus doux, mais dans la quelle l'indifférentisme ne peut être que très dangereux" (Tronchin to Puérari, 14 Dec. 1786; Archives d'Etat, Geneva). If TJ sent a covering letter with the Act, it has not been found.

From George Washington

Dear Sir Mount Vernon Augt. 1st. 1786.

The letters you did me the favor to write to me on the 4th. and 7th. of Jany. have been duly received.

In answer to your obliging enquiries respecting the dress, attitude &c. which I would wish to have given to the Statue in question, I have only to observe that not having a sufficient knowledge in the art of sculpture to oppose my judgment to the taste of Connoisseiurs, I do not desire to dictate in the matter; on the contrary I shall be perfectly satisfied with whatever may be judged decent and proper. I should even scarcely have ventured to suggest that perhaps a servile adherence to the garb of antiquity might not be altogether so expedient as some little deviation in favor of the modern custom,[1] if I had not learnt from Colo. Humphreys that this was a circumstance hinted in conversation by Mr. West to Houdon. This taste, which has been introduced in painting by West, I understand is received with applause and prevails extensively.

I have taken some pains to enquire into the facts respecting the medals of the Cincinnati, which Majr. L'Enfant purchased in France. It seems that when he went to Europe in 1783 he had money put into his hands to purchase a certain number, and that conceiving it to be consonant with the intentions of the Society, he purchased to a still greater amount—insomuch that a Committee of the General Meeting, upon examining his Account reported a balance due to him of Six hundred and thirty dollars which report was accepted. This money is still due, and is all that is due from the Society of the Cincinnati as a Society. General Knox has offered to pay the amount to Majr. L'Enfant, but as it has become a matter of some public discussion, the latter wished it might remain until the next General Meeting, which will be in May next.—In the meantime Genl. Knox (who is Secretary General) has, or will

[186]

1 AUGUST 1786

write fully on the Subject to the Marquis de la Fayette, from whom he has had a letter respecting the business.[2]

We have no news of importance and if we had, I should hardly be in the way of learning it; as I divide my time between the superintendance of opening the navigations of our rivers and attention to my private concerns.—Indeed I am too much secluded from the world to know with certainty, what sensation the refusal of the British to deliver up the Western posts, has made on the public mind.—I fear the edge of its sensibility is somewhat blunted.—Fœderal measures are not yet universally adopted. New York, which was as well disposed a State as any in the Union is said to have become in a degree antifœderal. Some other States are, in my opinion, falling into very foolish and wicked plans of emitting paper money.—I cannot however give up my hopes and expectations that we shall 'ere long adopt a more liberal system of policy. What circumstances will lead, or what misfortunes will compel us to it, is more than can be told without the spirit of prophecy.

In the meantime the people are industrious, œconomy begins to prevail, and our internal governments are, in general, tolerably well administered.

You will probably have heard of the death of Genl. Greene before this reaches you, in which case you will, in common with your Countrymen, have regretted the loss of so great and so honest a man. Genl. McDougall, who was a brave soldier and a disinterested patriot, is also dead. He belonged to the Legislature of his State, the last act of his life, was (after being carried on purpose to the Senate) to give his voice against the emission of a paper currency. Colo. Tilghman, who was formerly of my family, died lately and left as fair a reputation as ever belonged to a human character.—Thus some of the pillars of the revolution fall. Others are mouldering by insensible degrees. May our Country never want props to support the glorious fabrick!

With sentiments of the highest esteem and regard, I have the honor to be Dear Sir Yr. Most Obed. & very Hble. Serv.,

Go: Washington

RC (DLC: TJ Papers). FC (DLC: Washington Papers). Noted in SJL as received 25 May 1787.

[1] FC reads: "*costume.*"
[2] FC reads: "on the subject."

From Madame d'Anterroches

[*Puy d'Arnac, près Tulle, 2 Aug. 1786.* Noted in SJL as received 4 Sep. 1786. Not found.]

From Lafayette

MY DEAR SIR MalesHerbes August the 2d [1786]

I Have spoken with Baron de Grimm who, it Seems, Has No Notion to Continue the Monthly 25 guineas, and says He Has taken no other Engagement But to advance that sum once—for you must know, *Between You and me* that the 25 guineas exceeding this Sum Have Been delivered under his Name on my Account, which of course the Empress will Reimburse if She Accepts of the proposal. In the mean while Baron de Grimm advises our friend Ledyard not to Throw a way Any other opportunity that might offer.

Inclosed is a letter from Mr. Littlepage, and also a small Bill of exchange which Mr. Grand will Be more able than you or me to Have paid and forwarded to Mr. Livingston the one for whom I sent You a Letter. At the same time that I would be very sorry to meddle in an affair of that Nature, I would think myself very much to Blame, Was I to throw away dispatches and Monney sent to me to be forwarded, the more so as I don't know if they Contain Any thing Relative to that dispute. Adieu, Your sincere friend, LAFAYETTE

RC (DLC); without indication of the year, which has been supplied from internal evidence; see also TJ to Ledyard, 27 July 1786. Enclosures (DLC): (1) Lewis Littlepage to Lafayette, Warsaw, 10 June 1786, enclosing "a small bill of exchange, which your homme d'affaires will deliver to the Banker, and pardon the Liberty I take in troubling you to find some means of remitting the amount to Mr. Livingston who you know was kind enough to take charge of my affairs in New York" and asking Lafayette to inform him "whether Mr. Jefferson has received any advices from Virginia upon the subject of the affair which occasions me so much uneasiness." (2) The "small Bill of exchange" referred to by both Littlepage and Lafayette but not otherwise identified.

I SENT YOU A LETTER: Neither this letter nor its covering letter from Lafayette to TJ—if one was written—has been found.

From André Limozin

MOST HONORED SIR Havre de Grace 2nd August 1786

I have duely received the two Letters your Excellency hath honored me with; the 7 Packages for the Virginias States are in my Stores, but I have not heard a Single word from Messrs. Robt.

and Anthy. Garvey of Rouen about the parcells your Excellency hath consignd to their care to be forwarded to them, which is not astonishing because the Chief of that house is but very seldom at home, therefore punctuality, cant be expected as if the Master was looking upon his business.

I must observe your Excellency that it is impossible to dispatch the Seven Packages of Army's or Soldiers Furnitures, without you obtain leave from the Minister which the French Call Passeport. We have at present the American Ship the George & Patty Washington, Captn. Joseph Foulke, loading here for Baltimore; I suppose your Excellency would not wish that I should Ship on board of him the Seven here above mentioned Packages Soldjers Furnitures. I have the pleasure to inclose your excellency two large parcells arrived yesterday from Williamsburg under my Covert. I am most respectfully Your Excellency's Most obedient & very Humble Servant, ANDRE LIMOZIN

RC (DLC); endorsed. Noted in SJL as received 4 Aug. 1786. The "two large parcells" were not actually "enclosed"; one of them was an ill-fated box of seeds for Madame de Tessé (see TJ to Limozin, 8 Aug. 1786).

From Jean-Armand Tronchin

MONSIEUR à Paris le 2e. Aoust 1786.

J'ay reçu hier au soir la lettre dont vous m'avez honoré le même jour avec les 7 ffos. qu'elle contenoit. Je vais faire parvenir le tout à Messeigneurs du Conseil de Genève qui seront bien reconnoissans des égards que vous avez eu, Monsieur, à leur réquisition; et la famille de Mr. Gallatin bien contente d'aprendre son existence et la position avantageuse dans la quelle il se trouve.

Ce jeune homme a reçu l'éducation la plus soignée, at s'il fait souche dans vôtre Pays, j'espère qu'elle lui donnera comme dans le mien des hommes de mérite.

J'ay l'honneur d'etre avec la reconnoissance la plus parfaite de vos bons offices et les sentimens de respect et de la plus haute estime Monsieur Votre très humble et très Obeissant serviteur,
TRONCHIN

RC (MoSHi); endorsed.

From G. K. van Hogendorp

My dear Sir   Leyden August the 2 1786

As I am informed of your returning from London to Paris I venture to send you this letter, whose content any one at the Post house might know, for I care not the whole world's knowing how much I do esteem and belove you.

Your Friend, Mr. William Short, has a right to expect from me a letter respecting our Constitution, which on my word is ready, and that up in my writing-box these six months past. Why? You must hear and judge me. I now study the law, and will within two months, after a seven month's stay at this University, be able to correct many faults and to add many important points in my letter. This reason alone would do, I think, but, dear Sir, I have an other one not less valuable. In former times, my letter as it now lies before me, would give your friend some pleasure, and by this way to myself likewise. But now, among dangerous civil dissensions, this very letter cannot be too cautiously written, not with a mind to hide truth in equivocal terms, I think too freely, in spite of any persecution, for concealing my real sentiments, but I want to express my mind with so much perspicuity and so concisely that it cannot be misconstrued. For you ought to know, my respectable friend, that though a friend to liberty, my principles do not agree with many who call themselves by the same denomination. I am writing a Dissertation De ratione Subsidii fœderatis debiti, and take the freedom to desire your answering without any delay the following Queries.

Which are at present the general interests of the United States?
What is the extent of the Congress's power in managing them?
Which are the expences of Congress?
Which the revenues.

In which way do the particular states contribute to the general expences?

Are general duties, to be levied by Congress, still expected to be acquiesced to by the States?
But if besides this you should know any thing relative to the matter I treat, be so kind as to add it to your answers.

Your Notes on Virginia have been read by a few men of understanding who got both instruction and amusement by the lecture.

How does your health, my dear Sir, and when will both your time and your inclination allow you a turn through Holland; for if you don't come very soon to me, you'll oblige me to set out for Paris in order to see you.

I embrace you very heartily. Yours for ever,
VAN HOGENDORP

A short but authentic account of the present state of the Bank of North America would be very acceptable to me.

RC (DLC); endorsed. Noted in SJL as received 8 Aug. 1786.

From Létombe

MONSIEUR   Boston, 3. auguste 1786.

J'ai L'honneur d'informer votre Excellence que J'ai remis à M. le Jay, aussitot mon arrivée à New york, les deux Lettres qu'Elle avoit bien voulu me confier. Je me suis acquitté de cette Commission avec Zéle, avec empressement Et Je desirerois trouver les occasions de vous donner, Monsieur, des Preuves de mon dévouement.

Je suis, avec Respect, de votre Excellence Le très-humble et très-obeissant Serviteur,
DE LETOMBE

RC (MoSHi); endorsed. An entry in SJL for 20 Sep. 1786 recording the receipt of a letter from Létombe, without place or date, evidently refers to the present letter. The DEUX LETTRES for Jay were doubtless those of 27 May 1786, which were written in haste in order to catch the French packet; the public letter of that date was transmitted by Jay to Congress on 2 Aug. 1786.

From John Bondfield

DR. SIR   Bordeaux 5 Aug. 1786

Since the advices I had the honor to transmit you the 15. ulto. I have received Eighteen Cases Arms from the manufactory at Tulle Nos. 51 to 68 with a Certificate from the Inspector General, the whole in good Order.

In mine of the 15th. I mention'd to you the difficulty I met with from the Intendant. I applied yesterday at the Intendants Office. The Subdelegate informd me that he could not grant a further permission without Instructions from the Intendant who resides in Paris or by a Special Order from the Minister, the Exportation being strictly Prohibited. We have two or three Virginia Ships in this Port. If a permission comes down the Cases at hand may be forwarded by them. I also transmitted you a State of the Duties to which these articles are subject as also the Bonds I have entered into to present in due time the Certificates of the Landing of the Arms in America.

Five large Ships with Tobacco for the farmers General in compliance with their Contract with Mr. Morris arrived lately. It appears Mr. Morris exerts his utmost Efforts to compleat his Contract which is too lucratif to neglect. With respect I have the honor to be Sir your most obedient Humble servant, JOHN BONDFIELD

RC (DLC); addressed and endorsed. Noted in SJL as received 9 Aug. 1786.

From Schweighauser & Dobrée

SIR   Nantes 5. August 1786

In hopes of obtaining from you the justice which has been so long denied us, we beg leave to inclose copy of the letter our late Partner and parent Mr. J. D. Schweighauser wrote to Congress the 30. Novr. 80 which will give you ample informations of our claims for our advances for the Continental frigate Alliance to which we join copy of the resolve which it produced. Mr. Johnson persisted in his refusal of examining our accounts as no longer Auditor general and Dr. Franklin refused the payment of them as not having been examined by this gentleman. We repeatedly sollicited that he would name a committee for that purpose but to elude satisfying us he would not adopt this measure.

We have since laid these accounts and their vouchers before Tho. Barclay Esqr. who has seen every one of them and is perfectly convinced as was Dr. Franklin himself of their exactness. Permit us earnestly to request as an act of justice and friendship that you would put us in the way of obtaining our payment and to assure you of our acknowlegement and gratitude. We have still a parcel of arms &ca. on hand belonging to Congress which our co-partners in the house of Puchelberg & Co. in L'Orient have laid an attachment on, to assure them and us our due or at least part of it for we know not the value of them and not being yet authorized to sell them they are of no utility to us and we fear that warehouse rent of them will absorb one day their whole amount which without that will be greatly reduced by the want of having them cleaned which permission we have so often vainly sollicited. If you could give us directions to sell them it would be securing to the States a value which is now daily diminishing and will by further delays be absolutely eat up.

7 AUGUST 1786

We submit the whole to your justice and have the honor to be respectfully; your Excellency's &c.

SCHWEIGHAUSER & DOBREE

Tr (DNA: PCC, No. 87, I); in Short's hand. PrC (DLC). Tr (DNA: PCC, No. 107). Noted in SJL as received 8 Aug. 1786. Enclosures: (1) Schweighauser to Congress, 30 Nov. 1780. (2) Resolution of Congress, 24 Aug. 1781, authorizing Joshua Johnson to "examine, audit and settle the accounts of T. D. Schweighauser, against the frigate *Alliance*" and directing the American minister to France "to pay the balance that may be found due" (JCC, XXI, 907; see also, JCC, XX, 590, 649).

From John Banister, Jr.

[*Pons, 6 Aug. 1786.* Entered in SJL as received 12 Aug. 1786. Not found; but see TJ to John Banister, 14 Aug. 1786.]

To Achard Frères

GENTLEMEN   Paris August 7. 1786.

I have been duly honored with your favor of the 2d. instant, and thank you for your attention to the wine forwarded for me by Messrs. le freres Roussac. I expect every moment to receive a proper order to the Douane of Rouen to permit these wines to pass on to Paris free of duty, which order shall accompany this letter, or be sent directly to the officers of the Douane at Rouen. I will beg the favour of you to forward the wine by water, addressed to me at Paris at the grille des champs elysées, notifying me of any expence you may incur which shall be paid to your order. I have the honour to be with sentiments of much esteem Gentlemen your most obedient humble servt.,   TH: JEFFERSON

PrC (MHi); endorsed; at foot of text: "Messrs les freres Augt. 3." YOUR FAVOR: Not found, but recorded in SJL as received 3 Aug. 1786.

To Anthony Garvey

SIR   Paris Aug. 7. 1786.

Some time in the month of June I sent by one of the vessels which pass between this place and Rouen a box containing the model of a house made in plaister. This box was directed to the Governor of Virginia, to your care at Rouen, and to the care of Mr. Limousin at Havre. Mr. Limosin writes me word it is not come to his hands.

[193]

Fearing it may be stopped at Rouen, without your having notice of it, I take the liberty of asking your enquiries after it, and to send it on to Mr. Limosin, by water, and under the strictest charge to the porters to handle it gently, lest it should be broke.

A mercantile house in Lisbon has sent me some wines to the address of Messrs. Achards freres at Rouen, which are arrived at Rouen. I expect to forward herewith an order to the Douane to suffer them to pass free of duty. I do not know that there will be any difficulty in procuring them to be forwarded, but if there should, any assistance which you will be so good as to give will oblige Sir Your very humble servant, TH: JEFFERSON

PrC (DLC).

From Ferdinand Grand

MONSIEUR Paris Le 7 aout 1786.

Je vous prie d'agréer mes excuses du retard des comptes que vous m'avés fait l'honneur de me demander et que différentes occupations pressantes m'ont fait différer. Vous les trouverés Monsieur, cy joints, Savoir

Le compte des Etats Unis soldé au 31 mars 1786 par £.22447. 14. que me restoient dues à cette époque.

Le Votre, Monsieur, au débit duquel j'apperçois qu'on a porté divers articles qui concernent les Etats Unis et qui devront sans doute en être retranchés.

Enfin celui des objets payés des fonds de L'Etat de Virginie.

Veuillés, Monsieur, avoir la bonté de marquer sur ces deux derniers comptes les articles qui doivent être ajoutés au débit de celui des Etats Unis. Il sera facile alors de les Solder au moyen des fonds que j'ai reçus de Monsieur Jones et j'aurai l'honneur de vous transmettre ensuite la notte de ce qui restera au crédit des Etats Unis, ainsi que vous le désirés. Je vous demande pardon de la peine que je vous donne par cet examen.

Je Suis avec une considération respectueuse, Monsieur, Votre très humble et très obt. Serviteur, GRAND

RC (DLC). Enclosures (DLC): (1) Statement of account bearing TJ's endorsement: "Grand & Co. account against US. 1784. Aug. 20—1786. July 11." (2) Statement of account of funds of Virginia with Grand & Co., to 27 July 1786. (3) Statement of TJ's account with Grand & Co., 20 Aug. 1784 —11 July 1786. These accounts were checked and annotated by TJ as requested; they will be printed among Accounts, Second Series. See also Grand to TJ, 25 May 1793.

From William Macarty

SIR   L'orient 7th. Augst. 1786

I have just finish'd the delivery of 750 Hhds. Tobacco to the Farmers General, in consequence of the Decission of the Committé. But to my great surprise, their Director here pretends to pay only 34.<tt>#</tt>10s for the first quality of Virginia Tobacco 34.<tt>#</tt>2s. for the second quality and 33.<tt>#</tt>10s. for the 3d. quality, those prices being far less, than Mr. Morris's contract, and less than we expected from the spirit of the Decission. I have therefore refused to recieve payment at those prices altho I am in great want of the money.

At this rate we shall lead our friends again into an error, which may be fatal to some and injure the commercial connections between the two countries.

I have thought it my duty to lay before your Excellency a Sketch of the Reception and manner the Director proposes paying, and take the Liberty to request your influence to have the matter ascertain'd for the Security of our Tobacco Trade.

I cannot help observing to your Excellency that the Director here has offer'd, and continues to offer, even a much less price and other Conditions to some persons who have small quantitys. This appears contradictory to the Intentions of Government. Every Individual having, undoubtedly, a right to the same favour. I have the Honor to be with the greatest Respect Your Excellencys Most Humble and obedt. Servant,   WM. MACARTY

Note of Tobacco Delivered to the Farmers General

[Wei]ght tobo. 36#10.

367	Hhds. first quality of Virginia W.F.	343146 ℔. Net @	34.# 10
148	do. Second do.	133326	34. 2
106	do. 3d do.	91723	33. 10
91	do. first quality Maryland	77441	32. 10
38	do. second do.	31237	32.
750	Hhds. weighing	676873 ℔.	

RC (DLC); addressed and endorsed; calculations in TJ's hand at head of text. Noted in SJL as received 11 Aug. 1786.

To John Adams

DEAR SIR   Paris Aug. 8. 1786.

Your favour of July 16. came duly to hand by Mr. Trumbul. With respect to the whale oil, tho' this country has shewn a desire to draw it hither, and for that purpose have reduced the duties to about four guineas on the English ton, yet I do not see a probability of a further reduction at this moment. It has been much pressed, and I expect every day to receive a final determination. Should it not be obtained now we have reason to expect some years hence an abatement of one third, as a promise was given to the people that the imposition of 10. sous per livre should not be renewed at the expiration of the term for which it was laid on, which will be about half a dozen years hence. I inclose you copies of letters received from Mr. Carmichael, O'Brian, and Lamb. Be so good as to say what answer we shall give the last about his settlement. Shall we undertake the settlement? If so, where shall it be done? I will join in any thing you please as to this. Taking for granted, from a message delivered by Mr. Trumbul, that you are now in Holland, I will only add a request to send me some copies of the ratified treaty with Prussia (which will be I hope in both languages,) and assurances of the sincere esteem and respect with which I have the honour to be Dear Sir your most obedt. humble servt.,

TH: JEFFERSON

RC (MHi: AMT); endorsed by Smith; also, in part, by Adams: "answered Septr. 11. 1786." PrC (DLC). Enclosures: Copies of letters from Carmichael, 15 and 18 July; from Lamb, 18 July; from Richard O'Bryen, 12 July 1786.

To John Bondfield

SIR Paris Aug. 8. 1786.

I have now before me your several favors of May 27. June 10. 24. and July 15. I know of no appointment of agents in the ports of Rochfort, Rochelle or Bayonne, made by Mr. Barclay, nor, till the receipt of your letter did I know that you had been so kind as to extend your cares to those ports. In consequence of this, I had inclosed a copy of the order of Council of Berny to a Mr. Louis Alexander, with whom I had had a correspondence on another occasion. I am sensible of the inconveniencies which attend the want of arrangement in the department of our commerce here. This is owing to the load of business before Congress which prevents their concluding a system of consular establishment which they have under contemplation. We expect this daily, which is the reason Mr. Barclay has not made arrangements finally. Your bill for the disbursements on account of arms was paid on sight. I have not applied for a license to export arms, because I am solliciting a general regulation on that subject. The wine is come to hand, and the cost of it shall be paid when you please. We find the red wine excellent. The Grave is a little hard. I am much obliged by your attention to the several objects public and private with which I have troubled you, and am with great respect & esteem, Sir, Your most obedient humble servt., TH: JEFFERSON

PrC (DLC).

To Stephen Cathalan, Jr.

SIR   Paris Aug. 8. 1786.

I have been duly honoured with your favor of July 28. I have in consequence thereof re-considered the order of council of Berny, and it appears to me to extend as much to the Southern ports of France as to the Western, and that for tobacco delivered in any port where there is no manufacture, only 30. sols per quintal is to be deducted. The farmers may perhaps evade the purchase of tobacco in a port inconvenient to them by purchasing the whole quantity in other ports. I shall readily lend my aid to promote the mercantile intercourse between your port and the United states whenever I can aid it. For the present it is much restrained by the danger of capture by the pyratical states. I have the honor to be with much respect, Sir, your most obedient & most humble servant,

TH: JEFFERSON

P.S. If very good Frontignac wine can be procured at Marseilles I would be obliged to you for six dozen bottles, the price of which I will pay on your bill.

PrC (DLC).

To André Limozin

SIR   Paris Aug. 8. 1786.

I am honoured with your favor of the 2d. inst. but of the two packages that you mentioned as accompanying it, only one came to hand. The other should have contained seeds from America. I mention this, that if it escaped your notice when you forwarded the other, you may be so kind as to do it now, or if it was forwarded you may advise me how to trace it. I have written to Mr. Garvey to ask his enquiries after the box sent in June to his and your care.

With regard to the passport for the cartridge boxes for Virginia, I would observe to you that having lately shipped a number of muskets from Bourdeaux for Virginia, they asked only a bond that they should be carried to America, and that proofs should be sent from thence that they were actually for the use of that country. This bond being given they permitted the arms to be exported. I should rather give a like bond as to the cartouch-boxes than ask a passport from the minister. I will be obliged to you therefore to ask whether this would be sufficient. If it would, and they will be so good as to send me a form of a bond, satisfactory to them, I will sign it. If nothing but a passport will do, and you will be so kind as to write me again, I will endeavor to obtain one. Mr. Mazzei, of whom I once wrote to you, asks an answer to a letter with which he took the liberty of troubling you. I have the honour to be with much respect & esteem, Sir, your most obedient humble servt.,

TH: JEFFERSON

PrC (DLC).

To John Paradise

DEAR SIR   Paris Aug. 8. 1786.

I have been honoured with your favour of July 20. and it's duplicate of July 28. I am glad you concur in the opinion that a trip to Paris will be adviseable as I shall be happy in the pleasure of your company here and in every occasion of serving you. Perhaps you will find it convenient to come on the return of Dr. Bancroft whom you will have seen in London before this. We have obtained a regulation here obliging the farmers general to buy, from such individuals as offer, 15,000 hhds. of tobacco a year at 34.^{tt} 36.^{tt} and 38.^{tt} the quintal, according to it's quality. If you could send your tobacco here in a *French* vessel it might obtain you that price which I apprehend to be more than is given in London. A port where there are manufactories of tobacco would be best, as there would be an abatement of 1^{tt}-10s the quintal in any other port. I have lately received a letter dated May 12. 1786. from my friend Colo. Madison of Orange to whom I had written on your affairs. It contains the following paragraph. 'Doctr. Bancroft's application in favor of Mr. Paradise, inclosed in your letter, shall be attended to as far as the case will admit; though I see not how any relief can be obtained. If Mr. Paradise stands on the list of foreign creditors, his Agent here may probably convert his securities into money without any very great loss, as they rest on good funds, and the principal is in a course of paiment. If he stands on the domestic list, as I presume he does, the interest only is provided for, and, since the postponement of the taxes, even that cannot be negociated without a discount of ten per cent at least. The principal cannot be turned into cash without sinking three fourths of it's amount.'

The question, you see then, is whether you be considered as a citizen or a foreigner? In *mind* I know you to be zealously a citizen, but in *body*, the law will consider you as a foreigner; because that has not only prescribed that the oath of fidelity shall be taken, but that it shall be taken before some *magistrate in the country*. This you have never had an opportunity to do. As you are therefore subject to any loss which the character of a foreigner might bring on you, so you ought to avail yourself of any benefit which it may bring. Mrs. Paradise's being born a citizen, saves the estate from confiscation. Your being a foreigner entitles you to prompt paiment of the debt due to you. I would therefore press you strongly to avail yourself of this circumstance and to instruct your agent to claim paiment for you as a foreigner. He may safely apply to Mr. Madison (of Orange) for advice, and cannot obtain better advice. Get paiment as a foreigner first, and then reward our country by becoming it's citizen. Present me affectionately to Mrs. and Miss Paradise and be assured of the esteem with which I have the honour to be Dear Sir your friend & servt., TH: JEFFERSON

PrC (DLC).

To Lefévre, Roussac & Cie.

GENTLEMEN   Paris Aug. 8. 1786.

Your favors of the 1st. and 11th. of July came safely to hand. The wine you sent to the care of Messrs. Achards is arrived at Rouen. Your bill was presented to me three days ago, was accepted and shall be duly paid. When Mr. Pecquet was here I asked him if he would send me some very good Malvoisie de Madeire. He told me that by attending the sales of wine, after decease, he could purchase what was old and fine, and at a reasonable price. I therefore desired him [to do so.] Perceiving by your letter that there are only 30. bottles of Malvoisie de Madeire in the parcel sent, I will beg [the favor of you] to send me six dozen bottles more of that kind of wine of what is old and good. [Your] kind offer of service has induced me to take the liberty [of giving] you this trouble; I have the honour to be with sentiments of much esteem & respect Gentlemen your most obedient & most humble servt.,

TH: JEFFERSON

PrC (ViWC); MS faded and partly illegible.

To St. Lambert

Aug. 8. 1786.

Mr. Jefferson has the honour of presenting his compliments to Monsieur le marquis de St. Lambert, and of thanking him for his very excellent translation of the act of the Virginia assembly. An opportunity having occurred, before the receipt of it, of forwarding the act to some foreign courts where it was thought it would be well received, Mr. Jefferson had been obliged to print copies from a translation prepared for the Encyclopedie. He shall endeavor as soon as possible to avail the public of the better one of M. de St. Lambert. He begs leave to present to him, and also through him to Madame la Comtesse d'Houditot the homage of his respects.

PrC (DLC).

St. Lambert's translation of the Act for Establishing Religious Freedom may have been enclosed in his to TJ of 27 July 1786, though it is not mentioned therein. The translation prepared by Démeunier for the *Encyclopédie* (see notes to Démeunier's article on the United States, printed under 22 June 1786) that TJ sent TO SOME FOREIGN COURTS must have been printed and dispatched to the unnamed embassies during July; subsequently TJ caused St. Lambert's translation to be printed separately for similar use. He also obtained an Italian translation (perhaps through Mazzei) and sent it to some foreign ministers (see note to TJ to Tronchin, 1 Aug. 1786).

To Dumoulin de Seille & Son

GENTLEMEN   Paris Aug. 8. 1786.

I am duly honoured with your favor of July 24. and sensible of the kind offer of services therein made to the United states of America. With respect to the appointment of vice-consuls and agents that power rests at present with Mr. Barclay the Consul general of the United states for France. Having appointed Mr. Bondfeild at Bourdeaux, I beleive Mr. Barclay has not made any appointment for Royan. Should any occasion arise, I will take the liberty of asking your friendly offices to the citizens of the United states whom I may hereafter know to be under difficulties at your port, and have the honour of being with sentiments of much

8 AUGUST 1786

esteem and respect Gentlemen Your most obedient & most humble servt., TH: JEFFERSON

PrC (DLC); endorsed.

From John Stockdale

SIR   Piccadilly 8th. Augt. 1786.

I duly received your two Orders for which I return you my sincere thanks, the whole of which is executed excepting one Copy of McIntosh['s] Travells, which is entirely out of print. The List of the Books sent in a Box directed to you at Paris, is on the other side, which I have Book't at the Mess. Beam, Piccadilly, this day and they will set out for Paris to Morrow. There is no more of Soulés History of the War, except 2 Volumes, nor is it at all likely that there will ever be any more. I have had some thoughts of printing your Work in England, which is highly spoke of except those parts that relate to our Country, but I had some doubts wether it wou'd sell sufficient to defray the expences. At a convenient oppertunity shall be glad to have your opinion on it. I am with great Respect, sir Your much oblig'd & very hble. Servt.,

JOHN STOCKDALE

His Excy. Thos. Jefferson
1786.   Dr. to John Stockdale

Aug. 18th.	Homers Ilias & Odyssia Greek 2 vols. folio bd.	2	4
	Schrevellii Lexicon		7 6
	2 Capper's Travels bound		12
	1 McIntosh's Travels bd.		18
	Price's Observations on do.		2 6
	Andrew's History of the War 4 vols. bds.	1	10
	Bells Shakespeare No. 25 to 32		12
	Cooke's Littleton Pt. 4		7 6
	American War No. 25 to 28		4
	Jeffery's Historical Chart		10 6
	Priestley's Biogl. Chart		10 6
	Description of do.		— — —
	Evans's Map of the Middle Colonies		2
		8	0 6

N.B. The Bookseller will not sell the description of the Chart separate, nor will he make the book perfect, but if you will at

[201]

another opertunity specify the Pages Wanting I will endeavour myself to get them at the booksellers. J.S.

RC (MHi); endorsed. Noted in SJL as received 13 Aug. 1786.

To Abigail Adams

DEAR MADAM   Paris Aug. 9. 1786.

It is an age since I have had the honor of a letter from you, and an age and a half since I presumed to address one to you. I think my last was dated in the reign of king Amri, but under which of his successors you wrote, I cannot recollect. Ochosias, Joachar, Manahem or some such hard name. At length it is resumed: I am honoured with your favor of July 23. and I am at this moment writing an answer to it. And first we will dispatch business. The shoes you ordered, will be ready this day and will accompany the present letter. But why send money for them? You know the balance of trade was always against me. You will observe by the inclosed account that it is I who am to export cash always, tho' the sum has been lessened by the bad bargains I have made for you and the good ones you have made for me. This is a gaining trade, and therefore I shall continue it, begging you will send no more money here. Be so good as to correct the inclosed that the errors of that may not add to your losses in this commerce. You were right in conjecturing that both the gentlemen might forget to communicate to me the intelligence about Captn. Stanhope. Mr. Adams's head was full of whale oil, and Colo. Smith's of German politics (—but don't tell them this—) so they left it to you to give me the news. De tout mon coeur, I had rather receive it from you than them. This proposition about the exchange of a son for my daughter puzzles me. I should be very glad to have your son, but I cannot part with my daughter. Thus you see I have such a habit of gaining in trade with you that I always expect it.—We have a blind story here of somebody attempting to assassinate your king. No man upon earth has my prayers for his continuance in life more sincerely than him. He is truly the American Messias. The most precious life that ever god gave, and may god continue it. Twenty long years has he been labouring to drive us to our good, and he labours and will labour still for it if he can be spared. We shall have need of him for twenty more. The Prince of Wales on the throne, Lansdowne and Fox in the ministry, and we are undone! We become chained by our habits to the tails of those

[202]

who hate and despise us. I repeat it then that my anxieties are all alive for the health and long life of the king. He has not a friend on earth who would lament his loss so much and so long as I should.—Here we have singing, dauncing, laugh, and merriment. No assassinations, no treasons, rebellions nor other dark deeds. When our king goes out, they fall down and kiss the earth where he has trodden; and then they go to kissing one another. And this is the truest wisdom. They have as much happiness in one year as an Englishman in ten.—The presence of the queen's sister enlivens the court. Still more the birth of the princess. There are some little bickerings between the king and his parliament, but they end with a sic volo, sic jubeo. The bottom of my page tells me it is time for me to end with assurances of the affectionate esteem with which I have the honor to be, dear Madam, your most obedient & most humble servant, TH: JEFFERSON

Mrs. Adams to Th:J.   Dr.

85. June	2. To paid Petit		173ℓt- 8s
Aug.	17. To pd. Mr. Garvey's bill		96 -16 - 6
Nov.	To cash by Colo. Smith		768 - 0 - 0
86. Jan.	5. To pd. Bazin for Surtout de dessert & figures &c.		264 -17 - 6
Feb.	27. To pd. for shoes for Miss Adams		24 -
Mar.	5. To pd. for sundries viz.		
	12. aunes de dentelle	96.ℓt	
	une paire de barbes	36.	
	4. aunes of cambric	92.	
	4. do.	60.	284 - 0 - 0
	(reckoning 24. livres at 20/ sterl.)		1611 - 2 - 0 being £67- 2 - 7
Mar.	9. To balance expences of journey between Mr. Adams & myself		8- 9 - 4
			75-11 -11

9 AUGUST 1786

Cr.

1785 Oct.	12.	By pd. insurance on Houdon's life		£32-11s-
1786 Jan.	10.	By damask table cloth & napkins		7- 0 -
		2. pr. nutcrackers		4 -
		2 peices Irish linen		
		@ 4/	£8 -14s	
		making 12. shirts	1 -16	
		buttons, thread, silk	3	
		washing	3 -6	
		a trunk	1 - 1	11-17 -
Apr.	9.	By pd. for 9 yds. muslin @ 11/		4-19 -
	12.	By do. for 21 yds. Chintz @ 5/6		5-15 -
		By pd. for 25 yds. linen @ 4/ ⎫	£5. ⎫	
		for making 7. shirts ⎭	1-6-6 ⎭ for Mr. Short	6- 6 -
		By pd. for altering 12. shirts		6 -
		Balance		6-11 -1
				75-11 -1

RC (MHi: AMT); endorsed. PrC (DLC). Enclosure (MHi: AMT; PrC in DLC).

Abigail Adams' incomplete attempt at stating the account is to be found in MHi: AMT in two fragments, one of which is quoted in the note to her letter to TJ, 11 Feb. 1786. The other agrees with the items credited to her by TJ, save that she omitted the pair of nutcrackers and stated the cost of the two pieces of Irish linen at £8 10s. instead of £8 14s.

From Paul Bentalou

Sir Bayonne August the 9th 1786

After a Long and Tedioux passage of seventy seven Days from Baltimore, I Embrace this first Opportunity To forward your Excellency The Inclosed from Mr. James McHenry, and if Deprived of the Honour of Delivering it my self, I am happy of having in my power, to offer you, the favourable Opportunity of the Brigantine The Heart-Wig Capn. Richd. Barry; which is to sail from this port in the Course of this Month; and above all My Most Devoted Zeal To fulfill such Orders as you may be pleased to Intrust me with and which I'll be proud to Receive at the House of My Correspondents here Messrs. Pre. & Leon Batbedat.

[204]

Although I had the Honour of being Introduced to your Excellency at Williamsburg, while I Remained in that place, with the Troop of Dragoons, of Late Pulasky's Legion, which I had the Honour to Command; I Can not presume that My Little Individual should be Reminded; but as I flatter my self that before I Depart from my Native Land, it will be in My power to Go to Paris; I shall be happy to have the honour Granted of Paying My Due Respects and Receive Orders from the Minister of a Contry which I have adopted, that I had the Honour to serve and for which I'll never Cease to be Devoted in My Little Capacity, Glorying My self of being one of its Best Citizens.

Your Excellency's Benevolence is so well known that I am Imboldened to Intreat your Patronage, in Order to Obtain a permission from the french Ministry for Mrs. Bentalou, who hath accompanied me in this voyage, to keep her Little Negro-Boy, while she Remains in the Kingdom, which will not Exceed Eighteen Month! and I'll be Ready to Give security if Required for the Complyance thereof. The boy is between Eight or Nine years Old, not only very usefull to Mrs. Bentalou here, as at sea when she'll Return to America but her feelings would be very much Hurt was she Obliged to send him back and Expose him to be used Ill by a Captain if not spoiled out of her sight by the Bad Example of sailors. But I am In hopes that the Request will be Granted if Made by the American Embassador, for an american Lady and when Considered that the youth is Incapable of Causing what the Law will wisely prevent; Mrs. Bentalou adds her Entreaty to Mine, and Reposing Our selves on your Condescendence, I have the Honour to assure you the Right you have to Expect from my Duty My Most Unbounded Devotion which a Multitude of Considerations oblige me to be of your Excellency The Most Obedient & Most Humble servant,

PAUL BENTALOU

RC (DLC); endorsed by TJ: "Bentalou Capt." Noted in SJL as received 22 Aug. 1786. Enclosure: McHenry to TJ, 12 May 1786.

To Jean Jacques Bérard & Cie.

GENTLEMEN   Paris Aug. 9. 1786.

Mr. Lewis of New-York informed me by a letter which came in the French packet which left New York the 11th. of May and [arrived] at L'orient about the 20th. of June, that he had by the same packet sent me a pipe of Madeira wine addressed to your care. I trust it has arrived safely and must sollicit your attention to it, and to be so good as to have it brought on to Paris. I imagine it will be best to send it round by water to Havre or Rouen, to the care of Mr. Limozin at the former place or Messrs. Garvey at the latter. I shall be very thankful for your goodness on this occasion, and will pay to your order on sight whatever expences you may incur. I have the honour to be with great respect Gentlemen Your most obedient & most humble servt., TH: JEFFERSON

PrC (DLC); endorsed.

To Pierre Dessin

SIR   Paris Aug. 9. 1786.

Having desired my friend Colo. Smith in London to procure me some chariot harness, plated, and to send them on to Paris by the Diligence, I have taken the liberty of desiring him, in case that the master of the Diligence cannot send them on to the Douane at Paris, to direct an application to be made to you at Calais. I take the liberty of asking you, in case of any difficulty, to be so good as to have them plumbed, and to give your acquit à caution in order that they may come on, under an assurance that I will immediately have your acquit à caution returned to you, so that you shall have no other trouble with it but the signing it. I take for granted you received duly those which you had been so kind as to give for me before, and which were immediately redeemed here. Your favour on this occasion will much oblige Sir Your most obedient humble servt.,
TH: JEFFERSON

PrC (DLC); endorsed.

To the Governor of Virginia

SIR   Paris Aug. 9. 1786.

I have duly received the honour of your Excellency's letter of May 17. 1786. on the subject of Captn. Greene supposed to be in captivity with the Algerines. I wish I could have communicated the agreeable news that this supposition was well founded, and I should not have hesitated to gratify as well your Excellency as the worthy father of Capt. Greene by doing whatever would have been necessary for his redemption. But we have certainly no such prisoner at

9 AUGUST 1786

Algiers. We have there 21. prisoners in all. Of these only 4. are Americans by birth. Three of these are captains, of the names of O'Brian, Stephens and Coffyn. There were only two vessels taken by the Algerines, one commanded by O'Brian, the other by Steevens. Coffyn, I beleive, was a supercargo. The Moors took one vessel from Philadelphia, which they gave up again with the crew. No other captures have been made on us by any of the pyratical states. I wish I could say we were likely to be secure against future captures. With Marocco I have hopes we shall; but the states of Algiers, Tunis and Tripoli hold their peace at a price which would be felt by every man in his settlement with the tax gatherer. I have the honor to be with sentiments of the highest respect, Your Excellency's most obedient & most humble servt.,   TH: JEFFERSON[1]

P.S. Aug. 13. 1786. I have this morning received information from Mr. Barclay that our peace with the Emperor of Marocco would be pretty certainly signed in a few days. This leaves us the Atlantic free. Algiers, Tunis and Tripoli however, remaining hostile, will shut up the Mediterranean to us. The two latter never come into the Atlantic; the Algerines rarely, and but a little way out of the streights. In Mr. Barclay's letter is this paragraph. 'There is a young man now under my care, who has been a slave some time with the Arabs in the desert. His name is James Mercier, born at the town of Suffolk, Nansemond county Virginia. The king sent him after the first audience, and I shall take him to Spain.' On Mr. Barclay's return to Spain he shall find there a letter from me to forward this young man to his own country, for the expences of which I will make myself responsible.[2]

RC (NN); at foot of text: "H.E. Govr. Henry." PrC (DLC).

The present letter was in response to Henry's of 17 May (missing), but it was received by Gov. Edmund Randolph who in the meantime had succeeded Patrick Henry. I HAVE THIS MORNING RECEIVED INFORMATION FROM MR. BARCLAY: There is no entry in SJL for a letter from Barclay under 13 Aug. but at the foot of the page following the entry for 16 Aug. there is the following: "about the 11th. received T. Barclay's Marocco June 26." TJ did not acknowledge Barclay's letter until 31 Aug. 1786 and in that letter he did mention JAMES MERCIER. Probably the LETTER FROM ME TO FORWARD THIS YOUNG MAN TO HIS OWN COUNTRY was one to Mercier himself, perhaps enclosed in one to Barclay or Carmichael; if there was such a letter, it has not been found. See Randolph to TJ, 28 Jan. 1787.

[1] Beneath the signature, at the bottom of the first page, TJ wrote: "turn over," then added the postscript of 13 Aug. at the top of the second page.

[2] At this point TJ wrote, then deleted: "in confidence that the state or his relatives will take it on themselves or at any rate that I shall have paid a good tribute to humanity."

From John Paul Jones

Sir *Paris, August 9th, 1786.*

As it now appears by the reply I have just received from Mr. Adams, dated London the 17th of last month, which I had[1] the honor to communicate to you, that his letter to the Baron de Waltersdorff, respecting my prizes delivered up to the English at Bergen in Norway, in the year 1779, by the court of Denmark, has not been answered; and as the Baron de Waltersdorff is now gone to the West Indies, and Mr. Adams advises me in his letter, to apply to the Danish Minister at his court; it now becomes my duty to ask your advice and assistance in the steps that remain to be pursued, to obtain a compensation from the government of Denmark for those prizes.

And in order to give you the necessary information on this subject, I here subjoin some extracts from the papers left in my hands by Mr. Franklin, to wit:

No. 1. Extract of a letter from Monsieur Duchezaulx, Consul of France, to M. Caillard, Charge des affaires du Roi á Copenhagen, dated á Berghen en Norvege le 14 July 1779.

"Les deux dites prises sont considérables; elles etoient armeés en guerre et en marchandises, et les commandants pourvus de commissions aux Lettres de Marque; savoir *L'Union* de Londres, du port de 400 tonneaux armé de 22 canons de 6, et 4 livres de balle, plusieurs pierriers et autres armes; chargé de cables, cordage, et toile a voile, enfin tout ce qu'il faut en ce genre pour le grément de sept Batiments de guerre, avec plusieurs autres effets, destinés pour Quebec; et le *Betsey* de Liverpool, du port de 350 tonneaux armé de 20 canons de 6, et de 2 de 9 livres de balle, 12 pierriers et autres armes, chargé de fleur de farine, bœuf, et lard salés, et autres provisions et marchandises destinés pour la Nouvelle York, et la Jamaique. Les deux cargaisons peuvent être évaluées au moins un million de livres."

No. 2. Extract from a letter written by the Consul of France, before mentioned, to Dr. Franklin, minister of America at the court of France, dated á Berghen le 26 Oct. 1779.

"Il m'est douloureux au de la de toute expression, d'avoir a vous informer aujourdhui, que les deux prises the *Betsey* and the *Union*, ont eté ces jours ci restituées aux Anglais, en vertû d'une résolution emanée du Roi de Danemark: Résolution injuste et contraire au droit des gens."

No. 3. Extract from the same letter.

9 AUGUST 1786

"La valeur de ces deux prises que l'on vous enleve injustement, est au moins de 40,000*l* sterling, indépendamment des Frais et l'argent deboursé par les banquiers M. M. Danekert and Krohn, dont je vous remettrai le compte."

No. 4. Extract of a letter from all the American officers in Norway to Dr. Franklin, minister of America in France, dated Bergen, Jan. 4th, 1780.

"The Brigantine *Charming Polly*, which arrived 14 days after us, was likewise delivered up in the same manner."

No. 5. Extract of a letter from the same officers to Dr. Franklin, dated at Bergen, April 11th, 1780.

"Our expenses while on board the ships, were paid by the English Consul; and those since, by the King of Denmark; which enables us to proceed without drawing bills upon France. We have also the protection of the Danish flag till our arrival in France."

After my return here from L'Orient, you remember I was prevented, by circumstances, from pursuing the application to the Court of Denmark, in person. The bills I had received were not yet payable, and I thought it would be necessary for me to go to America in the spring, to deposit the prize-money received from this government, in the Continental treasury; so that I was prevented from going to the Court of Denmark. And there being no Danish minister here, nor expected here during the winter, you remember your having approved of my deputizing Dr. Bancroft to solicit the Court of Denmark, through the Danish minister in London; and that you was so obliging as to join me in requesting Mr. Adams to support that application.

But as experience has now shewn that this method is slow and uncertain; and as the late order of the Board of Treasury respecting the prize-money I have recovered, makes my return to America, on that account, at present unnecessary; I presume the best thing I can do will be to proceed to Copenhagen, and there make application to that court. If you approve of this, it would be useful for me to have a letter from the Count de Vergennes to the Baron de la Houze, minister of France at the Danish Court, directing him to support my reclamation. The interference of this government may be asked for with propriety, because the King had the gallantry to support under the flag of America, the squadron I commanded in Europe. It is also to be wished that I could carry letters with me from the Danish minister at this court, and it is therefore very unlucky that he is now absent at the waters. If you think fit to write to him, I can at the same time, obtain and forward a letter from

9 AUGUST 1786

his particular friend the minister of the Duc de Wertemburg; which may have a very good effect. I am persuaded that the Count de Vergennes, on my own application to him, would immediately give me a proper letter to the Baron de la Houze; but it will be more official to obtain it through your application, which I therefore request.

As I flatter myself that the Danish Court is still disposed to make a compensation, it is necessary for us now to determine on the lowest sum to be accepted. Doctor Franklin, in his letter to me from Havre, says the result of his letter to a broker in London was, that those Quebec ships were worth 16 or 18 thousand pounds each. I have reason to believe that the two ships delivered up, with their cargoes and armament, worth a greater sum. And besides, you will observe that the brigantine *Charming Polly*, was also delivered up. I cannot judge of the value of this last prize; and perhaps it may be necessary for me to write to Bergen to obtain information. I am, with respect, &c.

MS not located. Text printed from Sherburne, *John Paul Jones*, p. 270-3. Noted in SJL as received 10 Aug. 1786. Enclosure (DLC): Adams to Jones, 17 July 1786 (see note below); this letter was carried to Paris by John Trumbull, who arrived at least as early as 2 Aug., for on that day TJ received letters from John and Abigail Adams (16 and 23 July), Smith (18 July), and Paradise (28 July), all of which were evidently brought by him; in it Adams said: "Cash, I fancy, is not an abundant article in Denmark, and your claim has probably delayed and suspended all negotiations with Mr. Jefferson and me respecting a commercial treaty, for which three years ago there was so little zeal. This however is only conjecture, in confidence."

[1] Evidently a misreading of "have"; Adams' letter of 17 July had just been received by Jones and was evidently enclosed in the present letter.

To Francis Lewis

Sir   Paris Aug. 9. 1786.

I am now to acknowlege the receipt of your favors of May 9. and 11. and to return you many thanks for the ready attention you were pleased to pay to my request for the Madeira wine. Your bill for 1075^{tt}-10s has been presented and paid. I have not yet heard from Monsr. Berard & Co. but I take for granted the wine arrived by the same packet with the letter, and that they are taking measures to forward it to me. I shall be happy in any occasion of shewing you how sensible I am of your kindness, and the sentiments of esteem and respect with which I have the honor to be Sir Your most obedient & most humble servt.,   TH: JEFFERSON

PrC (MHi); endorsed.

Essai d'Imprimerie

Présenté à l'Académie Royale des sçiences le 8 de février 1786 par M. l'Abbé ROCHON.

Mr. Hoffman a trouvé une Méthode d'Imprimer qui m'a paru offrir plusieurs Avantages considérables. l'œconomie du papier est sans-doute, le plus précieux de tous ces avantages. un Auteur, qui ne peut jamais sçavoir au-juste, le nombre d'Exemplaires, dont son ouvrage est susceptible, se trouve privé du fruit de ses travaux, par des frais, & des avances de papier & d'impression, qui le mettent toujours, dans la dépendance absolue des libraires. Le Moyen d'imprimer, dont nous allons donner la description, n'aura aucun de ces inconvéniens. les seules Avances qu'il faudra faire, sont 1° le salaire du Compositeur: 2° l'Achat du Plomb & du régule d'Antimoine, pour former les planches, qui doivent servir au tirage de l'Ouvrage. Ces Frais sont in-évitables; mais alors, les auteurs ne feront plus dans la dépendance des libraires, pour l'impression & pour la vente de leurs ouvrages, puis qu'après toutes les planches qui servent au tirage, leur appartiendront en propriété.

Essai d'Imprimerie

Présenté à l'Académie Royale des sçiences le 8 de février 1786 par M. l'Abbé ROCHON.

Mr. Hoffman a trouvé une Méthode d'Imprimer qui m'a paru offrir plusieurs Avantages considérables. l'œconomie du papier est sans-doute, le plus précieux de tous ces avantages. un Auteur, qui ne peut jamais sçavoir au-juste, le nombre d'Exem-

Specimen pages of polytype printing. (See p. xxviii.)

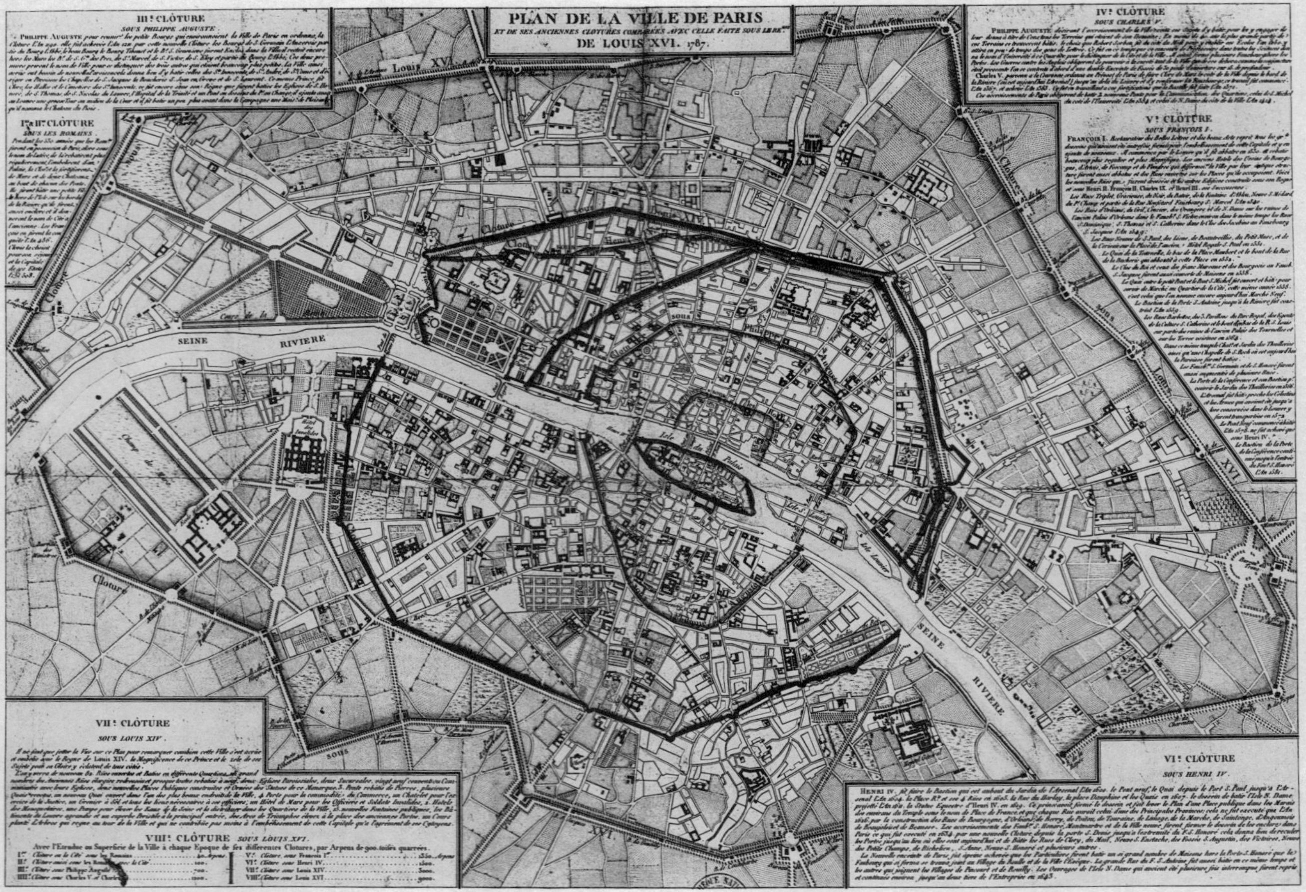
PLAN DE LA VILLE DE PARIS
DE LOUIS XVI. 1787.
III.e CLÔTURE
SOUS PHILIPPE AUGUSTE.
I.re & II.e CLÔTURE
SOUS LES ROMAINS.
IV.e CLÔTURE
V.e CLÔTURE
SOUS FRANÇOIS I.
VI.e CLÔTURE
SOUS HENRI IV.
VII.e CLÔTURE
SOUS LOUIS XIV.
VIII.e CLÔTURE SOUS LOUIS XVI.
SEINE
RIVIERE
Champ de Mars
Isle du Palais
Isle Louvier

To William Stephens Smith

Dear Sir Paris Aug: 9. [i. e., 10] 1786.

An opportunity will offer by Mr. Bullfinch of acknowleging the receipt of your favours of July 5. and 18. and as I mean by the same hand to write my American letters, the number of these obliges me to abridge with you. I therefore make this previous declaration that there shall be neither prayer nor compliment in this letter, nothing but a simple tho' sincere proffer of respect to Madame, which I desire to place here that I may not have to repeat it at the end of my letter. The things she desired will be ready to go by Mr. Bullfinch. Petit tells me he has transgressed her orders as to the cambrick by buying at a smaller price a better cambric than he could get at the place she named or any where else at the price desired. I wish he may be right, and that the execution of this commission may encourage her to continue her custom to us. I say, *to us*, being like other commanders in chief, willing to gobble up the credit due to the actions of my inferior officers.—But I forget myself and am writing about other people's business, when I had previously determined to write about my own only: to be absolutely selfish.—Imprimis. I have desired Mr. Grand to send me a letter of credit on his correspondent in London for 100. or 120. guineas, which I shall receive to-day and will inclose herein. This will cover your advances for me heretofore, and extend to other objects which I will explain.

Mr. Paradise and Dr. Burney are having a harpsichord made for me at Kirkman's. I must impose on you the trouble of taking the charge of paying for it and of ordering it's transportation from Kirkman's shop to Havre or Rouen to the care of Mr. Limozin at the former place, or Messrs. Garvey at the latter. I could wish the copying press from Woodmason to come at the same time, because I can have them covered by the same Passport, whereas if they come separate, I shall be obliged to sollicit two, and of course to feel disagreeably twice instead of once.

I will beg the favor of you to procure me a pair of Chariot harness, plated, of about 15. guineas price, which you say will get them handsome without being tawdry: also a harness for what is called here a Cabriolet, and we call a chaise or chair. It is for a single horse; and the traces of this must be fixed with spring swivels. I believe that is the name of the irons fixed at the end of the trace in this form ⊶ like those to a watch-chain. These harness I would have with breast plates, not collars. I have seen here some, the pads and other ornaments of which were somewhat octagonal, as thus ⌘ and thus ◗ and thus ⬤ &c. What think you of them? They appeared to me handsome, but it is you and not me who are to judge on this occasion. I would be obliged to you to send these by the diligence which comes weekly from London to Paris. They must be directed to me, which will facilitate their entrance at Calais; but I am not sure that it will ensure their coming on to Paris. Perhaps the owner of the diligence can take measures for their coming on to the Douan of Paris from whence I can easily obtain them; or, at the worst, I think that Monsr. Dessin at Calais will have them plumbed and give his acquit à Caution for me, as he did once before. I am not able to tell you from what part of London this Diligence comes; but there is but one there where seats can be taken weekly for Paris.

I send herewith a map, to be engraved by Samuel Neele engraver No. 352. near Exeter change, strand, with whom I spoke on the subject when in London. I shewed him the map, not then quite finished. He told me he would engrave it, in the best manner possible for from 20. to 25. pounds sterling. I must beg the favour of you to engage him to do it. Should he ask a few guineas more, I shall not stand about it. But nothing must be wanting in the execution, as to precision, distinctness, exactness, the form of his letters, and whatever else constitutes the perfection of a map. He told me it would take him six weeks. In fact the plate must be here by the middle of October, at which time the work will appear for which it has been constructed.

Still another commission about maps. Don Lopez, after a long residence in S. America, and infinite pains and expence on it's topography, made a map of that country, on 12. sheets, with a precision which qualifies it even to direct military operations in that country. The government of Spain at first permitted the map, but the moment they saw one of them come out, they destroyed the plates, seized all of the few copies which had got out and on which they could lay their hands, and issued the severest injunctions to call in the rest and to prevent their going abroad. Some few copies escaped their search. A friend has by good management procured me one, and it is arrived safe through all the searches that travellers are submitted to. Does Mr. Faden know anything of this map? Would he wish to publish it? If he will undertake to publish an accurate copy of it, I will send it to him, asking in return half a dozen copies for Congress, for it's bureaus, and for myself. I expect the copy I have has cost me from ten to twenty guineas. I have not yet received the account. This is more than half a dozen will be worth when they come to be in possession of the public.

One more request, that you will be so good as to send me copies of the joint letters written by Mr. Adams and myself to Congress while I was in London.

Have I been as good as my word? After the small deviation into which Mrs. Smith led me (for beauty is ever leading us astray) have I written one syllable which has any thing but self in view? That I may not break my promise at last I will conclude here with assurances of the perfect esteem with which I have the honour to be Dear Sir your friend & servt., TH: JEFFERSON

P.S. The engraver must absolutely have always before his eyes Hutchin's map of the Western country, Schull's map of Pennsylvania, Fry and Jefferson's map of Virginia, and Mouzon's map of N. Carolina. The two former I send herewith for him. The two latter I will be obliged to you to desire Faden to furnish him, which he will place against some of the new maps to be furnished him. The reason why there is an absolute necessity for the engraver to have these maps before him is that in many instances he will not be able to make out the letters of the manuscript map; he must in those cases have recourse to the maps abovementioned which are the basis of the M.S. map.—Send me if you please from Woodmason three reams of copying paper and proportionable supply of ink powder. Let it come with the harpsichord.

PrC (DLC); despite its date, this letter was written on 10 Aug., for the draft sent by Grand and the manuscript map returned by Morellet were both transmitted to TJ on that date. Enclosures: (1) TJ's manuscript map of the country between Albemarle Sound and Lake Erie (missing). (2) Thomas Hutchins' *Map of the Western Parts of Virginia, Pennsylvania, Maryland and North Carolina*; it is not possible to tell which of several editions of this map TJ sent. (3) Fry and Jefferson's *A Map of the most inhabited part of Virginia*; TJ may have sent the 1775 edition by Jefferys, but the edition cannot be identified with certainty.

MY INFERIOR OFFICERS: There is no mention here of the fact that Col. and Mrs. Smith had evidently desired to obtain the services of one of TJ's domestics. Three days earlier William Short, writing with TJ's knowledge and perhaps even at his dictation, had reported to Smith: "Espagnol has entered into Mr. Jefferson's service as a Valet de chambre; Petit is promoted to the Rank of maitre d'hotel. These changes took place about a month ago in consequence of embezzlements and depredations committed by Monsr. Mark the late Controller of Finances in his Department. Petit's honesty has long been well known and his abilities which alone were questionable at present stand acknowledged. He would have suited you à *merveille*; but I do not think that Espagnol, notwithstanding his honesty and his good dispositions are I am sure equal to Petits, would answer your purposes even if the service in which he is at present engaged permitted the subject to be mentioned to him. Mr. Jefferson is of the same opinion or I am sure he would relinquish any right he may have in your favor. I take it however that Espagnol though an excellent Valet de chambre is entirely without experience

10 AUGUST 1786

in the Line in which you would wish him to move. Would you not do better to get a Cook from Paris than a Maitre d'hotel? Determine this matter for yourself; i.e. in concert with her who makes with you but one and the same person, and give me your orders thereon. I will make every exertion Sir to produce for you such a Servant as you should wish —you have only to mark out the qualities that you would chuse in him" (Short to Smith, 6 Aug. 1786; DLC: Short Papers). Marc's "embezzlements and depredations" seem to have become apparent shortly after TJ's return from London, for in the Account Book under 2 May 1786 there appeared TJ's "Analysis of Marc's Accounts from Mar. 6 to April 23." which tabulated each item of account week by week for the period during which TJ had been absent; these showed a decline from normal expenditures, but not such as could have been expected under the circumstances (see Accounts, Second Series). TJ had employed Marc on 20 Aug. 1784 as "Valet de Chambre @ 40 Louis a year and he feeds himself"; on 1 Dec. 1784 he increased Marc's salary from 80 to 100 livres per month, at which figure it remained until 26 June 1786 when Marc was dismissed. Marc evidently had acted as maitre d'hotel almost from the beginning. Espagnol was employed as valet de chambre on 27 June 1786 (same).

DON LOPEZ, AFTER A LONG RESIDENCE IN S. AMERICA . . . MADE A MAP OF THAT COUNTRY, ON 12. SHEETS: The FRIEND who procured a copy for TJ was Carmichael, who had reported on 16 June 1786 that he had sent by Randall "a Map of Mexico which is not to be bought here" because the minister had stopped the sale of it some years earlier. Carmichael's reference to suppression by the minister seems to fit the circumstances of the map described by TJ in the present letter, as does the timing: Randall had arrived in Paris on 2 July. TJ's remark about the safe arrival of the map THROUGH ALL THE SEARCHES THAT TRAVELLERS ARE SUBMITTED TO would also seem to fit the requirements, for Randall, of course, travelled under a diplomatic passport and, though not exempt from search, would probably not have been subject to the scrutiny given by customs officials to ordinary travellers. If this assumption is correct—that the map of "Mexico" conveyed by Randall was in fact the map of South America here described by TJ—then it is possible that Randall himself may have been the source of some of the misinformation contained in the description. For there was some error in TJ's comment: (1) There is no evidence that Lopez was ever in South America; (2) no edition of a map of South America with which Lopez was associated can be found that was issued in twelve sheets; (3) the map that actually fits the other circumstances described by TJ seems to be one by Cruz Cano, published in 1775 on eight sheets (see TJ's observations on the republication of this map, following). Faden agreed to bring out the publication as suggested here by TJ, and on 22 Oct. 1786 TJ wrote Smith that he would send the "twelve sheet map . . . by the first good opportunity." The map was later carried to London by Franks who also conveyed another letter to Smith, in which TJ remarked: "For his gain he [Faden] will wish to make the map large, for that of the public and for their convenience I wish to debarrass it of all useless margin"—a remark that reflects the view set forth in TJ's observations on the republication of the Cruz Cano map in eight sheets. See Smith to TJ, 13 and 22 Sep. 1786; and 29 Jan. 1787; TJ to Smith, 22 Oct., 20 Dec. 1786. On 2 Feb. 1788 TJ wrote Smith: "Be so good also as to let me know who undertook the map of S. America, and even to get from him some acknolegement in writing of what he is to do." Smith did not mention the map in his reply to this inquiry. Soon thereafter, TJ, Adams, and Smith met in Holland, and the question of the map may have been discussed then. There seems to have been no further correspondence on the subject between Smith and TJ, and none between TJ and Faden.

The *Mapa Geográfico de America Meridional* by Don Juan de la Cruz Cano y Olmedilla was engraved and printed in Madrid in 1775; each of the eight sheets of the copy in the Map Division of the Library of Congress measures 22 x 34¾ inches. The DON LOPEZ to whom TJ referred does not appear in the title of the map nor is there in the lengthy "Advertencias para la inteligencia de esta mapa" across the lower margin any indication that he played a part in preparing it. But Don Tomas Lopez de Vargas Machucha (b. Madrid 21 Dec. 1731–d. same city, July 1802) and Don Juan de la Cruz Cano y Olmedilla (b. Madrid 6 May

[214]

1734–d. 13 Feb. 1790) were nevertheless associated briefly in the preparation of this rare and valuable map. In 1752 Lopez, Cruz Cano, and two other young students were sent by the Spanish government to Paris to study map engraving, ornamentation, and architecture. In 1755 Lopez and Cruz Cano jointly published a two-sheet chart of the Gulf of Mexico and in 1757 they collaborated in preparing a map of North America in two parts showing English and French claims respectively. In 1760 Lopez returned to Madrid and during the next forty years published more than 220 maps. A comprehensive but "probably still incomplete" list of maps published by Lopez was included by Gabriel Marcel in his "Le geographe Thomas Lopez et son oeuvre," *Revue Hispanique* (Hispanic Society of America), XVI (1907), 137-243. *This list includes no such edition in twelve sheets as that described by TJ.* After 1757 there is no further evidence of collaboration between Lopez and Cruz Cano until they became temporarily associated in the preparation of the 1775 Cruz Cano map of South America. That map and its preparation were described in detail in 1797 by Lopez himself. According to this account, Lopez and Cruz Cano had been asked (presumably about 1765) by the Marquis de Grimaldi, then Minister of State, to prepare a map of South America. Each was assigned a portion of the map to execute and they began their collaboration. But very soon Lopez discovered that there were wide differences in their conceptions of the task and he thereupon permitted Cruz Cano to assume full responsibility, turning over to the latter all of the data that he had in his possession. The task required ten years. When completed, the map was printed by the government and some copies distributed to ambassadors, ministers, and "influential persons." However, according to Lopez' statement in 1797, "the war with Portugal having been declared, it was observed that the map of Cruz Cano did not favor the Spanish claims in America. The government was thereupon moved to disclaim a work with which they had been wholly satisfied, and of which they had started distribution; and they even sought to recover the copies distributed and let it be known that it was very inaccurate, when the real trouble which they found with it concerned the boundaries, which were delimited by the map-maker with impartiality and with the sole objective of accuracy" (from Marcel's summary of Lopez' report of 1797, *Revue Hispanique*, XVI [1907], 179-80; Lopez' report is published in full in D. Cesareo Fernandez, *Armada española*, VII, 399-415; the Editors are indebted to Messrs. Burton W. Adkinson, Director, Reference Department, and Walter W. Ristow, Assistant Chief, Map Division, Library of Congress, for communications concerning the Cruz Cano map on which the foregoing account is based, including their translation of Marcel's summary of the Lopez report, and for their opinion—in which the Editors fully concur—that the map discussed by TJ in the present and subsequent letters was in fact the Cruz Cano map of 1775).

From these facts it appears obvious that TJ could only have transmitted to Smith for Faden's use a copy of the rare Cruz Cano map of 1775. Faden was evidently so eager to do the map that Smith was able—three months before he or Faden saw the map itself—to report a firm agreement with Faden according to the terms suggested by TJ and to urge that "the sooner you forward [the map] the better" (Smith to TJ, 22 Sep. 1786). The cause of Faden's failure to execute this understanding is not known, but these facts may be noted: (1) TJ had transmitted a rare and valuable map which had cost him personally FROM TEN TO TWENTY GUINEAS; (2) he asked on 2 Feb. 1788 for further word on the map and for a commitment in writing from the publisher; (3) this request evidently was not pressed further and there is no proof that the map belonging to TJ was ever returned; (4) Faden did in 1799 bring out an edition of the Cruz Cano map of 1775 with the statement that it was "una copia literal y exacta de un Mapa español mui raro; dispuesto y gravado en Madrid, año 1775"; and (5) he issued it in three sheets as TJ had suggested in the document following. In view of the fact that the suppression and subsequent rarity of the map was owing to political considerations, it is not unreasonable to suggest that Faden's failure to do the map and TJ's silence may also have been due to political factors. Faden was Geographer to the King, and, while TJ was undoubtedly motivated by a characteristic desire to advance knowledge, he was also an American minister. Unauthorized publication of a map in 1786 that responsible Spanish officials believed would affect Spanish boundary claims might very well

[215]

have affected also the fate of the recently negotiated treaty with Portugal and might have had an influence on relations between England and Spain. What may not have been possible or expedient in 1786-1787 when the European balance of power was precariously adjusted and when Spain and England were reluctantly on the brink of war could have been quite feasible a decade later when the political climate of Europe had been vastly altered. It is to be hoped that further study by cartographers will clarify some of the factors involved in TJ's relationship with the Cruz Cano map and may establish as fact what now can only be stated as a possibility—that the "mui raro" copy of the map that Faden utilized in 1799 was indeed the identical copy which had been procured for TJ with some difficulty and which, with a restraint rare in any collector and phenomenal in the most assiduous gatherer of Americana then living, he evidently allowed to go quietly and permanently out of his possession when he alone had title to ownership. There are three copies of the Cruz Cano map of 1775 in London in the following collections: (1) the Topographical Collection of George III, British Museum; (2) the Colonial Office series in the Public Record Office; and (3) the Library of the Colonial Office itself (communication from R. A. Skelton, The Map Room, British Museum, to the Editors, 28 May 1954). None of these maps has any MS notations on it, and all three are uncolored; Faden, as indicated in the list of symbols, must have utilized a copy in which the political boundaries were indicated by different colors.

Carmichael's reference to a map of "Mexico" and TJ's puzzling—and repeated—references to a map of South America in twelve sheets require a final comment that can be advanced at this time only as pure hypothesis. From the foregoing account it will be seen that Cruz Cano and Lopez also collaborated in producing two other maps, one of the Gulf of Mexico in two sheets and one of North America in two sheets. These, too, are quite rare maps. Carmichael evidently acquired the Cruz Cano map in Cadiz through an agent (Carmichael to TJ, 16 June 1786), and it is reasonable to suppose that any "influential person" having obtained custody of that map might also have had an interest in possessing these others by Cruz Cano and Lopez. If this supposition is correct and if Carmichael did in fact send to TJ all three maps, then this might help to explain his reference to a map of "Mexico" and TJ's reference to twelve sheets. Admittedly this is an inadequate explanation, for it seems unlikely that Carmichael would refer to maps of the Americas by the name of the least important area covered by the three, and it also seems unlikely that TJ would refer to A MAP OF THAT COUNTRY, ON 12. SHEETS in a context that could only mean South America if he had in fact meant to include the total number of sheets of maps covering all of the Americas. The problem is further complicated by the fact that TJ correctly designated the number of sheets in the Cruz Cano map in his suggestions about its republication (document following). But, at present, this seems to be not only the best but the only hypothesis that offers a plausible explanation for the discrepancy.

Jefferson's Suggestions for Republishing the Cruz Cano Map of South America

[ca. Aug. 1786]

Observations for the republication of the map of South America by Don Juan de la Cruz Cano.

The same scale should be preserved, and the Spanish names of places. The title, marginal explanations &c. may be in Spanish or English, as shall be thought best. The original is on 8 sheets of paper, numbered as below. Measuring the geographical part I

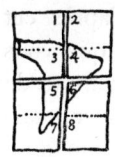

10 AUGUST 1786

find that it may be comprehended in a parallelogram 4. feet wide and 6.f. 1.Inch high. That is to say from Cape Blanco to Cape Saint Roque, those being the most Westwardly and Eastwardly points, and in the same parallel of 5° S. Lat: and from Cape horn to Cape de la Vela, the most Southernly and Northernly points, and nearly in the same meridian. It may then be put into 4. sheets of the size of those of the original, that is in half the space, and yet the same scale preserved. They must be thus arranged. No. 1. 3. in one sheet; 2. 4. in another; 5. 7. in a third; 6. 8. in a fourth as is seen above.

But I should like it better in 3. sheets, to wit 1. 3. in one; 2. 4. in another; and 5. 6. 7. 8. in a third sheet. This third sheet must be 38 I. by 30. I. Because this map is too large ever to be hung up as a single one: and for an Atlas it is more convenient to put 5. 6. 7. 8. into one sheet, getting rid of the margin. But if it be insisted to make two equal maps of it, then arrange them as first proposed, but place the graduations of latitude and longitude in the two Southern sheets close by the geographical outlines, so that those who chuse it, may paste the two bottom sheets together, and cutting off what is without the graduation, reduce it to the size of one sheet. In this case the scales and explanations, now in the S.W. corner of No. 7. must be put in No. 6. 8. between the outlines of the coast and the graduated lines. The plans of Lima, and of the Angostura, can be put into the N.E. corner of No. 2.

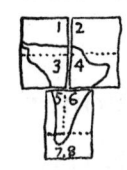

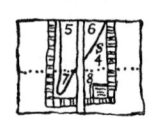

PrC (DLC); undated, but evidently written sometime between Randall's arrival in Paris on 2 July 1786 and the date when TJ dispatched the Cruz Cano map to London with his letter of 20 Dec. 1786 to Smith (see note to Smith to TJ, 9 Aug. 1786 for identification of this map and for facts concerning TJ's relationship with its intended publication by Faden). Tr (DLC: TJ Papers, 27: 4568); in the hand of H. A. Washington and dated by him "Dec. 1786" evidently because of TJ's letter to Smith of 20 Dec. 1786.

The SHEETS . . . OF THE ORIGINAL measure, if those of the copy in the Library of Congress may be taken as standard, approximately 22 by 34¾ inches; their margins are wide and elaborately decorated and part of the marginal space is devoted to inset maps of LIMA, AND OF THE ANGOSTURA.

From Ferdinand Grand

MONSIEUR Paris le 10 aout 1786.

J'ai l'honneur de vous envoyer la lettre de crédit de £120. que vous desiriés Sur Mr. Louis Teissier que j'ai prévenu que vous

[217]

tireriés cette Somme, Monsieur, en divers appoints. D'après cet avis qu'il aura reçu, peut être ne sera-t-il pas nécessaire que vous lui Fassiés présenter ma lettre et vos traittès Sur lui, à compte de cette Somme, Suffiroient. Dans ce cas, veuillés me la renvoyer, mais je vous prie de faire la dessus ce qui vous sera le plus commode.

M. Leroy de l'académie des Sciences m'a dit que M. Charpentier, Méchanicien dans la cour du Louvre, seroit peut être l'homme de tous le plus propre pour l'exécution de la Machine à copier. C'est lui qui a monté la grande Lentille de Mr. De Trudaine.

Je Suis avec une considération respectueuse, Monsieur, Votre très humble et très obt. Serviteur, GRAND

RC (DLC); in a clerk's hand, signed by Grand; endorsed. Enclosure missing; see TJ to Smith, 9 Aug. 1786.

John Lamb to the American Commissioners

Alicante August 10th. 1786

Finding my self unable to Imbark and Desiring to have my Decleration forwarded as soon as possible according to your Excellency orders; have sent the vessel to give the earlyst notice. She sailed the nineth of this Curt. with Every Transaction, together with my last orders from Your Excellencys. The vessel is insured and Doth not sail at publick expence. I should be glad if I could here if Mr. Randall had arived and had Delivered to your Excellency my Declaration which I forwarded by him: at the reception of your Excellencys last orders to me. I Stated my Situation[1] in Two letters one of the 15th July and the other of the 18th. Ditto, hope they have come safe to hand. I am with Due Respect Your Excellencys Most Obednt. Hmbe Servant, JOHN LAMB

RC (DLC); endorsed. Tr (DNA: PCC, No. 87, I); in Short's hand, with a few corrections in spelling and punctuation. Tr (DNA: PCC, No. 107). Noted in SJL as received 5 Sep. 1786.

YOUR ... LAST ORDERS: See Commissioners to Lamb 20 June and 29 June 1786 (the latter under 7 July).

[1] This is a good example of the manner in which Short occasionally corrected Lamb's punctuation and spelling, with the result that his letters as published make Lamb appear more literate than he actually was. This passage, as punctuated by Short and as published in *Dipl. Corr., 1783-89*, I, 816, reads: "I should be glad if I could hear if Mr. Randall had arrived and had delivered to your Excellency my declaration, which I forwarded by him. At the reception of your Excellency's last orders to me, I stated my situation," &c.

[218]

From Abbé Morellet

Monsieur   jeudy [10 Aug. 1786]

 En recevant le dernier billet que vous m'aves fait l'honneur de m'ecrire lorsque vous m'aves envoyé la carte que vous aves pris la peine de faire j'étois obligé de sortir au moment même et je n'ai pas eu le tems de vous parler de cette même carte. Je repare aujourd'hui cette omission. Je ne doute point que votre travail ne donne beaucoup de prix à nôtre edition. Une bonne carte est la chose la plus essentielle pour une description de pays aussi bien faite que celle que vous voules bien permettre que je rende publique mais par cette raison même il est bien essentiel que la carte soit prête pour la fin de l'automne. Vous pouves seul prendre les moyens necessaires pour la prompte execution puisque vous connoisses le graveur que vous en charges. Il fera plus pour vous que pour un libraire francois et s'il falloit que le mien traitat directement avec lui ce seroit un embarras dont nous ne nous tirerions point. Je sens pourtant fort bien qu'il faut que les frais soient faits ou du moins remboursés par le libraire qui vendra la traduction. C'est aussi l'engagement que je contracte pour lui envers vous en vous suppliant de vouloir bien faire l'avance de la petite somme que le graveur exigera et dont vous seres remboursé sur les premiers produits de la vente de l'ouvrage. Je suis obligé d'ailleurs de faire au libraire quelque avance car il a fort peu de fonds et sans cela je ne l'aurois pas determiné à se charger de ma traduction. Mais comme l'ouvrage enrichi d'une bonne carte sera certainement recherché nous aurons bientot retiré nos avances et nous aurons eu le plaisir de publier un ouvrage utile. J'ai eu l'honneur de vous ecrire qu'il falloit que la planche nous fut envoyée aussi tot qu'elle seroit gravée. C'est le seul moyen de la donner au public à un prix raisonnable car s'il falloit faire tirer et faire venir d'angletterre les cartes elles mêmes jamais nous ne sortirions de cet embarras nous serions à la merci du graveur anglois et le livre avec la carte reviendroient à un prix exorbitant. Je ne puis trop insister sur ce point sur lequel je vous supplie de vous expliquer clairement et positivement avec le graveur anglois en lui confiant votre carte manuscrite. J'attens avec beaucoup d'impatience un jour de liberté ou je puisse aller vous rendre mes devoirs dans la solitude que vous embellissés par tous les moyens que pline employoit lorsqu'il disoit qu'il n'étoit jamais moins seul que quand il etoit seul. Agrèes mes très humbles respects.

11 AUGUST 1786

J'oubliois de vous faire observer que lorsque la planche aura fourni le nombre d'exemplaires necessaire à notre edition elle vous reviendra pour en faire l'usage que vous trouveres convenable à moins que vous ne veuillies nous la laisser pour en traiter avec quelque geographe et pour etre par là même en etat de la vendre dans l'ouvrage à un prix plus modique.

RC (DLC); unsigned, addressed, and endorsed; undated, but Thursday fell on 10 Aug., TJ replied to this letter on 11 Aug., and the entry in SJL for 10 Aug. shows that a letter was received from the Abbé Morellet on that day. TJ's MS map of Virginia was returned with the present letter, and was enclosed in TJ to Smith, 9 [i.e., 10] Aug. 1786.

LE DERNIER BILLET: TJ's note written when the map was sent has not been found and is not recorded in SJL; it was, however, written perhaps on the 2d or 3rd in reply to Morellet's of 1 Aug.

Thomas Barclay to the American Commissioners

GENTLEMEN DAralbeyda 11th. Aug. 1786.

I arrived here today and shall Continue my Journey to Tangiers Early in the morning. The Plague being at Constantina occasions a Rigorous Quaranteen of 40 days (from Barbary) in Spain.—I shall therefore Endeavor to get into Ceuta which being in the hands of the Spaniards is an Exception to the above remark and I think the Quaranteen from thence is only twelve[1] days.

The Treaty shall be forwarded with all Expedition as soon as I arrive in Europe,[2] and in the mean time I am Gentlemen Your very Obed. Serv., THOS. BARCLAY

RC (DLC); endorsed by TJ. Tr (DLC); in Franks' hand, signed and marked "Triplicate" by Barclay; endorsed by TJ. Tr of Tripl (DNA: PCC, No. 87, I); in Short's hand. Tr (DNA: PCC, No. 107). Enclosed in TJ to Jay, 26 Sep. 1786. Noted in SJL as received 13 Sep. 1786.

Barclay wrote to Adams on this date informing him that he had drawn two bills totalling £750 sterling and repeating substantially the sentences of the present letter (MHi: AMT).

[1] This word interlined and "two" deleted in RC.
[2] In his letter to Adams, Barclay wrote: "The Treaty will be forwarded to Paris immediately on my arrival in Europe."

To John Jay

SIR Paris Aug. 11. 1786.

Since the date of my last, which was of July 8. I have been honoured with the receipt of yours of June 16. I am to thank you

[220]

on the part of the minister of Geneva for the intelligence it contained on the subject of Gallatin, whose relations will be relieved by the receipt of it.

The inclosed intelligence relative to the instructions of the court of London to Sr. Guy Carleton come to me thro' the Count de la Touche and Marquis de la Fayette. De la Touche is a Director under the Marechal de Castries Minister for the Marine department, and possibly receives this intelligence from him, and he from their ambassador at London. Possibly too it might be fabricated here. Yet weighing the characters of the ministers of St. James's and Versailles, I think the former more capable of giving such instructions, than the latter of fabricating them for the small purposes it could answer.

The gazette of France of July 28. announces the arrival of Peyrouse at Brazil, that he was to touch at Otaheité, and proceed to California, and still further Northwardly. This paper, as you well know, gives out such facts as the court are willing the world should be possessed of. The presumption is therefore that they will make an establishment of some sort on the North-west coast of America.

I trouble you with the copy of a letter from Schweighauser and Dobreé, on a subject with which I am quite unacquainted. Their letter to Congress of Nov. 30. 1780. gives their state of the matter. How far it be true and just can probably be ascertained by Doctr. Franklin, Doctr. Lee and other gentlemen now in America. I shall be glad to be honoured with the commands of Congress on this subject. I have enquired into the state of the arms mentioned in their letter to me. The principal articles were about 30,000 bayonets, 50,000 gunlocks, 30 cases of arms, 22 cases of sabres, and some other things of little consequence. The quai at Nantes having been overflowed by the river Loire, the greatest part of these arms were under water, and are now, as I am informed, a solid mass of rust, not worth the expence of throwing them out of the warehouse, much less that of storage. Were not their want of value a sufficient reason against reclaiming the property of these arms, it rests with Congress to decide whether other reasons are not opposed to this reclamation. They were the property of a sovereign body, they were seized by an individual, taken cognizance of by a court of justice, and refused, or at least not restored by the sovereign within whose state they had been arrested. These are circumstances which have been mentioned to me. Doctr. Franklin however will be able to inform Congress with precision as to what passed on this subject. If the information I have received be any thing like the truth, the discussion of this matter can only be with the court of Versailles, it would be very delicate, and could have but one of two objects; either to recover the arms, which are not worth receiving, or to satisfy us on the point of honour. Congress will judge how far the latter may be worth pursuing against a particular ally, and under actual circumstances. An instance too of acquiescence, on our part, under a wrong, rather than disturb our friendship by altercations, may have it's value in some future case. However I shall be ready to do in this what Congress shall be pleased to direct.

I inclose the dispatches relative to the Barbary negociations received since my last. It is painful to me to overwhelm Congress and yourself continually with these voluminous papers. But I have no right to suppress any part of them, and it is one of those cases, where for a want of well digested information, we must be contented to examine a great deal of rubbish in order to find a little good matter.

The gazettes of Leyden and France to the present date accompany this, which for want of direct and safe opportunities I am obliged to send by an American gentleman by the way of London. The irregularity of the French packets has diverted elsewhere the tide of passengers who used to furnish me occasions of writing to you, without permitting my letters to go through the post-office. So that when the packets go now, I can seldom write by them. I have the honour to be with sentiments of the highest esteem and respect, Sir, your most obedient & most humble servt.,   TH: JEFFERSON

RC (DNA: PCC, No. 87, 1). PrC (DLC). Tr (DNA: PCC, No. 107). Enclosures: (1) De la Touche to Lafayette, 28 July 1786 (RC in DLC; Tr, in Short's hand, and translation by John Pintard, in DNA: PCC, No. 87, 1; Tr in DNA: PCC, No. 107), transmitting (2) an "Extract of the new System of English Politics" respecting North America (RC in DLC; Tr, in Short's hand, and translation, in another hand, in DNA: PCC, No. 87, 1; PrC of Short's Tr in DLC; Tr in DNA: PCC, No. 107), stating that Gen. Carleton departed for Canada with precise instructions to plague the Americans as much as possible; that Joseph Brandt left England loaded with presents for himself and several other Indian chiefs who live near the borders of Canada; that the Americans should be informed that quarrels will be fomented against them to disturb their government; that the new states which are being formed will sooner or later put themselves under the protection of England. (3) Tr of the letter of Schweighauser & Dobrée to TJ, 5 Aug. 1786. (4) Tr of extracts of Carmichael's letter to TJ, 15 July 1786, and enclosures. (5) Tr of extracts from Carmichael's letter to TJ, 18 July 1786. (6) Tr of Lamb to TJ, 15 July 1786. (7) Tr of Lamb to TJ, 18 July 1786.

From André Limozin

Most Honored Sir [Havre de Grace 11th. August 1786]

I am indebted to your Excellency's most honored Favor, of the 8th inst. Our Customhouse officers will not admit the Shipment for America of the Cartridges boxes you have consigned me, unless I shew them an order from the Minister. Therefore I must beg of your Excellency to procure me such voucher, and to let me know if I could dispatch them by the way of Baltimore.

I have not as yet received any Letters from Mr. Mazzei, and I wish your Excellency could recollect in what time your Excellency hath mentionned him to me.

I have received no accounts as yet from Messrs. Garvey about what your Excellency forwarded them.

I have the honor to remain with the highest regard Your Excellency's Most obedient & very humble Servant,

André Limozin

My letter of the 2nd. inclosed two large parcells which I looked upon as papers directed to my Care, from a Mr. Oster French Consul at Richmond and if your Excellency found only one my Letter must have been opend in the post office.[1]

RC (MHi); without date which has been supplied from Dupl; postmarked "HAVRE"; addressed; endorsed. Dupl (MHi); unsigned, at head of text in Limozin's hand: "Copy"; endorsed. Dupl varies slightly in phrasing from RC. Noted in SJL as received 13 Aug. 1786; dupl enclosed in Limozin to TJ, 2 Sep. 1786.

[1] Dupl reads: "If you have received only one, I must think that my letter hath been opened, and one of the parcells taken away."

To James Monroe

Dear Sir Paris Aug. 11. 1786

I wrote you last on the 9th. of July and since that have recieved yours of the 16th. of June with the interesting intelligence it contained. I was entirely in the dark as to the progress of that negociation, and concur entirely in the views you have of it. The difficulty on which it hangs is a sine qua non with us. It would be to deceive them and ourselves to suppose that an amity can be preserved while this right is witheld. Such a supposition would argue not only an ignorance of the people to whom this is most interesting, but an ignorance of the nature of man, or an inattention to it.

11 AUGUST 1786

Those who see but half way into our true interest will think that that concurs with the views of the other party. But those who see it in all it's extent will be sensible that our true interest will be best promoted by making all the just claims of our fellow citizens, wherever situated, our own, by urging and enforcing them with the weight of our whole influence, and by exercising in this as in every other instance a just government in their concerns and making common cause even where our separate interest would seem opposed to theirs. No other conduct can attach us together; and on this attachment depends our happiness.

The king of Prussia still lives, and is even said to be better. Europe is very quiet at present. The only germ of dissension which shews itself at present is in the quarter of Turkey. The Emperor, the Empress, and the Venetians seem all to be pecking at the Turks. It is not probable however that either of the two first will do any thing to bring an open rupture while the K. of Prussia lives.

You will perceive by the letters I inclose to Mr. Jay that Lambe, under the pretext of ill health, declines returning either to Congress, Mr. Adams or myself. This circumstance makes me fear some malversation. The money appropriated to this object being in Holland, and having been always under the care of Mr. Adams, it was concerted between us that all the draughts should be on him. I know not therefore what sums may have been advanced to Lamb. I hope however nothing great. I am persuaded that an Angel sent on this business, and so much limited in his terms, could have done nothing. But should Congress propose to try the line of negociation again, I think they will perceive that Lamb is not a proper agent. I have written to Mr. Adams on the subject of a settlement with Lamb. There is little prospect of accomodation between the Algerines and the Portuguese and Neapolitans. A very valuable capture too, lately made by them on the Empress of Russia, bids fair to draw her on them. The probability is therefore that these three nations will be at war with them, and the possibility that, could we furnish a couple of frigates, a convention might be formed with those powers, establishing a perpetual cruize on the coast of Algiers which would bring them to reason. Such a convention, being left open to all powers willing to come into it, should have for it's object a general peace, to be guarantied to each by the whole. Were only two or three to begin a confederacy of this kind, I think every power in Europe would soon fall into it except France, England, and perhaps Spain and Holland. Of these there is only England who would give any real aid to the Algerines. Marocco, you perceive, will be at peace with us. Were the honour and advantage of establishing such a confederacy out of the question, yet the necessity that the U.S. should have some marine force, and the happiness of this as the ostensible cause for beginning it, would decide on it's propriety. It will be said there is no money in the treasury. There never will be money in the treasury till the confederacy shews it's teeth. The states must see the rod; perhaps it must be felt by some one of them. I am persuaded all of them would rejoice to see every one obliged to furnish it's contributions. It is not the difficulty of furnishing them which beggars the treasury, but the fear that others will not furnish as much. Every national citizen must wish to see an effective instrument of coercion, and should fear to see it on any other element but the water. A naval force can never endanger our liberties, nor occasion bloodshed; a land force would do both. It is not in the choice of the states whether they will pay money to cover their trade against the Algerines. If they obtain a peace by negociation they must pay a great sum of money for it; if they do nothing they must pay a great sum of money in the form of insurance; and in either way as great a one, and probably less effectual than in the way of force.—I look forward with anxiety to the approaching moment of your departure from Congress. Besides the interest of the Confederacy and of the State I have a personal interest in it. I know not to whom I may venture confidential communications after you are gone. *Lee*[1] *I scarcely know, Grayson is lazy,*[2] *Carrington is industrious but not always as discreet as well meaning yet* on the whole I believe *he would be the best.* If you find him *disposed to the correspondence engage him* to *begin* it. I take the liberty of placing here my respects to Mrs. Monroe and assurances of the sincere esteem with which I am Dear Sir your friend & servant,

TH: JEFFERSON

RC (NN); partly written in code and decoded by Monroe interlineally. PrC (DLC).

[1] This and the following words in italics are written in code and have been decoded by the editors, employing Code No. 9.

[2] TJ erroneously wrote the code numeral for "zeal" instead of "z"; this word not decoded by Monroe.

To Abbé Morellet

SIR Paris Aug. 11. 1786.

I am honoured with your letter of yesterday on the subject of the map. My original inducement to undertake the construction of it

12 AUGUST 1786

was to accomodate the bookseller who was engaged to publish the translation you have been so good as to make of my Notes; but I at the same time had in view to have as many maps struck off as might be necessary for the original edition in English, and even for a new edition in English, should one be ever printed. This therefore would render it necessary for me to retain the property of the plate, and of course to answer the expence of engraving it. What this will be I cannot tell. Faden the principal map seller in London asked me 50 guineas for the engraving, when the map was not near so much charged with writing as it is since. Be this what it will I shall pay it without expecting that your bookseller will be at all answerable, or do more than take the number of maps he may want at a rea[sonable price?]. This I suppose cannot be less than a livre; and I[1] [. . . . my] self the pleasure of waiting on you to pay you my respects but that in order to finish the map I have [allowed] the business of my office to get so far behind as to occupy me much. I have the honour to be with sentiments[2]

PrC (MoSHi); MS badly mutilated and a portion of the text entirely illegible. The Editors are indebted to Professor William A. Ringler, Department of English, Washington University, St. Louis, a scholar of high competence in the decipherment of difficult texts, for his attempts to restore that part of the text of this press copy where the chemical action of the ink has eaten quite through the paper and where the paper is otherwise mutilated. This press copy also exhibits a characteristic that may have followed from TJ's shortage of copying paper at this time: that is, the impression of the top half of the first page of the missing RC appears at bottom of PrC; when this was done, TJ made another impression at the top of the PrC of all of the remainder of the text save part of the complimentary close, which must have carried over to the second page of the RC.

[1] At least three and perhaps four lines missing at the top of page, as described above.

[2] Text of PrC ends at this point; see Vol. 9:217, note 1.

To Richard Cary

DEAR SIR   Paris Aug. 12. 1786.

Your favor of Dec. 22. 1785. came to hand eight days ago. I had taken the liberty of recalling myself to your memory by a letter I wrote on the 4th. of May, by Monsr. La Croix, by whom I sent you a copy of the new English edition of Linnaeus's finding. You are willing to enter into a botanical commerce, by an exchange of roots, plants and seeds. I accede to it cheerfully, and will undertake to send you whatever you desire in that way. As soon as the season permits I shall send you what I saw on your list in Mr. Mazzei's hands, that is to say, if I can find an opportunity, for that is the

12 AUGUST 1786

only difficulty against which I cannot provide. I will pray you in like manner to send me the articles noted hereon, that is to say, the plants. Havre would be the best port to send them to, where Monsieur Limozin will receive and forward them. Next to that is Lorient where Mr. Cairnes an American merchant will take care of them. To send them to any other port will be throwing them away, and I repeat it that Havre is much preferable to Lorient. These articles are intended for persons here, fond of botany, whose friendship I esteem, and whom I am desirous to oblige. You know how grateful offices of this kind are to amateurs. With respect to the method of packing, they give me the following directions which they pray may be observed literally. Take fresh moss, spread a layer of it, two inches thick, in the bottom of the box, lay on that a layer of plants, each labelled with sheet lead, or with wood on which the name is engraved (and not merely marked with ink). If the roots are of any size, they should be wrapped in moss particularly, then a layer of moss an inch thick, then one of plants, and so on till the box is well filled, observing to finish with moss. My promise to communicate their wishes literally will apologize for my doing it to you who would have known so well what to do, without this information. These plants should leave Virginia before Christmas.

Europe is so quiet that it furnishes nothing new. I shall therefore conclude with assurances of the esteem with which I am Dr. Sir your friend & servt., TH: JEFFERSON

*Andromeda arborea
*Azalea nudiflora
*Azalea viscosa
Acer Pensylvanicum
Cornus florida
Ceanothus americana
Cupressus disticha
Cupressus thyoides
Clethra
Campanula perfoliata
Campanula americana
Geranium maculatum
Geranium gibbosum
Guilandina Bonduc
Halesia tetraptera
Itea
Juglans cinerea

the Gloster hiccory
Laurus Benzoin
*Magnolia glauca
*Kalmia latifolia
*Kalmia angustifolia
Nyssa
Ptelea trifoliata
Ptelea pinnata
Populus heterophylla
*Quercus phellos
Quercus virginiana of Millar
*Rhododendron maximum
Rhus copallinum
Viburnum acerifolium
Viburnum nudum
*Bignonia sempervirens
 (yellow jasmine)

12 AUGUST 1786

Those marked * are desired in greater quantities and particularly in plants. The others to be in plants where the plant succeeds tolerably, and seeds of the whole or as many as can be got will be desireable. The reason of desiring plants is that they may be sooner enjoyed.

I send you some seeds of Ranunculus, Broccoli and Cauliflower and bulbs of the tulip. Having thought it best to put off getting the articles till the bearer of this was setting out, they have disappointed me of Carnations, Auricules, Tuberoses, Hyacinth and Belladonna lillies which I had ordered. The Arno pink seed can of course only be sent you by Mazzei from Florence if he should ever go there. The Alpine strawberry I expect you have got from Mr. Eppes. Muskmelons, such as are here, are worse than the worst in Virginia. There is not sun enough to ripen them, and give them flavor. The caper bush would require a better opportunity than the present. Therefore I have not enquired whether it can be got here. I do not know what the Nut bearing pine is. I have no Millar's dictionary here. You must therefore always give the Linnean names. Send me your list so that I may receive it by the latter end of summer, and I will send out the articles [by] the October packet. To what I have formerly written for, be so good as to add some cones of the Pinus foliis ternis of Clayton, which I want for the Duke de la Rochefoucault. Adieu.

PrC (DLC); endorsed.

To the Governor of Virginia

Sir   Paris Aug. 12. 1786.[1]

I had the honour of addressing your Excellency on the 9th. inst. in answer to your's of May 17. on the subject of Capt. Greene; and on the 22d. of July, I wrote you that 1500 stand of arms were then shipped at Bourdeaux, and some cartouch boxes were on their way to Havre. The arms went on board the ship Comte d'Artois Capt. Gregory bound to Richmond and addressed to your Excellency according to the bill of lading inclosed in my letter of July 22. The Cartouch boxes with their accoutrements were 2000 in number and are safely arrived at Havre in the care of Mr. Limozin, but no vessel has as yet occurred by which they can be sent. These articles are paid for, and your funds at this place stand in the following form, nearly.

12 AUGUST 1786

Received from Laval & Wilfelsheim		8,957₶- 11s
Lodged in Mr. Grand's hands by Mr. Barclay		166,666 - 13 - 4
		175,624 - 4 - 4
Paid towards the bust of M. de la Fayette	1,800₶	
towards Genl. Washington's statue	19,622 - 2 - 6	
for Arms	59,066 - 12 - 1	
for drawings and models of the public buildings	715 - 9	81,204 - 3 - 7
Balance on hand		94,420 - 0 - 9

I now receive advice that 18. cases more of arms are delivered to Mr. Bondfield at Bourdeaux. Mr. Barclay is at present at Marocco, and it is incertain whether he will return to America directly or by the way of Europe. The M. de la Fayette has been some time gone into the South of France for the summer. But I shall spare no pains in seeing that your intentions relative to the arms shall be completely fulfilled and as expeditiously as possible; and that to the extent directed by the assembly, not doubting but that funds will be lodged in time to comply with my engagements. I have taken the liberty of placing in your account an article of 715₶-9 paid for the directors of the public buildings in pursuance of instructions from Messrs. Buchanan and Hay. It simplified my accounts, and I thought would be easily settled on their part by their paying to your order that sum in Virginia. However, if it is preferred, they can remit the sum to me, and I shall transfer it to a separate account.

I have the honor to be, with sentiments of the most perfect esteem and respect Your Excellency's Most obedient & most humble servt.,

TH: JEFFERSON

RC (PHi); endorsed in part in the hand of Edmund Randolph: "Mr. Jefferson received by E. R. decr 3. 1786"; at foot of text: "H. E. the Gov. of Virginia." PrC (DLC).

[1] The date, as first written, read merely "Aug. 12." TJ then made the PrC, added "1786" to the dateline on RC, and failed to add it to PrC.

From James Madison

DEAR SIR   Philada. Aug: 12th. 1786

My last of the 19th. of June intimated that my next would be from N. York or this place. I expected it would rather have been from the former which I left a few days ago, but my time was so

12 AUGUST 1786

taken up there with my friends and some business that I thought it best to postpone it till my return here. My ride through Virga. Maryd. and Pena. was in the midst of harvest. I found the crops of wheat in the upper parts of the two former considerably injured by the wet weather which my last described as so destructive in the lower parts of those States. The computed loss where I passed was about one third. The loss in the Rye was much greater. It was admitted however that the crops of both would have been unusually large but for this casualty. Throughout Pena. the wheat was unhurt, and the Rye very little affected. As I came by the way of Winchester and crossed the Potowmac at Harpers Ferry I had an opportunity of viewing the magnificent scene which nature here presents. I viewed it however under great disadvantages. The air was so thick that distant objects were not visible at all, and near ones not distinctly so. We ascended the mountain also at a wrong place, fatigued ourselves much in traversing it before we gained the right position, were threatened during the whole time with a thunder storm, and finally overtaken by it. Had the weather been favorable the prospect would have appeared to peculiar advantage, being enriched with the harvest in its full maturity, which filled every vale as far as the eye could reach. I had the additional pleasure here of seeing the progress[1] of the works on the Potowmac. About 50 hands were employed at these falls or rather rapids, who seemed to have overcome the greatest difficulties. Their plan is to slope the fall by opening the bed of the river, in such a manner as to render a lock unnecessary, and by means of ropes fastened to the rocks, to pull up and ease down the boats where the current is most rapid. At the principal falls 150 hands I was told were at work, and that the length of the canal will be reduced to less than a mile, and carried through a vale which does not require it to be deep. Locks will here be unavoidable. The undertakers are very sanguine. Some of them, who are most so, talk of having the entire work finished in three years. I can give no particular account of the progress on James River, but am told it is very flattering. I am still less informed of what is doing with North Carolina towards a canal between her and our waters. The undertaking on the Susquehannah is said to be in such forwardness as to leave no doubt of its success. A negociation is set on foot between Pena. Maryd. and Delaware for a canal from the head of Chesapeak to the Delaware. Maryd. as I understand heretofore opposed the undertaking, and Pena. means now to make her consent to it a condition on which the opening of the Susquehannah within the limits of Pena. will depend. Unless this is permitted the opening undertaken within the limits of Maryland will be of little account. It is lucky that both parties are so dependent on each other as to be thus mutually forced into measures of general utility. I am told that Pena. has complied with the joint request of Virga. and Maryland for a Road between the head of Potowmac and the waters of the Ohio and the secure and free use of the latter through her jurisdiction. These fruits of the Revolution do great honour to it. I wish all our proceedings merited the same character. Unhappily there are but too many belonging to the opposite side of the account. At the head of these is to be put the general rage for paper money. Pena. and N. Carolina took the lead in this folly. In the former the sum emitted was not considerable, the funds for sinking it were good, and it was not made a legal tender. It issued into circulation partly by way of loan to individuals on landed security, partly by way of payment to the public creditors. Its present depreciation is about 10 or 12 per Ct. In N. Carolina the sums issued at different times has been of greater amount, and it has constantly been a tender. It issued partly in payments to military creditors, and latterly in purchases of Tobacco on public account. The Agent I am informed was authorized to give nearly the double of the current price, and as the paper was a tender, debtors ran to him with their Tobacco and the Creditors paid the expence of the farce. The depreciation is said to be 25 or 30 per Ct. in that State. S. Carolina was the next in order. Her emission was in the way of loans to individuals, and is not a legal tender. But land is there made a tender in case of suits, which shuts the courts of Justice, and is perhaps as great an evil. The friends of the emission say that it has not yet depreciated, but they admit that the price of commodities has risen, which is evidently the form in which depreciation will first shew itself. New Jersey has just issued £30,000 (dollar at 7/6). in loans to her Citizens. It is a legal tender. An addition of £100,000 is shortly to follow on the same principles. The terror of popular associations stifles as yet an overt discrimination between it and specie; but as this does not operate in Philada. and N. York where all the trade of N.J. is carried on, its depreciation has already commenced in those places and must soon communicate itself to N.J. New York is striking £200,000 (dollr. at 8s) on the plan of loans to her citizens. It is made a legal tender in case of suits only. As it is but just issuing from the press, its depreciation exists only in the foresight of those who reason without prejudice on the subject. In Rhode Island £100,000 (dolr. at 6s.) has lately been issued in loans to individuals. It is not only made a tender, but severe penalties annexed to the least attempt direct or indirect to give a preference to specie. Precautions dictated by distrust in the rulers, soon produced it in the people. Supplies were witheld from the Market, the Shops were shut, popular meetings ensued, and the State remains in a sort of convulsion. The Legislature of Massts. at their last session rejected a paper emission by a large majority. Connecticut and N. Hampshire also have as yet foreborne, but symptoms of the danger it is said begin to appear in the latter. The Senate of Maryd. has hitherto been a bar to paper in that State. The clamor for it is now universal, and as the periodical election of the Senate happens at this crisis, and the whole body is unluckily by their constitution to be chosen at once, it is probable that a paper emission will be the result. If in spite of the zeal exerted against the old Senate a majority of them should be reelected, it will require all their firmness to withstand the popular torrent. Of the affairs of Georga. I know as little as of those of Kamskatska. Whether Virga. is to remain exempt from the epidemic malady will depend on the ensuing assembly. My hopes rest chiefly on the exertions of Col. Mason, and the failure of the experiments elsewhere. That these must fail is morally certain; for besides the proofs of it already visible in some states, and the intrinsic defect of the paper in all, this fictitious[2] money will rather feed than cure the spirit of extravagance which sends away the coin to pay the unfavorable balance, and will therefore soon be carried to market to buy up coin for that purpose. From that moment depreciation is inevitable. The value of money consists in the uses it will serve. Specie will serve all the uses of paper. Paper will not serve one of the essential uses of specie. The paper therefore will be less valuable than specie. —Among the numerous ills with which this practice is pregnant, one I find is that it is producing the same warfare and retaliation among the States as were produced by the State regulations of commerce. Massts. and Connecticut have passed laws enabling their Citizens who are debtors to Citizens of States having paper money, to pay their debts in the same manner as their Citizens who are Creditors to Citizens of the latter States are liable to be paid their debts.—The States which have appointed deputies to Annapolis are N. Hampshire, Massts., R. Island, N.Y., N.J., Pena., Delaware and Virga. Connecticut declined not from a dislike to the object, but to the idea of a Convention, which it seems has been rendered obnoxious by some internal conventions which embarrassed the Legislative Authority. Maryd. or rather her Senate negatived an appointment because they supposed the measure might interfere with the plans or prerogatives of Congress. N. Carolina has had no Legislative meeting since the proposition was communicated. S. Carolina supposed she had sufficiently signified her concurrence in a general regulation of trade by vesting the power in Congress for 15 years. Georgia——Gentlemen[3] both within and without Congress wish to make this meeting subservient to a plenipotentiary convention for amending the Confederation. Tho' my wishes are in favor of such an event, yet I despair so much of its accomplishment at the present crisis that I do not extend my views beyond a Commercial Reform. To speak the truth *I*[4] *almost despair even of this.* You will find the *cause in a measure* now before *Congress of which you will receive* the *details* from *Col. Monroe.* I content myself with *hinting* that it is a *proposed treaty with Spain,* [in][5] one *article of* which *she shuts the Mississippi for twenty five or thirty years.* Passing by the other *southern States, figure* to yourself the *effect of such a stipulation* on the *assembly of Virginia* already *jealous* of *northern policy* and which will be composed of about *thirty members from the western waters;* of a majority of others attached to the *western country from interests* of their *own, of their friends, or their constituents* and of many others who though indifferent to the *Mississippi will zealously* play off the *disgust of* its *friends against federal measures.* Figure to yourself its effect on the *people at large* on the *western waters* who are impatiently waiting for a *favorable result* to *negociation with Guardoqui* and who will consider themselves as *sold by* their *Atlantic brethren.* Will it be an unnatural consequence if they consider *themselves as absolved* from every *federal tie* and *court some protection* for their *betrayed rights?* This *protection* will appear more attainable from the *maritime power* of *Britain* than any from *any other quarter;* and *Britain* will be *more ready than any other nation* to *seize an opportunity of embroiling our affairs.* What may be the motive *with Spain to satisfy her self* with a *temporary occlusion* of the *Mississippi* at the same time that *she holds forth* our *claim to it*[6] *as absolutely inadmissible is matter* of *conjecture only.* The *patrons* of the *measure in Congress* contend that the *Minister* who at present *governs* the *Spanish Councils* means only to *disembarrass himself at the expence* of *his successors.* I should rather suppose *he means to work a total* separation of *interest and affection between* the *western and eastern settlements* and to *foment* the jealousy *between the eastern and southern states.* By the former the *population of* the *western country* it may be expected will be *checked* and the

12 AUGUST 1786

Mississippi so far secured; and by both the general *security of Spanish America* be promoted. As far as I can learn the *assent of nine states* in *Congress* will not at this time be *got to the proposed*[7] *treaty*. But an *unsuccessful attempt* by *six or seven* will *favor the views of Spain* and be *fatal I fear* to an *augmentation of* the *federal authority* if not to the *little now existing*. My personal situation is rendered by this business particularly *mortifying*. Ever since I have been *out of Congress I have been inculcating* on our *assembly a confidence* in the *equal attention of Congress* to the *rights and* interests of *every part of the republic* and on the *western members* in particular, the necessity of making the Union *respectable by new powers* to *Congress* if they wished *Congress to negociate with effect for the Mississippi*. I leave to Col. Monroe the giving you a particular account of the Impost. The Acts of Penna. Delaware and N. York must be revised and amended in material points before it can be put in force, and even then the fetters put on the collection by some other States will make it a very awkward business.—Your favor of 25th. of April from London found me here. My letter from Richmd. at the close of the Assembly will have informed you of the situation in which British debts stand in Virga. Unless Congress say something on the subject I do not think any thing will be done by the next Session. The expectations of the British Merchants coincide with the information I had received, as your opinion of the steps proper to be taken by the Assembly do with those for which I have ineffectually contended. The merits of Mr. P.[8] will ensure every attention from me to his claim as far as general principles will admit. I am afraid that these will insuperably bar his wishes. The Catalogues sent by Mr. Skipwith I do not expect to receive till I get back to Virga. If you meet with "Græcorum Respublicæ ab Ubbone Emmio descriptæ," Lugd. Batavorum, 1632, pray get it for me.

My trip to N.Y. was occasioned chiefly by a plan concerted between Col. Monroe and myself for a purchase of land on the Mohawk. Both of us have visited that district, and were equally charmed with it. The soil is perhaps scarcely inferior to that of Kentucky, it lies within the body of the Atlantic States, and at a safe distance from every frontier, it is contiguous to a branch of Hudson's River which is navigable with trifling portages which will be temporary, to tide-water, and is not more than ten, 15 or 20 miles from populous settlements where land sells at £8 and £10 per Acre. In talking of this Country sometime ago with *General Washington* he considered it in the same light with Monroe and

12 AUGUST 1786

myself, intimating that if he had money to spare and was disposed to deal in land, this is the very spot which his fancy had selected out of all the U.S. We have made a small purchase, and nothing *but the difficulty of raising a* sufficient *sum restrained us* from *making a large one.* In searching for the *means of overcoming this difficulty* one has occurred which we have agreed that *I should mention to you*, and which if *you should think as we do* is recommended by the prospect of *advantage to yourself as well as to us.* We mention it *freely because we trust* that *if it does* not *meet your sanction you will as freely tell us so.* It is that the *aid of your credit* in *your private capacity* be *used for borrowing* say *four or five thousand louis* more or less on the *obligation of Monroe* and myself with *your suretyship*, to be laid out by *Monroe and myself* for *our triple emolument;* an *interest* not *exceeding six per cent* to be *paid annually* and the *principal within a term* not less than *eight or ten years.* To guard against accidents a private *instrument* might be *executed among ourselves specifying* all necessary *covenants.* We have not taken the resolution of *submitting this plan without well examining* the expediency of *your becoming a party to it* as well as the *prospect of its succeeding.* There can certainly be *no impropriety in your* taking *just means of bettering your fortune.* Nor can *we discover any in your doing this on* the *Mohawk*, more than *on James River.* For the prospect of *gain by the rise of* the *land beyond* the *interest of the money we calculate* on the present *difference of price* between the *settled and vacant land* far beyond any *possible* difference in the *real value.* The former as has been noted *sells for eight or ten pounds per acre.* The latter distinguished only by its being a little *higher up* the *river* and its being *uninhabited* was *bought by us for* one *dollar and a half* and there is little doubt that *by taking a larger* quantity, still *better bargains may be got.* This comparative *cheapness* proceeds from causes which are accidental and temporary. The *lands in question* are chiefly in the *hands of men who hold large quantities* and who are either *in debt* or *live in* the *city at an expence* for which *they have no other resource* or are *engaged in transactions* that *require money.* The scarcity of *specie which* enters *much into the cheapness* is probably but temporary also. As it is the *child of extravagance* it will become the *parent of economy* which will regain us our due share of the *universal medium.* The same vicisitude which can only be retarded by our *short lived substitutes of paper* will be attended also by such a *fall in the rate of exchange* that *money drawn by bills* from *Europe now* and *repaid a few years hence* will probably *save one years interest at least* and I will only add that scarce an instance has happened in which *purchases of new land of good quality* and *in good situations* have not *well rewarded the adventurers*. With these remarks which determine *our judgments, we submit to your better one* the *project to which they relate*.—Wishing you every possible happiness I remain Dr. Sir your affectionate friend & Servt.,

Js. Madison Jr.

Mrs. House and Mrs. Trist desire to be particularly remembered to yourself and Miss Patsy. I left with Col. Monroe letters for you both from Mrs. T. which will probably go by the same packet with this.

RC (DLC: Madison Papers); endorsed by Madison; partly in code and decoded interlineally by Short. Noted in SJL as received 22 Sep. 1786.

1 These two words interlined in substitution for "an example," deleted. Here and elsewhere it is not possible to tell whether Madison made this change in the course of writing or late in life.
2 This word interlined in substitution for "artificial," deleted.
3 Thus in MS.
4 This and subsequent words in italics are written in code and were decoded interlineally by Short; his decoding has been verified by the Editors, employing Code No. 9; several errors of encoding and decoding have been corrected silently.
5 Madison omitted this word.
6 As first written, this passage read: "... *she* holds forth *a* compliance with our *claim to it*," &c. The words "compliance with" were deleted, but not the symbol for "a" and Short decoded it.
7 This word was correctly encoded, but Short's decoding appeared illegible to Madison when he read the letter over late in life, and so he interlined the word "projected," which was not a correct decoding of the symbols employed but which Hunt followed (Madison, *Writings*, II, 264).
8 Madison, late in life, wrote interlineally: "[Paradise]."

From Abbé Morellet

Monsieur   ce samedi [12 Aug. 1786]

Rien n'est plus juste et plus raisonnable que ce que vous me mandes au sujet de la carte. Ce que je vous ai ecrit à ce sujet n'etoit que dans la supposition que vous n'eussies aucun autre usage à faire de la carte que pour une edition francoise mais puisque vous faites imprimer votre ouvrage en anglois soit à londres soit à paris il faut bien que la planche fournisse aux deux editions et que vous vous la reservies. Je reconnois aussi dans les facilités que vous voules bien donner à mon libraire toute votre bonté. J'aurai l'honneur d'aller vous en remercier incessamment, agrées mes très respectueuses civilités.

L'abbé Morellet

RC (DLC); endorsed; undated, but evidently written on the 12th which was the first Saturday after TJ's letter of 11 Aug. 1786, to which it is a reply.

To the Commissioners of the Treasury

GENTLEMEN Paris Aug. 12. 1786.

Your favor of May 9. came to hand on the 25th. of June. I immediately communicated to the foreign officers the inability of the treasury at that moment to provide paiment of the interest due them, with assurances of your attention to them in the first possible moment. I communicated to Commodore Jones also your order for the balance in his hands. As he was entitled to a part of the money he had received, and it was reasonable to suppose he must have been living here on that resource, so that he could not be expected to pay the whole sum received, I desired him to state his account against that fund as he thought just himself, to pay me the balance on account, reserving to you a full right to discuss the propriety of his charges, and to allow or disallow them as you pleased, so that nothing that passed between us, should either strengthen or weaken his claims. He accordingly rendered me the account which I now inclose, balance 112,172.ᵗᵗ2.4. He desired me at the same time to forward to you the papers No. 1.-12, which will shew the objections and difficulties he had to encounter, and which could have been obviated by no body else. There certainly was no other person whose knowledge of the transactions so well qualified them to negotiate this business, and I do suppose that this fund would have lost some of it's capital articles in any other hands. This circumstance, with the real value of this officer, will I doubt not, have their just influence in settling his claims. There is no doubt but that he has actually expended the money charged to have been expended. Without this supply Mr. Grand would have been in advance for the U.S. according to a rough estimate which I make 42,281.ᵗᵗ16, besides 24,437.ᵗᵗ11 which, on the failure of the federal funds here, and on being apprised of Mr. Grand's advances, I had ventured to order him to take,[1] from a sum of money lodged in his hands for the state of Virginia for the purchase of arms. This liberty was taken in order that he might honour the draughts of Mr. Carmichael and Mr. Dumas, pay certain foreign officers who had not yet been paid pari passu with their brother officers, and answer my demands also. These two sums, amounting to 66,719.ᵗᵗ7 were first to be replaced and left a balance of 45,452.ᵗᵗ15.8. Tho' you had proposed to leave this in my hands for the calls of the diplomatic establishments in Europe, I ventured to have it paid with the residue of the mass into Mr. Grands hands, to avoid giving him umbrage and lessening his dispositions to advance hereafter, and also because it would have been very insecure in my house which stands on the outline of the city, separated from all others by a considerable interval, and therefore exposed to robbery. The insurance in this situation would have been worth much more than Mr. Grand's commission on it. From this detail you will perceive that there remains in hand about enough to answer the demands of the diplomatic establishment in France, Spain, England, and Holland for a quarter of a year from this date, which I have instructed Mr. Grand to apply solely to that purpose.

Commodore Jones will set out shortly for Copenhagen to settle the demand against that court, which done, he will return to America to close the matters which have been confided to him.

I have the honor to be with sentiments of the highest esteem and respect, Gentlemen, Your most obedient & most humble servt.,

TH: JEFFERSON

PrC (DLC). Tr (DNA: PCC, No. 138, I); at foot of text: "Compard with the Original in the office of the Board of Treasury. Wm. Duer Secy." Enclosures: (1) Account of John Paul Jones (see Jones to TJ, 7 July 1786, and Sherburne, *John Paul Jones*, p. 275). (2) The "papers No. 1-12" have not been identified, but they may have included various letters written by Jones to Castries from 1 Feb. 1784 to 10 July 1785 (texts printed in Sherburne, *John Paul Jones*, p. 250-64). See also Jones to TJ, 14 Aug. 1786.

A memorandum, entirely in TJ's hand, having at the head of the text: "Rough sketch stated to Commrs. of the Treasury Aug. 12 1786," gives in tabular form the figures contained in this letter and has the following note at the foot of the table: "This is about the amount of the diplomatic establishment in France, Spain, England and Holland for one quarter of a year" (DLC: TJ Papers, 23: 3982).

[1] At this point TJ wrote, then deleted: "for federal purposes."

To John Adams

DEAR SIR Paris Aug. 13. 1786.

The inclosed came to hand this morning. Mr. Carmichael you observe, and Mr. Barclay suppose something may yet be done at Algiers. It remains for us to consider whether the conduct of the Dey of that country leaves any room to hope that any negotiator can succeed without a great addition to the price to which we are confined? And should we think in the negative, yet whether the expences of Mr. Barclay's going there may not be compensated by additional information, by the possibility that he may get at their ultimatum, by the importance of possessing Congress of this ultimatum, that knowing their ground, they may not suspend a decision. Spain having made it's peace with Algiers, we may see whether their interference can count as money, as it has done at

[238]

Marocco. Hostilities too may possibly be suspended or slackened a while longer. These are all chances on which I acknolege I build very little; yet as nothing weighs against them but the expence of Mr. Barclay's journey, they might be tried. If you are of that opinion, send me the necessary papers for Mr. Barclay ready signed by you, and I will sign them and forward them.—There is lodged in Mr. Grand's hands money enough to support the diplomatic establishment of our country in Europe three months, on which your draughts and Colo. Smith's shall be honoured if you think proper to make them. I am with sincere esteem Dear Sir, your friend & servt., TH: JEFFERSON

RC (MHi: AMT); endorsed by Adams, in part: "ansd Sept. 11. 1786." PrC (DLC). Enclosures: (1) Barclay to Commissioners, 26 June 1786. (2) Carmichael to TJ, 31 July 1786.

From Madame de Grégoire

MONSEIGNEUR   paris le 13 aoust 1786

La dame de Gregoire Reclame, chès les Etats unis, une Concession de terre faite par le Roy Louis. 14. à antoine de lamotte Cadillac son Grand pere, elle se transporta a londres, pour faire Cette Reclamation, il luy fut dit par Mr. Eliot, au Bureau du departement de L'Amerique, que par la ligne tirée, qui separe Aujourdhuy, les Anglais, des Etats unis, cette terre se trouve etre ches ses derniers. Mr. le Docteur Franklin, auquel la dame de Gregoire presenta ses titres, luy Repondit, que sa demande étoit juste, qu'il faloit presenter un Memoire, a Mr. hankoke Gouverneur, et à Mr. de Letombe, Consul de france, et qu'il se chargeoit de leur faire parvenir le tout, Ce qu'il fit. La dite Dame obtint de Mr. le Comte de Vergennes Ministre une lettre de Recommandation, pour une affaire qui luy parut si juste, qu'il Envoya à Mr. Marbois, et apres luy, à Mr. Otto, son Envoyè Resident à Newyork, lequ'el devoit la Notifier à Mr. de letombe, et par interim à Mr. toscan, Residant a Boston.

La Dame de Gregoire, voyant que Mr. de letombe et toscan, ne mettent pas toute la vigilance, dont ils sont chargès par le Ministre à Cette affaire, et que depuis trois ans, on luy dit toujours, que la Multiplicité des affaires, empeche les Congrès de s'en occuper, à Resolu de passer la Mer, et de s'y Rendre. Comme Mr. de la fayette luy veut beaucoup du Bien, et qu'il desire que la dite dame Rentre dans une Reclamation si juste, luy à tres fort Conseillé, de s'y transporter, et luy à donné, des lettres de Recommandation, pour this excelincy james Baudouin Governoris has nuti of Massachuset, Bay Boston, et pour the honorable major general Knix Secretariat har à Newyork, et la en meme tems pressèe de se Rendre aupres de votre Excellence, pour la supplier de vouloir bien aussi, luy donner, qu'elque lettre, affin que prompte justice luy soit faite. Comme la dame de Gregoire Sçait avec toute la terre, qu'e l'humanitè, la Bienfaisance, et toutes les vertus morales, siegent ches vous, elle ose esperer, que vous ne luy Refuserès pas cette Grace, et elle ne Cessera de faire des voeux pour la santè et prosperitè de votre Exellence

MADAME DE GREGOIRE NÈE DE LAMOTTE CADILLAC

RC (DLC); endorsed.
POUR THIS EXCELINCY JAMES BAUDOUIN . . . GENERAL KNIX: Mme. de Grégoire was evidently copying from Lafayette's letters, which doubtless read: "His Excellency James Bowdoin, Governor of the state of Massachusetts Bay, Boston," and "the honorable Major General Knox, Secretary at War, at New York."

To Benjamin Hawkins

DEAR SIR   Paris Aug. 13. 1786.

Your favor of June 14. is come to hand and I am to thank you for your attention to my queries on the subject of the Indians. I have sent many copies to other correspondents, but as yet have heard nothing from them. I shall proceed however in my endeavors particularly with respect to their language and shall take care so to dispose of what I collect thereon as that it shall not be lost. The attention which you pay to their rights also does you great honor, as the want of that is a principal source of dishonour to the American character. The two principles on which our conduct towards the Indians should be founded are justice and fear. After the injuries we have done them, they cannot love us, which leaves us no alternative but that of fear to keep them from attacking us. But justice is what we should never lose sight of, and in time it may recover their esteem.—Your attention to one burthen I laid on you encourages me to remind you of another, which is the sending me some seeds of the Dionaea muscipula, or Venus's fly-trap, called also with you, I believe, the sensitive plant. This can come folded in a letter.—Europe is in a profound calm. The Venetians, Russians, and Austrians indeed are pecking at the Turks, but I suppose it is only to keep alive pretensions which may authorize the commencement of hostilities when it shall suit them. Whether this will be

[240]

immediately on the death of the K. of Prussia or some time after, cannot be said. That event may be daily expected. It seems as if this court did not fear a land war, and they are possessed of the best materials of judging. My reason for thinking they do not expect a disturbance of their tranquillity on this continent, is that their whole attention is bestowed on marine preparations. Their navy is growing, and the practicability of building a seaport is no longer problematical. Cherburg will certainly be completed, will be one of the safest and most commodious ports in the world and will contain the whole navy of France. It will have the advantage over the English ports on the opposite shore, because they leave two openings, which will admit vessels to come in or go out with any wind. This port will enable them in case of a war with England to invade that country, or to annihilate it's commerce and of course it's marine. Probably too it will oblige them to keep a standing army of considerable magnitude.—We are tolerably certain of establishing peace with the Emperor of Marocco, but Algiers, Tunis, and Tripoli will still be hostile. Marocco however lying on the Atlantic, was the most important. The Algerines rarely come far into that and Tunis and Tripoli never. We must consider the Mediterranean as absolutely shut to us till we can open it with money. Whether this will be best expended in buying or forcing a peace is for Congress to determine.—I shall be glad often to hear from you and am with much esteem, Dr. Sir, your friend & servt.,
TH: JEFFERSON

PrC (DLC).
SOME SEEDS OF THE DIONAEA: These were evidently those intended for Madame de Tessé (see Gilmer to TJ, 11 Dec. 1785, note; Madame de Tessé to TJ, 30 Mch. 1787).

To John Jay

SIR   Paris Aug. 13. 1786

The inclosed letter from Mr. Barclay, and one from Mr. Carmichael, of which I send you extracts, are come to hand this morning, which is in time for them to go by the same gentleman who carries my letter of the 11th. I observe what Mr. Carmichael says on the subject of the Portuguese treaty, and am sorry it meets with difficulties. I doubt however whether he ascribes them to their true cause, when he supposes they are occasioned by M. del Pinto's being of a party opposed to that of the minister at Madrid. The cause is not proportioned to the effect. The treaty between

France and England has lately been thought to have become stationary. This is conjectured from the rigour of the custom houses, much increased by late orders, as also from some other circumstances. The overtures between England and Portugal are animated in proportion; and in the same degree I suspect that the latter lessens her care about us. If her wines were to become superfluous at the English market she wished and hoped to find a great one with us, open to receive them. M. del Pinto's courier, which carried the treaty to Falmouth, arrived a few hours too late for the Lisbon packet boat. This lost a month in the conveiance, and that month, by producing new prospects, has been critical. There is not a want of probability that del Pinto himself will succeed to the deceased minister in Portugal. This would be favourable to our treaty, and fortunate for us in proportion to the value of a connection with that nation. He is sensible, candid, and has just ideas as to us, and favourable dispositions towards us.

I expect that Mr. Adams is at this moment at the Hague, as he intended there to take leave of that court, and, at the same time, to exchange the ratifications of the Prussian treaty. But I send on to London copies of the inclosed, in hopes he will speedily be returned there. I shall propose to him that we consider whether the conduct of the Dey of Algiers leaves any hope that any negotiator whatever could obtain his peace without a prodigious addition to the price we had thought of? If we conclude on the negative, still it will remain to decide Whether the expence of Mr. Barclay's going there may not be compensated by additional information, by the possibility that he might find their ultimatum, and the advantage of relieving the mind of Congress from all suspence by possessing them of this ultimatum. The peace of Spain too being concluded, it is to be seen whether their interference can weigh as money. It has done so at Marocco. But Algiers is a fiercer power.

I have the honour to be, with sentiments of the highest respect & esteem, Sir, Your most obedient & most humble servant,

TH: JEFFERSON

RC (DNA: PCC, No. 87, i). PrC (DLC). Tr (DNA: PCC, No. 107). Enclosures: (1) Extracts of Barclay to Commissioners, 26 June 1786. (2) Carmichael to TJ, 31 July 1786.

To John Stockdale

[*Paris, 13 Aug. 1786.* An entry in SJL under this date reads: "Stockdale J. inclosing Dr. Priestly's pamphlet." Neither the letter nor the pamphlet has been found; the latter may have been one of Priestley's annual defenses of unitarianism, and it was possibly a French translation of the pamphlet; TJ received Stockdale's letter of 8 Aug. on 13 Aug.]

To George Wythe

Dear Sir   Paris Aug. 13. 1786.

Your favors of Jan. 10. and Feb. 10. came to hand on the 20th. and 23d of May. I availed myself of the first opportunity which occurred, by a gentleman going to England, of sending to Mr. Joddrel a copy of the Notes on our country, with a line informing him that it was you who had emboldened me to take that liberty. Madison, no doubt, informed you of the reason why I had sent only a single copy to Virginia. Being assured by him that they will not do the harm I had apprehended, but on the contrary may do some good, I propose to send thither the copies remaining on hand, which are fewer than I had intended, but of the numerous corrections they need, there are one or two so essential that I must have them made, by printing a few new leaves and substituting them for the old. This will be done while they are engraving a map which I have constructed of the country from Albemarle sound to Lake Erie, and which will be inserted in the book. A bad French translation which is getting out here, will probably oblige me to publish the original more freely, which it neither deserved nor was ever intended. Your wishes, which are laws to me, will justify my destining a copy for you. Otherwise I should as soon have thought of sending you a horn-book; for there is no truth there that is not familiar to you, and it's errors I should hardly have proposed to treat you with.

Immediately on the receipt of your letter, I wrote to a correspondent at Florence to enquire after the family of Tagliaferro as you desired. I received his answer two days ago, a copy of which I now inclose. The original shall be sent by some other occasion. I will have the copper plate immediately engraved. This may be ready within a few days, but the probability is that I shall be long getting an opportunity of sending it to you, as these rarely occur. You do not mention the size of the plate but, presuming it is intended for labels for the inside of books, I shall have it made of a proper size for that. I shall omit the word $\alpha\rho\iota\sigma o\varsigma$,[1] according to the license you allow me, because I think the beauty of a motto is to condense much matter in as few words as possible. The word omitted will be supplied by every reader.

The European papers have announced that the assembly of Virginia were occupied on the revisal of their Code of laws. This, with some other similar intelligence, has contributed much to convince the people of Europe, that what the English papers are constantly publishing of our anarchy, is false; as they are sensible that such a work is that of a people only who are in perfect tranquillity. Our act for freedom of religion is extremely applauded. The Ambassadors and ministers of the several nations of Europe resident at this court have asked of me copies of it to send to their sovereigns, and it is inserted at full length in several books now in the press; among others, in the new Encyclopedie. I think it will produce considerable good even in these countries where ignorance, superstition, poverty and oppression of body and mind in every form, are so firmly settled on the mass of the people, that their redemption from them can never be hoped. If the almighty had begotten a thousand sons, instead of one, they would not have sufficed for this task. If all the sovereigns of Europe were to set themselves to work to emancipate the minds of their subjects from their present ignorance and prejudices, and that as zealously as they now endeavor the contrary, a thousand years would not place them on that high ground on which our common people are now setting out. Ours could not have been so fairly put into the hands of their own common sense, had they not been separated from their parent stock and been kept from contamination, either from them, or the other people of the old world, by the intervention of so wide an ocean. To know the worth of this, one must see the want of it here. I think by far the most important bill in our whole code is that for the diffusion of knowlege among the people. No other sure foundation can be devised for the preservation of freedom, and happiness. If any body thinks that kings, nobles, or priests are good conservators of the public happiness,[2] send them here. It is the best school in the universe to cure them of that folly. They will see here with their own eyes that these descriptions of men are an abandoned confederacy against the happiness of the mass of people. The omnipotence of their effect cannot be better proved than in this country particularly, where notwithstanding the finest soil upon earth, the finest climate under heaven, and a people of the most benevolent, the most gay, and amiable character of which the human form is susceptible, where such a people I say, surrounded by so many blessings from nature, are yet loaded with misery by kings, nobles and priests, and by them alone. Preach, my dear Sir, a crusade against ignorance; establish and improve the law for educating the common people. Let our countrymen know that the people alone can protect us against these evils, and that the tax which will be paid for this purpose is not more than the thousandth part of what will be paid to kings, priests and nobles who will rise up among us if we leave the people in ignorance.—The people of England, I think, are less oppressed than here. But it needs but half an eye to see, when among them, that the foundation is laid in their dispositions, for the establishment of a despotism. Nobility, wealth, and pomp are the objects of their adoration. They are by no means the free-minded people we suppose them in America. Their learned men too are few in number, and are less learned and infinitely less emancipated from prejudice than those of this country. An event too seems to be prospering, in the order of things, which will probably decide the fate of that country. It is no longer doubtful that the harbour of Cherbourg will be completed, that it will be a most excellent one, and capacious enough to hold the whole navy of France. Nothing has ever been wanting to enable this country to invade that, but a naval force conveniently stationed to protect the transports. This change of situation, must oblige the English to keep up a great standing army, and there is no king, who, with a sufficient force, is not always ready to make himself absolute.—My paper warns me it is time to recommend myself to the friendly recollection of Mrs. Wythe, of Colo. Taliaferro and his family and particularly of Mr. R. T. and to assure you of the affectionate esteem with which I am Dear Sir your friend & servt.,

TH: JEFFERSON

PrC (DLC). Enclosure: Tr of Giovanni Fabbroni to TJ, 20 July 1786.

Mr. R. T.: Richard Taliaferro. I WILL HAVE THE COPPER PLATE IMMEDIATELY ENGRAVED: On 25 Oct. 1786 Short wrote to William Nelson: "This will be delivered to you by Major Martin of Williamsburg. He has been in Paris a few days and leaves it immediately to return to America by the way of London. Mr. Jefferson sends by him also the Arms of the Family of Tagliaferro as received from Italy" (DLC: Short Papers; see also TJ to Short, 7 Apr. 1787; TJ to Wythe, 16 Sep. 1787).

The original copperplate of the Taliaferro arms is owned by Colonial Williamsburg, Inc., and is in the Wythe House, Williamsburg.

[1] Thus in MS; TJ followed Wythe's use of the word literally, both as to the erroneous spelling and as to the form of the first sigma; see Wythe to TJ, 10 Jan. and 10 Feb. 1786.

[2] The preceding seven words were interlined in substitution for: "could give any aid towards their preservation," deleted.

To John Banister, with a Note to Anne Blair Banister

Dear Sir   Paris Aug. 14. 1786.

Your favor of May 12. 1786. came to hands a few days ago, and I am to thank you for the trouble you have taken in the affair respecting Mr. Mark. When he shall have delivered you the state he had promised, you will have the goodness to forward it. The health of your son is not yet established. He had proposed to come and try for some time the climate of Paris, and set out from Bourdeaux with that view. He had a relapse however at Libourne which prevented his pursuing his journey to this place. From thence he wrote me that he had found so little benefit from the climates of Europe that he thought it would be better for him to return to Virginia, and asked my advice on the subject. As I had not seen him since he was first at Paris, I thought himself alone the only competent judge; but as, when here, he seemed to be almost in perfect health, and that this had been obtained while he was in England, I suggested to him the expediency of a visit to that country, before his return, to see whether it's climate or it's physicians might not have again the same happy effect. I think he will accordingly go there. I have a letter from him dated Pons the 6th. inst. by which he informs me he is well enough to be on his way to Nantes. Europe is in a state of quiet at present. We are always in expectation of the K. of Prussia's death. Some think that will be the signal of war. I suppose that before this our peace is signed with Marocco. But Algiers, Tunis and Tripoli are still hostile. Nothing but force, or a very great sum of money will procure us the peace of Algiers. They come little however into the Atlantic, and Tunis and Tripoli not at all.

I am with sincere esteem Dear Sir your friend & servt.,

TH: JEFFERSON

Mr. Jefferson's compliments to Mrs. Bannister. It is a great gratification to him that, at such a distance of time and place, she yet recollects him. His daughter is well, and returns her thanks for Mrs. Bannister's notice. Mr. Jefferson will be very happy on his return to his native country, to renew an acquaintance which he has always held among the most precious of those he has ever made. In the mean time he begs her to be assured of his most perfect esteem and respect.

PrC (DLC); endorsed.

Anne Blair Banister was the daughter of John Blair of Williamsburg; one of her sisters married Wilson Miles Cary, and another was Elizabeth Thompson whom TJ had called upon but had missed at Titchfield in 1784 (see Elizabeth Thompson to TJ, 10 Jan. 1787). TJ had known Anne Blair and her family at least since his college days; one of her letters, dated 21 Aug. 1769, is to be found in WMQ, 1st ser., XVI (1907-1908), p. 174-80; among other charming incidents, it describes a visit of Governor Tryon and his lady to Williamsburg and a moonlit evening when Lord Botetourt joined a group singing on the steps of the Blair house.

To Benjamin Franklin

DEAR SIR Paris Aug. 14. 1786.

I received your favor of March 20. and much satisfaction from it. I had been alarmed with the general cry that our commerce was in distress, and feared it might be for want of markets. But the high price of commodities shews that markets are not wanting. Is it not yet possible however that these high prices may proceed from the smallness of the quantity made, and that from the want of labourers? It would really seem as if we did not make produce enough for home consumption, and of course had none superfluous to exchange for foreign articles. The price of wheat for instance shews it is not exported, because it could not at such a price enter into competition at a foreign market with the wheat of any other nation.

I send you some packets which have been put into my hands to be forwarded for you. I cannot send your Encyclopedie by the same conveyance, because it is by the way of England. Nothing worth reading has come from the press I think since you left us. There are one or two things to be published soon, which being on the subject of America, may be grateful to you, and shall be sent.

Europe enjoys a perfect repose at present. Venice and the two empires seem to be pecking at the Turks, but only in such a degree as may keep alive certain pretensions for commencing war when they shall see the occasion fit. Whether this will be immediately on the death of the K. of Prussia remains to be seen. That event must happen soon. By the little attention paid by this country to their land army it would seem as if they did not apprehend a war on that element. But to the increase and arrangement of their navy they are very attentive. There is no longer a doubt but that the harbour of Cherbourg will be completed, will be a most excellent one and capable of containing the whole navy of France. By having two outlets, vessels may enter and sally with every wind, while in the opposite ports of England particular winds are necessary.—Our peace with Marocco is probably signed by this time. We are indebted for it to the court of Spain. Algiers, Tunis and Tripoli will continue hostile according to present appearances.

Your friends here, within the circle of my acquaintance, are well, and often enquire after you. No interesting change that I recollect has taken place among them. Houdon has just received the block of marble for Genl. Washington's statue. He is married since his return. Trumbul, our young American painter is come here to have his Death of Montgomery and Battle of Bunker's hill engraved. I will beg leave to place here my friendly respects to young Mr. Franklin and assurances of the esteem and regard with which I have the honour to be Dear Sir your most obedient & most humble servant, TH: JEFFERSON

PrC (DLC). The "packets" that TJ presumably sent with this letter have not been identified.

From Plowden W. Garvey

SIR Rouen the 14 August 1786

We received the letter your Excellency honored us with 7 current only yesterday, the one it enclosed for Messrs. Achard was immediately delivered, and we told them if we could be of any Service in helping or giving dispatch to the Wine for you, we were willing to do it, wishing on all occasions to shew the respect we have for your Excellency.

The Box containing the Model of a House is in our Store; had we known who it came from, or to whom to send it, should long er this have sent it to Mr. Limozin of Havre. It is to be loaded this evening, our expences Shall be taken on him. We are on all your Commands with respect and very true regard sir Your Excellency's most humble and very obedient Servants

by procn. de RT. & AT. GARVEY
PLOWDEN W. GARVEY

RC (MHi); endorsed. Noted in SJL as received 15 Aug. 1786.

To Francis Hopkinson

DEAR SIR Paris Aug. 14. 1786

Your favours of Mar. 8. 28. and May 1. have come to hand since the date of my last which was of May 9. That of Mar. 8.

[248]

14 AUGUST 1786

begins with these words. 'I cannot at present lay my hands upon your last but recollect it was of an old date.' This seems to imply a charge of my being behind-hand in the epistolary account. Turning to my epistolary ledger I find our account since my arrival in Europe to stand thus.

My letters are of	Yours are of
1784. Nov. 11.	1784. Nov. 18.
1785. Jan. 13.	1785. Mar. 28.[1]
July 6.	April 20.
July 8.	July 23.
Sep. 25.	Sep. 28.
1786. Jan. 3.	Oct. 25.
Jan. 26.	Dec. 31.
May. 9.	1786. Mar. 8.
Aug. 14.	Mar. 28.
	May 1.

After the present then I shall still be a letter in your debt. One would think that this balance did not justify a scold. The manner of curing the Essence d'Orient is, as you are apprised, kept secret here. There is no getting at it therefore openly. A friend has undertaken to try whether it can be obtained either by proposing the partnership you mention, or by finding out the process. You shall have the result of these endeavors. I think I sent you in January the 5th. and 6th. volumes of the Bibliotheque physico-œconomique, which are the last published. I have for yourself and Dr. Franklin the 17th. and 18th. livraisons of the Encyclopedie, and expect the 19th. will come out very soon. These will form a respectable package and shall then be forwarded. I will send, as you propose, copies of my Notes to the Philosophical society, and the City library as soon as I shall have received a map which I have constructed for them, and which is now engraving. This will be a map of the country from Albemarle sound to Lake Erie, as exact as the materials hitherto published would enable me to make it, and brought into a single sheet. I have with great impatience hoped to receive from some of my friends a particular description of the Southern and Western limits of Pennsylvania. Perhaps it might still come in time if you could send it to me in the moment almost of your receiving this. Indeed it would be very desirable if you could only write me an answer to these two queries, viz. How far Westward of F. Pitt does the Western line of Pennsylvania pass? At what point of the river Ohio does that line strike it? Should this arrive even after they shall have begun to strike off the map, I can have the plate altered so as that the latter copies shall give that line right. Mr. Rittenhouse will have the goodness to furnish you answers to these queries. Could you prevail on him to answer this also, When will the Lunarium be done?—I envy your Wednesday evenings entertainments with him and Dr. Franklin. They would be more valued by me than the whole week at Paris.—Will you be so good as to send me a copy of a Botanical book published by some person in the country not far from Philadelphia, whose name I have not heard? It is a description of the plants of Pennsylvania. I have nothing new to communicate to you either in the arts or sciences. Our countryman Trumbul is here, a young painter of the most promising talents. He brought with him his Battle of Bunker's hill and Death of Montgomery to have them engraved here, and we may add, to have them sold; for, like Dr. Ramsay's history, they are too true to suit the English palate. He returned last night from examining the king's collection of paintings at Versailles, and acknoleges it surpassed not only every thing he had seen, but every idea he had ever formed of this art. I persuade him to fix himself here awhile, and then proceed to Rome. My daughter is well and joins me in respects to her and your common mother, to your lady and family also, as well as to our friends of the other house, meaning Mr. Rittenhouse's. Be assured yourself of the perfect esteem with which I am Dear Sir your friend and servant,

Th: Jefferson

PrC (DLC); endorsed.
I SHALL STILL BE A LETTER IN YOUR DEBT: This is by counting, as TJ did, the postscript to his letter of 6 July 1785 as a separate letter. The copy of *Notes on Virginia* promised for the American PHILOSOPHICAL SOCIETY was not sent until 1805 (see TJ to John Vaughan, 2 May 1805). That for the CITY LIBRARY (The Library Company of Philadelphia) was evidently never sent. The BOTANICAL BOOK PUBLISHED BY SOME PERSON . . . WHOSE NAME I HAVE NOT HEARD was Humphrey Marshall's *Arbustrum Americanum: the American grove, or, An Alphabetical catalogue of forest trees and shrubs, natives of the American United States* (Philadelphia, Joseph Crukshank, 1785; Sowerby, 1078).

[1] That is, 20 Mch. 1785 (see Vol. 8: 50-2).

To David Humphreys

Dear Sir   Paris Aug. 14. 1786.

I wrote you on the 7th. of May, being immediately on my return from England; and have lately received your favor of June

5. and thank you for the intelligence it contains. Every circumstance we hear induces us to beleive that it is the want of will, rather than of ability, to furnish contributions which keeps the public treasury so poor. The Algerines will probably do us the favour to produce a sense of the necessity of a public treasury and a public force on that element where it can never be dangerous. They refuse even to speak on the subject of peace. That with Marocco I expect is signed before this time; for which we are much indebted to Spain.

Your friend Mr. Trumbul is here at present. He brought his Bunker's hill and Death of Montgomery to have them engraved here. He was yesterday to see the king's collection of paintings at Versailles, and confesses it surpassed every thing of which he even had an idea. I persuade him to stay and study here, and then proceed to Rome.—Europe is yet quiet, and so will remain probably till the death of the K. of Prussia which is constantly expected. Whether this will be the signal of war or not, is yet to be seen. The two empires and Venice keep alive certain pretensions which may give colour to the commencement of hostilities when they shall think the occasion good. This country is much more intent on sea than on land preparations. Their harbour of Cherbourg will be completed and will hold their whole navy. This is putting the bridle into the mouth of England. The affairs of the United Netherlands have so long threatened civil war, that one ceases almost to believe any appearances. It must be confessed they cannot be stronger. Your friends here are well. La Comtesse d'Houditot asks kindly after you. The public papers continue to say favourable and just things of your poem. A violent criticism of Chastellux's voiages is just appearing. It is not yet to be bought. I am labouring hard with the assistance of the M. de la fayette to get the general commerce of the U.S. with this country put on a favourable footing, and am not without some hopes. The Marquis is gone into Auvergne for the summer. The rest of the beau monde are also vanished for the season. We give and receive them you know in exchange for the swallows.—I shall be happy to hear from you often, and to hear that you are engaged usefully to your country and agreeably to yourself, being with the most real esteem Dear Sir Your sincere friend & servt., TH: JEFFERSON

RC (Andre deCoppet, New York, 1949); endorsed. PrC (DLC).

YOUR FRIEND MR. TRUMBUL IS HERE: *The Autobiography of Colonel John Trumbull*, ed. Theodore Sizer (New Haven, 1953), an accurate and well-annotated edition of Trumbull's *Autobiography, Reminiscences and Letters* (New Haven, 1841), presents an excellent account of TJ's relations with

14 AUGUST 1786

Trumbull at this period: "Mr. Jefferson . . . had a taste for the fine arts, and highly approved my intention of preparing myself for the accomplishment of a national work. He encouraged me to persevere in this pursuit, and kindly invited me to come to Paris, to see and study the fine works there, and to make his house my home, during my stay.—I now availed myself of this invitation, and went to his house, at the Grille de Chaillot, where I was most kindly received by him. My two paintings, the first fruits of my national enterprise, met his warm approbation, and during my visit, I began the composition of the Declaration of Independence, with the assistance of his information and advice" (Sizer, *Autobiography*, p. 92-3; see illustration in this volume). On Sunday 6 Aug., Trumbull had gone "with Mr. Jefferson and others to see the ceremony of crowning the *rosière* of Sarennes, a village near St. Cloud, four miles from Chaillot" (Trumbull gives the date as *"Sunday, August 5th,"* but it is evident that here and elsewhere in editing his Paris diary for publication he erred in assigning dates to the days of the week); the party evidently did not include Trumbull's friends the Richard Cosways, for TJ's Account Book shows that he bought only three "tickets to Suresne," one of them doubtless being for Short. TJ may have been present on Monday, 7 Aug., when Trumbull "Went with M. and Madame Houdon, to the *salon* on the Boulevards, to see his little Diana in marble"; he was almost certainly present on Thursday the 10th when Trumbull "Went to the Luxembourg palace with Mr. and Mrs. Cosway" and others; he evidently was not with Trumbull when the latter "Went to Versailles with Mr. and Mrs. Cosway, MM. D'Hancharville, Poggi, Bulfinch, Coffin, &c." The last expedition was on Sunday the 13th (the 12th by Trumbull's dating), and on Monday the 14th Trumbull "Dined, in company with Mr. Jefferson, at the Abbés Chassi [Chalut] and Arnout [Arnoux] in Passy; a *jour maigre*, or fast day, but the luxury of the table in soups, fish and fruits, truly characteristic of the opulent clergy of the times. After dinner visited Madame De Corny" (same, p. 98-9, 107, 118). Unhappily, Trumbull suffered the loss of one or two sheets of his diary toward the close of Aug. Under date of 19 Aug. (i.e., 20 Aug.) he wrote late in life: "I distinctly recollect, however, that this time was occupied with the same industry in examining and reviewing whatever relates to the arts, and that Mr. Jefferson joined our party almost daily; and here commenced his acquaintance with Mrs. Cosway, of whom very respectful mention is made in his published correspondence" (same, p. 120). A VIOLENT CRITICISM OF CHASTELLUX'S VOIAGES: This was Brissot de Warville's *Examen critique des "Voyages dans l'Amérique septentrionale de M. le Marquis de Chatellux"; ou lettre à M. le Marquis de Chatellux dans lequel on réfute principalement ses opinions sur les Quakers, sur les Nègres, sur le peuple et sur l'homme*, which had appeared in July (C. Perroud, *J.-P. Brissot, Correspondance et Papiers*, Paris, 1911, p. 90; although this title, like some others by Brissot de Warville, bears the imprint "Londres," it was in fact printed in Paris—a device made necessary by the radical nature of the writings of the young *philosophe*. At the conclusion of 135 pages of criticism of Chastellux' *Voyages*, Brissot declared that there was no Frenchman nor American who would not derive pleasure from re-reading "les portraits de Washington, du savant M. Jefferson, et de ce jeune et brave François que vous caractérisez si bien comme l'espérance de notre Nation, *spes altera Romæ*, dont le nom sera cité à jamais à côté de celui de son père, de son ami Washington, dans les Annales des Etats-Unis"—a tribute that Lafayette must have read with pleasure (see Lafayette to TJ, 30 Aug. 1786). THE PUBLIC PAPERS CONTINUE TO SAY FAVOURABLE AND JUST THINGS OF YOUR POEM: The issue of *Mercure de France* for 5 Aug. 1786 contained a tribute to Chastellux' translation of "un Poëme d'un Officier Américain, qui peut disputer de verve et de beautés avec les meilleures pièces de vers Angloises" (p. 40).

[252]

From John Paul Jones

Dear Sir   Paris August 14th. 1786

I send you herewith the Rolls of the Bon-Homme-Richard and Alliance; with Copys of the other Papers in French respecting the Prize-Money of the Squadron I commanded. They are numbered from 1 to 23, and I have left them open for your inspection. I rely on the good effect of your Observations that will accompany them, with the Papers in your Hands, to Congress, and have no doubt but that my conduct will in consequence be approved. The second set of Papers are not yet finished, but will be ready in a few days so as to be forwarded by the next good opportunity, with the second set of the Papers in English now in your Hands.

I have the honor to be, with very great esteem and respect, Dear Sir, your most obedient and most humble Servant,

J Paul Jones

RC not found; text from facsimile in Catalogue of the Boyle Sale, Anderson Galleries, 19-20 Nov. 1923, Lot 144. Enclosures not identified; see TJ to Commissioners of Treasury 12 Aug. 1786.

From André Limozin

Most Honored Sir   Havre de Grace 14th August 1786

I had the honor of writing your Excellency the 11th Instant: this is on a Serious Matter, and I take the Freedom to beg of your Excellency to advise me how I must act on that occasion.

One Captn. Robertson master of a Swedish Vessell sailing under American Colors called Le Couteulx, and which brought here a Cargoe of Tobacco from Norfolk, dyed at Sea. He had with him one of his youngest Sons. He is about 17 years old. The deceased had shipped on board of his said ship for his own account a parcell of Tobacco and Staves. When the young man came ashore knowing that his Father leaves a very handsome Fortune, he hath purchased a Suit of Mourning Cloathes. He applyed to one Mr. Ruelon for the payment of that expence but that Merchant hath refused to comply with his demand, altho the young man represented that he had taken possession of his deceased Father's Property to which he had no right. But Mr. Ruelon gave him a very disagreable answer. When the young man saw that he could have no money to pay the expence of that Mourning Suit, he applyed to a Lawyer for advice, who said Mr. Ruelon is not intitled neither to keep nor to dispose of a deceased American Subject. Mr. Limozin is the only person to whom you can apply to procure you[r] right, because he hath an appointment from Mr. Barclay to act for him in that Case, but as that apointment hath not as yet received a legal Sanction, you must desire Mr. Limozin to apply to his Excellency the Ambassador of the United States in order to give him authority to act in that Circumstance under his seal and under his hand.

I have taken proper informations on the account of that young Robertson. He bears a good repute, he looks to be a very decent sober honest young man. He was introduced at my house, by sundry American Masters who beg'd of me to assist him and to not permit any American Subjects to be so ill used. It seems that they were all very angry against the proceedings of that Merchant. My intention is to do nothing unless I am directed intirely by your Excellency in that occasion. I have very often Kept silence on such like occasions, and I must say that it is very unhappy for the American Subjects in general that there is no American Consul legally appointed in this Port, for you cant imagin how much they are imposed upon. In expectation of your orders I have the honor to remain with the highest regard Your Excellency's Most obedient & very Humble Servant, ANDRE LIMOZIN

RC (MHi). Noted in SJL as received 16 Aug. 1786.

From Zachariah Loreilhe

SIR L'Orient August 14th. 1786

Having been advised by Mrs. Barclay of the safe arrival of Mr. Barclay at Magadore the 10th. of June last and of the Distinguished honour he met there by order of the Emperor, I made Monsieur Thevenard, Chef Descadre and Commandant in this Port, acquainted with it, Knowing the Esteem he Entertains for Mr. Barclay and the great Interest he takes in every thing that concerns the honour and Prosperity of the United Estates, and he has made it his request that I wou'd present his Compliments to your Excellency and to inform you that he has received this account with the greatest Satissfaction, and with his Wishes that Mr. Barclay's Mission may end to the honour and advantage of the United Estates of which he will be happy to be Informed. I have the honour of offering you a continuation of my best services, I remain with great respect sir your most obedt. humble servt.,

Z: LOREILHE

RC (DLC); endorsed.

From Champagne

Chalons, 15 Aug. 1786. Transmits a statement of the Chevalier de Borre, dated 16 Mch. 1786, that a man named Champagne had left him in Charleston in 1778; that the said Champagne presumably went to Savannah where he kept a shop; that the shop was looted and the owner wounded by the British; that he is said to be dead. The present "Champagne" asks "Monsieur j'iemesomme" to look into this matter since it refers to family business and the right of succession and settlement.

RC (DLC: TJ Papers, 24:4071); in French; 1 p.; at foot of text in TJ's hand: "Aug. 25. 1786. wrote to del. of Georgia. s.c."; endorsed by TJ: "Gaspard." Not recorded in SJL. The letter from TJ to the Georgia delegates in Congress, 25 Aug. 1786, has not been found; but there is a record entry in SJL under that date reading: "Delegates of Georgia s[ee] c[opy]. (Champagne's case)."

The CHEVALIER DE BORRE was in the "regiment de Champagne" (Lasseray, *Les Français sous les Treize Etoiles*, I, 367). He served in America from 1776 until Sep. 1777, and sailed from Charleston in Jan. 1779. The Champagne who left the Chevalier de Borre in Charleston was probably a servant; Gaspard, the name which TJ endorsed on Champagne's appeal, was a servant employed by TJ in the Hôtel d'Orleans, where TJ had stayed during Sep. 1784, before moving to the Cul-de-Sac Taitbout. Champagne, therefore, may have been a friend or relative of TJ's Gaspard.

From Lucy Ludwell Paradise

DEAR SIR   London Charles St. August the 15th. 1786

I had the honour to receive your Excellency's kind and friendly letter of the 29th. of May, for which I return you a thousand thanks. The present situation of our affairs is truly distressing, as a debt of such an enormous size is not easily discharged. The Ship we expected arrived a few weeks ago, and brought only 44 Hogshd. of tobacco. I say only 44 as it is not enough to pay the creditors and at the same time to support the family. The very valuable library we had has at different times been sold, and the last of them were disposed of about a month ago. Mr. Paradise received your Excellencys letter, and likewise the letters for the gentlemen in Virginia, for which he told me, he was greatly obliged to you, and that had he had money he would have set out immediately on receiving your kind invitation. He has told me and our dear friend

Dr. Bancroft that he would positively go in the Spring and take his family with him. There are many months to the Spring, therefore if he could be advised, and prevailed upon to go in October, and he would go, I think it would be the wisest action he ever did. The merchant we have now got, is a very proper one, as he is perfectly acquainted with all my relations and likewise with our property. His name is Gist and he lives in America Square Crutched friers. To this gentleman if I was Mr. Paradise I would lay open the whole of the debt I owed, and ask him if he would become the only creditor. I mean by that, if he would advance the whole of the money that would be necessary to pay all the creditors. I am of opinion he would, and then Mr. Paradise could go very easily in October; For the longer he stays here the greater the distresses he must necessarily draw himself and his family into. This letter will be delivered into your Excellencys hand by Mr. Voss a very amiable honest and good young gentleman and a native of Virginia. He has promised to deliver it to you himself and if it will not be intruding upon your precious moments, he will bring me your Excellencys Answer at his return. The truly kind and friendly part you take in my affairs I never shall forget, as long as I live, and I beg you will believe me when I assure you that if there is an thing in this World I can be of service to you, or your amiable daughters, you have only to let me know it, and I will do it to the utmost of my poor abilities, And remain Your Excellencys Most Obliged humble Servant, LUCY PARADISE

P.S. I beg no mention may be made of this letter to Mr. P.

RC (DLC); endorsed. Noted in SJL as received 21 Aug. 1786.

To John Banister, Jr.

DEAR SIR   Paris Aug. 16. 1786.

Your favor of the 6th. inst. gave me the agreeable intelligence of your being well enough to proceed on your journey. Your bill for ten guineas has not been presented. It shall be honored whenever it is, as well as those for any other sum you may have occasion for. I now inclose you the only letter I have on hand for you. I have received a letter from your father dated May 12. He was then well. He proposed your passing a year at Rome. I have written to him that you rather thought it adviseable to return to America, and that I had ventured to propose your passing by the way of

England, to see whether it's air, or it's medicine, whichever it was, might not produce a second time the good effect it had done the first. I shall be glad to hear from you from time to time while you are in Europe, and not less so when you are in America, a scene much more interesting to me. I am with sincere esteem Dr. Sir Your friend & servt.,
              Th: Jefferson

RC (DLC: Shippen Papers). PrC (DLC: TJ Papers); endorsed.

From André Caron

paris ce 16. aoust 1786.
Monseigneur Rue des moulins Butte St. Roch No. 9.

 Le Nommé andré Caron a Eté Embarqué le 10 Juillet. 1780. Sur La frégate L'arielle à L'orient, Commandé par Le Commodor paul Jones. Il est resté Sur cette fregate Jusqu'au 4 *avril 1781.*, Epoque a la quelle Monsieur Le Comte de la touche L'a fait debarqué, Etant arrivé à philadelphie, pour Le Transferé sur L'hermione; de là, fait passé sur Le Vaisseau du Roy Le Conquérant, après avoir promis, et même Monsieur Le Chevalier de La Luzerne pour lors Ambassadeur a philadelphie, que L'on auroient fait passé entre Les mains du Major Général de L'armée ce qu'il revenoient de nos mois.

 Le supliant Etoit Embarqué Sur La frégate L'arielle comme caporal des Volontaires à la paye de 36.ᵗᵗ par mois, ce qui fait en tout huit mois 24 jours, Ensemble 316.ᵗᵗ 16. Il n'a été payé que de Deux mois, il revient 244. 16. dont il n'a pas encore Touché un Sols.

 Il a L'honneur de se retirer vers vous, Monseigneur, pour vous prier de vouloir Bien ordonné qu'il soit payé.

 Il ne cessera de prier Le Seigneur pour La Conservation de Vos jours précieux. Et a L'honneur d'etre avec un tres profond respect, Monseigneur, Le plus humble et Le plus soumis de Vos Serviteurs,
                A. Caron

RC (DNA: PCC, No. 87, I; accompanied by translation by John Pintard); without indication of name of addressee. Tr (DNA: PCC, No. 107). Although this letter has no address-leaf and is not recorded in SJL, it was received by TJ (see Jones to TJ, 16 Aug.; TJ to Jay, 31 Dec. 1786).

From John Paul Jones

Sir Paris August 16th. 1786

Having no Roll of the Ariel in my Possession, I am unable to determine the legality of the claim expressed in the Paper you did me the Honor to send for my opinion. The Papers of that Frigate were deposited in the Admiralty at Philadelphia, I think, in April or May 1781, and I remember that some arrangement with Mr. Holker was spoke of by the Board, for the Wages due to the Marines; who being French subjects were claimed by the Chevalier de La Luzerne and sent to join Monsieur des Touches at Rhode Island. As this happened in the moment when paper Money was going out of circulation, perhaps the Men have not been paid? The truth can only be known by writing to America, unless you think fit to consult the Count de la Touche, with whom they embarked at Philadelphia for Rhode Island.

I am, Sir, with great esteem & respect, Your most obedient and most humble Servant, J Paul Jones

RC (DNA: PCC, No. 87, i). Tr. (DNA: PCC, No. 107).
THE PAPER YOU DID ME THE HONOR TO SEND: See André Caron to TJ, 16 Aug. 1786.

To John Ledyard

Sir Paris Aug. 16. 1786.

I saw Baron de Grimm yesterday at Versailles, and he told me he had received an answer from the Empress, who declines the proposition made on your account. She thinks it chimærical. I am in hopes your execution of it from our side of the continent will prove the contrary. I thought it necessary to give you this information that you might suffer no suspence from expectations from that quarter. I wish you success in whatever enterprize you adopt and am Sir Your most obedt. humble servt., Th: Jefferson

PrC (DLC).

From John Ledyard

Sir London August 16th 1786

Whenever I have occasion to write to you I shall not want to say so much on the score of Gratitude, that if I do not tire you with

16 AUGUST 1786

the Repetition of my thanks, I shall at least do injustice to the other Parts of my Letters unless you will be so good as to accept of a single honest heartfelt *Thank You* for the whole. In that case I shall always proceed to plain narration.

The same Sir James Hall that made me the remarkable visit at St. Germains is my friend here. I have arrived most opportunely indeed. An English Ship sails in three days for *Nootka Sound*. I am introduced by Sir James Hall to the Merchants who welcome me to a passage there and as one of them goes himself thank me for my comp[any.] I shall go on board to morrow. An Officer of Capt. Cooks goes also. He is highly pleased at my accompanying them. Sir J. Hall presented me with twenty Guineas Pro Bono Publico.—I bought two great Dogs, an Indian pipe and a hatchet. My want of time as well as more money will prevent my going otherwise than indifferently equipped for such an Enterprise; but it is certain I shall be more in want before I see Virginia. Why should I repine? You know how much I owe the aimiable La Fayette, will you do me the honor to present my most grateful thanks to him?—If I find in my Travels a mountain as much above the Mountains as he is above ordinary men I will name it La Fayette.—I beg the honor also of my compliments to Mr. Short who has also been my friend and like the good Widow in Scripture cast in not only his mite but more than he was able, to my assistance. Adieu.

I have the honor to be Sir your most grateful and most Obedt huml Servt.,
JOHN LEDYARD

Tr (Mrs. Jane Ledyard Remington, Cazenovia, N.Y., 1951). Noted in SJL as received 3 Oct. 1786.

In a letter written to a friend, dated at St. Germain 8 Aug. 1786, Ledyard gave an account of an incident involving THE SAME SIR JAMES HALL: "About a fortnight ago, Sir James Hall, an English gentleman, on his way from Paris to Cherbourg, stopped his coach at our door, and came up to my chamber. I was in bed at six o'clock in the morning, but having flung on my *robe de chambre*, I met him at the door of the antechamber. I was glad to see him, but surprised. He observed, that he had endeavored to make up his opinion of me, with as much exactness as possible, and concluded that no kind of visit whatever would surprise me. . . . In walking across the chamber, he laughingly put his hand on a six livre piece and a louis d'or, that lay on my table, and with a half stifled blush, asked me how I was in the money way. Blushes commonly beget blushes, and I blushed partly because he did, and partly on other accounts. 'If fifteen guineas,' said he, interrupting the answer he had demanded, 'will be of any service to you, there they are,' and he put them on the table. 'I am a traveller myself, and though I have some fortune to support my travels, yet I have been so situated as to want money, which you ought not to do. You have my address in London.'" (quoted in Sparks, *Life of John Ledyard*, p. 168-9). Sir James was almost a total stranger, but Ledyard accepted the money "without any hesitation, and told him I would be as complaisant to him, if ever occasion offered." TJ, though in a more conventional manner, was also among the "vice-consuls, consuls, ministers, and plenipotentiaries" who, according to Ledyard, had been "tributary to" him (same, p. 167). On 15 Feb. 1786, according to his Account Book, TJ "lent Ledyard 48f"; on the 20th of that month he received of "M. de la Fayette to be paid to Ledyard on account of Empress of Russia 600 f"; on 4 Aug. he "gave Ledyard 132f"; and again on 7 Aug. he "gave Ledyard 96f" —both of the last being, according to Ledyard's own account, within a fortnight after he had received fifteen guineas from Sir James Hall.

From Thomas Mann Randolph, Jr.

DEAR SIR Edinburgh August 16 1786

I am afraid by delaying so long a time to answer your letter I have deservedly forfeited the advantages which might be derived from such a correspondence, but still hope that as I wish to make amends for my fault your goodness will incline you to forgive it. By the reestablishment of my health in great measure, a removal to the continent has become unnecessary, at least before the time which is generally thought sufficient here for the completion of an academical education is elapsed. The first winter of my abode in Edinb. I turned my attention to the languages and Mathematics only, being allmost entirely ignorant of both on my arrival; since however I have been engaged in more intellectual pursuits, and have tasted of the exquisite pleasure which the mind derives even from the first insight into Philosophy. I have all along felt a particular attachment to the Study of Natural History, and the two *summers* of my residence here have made it the chief object of my attention; the necessary instructions to enable me to read with advantage on the subject I have received from Dr. Walkers lectures, who is no less famous for his extensive information with respect to this science than the enthusiastic pleasure which he takes in propagating the knowledge of it. As yet I have entered on no pursuit immediately relating to my intended profession, being convinced that to begin at my time of life the investigation of intricate points of law, before a proper foundation had been laid to proceed on by an intimate acquaintance with history and Mathematics would not only be fruitless but tend to create an unwillingness to prosecute farther a subject which exhibited at first view such apparently insurmountable difficulties. It is my intention to attend this winter the lectures on Natural philosophy and civil history, perhaps likewise on Anatomy, for I have a great desire to obtain some knowledge of the structure of the human body, but am uncertain whether it would not be more advantageous to defer it some time yet. Your advice not only on that particular but the whole course of my education would be extremely acceptable, and shall be implicitly followed. My Brother and my self are to spend the next year I believe in France, but will remain some months at a provincial town to get a little acquainted with the language before we shall have the honor of seeing you at Paris. He and Mr. And. Randolph desire to be remembered to you. My compliments to Miss Jefferson. Your leisure time, if you have any from your important function, cannot be employed where it will be more thankfully received than in writing to Your most obedt. humble servt.,

T. M. RANDOLPH

RC (MHi); endorsed. Noted in SJL as received 26 Aug. 1786.

To Vergennes

SIR   Paris Aug. 16. 1786.

I take the liberty of repeating what I had the honor of mentioning to your Excellency yesterday, that, by order of the state of Virginia, a contract has been made in France for 3400. stand of arms, as many cartouch boxes with their accoutrements, and that I am yet to purchase as much gunpower, gunflints and Cartridge paper as will, with the arms and cartouch boxes, employ the sum of 180,000 livres, to which this purchase is directed to extend in the whole. I am now to ask the favor of a permission to export these articles from the port of Bourdeaux, except the Cartouch boxes which, being made at Paris, will be exported from Havre.

Permit me here also to ask the letter to his majesty's minister at Copenhagen to support the application of the Chevalier Paul Jones to that court for satisfaction for the prizes taken by him, carried into a port of Denmark, and delivered by the order of that court to the English.

I have the honour to be with sentiments of the most perfect esteem & respect, your Excellency's most obedient and most humble servant,   TH: JEFFERSON

RC (Arch. Aff. Etr., Corr. Pol., E.-U., XXXII); at head of text: "M DeR[ayneval]"; and "Envoyé copie à M. de Ségur et à M. de Calonne le 5. 8bre. 1786"; attached to RC is a translation in a clerk's hand.

To Brissot de Warville

SIR   Paris Aug. 16. 1786.

I have read with very great satisfaction the sheets of your work on

16 AUGUST 1786

the commerce of France and the United states which you were so good as to put into my hands. I think you treat the subject, as far as these sheets go, in an excellent manner. Were I to select any particular passages as giving me particular satisfaction, it would be those wherein you prove to the United states that they will be more virtuous, more free, and more happy, emploied in agriculture, than as carriers or manufacturers. It is a truth, and a precious one for them, if they could be persuaded of it. I am also particularly pleased with your introduction. You have properly observed that we can no longer be called Anglo-Americans. That appellation now describes only the inhabitants of Novas Scotia, Canada, &c. I had applied that of Federo-Americans to our citizens, as it would not be so decent for us to assume to ourselves the flattering appellation of Free-Americans.

There are two passages in this work on which I am able to give you information. The first is in page 67 'ils auront le coton quant ils voudront se livrer à ce genre de culture,' and the note 'l'on voit dans la baie de Massachusets &c.' The four Southernmost states make a great deal of cotton. Their poor are almost entirely clothed in it in winter and summer. In winter they wear shirts of it, and outer clothing of cotton and wool mixed. In Summer their shirts are linnen but the outer clothing cotton. The dress of the women is almost entirely [made of] cotton manufactured by themselves, except the richer class, and even many of these wear a good deal of home-spun cotton. It is as well manufactured as the calicoes of Europe. Those 4. states furnish a great deal of cotton to the states North of them, who cannot make it, as being too cold.—There is no neighborhood in any part of the United states without a water-grist-mill for grinding the corn of the neighborhood. Virginia, Maryland, Delaware, Pennsylvania, New Jersey, New York, abound with large manufacturing mills for the exportation of flour. There are abundance of saw-mills in all the states. Furnaces and forges of iron, I believe in every state, I know they are in the nine Northernmost. There are many mills for plating and slitting iron, and I think there are many distilleries of rum from Norfolk in Virginia to Portsmouth in New Hampshire. I mention these circumstances because your note seems to imply that these things are only in the particular states you mention.

The second passage is page 101. and 102. where you speak of the 'ravages causés par l'abus des eaux de vie' which seems, by the note in page 101. to be taken on the authority of Smith. Nothing can be less true than what that author says on this subject; and we may say in general that there are as many falshoods as facts in his work. I think drunkenness is much more common in all the American States than in France, but it is less common there than in England. You may form an idea from this of the state of it in America. Smith saw every thing thro' the medium of strong prejudice. Besides this he does not hesitate to write palpable lies, which he was conscious were such.—When you proceed to form your table of American exports, and imports, I make no doubt you will consult the American traveller, the estimates in which are nearer the truth than those of Ld. Sheffield and Deane, as far as my knowlege of the facts enables me to judge. I must beg your pardon for having so long detained those sheets. I did not finish my American dispatches till the night before last, and was obliged yesterday to go to Versailles. I have the honour to be with very great respect, Sir, your most obedient & most humble servant,

TH: JEFFERSON

PrC (DLC).
The number of SHEETS OF YOUR WORK that Brissot de Warville sent to TJ cannot be determined; the volume of which he was joint author with Etienne Clavière was not published until 1787 and was entitled: *De la France et Des Etats-Unis, ou de l'Importance de la Révolution de l'Amérique pour le bonheur de la France, des Rapports de ce Royaume & des Etats-Unis, des avantages réciproques qu'ils peuvent retirer de leurs liaisons de Commerce, & enfin de la situation actuelle des Etats-Unis*; it was dedicated to Congress "et aux amis des Etats-Unis, dans les Deux Mondes." The INTRODUCTION that pleased TJ so much pointed out that, no sooner had England lost the colonies than her writers (Sheffield and others) began to emphasize the importance of restoring American commerce to its former channels; that, despite the great value of American commerce to France, there was in general little public interest in the subject; and that one of the chief causes of this indifference was the absence of freedom of the press, whereby discussion of political questions was curtailed and many political advantages lost. As finally published, the work revealed many traces of TJ's influence. It included (p. 330-6) the text of Calonne's letter to TJ of 22 Oct. 1786 and the Act for Establishing Religious Freedom (p. 336-9). In addition, the concluding chapter—a vigorous refutation of the idea that anarchy prevailed in America because of Shays' rebellion, the clamors for paper money, and other evidences of popular discontent—contained some materials that could evidently have been furnished only by TJ. In respect to the adoption of a money unit by Congress, the authors observe: "On a suivi pour ce réglement le plan proposé par le judicieux et savant M. Jefferson. Une des parties les plus frappantes de ce plan est de réduire tous les calculs sur les monnoies à la raison décimale" (p. 321). Also, the allegation that England had declined to negotiate a treaty of amity and commerce on the ground that the constitutions "n'étoient pas encore assez fixes" (p. 327) must have come from him. His influence seems discernible, too, in the substance if not the phraseology of the eloquent passage at p. 320-4, reflecting arguments that TJ had been employing for months past: "Observez en effet tout ce qui s'est passé dans les Etats-Unis depuis le retour de la paix, et vous retrouverez cet esprit public, dans tous leurs actes législatifs, dans toutes leurs réformes, dans toutes leurs améliorations, dans tous leurs développemens.—Vous le retrouverez dans cette cession généreuse & sans exemple dans l'histoire, que divers Etats ont faite au congrès, de leurs territoires trop étendus; cession bien propre à disculper ces républiques des vues d'ambition et d'aggrandissement qu'on leur prête; cession qui affermit leurs bases en circonscrivant à jamais leurs limites.—Vous le

retrouverez dans la volonté unanime et déclarée de tous les Etats, de payer la dette publique, et dans leur intention d'acquiescer aux moyens infaillibles qui doivent l'éteindre. Il est du devoir des vrais amis des Américains libres d'insister sur ce concert, pour rassurer les François et les autres Européens qui sont leurs créanciers.—Vous le retrouverez dans ce réglement du congrès qui simplifie les monnoies, qui les réduit à des divisions faciles pour le commerce; qui donne à l'Europe un grand exemple, l'exemple de plusieurs Etats indépendans les uns des autres, occupant une vaste étendue, et n'ayant cependant qu'une même monnoie, comme un même poids, de mêmes mesures, un même language. . . . Vous le retrouverez cet esprit public dans l'accord de tous les Etats pour n'avoir qu'une régle commune relative au commerce extérieur, et pour réformer les abus qui peuvent s'être glissés dans le système fédéral.—Vous le retrouverez dans la disposition générale de tous les Etats à bien accueillir les étrangers, dans ce traité de paix et d'amitié entre eux et la Prusse; où, pour la premiere fois, on abjure les préjugés ridicules qui souillent encore la diplomatique de nos jours; où l'on convient enfin, que la guerre ne frappera plus ni sur l'agriculture ni sur l'industrie, ni sur le commerce.—Vous le retrouverez dans cette anxiété qu'éprouvent tous les Américains vertueux à la vue du luxe qui s'accroît chez eux; dans les moyens qu'ils prennent pour l'arrêter & pour conserver leur première simplicité.— Vous le retrouverez dans toutes les loix passées par les divers Etats; dans celle qui rappelle les loyalistes; car l'esprit public ne connoît point de vengeance implacable; dans cette autre loi qui supprime les confiscations de biens des coupables; pratique barbare, enfantée dans les tems désastreux des proscriptions Romaines, conservée par l'esprit de rapine de la féodalité.—Vous le retrouverez dans ces réglemens sur la religion, qui établissent par-tout une tolérance civile et religieuse; tolérance si nécessaire à l'harmonie et dont l'ignorance seule ou les préjugés peuvent combattre les avantages évidens.—Vous le retrouverez dans toutes les loix qui sanctionnent l'établissement de maisons d'éducation, de grands chemins, de canaux, et de tout ce qui peut contribuer à la commodité et à l'aggrandissement du commerce intérieur." CONSULT THE AMERICAN TRAVELLER: That is, Alexander Clunie's *The American Traveller: or, observations on the present state, culture and commerce of the British Colonies in America, and the further improvements of which they are capable; with an account of the exports, imports and returns of each Colony respectively* (London, 1769; Sowerby No. 3611).

To Samuel Adams and John Lowell

DEAR SIR Paris Aug. 17. 1786.

This will be delivered you by a Madame de Gregoire a lady of this country who goes to America to sollicit from the state of Massachusets a claim which she has to certain lands in the province of Maine. These lands had been long in the occupation of her family under a grant from the crown of France, while it held the colony of Acadie. Subsequent events threw this territory under the British government, and lastly within the lines ceded by that government to the United states. As her claim stands on singular ground, the indulgence can do little injury as a precedent which may be extended to it either in consideration of her just right, or in proof of our dispositions to favor her nation, and to bind it's individuals to us by every possible tie, as well as it's government. On the footing of the acquaintance I have had the honor of having with you, I presume to recommend her to your patronage, and to ask for her your counsel and assistance, so far as justice, or motives of sound policy may authorize you to yield them. I take this liberty with the more good will as it gives me an opportunity of recalling myself to your recollection, and of renewing to you assurances of the perfect esteem and respect with which I have the honour to be, Dear Sir, your obedient & most humble servant,

TH: JEFFERSON

RC (Mrs. Howard B. Field, Durham Center, Conn., 1944); the name of the recipient (John Lowell), at the foot of the page, has been cut away. PrC (DLC); at foot of text: "S. Adams J. Lowel esq." The RC addressed to Adams has not been found.

From William Carmichael

SIR St. Ildefonso 17th. Augt. 1786

I had the honor to transmit on the 15th. July to your Excellency a copy of a note to me from his Excy. The Ct. of Florida Blanca dated the 13th. Dto. inclosing Extracts of a Letter from the Spanish Consul General in Morocco and of one from the Principal Minister of his M.M. relative to Mr. Barclay's negociation. On the 11th. Inst. I received a note from the Ct. of F.B. with a copy of the Treaty in Spanish which I forwarded to Mr. Jay viâ France, by the Last Post. The Ct. of F.B. having requested me to return the Copy he sent me for my perusal, I had not time to make out a second for my own use, and as I perceived by a Letter which I lately sent you from Mr. Barclay and which that Gentleman left open for my perusal, that all but one Article of his propositions had been accepted, I do not so much regret my want of time to transcribe a copy for you. I think it however proper to submit to your perusal the Translation of a Letter from his Marroccan Majesty to the Consul General of Spain, which proves the Essential Services that the Interference of his C.M. hath rendered the U.S. on this occasion. It is as follows.

"Gracias á Dios uno solo, no hay fuezza ni pedor sino en Dios. (L.S.) Al Consul Espanol. Par al que signe el verdadero Camino. Despues nos ha llegado esta tu Carta, y sobre lo que nos escribes a cerca de los Americanos, Elles se han presentado, y trayeon del Rey Carlos una carta y *en atencion a ella* lo hemos concedido quanto han pretendido firmando los Tratados de par que nos pidieron y hemos aceptado, y a qui te embiamos una copia de Ellos para que la mandos al Rey de España, y tu quando estes prento para venir à

17 AUGUST 1786

neustra presencia, notificando, para embiarte los Caballos que han de acompanar y Salud. A onze dias de la Luna de Ramadan ano de 1200 (que correspondeci a 8 de Julio 1786)."

Yesterday morning I received the inclosed Letter from Mr. Barclay, which your Excellency will receive by a Courier dispatched from hence to the Ct. d'Aranda and the Chevalier Del Campo. This Messenger carries the ratification of the Convention relative to the Mosquito Shore signed the 14th. of July by the Latter and the Marquis of Carmarthen. I have in my possession an extract of this Convention, but as I presume Mr. Adams must have already furnished you with a copy of it, I forbear transmitting it. It has given great satisfaction here. The King manifested in a particular manner to the British Minister the pleasure the conclusion of this Affair gave him. It seems to be the System of G.B. to court Spain, and their Minister here is well qualified to execute their plans. On the 14th. of June a Treaty was signed between Spain and Algiers. It is not however yet ratified owing to the bad State of health of the Ct. of F.B. I have sent to Mr. Jay a copy of this Treaty. I have such a firm reliance on the repeated promises of the Ct. de F.B. from the experience of this Minister's punctuality and regard to his word in all the Transactions that I have had with him during my mission here, that I think I can safely assert that we may depend on the best offices of this court whenever it may be judged proper to renew our overtures to Algiers. [I beg you to have the goodness to charge one of your Servants with the Delivery of the inclosed Letters. If you chuse to be acquainted with two Amiable Ladies, you may avail yourself of this opportunity. They are from Mr. Celesia The Genoese Minister at this Court. We live together at this Residence and he will with pleasure write to these Ladies in favor of a Republican.][1] His republic[2] is doing what its limited finances will permit it to protect its Commerce. I am told That the King of Sardinia is doing the Same. The Portuguese and Neapolitan Envoys have gone to Algiers. Their Success is problematical. If I was informed of the Obstacles attending our Treaty with Portugal, I flatter myself that I might be of some Utility. It is not improbable that the Portuguese Ambassador at this court will be nominated Minister of State. I tell you before hand that he is Antigallican. I beleive he is of a party opposed to the Chevalier Pinto. [He has offered repeatedly to me, In case the Treaty should take place, to procure an intimation from the Queen that my Nomination would be agreable to her Majesty.][1] I am assured by *what* ought *to be good authority* that the Affairs of the Court of Naples are in a good train. This appears to want Confirmation. I write freely and fully to you and I hope you will have the same confidence with respect to your Excellency's[3] Most Obedt. & Humble Sert.,

WM. CARMICHAEL

P.S. Mr. Lamb is at Alicant, he has sent the vessel he purchased to America.

RC (DLC); endorsed. Tr (DNA: PCC, No. 87, 1); headed, in Short's hand: "Extracts of a Letter from Mr. Carmichael." PrC (MHi: AMT). Tr (DNA: PCC, No. 107). Noted in SJL as received 24 Aug. 1786. Enclosures: (1) Barclay to Commissioners, 16 July 1786. (2) Probably letters to the two unidentified ladies "from Mr. Celesia."

[1] Brackets in MS; the bracketed passage is omitted from Tr.
[2] Tr reads: "The Republic of Genoa."
[3] Tr ends at this point.

To Dangirard & De Vernon

Paris. Aug. 17. 1786.

There appears to be due to Mark & co. for Messrs. de Vernon & Danguard

	Principal	Interest to Dec. 31. 1785	Principal in livres	Interest to Dec. 31. 85
From the treasury of the United States	$4691\frac{7}{90}$	281.46.d.	₶ s 24,628. 4	₶ s 1,477.13
From the treasury of Virginia	£ s d 1823.5.4	£ 632.16	32,818.16	11,390. 8
			57,477.	12,868. 1

Besides this, Mark & co. have received from the treasury of the U.S. the interest on $4891\frac{7}{90}$D from the respective dates at which the sums were placed therein up to the 31st. Dec. 1784. amounting to 1550 Dollars or 8137₶-10s. As to the $4691\frac{7}{90}$ Dollars = 24,628₶-4s due from the U.S. it bears an annual interest of 281.46 Doll. = 1477₶-13s which appears to have been regularly paid. As to the 1823£-5s-4d = 32,818₶-16s principal and 632£-16s = 11,390₶-8s. interest due from the state of Virginia, I know not the reason why the whole interest and a part of the principal have not been paid; as it appears by the letter of Mr. Bannister and other information I have received that the principal of that debt is in a course of paiment. The whole will probably be

[267]

17 AUGUST 1786

discharged in a very few years. I would advise Messrs. Danguard and DeVernon to execute a power of Attorney in the form I send them, leaving a blank for the attorney's name. That I will send to Mr. Bannister praying him to insert the name of some trust-worthy attorney. This will authorize that attorney to call Messrs. Mark Nephew & co. to account, and in the mean time stay the paiment of any more money to them. If Mark, nephew & co. have not made themselves citizens of any of the American states, this matter will be determined summarily before Mr. Oster the French consul residing in Virginia; but if Mark has made himself a citizen, it must be decided in the courts of justice of the country, in which case it may require a couple of years to settle it. The power of attorney, of which I send a form, must be signed by Messrs. Danguard & de Vernon before a Notary, and there must be a certificate that the person is a Notary, which certificate must be signed by the Prevot de Marchands of Paris with the seal of his office. Besides this, these gentlemen should draw up a full state of their case, and prepare authentic vouchers to support it, and send them to their attorney. TH: JEFFERSON

ENCLOSURE

Know all men by these presents that we [here insert the name of Messrs. Danguard & de Vernon][1] subjects of his most christian majesty the king of France, and inhabitants of the said kingdom, have constituted and appointed   of the commonwealth of Virginia our lawful attorney, for us and in our names to sue for, recover, and receive all sums of money or other property of ours in the hands of Messrs. Marc. nephew & co. as also to sollicit from the Loan Office of the United states of America and from the Loan office of the commonwealth of Virginia all sums of money lodged in either of them, in our own names, or in the names of Marc nephew & Co. or in any other name in our behalf, and all sums of interest due or to become due thereon; and for such monies or other property recovered or received from the said Marc nephew & co. or from either of the said loan offices to give sufficient acquittances on our behalf: and we hereby confirm whatever our said attorney shall do by virtue of this power as fully as if done by ourselves; hereby revoking all former powers given to the said Marc, nephew & co. or to any other person touching the premises. In witness whereof we have hereto set our hands and seals at Paris in the kingdom of France this   day of   1786.

PrC (MoSHi). Enclosure: PrC (MoSHi); entirely in TJ's hand. There is the following entry in SJL under this date: "Arnoud for du Vernon. s.c. [see copy] to du Vernon"; presumably TJ sent copies of this statement, therefore, to both the Abbé Arnoux and Dangirard & De Vernon.

THE LETTER OF MR. BANNISTER: See Banister to TJ, 12 May 1786.

[1] Brackets in MS.

To R. & A. Garvey

[*Paris, 17 Aug. 1786.* An entry in SJL, under this date and immediately below the entry for the (missing) letter to André Limozin of this date, reads: "Garvey. do." Not found.]

To André Limozin

[*Paris, 17 Aug. 1786.* An entry in SJL under this date, partly illegible, reads: "Limozin [Introduct]ion of Bassville and Morrises." Letter not found; but see Bassville to TJ, 18 Aug., and Limozin to TJ, 2 Sep. 1786.]

Deposition of Richard Riddy

Paris in the Kingdom of France, to wit.

Richard Riddy esq. merchant of the commonwealth of Pennsylvania, but now resident at Nantes in the kingdom of France aforesaid made oath before me Thomas Jefferson minister plenipotentiary for the U.S. of America at the court of Versailles, that in the month of January in the year 1783 he was taken prisoner on the high seas by the English, and carried to New York; that while he was there, David Sproate Commissary general of prisoners to the British army informed him that upwards of eleven thousand American prisoners had died on board the prison ship the Jersey, and shewed him the registers whereby it appeared to be so.

Given under my hand and seal at Paris aforesaid this 17th. day of August 1786.

MS (DNA: PCC, No. 107, II); entirely in TJ's hand; on verso, in the hand of Henry Remsen: "No 72 There is a person living now on Long Island, who informed me that the number of american prisoners who were buried from on board the Jersey prison ship, along the shore on his land, could not be less in number than 10,000.—H.R. Junr." MS is torn at bottom, and signature may have been removed thereby. This and the draft of a letter from the Commissioners to the King of Spain (undated) are the only MSS in TJ's hand in PCC, No. 107, which is made up otherwise of transcripts of TJ's letters to Jay, 1785-1787.

From Hugon de Bassville

Monsieur   paris le 18 aout 1786

J'ai recu hier Le paquet que vous avez eu La bonté de M'envoier. J'avais oublié de vous demander un passeport qui nous est absolu-

[269]

ment nécéssaire pour sortir du Roiaume, j'espère que vous voudrez bien me le faire passer à abbeville ou nous serons, jusqu'au 12 7bre, avec les lettres de recommandation pour les Ministres, de la part de Mr. de Vergennes.

Il faut que le passeport soit pour Mrss. Morris, pour moi, pour un valet de chambre et un domestique.

J'ai Lhonneur d'etre tres respectueusement Monsieur Votre tres humble et tres obeissant serviteur,   Hugon de Bassville

RC (DLC); endorsed.

For Hugon de Bassville, see F. Masson, *Les Diplomates de la Révolution: Hugon de Bassville à Rome* (Paris, 1882). "Nicolas-Joseph Hugon de Bassville fut gouverneur des fils de M. Morris, de Philadelphie, qui devaient visiter l'Europe. Il fit avec eux le tour de France, parcourut la Belgique, demeura en Hollande, traversa l'Allemagne, et connut par la même la Suisse. On connait une de ses lettres de juillet 1785 où il parle de la vie que les trois voyageurs menaient en Suisse, avec suite de domestiques et de chevaux. Monsieur Morris au retour de voyage se déclare satisfait du voyage et lui fit une pension de trois mille livres par an" (L. Vecchi, *Les Français à Rome*, p. xxxix-xc). LE PAQUET that Hugon de Bassville received the day before may have included letters of introduction to persons in Holland, including one to Dumas; if TJ sent the packet with a letter, as is probable, it has not been found.

To De Blome

Sir   Paris Aug. 18. 1786.

Dr. Franklin, during his residence at this court, was instructed by Congress to apply to the court of Denmark for a compensation for certain vessels and cargoes taken from the English during the late war by the American squadron under the command of Commodore Paul Jones, carried into a port of Denmark, and, by order of the court of Denmark, redelivered to the English. Dr. Franklin made this application through the Baron de Walterstorf, at that time charged with other matters relative to the two countries of Denmark and the United states of America. Baron de Waltersdorf, after having written to his court, informed Dr. Franklin that he was authorized to offer a compensation of ten[1] thousand guineas. This was declined, because it was thought that the value of the prizes was the true measure of compensation, and that that ought to be enquired into. Baron de Waltersdorf left this court some time after, on a visit only, as he expected, to Copenhagen, and the matter was suffered to rest till his return. This was constantly expected, till you did me the honour of informing me that he had received another destination. It being now therefore necessary to renew our application, it is thought better that Commodore Paul Jones should repair in person to Copenhagen. His knowlege of the whole transaction will best enable him to represent it to that court, and the world has had too many proofs of the justice and magnanimity of his Danish majesty to leave a doubt that he will order full justice to be done to those brave men who saw themselves deprived of the spoils, won by their gallantry, and at the hazard of their lives, and on whose behalf the justice and generosity of his majesty is now reclaimed.

I am now, Sir, to ask the favor of you to communicate this application to your court, to inform them that Commodore Paul Jones, who will present himself to them, is authorized to sollicit and arrange this matter, and to ask your good offices with his Majesty and his ministers, so that the representations of Mr. Jones may find their way to them, which we are assured is all that is necessary to obtain justice.

I have the honour to be with sentiments of the most perfect esteem and respect, Sir, your most obedient and most humble servant, TH: JEFFERSON

PrC (DLC); at foot of text: "Baron Blome M.P. for Denmark." Tr (DNA: PCC, No. 168, II).

[1] This word interlined in substitution for "five," deleted; see Jones to TJ, 21 Aug. 1786.

From John Jay

DR SIR New York 18th. August 1786

My last to you was dated the 14th. of last Month, since which I have received and laid before Congress your several Letters of 12th. 22d. 23d. two of 27th. and one of 31st. May last, with the Papers enclosed with them.

It has happened from various Circumstances, that several Reports on foreign Affairs still lay before Congress undecided upon. The want of an adequate Representation for long Intervals, and the Multiplicity of Business which pressed upon them when that was not the Case, has occasioned Delays and Omissions which however unavoidable are much to be regretted. It is painful to me to reflect that altho' my Attention to Business is unremitted yet I so often experience unseasonable Delays and successive Obstacles in obtaining the Decision and Sentiments of Congress, even on Points which require Dispatch. But so it is, and I must be content with leaving nothing undone that may depend upon me.

The consular Convention is now as it has long been, under the consideration of Congress, and I have Reason to hope they will soon enable me to send you full Instructions on that Subject.

I have long thought and become daily more convinced that the Construction of our fœderal Government is fundamentally wrong. To vest legislative, judicial and executive Powers in one and the same Body of Men, and that too in a Body daily changing its Members, can never be wise. In my Opinion those three great Departments of Sovereignty should be for ever separated, and so distributed as to serve as Checks on each other. But these are Subjects that have long been familiar to you and on which you are too well informed not to anticipate every Thing that I might say on them.

I enclose a late Ordinance of Congress for Indian Affairs, and their Requisition for the ensuing Year. Those Subjects have consumed much Time. They are however important ones and the Attention of Congress to them could not with Propriety have been postponed.

[I have advised Congress to renew your Commission as to certain Powers. Our Treasury is ill supplied; some States pay nothing and others very little. The Impost not yet established. The People generally uneasy in a certain Degree, but without seeming to discern the true Cause, vizt., want of Energy both in state and fœderal Governments. It takes Time to make Sovereigns of Subjects.][1]

I am, Dr. Sir, with great Esteem & Regard, &c.   JOHN JAY

FC (DNA: PCC, No. 121); written partly in code. Dft (NK-Iselin). Noted in SJL as received 22 Sep. 1786. Enclosures: (1) Ordinance for the regulation of Indian affairs, 7 Aug. 1786 (printed in JCC, XXXI, 490-3). (2) Requisition for 1786, 2 Aug. 1786 (same, p. 461-5).

Jay's report to Congress on THE CONSULAR CONVENTION was submitted on the day that he wrote the present letter; it was adopted almost verbatim on 3 Oct. 1786 (see Jay to TJ, 3 Oct. 1786). The report is printed in JCC, XXXI, 647-9.

[1] The paragraph in brackets (supplied) is underscored in Dft and has "cyphers" written in margin; in FC and, of course, in the missing RC this paragraph is encoded (Code No. 10 being employed); also in FC the paragraph is set forth below the code symbols and opposite it the word "Explication" is written.

To Schweighauser & Dobrée

GENTLEMEN   Paris Aug. 18. 1786.

I have duly received your favor of Aug. 5. Being entirely uninformed and uninstructed on the subjects thereof, I could do no more than forward them to my constituents. This I have accordingly done, and will do myself the pleasure of informing you of their decision so soon as it shall be communicated to me. I have the honour of being with much respect Gentlemen your most obedient and most humble servt., TH: JEFFERSON

PrC (DLC).

From the Abbés Arnoux and Chalut

Passy 19 Aoust [1786]

Les Abbés Chalut et Arnoux présentent Leurs civilités à Monsieur Jefferson: ils auront l'honneur de se rendre à son invitation Lundi prochain 21 du Courant.

RC (MHi); addressed. The year 1786 has been supplied in the date line because it was the only year during TJ's stay in France in which 21 Aug. fell on Monday.

To André Limozin

SIR Paris Aug. 19. 1786.

I have duly received your favor of the 14th. inst. Had Congress made appointment of Consuls regularly in the several ports, the difficulty would not have happened which is the subject of your letter. But their other business has as yet prevented the final completion of arrangements for that department. In the mean while we must conduct the business as well as we can, the Agents in the several ports undertaking to act where there is no legal opposition made. In the present case I suppose that Mr. Ruilon will make opposition, and therefore I have taken the advice of an eminent Avocat au parlement as to the matter. He says that application must be made to the Amirauté who are authorized to decide as to the person who shall take possession of the effects of the deceased Mr. Robertson. He thinks they will not give possession to the son because of his minority, but that they will give it to you as having the substantial, tho' not the formal appointment to take care of all matters in which a citizen of the United states is interested. It is a better authority than M. Ruilon can shew, as I presume. You do not mention on what pretensions he has taken possession. I should therefore advise your application to the Amirauté, having no authority to act in it myself. I have the honour to be with much respect Sir your most obedient humble servt., TH: JEFFERSON

PrC (DLC).

To William Macarty

Sir   Paris Aug. 19. 1786.

On the receipt of your letter of the 7th. inst. I called on one of the Farmers general who is of my acquaintance, and asked from him explanations of the reasons for the low prices offered for tobacco. He said they considered themselves as bound to purchase the quantities directed by the order of Berny, and at the prices therein ordered, which quantities they apportioned among the ports according to their wants, allotting certain quantities to be bought weekly or monthly, that when greater quantities offered they thought themselves at liberty to buy them, at a lower price if the holder would take it, that this was done by a previous contract. I gave him an extract of the letter, and he promised to enquire into it, and to use his influence that justice should be done you.

If you made an express contract for the prices you mention, without doubt you will be held to them. If you did not make a contract, I think it as certain you will be entitled to the prices fixed by the government. Should they refuse justice I am told you may have redress by application to a court on the spot, or to a tribunal at Paris which takes cognisance of whatever relates to the farms. But I beleive also that the Committee, who proposed this regulation, are authorised to take cognisance of all infractions of it. As soon as I obtain an answer from the farmer general I will do myself the pleasure of communicating it to you. I am with much respect Sir your most obedient & most humble servt.,

Th: Jefferson

PrC (DLC).

ONE OF THE FARMERS GENERAL WHO IS OF MY ACQUAINTANCE: This may very well have been Chalut de Verin, with whom TJ had sometimes dined at the home of Chalut de Verin's brother, the Abbé Chalut (see the Abbés Arnoux and Chalut to TJ, 11 Nov. 1785).

From James Monroe

Dear Sir   New York Augt. 19. 1786.

My last advis'd you of the *progress*[1] *of Spanish negotiation. Until that time the reference of Jay's letter to a committee was,* I believe, the point at which *it rested;* but to enable you to form a satisfactory opinion *of the object of that letter I transcribe you only* operative *paragraph* in it. "*I take the liberty therefore of* sub-

[274]

mitting to the *consideration* of *Congress whether it might not be adviseable to appoint a committee with power to instruct and direct me on every point and subject relative to the proposed treaty with Spain."* You are to observe *his only ultimata were* respecting *the Mississippi and the boundaries; the committee*, consisting of *a member from Massachusetts, Pennsylvania*, and *myself, kept it about two months* and at length two of them *reported that they be discharged, the letter referred to^2 a committee of the whole and himself ordered to^2 attend.* It was agreed to with this alteration that *he attend Congress* to explain *the difficulties stated in his letter* and to lay *before them a state of the negotiation. He accordingly came and being aware objections would be made to^2 his entering into debate, produced a long written speech which he read by^3 virtue of his office* and which was *in substance as follows. France against our right of the navigation of the Mississippi and, in case of a variance with Spain upon that point, against us.* Well to be on good terms with *Spain* therefore on that account as well as to avail ourselves of her *influence in the councils* of *Portugal, the Italian States* and *the Barbary Powers, as also* in *those* of *France herself.* That *Great Britain would rejoice* to see *us at variance* with *Spain*, and therefore would *foment dissentions* between us that in case *this treaty failed, Spain, mortified and disappointed* in the eyes of *all Europe* would enter into engagements with *Britain* (or in resentment) *so as to exclude us from her ports.* For *these reasons* and fully to obtain the confidence and good wishes of *that power*, as also *her* good services in the lines abovesaid, he *thought it wise to forebear the use* of *the navigation of Mississippi* for *twenty-five years* or *thirty*, if necessary, as a condition to obtain at the same time the following *liberal articles* as the *basis* of a *commercial treaty.—*1. *All commercial regulations shall be reciprocal, Spanish merchants* in the *ports of* [America][4] and *American merchants* in those of *Spain* and *the Canaries* to have the *rights of native merchants* of *the* two *countries.* 2. To establish *consuls* in *their respective countries.* 3. *The bona fide manufactures and productions* of both parties, *tobacco excepted*, to *be admitted* in *the ports aforesaid* in *the vessels* of both parties upon the *same footing* as if they were their *own manufactures* and *productions*; and further that all *such duties* and *imposts* as *may mutually* be thought necessary to *lay* on them *by either party* shall be regulated on *principles of exact reciprocity* by a *tariff* to be form'd within one *year after the ratification of this treaty*, and in the mean time they shall severally *pay in the ports of each other*

19 AUGUST 1786

those of natives only. 4. Masts and *timber for the navy* to be *bought, provided* they be as *cheap* as in *other countries.* This was the amount of his communications as to *the project* which *he urged our adopting by all the arguments he could think of,* such as, *we cant obtain the use,* and therefore of no consequence; *we must now decide*; must terminate in accomodation, *war, or disgrace, the last the worst, the second unprepar'd for, the first*[5] *the preferable course*; that we should avail ourselves of *the moment or Britain would*; therefore no *time to lose* with others of the same kind. This *subject* hath, since the above *communication, engaged the attention of Congress* for *ten days past.* The *delegates of Massachusetts* who *are his instruments on the floor* moved *in committee* to *repeal his ultimata* with a view of suffring *him to proceed at pleasure,* and upon this point hath *the debate turn'd.* It hath been manifest *they have had throughout seven states and we five. They, to Pennsylvania inclusive,* and *Delaware* being *absent,* the *rest against him.* We deny *the right* in *seven states* to *alter* an *instruction* so as to make it *a new one* but they will proceed, *be that* as it may, *the treaty* in that event be form'd and soon *presented for ratification.* To prevent this we *have told them we would* give notice to *the secretary* of the incompetency of his *powers* as also to *the resident* of *Spain* to *justify Congress* in *refusing* to ratify, if they should chuse it. In this state it *remain'd* without any new *proposition* untill yesterday, being friday. *We stated however in the close of the day* that *we* would agree that *a treaty* be *form'd upon the following conditions. That exports be admitted thro the Mississippi, paying at New Orleans a duty* of *two* and *half per cent ad valorem to Spain,* to be carried thence in *Spanish American* and *French bottoms.* That *imports* be *prohibited* in that line. If this should be adopted *we propose* to *change the scene of negotiation* and to carry it to *Madrid,* to take it out of the present and put it into *yours* and *Adams's* hands. We fear however and with too much reason that this will fail. Nothing *could have been more unfortunate than even the* agitation of this subject. *It hath lessen'd the* ground on which we stood and *given Spain* hopes *she had no* reason to calculate on. What prospects to *the general interest* might be calculated on as resulting from the *deliberations of the convention* at *Annapolis* must be *diminished.* In short *the measure* strikes me as every way *highly injurious.* I am *sorry* to *inform you* that *our affairs* are *daily falling into a worse situation,* arising more from *the intrigues of designing men than any real defect in our system or distress of* our *affairs.* The same *party* who *advocate* this business have certainly *held* in this *city committees* for *dismembering the confederacy* and throwing *the states eastward the Hudson into* one *government*. As yet this business hath *not gone far* but that there should be a *party in its* favor, and *a man*, heretofore *so well respected* but in my opinion so little known, engag'd in it *is to me very alarming*. Congress have again requir'd money for the insuing year, including that part of the principal of the foreign loans that becomes due in that time. All the States except New York and Pena. have acceded to the impost to the acceptation of Congress, the former hath granted the revenues accruing from it but hath not made the collectors so amenable to Congress as the system requires and the other states have done; and Pena. hath granted the impost but suspended its operation untill all the states shall have granted the supplemental funds. A committee is appointed to attend the legislature of Pena. on this subject, and recommendation pass'd to the Executive of New York to convene the legislature to take the said system again into consideration. They meet in the usual term in the fall or commencment of the winter. They have pass'd an ordinance regulating the coin. I have been appriz'd of the arrival of the Encyclopedie at Baltimore upon the cover of a letter address'd from Mr. Mazzai, forwarded thence here, but have not heard in whose ship or under whose care it is except from your letter. I have since my last received yours of the 10. of May. Your late communications on the commercial subject have given great satisfaction to Congress. We hope the monopoly of our tobacco in hands of the farmers general will ultimately be abolish'd. The services of Monsr. La Fayette are acknowledg'd with gratitude by Congress. I shall leave this after the first of Octr. for Virginia, Fredricksburg. Believe me I have not relinquish'd the prospect of being your neighbour. The house for which I have requested a plan may possibly be erected near Monticello. To fix there and to have yourself in particular with what friends we may collect around for society is my chief object, or rather the only one which promises to me with the connection I have form'd real and substantial pleasure, if indeed by the name of pleasure it may be call'd. I inclose you some letters for yourself and Miss Patsy to whom be so kind as make my best respects. I am Dear [Sir] very affectionately yr. friend & servant,

JAS. MONROE

RC (DLC); written in part in code and decoded interlineally by Short. Noted in SJL as received 22 Sep. 1786. The full extent of Monroe's alarm over the Jay-Gardoqui negotiations and the nature of his maneuvers in Congress to CHANGE THE SCENE OF NEGOTIATION can best be appreciated in the light of two other letters written about this time, both perhaps the product of Monroe's urging—Madison to TJ, 12 Aug. 1786 and Otto to Vergennes, 23 Aug. 1786. Madison was in New York consulting Monroe about their land speculation in the Mohawk valley when Jay, on 3 Aug., so violently aroused the feelings of the Virginia and other delegates from the south with his LONG WRITTEN SPEECH proposing that the navigation of the Mississippi be yielded for a period of years. Monroe at once put him in possession of the facts and began to develop "the plan in conformity with the Idea" that he then suggested to Madison (Monroe to Madison, 30 Aug. 1786; Burnett, *Letters of Members*, VIII, No. 492). Madison departed from New York before the week was out, stopped in Princeton to discuss the alarming situation with President Witherspoon, and, undoubtedly as agreed upon with Monroe, set forth his own views in the letter to TJ. Monroe had for months entertained a fierce resentment toward Jay because of his conduct of the Spanish negotiations, and he genuinely feared that, having been captured by the northern interest, Jay was knowingly engaged in a course that would result in a DISMEMBERING [OF] THE CONFEDERACY. Madison was less violent, but he believed, with others, that Jay's proposal would be "fatal . . . to an augmentation of the federal authority"; it was also "particularly mortifying" to him as leader of the Virginia Assembly because he had endeavored to gain support of western members for federal measures by assuring them that Congress would deal effectively with their claim to a right to free navigation of the Mississippi (Madison to TJ, 12 Aug. 1786). Monroe, writing without benefit of code but so alarmed that he was willing to risk it, gave Gov. Henry a secret but full account of the critical situation, assuring him that the Virginia delegation had and would continue to "throw every possible obstacle in the way of the measure" since the opposition controlled the votes of seven states and would "go on under 7 states and risque the preservation of the confederacy on it." He did not, however, inform Henry of the nature of the obstacle he had in mind, and in his letters to Monroe he referred only guardedly to "the Idea I suggested to you" (Burnett, *Letters of Members*, VIII, Nos. 463-492). That idea was developed in speeches by Monroe, Carrington, and Grayson in the two weeks after Madison left New York, but it was disclosed fully only in the long letter to Vergennes that Otto finished hurriedly in the last few hours before the August packet sailed (same, Nos. 467, 472, 474, 480). A few of the southern leaders, Monroe doubtless at their head, called upon Otto, declared that the delegates of the five southern states had formed a league to break off the Jay-Gardoqui negotiations entirely, and confidentially informed him of their desire to obtain the good offices of Vergennes in promoting other proposals at Madrid. They laid stress upon the danger that an occlusion of the Mississippi by Spain might drive the western inhabitants into the arms of Great Britain, in which case it would be easy for that nation to trade Gibraltar for West Florida and thus bring the whole interior of North America under her dominance; they also claimed to have the support of seven states on their side and held forth the possibility of gaining two others. They declared: " 'Il n'y a que M. le Comte de Vergennes qui puisse nous procurer les avantages que nous desirons; nous en avons ecrit à M. Jefferson en lui recommandant le secret et nous voulons que notre traité se fasse par Votre cour ou qu'il ne se fasse pas du tout.' " Outlining to Otto the terms they proposed for the negotiation—including payment of 2½% ad valorem duty at New Orleans; re-exportation in French, American, and Spanish bottoms; prohibition of all importations; residence of French and American merchants at New Orleans; and participation by France in this commerce in compensation for her mediation—the Southern leaders asked him to communicate immediately with Vergennes. At the same time they urged him to maintain absolute secrecy vis-à-vis Gardoqui or anyone else. Remembering Vergennes' orders about the need for discretion in intervening in Spanish-American affairs, Otto assured the delegates that they could rely upon him to be discreet and promised to give Vergennes an account of their "conversation confidentielle." The delegates then informed Otto of their plans for the conduct of the negotiations: "Ils desirent de faire donner des pouvoirs à M. Jefferson de negocier le traité à Madrid, mais de lui prescrire de la manière la plus positive de se diriger entierement d'après Vos Conseils et de ne pas faire un pas sans Votre agrement. Ils ont deja sept Etats de leur coté et s'ils peuvent en gagner encore deux ce qui est très vraisemblable M. Jefferson recevra sur le champ ses instructions" (Otto to Vergennes, 23 Aug. 1786; Arch. Aff. Etr., Corr. Pol., E.-U., XXXII; Tr in DLC; translation in Burnett, *Letters of Members*, VIII, No. 475, note 3). On Friday, 18 Aug., the Virginia delegates IN THE CLOSE OF THE DAY introduced a motion that "the Chargé des Affaires at the court of Spain" be directed to state the desire of the United States to negotiate a treaty "upon the subject of the Mississippi" in accordance with certain terms, which were substantially the same as those set forth in Otto's report to Vergennes (same, No. 475). Over the weekend Monroe wrote the present letter and another to Washington asking his opinion about putting the negotiations for the treaty "in the hands of Mr. Jefferson and Mr. Adams" and sending "the former . . . to Madrid under the mediation of France for that purpose in the character of Envoy Extraordinary" (same, No. 479). On Monday the 21st the Virginia delegates moved that a minister or envoy be sent to Spain to propose that New Orleans be a free port for the produce of the upper Mississippi. On the 22d their motion was amended—perhaps by returning to the motion that the subject be opened in Madrid by Carmichael and that "2 Com'rs be added to him" to negotiate a commercial treaty—and Monroe, supported by Carrington, made "a long sp[eech]" in support of it (same, Nos. 475, 479, 481; see Monroe to TJ, 12 Oct. 1786). From the foregoing it is probable that the secret meeting with Otto took place as late as the 22d—he wrote only a few hours before the packet departed—when the Southern leaders, fearing defeat, threw a last desperate obstacle in Jay's path. The packet made a quick voyage, and Vergennes received Otto's letter on 22 Sep. 1786, the very day that TJ, confined to his quarters with a painful wrist, received the present letter and also Madison's of 12 Aug. Long before then, as Monroe reported to Madison, the Virginia motion was lost: "it now remains," he asked, "will Mr. Jay proceed? . . . I apprehend he will not" (30 Aug. 1786; Burnett, *Letters of Members*, VIII, No. 492). The complicated issue remained, but Jay had been given such a blow by the vigor and resourcefulness of Monroe's attack that, for the moment, the danger of disunion subsided, and attention became focussed upon the more hopeful discussions of the Annapolis Convention.

[1] This and subsequent words in italics are written in code and were decoded interlineally by Short, whose decoding has been corrected and verified by the Editors, employing Code No. 9. A number of errors made in encoding and decoding have been silently corrected; others are indicated below.

[2] Here and elsewhere Monroe wrote *707*, the symbol for "d," instead of *770*, the symbol for "to."

[3] Monroe erred in writing *461*, the symbol for "nine," and Short so decoded it; what Monroe intended to write was *1461*, the symbol for "by."

[4] The symbol for "America" was omitted, but obviously intended.

[5] Monroe wrote the symbol for "third" and Short so decoded it, a reading followed by Burnett, *Letters of Members*, VIII, No. 477, and others. This is an error, for Monroe, in accordance with Jay's statement, intended to write the symbol for "first." Jay's speech is printed in *Secret Journals of Congress*, IV, 44-57.

From Dangirard & De Vernon

[ca. 20 Aug. 1786]

Monsieur Jeffersonne peut il procurer a M.M. Dangirard et De Vernon une lettre de recommandation pour Mr. Barnister a qui çes M.M. écriroient alors sous les auspiçes de Monsieur L'ambassadeur.

M. Barnister pourroit il se charger de la procuration de çes M.M. et Monsieur Jeffersonne veut il bien nous faire passer la note de ses noms de baptême qualité et demeure.

21 AUGUST 1786

La somme principale duë aujourd'huy par les Etats unis annonçée s'elever a Dollars 4691. 7/90. est elle celle a laquelle s'est trouvée réduite La créançe de la société Thomas sur les dites Etats, et pareillement celle duë par le Tresor de la Virginie. Et N'y a t il rien a esperer audela des dites réductions de la part du Tresor des Etats unis et de celui de la Virginie.

Dans le cas où Monsieur L'ambassadeur ne croiroit pas que M. Barnister put se charger de la procuration de ces M.M. trouve t'il quelqu'inconvenient a la faire faire toujours au nom de M. Barnister avec pouvoir de substituer procureur afin que çes M.M. ne soient point obligés de la faire faire en blanc.

RC (MHi); endorsed by TJ: "Du Vernon."; without date and not recorded in SJL, but assigned to this date because it is a reply to TJ's letter to Dangirard & De Vernon of 17 Aug. and because TJ's letter to the same, 25 Aug., is a reply to the present letter.

To Edward Bridgen

Sir   Paris Aug. 21. 1786.

I must beg your pardon for being so long acknowleging the receipt of your favor of June 17. In the moment of my perusing it, it got misplaced so as to escape my recollection till yesterday. With respect to the book which accompanied it, I doubt whether I could with propriety offer it to the queen, and must therefore beg leave to decline it, however desirous I am of doing homage to the author, and of shewing how much I respect your application. If the author could write to the English minister to desire him to present it, I will deliver it to him or to any other person whom he shall think proper to direct. I have the honor to be with sentiments of the highest respect Sir, Your most obedt. & most humble Servt.,   Th: Jefferson

PrC (DLC); endorsed.

From the Georgia Delegates in Congress

Sir   New York August 21. 1786.

We have received your Letter wherein you mention that the Chevalier de Merceres, as Heir of the late General Oglethorp, claims land lying in Georgia which has been sold by virtue of an Act of the Legislature of that State.

[280]

We have in consequence made every enquiry respecting this matter, and can inform you with certainty that no land or any other property has been sold in that State as belonging to the late Genl. Oglethorp, nor can we hear of any Estate he had there.

Had the case been as you was informed, we should with pleasure have interested ourselves in forwarding your request, and have no doubt but it would have been immediately complied with by the Legislature of the State, as the memory of the late Genl. Oglethorp is much respected in that Country, and we are well assured that any just claim of the Chevalier de Merceres as his Heir would readily be admitted. We are Sir With great respect Your most Obed. & most hum Servts.,

Wm. Houstoun
W. Few
Delegates In Congress

RC (DLC); in clerk's hand, signed by Houstoun and Few. Tr (Arch. Aff. Etr., Corr. Pol., E.-U., XXXII). Tr (DLC). Noted in SJL as received 6 Dec. 1786.

From John Paul Jones

Sir *Paris Aug. 21st, 1786.*

I am much obliged by the letter you sent me from the Count de Vergennes to Baron de la Houze, with your own to the Baron de Blome. An indisposition, that has confined me close for three days, has prevented me from observing to you sooner, that Dr. Franklin, in the letter he wrote me from Havre, says, the offer made by the Baron de Waltersdorff was ten thousand pounds sterling. As you have misapprehended the amount of that offer, I take the liberty to return your letter to the Baron de Blome, praying you to alter the word five with your own hand. I should be glad to be favored with your opinion whether I ought to accept of any sum less than what was offered to Dr. Franklin? It is very improbable that a less sum will be offered by the Danish ministers; but supposing them less favorably disposed now than formerly, it is necessary for us to be determined beforehand.

I have the honor to be, &c.

MS not found. Text printed from Sherburne, *John Paul Jones*, p. 273. Noted in SJL as received 21 Aug. 1786. Enclosure: TJ to Blome, 18 Aug. 1786.

THE LETTER . . . FROM THE COUNT DE VERGENNES: a copy of the formal letter from Vergennes to Baron de la Houze, 15 Aug. 1786, asking the latter to receive Jones "favorably" and to assist him with "counsels" and "good offices" (printed in *Dipl. Corr.*, 1783-89, III, 697; also, Sherburne, *John Paul Jones*, p. 280). TJ was at Versailles on 15 Aug. and may have obtained this letter from Vergennes at that time; if so, he probably forwarded it immediately to Jones; no covering letter of transmittal has been found and none is recorded in SJL. Franklin, in THE LETTER . . . FROM HAVRE, 21 July 1785, said that the OFFER MADE BY THE BARON DE WALTERSDORFF "was to give us the sum of ten thousand pounds sterling as a compensation for having delivered up the prizes to the English. I did not accept it, conceiving it much too small a sum, they having been valued to me at fifty thousand pounds" (*Dipl. Corr.*, *1783-89*, III, 698). In DLC: TJ Papers, 4: 624-6, there is a PrC in Short's hand of a letter, signed Dechesaulx, French consul at Bergen, Norway, 26 Oct. 1779, reporting the transfer to the English of the two prizes captured by *The Alliance* and stating: "La valeur de ces deux prises que l'on vous enleve injustement est au moins de £40,000 sterling indépendamment des frais, et l'argent deboursé par le banquier M. Dankert DtKrohn, dont je vous remettrai le compte."

To John Paul Jones

Aug. 21. 1786.

Mr. Jefferson's compliments to Commodore Jones. His memory had deceived him as to the sum offered by the court of Denmark to Doctr. Franklin. He has accordingly corrected it in his letter to Baron Blome. He is of opinion, that according to the instructions of Congress, any sum, however small, must be accepted, which shall be offered by that court. He does not apprehend however they will offer less than formerly, on the contrary, he would hope more. He is glad to hear that Commodore Jones is getting better.

PrC (DLC).

To Dorcas Montgomery

MADAM   Paris Aug. 21. 1786.

Your letter of the 18th. inst. came to hand yesterday. I am sorry it is not in my power to direct the paiment of the bills therein inclosed, as that would probably be more agreeable to you. Doctr. Franklin was the last of the American commissioners in Europe authorized to pay those bills. This he did as long as he staid which was for six years after the date of the bills. Those not presented in that time have been obliged to be sent to America for paiment. I send the bills to Mr. Grand according to your desire.—I have letters and papers from America as late as the middle of June, but they contain little interesting. The death of Mrs. Wilson you have probably heard of. Mrs. Barclay and her family are well at St. Germains. Mr. Barclay was also well at Marocco the middle of June which is the date of my last letter from him. I have the honour to be, with sentiments of the highest respect Madam your most obedient & most humble servt., TH: JEFFERSON

PrC (ViWC); endorsed by TJ: "Mrs. Montgomery."
YOUR LETTER OF THE 18TH: Not found, but recorded in SJL as received 20 Aug. 1786. Mrs. Montgomery was a native of Philadelphia, a friend of the Bache family, and had gone to France in 1780 or 1781; in 1785 she informed Franklin that her son was in college at Abbeville (Mrs. Montgomery to Franklin, 23 June 1785, PPAP; see also Mrs. Montgomery to TJ, 16 May 1788). THE DEATH OF MRS. WILSON: Mrs. James Wilson had died on 14 Apr. 1786 (*Penna. Gazette*, 19 Apr. 1786).

To Mirabeau

[21 Aug. 1786]

'Il n'est pas un pays sur la terre, je n'en excepte pas les nouvelles republiques Americaines, ou il suffise à un homme de pratiquer les vertus sociales pour participer à tous les avantages de la societé.' Lettre de M. le comte de Mirabeau sur M. de Cagliostro pa. 48.

A person who esteems highly the writings and talents of the Count de Mirabeau, and his disposition to exert them for the good of mankind takes the liberty of inclosing him the original and a translation of an act of one of the legislatures of the American republics, with which the Count de Mirabeau was probably not acquainted when he wrote the above paragraph. It is part of that general reformation of their laws on which those republics have been occupied since the establishment of peace and independance among them. The Count de Mirabeau will perhaps be able on some occasion to avail mankind of this example of emancipating human reason.

PrC (DLC); without date, which has been assigned from internal evidence and an entry in SJL under this date; Ford, IV, 283, assigns the date 20 Aug., but gives no evidence. Enclosure: A printed copy (French and English text) of the Act for Establishing Religious Freedom (see Vol. 2: 550; Sowerby No. 2566).

From Robert Robertson

MOST HONORED SIR Havre de Grace 21st. August 1786.

I take the freedom to beg your Excellency's assistance. I had the misfortune to Loose my father commander of a very Large ship call'd LeCouteulx upon her passage from Norfolk to Havre de Grace. My father was one of the oldest Captains out of Philadelphia. If you have made any stay in that place, his name, his

Caracter and fortune, will be wellknown to Your Excellency. I am turnd out of the ship as if I was a common sailor by the merchant to whom the ship is consign'd. I cant get neither Victels, nor Wages, nay even one single part of my own Cloathes, because they were in the Same Trunk as those of my father, who had Tobacco and staves in the said ship on his account, and of which the Same merchant has taken possession without my Consent.

I thought Decency and the Respect to Such a good father requird that I should mourn for him. I have in consequence got a black mourning Suit, but being without money and that merchant refusing to supply me with some I cant pay its amount altho of no great consequence.—It is impossible to discribe to Your Excellency how I have been us'd by that merchant, who promisd me at first very fair things, but at last us'd me very ill. I have applyd to The american Agent Andrw. Limozin Esqr. who hath done much in the behalf of the american Nation, but he Saith, he is not properly entitled to assist me in Such Occasion. Therefore I am oblig'd to trouble your Excellency and to beg his assistance.

I remain with the highest Regard Your Excellency's Very humble & most Obedient servant, ROBERT ROBERTSON

RC (ViWC); endorsed. Noted in SJL as received 23 Aug. 1786.

To William Carmichael

SIR   Paris Aug. 22. 1786.[1]

Your favors of June 16. July 15. 18. and 31. I have the honour now to acknowlege. I have been for a month past so closely employed that it has been out of my power to do myself the pleasure sooner of writing to you on the several subjects they contain.— I formerly wrote you the reason why Mr. Grand had not paid your bills, that is to say, the want of a letter of advice. As to the notary's calling on me as inserted[2] in the protest, I do not remember that he did. Persons calling on me with demands on account of the U.S. I generally refer to Mr. Grand, with information that I have not anything to do with the monies of the United States. Mr. Grand, by refusing to make paiments without my order in many cases, has obliged me to interfere till I could obtain instructions to him from the treasury as to the manner in which he should govern himself. With respect to your bill I am thoroughly satisfied he had no reason for not paying it but the want of a letter of advice. Had there been one, I would have ordered the paiment, but this being a caution required between private individuals, it was less to be dispensed with in the case of the public. I believe I may venture to assure you that if you will always write a letter of advice with your bills, they will always be honoured. If the mode of doing business at Madrid would admit their being drawn at so many days sight, it would be better, because it would allow time to consult you if the letter of advice is miscarried. Your bills, tho' drawn at 60 days from the date have been kept up by your correspondent till they were become payable. The first notice of them has been the demand of paiment. However this is not essential nor any thing else except the letter of advice, not even the having money in our funds here, for this sometimes happens. I had your last bills, those of Mr. Dumas, and some other federal demands paid out of a sum of money lodged here by the state of Virginia for the purchase of arms. However we have at present three months supplies on hand.

I am to thank you for the map which I recieved by Mr. Randall. Mr. Barclay has sent from Cadiz some of the books purchased there. Should you at any time meet with any of the others named in my Catalogue, at reasonable prices, I will thank you to think of me. I paid Mr. Barclay's draught for those coming from Cadiz, and will answer yours, or find means of remitting the money to you for the map and such other books as you may be so good as to purchase for me.—I return you, according to your desire, O'Bryan's letter, having sent copies of that and the other papers you have forwarded me from time to time, as also extracts from your own letters on the Barbary affairs to Congress and to Mr. Adams. Mr. Adams left London about the 3d. or 4th. inst. for the Hague, to exchange ratifications of our treaty with Prussia with the Baron de Thulemeyer, and also to take leave of their High mightinesses, which he had not done before. I suppose by this time he is returned to London. It is inconceivable to me what difficulties can have arisen in our treaty with Portugal. However the delay of the signature indicates that there are such. You intimate the expediency of the mutual appointment of Consuls between Denmark and us. But our particular constitution occasions a difficulty. You know that a Consul is the creature of a convention altogether, that without this he must be unknown and his jurisdiction unacknoleged by the laws of the country in which he is placed. The will of the sovereign in most countries can give him a jurisdiction by a simple order. With us, the confederation admitting Congress to make treaties with foreign powers, they can by treaty or convention provide for the admission and jurisdiction of Consuls, and the Confederation and whatever is done under it being paramount to the laws of the states, this establishes the power of the Consuls. But without a convention, the laws of the states cannot take any notice of a Consul, nor permit him to exercise any jurisdiction. In the case of Temple the Consul from England therefore, Congress could only say he should have such powers as the law of nations and the laws of the states admitted. But none of the states having passed laws but for nations in alliance with us Temple can exercise no jurisdiction nor authority. You ask in what state is our treaty with Naples? Congress gave powers to Mr. A., Dr. F. and myself to form treaties of alliance and commerce with every nation in Europe with whom it could be supposed we should have an intercourse of any sort. These powers were to continue two years. We offered to treat with all those nations. Prussia made a treaty with us. Portugal we expect does the same. Tuscany exchanged propositions backwards and forwards with us, but before they could be compleated, our powers expired. The Emperor somewhat the same. But all the other nations made professions of friendship and said they supposed a commerce could be carried on without a treaty. Spain you know treats at New York. At present therefore we stand thus. France, the U. Netherlands, Sweden, and Prussia are connected by treaty; Spain and Portugal will probably be so. Perhaps the powers may be renewed for the Emperor and Tuscany, but as to every other nation of Europe, I am persuaded Congress will never offer a treaty. If any of them should desire one hereafter, I suppose they will make the first overtures. In fact, the exclusion of our vessels from the English and Spanish American possessions in America, and the modified reception of them in the French islands, may render regulations on our part necessary, which might be embarrassed by a multiplication of treaties with other nations. I think therefore that at present Congress would not wish to make any other treaties than those actually in agitation with Spain and Portugal. A Commercial Congress is to meet to prepare an article defining the extent of the powers over commerce which it may be expedient to give to the U.S. in Congress assembled. Every state has appointed deputies to meet for this purpose, except Maryland, which declined it because they thought the established Congress might propose an article. It is thought they will still appoint, but that at any rate they will accede to what shall be done. Congress being once invested with these powers, will be the less embarrassed in their system in proportion as their hands are less tied up by engagements with other powers.—While Mr. A., Dr. F. and myself were here together, it was made a question whether we should send agents to the Barbary powers, or receive their agents here. As these would expect to be supported we thought the former the more œconomical plan. An Agent from Algiers to Madrid must have great presents and be pompously supported. This induced us to send Mr. Lamb to Algiers. The possibility[3] that mal-adroitness in him may leave something yet practicable by Mr. Barclay may perhaps occasion a mission of this latter gentleman to Algiers. On this I expect to hear from Mr. Adams as soon as he returns from the Hague. As to myself I confess I expect nothing from Algiers, were we to send an Angel, without more money than we are authorised to give them.—We desired Mr. Lamb to repair to Congress that he might, by his information, aid them in their decisions. He answers us by resigning his commission, saying that his health will not permit him either to go to Congress or to come to us; yet he desires we will settle his accounts. It should seem then as if he meant to live at Alicant, Carthagene or somewhere there. Certainly we cannot go to him. If he has still money in your bankers' hands belonging to the U.S. and you judge from any circumstances that it ought to be stopped, be so good as to write to us on the subject, and in the mean time to stop it.—You observe that I do not write to you on foreign subjects. My reason has been that our letters are often opened; and I do not know that you have yet received the cypher Mr. Barclay was to leave with you. If you have not, be so good as to ask a copy of his, which being already in the hands of Mr. Jay, Mr. Adams, and myself, will enable you to write in cypher to any of us. Indeed I wish you could get the one from Mr. Lamb, which is a copy.—I have seen the Chevalier de Burgoyne two or three times, and was much pleased with him. He expressed great friendship for you. I have not yet seen Mr. Galvez, but shall surely pay all the attention I can to him, as well as to any other person you may be so kind as to recommend.

My letters and papers from America come down to the last week in June. They inform me that treaties are concluded with most of the Indian nations within our boundaries, that lands are purchased of them, and Hutchins, the surveyor for the U.S. gone out to lay them off. Straggling Indians however still molest our settlements. But it is neither in the general disposition, nor in the power of those tribes to do us any serious ill. All the states have agreed

22 AUGUST 1786

to the impost. But N.Y. has annexed such conditions as that it cannot be accepted. It is thought therefore they will grant it unconditionally. But a new difficulty has started up. Three or four of the states had coupled the grant of the impost with the grant of the supplementary funds asked by Congress at the same time, declaring that they should come into force only when all the states had granted both. One of these, Pennsylvania, refuses to let the impost come into being, alone. We are still to see whether they will persist in this. I inclose you the copy of an act of the Virginia assembly for religious freedom, which I have had translated here into French and Italian. It is one chapter only of the revised code of the laws of that state which their assembly began to pass at their last session and will finish at their next. Pennsylvania is proposing a reformation of their criminal law; N.York of their whole code. I send you also the article 'Etats Unis' of the Encyclopedie Methodique which came out two or three days ago only. They have printed some copies of this article by itself. The two first sections you will find bad; in the others are several errors; but there are a great number of details made on authentic materials, and to be relied on.—Remarkeable deaths in America are Genl. Cadwallader, Colo. Tilgham (Tench), Genl. McDougal, and Mrs. Wilson wife of the member of Congress. Mr. Telfair is Governor of Georgia, Collins of Rhode island and S. Huntington of Massachusets. I observe that S. Adams is not re-elected president of the senate of Massachusets. I know not the reason of this. Recollecting nothing else material, and having sufficiently fatigued you already, I shall conclude with assurances of the esteem and respect with which I have the honour to be Dear Sir your most obedient & most humble servant, TH: JEFFERSON

PrC (DLC). Enclosure: (1) O'Bryen to Carmichael, 11 July 1786. (2) Printed copy of the Act for Establishing Religious Freedom. (3) Démeunier's separately printed article on the United States (see under 22 June 1786).

[1] Here and elsewhere in this and other press copies by TJ, someone in the 19th century, probably employing a sharp steel pen, traced over the faint and fading lines. The motive was laudable, but the execution was often demonstrably faulty. When such retouching of a PrC raises doubt as to accuracy of the text the fact will be indicated. H. A. Washington was one of those who was responsible for retracing faded parts of press copies.

[2] This word retraced in the manner indicated in note 1; TJ undoubtedly wrote "asserted."

[3] TJ first wrote: "perhaps his maladroitness," &c., and then altered the phrase to read as above.

From John Richard

Sir 22 August 1786

I have the honour to inform your Excellency that the Packet from Lorient will sail without fail the 1st. September, for New York.

The Duties on Pot ash are very considerable and a mitigation would much encourage the Importation. On a parcell of 32 Casks sold lately at Rouen was paid

Droits de Romaine sur 10995 ℔. brut a 7s.6d & 10s p. ℔.	62	5
Octroy sur Id. a 22s & 10s p. Livre et acquit	190	10
	252	15

The value was £3800 so that the duties amount to near 84%. Spermaceti Candles are prohibited but as the Importation of Oil is favourd, it is to be wish'd that the Importation of Candles might be allowd. M. Barrett has a parcell arrivd at Havre, which can not be landed. I have the honour to be Respectfully Your Excellency's Most Obedient Servant, John Richard

RC (DLC); endorsed in part by TJ: "from Richard. Potash. cost in Boston 32/ lawful sold here 42^{lt}-10s duties of several kinds paiable here amounting to about 10. p. cent. for bleaching linen."

From Sarsfield

Rennes le 22 aout 1786 qui est mon adresse constante
de quelque lieu que J'ecrive

Je vous prie, Monsieur, D'avoir la bonté de faire passer cette lettre a M. Adams que la Gazette m'a appris Etre actuellement a La Haie avec une destination pour L'Espagne. Il faut que les ordres qu'il a recus aient ete bien pressans car Sa lettre alaquelle Je repons n'a pas plus de Six semaines de datte: Je souhaite qu'il retourne en angleterre, car Je n'irai Surement pas le Chercher a Madrid.

J'ay vu avec grand plaisir cette occasion de me rappeller a l'honneur de votre Souvenir. Je serois tres aise que mon Sejour dans cette Province put me mettre aportée De vous etre bon a quelque Chose ou a vos amis. Il est vray que Je vais passer 2 a 3 mois dans une Campagne fort retirée mais Je serai a Brest du 20 au 30 7bre Et Rennes dans le mois de novembre Et Je pourois peut etre quelque chose par lettres.

J'ay l'honneur d'Etre avec un tres Sincere attachemt. Monsieur Votre tres humble et tres obeist Servitr, SARSFIELD

RC (MHi); endorsed. Noted in SJL as received 27 Aug. 1786. Enclosure: Presumably a letter from Sarsfield to Adams, forwarded by TJ to Adams on 27 Aug.

From Jean Jacques Bérard & Cie.

SIR Lorient 23d. Augt. 1786.

We have received the letter your Excellency favoured us with the 9th. Insste. We did receive by the Packet boat Courier de l'Europe, Captn. Sionville, a Pipe of Madeira Wine shipp'd by Mr. Lewis and directed to us by Mr. Otto, his Majesty's consul General at New yorck, which he desired us to have forwarded to your Excellency. It has been effectuated, and shipped here on board the Brig Magnifique, Captn. Letellier, bound for Rouen, directed to Messrs. LeCouteulx & Co. merchants there, to whom we sent the advice and bill of loading for the same the 10th. July past, with order to make the further Expedition of that Pipe to your Excellency in Paris as soon as it would have reached to their Port.

We think that Ship has met with some retardment in her voyage otherwise Messrs. LeCouteu[lx] & Comp. of Rouen would have advised your Excellency of its arrival.

We shall Esteem ourselves very happy to have some occasion to be of any use to your Excellency and beg leave to Subscribe our Selves with great respect Sir Your most obedient and most humble Servants, J. J. BERARD & COMP.

RC (DLC); endorsed. Noted in SJL as received 27 Aug. 1786.

From Zachariah Loreilhe

SIR L'Orient august 23d. 1786

I beg leave to acquaint your Excellency that Mr. Thos. Barclay has Informed me that before he left Paris he had Contracted for arms to be delivered at Bordeaux about the month of September next for the use of the State of Virginia. Mr. Barclay's desires are that in case he should be prevented from attending the receiving and shipping of them himself that I should take the care of it myself, which I shall do with the greatest pleasure if your Excellency aproves of it. I do not know whether Mr. Barclay will be in france at that time, but if he was I doubt if he could attend on that business himself, therefore I would beg leave to observe, on a Supposition that you will have no objections to my attending on that business, that it would be necessary for me to be furnished with proper Instructions relative thereto, that I might correspond with the person that contracted with Mr. Barclay to be informed of the time they will be delivered a Bordeaux to the end that a Vesell may be provided to receive them on their arrival and thus avoid the very high expence of storage &c. &c. It would also be necessary that I should be made acquainted with the Nature of the Contract that I may be Enabled to Judge if the Conditions have been faithfully attended to. May I beg the favour of an answer on this Subjet.

I have the honour to be with great respect your Excellency Most obedt. & faithfull serv., Z: LOREILHE

RC (DLC); endorsed. Noted in SJL as received 27 Aug. 1786.

From William Stephens Smith

DR. SIR London August 23d. 1786.

I replyed fully to yours of the 9th. Ulto. on the 18th. of the same since which I have not had the pleasure of hearing from you. Mr. Dilley informs me the Books are shiped agreable to the inclosed Bill of Lading accompanied with the account ammounting to £25/14.0 sterg. I have also the honor of forwarding a Copy of a Letter received this morning from Mr. Barclay at Morocco of the 26th. of June. Mr. Adams not having returned from the Hague, I have forwarded a Copy to Mr. Jay by the way of Boston, and being convinced that observations on this subject, from me to you, are unnecessary, I shall only subscribe myself your Excellency's most Obedt. & very Humble Servt.,

W. S. SMITH

RC (MHi); endorsed. Noted in SJL as received 30 Aug. 1786. Enclosures: Bill of lading for "One Case of Printed Books," shipped by Charles Dilly on board the *Adventurer*, Captain Damon, dated 7 Aug. 1786 (MHi); bill for 50 copies of *History of South Carolina*, drawn to the credit of David Ramsay, for £25.14.0, dated 7 Aug. 1786 (MHi); Tr of Barclay to Commissioners, 26 June 1786.

From St. Victour & Bettinger

Monsieur   Paris le 24 aout 1786

Nous avons l'honneur de vous remettre cy joint copie du Certificat expedié par l'officier d'artillerie en residence a la Manufacture de Tulle en datte du 14 Juillet dernier pour 18 caisses contenant 540 Fusils a 27.ᵗᵗ 10 piece prix du Roy, compris les frais d'emballages et de transport montant a 14850.ᵗᵗ

Nous y joignons copie de la lettre de M. John Bondfield de Bordeaux en datte du 15 de ce mois, par laquelle il nous accuse la reception de l'expedition de 18 caisses contenant 540 fusils mentionnés au Certificat de M. Dubois Descordal: no.

Nous vous prions, Monsieur, de vouloir bien nous faire passer le montant de cette livraison; nous remettrons a la Personne qui en sera chargée, la quittance de M. Bettinger autorisé a cet effet ainsi que l'original du certificat qui prouve l'expedition et la lettre de M. John Bondfield qui constate la reception.

Nous avons l'honneur d'etre avec un tres respectueux attachement Monsieur Vos tres humble et tres obeissants Serviteurs,

BETTINGER ET COMPAGNIE

RC (Vi). Noted in SJL as received 26 Aug. 1786. Enclosures (Vi): (1) Certificate signed by Dubois Descordal, Tulle, 14 July 1786; endorsed by TJ: "Bettinger & St Vic 1786. Aug. 15. 14850ᵗᵗ Aug. 24. 14850 29700; endorsed by J. Latil: "I do Certify that the two within accounts amount to Livres 29700—for arms. Decemb. 9th. 1789." (2) Tr of a letter of Bondfield to Bettinger, Bordeaux, 15 Aug. 1786, acknowledging the receipt of cases of arms numbered 51 to 68. RC and MS of both enclosures are also in Vi.

To Pierre Dessin

Sir   Paris Aug. 24. 1786.

On the receipt of your letter I sent to the Douane to inquire for your other acquit à caution, and I this moment receive from thence the inclosed paper which they assure me will indemnify you. I should not have failed to have sent you both as soon as I arrived here, but the person who had brought the other articles said he was responsible for the return of the acquit à caution and would not trust to me to send it. I am Sir your most obedient and most humble servt.,   TH: JEFFERSON

PrC (DLC); endorsed. Enclosure not found.

To Lafayette

Dear Sir   Paris Aug. 24. 1786.

Your other friends here being so much better qualified to give you the transactions of this metropolis during your absence, it would be presumption in me to touch on them. I assume therefore the office of your correspondent for American affairs, in the discharge of which I may stand a chance to communicate to you details which you cannot get in the ordinary course of your correspondence, and which the interest you are so good as to take in our affairs will sometimes render agreeable to you. My letters and papers from America come down to the 16th. of July. The impost then wanted the accession of New York only; but another difficulty had started up. Three or four of the states had coupled together the impost and the Supplementary funds, so as that neither could take place till all the states had granted both. Pennsylvania was of this number, and tho' desired by Congress to suffer the impost to be established unconnected with the Supplementary funds, they have refused; saying that should the interest of the foreign debt get into a course of regular paiment separately from that of the domestic one, the other states will be the less ready to provide for the latter. Some of the other states have hereupon provided the supplementary funds. It remains to see whether it will be easiest to get all the states to do this, or to prevail on Pennsva. to recede. All the states have come into the Virginia proposition for a Commercial convention, the deputies of which are to agree on the form of an Article for giving to Congress the regulation of their commerce. Maryland alone has not named deputies, conceiving that Congress might as well propose the article. They are however for giving the power, and will therefore either nominate deputies to the Convention or accede to their measures. Massachusets and N. Hampshire have suspended their navigation acts. The English encroachments on the province of Maine become serious. They have seised vessels too on our coast of Passimaquaddy, thereby displaying a pretension to the exclusive jurisdiction of the bay of Fundi which separates Nova Scotia and Le Maine, and belongs as much to us as them.—The Spaniards have not yet relinquished the fort of the Natches, and our arrangements with them hang on a great obstacle, indispensable with us, and of which they are unjustly and unwisely tenacious. The Indians, both Northern and Southern within our boundaries have made peace, except the Creeks, who have made a formidable attack on

24 AUGUST 1786

Georgia. Scattering parties of the Northern Indians too have killed some people at Kentuckey. They are unacknowleged however by their nations. I observe that Sam. Adams is not elected president of the Senate. I cannot conjecture the reason of this. General Sullivan is made president of N. Hampshire. Generals Greene, McDougal and Williamson are dead.—There have been for some time 12. states present in Congress. By a letter from Mr. Barclay of July 16. I expect our peace with Marocco is signed. For this we are indebted to the honest offices of Spain. Your letter to some friend in Boston inclosing M. de Calonne's of Nov. 19. 1785. on the subject of whale oil is printed at length in our papers. Your name is to it, but not that of the person to whom addressed, nor any date. It will do you just service there: the only question is whether it may not disarm you here. I have as yet not heard a tittle from M. de Calonnes on the subject of our commerce. I have received for you from London Andrew's history of the war and Capper's travels. McIntosh's is not to be bought, the whole edition being exhausted. Our Madeira will be in Paris to-day or tomorrow. I shall be able to have a small copying press completed for you here in about three weeks. Must it wait your return or will you have it sent to you?—Adhering to my promise of saying nothing to you of what I know so imperfectly as the affairs of this country, I shall conclude with assurances of the sincere esteem and respect with which I have the honor to be Dear Sir your most obedient & most humble servant,
TH: JEFFERSON

PrC (DLC).

MY LETTERS . . . FROM AMERICA: On 22 Aug. TJ had received letters from McHenry (12 May), Madison (19 June), Thomson (8 July), Jay (14 July), and Monroe (16 July). YOUR LETTER TO SOME FRIEND IN BOSTON: This letter was printed in *Penna. Packet*, 24 June 1786; Gottschalk conjectures that it may have been one addressed to Samuel Breck dated 3 Dec. 1785 (*Lafayette, 1783-89*, p. 165, 245). At the very moment TJ was writing this gentle warning to Lafayette, John Jay was about to send out the circular that resulted in the publication of TJ's confidential dispatch, to his own acute embarrassment (see note to TJ to Jay, 27 May 1786). OUR MADEIRA: On 2 Aug. 1786 TJ made the following entry in his Account Book: "paid Fras. Lewis's bill of exchange on me for a pipe of Madeira 1075f10. Note one half is for the M. de la fayette."

To Robert Robertson

SIR   Paris Aug. 24. 1786.

Mr. Limozin having been so kind as to write to me on your subject, I consulted with an advocate here, and informed Mr. Limozin by letter of the 19th. inst. that an application from him

[294]

to the Admiralty was thought the most adviseable measure; and that the admiralty would probably put him into possession of your father's property. It will then be in his power to pay your reasonable expences. Matters of this kind belonging altogether to Mr. Barclay and the Consular department, I can only advise, having myself no authority to require any thing from the government.

I have the honour to be Sir Your most obedient humble servt.,

TH: JEFFERSON

PrC (DLC).

From Valade

[*Without place*, 24 *Aug.* 1786. Recorded in SJL as received 3 May 1787. Not found.]

From Hugon de Bassville

[25 Aug. 1786]

Monsieur De jéfferson aura La Bonté de faire demander à Mr. le Comte de Vergennes, des Lettres de recommandation pour les Ministres de france à La haye, et dans toutes les Cours de L'allemagne, pour Mrs. Morris de philadelphie, qui sont accompagnés par Mr. de Basseville de L'académie de Lyon.

Si Mr. de jéfferson à La bonté de nous donner des Lettres particulieres pour Rouen et le havre, nous les recevrons a paris hôtel d'orleans rüe de richelieu.

Quant au paquet de Lettres de Versailles ou autre qui arriverait apres notre départ Mr. de jefferson pourrait l'envoyer à *Mr. de Basseville poste restante à abbeville* jusqu'au 10 7bre.

RC (DLC); some figures on verso in TJ's hand. Not recorded in SJL; see TJ's reply, following.

To Hugon de Bassville

SIR   Paris Aug. 25. 1786.

I have now the honor to inclose to you a letter of introduction to Mr. Dumas, who is charged with the affairs of the United states at the Hague. I have therein desired him to present yourself and the two Mr. Morrises to the French ambassador, which, on reflection I thought was a more proper step for me, than that thro' the channel of M. de Vergennes. I inclined to it too the more readily, knowing that Mr. Dumas is particularly honoured with the esteem of the Ambassador of France at the Hague, and as it gave me an opportunity of stating myself your right to these attentions. I have the honour to be with sentiments of esteem & respect Sir Your most obedient & most humble servant,

TH: JEFFERSON

PrC (DLC); endorsed. Enclosure: TJ to Dumas, this date.

To Paul Bentalou

SIR   Paris Aug. 25. 1786.

I am honoured with your favour of the 9th. inst. and am to thank you for your care of the packet from Mr. McHenry, and congratulate yourself and Mrs. Bentalou on your safe arrival in France. I have made enquiries on the subject of the negro boy you have brought, and find that the laws of France give him freedom if he claims it, and that it will be difficult, if not impossible, to interrupt the course of the law. Nevertheless I have known an instance where a person bringing in a slave, and saying nothing about it, has not been disturbed in his possession. I think it will be easier in your case to pursue the same plan, as the boy is so young that it is not probable he will think of claiming freedom. This plan is the more adviseable, as an unsuccessful attempt to procure a dispensation from the law might produce orders which otherwise would not be thought of. Nevertheless should you find that you shall lose the possession of the boy unless protected in it, if you will be so good as to inform me of the facts, I will try whether a dispensation can be obtained. I would rather avoid asking this if you can, by any means, keep the boy without it. I have the honour to be with sentiments of much respect, Sir, your most obedient humble servant,

TH: JEFFERSON

PrC (DLC); endorsed.

TJ spoke on good authority when he said that he had known of A PERSON BRINGING IN A SLAVE, AND SAYING NOTHING ABOUT IT: that person was himself and the slave that he brought in was James Hemings, "one of his slaves, whom he subsequently had trained in Paris to become the cook at Monticello, and later freed" (Marie Kimball, *Jefferson: The Scene of Europe*, p. 3). According to French law, even TJ's status as a diplomat would not have permitted him to retain ownership of a slave on French soil if the issue had been raised. James was freed by TJ on 5 Feb. 1796 (Edwin M. Betts, ed., *Thomas Jefferson's Farm Book*, Princeton, 1953, p. 15).

To C. W. F. Dumas

Sir   Paris Aug. 25. 1786.

This will be delivered you by the two Mr. Morrises, and Mr. Basseville; the former are sons of our late financier which will be a sufficient voucher to you of their condition and that they are objects of just respect and attention. The latter is their tutor, a gentleman of letters, of reputation and of merit. I take the liberty of introducing them to your notice, and of asking your attentions to them during their stay at the Hague which will be short. Not having the honour of an acquaintance with the Ambassador of France, I will beg the favour of your presenting them to him. I am induced to ask this from a desire that our citizens may always consider it as their duty to pay their respects to the ambassadors and ministers of France, as to their own; and also from a wish that no opportunity may be lost of attaching to that country persons whose station, wealth and talents are likely to have influence in the government of the United states. I have the honor to be with sentiments of the most perfect respect, Sir, your most obedient & most humble servant,

Th: Jefferson

PrC (DLC); endorsed.

To G. K. van Hogendorp

Dear Sir   Paris Aug. 25. 1786.

Your favour of the 2d. instant has been duly received, and I employ the first moment which has been at my disposal to answer it. The author of the part of the new Encyclopedie which relates to Political oeconomy having asked of me materials for the article Etats-unis, and stated a great number of questions relative to them, I answered them as minutely and exactly as was in my power. He has from these compiled the greatest part of that article. I take the liberty of inclosing you one of these as it will give you all the details to which your letter leads, as exactly as it is in my power to furnish them. I can even refer you to the passages which answer your several questions.

What is the extent of the Congress's power in managing the interests of the U. States? The 6th. and 9th. articles of the Confederation define their powers. Those which it is thought they still need you will find indicated in this pamphlet pa. 29. 30. and in page 31.b. their powers of coercion?

Qu. Which are the expences of Congress?

Ans. pages 42.b. and 43.b.

Qu. Which the revenues?

Ans. As yet they have no standing revenues; they have asked standing revenues as shall be noted under a subsequent question. In the mean time they call annually for the sums necessary for the federal government. See pages 43. 44.

Qu. In which way do the particular states contribute to the general expences?

Ans. Congress once a year calculate the sum necessary the succeding year to pay the interest of their debt, and to defray the expences of the federal government. This sum they then apportion on the several states according to the table page 44.a. and the states thereon raise each it's part by such taxes as they think proper.

Qu. Are general duties, to be levied by Congress, still expected to be acquiesced to by the states?

Ans. See page 30.a. New York the only state which had not granted the impost of 5. per cent, has done it at a late session; but has reserved to herself the appointment of the collectors. Congress will not receive it upon that condition. It is beleived that New York will recede from the condition. Still a difficulty will remain. The impost of 5. per cent not being deemed sufficient to pay the interest of our whole debt foreign and domestic, Congress asked at the same time (that is in 1783) supplementary funds to make good the deficiency. Several of the states have not yet provided those supplementary funds. Some of those which have provided them have declared that the Impost and Supplementary fund shall commence only when all the states shall have granted both. Congress have desired those states to uncouple the grants, so that each may come into force separately as soon as it is given by all the states. Pennsylvania has declined this, saying that if the impost be granted alone, as that will do little more than pay the interest of the foreign debt, the other states will be less urgent to provide for the interest of the domestic debt. She wishes therefore to avail herself of the general desire to provide for foreign creditors in order to enforce a just attention to the domestic ones. The question is whether it will be more easy to prevail on Pennsylvania to recede from this condition or the other states to comply with it. The treaties with the Indians have experienced a greater delay than was expected. They are however completed, and the Surveyors are gone into that country to lay out the land in lots. As soon as some progress is made in this, the sale of lands will commence, and I have a firm faith that they will in short time absorb the whole of the certificates of the domestic debt.

The Philadelphia bank was incorporated by Congress. This is perhaps the only instance of their having done an act which they had no power to do. Necessity obliged them to give this institution the appearance of their countenance, because in that moment they were without any other resource for money. The legislature of Pennsylvania however passed an act of incorporation for the bank, and declared that the holders of stock should be responsible only to the amount of their stock. Lately that legislature has repealed their act. The consequence is that the bank is now altogether a private institution and every holder is liable for it's engagements in his whole property. This has had a curious effect. It has given those who deposit money in the bank a greater faith in it, while it has rendered the holders very discontented, as being more exposed to risk, and has induced many to sell out, so that I have heard (I know not how truly) that bank stock sells somewhat below par. It has been said $7\frac{1}{2}$ per cent; but as the publication was from the enemies of the bank, I do not give implicit faith to it.—With respect to the article (Etats unis) of the Encyclopedie now inclosed I am far from making myself responsible for the whole of the article. The two first sections are taken chiefly from the Abbé Raynal, and they are therefore wrong exactly in the same proportion. The other sections are generally right. Even in them however there is here and there an error. But on the whole it is good; and the only thing as yet printed which gives a just idea of the American constitutions. There will be another good work, a very good one, published here soon by a Mr. Mazzei who has been many years a resident of Virginia; is well informed, and possesses a masculine understanding. I should rather have said it will be published in Holland, for I believe it cannot be printed here.—I should be happy indeed in an opportunity of visiting Holland; but I know not when it will occur. In the mean time it would give me great pleasure to see you here. I think you would find both pleasure and use in such a trip. I feel a sincere interest in the fate of your country, and am disposed to wish well to either party only as I can see in their measures a tendency to bring on an amelioration of the condition of the people, an increase in the mass of happiness. But this is a subject for conversation. My paper warns me that it is time to assure you of the esteem & respect with which I have the honour to be Dear Sir your most obedient humble servant, TH: JEFFERSON

RC (Rijksarchief, The Hague, Hogendorp Papers). PrC (DLC). Noted in SJL under 26 Aug. but the date on the letter itself is 25 Aug. Enclosure: Démeunier's *Essai sur les Etats-Unis* (see under 22 June 1786).

This was the last letter in the exchange between TJ and Van Hogendorp, and they evidently did not meet when TJ was in Holland in 1788.

To De Vernon

ce 25me. Aout 1786.

Par les papiers que M. de Vernon a eu la bonté de me remettre il me semble que le tresor du Congrés lui devoit $4691\frac{7}{90}$ Dollars de principal, et 281. Dollars d'interet au fin de l'année passée; et que le tresor de l'etat de Virginie lui devoit 1823£.5s.4d. principal et 632£.16s. interet au meme jour. Ces sommes valent ensemble 70,315 livres tournois. Pour determiner la valeur du papier-monnoie on a cherché à quel prix, en argent blanc, ce papier-monnoie a eté acheté et vendu à chaque année et à chaque mois de l'an. On a fixé ladessus une table des vrais valeurs selon laquelle on paie tout le monde. La valeur des effets en papier de M. de Vernon ayant eté reglée par cette table, il n'y a aucun moyen de la changer.

M. Jefferson croit qu'il seroit mieux de laisser les lettres de procuration en blanc, et de prier M. Bannister d'y mettre le nom d'un procureur sur lequel on peut conter. Il se chargera de faire cette priere à M. Bannister et aussi pour qu'il continue d'y surveiller luimeme. M. Jefferson se chargera toujours de faire passer les lettres, instructions &c. de M. Vernon.

M. Jefferson a l'honneur de souhaiter le bon jour à M. de Vernon et de lui renouveller l'offre de ses services.

PrC (MoSHi); endorsed.

To St. John de Crèvecoeur

Dear Sir   Paris Aug. 26. 1786.

I have duly received the honour of your letter of the 20th. inst. Mr. Barclay has been long gone to Marocco, with which power he was by his last letter about signing a treaty of peace. This must apologize for your not having heard from him. If you will inform me to whom (in Paris) the 55^{lt}-16s can be paid I will order it to be paid.—I have letters and papers from America to July 16. They inform us of the deaths of Generals Greene, McDougal and Williamson, also that Genl. Sullivan is President of N. Hampshire. S.

Adams is no longer president of the Senate of Massachusets. I cannot conceive the reason of this. The Creeks have made a formidable invasion of Georgia. Some scattered Indians have done mischeif at Kentucke; they are however disavowed by their tribes. The Commercial Convention is likely to take effect and will prepare an article for giving Congress a power over our Commerce. John Collins is Governor of Rhode island, Huntingdon of Connecticut. N. Hampshire and Massachusets have suspended their navigation acts. This being every thing material of our American news, and your other friends here in a better situation to give you what relates to this country, I shall only add assurances of the esteem with which I have the honor to be Dear Sir your most obedient & most humble servt.,

TH: JEFFERSON

RC (Louis St. John de Crèvecoeur, Montesquieu-sur-Losse, France, 1947). PrC (DLC); endorsed.

YOUR LETTER OF THE 20TH: Not found, but recorded in SJL as received 25 Aug. 1786 and as written from Caen.

From V. & P. French & Nephew

DR. SIR   Bordeaux 26 August 1786

Mr. J. Banister Junr. of Petersbourg Virginia on his departure some time ago gave us a small bill dated the 27 Ulto. for £240 Tours. on you which we Kept by us untill now, that our occasions of making remittances to our Bankers Tourton & Ravel make it necessary and we pray you to accept and pay it in course. Mr. Banister thought convenient to ride to Paris for the benefit of his health making easy journeys, passing thro' Rochefort, La Rochelle, Nantes &c., Towns he seemed curious to see and we recommend him to our friends in each. He is a worthy young fellow meriting esteem wherever he goes. He has, tis hoped, ere now arrived safe in Paris, or will shortly and give us pleasure to hear. His letter on his leaving this we enclose you, also the copy of one we wrote to the Minister Mr. De Calonne concerning one of the american Traders to our address, the Contents of which is literally true, to which we beg leave to refer you. The minister made no reply to it, and if you will be so obliging to solicite one, the act will be meritorious in itself, serve your Country man and Confer obligation on Dr. Sir, Your obedt. humble Servts.,

V. & P. FRENCH & NEPHEW

RC (DLC); endorsed. Noted in SJL as received 30 Aug. 1786. Enclosures missing.

To John Adams

Dear Sir   Paris Aug. 27. 1786.

Your favour of July 31. was lately delivered me. The papers inform me you are at the Hague, and, incertain what stay you may make there, I send this by Mr. Voss who is returning to London by the way of Amsterdam. I inclose you the last letters from Mr. Barclay and Mr. Carmichael, by which we may hope our peace with Marocco is signed, thanks to the good offices of a nation which is honest, if it is not wise. This event with the naval cruises of Portugal will I hope quiet the Atlantic for us. I am informed by authority to be depended on, that insurance is made at Lorient, on American vessels sailing under their own flag, against every event, at the price usually paid for risks of the sea alone. Still however the most important of our marts, the Mediterranean, is shut. I wrote you a proposition to accept Mr. Barclay's offer of going to Algiers. I have no hope of it's making peace; but it may add to our information, abate the ardor of those pyrates against us, and shut the mouths of those who might impute our success at Marocco and failure at Algiers to a judicious appointment to the one place and an injudicious one at the other. Let me hear from you as soon as possible on this, and if you accede to it send me all the necessary papers ready signed. I inclose you the article 'Etats Unis' of one of the volumes of the Encyclopedie, lately published. The author, M. de Meusnier, was introduced to me by the D. de la Rochefoucault. He asked of me information on the subject of our states, and left with me a number of queries to answer. Knowing the importance of setting to rights a book so universally diffused and which will go down to late ages, I answered his queries as fully as I was able, went into a great many calculations for him, and offered to give further explanations where necessary. He then put his work into my hands. I read it, and was led by that into a still greater number of details by way of correcting what he had at first written, which was indeed a mass of errors and misconceptions from beginning to end. I returned him his work and my details; but he did not communicate it to me after he had corrected it. It has therefore come out with many errors which I would have advised him to correct, and the rather as he was very well disposed. He has still left in a great deal of the Abbé Raynal, that is to say a great deal of falsehood, and he has stated other things on bad information. I am sorry I had not another correction of it. He has paid me for my trouble, in the true coin of his country, most unmerciful compliment. This, with his other errors, I should surely have struck out had he sent me the work, as I expected, before it went to the press. I find in fact that he is happiest of whom the world sais least, good or bad.—I think if I had had a little more warning, my desire to see Holland, as well as to meet again Mrs. Adams and yourself, would have tempted me to take a flying trip there. I wish you may be tempted to take Paris in your return. You will find many very happy to see you here, and none more so than, Dear Sir, your friend and servant, TH: JEFFERSON

RC (MHi: AMT). PrC (DLC). Enclosures: (1) Barclay to Commissioners, 16 July 1786. (2) Carmichael to TJ, 17 Aug. 1786. (3) Démeunier's *Essai sur les Etats-Unis* (see under 22 June 1786).

From John Banister, Jr.

DEAR SIR			Nantes August 27th 1786

I arrived here some days since after a very leisurly ride along the sea coast which lies between this and Bordeaux, in which I have made it my business to acquire every information respecting the productions manufactures and commerce of this part of France. The objects of manufacture are numerous but they are in a state of infancy almost inconceivable. I am however of opinion that when our commerce has acquired a little more stability; we, particularly in Virginia, shall find a market for many of our raw materials at present in no estimation. This will lay open numberless resources to the possessors of lands in America of which they have at present no idea. Our wool and cotton, for instance, require little labor in cultivating, and are in no kind of estimation because no one has ever made trial of them in foreign markets. I mention these as instances where twenty others might be adduced of much more immediate consequence. Since my arrival here I have been again unwell which will lengthen my stay. Could my health permit I should relish greatly my fathers plan of my passing some time in Italy and I still have some hopes as I am certainly better than when I left England. Accept Dear Sir my warmest acknowlegment for your friendly offers of which I shall ever entertain the highest sense. I am with the greatest respect Yours,   JNO. BANISTER JUNR.

P.S. Be pleased to direct to the care of Mr. Carnes.

RC (DLC). Noted in SJL as received 30 Aug. 1786.

To Zachariah Loreilhe

Sir   Paris Aug. 27. 1786.

I am honoured with your letter of the 14th. instant on the subject of Mr. Barclay. I have received one from him of the 16th. of July. He expected to sign our treaty with Marocco in a few days. The interest which M. de Thevenard takes in whatever relates to us is a proof of his goodness; and I consider it as fortunate that the port, to which so great a proportion of the American commerce comes, should be under the care of a person so friendly disposed to our nation. It is good for both countries to cherish a connection commercial, political, and social.—I undertook to have the picture of Genl. Washington copied for M. Thevenard. I engaged Mr. Houdon to find a good hand to execute it and to superintend it himself. I have put off answering your letter two or three days that I might be enabled to inform M. de Thevenard that the picture is finished. I received this information myself last night, and therefore I will beg the favor of you to communicate it to him, and to ask him by what conveyance he would wish me to send it. By rolling it up we might get it into a smaller and lighter box, but a painting sustains some injury by being rolled, as it is apt to crack. His orders shall be implicitly followed, and I shall be happy to receive them as soon as convenient to him. I have the honour to be with much respect Sir your most obedient & most humble servant,

                                                                    Th: Jefferson

PrC (ViWC); endorsed.
The identity of the good hand employed by Houdon in copying Wright's portrait of Washington has not been established. See Vol. 7: xxvii, 133.

To Lucy Ludwell Paradise

Dear Madam   Paris Aug. 27. 1786.

I am honoured with your letter of the 15th. inst. by Mr. Voss. I concur with you in opinion that it is for Mr. Paradise's interest to go as soon as possible to America, and also to turn all his debts into one which may be to Mr. Gist or any other: upon condition that the person giving him this credit shall be satisfied to receive annually his interest in money and shall not require consignments of tobacco. This is the usual condition of the tobacco merchants. No [burthen][1] can be more oppressive to the mind or fortune, and long experience has proved to us that there never was an instance of a man's getting out of debt who was once in the hands of a tobacco merchant, and bound to consign his tobacco to him. It is the most delusive of all snares. The merchant feeds the inclination of his customer to be credited till he gets the burthen of debt so increased that he cannot throw it off at once. He then begins to give him less for his tobacco and ends with giving him what he pleases for it, which is always so little that let the demands of the customer for necessaries be reduced ever so low in order to get himself out of debt, the merchant lowers his price in the same proportion so as always to keep such a balance against his customer as will oblige him to continue his consignments of tobacco. Tobacco always sells better in Virginia than in the hands of a London merchant. The confidence which you have been pleased to place in me induces me to take the liberty of advising you to submit to any thing rather than to an obligation to ship your tobacco. A mortgage of property, the most usurious interest, or any thing else will be preferable to this. If Mr. Paradise can get no single money lender to pay his debts, perhaps those to whom he owes might be willing to wait on his placing in the hands of trustees in London whom they should approve, certain parts of his property, the profits of which would suffice to pay them within a reasonable time. Mr. Voss was in hopes of seeing Mr. Paradise here. I shall not fail to give him such information as my knowlege of the country to which he is going may render useful; nor of availing myself of every occasion of rendering him, yourself and family every service in my power, having the honour to be with sentiments of the most perfect esteem & respect, Madam, your most obedient & most humble servant,

TH: JEFFERSON

PrC (DLC); endorsed.
1 PrC faded; Ford, IV, 288, and Shepperson, *John Paradise and Lucy Ludwell*, p. 242, read, erroneously: "No other law. . . ."

To Thomas Mann Randolph, Jr.

DEAR SIR Paris Aug. 27. 1786.

I am honoured with your favour of the 16th. instant, and desirous, without delay, of manifesting my wishes to be useful to you, I shall venture to you some thoughts on the course of your studies which must be submitted to the better advice with which you are surrounded. A longer race through life may have enabled me to seise some truths which have not yet been presented to your

27 AUGUST 1786

observation. A more intimate knowlege of the country in which you are to live and of the circumstances in which you will be placed, may enable me to point your attention to the branches of science which will administer the most to your happiness there. The foundations which you have laid in languages and mathematics are proper for every superstructure. The former exercises our memory while that and no other faculty is yet matured, and prevents our acquiring habits of idleness; the latter gives exercise to our reason, as soon as that has acquired a certain degree of strength, and stores the mind with truths which are useful in other branches of science. At this moment then a second order of preparation is to commence. I shall propose to you that it be extensive, comprehending Astronomy, Natural philosophy (or Physics) Natural history, Anatomy, Botany and Chemistry. No inquisitive mind will be content to be ignorant of any one of these branches. But I would advise you to be contented with a course of lectures in most of them, without attempting to make yourself completely master of the whole. This is more than any genius, joined to any length of life is equal to. You will find among them some one study to which your mind will more particularly attach itself. This then I would pursue and propose to attain eminence in. Your own country furnishes the most aliment for Natural history, Botany and Physics, and as you express a fondness for the former you might make it your principal object, endeavouring however to make myself more acquainted with the two latter than with other branches likely to be less useful. In fact you will find botany offering it's charms to you at every step, during summer, and Physics in every season. All these branches of science will be better attained by attending courses of lectures in them; you are now in a place where the best courses upon earth are within your reach, and being delivered in your native language, you lose no part of their benefit. Such an opportunity you will never again have. I would therefore strongly press on you to fix no other limitation to your stay in Edinburgh, than your having got thro this whole circle. The omission of any one part of it will be an affliction and a loss to you as long as you live. Besides the comfort of knowlege, every science is auxiliary to every other. While you are attending these courses you can proceed by yourself in a regular series of historical reading. It would be a waste of time to attend a professor of this. It is to be acquired from books, and if you pursue it by yourself, you can accomodate it to your other reading so as to fill up those chasms of time not otherwise appropriated. There are portions of the day too when the mind should be eased. Particularly after dinner it should be applied to lighter occupations. History is of this kind. It exercises principally the memory. Reflection also indeed is necessary, but not generally in a laborious degree. To conduct yourself in this branch of science you have only to consider what aeras of it merit a general and what a particular attention, and in each aera also to distinguish between the countries the knowlege of whose history will be useful, and those where it suffices only to be not altogether ignorant. Having laid down your plan as to the branches of history you would pursue, the order of time will be your sufficient guide. After what you have read in Antient history, I should suppose Millot's digest would be useful and sufficient. The histories of Greece and Rome are worthy a good degree of attention. They should be read in the original authors. The transition from Antient to modern history will be best effected by reading Gibbons, then a general history of the principal states of Europe, but particular ones of England. Here too the original writers are to be preferred. Kennet published a considerable collection of these in 3. vols. folio but there are some others, not in his collection, well worth being read. After the history of England, that of America will claim your attention. Here too original authors, and not compilers, are best. An author who writes of his own times, or of times near his own, presents in his own ideas and manner the best picture of the moment of which he writes. History need not be hurried, but may give way to the other sciences; because history can be pursued after you shall have left your present situation, as well as while you remain in it.

When you shall have got thro' this second order of preparation, the study of the law is to be begun. This, like history, is to be acquired from books. All the aid you will want will be a catalogue of the books to be read, and the order in which they are to be read. It being absolutely indifferent in what place you carry on this reading, I should propose your doing it in France. The advantages of this will be that you will at the same time acquire the habit of speaking French which is the object of a year or two, you may be giving attention to such of the fine arts as your taste may lead you to, and you will be forming an acquaintance with the individuals and character of a nation with whom we must long remain in the closest intimacy, and to whom we are bound by the strong ties of gratitude and policy; a nation in short of the most amiable dispositions on earth, the whole mass of which is penetrated with an affection for us. You might, before your return to your own country, make a visit to Italy also.

27 AUGUST 1786

I should have performed the office of but half a friend were I to confine myself to the improvement of the mind only. Knowlege indeed is a desireable, a lovely possession, but I do not scruple to say that health is more so. It is of little consequence to store the mind with science if the body be permitted to become debilitated. If the body be feeble, the mind will not be strong. The sovereign invigorator of the body is exercise, and of all the exercises walking is best. A horse gives but a kind of half exercise, and a carriage is no better than a cradle. No one knows, till he tries, how easily a habit of walking is acquired. A person who never walked three miles will in the course of a month become able to walk 15. or 20. without fatigue. I have known some great walkers and had particular accounts of many more; and I never knew or heard of one who was not healthy and long lived. This species of exercise therefore is much to be advised. Should you be disposed to try it, as your health has been feeble, it will be necessary for you to begin with a little, and to increase it by degrees. For the same reason you must probably at first ascribe to it hours the most precious for study, I mean those about the middle of the day. But when you shall find yourself strong, you may venture to take your walks in the evening after the digestion of the dinner is pretty well over. This is making a composition between health and study. The latter would be too much interrupted were you to take from it the early hours of the day, and habit will soon render the evening's exercise as salutary as that of the morning. I speak this from my own experience, having, from an attachment to study, very early in life, made this arrangement of my time, having ever observed it, and still observing it, and always with perfect success. Not less than two hours a day should be devoted to exercise, and the weather should be little regarded. A person not sick will not be injured by getting wet. It is but taking a cold bath, which never gives a cold to any one. Brute animals are the most healthy, and they are exposed to all weather, and of men, those are healthiest who are the most exposed. The recipe of those two descriptions of beings is simple diet, exercise and the open air, be it's state what it will; and we may venture to say that this recipe will give health and vigor to every other description.—By this time I am sure you will think I have sermonized enough. I have given you indeed a lengthy lecture. I have been led through it by my zeal to serve you; if in the whole you find one useful counsel, that will be my reward and a sufficient one. Few persons in your own country have started from as advantageous ground as that whereon you will be placed. Nature and fortune have been liberal to you. Every thing honourable or profitable there is placed within your own reach, and will depend on your own efforts. If these are exerted with assiduity, and guided by unswerving honesty, your success is infallible: and that it may be as great as you wish is the sincere desire of, Dear Sir, your most affectionate humble servant, TH: JEFFERSON

P.S. Be so good as to present me affectionately to your brother and cousin.

RC (DLC). PrC (DLC).

From Madame de Lafayette

Lundy 28 [Aout 1786]

Mde. De La Fayette, desire bien vivement de se dedomager du plaisir dont La timidite de Melle. Jeffersson La prive pour demain, et elle a bien de Lempressement de se rendre a Linvitation de Monsieur Jeffersson. Elle sera charmee d'avoir lhonneur de faire connoissance avec Mr. trumbull, et d'admirer des ouvrages, du merite desquels elle a deja entendu parler, et dont Les sujets, et Lauteur, reunissent plus dune maniere, de L'interesser. Elle auroit bien du plaisir a Le recevoir ches elle, mais ce seroit pour Lui et pour Monsieur Jeffersson une importunite de venir La chercher, et elle repart demain pour Châville, d'asses bonne heure. Elle supplie donc Mr. Jeffersson de remettre a Jeudy, et elle ira Lui demander a dîner en famille puisqu'il veut bien Le Lui permettre. Mde. De tessé comme un peu americaine, et Mde. De tott comme artiste, demandent en grace a Monsieur Jeffersson de Leur amener, un jour Mr. trumbull dîner a Chaville. Elles se plaignent un peu de La severite de Mademoiselle Jeffersson, et offrent ainsi que Mde. De La fayette, Leur tendre hommage a monsieur Son pere.

Si ce pouvoit être mercredy que Monsieur Jeffersson vînt dîner avec Mr. trumbull a Chaville, Mde. De La fayette y seroit encore et elle sen feliciteroit de bien bon coeur.

RC (DLC); addressed to TJ, "rue neuve de Bery pret la grille de Chaillot."

To Zachariah Loreilhe

SIR   Paris Aug. 28. 1786.

Your favor of the 23d. came to hand yesterday. Mr. Barclay had contracted for the delivery of the arms for Virginia at the port of Bourdeaux, and, if I mistake not, had charged Mr. Bondfeild there with the receipt of them. On this presumption, as soon as I was informed of their arrival at Bourdeaux I desired [Mr.] Bondfeild to ship them from thence directly to Virginia. He has accordingly sent the first parcel of 1500. and has received 500 more to be forwarded immediately. I imagine this to be the least expense of course. I thank you however for your kind offers of service in this business, and shall not fail to avail the public of them whenever occasion shall offer. I had the honour of writing you yesterday on the subject of a picture for M. Thevenard, and have now that of being with the most perfect respect Sir Your most obedient & most humble servt., Th: Jefferson

PrC (MHi); endorsed.

From Achard Frères

[*Rouen, 29 Aug. 1786.* Recorded in SJL as received 2 Sep. 1786. Not found.]

From Lafayette

My dear Sir   Luneville August the 30th 1786

I Have been Honoured with your welcome favour of the 24th just as I Had set down at Luneville with an Intention to write to you, and give you an account of my Round about journey, which shall be at an End By the 20th of the Next Month.

In an official, and a private letter June the 16th, General Knox acknoledged the Receipt of our letters inclosing a Note from Count d'Estaing and Says He Has laid them Before Congress.

My intelligences from Mount Vernon are dated May the 10th and the 23d, and June the 8th and are Expressive of Hopes that Matters will soon take a favourable turn in the federal Constitution.

By a letter dated June the 16th, Mr. Jay says that the Spaniards do not Consider themselves as positively Engaged By Count de Florida Blanca's letter to me Respecting the limits. But as the Count Has Been pleased to approve the Whole tenor of it with His own Hand, in presence of Count de Montmorin, the Matter May Be easily Explained to Mr. Gardoqui—Besides Which the friendly Conduct of the Spanish Court with Respect to the Algerines Cannot fail to obtain the Gratitude of the United states, and at the same time to Convince the Spanish Envoy that far from Receding from the positive Engagement taken with me to Adopt the English limits His Catholic Majesty Means to Give further proof of His good dispositions.

General Parsons writes to me on His Return from the Banks of the Ohyo, and Gives me Very Good Reasons to Make New orleans a free, or a french port. I keep the Above Mentioned Papers for you But do not send them by post as they are too Voluminous.

I also keep for Your perusal some intelligences from England full of the Mischievous intentions of Great Britain Against the trade, the federal Union, the Navigation, and the peace of America. They are But a Confirmation of what we already know, and the Informant Advises Very spirited Measures to be taken Against that Haughty, and ill designing Nation.

In the Mean While that I send you my old Intelligences I most Heartily thank you for the later ones you Have Been pleased to impart. I Confess I am very partial to the domestic debt, and altho' Policy Urges the payement of the foreign one, altho' National Honour calls for it, I Cannot lament a few Months delay, provided it Gives the Means to attend to a debt very Sacred too, Very Urging, the domestic debt in which so many Valuable Men, Gallant Soldiers, patriotic Citizens Wholly depend for the Subsistence of their families.

In a late letter of a private Nature, Gnl. Knox Has Acquainted me with the Sad, and so much to Be lamented Account of the death of our friend General Greene. It is a Great loss for the United states to which He Has Been an Useful servant, and I May add a Great Ornament. I Have personally lost a friend, and Heartily Mourn for Him. Gnl. McDougall Had faithfully and ably served during the Revolution. He Had a friendship to me and when Ever Any of My Good Brother Soldiers are Mowed By the Sword of Death, it seems to me I feel the Blow. Poor Greene! His last letter was particularly affectionate to me, particularly Expressive of His Concern in the affairs of His Country.

I Request You will keep for me the letter to which You allude. It is possible, as there is no date, nor direction, that it Has Been Made by an Unfriendly Hand on purpose to set me up as a Man Blinded By partiality. I will see it at once, when we are together. I Have not Heard Any thing, as yet from M. le noir Respecting some favourable dispositions of the Ministry, which were to be digested before they are officially Announced.

I am sorry, My dear Sir, not to Have Been in Paris to Welcome Mr. Trumbul and offer Him what little Services May lay in My power. I Requested Mde. de tessé to invite Him to Chaville, Hoping she May Assist Him in His Visits to the french Artists, or french Cabinets. I Earnestly Hope He will not Be Gone Before the 20th of September. It will Be a Sincere Satisfaction for me to see a Gentleman who does Honour to America, whose family and person I Have a Great Regard for, and whose talents are Employed, in the very way I wanted. Be pleased to present My Compliments to Him and tell him I hope and wish to see Him before He goes. I think it would Be well to print Count de Florida Blanca's letter to me in American papers. Had it Been done sooner, the people would Have Conceived a Better opinion of the friendly dispositions of Spain in their Behalf, and Spain would Have found Herself more Engaged. Motives of personal delicacy Have prevented me from Recommending the Measure which would Have Had an air of Vanity. But I think it is not a Bad one and is a further proof of the Efforts of the french ambassador at that court in favour of America.

There is a Most Severe Criticism popping out Against our friend Chastelux, the author of which is M. de Warville Whom you will know. As you have probably Read the Book I Need not add any Comments.

Be so kind as to keep for me what you Have Been pleased to gather. I would also like to Have a large press, Besides the Small one.

I Have Been on the Road Very Agreably Employed in perusing Again your Notes on Virginia. While I Had the Pleasure Once more to Admire your Sentiments, Very Similar to mine, on the Spoken of dictator ship in the Year 1781, I Could not Help Regretting that I was not Enabled to give a public testamonie of my opinion on that Head, which would Have Conspicuously taken place in Case the dictatorship Had Been offered for the Campaign to the Commander of the Army in Your State, or in the less pleasing opportunity that would Have offered, Had an Unfortunate Capture at Charlotteville so strangely Situated me as to Make me the instrument to Call a Conventi[on].

Adieu, My dear Sir. Remember me Most Respectfully to Miss Jefferson. My Compliments wait on Mr. Short, with every Sentiment of affection and Respect I have the honour to be Yours,

LAFAYETTE

I Beg You will send the Inclosed to Clel. Smith By a safe Hand as I answer to some intelligences He gave me Respecting British and irish affairs.

RC (DLC); endorsed. Noted in SJL as received 3 Sept. 1786. Enclosure missing.

OUR LETTERS: See Lafayette to TJ under 6 Mch. 1786 and notes there; also JCC, XXX, 315, note. For FLORIDA BLANCA'S LETTER to Lafayette of 19 Feb. 1783 and Jay's comment thereon in his report to Congress of 17 Aug. 1786, see JCC, XXXI, 542-3. The INTELLIGENCES FROM ENGLAND may have been the same as those which TJ forwarded to Jay on 11 Aug. 1786. M. LE NOIR: Councillor of State in the Department of Finance, who was at this time corresponding with Lafayette about the negotiations in the American Committee which culminated in the policy set forth in Calonne's letter to TJ, 22 Oct. 1786 (Gottschalk, *Lafayette, 1783-89*, p. 249).

To Thomas Barclay

DEAR SIR Paris Aug. 31. 1786.

The incertainty of getting a letter to you while on the other side of the Mediterranean prevented my writing to you and the rather as no circumstance occurred which rendered it necessary for Mr. Adams and myself to make any change in our plan. The instructions given you having been jointly agreed on, and being, before this, executed, I have no matter, even now, for an official letter. I have written to Mr. Adams a proposition to avail ourselves of your kind offer to go to Algiers, where, as you will have heard before you receive this, Mr. Lambe's efforts have failed. Mr. Adams having gone to the Hague to exchange the ratifications of the Prussian treaty, and to take his leave of their high-mightinesses, which he had never yet done, will occasion a delay in the conveiance of my letter. I expect an answer however shortly and you shall immediately know what it is. In the mean time I think it so probable he will concur with me, that I would wish you to remain in Spain till you receive a definitive letter on the subject. Having, as I before mentioned, nothing official to write you, I will acknolege the receipt of your letters from Madrid Apr. 10. Cadiz May 23. and 26. Mogadore June 10. Marocco June 26.[1] and July 16 and proceed to give you such news as I imagine will be interesting to you. And first of all Mrs. Barclay and your family are in good health. I have American letters and papers to the 16th. of July. The impost is not yet given by N. York in an admissible form; when they shall have given it as they should do it will remain for the two or three states who have coupled together the impost and supplementary funds to uncouple them. Pennsylvania, one of these, has refused to do this, saying that if they permit the Impost to take effect alone, the other states seeing the foreign debts provided for, will be less likely to grant the supplementary funds on which the domestic debts are principally to rely. The Commercial convention proposed by Virginia

[313]

31 AUGUST 1786

takes place. It's object is to prepare an article for defining the powers which Congress shall have over our Commerce. Maryland, thinking Congress itself might as well propose this article, did not name members to the Convention, but as she was a friend to the main object she will probably either name members, or accede to what the Convention shall do. The purchases of Indian lands are completed, and treaties made with them. Some lawless individuals among them have committed hostilities at Kentuckey; but they are disavowed by their nations. The Creeks alone, as a nation, have commenced war in a more serious form. As they are between the Spaniards and us, it has been much believed that they were spirited on by the Spaniards. I have a different opinion of the wisdom of that nation. Because if the Spaniards really apprehend danger to their possessions from us at some future day, and from that apprehension might wish us annihilated, they must be sensible we cannot be annihilated. They have therefore but one or two plans to follow, either to prevent our growth, by making open and eternal war on us, or to cultivate our friendship and endeavor to bind us by ties of gratitude. The former plan is neither consistent with their spirit, nor could it possibly succeed. It would only hasten the events it would propose to prevent or retard. Conciliation then is the most probable plan; it is the most likely to have effect, and I think, from the conduct of that court towards us, it is the plan they have adopted. The instigating the Indians to make war on us therefore, is inconsistent with this plan. It would be at the same time impotent and irritating and, in my judgment, I clear them of it.—The Assembly of Pensylva. has refused to repeal the law which had taken away the charter of the bank. Promotions are Telfair Governor of Georgia, Collins of Rho. isld. S. Huntington of Connecticut and Genl. Sullivan of N. Hampshire. Remarkeable deaths are Generals Greene, McDougal and Williamson, Mrs. Wilson and Mrs. Clarkson, the former the wife of the member of Congress, the latter of the Gentleman who came to France in 1784.—To these we must add in Europe the death of the k. of Prussia. The council here have ordered the Farmers general, during their contract with Mr. Morris, to purchase over and above that, 12, or 15,000 hhds. of tobacco from individual merchants who shall bring it in French or American vessels, at 38.^{tt} 36.^{tt} and 34.^{tt} the quintal for 1st. 2d. and 3d. qualities.—Expecting shortly to address you again I close here with my compliments to Colo. Franks and assurances to yourself of the perfect esteem with which

[314]

1 SEPTEMBER 1786

I have the honour to be, Dear Sir, your most obedient humble servt.,

TH: JEFFERSON

PrC (DLC); altered in places by overwriting; see TJ to Carmichael, 22 Aug. 1786, note 1.

[1] The person who altered the PrC by overwriting erred by making the date 28 June: there was no letter of that date, for TJ on 16 July refers to Barclay's of 26 June as the last.

From William Stephens Smith

SIR   London Septr. 1st. 1786.

I have the honor of forwarding to your Excellency a Copy of a Letter I received this day from Mr. Barclay at Morrocco dated the 16th. of July ulto. I have sent a Copy to Mr. Jay and shall forward a duplicate by the next Vessel. I am your Excellency's most Obedt. Humble Servt.,   W. S. SMITH

RC (MHi): postmarked; addressed. Noted in SJL as received 23 Sep. 1786. Enclosure: Barclay to Commissioners, 16 July 1786.

Smith did, on this date, send A COPY TO MR. JAY, but the chief burden of his letter of transmittal was that of informing Jay about John Ledyard's plans: "During my tour on the Continent the last season, I formed an acquaintance with a Mr. Ledyard, a Gentleman from Connecticut, who accompanied Capt. Cook on his last Voyage to Kamtschkatka; he was about offering his services to the Empress of Russia, for exploring the western Coast of America, which it is the received opinion is not very distant from the back parts of Siberia and the place abovemention'd. He has been disappointed in his pursuits, notwithstanding in Paris, he was much countenanced and protected by Mr. Jefferson and the Marquis de Lafayette, in his negotiations with the Russian Ambassador &c. &c. After meeting with various impediments he gave up all thoughts of bringing the subject to that beneficial point of operation, which he at first expected, and in consequence of some allurements from an English nobleman at Paris, he came here with an intention of entering into the service of this Country for the purpose of visiting and exploring that Coast and Country.—Upon being acquainted with his pursuits, I endeavour'd to convince him, that it was his duty as an American Citizen, to exercise his talents and Industry for the immediate service of his own Country, and if the Project he was upon, could be beneficial to any, his Country upon every Principle was entitled to those services.—After a few conversations on the subject, he consented to move independent of this Court, and a Vessel being on the point of sailing for that Coast, after supplying himself with a few necessary articles for his Voyage, and march, he procured a Passage, with a promise from the Captain to land him on the Western Coast, from which he means to attempt a march thro' the Indian nations, to the back parts of the Atlantic States, for the purpose of examining the Country and its Inhabitants, and expects he will be able to make his way thro', possessed of such information of that Country and its produce, as will be of great advantage to ours. This is to be proved. It is a daring, wild attempt, and I have my doubts of his success. But finding him determined to pursue the subject, I thought he had better do it in the way he now is, than bind himself in any manner to this people. He embarked the last week *free and independent of the World*, pursuing his plan unimbarassed by Contract or obligation. If he succeeds, and in the Course of 2 or 3 years, should visit our Country by this amaizing Circuit, he may bring with him some interesting information, if he fails, and is never heard of, which I think most probable, there

[315]

is no harm done. He dies in an unknown Country, and if he composes himself in his last moments with this reflection, that his project was great, and the undertaking, what few men are capable of, it will, to his mind, smooth the passage. He is perfectly calculated for the attempt; he is robust and healthy, and has an immense passion to make some discoveries which will benifit society and insure him, agreable to his own expression, 'a small degree of honest fame.' The Vessel sails round Cape Horn, bound to Nootka sound in the Pacific ocean, situated on the northwest Coast of America in Lat. 40° No. At this place he intends to land, and begin his march nearly a south East course. It may not be improper for your Excellency to be acquainted with these Circumstances, and you are the best judge of the propriety of extending them further" (Smith to Jay, 1 Sep. 1786; DNA: PCC, No. 92, p. 136-9).

To Ezra Stiles

Sir
Paris Sep. 1. 1786.

I am honoured with your letter of May 8. That which you mention to have written in the winter preceding never came to hand. I return you my thanks for the communications relative to the Western country. When we reflect how long we have inhabited those parts of America which lie between the Alleghaney and the ocean, that no monument has ever been found in them which indicated the use of iron among it's aboriginal inhabitants, that they were as far advanced in arts, at least, as the inhabitants on the other side the Alleghaney, a good degree of infidelity may be excused as to the new discoveries which suppose regular fortifications of brick work to have been in use among the Indians on the waters of the Ohio. Intrenchments of earth they might indeed make; but brick is more difficult. The art of making it may have preceded the use of iron, but it would suppose a greater degree of industry than men in the hunter state usually possess. I should like to know whether General Parsons himself saw actual bricks among the remains of fortification. I suppose the settlement of our continent is of the most remote antiquity. The similitude between it's inhabitants and those of the Eastern parts of Asia renders it probable that ours are descended from them, or they from ours. The latter is my opinion, founded on this single fact. Among the red inhabitants of Asia there are but a few languages radically different. But among our Indians the number of languages is infinite which are so radically different as to exhibit at present no appearance of their having been derived from a common source. The time necessary for the generation of so many languages must be immense.—A countryman of yours, a Mr. Lediard who was with Capt. Cook on his last voiage, proposes either to go to Kamschatka, cross from thence to the Western side of America, and penetrate through the Continent to our side of it, or to go to Kentucke, and thence penetrate Westwardly to the South sea. He went from hence lately to London, where if he found a passage to Kamschatka or the Western coast of America he would avail himself of it; otherwise he proposed to return to our side of America to attempt that route. I think him well calculated for such an enterprize, and wish he may undertake it. Another countryman of yours, Mr. Trumbul, has paid us a visit here, and brought with him two pictures which are the admiration of the Connoisseurs. His natural talents for this art seem almost unparalleled. I send you the 5th. and 6th. vols. of the Bibliotheque physico-oeconomique, erroneously lettered as the 7th. and 8th. which are not yet come out. I inclose with them the article 'Etats unis' of the new Encyclopedie. This article is recently published, and a few copies have been printed separate. For this twelvemonth past little[1] new and excellent has appeared either in literature or the arts. An Abbé Rochon has applied the metal called platina to the telescope instead of the mixed metal of which the specula were formerly composed. It is insusceptible of rust, as gold is, and he thinks it's reflective power equal to that of the mixed metal. He has observed a very curious effect of the natural chrystals, and especially of those of Iceland; which is that lenses made of them have two distinct focuses, and present you the object distinctly at two different distances. This I have seen myself. A new method of copying has been invented here. I called on the inventor, and he presented me a plate of copper, a pen and ink. I wrote a note on the plate, and in about three quarters of an hour he brought me an hundred copies, as perfect as the imagination can conceive. Had I written my name, he could have put it to so many bonds, so that I should have acknoleged the signature to be my own. The copying of paintings in England is very inconceivable. Any number may be taken, which shall give you the true lineaments and colouring of the original without injuring that. This is so like creation, that had I not seen it, I should have doubted it.—The death of the K. of Prussia, which happened on the 17th. inst.[2] will probably employ the pens, if not the swords of politicians. We had exchanged the ratifications of our treaty with him. The articles of this which were intended to prevent or mitigate wars, by lessening their aliment, are so much applauded in Europe that I think the example will be followed. I have the honour to be with very sincere esteem, Dear Sir, your most obedt. humble servt.,   TH: JEFFERSON

RC (Lewis Gannett, New York, 1944); endorsed by Stiles: "Received Aug 11 1787." PrC (DLC).

Stiles' letter WRITTEN THE WINTER PRECEDING has not been found. William S. Smith's account of the plan of MR. LEDIARD, as reported to Jay, differs somewhat from TJ's; see note to Smith to TJ, preceding. For the NEW METHOD OF COPYING . . . INVENTED HERE, see the group of documents following. Stiles made an extended summary of TJ's letter in his diary, particularly in respect to the new method of copying (MS diary, CtY). On THE COPYING OF PAINTINGS IN ENGLAND, see *An Address to the Public, on the Polygraphic Art, or the Copying or Multiplying Pictures in Oil Colours, by a Chymical and Mechanical Process, the invention of Mr. Joseph Booth, Portrait Painter* (London, The Logographic Press, 1788); see also Dickinson, *Matthew Boulton*, p. 104-7; *Printing Review*, III (1933), 61, 131, 175.

[1] This word interlined in substitution for "nothing," deleted.
[2] TJ meant "ult."

Polytype and Other Methods of Printing

[1786]

I. INVITATION TO DAVID HARRIS PRINTED BY POLYTYPE
II. ESTIMATE FOR PRINTING *NOTES ON VIRGINIA* BY POLYTYPE
III. NOTES ON THE ABBE ROCHON'S METHOD OF ENGRAVING

EDITORIAL NOTE

New discoveries and inventions in the arts and sciences had a powerful appeal for Jefferson because of their promise of the improvement of society in general, but none had so immediate or so personal an impact as those affecting the multiplication of copies of the written word. The enthusiasm with which he presented to friends in America and Europe copying presses for making duplicates or triplicates of letters, memoranda, reports, and other writings that consumed so much clerical labor is one index of this interest. Another is the excitement with which he hailed the new method of printing of one François Hoffman, an Alsatian, whose "Imprimerie Polytype" was located in the rue Favart, "opposite the Rue Grétry" and across the street from the Théâtre des Italiens.

"Hoffman's method of engraving with ink was, I believe, known to you," Jefferson wrote to Franklin on 27 Jan. 1786 (see also TJ to Rittenhouse, 25 Jan. 1786; TJ to Madison, 8 Feb. 1786; TJ to Currie, 28 Jan. 1786; TJ to Stiles, 1 Sep. 1786). Franklin had indeed become acquainted as early as 1783 with what Jefferson considered "a pleasing method of engraving, such as would be useful to any gentleman." On 24 Apr. of that year Hoffman had demonstrated his method to Franklin and Franklin had written on one of Hoffman's plates: "A Wit's a Feather, and a chief is a Rod; an honest Man's the noblest work of God. Pope. Passy, April 24 1783. B.F." M. Adhemar, Curator, Cabinet des Estampes, Bibliothèque Nationale, discovered a copy of this early

[318]

EDITORIAL NOTE

specimen of polytype printing among other examples of Hoffman's work (Bibliothèque Nationale, Cabinet des Estampes, A d 11; see also a catalogue of an exhibit issued in 1951 by the Bibliothèque Nationale, *Diderot et l'Encyclopédie*, No. 560). According to a contemporary comment accompanying this specimen (and possibly written by the inventor himself) "aussitôt que son operation fut faite, il [Hoffman] lui donna a choisir ou de son original [sic], M. Francklin y fut trompé." How Franklin could have been at a loss about the identity of "son original" when that original necessarily was written on a metal plate is not made clear. Franklin was perhaps only being his usual diplomatic self, but Jefferson in his enthusiasm for the possibilities of the new invention stretched credibility even further in his account to Stiles: "I called on the inventor, and he presented me a plate of copper, a pen and ink. I wrote a note on the plate, and in about three quarters of an hour he brought me an hundred copies, as perfect as the imagination can conceive. Had I written my name, he could have put it to so many bonds, so that I should have acknoleged the signature to be my own" (TJ to Stiles, 1 Sep. 1786). In giving this account, and particularly in referring to the number of copies struck off, Jefferson may have furnished indirect evidence of what it was that he "wrote . . . on the plate."

It is very probable that the item produced in one hundred copies on this occasion was the form of dinner invitation presented here as Document I. Jefferson had described the process some months earlier in such a way as to indicate that he had already called upon the inventor and had witnessed an experiment with the new method: his letter to Madison of 8 Feb. 1786 was written the very day that Abbé Rochon reported on polytype printing to the Académie des Sciences. A hundred copies would not have been needed for purposes of demonstration, and if such had been struck off at the time of his first acquaintance with the invention, Jefferson's letters of January and February 1786 would no doubt have mentioned the fact. In December 1785 Hoffman and his son had obtained a royal license permitting them to operate their "Imprimerie Polytype." In February 1786 they began to publish the *Journal Polytype des Sciences et des Arts*, for which Jefferson immediately subscribed (Account Book, 12 Feb. 1786; Sowerby, No. 1096). During this same month Jefferson was assisting Lafayette in the preparation of materials for the American Committee and he may have suggested the use of Hoffman's method for duplicating copies of Lafayette's "Avis au Comité" (TJ to Lafayette, 20 Feb. 1786; Lafayette to TJ, 19 Mch. 1786). In view of this chronology, it is unlikely that the form of a dinner invitation was printed until after Jefferson had returned from England. With the arrival of Trumbull early in August and with the beginning of an acquaintance with the Cosways and the resultant social activity in which he became engaged, Jefferson may have thought it desirable to have such a printed or engraved invitation form as he was later to use in a variety of formats. This was precisely one of the ways in which the Hoffman method recommended itself as being "useful to any gentleman." Thus the invitation form may have been produced shortly before he wrote to Stiles on 1 Sep. The form here presented—evidently the only one that has survived—is dated 27 Sep. 1786, a fact which also supports the supposition.

Another allusion in the Stiles letter suggests an interesting possibility. If, as seems almost certain, the "hundred copies" did in fact represent a printing order and not a demonstration, why did Jefferson wait "about three quarters of an hour" for Hoffman to bring these copies? Could they have represented *both* a printing order and a demonstration? Jefferson's letter to Stiles mentions only that he called on the inventor, but this does not necessarily mean that others were not present. Nothing would have been more natural than that he should have taken Trumbull and the Cosways to see this new method of engraving during the time that they were all engaged in seeing the sights of Paris and were in the neighborhood of the Théâtre des Italiens. All were artists and both of the Cosways had practised engraving; the Hoffman method was therefore likely to be of considerable interest to them. This, of course, is a conjecture that might only be validated in the improbable event of the discovery of Trumbull's lost diary covering his stay in Paris, but it is both natural and likely that such a visit should have taken place. The circumstance of Jefferson's waiting three quarters of an hour makes this all the more probable, for it is certain that he could not have written on the plate in the rue Favart and have received the copies from Hoffman at the Hôtel de Langeac within forty-five minutes.

Perhaps in an effort to call attention to the new method of engraving, perhaps to encourage Hoffman, perhaps to make explicit the distinguishing feature of the method, Jefferson wrote the invitation form in his own hand and included in it the words "Imprim. Polyt." For what was really new in the Hoffman method was that it permitted anyone who could write, draw, or make diagrams to be his own engraver—that is, to multiply copies of writings, drawings, or other line images without having an engraver with a burin copy the result on a plate in reverse. "*Le Polytype*," declared the inventor, "*est l'Art de multiplier les originaux.*" Anything drawn or written on a metal plate with "une encre d'une composition particulière . . . peut se reproduire dans le même sens sur le papier un très-grand nombre de fois par les procédés de cet Art." Hoffman's public description concealed the secret but emphasized the difference between this and previous methods of engraving: "avec cette planche écrite dans le sens droit, nous obtenons, par une operation qui constitue notre secret, une planche gravée en creux dans le sens contraire, et . . . de cette planche, nous tirons des épreuves par les procédés connus de l'Imprimerie en Taille-douce. Comme dans cette opération le dessin lui-meme se reproduit sans l'intervention d'aucun Artiste, ces épreuves doivent être la parfaite image du dessin original, et l'on peut à juste titre les nommer des *dessins originaux multipliés*" (*Journal Polytype des Sciences et des Arts*, "Partie des Arts Utiles," p. 104-5).

But while calling the result multiplied original drawings (or writings) and while making much of the fact that the writing on the plate could be done by anyone without the intervention of an engraver, Hoffman at the same time felt called upon to dispel a rumor that had been spread abroad by some "personnes mal instruites." These misinformed persons had stated that this process of reproducing handwriting with the most exact fidelity might become dangerous by permitting the multiplication of signatures. Jefferson's enthusiastic letters to Madison and Stiles furnish a good example of the manner in which such a rumor might have been started. Hoffman therefore felt it necessary to say, in a footnote, that such fears were ill-founded for two reasons: (1) no one would be foolish enough to write promissory notes on copper-plates, and (2) the process of printing with intaglio plates could be carried out only with inks having an oil base, a fact which made it easy to verify the difference between such an engraving and handwriting by employing the ordinary test using nitric acid (same, p. 104-5). In brief, Hoffman thought himself justified in calling his productions "dessins originaux multipliés," but prudence suggested the necessary precaution of informing the public that the distinction between such "originals" and true originals could easily be established! Regardless of this nice dilemma, Hoffman had made it possible for an individual to do what Jefferson did in the case of this invitation form: to obtain a facsimile reproduction of handwriting without having an engraver make an intaglio plate which contained a copy of the handwriting in reverse. The method was simply that of taking a highly-polished copper-plate (Jefferson called it a brass plate in his letter to Madison) and having the writing or drawing or design traced on it in a special ink composed of an earthy substance ("avec une couleur terrestre"). Meanwhile an alloy of lead, tin, and bismuth had been heated. Just as this began to cool, the copper-plate was placed face down on it and subjected to heavy pressure. The raised lines drawn on the copper-plate were impressed into the warm metal sheet. This plate thus became an intaglio plate with the image in reverse ("une planche gravée en creux dans le sens contraire"). Obviously a plate made by such methods would lack the fineness of line and the sharp definition that could be achieved by an intaglio plate etched or incised with a burin and it would lack, too, the delicacy of line of handwriting with the use of ordinary pen and ink.

There is, therefore, no need of applying the nitric acid test that Hoffman recommended: in the invitation form and in the pages of Lafayette's "Avis au Comité" the difference between handwriting and polytype printing is discernible at a glance, the latter being uniform as to impression but varying from dullish-gray to black in color. In the ten pages of Jefferson's copy of the "Avis au Comité" there are considerable variations of impression. Since only one copy of the invitation form appears to have survived, no comparisons can be made, but the lines printed by polytype have the appearance of being much thicker and blunter than Jefferson's ordinary writing. He and Hoffman were not the only ones to make extravagant claims, however. Thiéry, *Guide des Amateurs*, I, 719, stated that polytype printing was neither printing nor engraving, but produced the same results with greater speed and less expense—indeed, that the French language was unable to provide terms sufficiently precise to describe this new art, so that the inventor had had to fall back on the Greek to obtain a name meaning "several originals" ("plusieurs originaux").

Hoffman had originally hoped to apply the invention primarily to the production and sale of drawings by artists, but the result was disappointing. He claimed that he was able to reproduce faithfully every design traced by an artist on a metallic plate, but that, working in such a medium, the artist was unable even with laborious effort to achieve the degree of perfection expected by the public. After making many attempts and employing the drawings of some of the best known artists, he gave up the effort to reproduce drawings ("Polytypage des Dessins") sometime around 1784 and began to apply the invention to the reproduction of manuscripts and writings ("Polytypage de l'écriture"). Hoffman saw possibilities in copying more faithfully the splendid manuscripts that existed before the invention of printing and of which printing itself was only an imitation. But this dream of a return to the manuscript also proved illusory, owing to the fact that printing had driven the medieval scribes out of existence and none could be found to copy their beautifully-shaped letters.

As Jefferson's invitation form and Lafayette's "Avis au Comité" prove, Hoffman had not given up the idea of applying the invention to the reproduction of handwriting, but by 1786 he had begun to concentrate his experiments on what was later to be called stereotype printing. Others had preceded Hoffman—Valleyrie in France and Ged in Scotland, for example—but his activities in this direction gave new impetus to the perfection of this form of printing. Both Hoffman and the inspectors who examined his method in September 1785, and on whose report he received a monopoly of the invention for fifteen years, claimed that the use of polytype to reproduce the printed page was the application of the same invention operating under the same principle as that used to reproduce drawings or handwriting ("un procédé qui tient absolument aux mêmes principes que celui qui repète les Dessins"). But the two processes had, in fact, only the alloy in common. Reproduction of drawings and handwriting could not be made unless drawn with Hoffman's special ink on a metal plate; a drawing or writing on paper would not suffice ("ne peut pas se répéter"). But "polytype" as applied to printing types meant the composition of a page (or part of a page) in movable types. This page was then impressed in a matrix of clay mixed with plaster, to which was added a gelatinous paste composed of gum syrup and potato starch. The alloy of lead, tin, and bismuth was then poured at the moment of cooling into the matrix which had been heated in order to prevent too sudden or unequal hardening. The result, as Jefferson somewhat inadequately described it in his letter to Madison of 8 Feb. 1786, was that Hoffman's "types for printing a whole page are all in one solid piece. An author therefore only prints a few copies of his work from time to time as they are called for. This saves the loss of printing more copies than may possibly be sold, and prevents an edition from being ever exhausted." Such advantages as these—together with the ease of storing stereotyped plates; the economy in printing classics, Bibles, and other works for which there was a steady demand over a long period of

EDITORIAL NOTE

time; the ability to ship plates from place to place for printing; and savings in type-composition—were all pointed out by Hoffman and other contemporaries and have since become commonplace (*Journal Polytype*, I, 105-14; A. G. Camus, *Histoire et Procédés du Polytypage et de la Stéréotypie*, Paris [1801], p. 45-51). Abbé Rochon, who described the Hoffman process to the Académie des Sciences on 8 Feb. 1786, considered the economy in paper to be "sans-doute, le plus précieux de tous ces avantages" (see illustration in this volume of a page printed by the polytype method, from DLC: TJ Papers, 19: 3261-2).

The inspectors who examined Hoffman's process were convinced that it could not produce the finished results that were already being achieved by established methods of printing from movable type. Hoffman challenged the skeptics by inserting two extra pages in the 29 Mch. 1786 issue of the *Journal Polytype* ("Partie des Arts Utiles"), the one printed by customary methods and the other by use of a polytype plate. These were numbered 1 and 2 and the readers were given the opportunity to identify each plate by its method. If anyone should be unable to distinguish them or should make the wrong choice, the Hoffmans declared, their error would be taken as compliment and as answer to critics; the solution appeared in the next number. The text of the page illustrated in this test was from a work then in progress at Polytype Imprimerie: Chenier's *Recherches historiques sur les Maures*, which was published in three volumes in 1787 entirely from polytype plates.

Such experiments aroused considerable interest in the circles frequented by Jefferson. Lavoisier, for example, published in the *Journal Polytype* for 27 Feb. 1786 ("Parties des Sciences") his epoch-making account of the large-scale synthesis of water (Denis I. Duveen, *Catalogue of Printed Works and Memorabilia of Antoine Laurent-Lavoisier* [New York, Grolier Club, 1952], No. 33). It now appears that Jefferson at one time considered the possibility of printing an edition in English of *Notes on Virginia* by this method, as evidenced by a price estimate obtained from Hoffman (see Document II). This estimate for printing Jefferson's work with "Planches polytypées rendues en toute proprieté" is revealing, but, since one of the advantages of stereotype printing was, as Jefferson stated, that "an author . . . only prints a few copies of his work . . . as they are called for," it is puzzling that he should have asked for an estimate for printing such a relatively large edition as fifteen hundred copies. It is not certain when Jefferson requested this estimate, but it must have been during the latter part of 1786. It was certainly before 1 Nov. 1787 when an arret was issued suppressing Hoffman's privilege. Nothing further came of this exploratory effort, though Jefferson continued to be interested in Hoffman's researches and in the efforts of Pierre Didot and others which resulted in the successful establishment of stereotype printing toward the end of the century.

Document III represents still another experimental process of printing which was neither polytype nor stereotype, but which seems to have had its origin in Benjamin Franklin's effort to reproduce handwriting directly or, as Abbé Rochon expressed it, "imprimer aussi vite qu'on écrit" (Camus, *Histoire*, p. 34). Before coming to France Franklin had carried on some experiments with this object in view. His method consisted in writing on a piece of paper with gummed ink which was then powdered with very fine sand or with sifted iron filings. This sheet of paper was then placed between two plates, of which the one in contact with the writing had to be of a soft metal such as copper, and the other of stone or iron. When the plates were run through a roller press, the hardened ink would be forced into the copper-plate, which thereupon became an intaglio plate for printing as many facsimiles of the writing as were needed ("autant d'exemplaires que la profondeur de la gravure le permettra"). Franklin described his attempt to Abbé Rochon, who evidently repeated the experiments, for he reported that the reproductions of handwriting obtained by this method —which was not essentially different from that of Hoffman—were not pleasing. In an effort to improve upon Franklin's device, he finally announced the method of engraving which Jefferson summarized in the notes here presented as Document III. While utilizing the ordinary practice of engraving a plate with nitric acid, Rochon's method, in its final stage, appears to be a crude forerunner of what today would be called offset printing. Abbé Rochon gave Franklin full credit for having stimulated him to achieve this result, declaring in fact that if it had not been for Franklin he would never have become interested in the art of engraving. Abbé Rochon's method was devised between 1777 when Franklin arrived in France and 1781 when he reported his own improvement upon it to the Académie des Sciences. The description of his method was published in Paris in 1783 in *Receuil de mémoires sur la mécanique et la physique*, p. 323-47. Abbé Rochon's intaglio plate produced a negative or reverse impression of the writing or design ("ces épreuves sont à contre-sens"), but by striking off as many copies as were desired and by interleaving these negative impressions with moistened sheets of fine paper while the ink was still fresh and by running the whole through a roller press, it was possible to obtain offset impressions at a single stroke that would be both positive and legible ("contre-épreuves très-propres et très-lisibles"). Rochon was well aware of the limitations of his method and frankly acknowledged that it would never equal ordinary engraving for general purposes, but he did claim that it would be very useful in cases where it was necessary to make a few copies quickly—as, for example, in the case of Lafayette's "Avis au Comité" (Camus, *Histoire*, p. 31-4). It is not known when Jefferson made his notes of Rochon's method: they could have been set down at any time after 1783, but were almost certainly made after his arrival in Paris in 1784 and were probably written in 1785 or 1786.

I. Invitation to David Harris

Mr. Jefferson begs the honour of Mrs. Harris's company to dinner on Sunday the 1st. of October

Imprim. Polyt.

Rep. S.V.P.

Sept.r 27h. 1786

RC (Mrs. H. Cavendish Darrell, Riderwood, Baltimore co., Md., 1945); addressed. The parts in polytype printing are in TJ's hand; the name, dates, and address are in the hand of William Short. Not recorded in SJL.

The Editors are indebted to Dr. J. Hall Pleasants, Baltimore, for his kindness in bringing this apparently unique specimen of polytype printing to their attention, as also for the identification of the recipient as David Harris (c. 1752-1809), a prominent merchant and banker of Baltimore.

II. Estimate for Printing *Notes on Virginia* by Polytype

L'Ouvrage de Monsieur Jefferson, pourra revenir en Composition en anglois, in Octavo, Tirage de Quinze Cents Exemplaires, Planches polytypeés rendues en toute proprieté, *Cinquante huit* livres la feuille, s'il n'y a pas de Nottes et *Soixante* livres s'il y en a. Le Papier est un objet Separé et le prix sera relatif à sa beauté.

MS (MHi); endorsed by TJ; "Printing Polytype printing." The handwriting seems to be the same as that employed in the polytype printing of Lafayette's "Avis au Comité" (see Lafayette to TJ, 19 Mch. 1786) and very probably is that of Hoffman himself. The document is not dated, but must have been written during the latter part of 1786 when TJ was contemplating an English edition of *Notes on Virginia*. See TJ to Stockdale, 8 Dec. 1786.

III. Notes on Abbé Rochon's Method

To prepare the plate of copper.
If it be new, sprinkle on it some blanc d'Espagne, and water, and

[325]

rub it, holding it over a chaffing dish. This is to absorb any grease which might have remained on the plate and which would injure the subsequent process.

If it be an old plate it must be rubbed.
1. with a crooked file, till the old letters are well effaced.
2. with pounce and water.
3. with [. . .]¹ charcoal and water.

To varnish the plate. Hold it over a chaffing dish of coals and ashes. Rub on it the varnish bag. Then dab it all over with the cotton puff or bag till the varnish is equal every where. Then hold it over a bougie to smoke it all over.

Write with a point as with a pen. Take care of the order of the pages. Make a border of engravers wax all round the writing. Pour in pure aq. fort. Let it stay on from   to 20' according to the strength of writing you desire. Pour off the aq. fort. and wipe the plate.⁽ᵃ⁾ Ink it with printer's ink and wipe it with a bit of linnen dipped in soap and water. Strike off a proof on thick paper properly moistened. Wipe your plate and ink it as before and strike off again, and so on till you have the number of proofs you desire. Then put a peice of fine paper properly moistened on the face of every proof, and pass the whole together thro' the press. The counterproofs will be written the direct way.

(a) Pour a little oil on the plate, and with a bit of linen wipe off all the varnish, to facilitate which it must be held over the chaffing dish. Rub the letters with oil and crumb of stale bread.

MS (DLC: TJ Papers, 234: 41866); entirely in TJ's hand; at head of text: "For engraving in the Abbe Rochon's method."
¹ Three or four words deleted and apparently written over, but now illegible.

From Paul Bentalou

SIR   Bayonne the 2d. of Sepber. 1786.

I should be wanting to the feelings of Gratitude with which I am Impressed, was I to Miss the first opportunity to acknowledge the Receipt of the Letter your Excellency Hath been Pleased, to Honour me with, the 25th Ulto and add my Respectfull Thanks, for the Informations you have been so Condescending as to give me on the Subject of Mrs. Bentalou's Negro Boy! She sympathizes Warmly with me, in Sentiments of the Deepest Impressions for your Kind Benevolence.

I should not have Disturbed your Excellency any further on any

2 SEPTEMBER 1786

Subject, Was it not for the Conviction in which I am, and every merchant in this free port is; that We are all Indebted to your Publick Character, for the Salutary Measures, Adopted by the Committee held at Berni the 24th of May Last, for the Revisal of the Farmers Generals Contract for Tobacco; we understood that the Report of said Committee, which you was pleased to Transmit here, Entitled Every American Merchant, to Claim of the farmers, the price Agreed by their Contract! In Consequence of which, I Requested My friends here Messrs. Pre. & Leon Batbedat, to offer the parcel I have Got on Hand, to their Agents in this port; but to Our Great surprise, they Made a Refusal of it! Saying that they had Orders to the Contrary. If we don't mistake the Interpretation of the Report, we Think we have a Right to Compel them; but it is Difficult for an Individual, to find out, in what Manner he is to proceed, in Order to have Justice Done him. Your Excellency's Oppinion on the Matter, would be a Direction, for any Other Citizen of the united-states, who May be Under My present predicament, as also for the Merchants of this an Other freeports, who may Receive Consignments from the United states.

The Brigantine *Heart-wig*; which Conveyance I had the honour to offer you by My Preceding! will sail by the Last of Next week; your silence on that subject, Induces Me to Think, that you had no Orders to Give me for that favourable Opportunity. In order Not to Take any more of your Excellency's Time, by any succeeding Letter I have the Honour to Inform you now, that I Intend to set off for Bordeaux, by the Last of Next week, where I Expect a ship, the Maryland, which in a short Time after her arrival, will sail again for Baltimore. Therefore, if it so happens, that you should have any Orders, to Intrust me with! be Pleased to honour me with them at my friend's there, Mr. Pre. Changeur, Rue Rousselle, and I will Think My self happy, and in the Line of My Duty, to fulfill with Zeal, what-ever Can be in My power, in My Little Capacity.

Having the Honour to subscribe My self Of your Excellency The Most Obedient & Most Humble Servant,

PAUL BENTALOU

RC (DLC); endorsed. Noted in SJL as received 9 Sep. 1786.

From André Limozin

MOST HONORED SIR   Havre de Grace 2nd Septembr 1786.
I am indebted to the two Letters your Excellency hath honored

2 SEPTEMBER 1786

me with the 17th and 19th ultimo. I have given hint of the Contents of the first to the young Robertson, who ever since he received that and which your Excellency wrote to him, promised to call again upon me, but never did it before this day to make again more and more complaints on Mr. Ruelon's behavior towards him. I am not all surprised about it, because such is the Case with almost all the American Ships which come here with Tobacco belonging to the Contract of Mr. Robt. Morris. He refuseth to allow no other Liquor to drink to the Sailors of the Ship Le Couteulx but water, when they are even working from Morning to night, and he hath got liberty from the Admiralty to lodge and confine in the gaol those who refuse to work because it is customary to give them a Small allowance of Spirit, when the owners dont give them Small Rum or Small Syder to drink and some of these poor People are confined, because they have no body whose protection they are intitled to claim for their defense. I am told that they are to remain there so long as the Ship sails, and after that they will have the liberty to look out for some other Ship. Such behavior is quite contrary to the instructions and orders sent to me by Mr. Thoms. Barclay, which I am not intitled to comply with. I am indeed very sory to see these Poor fellows vexed, and they think that I refuse to assist them in their distress. I had the misfortune to be yesterday on the way for some Mercantile business when your Second was brought to my House by Mr. Bassville. I did my self the honor to call this day at his Lodgings to have the honor to pay him my visit and likewise to both Mr. Robt. Morris's sons. But I was informed that they arrived in this Town the 31st August in the Evening and had left it this Morning very early towards 6 oClock. Thus I was very much disapointed to be Deprived of the pleasure to make their acquaintance and to shew them the most particular regard I pay to your recommendation.

Being this day very busy I have desired the young Robertson to call tomorrow upon me and I should look out to see how to procure him justice, for he complains sadly how ill he is used.

Having received no answer from your Excellency to my Letter of the 11th instt. I am afraid it did not reach you therefore take the freedom to send a Copy of it.

I remain with the highest regard Your Excellency's Most obedient & very Humble Servant,   ANDRE LIMOZIN

RC (MHi). Noted in SJL as received 4 Sep. 1786. Enclosure: Dupl of Limozin to TJ, 11 Aug. 1786.

THE FIRST . . . YOUR SECOND: Limozin has confused the "first" and "second" letters; on 17th TJ wrote about Bassville and Robert Morris' sons; on the 19th he wrote about Robertson's complaint. The latter was probably received first.

[328]

From John Paul Jones

Sir   Paris, Sept. 3d, 1786.

Since I had the honor of hearing from you last, my health has not permitted me to set out for Denmark. From the information I took at the Hotel of the Baron de Blome, I understood he was to arrive from the waters the 30th ult., so that I thought it better to wait till I could see him than to forward your letter. His servants arrived at the time that he was himself expected, and informed that the Baron had made a little jaunt to Geneva and would be at Paris the 15th of this month. I now have the honor to send you the second copy of the rolls, &c., that you lately forwarded to the Board of Treasury. There is a sure opportunity for London tomorrow at two o'clock. If you have any letters to send, or if you think fit to forward the papers respecting the prize-money, I will give them in charge to the person who will safely deliver them in London.

I am, Sir, with great esteem and respect, yours, &c.

MS not found; text printed from Sherburne, *John Paul Jones*, p. 273-4. Noted in SJL as received 3 Sep. 1786. Enclosures: Dupl of papers transmitted by TJ to Commissioners of Treasury, 12 Aug. 1786.

From William Carmichael

Dear Sir   Sn. Ildefonso 4th Septr. 1786

Since I had the honor to inform your Excellency of the Success of Mr. Barclays mission of which I was advised by his Excy. the Cte. de Florida Blanca, The Treaty of this Court with Algiers has been ratified by his Catholic Majesty. This ratification was signed the 27th. Ulto. The Ct. D'Expilly will set out for Algiers in a few weeks with the presents given on this occasion to the Dey and the principal Officers of the Regency. The ransom of the Spanish Prisoners is left for a distinct negotiation. There are also some arrangements to be taken with the Bey of Mascara or Constantine that demand patience and money.

I am assured by the Cts. de Florida Blanca and D'Expilly that until we have a treaty with the Port, It will answer no purpose to Attempt a Negotiation with Algiers.[1] On the 23d Ulto. The Dutch Ambassador signed a Memorial addressed by order of the States to this Court against the Navigation of the Vessels of the Phillippine company by the Cape of Good hope.

I beleive it was presented on Tuesday last. I have a copy of

4 SEPTEMBER 1786

it. The objections are founded on the 5th Article of the Treaty of Munster, confirmed by the 34th Article of the Treaty of Utrecht, and a memorial presented to the Court of G.B. by the Marquis de Pozo Bueno in name of Philip the Vth. the 26th of April 1724. The States of Holland seem to have been rather dilatory in taking up this business. The Philippine Company was established 14 Months ago and one of its vessels has actually been well received at the Cape of good Hope. I have some reason to beleive that ulterior propositions have just been sent to Mr. Gardoqui on the Subject of the Obstacles to our Treaty with this Country. But as I am kept in the Dark with respect to the progress of the Negotiation, I cannot without much impropriety attempt to speak to the Minister on this Subject. The plan proposed by the Court of Versailles for a reconciliation between this and that of Naples seems to encounter difficulties. Unless this reconciliation takes place, the Rupture will be Attended with much Eclat and perhaps Important consequences. By the best Intelligence I can procure, I think it highly probable that the Imperial Courts are preparing to execute their projects with the Ottoman Empire. I should deem it a particular favor if you would favor me with any Intelligence on this Subject. I also would be glad to know whether the Dutch have sollicited the Court of G. B. to support their remonstrances against the Navigation by the Rout abovementioned. The desire of Information on these Subjects may appear to you rather singular in my situation; But this Information will serve me as a Line to guide me to other Intelligence. I have been repeatedly asked here whether we are advanced in a negotiation with Naples? I do not know what to answer. I beg you to excuse the freedom with which I address you and beleive me With great respect & Esteem Your Excellencys Most Obedt Humble Sert, WM. CARMICHAEL

RC (DLC). Tr of an Extract (DNA: PCC, No. 87, i); in Short's hand. Tr of an Extract (DNA: PCC, No. 107). Noted in SJL as received 17 Sep. 1786. Enclosed in TJ to Jay, 26 Sep. 1786.

[1] TJ drew a line in RC at this point to indicate the end of the extract to be copied; Tr ends at this point. The omission is significant, especially when taken in context with other omissions in Carmichael's letter to TJ of 17 Aug. 1786. It must have become apparent to TJ by the time the present letter was received that Carmichael's persistent questioning about diplomatic events, his ready access to Floridablanca, and his standing in Madrid may have been due in part to information he was able to supply and wished to pass on to Spanish officials. TJ continued to have confidence in him, but ignored many of his requests for information; his failure to give replies to the indiscreet questioning in Carmichael's letters of 17 Aug. and 4 Sep. 1786 can scarcely have been due solely to the injury to his wrist (see TJ to Carmichael, 22 Sep., 26 Dec. 1786).

From Zachariah Loreilhe

Sir   L'Orient Septr. 4th. 1786

On the first Instant I received the letter your Excellency honoured me with the 27th. Ulto. on the Subject of a Picture for Mr. Thevenard which I Should have done myself the honour of answering the Same day but Mr. Thevenard being detained in his bed by a fitt of Sickness I could not comunicate to him the content of it untill the day following. I am desired by Mr. Thevenard to return you his thanks for your kind attention in procuring him the Picture of General Washington, and to request it of you that you will be so obliging as to order it to be put in a long Box properly conditioned that the Painting may not Sustain any Injury, and to forward it as Soon as possible by the Mesagerie.

Yesterdays post brought me your honoured letter of the 28th. past which Informs me that my Services will not be wanted at Bordeaux in the Shipping the arms for Virginia which Mr. Barclay had contracted for, Mr. Bondfield having been charged by your Excellency with that Commission. When Mr. Barclay wrote me from Magadore on this Business he did not intend that by employing me any additional expence Should be incured to the State of Virginia. I was to transact it at his desires without making any charges for my trouble or expence against Said State; when ever I Can be usefull to Congress or to any particular State I Shall think myself happy to devote my time and Service to them.

I Shall Set out for Bordeaux in a very few days, Some family affairs requiring my presence at Bergerac. If I can be of any Service to your Excellency at either place, I Shall think myself highly honoured by receiving your Commands, which Shou'd occasion offer I beg you will address them at Bergerac.

I have the honour to be with great respect your Excellency most humble & most obedient Servant,   Z: Loreilhe

RC (DLC); endorsed.

From Badon

[*Before 5 Sep. 1786.* Entry in sjl under this date reads: "Badon pere. Ancien capitaine d'infanterie à Montpellier." Not found.]

To John Banister, Jr.

Dear Sir   Paris Sep. 7. 1786.

Your favour of Aug. 27 came duly to hand. Since that I have received the inclosed letters for you. I am glad to hear you think yourself so much better as to open a prospect of your visiting Italy. Such a trip will certainly furnish you pleasing reflections through life. About the first of the next month I shall accompany the court to Fontainebleau and after a short stay there, make a tour to Lyons, Toulon, Marseille &c. the canal of Languedoc, Bourdeaux &c. to Paris. This will be more agreeable and more useful than lounging six weeks at Fontainebleau. Should your plans lead you to Paris I hope it will be before my departure. I have letters from America to the middle of July, but they give nothing interesting except the deaths of Generals Greene and McDougal. I should be glad to hear from you before I leave this place, as it will be a satisfaction to me to know your plan, and to render you any service I can, being with sincere esteem Dear Sir Your friend and servant,

Th: Jefferson

RC (DLC: Shippen Papers). PrC (DLC); endorsed. Enclosures: Several unidentified but "very satisfactory letters from America" (Banister to TJ, 16 Sep. 1786).

From —— to Madame d'Enville

paris ce 8 7bre 1786

Ma belle soeur, madame la Duchesse, vient de me mander que son jardinier attendroit le moment où vous seriez à Chaillot pour vous montrer en detail tout ce qui est dans son jardin. La maîtresse de la maison croit vous faire sa cour en ne paroissant pas. Elle m'assure que toutes les personnes que vous voudrez envoyer chez elle seront reçeues à toutes les heures. Recevez avec bonté les assurances de mon respect.

RC (MHi); endorsed by TJ: "lettre à Madame la duchesse Danville." The identity of the author has not been established; the handwriting seems to be feminine, but the author could have been a man. All that is certainly known is that the correspondent had a sister-in-law who had a house and garden in the neighborhood of Chaillot; it is evident, too, that the writer was an acquaintance of the Duchesse d'Enville and was on terms reflecting approximate equality of station. It is possible that the writer may have been the Comtesse de Marbeuf, who at this time owned a distinguished garden near Chaillot that was landscaped in the English manner (Thiéry, Guide des Amateurs, I, 42-3). The letter may have been handed to TJ when he called at Madame d'Enville's residence, the Hôtel de La Rochefoucauld. The fact that it was written at the time that TJ and Maria Cosway were making their tours of the environs of Paris suggests that he may have sought permission to see some gardens that interested them. On the 7th, for example, he and Maria Cosway had been to see the gardens at Marly, and on the 16th they went to the Désert de Retz, a garden some four miles from St. Germain (Marie Kimball, *Jefferson: The Scene of Europe*, p. 164-8).

From Pierre Dessin

Monsieur   Calais le 9 7bre. 1786.

Le duplicata de L'acquit à Caution que vous avez eû la bonté de m'Envoyer par L'honneur de votre Lettre du 24 août, Opére parfaitement bien ma décharge. En conséquence Je vous remercie de votre attention, et vous prie de vous en rapporter entierement à mes Soins pour toutes les Commissions dont Il vous plaira me charger.

Je suis avec un parfait dévouement, et le plus profond respect Monsieur Votre très humble et très obéissant serviteur,

                                                PIERRE DESSIN

RC (DLC); endorsed. Noted in SJL as received 13 Sep. 1786.

From Abbé Morellet

                             Samedi [9 Sep.? 1786]

J'ai recû Monsieur avant hier votre morceau. Je l'ai traduit hier et j'apprens ce matin ou plutot je vois en recevant des feuilles de l'imprimeur que l'endroit auquel ce changement est relatif est *tiré* ainsi que deux feuilles suivantes qu'on a *tirées* toutes à la fois parce qu'on en avoit accumulé plusieurs. Je ne vois plus de moyen d'employer ce que vous m'envoyés qu'en le mettant en postscriptum ou addition à la fin du volume. Je vous l'envoye en attendant, pour que vous jugies si j'ai bien saisi votre idée. J'ai été forcé aussi d'adoucir l'endroit des theologiens dans la crainte de nos censeurs qui me refuseroient la permission d'imprimer des choses trop claires. Vous etes bien heureux d'etre citoyen d'un pays libre et de pouvoir travailler vous même comme vous faites à etendre sa liberte. Ayes la bonté de me faire parvenir l'original anglois de l'acte de tolérance afin qu'il trouve sa place à l'article ou vous traités si bien ce sujet dont il me paroit que l'imprimeur s'approche beaucoup après m'avoir fait languir si longtems. Agrées mes très humbles respects et les sentimens que vous merités de tous ceux qui aiment et admirent les talens et les vertus employés à faire le bonheur des hommes.

RC (DLC); without signature or date; endorsed by TJ: "Morellet, l'Abbé de." The assigned date is conjectural and must be considered in connection with Morellet's letter printed under 11 Sep. 1786 which was in reply to TJ's "lettre du 9." This exchange must have taken place not long after that between Morellet and TJ of 1, 10, 11, and 12 Aug., and not too long after TJ's letter to St. Lambert of 8 Aug. 1786. See also TJ to Wythe, 13 Aug. 1786. Since the French edition of *Notes on Virginia* was published in 1786, TJ's "lettre du 9" could only have been written on the 9th of Sep., Oct., Nov., or Dec. The first of these possibilities seems to be most plausible in view of all the circumstances.

VOTRE MORCEAU: This (returned with the present letter) was an addition to TJ's ideas on the theory of the earth; see Morellet to TJ, under 11 Sep. 1786. If the conjectured date for the present letter is correct, TJ replied the same day, returning the additional matter to Morellet, who received it on his return from the country and responded on Monday the 11th.

Thomas Barclay to the American Commissioners, with Enclosure

GENTLEMEN   Tangier 10th. September 1786.

I am at present waiting for a fair wind to embark for Ceuta to avoid the quaranteen in Spain, and I embrace the Delay occasion'd by the Strong Easterly Winds that have prevail'd for some time, to reply to the Queries with which you honour'd me at parting. You put them respecting the Barbary States generally but as my business has been with the Emperor of Morocco only, I shall confine myself to what relates to his Dominions, and will state the answers in the order you put the Queries.

Commerce. The articles exported from this country are the Gums arabic, Sandrach and Senegal, Bees-wax, Copper in Blocks, Morocco Leather, Almonds, Dates, Figs and Walnuts, and Lemmons and Oranges might be had, was there wood in the Country to make Cases to pack them in. Great quantities of olive oil and oil of Argan (a fruit somewhat resembling an olive) are exported particularly to Marseilles, where it is used in making Soap. Mules are exported to Surinam and to other parts of America both on the Continent and among the Islands. Many of these animals passing from Constantina to Mogadore by land, being a journey of 1000 miles. Elephants teeth, Gold Dust and Ostrige feathers are brought from the Southward by the People who trade as far as to the River Nigre, and are sold and shipped at Mogadore the most Southerly Port in the Empire except Santa Cruis, from which last place the Emperor has forbid any foreign Trade to be pursued, and from Mogadore and Daralbeyda the export of wheat is very great. Morocco imports from Spain, Portugal, and Italy, several of the manufactures of these Countries, particularly Silks, Linnens, and woolen Cloths. With England and Holland the trade is more general and comprehends not only the same kind of Goods, but a variety of others such as Iron ware of various sorts, including tools made use of by Workmen, Tin ware, Steel, Iron in bars, Copper Utencils, Ship Chandlery, and Cordage for the repairing Dificiencies in merchant Vessels; Wine and Spirituous Liquors for the use of the Christians may be Imported from any part of the World Duty free, but the use is forbidden to the Mahometans; nor is there any thing in the Country sold by measure but Grain. They import Rice from the Levant which is of an inferior quality to the American Rice, and I believe a little of this article might answer and perhaps the Consumption increase, but this is conjecture for there is no answering for the taste of the Moors. Flour they have much cheaper than the price at which we coud supply them. They raise a good deal of Tobacco themselves, and some pretty good about Fez and Mequinez, none of it however is equal to our's but the Consumption of American tobacco wou'd be confin'd to the Europeans and consequently it wou'd not prove of much consequence. Furs are not used here and they want neither fish nor oil, provisions of all kinds are Cheap and their Seacoast furnishes them with abundance of fish for common uses. And their Ramadan or Lent does not permit the use of Fish more than of Flesh, being a strict abstinence from all kind of food or Drink for about sixteen hours of the twenty four. There is no demand for tar or turpentine. Each Merchant ship brings as much as is likely to be wanted for the voyage, and the Emperor is supply'd from the Baltic. Ship timber wou'd certainly be a most agreeable object to the Emperor, but he is the only person in his Dominions who wou'd purchase it, and the price wou'd be made by himself, he was anxious to know whether we had that article in America. Ready built Ships, that is, Frigates properly fitted out for sea and arm'd, wou'd prove the most acceptable article that cou'd be sent to him, but his making a purchase of any wou'd depend on the opinion he had of the value. He some time ago encouraged the building of one at Genoa and when she arrived at one of his Ports, He rejected her on account of the price.

 The Duties of Goods imported with a few exceptions is a tenth part of the Goods. Foreign Hides pay 3 Dollars and Iron and Steel four Dollars p. quintal. Cochineal and Alkermes are monopolized by the Emperor, and sold at a great advance in the price. The former is used in Dying the Morocco Skins and the latter in Dying the caps such as the soldiers and many of the inhabitants wear.

10 SEPTEMBER 1786

Ostrige feathers are a monopoly in the hands of a Jew at Mogadore without whose permission none can be exported. Offences committed against the interest of the Revenue are punish'd by fine impos'd by the Emperor sometimes with great severity, never with less than the crime deserves. All countries pay the same Duties but the King will sometimes favor an Individual by the remission of part of the ordinary Duties in return for some service, or as a mark of his approbation. The Moors are not their own carriers, nor is there any trading Vessels under the Colours of the Emperor. From this short state it will appear that few of the articles produced in Morocco are wanted in our parts of America, nor cou'd any thing manufactur'd here find a sale there except a little Morocco leather, which is very fine and good and the consumption of it in the Empire almost incredible. They make some Gold and Silk thread at Fez and in various parts of the Country coarse and fine stuff for Alhaigues, a good many Carpets, some coarse Linnen and a Great many red woolen Caps, and these articles I think compose the whole of their manufactures, which from the unskilfulness of the people who work at them, the Leather excepted, are too Dear for Exportation. Still this Country holds out objects to the Americans, sufficient to make a treaty of Peace and commerce a matter of consequence. Our Trade to the Mediterranean is render'd much the securer for it, and it affords us Ports where our ships may rest if we shou'd be engaged in a European War, or in one with the other Barbary States. Our Vessels will certainly become the Carriers of Wheat from Morocco to Spain, Portugal and Italy, and may find Employment at times when the navigation of our own country is stop'd by the winter Season, and we shall resume our old mule trade from Barbary to Surinam and possibly to some of the West India Islands. With respect to the prices of the exports of this country I will add a list of them together with one of the Duties.

Ports. I will enlarge a little on this subject by giving you a General Idea, not only of the best ports in the Empire, but of all that are of any consequence omitting Waladia Azamoz and some others which, in no Degree, in my opinion, deserve to be ranked in the number. I will begin with the most Southerly which is the only one of them which I have not seen.

Santa Cruz. Is the only Seaport in Sus, and is situated about Ninety miles to the Southward of Mogadore, and six from the western extremity of Mount Atlas, being between the end of that mountain and the sea, from which it is distant half a mile. It is placed on the declivity of a Hill and cannot be injur'd by any

10 SEPTEMBER 1786

shipping. There are no Fortifications nor any Guns mounted except two for signals. The Road for Vessels is open but the anchoring good, being a hard sandy Bottom, and the depth of water so gradual that ships may anchor in such as suits them best. There are about Two Thousand Houses in the Town and the Trade was very considerable until the Emperor order'd the Port to be shut up. It was the mart for all the Commodities of Tafila and Suz, and is the thoroughfare through which the Inhabitants of the Sea Coast pass to those Kingdoms, or to the Sahara. The trade is now remov'd to

Mogadore. A Town built by order of the present Emperor containing two thousand Houses and Eleven thousand Inhabitants as appears by an account taken previous to a Distribution of Corn being made a few months ago by order of the Emperor. About a mile from the Shore runs a tongue of Land called the Island of Mogadore, and between the Land and the Island the Ships anchor and may pass in safety if they draw no more than fifteen feet water. Some say sixteen feet. The Island proves a considerable Shelter for them, but a strong southerly or southwest wind incommodes them much, occasioning a swell in the Channell which is sometimes dangerous. The Bottom is hard and rocky and it is necessary to put Buoys to the cables to prevent them from Cutting. The Town is defended by Two Batteries, one of 9 Iron and 33 Brass cannon, 20 of which are fine Spanish Guns left at Gibraltar, in the last seige, the other of either five or six Iron guns and 20 Brass, and 33 more may be mounted. On a rock to the Northward of the Town is a Battery of ten guns, and on the main Land to the southward, one of 16. Another for ten Guns is now building and on the Island are five little forts of five Guns each. The Moors consider Mogadore as a strong place though some people think that all the Batteries being of Stone is a great disadvantage. Many of the Guns, all of which are about eighteen pound cannon, are yet unprovided with carriages. But the Town being a place much esteem'd by the Emperor, He is doing every thing in his Power to strengthen and improve it. The number of Guns actually mounted is 118 or 119.

Safia. This town is situated on the side of a Hill, about 2 miles from the southerly point of Cape Cantin. It was once a place of importance, but is now decaying fast, and at present the inhabitants are interdicted from all foreign trade. The anchoring ground is very good in water which varies in depth from 25 to 40 fathoms, but there is little Shelter (indeed almost none) and if it blows hard, as it sometimes do's in winter, ships must put out to sea for security. The Principal fortification is founded on a Rock, and capable of

10 SEPTEMBER 1786

mounting a Great number of Cannon, there are three iron and five Brass Guns mounted of about 18 pound Shot. The Brass Guns were made at Constantinople and ten or twelve small Guns lye unmounted. It is a place of little Strength as it now stands, and is reduced from 4000 Houses which it is said to have contain'd to about eight hundred.

Masagan. Was one of the strongest places in Barbary, when in the hands of the Portuguese about eithteen years ago. The Emperor learning that orders were come from Lisbon that the Town shou'd be evacuated, and the fortifications destroy'd, marched with a considerable Army and a train of Artillery, and while the Inhabitants were executing the instructions from their Court, bombarded the place, so that between the two parties it was left in a state of Desolation. Of 1500 houses, it retains about 400 of the meanest that were most easily repair'd. The Ruins, however shew that it was a place of Consequence. Ships of any Draught of water may lye at some Distance from the Town, the Soundings being gradual and the anchoring Ground good. But there is no shelter and if it blows hard the Ships must run out to sea.

Daralbeyda. Is at present remarkable for the great export of Wheat which has taken place there within twelve months, and which has amounted perhaps to half a Million of Bushells. It is a poor place, containing four or five hundred miserable Huts. The anchoring ground is good in some parts, with a sandy Bottom, in twelve fathom water, in other parts the Bottom is Stoney and rocky and in winter it is dangerous.

Rabat. Is built on the Banks of the Buragrag where that River enters the sea, and divides it from Salè which is on the opposite shore at about a mile Distance. Rabat contains about 2500 Houses, and is one of the best looking Towns I have seen in Barbary. The entrance into the River is much obstructed by a Bank of sand which runs across the mouth of it, and which is constantly shifting. At ordinary Tides vessels drawing 8 feet water may pass and at spring Tides those of twelve, but sometimes loaded vessels in the River are oblig'd to remain there three or four months for a passage out, which they can only have by the shifting of the sands. There are three forts at this place, one on a point which commands the entrance of the River of 10 Guns, and two on the sea shore, one of which is of eight, and the other intended for 16 Guns, of which three only are mounted. There is also a Castle or Fort without Guns upon the Hill on which the Town is built.

Salè. Is Built on an Eminence on a point of the Burregreg, at it's

10 SEPTEMBER 1786

entrance into the Ocean opposite to Rabat. It is defended towards the sea by a Battery of 8 pieces of Cannon, and is surrounded by a double Wall. The streets are narrow and dirty and the Houses mean, the number being about 2500. As the Navigation is in common with Rabat what has been said in the last article need not be repeated. This place which has been long famous for its depredations against the Christians, seems to be declining fast, but the same observation was made on it some centuries ago.

Mamora. Is situated on a high rock on the southern side of the River Cebu, a mile above its entrance into the sea and where the River is about a half a mile broad. It was formerly a place of considerable importance, but is now in the last stage of Desolation. There are the remains of two fortifications almost intire, and which seem to be built since the Town has been destroy'd. One of them is near the sea shore and on the declivity of the Rock, once mounted 12 Guns, and at present has three of Brass and one of Iron mounted. The other Fort stands higher up, was once of the same strength with the former but is now without Guns. The remains of the walls, ditches and Defences, shew that this was once deem'd a place of consequence, though a Bar runs across the mouth of the River that prevents the entrance of large Vessels as the Portugueze experienced in an expedition which they made against it in the year 1515.

Laracha. Is a strong place but not of considerable extent situated on the Top and Declivity of a Hill facing the port where the ships lye. It is a Bar harbour with a narrow Channell sufficient for one Vessell to pass, and ships bound in must keep the shore, as a seaman wou'd term it, close on board on the starboard hand. At common tides there are 12 feet water on the Bar, and in spring tides Depth sufficient for any Vessel which can lye safe in the Port, well Defended from any winds and where 60 or 80 sail may take the Ground in soft mud without Injury. The Channell is defended by three forts. The one farthest from the Town of 8 Guns, the next of 9, and the other of three, and every vessel going into the Harbour must pass along close by these Guns. On the entrance into the Harbour is a pile of Batteries rais'd over each other in three stories. Each Battery consisted of 20 Guns, but the only ones mounted are 16 Brass of about 16 pound ball which Guns are in the middle Battery. This pile has an Air of Great strength, but part of the middle Battery having sunk near 2 feet, I think the whole work must be greatly weaken'd by this misfortune. On a parallel with this middle Battery runs a small one of three Guns, on an Angle one of eleven, and below nearly on a level with the sea, one of nine;

10 SEPTEMBER 1786

so that the number of Batteries are nine, and that of the Guns, if all were mounted wou'd be 103, but of these perhaps 50 are wanting. There are, however, a considerable number of Guns scatter'd about without carriages, and from appearances there seems to be little apprehensions of a necessity of using any. The last attack on this place was made by the French in 1768 or 1769, when they forced their way in Boats under the cover of their ships into the harbour, with a Design to destroy the shipping, but the Tide going out, left them a prey to the Moors who never make prisoners on such occasions. I think the French lost 413 men being about one half of their whole number, the rest remaining on board the ship and the Emperor order'd their heads to be sent to Morocco, where he paid 2 Ducats a piece for about 200 that were preserv'd for him. I saw ten or twelve Moors at Laracha who assisted in repelling this Invasion and who spoke of it with great seeming pleasure. The people suppos'd the French were come to possess themselves of the Country, and took up arms very generally to oppose them. A strong Citadel once commanded the Harbour. It is situated on a Hill with a Ditch surrounding a part of it, but it is tumbling to Ruins. The inside of the walls contain nothing but narrow alleys across which a great number of low arches are turn'd, the use of which I cou'd neither learn nor conjecture, and a great many miserable Huts.

Arzilla. Is a little wall'd Town that has seen better days. The houses in number two or three hundred, are going fast to decay, as well as the fortifications. The walls have been strong and are encompassed with a Ditch. There are three or four guns mounted, and on a fort which lyes some distance from the town, six or eight, over one of the Gates is the Arms of Spain. A Reef or ledge of Rocks runs along the coast, but it is broken so as small vessels may pass in, and large ones may anchor on the outside in ten fathom water, but there is neither Port nor Shelter.

Tangiers. Is one of the most ancient Cities in Barbary, it has undergone many revolutions and was once a place of splendor and commerce. The whole Country distinguishing itself from the name of the City.

The King of Portugal took it in 1471, and in 1662 it was deliver'd to Charles the Second of England as part of his Wifes Dowry, and it was by that Monarch improv'd at an expence of two millions Sterling. In 1684 it was Destroy'd and abandon'd by the English. The Mole where a first rate Man of War cou'd ride in safety, was with incredible labor destroyed. The fortifications and walls were not only blown up, but the ruins tumbled into the

10 SEPTEMBER 1786

Harbour. In short in about 6 months, the English made a considerable progress in the destruction of the Port, which has since remain'd in the quiet possession of the Moors. The town is placed on the right hand side of the entrance into the Bay on a Hill two miles from the sea and about 5 miles distant from an opposite point on which a Battery of ten guns is placed. The form of the Bay is that of the third part of a Circle, and the number of Houses in the Town about 800, said to be half as many as were in it when the English had possession. At present small vessels may come in, and lye ashore on a soft Beach, without Danger. But large ones must anchor at a Distance in the Bay, and in case of blowing weather put to sea for safety. The Batteries here are, one almost level with the sea, and consisting of 13 Guns of 12 or 14 pound ball, the rest are on the Hill vizt. One of 9 Brass Guns, of about 24 pound shot cast in Portugal and three more may be mounted. A second of 12 new iron Guns of 24 pound shot, cast in England, and seven more may be mounted, and another of seven Iron Guns, of 12 or 14 pound shot; exclusive of these are two little Batteries of two Guns each. The Battery which was situated on the top of the Hill near the Castle where the Basha resides, and which contain'd 18 Guns of 16 pound ball, was totally destroy'd about twelve months ago by the blowing up of the Magazine where the Emperor's powder was stor'd. All the fortifications are going to Decay and seem very unequal to a Contest of any consequence. Tangiers is about 7 miles from Cape Spartel and consequently may be said to be within the Streights leading to the Mediterranean.

Tetuan—Is situated to the eastward of Ceuta, which lyes between Tangier and that place, but being in the hands of the Spaniards (as well as Melilla and Peñon de Velez) does not come under my notice. Tetuan lies on the River Marteen, about 5 miles from the Mediterannean sea, the Custom House at Marteen being about half way between the City and the sea. Across the mouth of this river also runs a Bar on which there is only six feet water, and as there is little tide here, the depth never exceeds 8 feet, and seldom is so much. Vessels must therefore lighten on the outside of the Bar, and can then pass up the Bay and River three miles to the Custom House, and from thence to Town. No boats, but small ones with fruit can go, owing to the shallowness of the River. The Town is built on a Hill, at the foot of a Mountain, and has only one fort or Citadel flank'd with four towers, and mounting 20 Cannon to defend it. The Houses are said to be about two thousand five Hundred, and the Inhabitants exclusive of Jews twenty thousand. But the estimation a few years ago was Double this number. No Christian is permitted to enter the City, and therefore this account of it depends on the Veracity and Knowledge of some jews, who visited me at my encampment near it. On the River Marteen, within half a mile of the Mediterannean, is a square Castle, at which Five Guns of sixteen pound ball are mounted.

From this view of the ports belonging to the Emperor, it will be seen that none of them are good, that Laracha is the best, next to which are I think Salè and Tetuan, but I believe the place from whence I write, might, with great abilities and Industry, and at a great Expence, be made a most valuable seaport. I think also that Masagan might be made a place of great Importance.

Naval force. The whole naval force of this Country consists of ten Frigates carrying 170 Guns, which at present are employ'd in this manner,

- 1. at D'aralbeyda of 18 Guns, six pound ball.
- 4. Sail'd from Laracha for Daralbeyda of 16 Guns to Load Corn and Barley for the Emperor to Distribute among his Subjects.
- 1. at Laracha of 22 Guns ⎫
- 1. at Do. of 14 do.   ⎬ 6 pound Shot
- 1. at Do. of 12 do.   ⎭ 4 pound do.
- 2. gone to Constantinople, with presents of Salt Petre and Silver, to the Grand Seignier, of 20 Guns each.

This is the State of the Emperor's fleet at present, and the five frigates, which are to take in Grain at D'aralbeyda are those the Commodore inform'd me some time ago were to go on a Cruize. His Ten half Galleys which I saw at Marteen are laid up on shore irrecoverably perish'd. He has however given orders for building some Galleys and half Galleys, two of which are on the Stocks here. The number of seamen Employ'd is about 798 men, and 1000 apprentices and he can increase the number as much as he pleases by ordering his Governors to put others on board his Vessels. A few days ago he made a general request to all the foreign Consuls, that each of their Nations shou'd send ten Seamen to improve his people in the Art of Navigation, promising to pay each person who will come half as much more as he receives in his own Country. He has not any Treaty of Peace with Russia, Hamburg, Dantzic or Malta, but he wrote some days ago to the sea Ports that he was not at Hostilities with any Nation whatever except the United States. The resources for encreasing his Navy are not internal, at least they depend chiefly on his Neighbours. He has a good deal

10 SEPTEMBER 1786

of small live oak and Corkwood, which last is esteem'd very good Wood, when cut in a proper time and season'd and the properties of the former are well known. The Prizes that are brought in, also furnish Timber for building and are broke up for that purpose. The Rigging, Sail Canvas, Anchors, Ship Chandlery, Tar, Pitch and Turpentine, are furnish'd by Holland, England, and Sweden, and His Frigates are often repair'd at Gibraltar without any expence to Him, and one return'd from thence since we left Morrocco, the fitting out of which cost the British seven thousand pounds Sterling. The season for cruizing is in the summer or rather from April to September, and the Grounds, to the Northward as far as the Coast of Portugal, to the Westward off the Canary, and Western Islands, and in the Mediterannean, His frigates are in good order and his Seamen neither very excellent nor despicable.

Prisoners. There are not any Prisoners or Christian Slaves in the Empire of Morocco, except Six or Seven Spaniards, who are in the Sahara or Desert, and which, the Emperor is endeavouring to procure that they may be deliver'd to their Country. This Part is not in Strict obedience to the King, though govern'd by his Son Abderhammon, from whom it is somewhat difficult to procure the release of Europeans that are cast away in those parts, and his Majesty has no way to get them but by encouraging the Southern Traders to purchase and bring them to Morocco, or to prevail on his Son to send them. And here it will be doing a piece of justice to the Emperor which he well Deserves to say that there is not a man in the World who is a greater Enemy to Slavery than He is. He spares neither money nor pains to redeem all who are so unfortunate as to be cast away, whom he orders to be fed and cloth'd, untill they are return'd to their Country. The Venetian Consul told me that the King being some time ago posses'd of Sixty Christians the Consul had a commission sent to him to redeem them, at an expence of 1000 Dollars each, but when his Majesty was applied to, he answer'd that he woud not sell them, but that the Grand master of Malta (with whom he was *not* at Peace), having liberated some Moors these Christians shou'd be deliver'd up as a Compliment to him. At another time his majesty made a purchase of Moorish Slaves, who were in the possesion of the Christian Powers, on the Coast of the Mediterranean for which he paid 160 thousand Dollars, without shewing any regard to which of the Barbary States they belonged and set them all at liberty without any condition whatever. The Expence of redeeming Slaves in the days of the

10 SEPTEMBER 1786

Muley Ishmael and Muley Abdallah was about 1000 Dollars a Head or three Moors for 1 Christian.

Treaties. I do not think there is any danger of the present Emperor's breaking any of his Treaties intentionally, or in matters of Consequence. He sometime ago however settled the Duty on the export of Barley by treaty with the British and soon after increas'd it. The English Merchants at Mogadore intended representing this matter to the Emperor, and did not Doubt but it wou'd be put to right. He said not long ago that if an European Vessel took on board any of his Subjects, who went on a pilgrimage to Mecca and landed them any where but in his Dominion He wou'd go to war with the nation to whom the Vessel belong'd, and on being told that there was nothing in any of the treaties to prevent a European Vessel from doing this, He reply'd, if that was the case, He wou'd not break the peace, but it wou'd be a Peace without friendship. When this Emperor dies, there will probably be g[reat] Contentions, and I suppose treaties will avail little either at Sea or Land until these contentions are adjusted.

Land Forces. The Grandfather of the present King rais'd an army of 100,000 Negros from whose Descendents, the Army has ever since been recruited. But these Standing forces at different times and for various reasons have been reduced to the number 14767, four thousand of whom are station'd at Morocco and the remainder in Seven Regiments in the different Provinces. Their pay including the maintenance of a Horse is one Ducat p. month, 10 Fanegas of Wheat, 14 of Barley, and 2 Suits of Cloaths annually and the King frequently makes distributions among their families, and whenever he sends any of them on particular business, such as Conducting foreigners through the Country, they are well paid. At the Commencement of a Campaign, He generally gives them ten Ducats, and at the end of it five and it is His Inclination and endeavours to keep them Satisfy'd. All his Male Subjects are born Soldiers, and in case of Necessity, all who are able, are oblig'd to attend him in the field. I suppose the Emperor has fifty thousand Horses and Mules distributed through his Dominions, which he recalls when he pleases and places at pleasure in the hands of others. These are all consider'd as obliged to take the field at a moments warning, and I have often heard, and I believe it to be true that in a few weeks, shou'd an Invasion from the Christians be dreaded (the fear of which is always accompanied by an Idea that they come to take possession of the Country) the Emperor cou'd bring into the field two hundred thousand men. But

I doubt much whether He cou'd equip half the number. The Strength of this Country certainly lyes in his Land Forces, on their own Ground which wou'd ever prove formidable in case of an invasion. Both regular troops and Militia are extremely expert in manuv'ring on horseback, at skirmishing, at sudden attacks and at sudden retreats, but I apprehend they wou'd cut but a bad figure in an open field against European troops. On this subject I can only add that when the Emperor wants soldiers, He orders such of the Bashas to join him as he thinks proper with the number of men wanted. The present Emperor has not had much occasion to call forth the Strength of His Country. In 1774, He went against Millila with 80,000 Militia, which I think was the greatest Draught he ever made.

Revenue. The amount of this article is very fluctuating, and uncertain. It consists of the following articles.

Duty on Exports which varies according to the will of the Emperor.

Duty on Imports which is in the same State, but at present taking them generally is 10 p. Cent.

Tax of 10 p. Cent on all the Grain us'd in the Country, on the Cattle and other moveable Property, which however is rated so much in favour of the proprietors that it does not produce one half the value.

Tax on each City according to its abilities.

Tax on Tobacco brought into the Cities of little consequence being farmed at 3000 Dollars ⅌ annum.

Fines on the Bashas or other public Officers for offences of any kind.

Fines for Smugling Goods which are arbitrary.

Fines impos'd on Towns or Provinces for revolting, quarreling with each other, or for offences commited by Individuals when the offenders are not discover'd.

Property, which falls into the hands of the Emperor at the Death of any Public Officer whose account with the public is unsettled.

Proportion of Prizes made at Sea.

Profit on Cochineal and Alkermes.

Presents from Foreign Nations and from his own Subjects.

There are a few other articles, such as coining money &c.; not worth enumerating nor does my knowledge of these which I have mention'd enable me to write as particularly about each as I cou'd wish. The sum of four Millions of Mexican Dollars is by many thought a high rate to State his annual revenue at, but Mogadore and D'aralbeyda will pay between them one million of Dollars in Duties for the last year, and I think the other places and other articles will certainly produce three times as much, though he receives no taxes from Tafilet and little from Sus.

Language. The common Language spoken in the sea ports is the Moorish which is a Dialect of the Arabic, the difference either in speaking or writing between the two being very little. A Language is spoken in the mountains and in the eastern part of the Empire, called the Berebere (or as it is usually pronounced, the Breber) tongue, and the European language that is best known is the Spanish for all the Jews, who are very numerous, speak it. French, Italian, and English are pretty equally understood and rank after the Spanish.

Government. The Government is that of Absolute Monarchy without limitation. The Emperor is the Supreme executive Magistrate, in whom is united all Spiritual and temporal Power, and his People hold their lives and property totally at his will and pleasure. The life of the meanest of his Subjects cannot be touch'd, except in an emergency, but by his own order, or by the order of some Basha to whom he has deligated the power of life and Death, a power he rarely places out of his own hands. Criminals from the most distant provinces are sent to Morocco, where the King hears the Complaints against them, and as soon as he pronounces Sentence, it is executed on the Spot, and this is always at an audience. When we left Morocco no execution had taken place for four months. This Court does not depend in any degree on the Ottoman Porte, nor on any other Power whatever. But there is a strict friendship between the Grand Seignior and the Emperor, and as there is a possibility of a war between the Turks and Russians, the Emperor thinking it a kind of common cause, being between Christians and Muslemans has shewn his disposition lately to aid the Grand Seignior by sending him two twenty Gun frigates with Saltpetre and Silver to a very considerable amount.

Religion. The Moors of the Empire of Morocco profess the Mahometan religion and obedience to the precepts of the Koran. But the Emperor holds the power of dispensing occasionally with such as he thinks propper. Thus the exportation of Corn which is prohibited by the Koran, is permitted by the King. With respect to their Piracies, I believe they do not proceed from any religious principle. It seems to be the general opinion that they took rise on the expulsion of the Moors from Spain in the reign of Phillip the 3d. when 700,000 were banish'd from that Country—that neces-

10 SEPTEMBER 1786

sity and revenge first instigated them to commit depredations on the Europeans, and their hands were strengthen'd and hatred encreas'd by the final Expulsion in the reign of Ferdinand and Isabell when 17000 families join'd their friends on the Sea coast on this side of the Mediterannean. A Piratical War, begun against the Spaniards, was extended to the other Christian Powers, And all the Barbary States have been enabled to support this war from the Supplies given them by the Maritime Powers of Europe, many of which seem contending with each other which shall enable the Moors most to injure the Trade of their Neighbours.

What I have said on this article, I give as the best information I can procure but it is not Satisfactory, and I am persuaded the Origin of these Depredations, of a much older date, for early in the Seventh Century the Spaniards made a Decent on the Town from which I write to revenge the Piracies commited by the People of this Country.

Captures. No American Vessel has been taken by the Emperor but one, which was commanded by Captain Irwin, and bound from Cadiz to Virginia. She lyes on the Beach at this place, and the Emperor order'd the Basha to deliver her and the cargo to me, but as I understood she had been Insur'd in Spain, I did not chuse to take her under my care.[1] The Emperor has no Treaty with Russia, Germany, Hamburg, Dantzic or Malta. But there seems to be a Cessation of Hostilities with all the world. He had order'd five frigates to be fitted for Sea, and I think it more than probable they were intended to Cruize against the Americans.

Having thus answer'd the queries which you were pleas'd to make. I shall at present conclude with the assurance of my being always with great respect and Esteem, Gentn. Your most obedt hble. Servt., THOS BARCLAY

ENCLOSURE

Prices of Goods in Mogadore in June 1786.

Wheat 5 to 6 ounces the Sal	Duty 1 Spanish milled Dollar and 1 Barbary ounce ℔ fanega
Olive Oil 34 Ounces ℔ Quintal	Duty 2 Dollars 1 Ounce ℔ Quintal
Wool 5 Ducats ℔ Quintal	Duty 2 Dollars
Elephants teeth 30 Ducats ℔ Do.	Do. 4 Do.
Bees Wax 27 Ducats the great Quintl: of 150 pounds	Do. 15 Do.
Gum Arabic 10 Ducats	Do. 2 Do. & one ounce
Senegal 14 Do.	Do. the Same
Sandrach 6½ Do.	Do. the Same
Copper in Blocks 11 Do.	5 Dollars

Shelled Almonds 6 Do.   1 Do. & one ounce
Mules for Exportation 30 to 35 Do.   10 Dollars
Red Morocco Skins as in quality,
  (about 10 Ounces ℔ Skin)   Duty free

Coins

The Gold Ducat 16 Ounces   value nearly 7/8 Sterg.
    Silver Do. 10 Do.   4/9½ do.
The ounce of 4 Blanquils a Silver coin worth nearly 5¾ do.
The Blanquil of 24 Fluces. Do. value about 1½ do.
The fluce a Copper coin value about one quarter of a farthing Sterg.
  Note. when the Ducat is mention'd in the prices of Goods the Silver Ducat is understood.

Weights

1¼ Mexican Dollars make one ounce
16 ounces or 20 Dollars a Pound
100 Pounds or 2000 Dollars the Small quintal
15 Pounds or 3000 Do. the great Do.

Measure

The Condre or Calà 2¼ of which make a french Aun, or 1¾ an English Ell nearly. Measures for Liquids, none.

RC (DNA: PCC, No. 91, 1); in a clerk's hand, signed and directed to Adams and TJ by Barclay; also in Barclay's hand: "No. 8" (i.e., enclosure No. 8 in Barclay to Commissioners, 2 Oct. 1786); the following appears on the margin of the final page of the letter, in the hand of Charles Thomson: "Copy of this to be given to the delegates of Virginia. C. Thomson." PrC of a Tr (DLC); in the hand of William Short. Enclosure (DNA: PCC, No. 91, 1): in a clerk's hand, endorsed by Barclay: "No. 8 Answer to the Queries put by Mr. Adams and Mr. Jefferson." PrC of Tr (DLC); in the hand of William Short.

[1] The first two sentences of this paragraph are bracketed in RC and, in the margin, there is the note by Thomson quoted above.

From John Adams

DEAR SIR   Grosvenor Square Septr. 11. 1786.

On my Return from Holland on the Sixth instant I found your Favours of the 8. and 13. Aug. On my Arrival at the Hague The Exchange of Ratifications was made on the 8. of August with The Baron De Thulemeier, and I had it Printed. It is only in French. Copies shall be Sent you as soon as I can find an Opportunity. We were present at Utrecht at the August Ceremony of Swearing in their new Magistrates. In no Instance, of ancient or modern History, have the People ever asserted more unequivocally their own inherent and unalienable Sovereignty.—But whatever Pleasure I might have in enlarging upon this Subject, I must forbear.

[348]

11 SEPTEMBER 1786

The Affair of Oil has taken a turn here. The Whale men both at Greenland and the southward, have been unsuccessful and the Price of Spermacæti Oil, has risen above fifty Pounds a Ton. Boylston's ship arrived with two or three hundred Ton, and finding he could pay the Duties and make a Profit of five and twenty Per Cent, he sold his Cargo here, instead of going again to France as he intended. This Circumstance will oblige the French Court, or the French Merchants or both to take other Measures, or they will loose this Trade. The Price of Oil will rise in Boston, so much that I am afraid Mr. Barrett's Contract must be fullfilled at an immense Loss.

As to Mr. Lambs Settlement, I still think he had better embark forthwith for New York from Spain. If he cannot he may transmit to you and me his Account, and remit to us the Ballance in favour of U.S.

Mr. Barclays Proposal, of going to Tunis and Tripoli, I suppose appears to you as it does to me, from what We learned from the Ambassador from Tripoli in London, to be unnecessary, at least till We hear farther from Congress. It seems to me too, very unlikely that any Benefit will be had from a Journey to Algiers. I wish to see the Treaty with Morocco, and to know the Particulars of that Affair, first. At present I believe We are taken in, and that We shall be plagued with Demands for annual Presents. I confess, I have no Faith in the Supposition that Spanish Interference has counted for Money, or at least that it will pass long for it.

If however you are clearly in favour of sending Mr. Barclay to Algiers, I will make out a Commission, and send it to you, for your Signature, Signed by my self, because I would not set up my own Judgment against yours, Mr. Carmichaels and Mr. Barclays: but I confess, at present I cannot see any Advantage in it, but on the contrary Several Disadvantages. Mr. Randall is gone to Congress, and We may expect their further orders, e'er long.

With Sincere Affection I am, dear sir, your Friend and servant,
JOHN ADAMS

Inclosed is a Project of an Answer to Mr. Lamb, if you approve it, you will sign and send it.   J.A.

RC (DLC). FC (MHi: AMT); in Smith's hand, with some slight variations in phraseology. Noted in SJL as received 19 Sep. 1786. Enclosure: Commissioners to Lamb; see under 26 Sep. 1786, the date it was signed and forwarded by TJ.

From Abbé Morellet

Monsieur   Lundi soir [11 Sep.? 1786]

    Depuis votre lettre du 9 que j'ai recüe aujourd'hui en revenant de la campagne je n'ai pas perdu de tems pour satisfaire s'il etoit possible le desir que vous avies de voir inserée dans votre ouvrage l'addition que vous me renvoyes mais vous jugeres vous même de l'impossibilité de faire cette insertion en jettant les yeux sur les feuilles que je vous envoye et qui sont tirées au nombre de 4 toutes suivant celle où se trouve le morceau sur les coquilles sans compter une cinquieme qu'on tiroit encore ce matin. De sorte qu'il faudroit perdre et recommencer cinq feuilles. La raison de ce contre tems est que ce même imprimeur qui a fait trainer pendant quatre mois l'impression de 4 feuilles et à qui je m'etois plaint amerement de cette lenteur a tout à coup pressé le travail et fait tirer toutes à la fois 4 ou cinq feuilles qu'il avoit toutes composées. Voilà l'etat des choses et l'obstacle insurmontable que je vois à faire ce que vous desiries: mais permettes moi de vous faire observer que l'inconvenient auquel vous voulies remedier n'existe plus. Le petit paragraphe de 25 à 30 lignes ou vous semblies presenter l'opinion de Voltaire comme aussi raisonnable que toute autre se trouve retranché; ainsi vous aures contenté Mr. Rittenhouse et j'ose dire moi même et vous n'aures point de querelle avec nos naturalistes et quant à l'addition que vous m'envoyes et que je trouve fort bonne si vous le juges convenable on la placera à la fin avec renvoi à l'endroit qu'elle eclaircit.

    Votre observation sur le mot *a knowledge of the first order* est juste: cependant je vous dirai qu'il s'agit icy bien moins de l'importance et de la dignité de la connoissance que de son caractere principal qui est d'etre fondée *sur ce qu'on a vû*. Ce qui pourroit se dire de connoissances qui n'ont *nor value nor dignity*. Le mérite d'une connoissance de ce genre est d'etre la premiere d'etre le 1er pas d'après lequel on en peut faire un second mais comme vous l'expliques si bien non pas un troisieme parceque dès lors on tombe dans le vague et dans le pays de l'imagination.

    L'acte de Tolerance est vraiment admirable mais je doute qu'on nous permette de l'imprimer. Je le tenterai pourtant. Il est vrai que c'est un simple fait un recit de ce qui se passe en Amerique mais depuis que vous habites ce pays vous aves bien observé qu'il y a des verités que nous n'aimons pas qu'on dise même à mille lieues de chès nous. Receves mes très humbles respects.

11 SEPTEMBER 1786

Je vous prie de me renvoyer les feuilles qui me servent pour me guider dans la distribution du manuscrit.

RC (DLC); without signature, name of addressee or date. Enclosure: see below.

VOTRE LETTRE DU 9: Not found, but it was in reply to that of Morellet, printed above under 9 Sep. 1786. None of these letters is recorded in SJL. The English text of the Act for Establishing Religious Freedom (L'ACTE DE TOLERANCE) was enclosed in TJ's letter of the 9th. LES FEUILLES QUE JE VOUS ENVOYE: The passage on shells occurs at page 75 in signature E of the French edition; consequently the four sheets that Morellet enclosed in the present letter—all of them printed and following the sheet in which the passage on shells occurred—were signatures F, G, H, and I; the fifth, which was being printed CE MATIN, was signature K, which carried the volume down through page 160, or somewhat less than half through the volume. TJ must have replied to the present letter by agreeing to Morellet's suggestion for putting L'ADDITION QUE VOUS M'ENVOYES at the end of the volume, for in his *Avertissement* Morellet stated: "L'Auteur ayant fait une addition à quelques idées qu'il expose sur la Théorie de la terre, dans les pages 72, 73, &c. et cette addition étant parvenue trop tard au Traducteur, on l'a placée à la fin de l'Ouvrage" (p. ii-iii); and the addition, which included Voltaire's hypothesis, is accordingly to be found at p. 387-90. TJ's subsequent reply to this suggestion has not been found, however. One of the principal reasons for TJ's displeasure over the inadequacy of the French edition of *Notes on Virginia* must have been the omission of the text of the Act for Establishing Religious Freedom. Morellet's arguments must have seemed unconvincing in light of what Démeunier and others had done; as TJ reported to Wythe on 13 Aug. 1786: "Our act for freedom of religion is extremely applauded. . . . it is inserted at full length in several books now in the press; among others, in the new Encyclopedie."

From Benjamin Putnam

[*Portsmouth?, Va., before 11 Sep. 1786*]. Visited Marseilles in 1783 in connection with his claim "against Count d'Arbaud, late governor of Guadeloupe, for a certain sloop, taken from me, together with her Cargo of Peas and 13. Negroes, estimated at 1130 half Joes"; the claim was not decided by the admiralty of France because of the press of other business and because the admiralty wished to obtain information from Count d'Arbaud; left his affairs in the hands of Matthew Ridley, then resident at Paris, who promised to assist him; Ridley wrote him later in 1783, from London, concerning a decree of the admiralty in regard to a schooner which had been condemned to his benefit, the schooner having been taken a year after the affair of the sloop occurred. At that time Ridley informed him that he had left Paris; that nothing had been decided about the sloop; but that the matter had been left in competent hands. Has not heard from Ridley since and does not believe he is in France. The suits for the schooner and the sloop were presented at the same time; in connection with the sloop, he had "obtained Congresses demand on the Court of France, which Resolution accompanied by Letters of Mr. Wm. Bingham then Agent at Martinique and Cte. d Estaing then at the same Island were committed to the Charge of Mr. Gerard late Minister at the United States"; Franklin had told him that he had never received the papers from Gerard but that he would try to obtain them; asks TJ to assist

[351]

11 SEPTEMBER 1786

him in his claim; supposes Barclay may be Ridley's successor; fears Ridley forgot him; thinks the claim may be decided and the money ready for him. His friends in Bordeaux will forward a letter to him by Capt. Blaney, of the ship *Louisa*, who brings this letter and will return to Virginia.

RC (DLC); 4 p.; addressed to TJ at Versailles and readdressed, in another hand, in part: "en son hotel a Paris ou a Passy"; endorsed; without place or date; the date has been assigned from an entry in SJL under 11 Sep. 1786 and TJ's reply of 8 Aug. 1787. MS mutilated by the removal of the seal, a few words being entirely lost.

Putnam's letters to Benjamin Franklin and William Temple Franklin concerning his claims are in PPAP (see *Cal. Franklin Papers*, II, 353, 419, 474, 510, 517; III, 111; IV, 112, 113, 116). His memorial to Congress is dated 24 Feb. 1781, and is in PCC, No. 42, VI, 258-60, but the resolution of Congress mentioned in Putnam's letter has not been found (JCC, XXI, 945).

From François Soulés

à l'abbaye de Livri près de Paris
le 11 sepbre. 1786

EXCELLENCY

I must return many thanks for the judicious remarks you were so obliging to send me. Due attention was paid to them. Conscious of your Excellency's great abilities, conscious that you are perfectly acquainted with most of the transactions in the American revolution, I will always have a proper deference for your opinion, and should think myself very happy, would your Excellency favour me with more observations on the rest of the work.

I will in the mean time beg leave to ask your Excellency a few questions:

What was the Exact number of Americans at Bunker's hill?

For what reason would not Mr. Campbell give up the command to Colonel Thompson after the death of Montgomery?

Is the speech to the Indians as related by Andrews a genuine one? Page 341.

Is what Andrews says of the old man's company page 357 true?

Was there an agreement between General Washington and Sir Wm. Howe at the evacuation of Boston?

Was not General Thomas with Arnold in the Canada expedition? Had not the Americans great confidence in him and did not he die of the smallpox in the retreat?

Is not Mr. Dumeunier greatly mistaken page 8, first when he says that the stamp act was passed in 1764? 2d. when he says—vainement leur dit-on que personne ne peut conteste à la grande Bretagne, &c., que ce soit dans l'ancien ou dans le nouveau-monde que ce tribut soit payé, ils comprennent que le nom, &c.

[352]

12 SEPTEMBER 1786

In my opinion the Colonies never objected to Great Britain's laying duties on goods exported from its Islands. It would have been as absurd as if they had been willing to prevent the grand Signor or the Emperor of China from taxing in their dominions merchandises that are to be exported out of them.

The Colonies objected to a tax laid on the importation of goods in America, I mean to an entrance duty to be paid and levied in America.

I am most Respectfully, Your Excellency's most obedt. and most humble servt., F. SOULÉS

RC (DLC); endorsed. Noted in SJL as received 13 Sep. 1786.
THE JUDICIOUS REMARKS: See under 13 Sep. 1786. ANDREWS: John Andrews, *History of the War with America*, France, Spain, and Holland, Vol. I (London, 1785). The page reference to DUMEUNIER is to the separate printing of Démeunier's *Essai sur les Etats-Unis*; see under 22 June 1786.

From Biron

Le 12. 7bre. 1786.

M.M. Les Ambassadeurs en france n'avoient autrefois aucune place marquèe pour leur voiture aux spectacles. Il a ensuite été décidé qu'il leur en seroit réservé une; mais cette distinction n'a été accordée qu'aux seuls ambassadeurs et non aux Ministres plenipotentiaires. Monsr. le Maréchal de Biron ne pouroit assigner de place à Monsieur de Jefferson sans un ordre particulier du Roy que M. de Vergennes Ministre des affaires étrangeres peut seul obtenir; autrement M. le Marechal donneroit lieu à tous les autres Ministres plénipotentiaires de se plaindre et de reclamer la même prétention. Tout ce que M. le Marechal de Biron peut faire, c'est de donner ordre d'avoir des ègards pour Monsieur Jefferson et de lui donner toutes les facilités que les circonstances pouront permettre. Il peut être persuadè que M. le Marechal sera fort aise de lui procurer en toute occasion les agrémens qui pouront dépendre de lui.

RC (DLC). Noted in SJL as received 13 Sep. 1786.
TJ must have made a formal request concerning privileges for carriages at theatres belonging to members of the diplomatic corps, but no copy of that request or of his reply to the present letter has been found; see under 14 Sep. 1786. TJ attended the theater often during the days that he saw so much of Maria Cosway; on Saturday, 9 Sep.—the day that Trumbull left Paris—he attended the Théâtre Italien to see "Richard Coeur de Lion" (Account Book).

From C. W. F. Dumas

MONSIEUR   La Haie, 12e. 7bre. 1786

Si j'ai différé de répondre à la Lettre dont Votre Excellence m'a honoré en date du 6 May à son retour d'Angleterre, ce n'est point par négligence, mais par la nature même et un concours de choses tant particulieres que publiques qui se passent ici, et dans lesquelles je suis tellement ou interessé ou initié, que je n'ai pu, sans risquer de compromettre cette République, ses Alliés, moi-même, et sans me rendre même suspect d'imprudence, écrire rien dans le lointain. D'ailleurs je me flattois toujours, au milieu des troubles journaliers, de les voir terminer paisiblement. Outre cela, ma santé a été fréquemment dérangée; moi-même avec ma famille, affligé de la perte d'une Belle-fille fort aimée de nous tous, morte inopinément à l'âge de 24 ans, et laissant mon Beau-fils Veuf avec deux petits Enfants. Joignez à cela, Monsieur, les embarras où me laisse toujours la Trésorerie des Etats-Unis, faute d'ordre pour pouvoir toucher mes Arrérages. Tout cela me fait espérer, que Votre Excellence me pardonnera ce long silence. Aujourd'hui, que la paix interne de la République paroît s'éloigner encore, je ne veux plus différer; [et je profite d'un Courier que Mr. le Ms. de Verac dépechera demain matin non seulement pour vous écrire la présente, mais aussi pour le charger d'un paquet séparé, où Votre Excellence trouvera un Exemplaire d'une Vie estimée de Mr. Turgot, pour Elle, et un autre pour Mr. Franklin à Philadelphie, que je La prie de vouloir bien lui acheminer promptement. J'en ai ajouté encore deux, l'un pour Mr. Jn. Jay, et l'autre pour Mr. Robert Morris.][1]

La Guerre civile vient enfin d'éclater. L'obstiné Stathouder désesperant d'engager, par toutes sortes d'artifices,[2] ses concitoyens dans quelques voies de fait [qui] lui donnassent au moins des prétextes pour attenter à leurs libertés, leve enfin le masque, et se permet toutes celles que la fureur et la lâcheté tyrannique peut suggérer. Votre Excellence pourra voir passablement par la Gazette de Leide, la plus véridique de toutes, ce qui se passe ici. Je n'entrerai donc dans aucun détail. J'ajouterai seulement, que toutes ces violences ont, non seulement augmenté prodigieusement la haîne et le nombre des Bourgeoisies patriotiques, mais aussi, ce qui est essentiel, rendu à peu près unanime l'Assemblée de Leurs Noblesses et Grands Pensionnaires où personne n'ose plus s'opposer aux Résolutions vigoureuses qui s'y prennent. Il y a apparence que celle de suspendre le Stathouder, Aggresseur de toutes ses fonctions dans cette Province, sera prise cette semaine. [Cinq villes, savoir Dordrecht, Gouda, Schoonhöven, Alkmar et Monnikendam sont déjà de cet Avis.]³ Et quant à l'Assemblée des Etats-Generaux, où jusqu'ici la pluralité des Membres, par des pratiques familieres à une longue usurpation, a été à la dévotion du Stathouder,⁴ la division ne pourra manquer de s'y mettre incessamment, par le parti que prennent leurs maîtres, notamment Overyssel, Groningue, Zélande et Frise, d'interdire, à l'exemple de la Hollande, aux troupes de leur répartition de se laisser employer.

Au moment où j'écris ceci, j'apprends que le simulacre tronqué des prétendus Etats d'Utrecht assemblés dans la petite Ville subjuguée d'Amersfort, n'ose plus insister auprès du Stathouder sur l'envoi, concerté avec lui, de troupes dans leur Province, et commence à parlementer pour obtenir l'intervention, ci-devant rejetée avec dédain, de la Hollande entre eux et la Ville d'Utrecht. Je prévois que la Majorité tyrannique des Etats de Gueldre se verra bientôt réduite à la même extrêmité. En attendant, leur moteur, le Stathouder, plein de terreur, se fait entourer dans son château du Loo par ce qu'il a pu ramasser de troupes, et se rend de difficile accès, crainte de quelque Harmodius ou Aristogiton. De ce côté-ci les troupes réglées les Corps Bourgeois francs, le Canon, les Munitions &c. de la Province d'Hollande continuent de marcher pour couvrir Utrecht, où d'ailleurs on est disposé à se battre s'il le faut à toute outrance; tandis que le Stathouder et les Oligarches Gueldrois qui lui sont devoués, n'osent dégarnir les grandes villes du pays comme Nimegue, Arnhem, et Zutphen, des troupes qu'ils y ont pour enbrider les Bourgeoisies.

Voilà le Tableau très-racourci, mais fidele des Affaires internes de la République. Celui que me fait Votre Excellence des termes où en sont les Etats-Unis vis-à-vis des Anglois, me plait autant pour le fond, que pour la maniere dont il est touché. Car j'ai été et suis toujours d'avis que la cordialité ne peut exister entre eux et nous, que lorsqu'ils ne pourront plus prétendre à aucune des supériorités qu'ils s'arrogent.

Je prendrai dans peu la liberté que Votre Excellence m'a permise, de tirer sur Elle à l'ordre de Mrs. Nic. & Jb. van Staphorst, pour le Semestre de mon Salaire annuel de 13 cents Dollars, échu le 19 Octobre prochain, la somme de 650 Dollars, ou 1625 florins courant d'hollande, La priant de vouloir bien faire honneur à ma Traite. Je suis avec un très-grand respect,⁵ De Votre Excellence, Le très-humble et très-obéissant Serviteur,   C W F Dumas

Des Amis m'ont prié d'acheminer les deux incluses pour Phila-[delphie.]

12 SEPTEMBER 1786

RC (DLC); endorsed. FC (Rijksarchief, The Hague, Dumas Papers; photostats in DLC); with numerous deletions and some differences in phraseology, some of which are indicated below. Enclosures: The "deux incluses" for Philadelphia have not been identified, but may have been from the sons of Robert Morris.

The VIE ESTIMÉE DE MR. TURGOT was Condorcet's *Vie de Monsieur Turgot*, of which several editions came out in 1786 (Sowerby, No. 217; see TJ to Dumas, 22 Sep. 1786).

[1] Text in brackets (supplied) does not appear in FC.
[2] FC reads: "mauvaises pratiques."
[3] Text in brackets (supplied) appears in margin of RC and is not in FC.
[4] FC reads: "d'un Parti."
[5] FC ends at this point.

From Lefévre, Roussac & Cie.

MONSIEUR   Lisbonne. 12. 7bre. 1786.

Nous sommes honorés de votre Lettre du 8. août qui nous accuse la reception de la facture du petit envoi de vin que nous vous expediâmes du montant duquel il est bien que vous ayez accueilli notre Traite; nous vous en remercions.

Pour nous conformer à vos intentions, nous vous remettons ci-inclus la facture des 6. douzaines bouteilles malvoisie de madere que vous Souhaités, qui sont chargées dans le navire français la Diligence, Cape. Denis, à la consignation de Mrs. Achard freres et Cie. a Rouen qui auront Soin de vous les faire parvenir. Nous vous debitons du montant en Rs.48,850., faisant au change de 426. rès pour 3^{tt}—£344.3d. dont nous nous remboursons sur vous, Monsieur, en notre Traite à 60 Jours de date ordre M. Valeur de Lavisse que nous recommandons à votre accueil.

Nous apprendrons avec beaucoup de plaisir que vous soyiez satisfait de ce vin ainsi que des qualités des precedents et lorsque nos Services pourront vous être agreables et a vos amis, nous vous réiterons qu'ils vous sont entierement acquis. C'est dans ces Sentimens que nous avons l'honneur d'être avec des Egards bien distingués Monsieur Vos très humbles et très obéissants Serviteurs,

LE FÉVRE ROUSSAC ET CIE

P.S. Notre Signature Sociale est Lefevre Roussac et Cie. et non Roussac freres.

RC (MHi); endorsed. Noted in SJL as received 30 Sep. 1786. There is in MHi a Sight draft at sixty days, dated Lisbon, 12 Sep. 1786, on TJ for 344.3d livres tournois; endorsements of payment on verso; also endorsed by TJ.

There is a Dupl (MHi) which lacks endorsements, but has the following, written in TJ's left hand: "Oct. 8. Accept[ed] Th: [Jefferso]n," the signature of acceptance having been torn out on payment.

From Lewis Littlepage

Sir   Warsaw. 12th. September. 1786.

Your silence upon the subject of the sum due from me to your Excellency upon the account of the State of Virginia, leaves too much room to apprehend some unforeseen embarrassment in the repayment of it to Mr. Henry. In consequence I have inclosed a bill of exchange to that amount to the Marquis de La Fayette, who will take up my bill in your Excellency's hands. I must at the same time intreat you, Sir, to accept an interest of six per cent upon the original sum, for the six months during which you have been deprived of it.

Should you hereafter receive assurances of it's having been settled in Virginia, you will be kind enough to return an equivalent of the sum to the Marquis, to be remitted to me.

With the highest sense of my obligation to you Sir, and the most profound respect, I have the honor to be Your Excellency's most obedient and most humble Servant,   Lewis Littlepage

RC (DLC); endorsed in TJ's left hand: "Littlepage Lewis." Noted in SJL as received 26 Sep. 1786. Enclosure missing.

Thomas Barclay to the American Commissioners

Gentlemen   Tangier 13th. September 1786.

Though in a letter written at this place, dated the 10th. instant, I gave you a long answer to the questions with which you charged me, I will now add some farther particulars on the Subject of this Country, which you will possibly be inclined to know.

The Emperor is on the most cordial and friendly footing with Spain. The presents, made him from that Court, have been uncommonly great; and among other valuable articles lately sent, were 80 thousand Dollars in Specie.

It was, sometime ago, debated in the Council at Versailles whether war shou'd not be declared against Morocco for the treatment which the Emperor gave Mr. Chinie the french Consul when he was last at Morocco. The fact was that the Emperor wrote to Rabat desiring to see the Consul at the Court from which Mr. Chinie excus'd himself on account of his health, which the Emperor was informed was very good. Some time after the Consul

13 SEPTEMBER 1786

went up to Morocco with a letter from M. De Castries, in answer to one which the Emperor had written to the King of France, but the Emperor was so much offended at the letter, not being from the King himself, and at Mr. Chinie for not complying with his Desire to go to Morocco, that, He wou'd not look at it, but ordered it, at the Public Audience, to be tied round the Consul's neck and dismissed him. The late ProConsul of France has been very successful in reconciling matters, and the present Consul was very well received while I was in Morocco—the Emperor however strongly advising him to avoid the ways of his Predecessor.

The Swedes are bound by treaty to send an Ambassador in two years, and the presents are considerable and very usefull to the Emperor.

The Danes are bound by treaty to pay an annual tribute of 25 Thousand Dollars.

The Venetians, by treaty also, are bound to pay ten thousand Sequins being about Twenty two thousand Dollars.

The presents from Holland are more considerable than those from any of the three last mention'd Powers, but they are not stipulated.

The English pay also very high without being bound to do so by treaty, and they enjoy at present very little of the Emperor's friendship or good wishes. There is not a Nation on earth of which he has so bad an opinion, and I have heard him say they neither minded their Treaties nor Promises. It wou'd be going into too long a Detail to mention all the particulars that gave rise to these prejudices which may very possibly end in a war.

The Emperor of Morocco has no Treaty with the Emperor of Germany and has given notice to the Imperial Consul at Cadiz that unless the Emperor of Germany sends him Three frigates, He will cruise against his Vessels.

With the Portuguese, He is very friendly. Their Men of War come into this bay to get Supplies of Provisions and other Necessaries, during their cruises against the Algerines, and a Man of War of 64 Guns which is lying at Anchor here for that purpose will sail in a few days to join the Portuguese Squadron of Six Vessels that are now in the Mediterranean to prevent the Algerine Cruisers from getting into the Atlantic. By the treaty between Portugal and Morocco the Emperor is not to allow his Vessels to Cruize to the Northward of Cape Finistre. My Information says Cape Finistre, but Probably it ought to be Cape St. Vincent, I cannot at present be certain about it.[1]

13 SEPTEMBER 1786

I have already mentioned the situation of the Emperor with the Porte. With Tunis and Tripoli he is on very good terms, but a Coolness has subsisted between Him and the Dey of Algiers for some time, which began I believe upon the Emperor's having made Peace with Spain without communicating with the Dey. I am told, however, that some late friendly overtures have been made from Algiers which will probably reinstate the Countries in their old situation.

The Dominions of the Emperor consist of the Kingdoms of Fez, Morocco, Tafilet and Sus, and his influence extends a great way into the Desert; Fez and Morocco are in many parts very fertile in corn, fruit and oil, and any quantity of wine might be raised but the use of it is prohibited. The last Harvest has produced an encrease of 40 for one, an assertion which from examination I know to be true, and 30. for one is not deem'd extraordinary. The resources of the Country are great, but the cultivation of those resources slovenly to a Degree. All the Arts and Sciences are buried in oblivion, and it appears almost impossible that these are the Descendants of the people who conquer'd Spain, ruled it for 700. years, and left some very striking memorials behind them in that country. The Streets and Houses in the City of Morocco are despicable beyond belief, with here and there the remains of something that, with the Mosques, shews the City was once of more consequence. There are Schools in all the Towns where reading and writing are taught and in some places arithmetic, and very rarely a little astronomy, and those branches comprehend the learning of the Moors. The people seem to be warlike, fierce, avaritious and Contemners of the Christians. The Arabs, who dwell in Tents, despise the Inhabitants of the Cities, but unite with them in their attachment to the Sovereign. The Emperor is 66 years of age according to the Mahometan reckoning which is about 64. of our years. He is of a middle Stature, inclining to fat, and has a remarkable cast in his right eye which looks blacker than the other; his Complexion is rather dark owing to a small mixture of Negro blood in him. He possessed in his early years all the fierceness of his ancestors, but being entrusted[2] by his father in Public matters, He turned his thoughts on the art of Government, and during his father's lifetime obtain'd absolute Dominion not only over the Country, but over his father who entrusted everything to his management, approving even of those acts which he did contrary to his instructions, and the most perfect friendship always subsisted between them. It is about 28 years since he ascended the Throne with-

13 SEPTEMBER 1786

out a Competitor, since which he has taken the utmost pains to conquer those habits and prejudices in which he was educated. One of his people, not long ago, making a Complaint of some ill treatment he had receiv'd, and not meeting such reddress as he expected broke out into some language that the Emperor was not accustomed to hear. His Majesty, with great temper, said "Had you spoke in such terms to my Father or Grandfather, what do you think wou'd have been the consequence?"

The king is fond of accumulating wealth and of distributing it. The sums he sends to Mecca are so extraordinary that they occasion conjectures that He may possibly retire there one Day Himself. He is religious and an observer of Forms, but this did not hinder him on a late journey from Salè to Morocco to strike out of the direct road and go to a Saint's House, where a number of Villains (about 300) had taken sanctuary, every one of which he order'd to be cut in pieces in his presence. He is a just man according to his Idea of Justice, of great personal Courage, liberal to a Degree, a Lover of his People, stern and rigid in distributing justice, and though it is customary for those people who can bring presents never to apply to him without them, yet the poorest Moor in his Dominions, by placing himself under a Flag which is erected every Day in the Court where the public Audiences are given, has a right to be heard by the Emperor in preference to any Ambassador from the first King upon earth, and to prefer his complaint against any subject be his rank what it may. His families which are in Morocco, Mequinez and Tafilet consist of 4 Queens, 40 Women who are not married, but who are attended in the same manner as if they were Queens, 243 Women of inferior Rank, and these are attended by 858 Females who are shut up in the seraglios, and the number of Eunuchs is great. The last Queen which He married two years ago, is now about 14 or 15 years of age, and his children are Sixteen Sons and Seven Daughters.

I shall conclude this letter with a short account of the two audiences I had. The first was a public one at which there were about one thousand people present. The Emperor came out on horseback, and we were presented by the Basha of Morocco. After enquiring what kind of Journey we had and whether we came in a frigate, He asked the situation of America with respect to Great Britain, and the Cause of our Separation. He then question'd me concerning the number of American Troops during the war and since the peace, of the religion of the white Inhabitants and of the Indians, of the latitude of the United States, and remarked that no person had sail'd farther than the 80th. Degree of North Latitude, and enquired whether our Country produced Timber fit for the construction of Vessels. He then asked for the letters, and ordering the [one] from the King of Spain to be open'd, He examin'd it and said He knew the writing very well. He then looked at an alarm watch which happened to strike, and asked several questions about it. He concluded by saying, "Send your Ships and trade with us, and I will do everything you can desire," at which he looked round to his Great Officers and people, who all cried out, "God preserve the life of our Master." He then ordered his Gardens to be shewn us and the American boy to be sent to me.

The second audience was in the Garden, when the King was again on horseback and as soon as we bowed to him he cried, bona! bona! and began to complain of the treatment he had reciev'd from the English. He examin'd a watch that was among the presents, and an Atlas with which he seemed very well acquainted, pointing out to Different parts of the World and naming them, though he cou'd not read the names as they were printed. He asked to see the Map of the United States, which was among the others, and after examining it, called for a pen and paper and wrote down the latitudes to which his Vessels had sail'd, after which he put down the latitudes of the Coasts of America, desiring to know which were the best ports, and said he wou'd probably send a Vessel there. I presented him with a book containing the constitutions of America and other public papers, and one of the Interpreters told him it also contained the reasons which induced the Americans to go to war with Great Britain. Let these reasons, said he, looking over the book, be translated into Arabic and sent to me as soon as possible. After some talk about Tobacco, the Day of the Month, and the Sun's Declination, and saying he woud order a Bag of herbs of Great and peculiar qualities to be sent me, I inform'd him that I wou'd appoint Mr. Francis Chiappi of Morocco, as an Agent to act in behalf of any American Citizens who coming to this Country may have occasion for his Service, or to transmit to His Majesty through Mr. Tahar Fenish any letters or papers from the Congress of the United States untill the farther pleasure of Congress shall be known.

In this account of the Audiences I have omitted some particulars which were of no consequence, and what I have related serves only to shew the turn of thinking which the Emperor possesses, and the objects that engross his attention. I have the honor to be gentn. your most obedt. hble. Servt.,   THOS. BARCLAY

RC (DNA: PCC, No. 91, I); in a clerk's hand, signed and amended by Barclay (see note 1 below); also in Barclay's hand: "No. 9" (i.e., enclosure No. 9 in Barclay to Commissioners, 2 Oct. 1786). PrC of a Tr (DLC); in hand of Short.

[1] This sentence added as footnote in hand of Barclay.
[2] Thus in RC and PrC; Barclay possibly intended to use the word "instructed" and the clerk erred.

To William Stephens Smith

Dear Sir   Paris Sep. 13. 1786.

I had the honour of addressing you on the 9th. of August and since that have received yours of Aug. 23. I have not yet heard of Mr. Adams's return to London, nor when that may be expected if it has not already taken place. I have nothing public and proper for the post. A letter from Mr. Barclay dated at Mogadore in July shews he was on his return. I impatiently wait an answer from Mr. Adams as to the further instructions for him. This court sets out for Fontainebleau about the 10th. of Octob. I propose to go there at the same time, to stay there about a week, and then employ the rest of the time of their continuance there in making a tour into the South of France, as far as the canal of Languedoc which I have a great desire to examine minutely as at some future time it may enable me to give information thereon to such of our states as are engaged in works of that kind. This will take me six weeks. I would wish Mr. Paradise to be informed of this movement, as it may influence his.

I inclose you a letter for Stockdale for some books, as also a list of others for Lackington, which I will pray you to send to him in the moment of receiving this, that my demand may be as little anticipated by others as possible. On you also I must put the trouble of paying Lackington and of contriving that his books and those of Stockdale may come in one package by the Diligence. Dr. Ramsay's book is much demanded here. Would it not be better that Mr. Dilley should send some copies by the Diligence as I proposed? As for those sent to Ostend I know no probability of their ever getting here unless Mr. Dilly has ordered them on from thence to Paris by some channel of conveyance with which he is acquainted. I know of none, have no correspondent or even acquaintance at Ostend, I therefore cannot intermeddle with them till delivered here. I am sensible my order from M. Grand on M. Tessier will fall short of it's objects. However if Mr. Tessier will be so good as to pay whatever may be requisite the moment he lets me know

13 SEPTEMBER 1786

the whole sum paid, I will send an order from Mr. Grand to cover it. Will you be so good as to direct your taylor to make me a couple of pair of breeches and two waist coats (Gilets double buttoned) of the same buff cotton which he made for me while in London. Dr. Bancroft will be so good as to bring them. I will also trouble you to call on the engraver and hurry him with my map, as the delay of it will be attended with extreme inconvenience. Trumbul left us three days ago. He will be a valuable recruit to you, as he will lighten the burthen of those numerous commissions which with great shame I impose on you. Present me affectionately to Mrs. Smith and be assured of the sincere esteem with which I am Dr. Sir your friend & servant, TH: JEFFERSON

RC (MB). PrC (DLC); endorsed. Enclosures: (1) TJ to Stockdale, 13 Sep. 1786. (2) List of books from Lackington's catalogue for 1787.

To François Soulés

SIR Paris Septemb. 13. 1786

Before the receipt of your favor of the 11th. inst. I had written the inclosed short notes on such parts of your work as I have yet been able to go over. You will perceive that the corrections are very trifling. Such as they are I will continue them, and forward them to you from time to time as I get along. I will endeavor also to answer such of the queries you propose in your letter as my memory will enable me to do with certainty. Some of them I shall be unable to answer, having left in America all my notes, memorandums &c. which might have enabled me to give you the information you desire. I have the honour to be with the most perfect esteem & respect Sir Your most obedient humble servt.,

TH: JEFFERSON

PrC (DLC). For the "inclosed short notes," see Editorial Note to TJ's comments on Soulés' *Histoire*, following.

Jefferson's Comments on François Soulés' *Histoire*

[July-Sep. 1786]

I. COMMENTS ON SOULES' *HISTOIRE*
II. ANSWERS TO SOULES' QUERIES

EDITORIAL NOTE

The assistance that Jefferson gave to the French historian François Soulés (1748-1809) was assumed by Ford, IV, 300, to have been based on "the MSS. or proof-sheets . . . which he submitted to Jefferson." Sowerby, I, 223, seems to imply that Jefferson employed page-proofs in making his comments, since he "probably had bound the two volumes that the author sent him for his corrections." There is, however, no evidence that Soulés requested Jefferson to make corrections; there is strong probability that these comments and corrections were undertaken by Jefferson on his own initiative; and it is certain that, in drafting them, he employed neither manuscript nor page-proofs but a previous edition of Soulés' work. The chronology of Jefferson's relation to this work and its author appears to be as follows.

During 1785 there was published in London a two-volume work by Soulés entitled *Histoire des troubles de l'Amérique Anglaise* (Sabin, No. 87291). It is not known when Jefferson acquired a copy of the *Histoire*—he may have obtained it while he was in London in the spring of 1786—but the fact that he had such a copy is proved by a letter he wrote Stockdale on 24 July 1786: "I have the two first volumes: if any more be come out, I shall be glad to receive them; or whenever they do come out." A fortnight after Jefferson wrote this letter he affixed the date of 3 Aug. 1786 to the commentaries on Soulés' work here presented as Document I. All of its page references are keyed to the pagination of the London edition, proving conclusively that these notes were compiled on a reading of those two volumes.

The inference that Jefferson may not have met the author at the time he wrote Stockdale or when he drew up these comments is based upon the fact that the comments exist in two states. There is in DLC: TJ Papers, 24: 4146 a two-page list of brief notes headed "Soulés" and containing references to various pages of the London edition of 1785. These page references go up to page 325 of Volume 1 and also include one going as far as page 6 of Volume 2. The last-named reference occurs at the bottom of the sheet (verso), and this may suggest the possibility that there were other parts of the memoranda covering the remainder of Volume 2 and that these may have become separated and lost. This is unlikely, for reasons given below. It is worth noting that this two-page list of topics is an original manuscript and not a press copy; that each of its topics is preceded by a check mark; and that, with a single exception (see note 7, Document I), each of its

EDITORIAL NOTE

items and page references is repeated in the more elaborate set of comments printed here as Document I. What is of particular interest, however, is the fact that its comments are briefer, blunter, and less tactful than those sent to Soulés.

What these facts suggest is that this two-page list of comments (referred to in the notes to Documents I and II as Dft) may have been made originally by Jefferson for his own use and without the intention of submitting the result to the author. That is to say, they may have been calculated to serve for him the uses that marginalia served for others. John Adams, Benjamin Franklin, John Dickinson, and others of Jefferson's compatriots often filled the margins of their books to such an extent as to result in a sort of running debate with the author. Jefferson never did. Only on extremely rare occasions did he make any memorandum in a book, but he sometimes made notes and comments on separate slips of paper. The brevity and bluntness of the document here referred to as Dft suggests that this was his purpose in the present instance, and that this document may have been drawn up sometime during July and may have inspired him to write Stockdale ordering any further volumes that had appeared or might appear. If Jefferson had known the author on 24 July when he wrote Stockdale, it is very unlikely that he would have been ignorant of the fact that no more volumes of the *Histoire* had appeared in London. He had just completed his long collaboration with Démeunier for the article on the United States to be published in the *Encyclopédie Méthodique*, and possibly because of this and of his growing reputation among French scholars as an unusually well-informed person on matters respecting America, he may have been sought out by Soulés, or he may have initiated the meeting himself through the intermediation of Lafayette, Crevecoeur, or some other friend. Démeunier, d'Auberteuil, and others whose letters he retained had appealed to him in writing for assistance. There is no such appeal from Soulés in the Jefferson papers, nor is there any reply to such an appeal.

It seems very probable, then, that Jefferson's collaboration in this instance began with a personal consultation. This may have occurred very shortly after he wrote to Stockdale. Possibly on meeting Soulés and on learning that he was preparing a new edition of his work, Jefferson drew up on the basis of his Dft a very much extended and more diplomatically phrased version of these notes. The resultant document occupies seven pages and must have been intended for presentation to Soulés; it is here printed as Document I. The original is missing, but Jefferson kept a press copy (DLC: TJ Papers, 23: 3934-40). On 11 Sep. Soulés thanked Jefferson for some "judicious remarks," asked for "more observations on the rest of the work," and submitted a few queries. Thus it is clear that in the six weeks after writing to Stockdale, Jefferson had learned that Soulés was at work on a revision of the two volumes that had appeared the previous year in London. Also, it is clear that after he had transmitted to Soulés the "judicious remarks," he had made additional "short notes" on such parts of the work as he had been able to go over. These "short notes" were enclosed in Jefferson's letter to Soulés of 13 Sep. 1786.

COMMENTS ON SOULÉS' HISTOIRE 1786

But what were these "short notes"? They could not have been the answers to Soulés' queries (Document II) because these were written before the queries themselves were set down. They could scarcely have been a copy of Dft, for the brevity of its notes would have made them generally unintelligible to anyone save their author—also, the comments (Document I) were only an amplification of the topics in Dft, paralleling their order and page sequence precisely, and it would have been needless to send both. Several possible explanations occur: (1) The "judicious remarks" acknowledged by Soulés referred to some missing set of observations by Jefferson, and the "short notes" could in consequence be the matter here printed as Document I. (2) Jefferson sent only a part of the amplifications he had made from Dft and included another part with his letter of 13 Sep. (3) The pages of press copies of both Documents I and II do not represent the true order of their originals and the parts covering matter between page 324 of Volume 1 and page 41 of Volume 2 of the London edition belong at the end of Document I—that is, that these final pages of Document II were the "short notes." There are difficulties with all of these explanations. The last seems to gain some force from the fact that the pages of both press copies are in fact disordered, those of Document II preceding those of Document I in TJ Papers as their text does in Ford, IV, 300-11. Also, the resumption of the page-by-page comment at page 324 of Volume 1 occurs at the top of a new page of the manuscript. But this explanation requires the assumption that the original of Document II ended with Jefferson's reference to the affair of The Cedars—an obstacle difficult to get around in view of the fact that Soulés' treatment of this incident in the second edition of the *Histoire* falls precisely after the point at which the matter covered by Document I ends and before the point at which that covered by Document II begins. The second possibility—that the matter represented by Document I was sent to Soulés in two parts at different times—is unlikely in view of the fact that there are no convenient breaks in the manuscript, each page ending with a catch-word or number for the succeeding page. A further difficulty with this possibility is that Jefferson stated the "short notes" to be "on such parts of your work as I have yet been able to go over." This was an inclusive description, evidently having reference to notes on Soulés' work from the beginning, not a mere continuation of comment to be added to something that had already been sent. On the whole, then, the first possibility seems the most plausible. The "judicious remarks" acknowledged on 11 Sep. may have been some general rather than specific comment designed to find out whether Soulés was receptive to the kind of assistance Jefferson had recently given to Démeunier. If this assumption is correct, then the "short notes" enclosed in the letter of 13 Sep. must have represented the seven pages embraced by Document I.

Jefferson, after giving an answer to Soulés' queries (Document II), had barely begun his resumption of the page-by-page commentary on the *Histoire* when he left off. So far as the record shows, he covered only the last few pages of Volume 1 and the first 41 pages of Volume 2 before ceasing. The reason is not difficult to establish. Trumbull

[366]

EDITORIAL NOTE

had just left Paris. Jefferson was seeing Maria Cosway and others of the Cosways' circle almost daily, and was giving less attention than usual to his paper work. And on 18 Sep. he suffered the accident to his wrist. Document II, being in his right hand, was therefore written between 13 and 18 Sep. 1786.

This, however, did not end Jefferson's effort to assist Soulés. He must have placed in his hands a copy of the *Essai sur les Etats-Unis*, for when the four volume edition of the *Histoire* appeared in Paris in 1787, Soulés included (IV, 179-255) a chapter on the general situation of the United States "fondée sur les Mémoires les plus authentiques: c'est un homme célèbre par ses talens littéraires, par la part qu'il a eue à cette révolution, le rang qu'il a tenu en Virginie, et qu'il tient à présent en France, qui a fourni à M. Démeunier les matériaux dont il s'est servi pour instruire le public de l'état des finances des Américains" (IV, 179). The materials followed closely those that Jefferson had supplied to Démeunier, and included "Loix criminelles de la Virginie depuis la revolution," summarizing the provisions of Jefferson's Bill for Proportioning Crimes and Punishments as if they had been enacted into law. These materials also included the text of the Act for Establishing Religious Freedom. Jefferson also submitted to Soulés some materials on the Battle of Wyoming that had been gathered by Crèvecoeur and that Soulés utilized in his work (TJ to Soulés, 19 Jan. and 2 Feb. 1787).

But it is not wholly accurate to suggest that Soulés adopted Jefferson's materials and statements in full or uncritically (see Sowerby, I, 224). He occasionally corrected his previous accounts in accordance with Jefferson's comments, and he drew freely from Documents I and II, from the *Essai sur les Etats-Unis*, and from other sources that Jefferson supplied. But, as the notes to the present documents indicate, he often rejected facts and opinions offered by Jefferson. In spite of his declaration that he loved liberty and was a friend of republican ideas (*Histoire*, IV, 265-6), Soulés was far less co-operative in adopting the American position as defined by Jefferson than Démeunier had been. In a concluding chapter he gave his own view: "On a vu les observations de M. Démeunier, sur les *Etats-Unis*; on a aussi pu voir, avant les siennes, celles de l'Abbé de Mably, et de plusieurs Ecrivains célèbres. Pleins de cette philanthropie qui distingue le siècle dans lequel nous avons le bonheur de vivre, ils ont parlé des Americains avec enthousiasme, et ont prédit que le Nouveau-Monde alloit fournir à l'ancien l'exemple d'une République de Philosophes; ils ont prédit que cette partie du Globe alloit servir de retraite à tous les êtres pensans, qui voudroient s'affranchir du joug de la tyrannie. La noble cause qui a produit la révolution, les a tous aveuglés. Ils regardoient sans doute les habitans de l'Amérique septentrionale, comme des hommes vertueux, éclairés, et qui agissoient tous suivant les mêmes principes. Ils n'ont point fait réflexion que le nombre de Sages et de véritables Patriotes, dans les treize Etats, étoit peu considérable, en comparaison de celui des ignorans, des gens intéressés, de ceux qui se laissent conduire sans connoissance de cause, et que l'on appelle, dans les Royaumes de l'Europe, la populace" (*Histoire*, IV, 263). Soulés went on to say that the members of the first Continental Congress would have done honor to Athens and Rome, but since then persons of mediocrity had come to the head of American affairs, proving that philosophy had not yet made great progress there and that the American electorate were already as corrupt as in the old world; that, long before the Revolution, European vices and prejudices had been carried to America; that the horrible monster of ambition, breeder of so many crimes, had existed there in the highest degree, and, though hidden, only wanted a favorable opportunity to make its appearance openly; that scarcely had independence been recognized when the order of the Cincinnati was proposed and "ces nouveaux Républicains, qui n'avoient pris les armes que pour abolir les dignités perpétuelles, pour rétablir l'homme dans ses justes droits; qui avoient fondé leur existence, comme *Nation*, sur ces paroles remarquables, *Nous tenons comme une vérité certaine et évidente, que tous les hommes sont créés égaux*, adoptèrent avec avidité cette proposition, et sans l'opposition de plusieurs Sénateurs célèbres, alloient jetter les semences d'une aristocratie, en voulant établir une democratie." Soulés further stated that all of the courts of Europe had been inundated with American ministers plenipotentiary who had exhibited a pomp and style scarcely compatible with the role of philosophers; that instead of cultivating the soil, establishing manufactures, and being content with their own homespun, Americans wanted to be clothed as the richest subjects of the greatest monarchies; that as a result they had contracted enormous debts, most of it to foreigners; that they had been unable to meet their financial obligations to the European powers; that they had not even been able to pay their own troops—those unfortunates who had been obliged to sell their certificates to usurers in order to maintain a miserable existence; that—and there could be little doubt in which direction this barb was aimed, since it was perfectly clear what source of information Démeunier had employed—Démeunier, in his opinion, had been badly informed on the subject of these soldiers' certificates; and that, as Washington had foreseen, America had become the plaything of European politics, which controlled its commerce at will.

Soulés' *Histoire* was primarily a military account of the Revolution, but these concluding observations struck at the heart of the political ends Jefferson had in view in this attempt to adapt history to the uses of diplomacy. Where Démeunier had repaid his effort with "unmerciful compliment" to him, Soulés repaid it with stinging comment upon his country.

I. Comments on Soulés' *Histoire*

Aug. 3. 1786.

Pa. 3.[1] 'Si dans son institution chaque individu avoit droit au gouvernement de l'etat, ou seulement ceux qui possédoient une certaine etendue de terre.' This is a luminous idea, and worthy of being

I. JEFFERSON'S COMMENTS

a little more developed. It places the question between Gr. Britain and America in the simplest form possible. No Englishman will pretend that a right to participate in government can be derived from any other source than a *personal* right, or a right of property. The conclusion is inevitable that he who had neither his *person* nor property in America could rightfully assume a participation in its government.

Pa. 17.[2] The seeds of the war are here traced to their true source. The tory education of the King was the first preparation for that change in the British government which that party never ceases to wish. This naturally ensured tory administrations during his life. At the moment he came to the throne, and cleared his hands of his enemies by the peace of Paris, the assumptions of unwarrantable right over America commenced; they were so signal, and followed one another so close as to prove they were part of a system, either to reduce it under absolute subjection and thereby make it an instrument for attempts on Britain itself, or to sever it from Britain so that it might not be a weight in the whig scale. This latter alternative however was not considered as the one which would take place. They knew so little of America that they thought it unable to encounter the little finger of Great Britain. M. de Soules has well developed this subject. He is best judge whether any thing more need be said on the subject.

Pa. 43.[3] 'Si le ministere Anglais avoit eu la patience d'attendre que ces marchandises fussent consommées &c.' Having seen and intimately known the positions of the Americans at that moment, I am certain that the conjecture would not have been verified. The determined resolution with which they met every effort of the Minister, whether made in the form of force, fraud or persuasion, gives us a moral certainty they would have been equally immoveable if tried in the way of privation here proposed.

Pa. 51.[4] 'pour accorder quelque chose &c.' The substitution of Gage for Hutchinson was not intended as a favor, but by putting even the civil government in military hands was meant to shew they would enforce their measures by arms. See pa. 109 where Congress make it one of their grievances.

Pa. 78.[5] A grand jury cannot be fewer than 12. nor more than 24. Some authors say it cannot be fewer than 13. nor more than 23.

Pa. 102.[6] 'Plusieurs criminels &c.' Notwithstanding the laws the English made, I think they never inclined to carry a single person to be tried in England. They knew that reprisals would be made and probably on the person of the governor who ventured on the measure.[7]

Pa. 140.[8] The fact that the English commenced hostilities at Lexington being proved beyond question by us and even acknowleged by the English, justice requires it should be plainly asserted, and left clear of doubt. Few of the facts, which history asserts and relies on, have been so well established.

Pa. 150.[9] 'L'humanité des Britons.' I doubt whether this is the character of the nation in general. But this history, and every one which is impartial must in it's relation of this war shew in such repeated instances, that they conducted it, both in theory and practice, on the most barbarous principles, that the expression here cited will stand in contradiction to the rest of the work. As examples of their Theory recollect the act of parliament for constraining our prisoners taken on the sea to bear arms against their fathers, brothers &c. For their practice, recollect their exciting the savages against us, insurrections of our slaves, sending our prisoners to the East Indies, killing them in prison ships, keeping them on halfrations and of the most unwholsome qualities, cruel murders of unarmed individuals of every sex, massacres of those in arms after they had asked quarter &c. &c.

Pa. 151.[10] 'A ce que l'on dit à 20,000 hommes.' It was of 22,000 men. I was in a situation to know the fact from Genl. Washington's own information.

158. 1. 8.[11] Strike out 'et probablement' and insert 'mais veritablement.' I remember the fact well and the leading persons of Connecticut, and particularly their delegates in Congress made no secret that their object was to over-awe N. York into it's duty.

159.[12] 'il fut resolu de la reduire [i.e. la Nouvelle York] en cendre.' This was proposed, and considered in Congress; but they refused to come to this resolution. Nor do I recollect that any other body resolved it.

163.[13] *Doctor* Franklin has been called by that title as early as 1760, within my own knowledge. I do not know how much longer.

His quality in France was that of Minister plenipotentiary, and not as Ambassador. We have never appointed an Ambassador. France offered to receive one.

Pa. 166.[14] The English set fire to Charlestown. Qu. as to the number of their killed.[15]

Pa. 180-181.[16] Gates was and still is an inhabitant of Virginia. He never lived in any other state.

Pa. 190.[17] M. Arnold avoit formé une entreprise &c. I never

I. JEFFERSON'S COMMENTS

understood that he formed this enterprise, nor do I believe he did. I heard and saw all General Washington's letters on this subject. I do not think he mentioned Arnold as author of the proposition; yet he was always just in ascribing to every officer the merit of his own works; and he was disposed particularly in favour of Arnold. This officer is entitled to great merit in the execution, but to ascribe to him that of the having formed the enterprize is probably to ascribe to him what belongs to Genl. Washington or some other person.

209.[18] 'et qu'il ne leur fut plus permis de lever la milice &c.' They had formerly had a law on the subject of invasions and insurrections which was of a perpetual tenor. They altered this law by one which was to be in force for a certain term of years only. That term of years affluxed at this time, the altering law expired, and therefore the old one resumed it's vigour. It was very imperfect; yet they chose to act under the colour of that rather than without any colour of law.

216.[19] 'dont elles se plaignoient.' This seems to be the proper place to rectify a small error in the arrangement of facts, and to state the answer to the conciliatory proposition, which was in truth the first work of the assembly. I have not here the journals of the assembly, but there are certain circumstances which render it impossible for my memory to lead me astray. I was under appointment to attend the General Congress: but knowing the importance of the answer to be given to the conciliatory proposition, and that our leading whig characters were then with Congress, I determined to attend on the assembly, and tho' a young member, to take on myself the carrying thro' an answer to the proposition. The assembly met the 1st. of June. I drew, and proposed the answer and carried it through the house with very little alteration, against the opposition of our timid members who wished to speak a different language. This was finished before the 11th. of June, because on that day, I set out from Williamsburgh for Philadelphia and was the bearer of an authenticated copy of this instrument to Congress. The effect it had in fortifying their minds, and in deciding their measures renders it's true date important because only Pennsylvania had as yet answered the proposition. Virginia was the second. It was known how Massachusets would answer it; and that the example of these three principal colonies would determine the measures of all the others, and of course the fate of the proposition. Congress received it therefore with much satisfaction. The assembly of Virginia did not deliver the answer to Ld. Dunmore till late in the session. They supposed it would bring on a dissolution of their body whenever they should deliver it to him, and they wished previously to get some important acts passed. For this reason they kept it up. I think that Ld. Dunmore did not quit the metropolis till he knew that the answer framed by the house was a rejection of the proposition, tho' that answer was not yet communicated to him regularly.

Pa. 231.[20] 'Quelques centaines de blancs.' These were composed principally of Scotch merchants and factors, and some few English who had settled in the country. I doubt whether there was a single native among them. If M. Soulés could therefore characterise more particularly who they were who joined Ld. Dunmore, it would be an agreeable act of justice to the natives.

Pa. 233.[21] 'Les Americains qui avoit joint Milord Dunmore.' The same observation applies to this.

Pa. 245.[22] 'Pendant l'eté le Congrés general avoit eté occupé a dresser un plan pour former une confederation.' It is necessary to set to rights here a fact which has been mistaken by every person who has written on this subject. I will do it from a perfect recollection of facts, but my memory does not enable me to state the date exactly. I was absent from Congress from the beginning of January 1776. to the middle of May. Either just before I left Congress, or immediately on my return to it (I rather think it was the former) Doctor Franklin put into my hands the draught of a plan of confederation, desiring me to read it and tell him what I thought of it. I approved it highly. He shewed it to others. Some thought as I did; others were revolted at it. We found it could not be passed, and that the proposing it to Congress as the subject for any vote whatever would startle many members so much that they would suspect we had lost sight of a reconciliation with Great Britain, and that we should lose much more ground than we should gain by the proposition. Yet that the idea of a more firm bond of union than the undefined one under which we then acted might be suggested and permitted to grow, Dr. Franklin informed Congress that he had sketched the outlines of an instrument which might become necessary at a future day, if the ministry continued pertinacious, and would ask leave for it to lay on the table of Congress, that the members might in the mean time be turning the subject in their minds, and have something more perfect prepared by the time it should become necessary. This was agreed to by the timid members, only on condition that no entry whatever should be made in the journals of Congress relative to this instrument. This was to con-

I. JEFFERSON'S COMMENTS

tinue in force only till a reconciliation with Great Britain. This was all that ever was done or proposed in Congress on the subject of a Confederation before June 1776, when the proposition was regularly made to Congress, a committee appointed to draw an instrument of Confederation, who accordingly drew one, very considerably differing from the sketch of Dr. Franklin.

Pa. 294.[23] 'il est à croire qu'il y avoit quelque convention.' It is well known there was such a convention. It was never made a secret of on our part. I do not exactly recollect it's terms, but I believe they were what M. Soulés states.

Pa. 301.[24] 'La petite verole.' I have been informed by officers who were on the spot, and whom I believe myself, that this disorder was sent into our army designedly by the commanding officer in Quebec. It answered his purposes effectually.

PrC (DLC: TJ Papers, 23: 3934-40); in TJ's hand. In this and the following document, page and volume references in the text are to the two-volume London, 1785, edition of Soulés *Histoire*; those in the notes are to the four-volume Paris, 1787, edition.

[1] Altered in a later hand by overwriting so as to read: "Vo. 3." This error on the part of the person who attempted to make the text more legible misled Ford who assumed it meant "Vo[lume] 3." and so printed it (Ford, IV, 306). The sentence quoted by TJ occurs in *Histoire*, I, 3; evidently Soulés adopted TJ's suggestion in part, for immediately following this sentence there is this development of the "luminous idea": "Il lui suffit de savoir que cela devoit être, qu'on n'a pu avec justice former son établissement sans l'une ou l'autre de ces méthodes, et que, si l'on a erré en quelque point, il n'est jamais trop tard de corriger ses erreurs. —Ce n'est point ici une assertion vague ou calculée pour servir de base à un système faux, mais une vérité évidente: un peuple ne sauroit être libre à moins qu'il n'ait part au Gouvernement, et il ne sauroit y avoir part que par un droit personnel ou par un droit de propriété." Soulés élabora this and then concluded: "Je me suis un peu étendu là-dessus, parce que c'est précisément l'origine des querelles qui subsistèrent entre la Grande-Bretagne et ses Colonies. Les Anglais prétendent qu'en quittant leur patrie, les habitans du nouveau monde ont renoncé à ses privilèges; et ces derniers au contraire soutiennent que leurs ancêtres, en prenant le nom de Colons, n'ont point abdiqué les droits d'Anglais. Je sais que la Constitution d'Angleterre n'est plus conforme à cette primitive institution dont je viens de parler; je doute même qu'elle le fût jamais: mais je suis certain qu'elle le devoit être, et cela me suffit" (*Histoire*, I, 3-5). In Dft TJ stated his intent more positively: "Introduction. The right to self-government in the British Constitution founded either 1. in right of person, or 2. right in lands. ⟨the author might have added . . .⟩ In either case the colonists had that right."

[2] *Histoire*, I, 10, contains the statement that the education of the Prince of Wales (later George III) "étoit confiée à un *Tory* des plus zélés; et c'est à lui qu'on attribue le présent système de Gouvernement." In Dft TJ wrote: "The education of the present king was Tory. He gave decisive victory to the Tories. To these were added sundry rich persons sprung up in the E.I. America would have been too formidable a weight in the scale of the Whigs. It was necessary therefore to reduce them by force to concur with the Tories."

[3] This passage (*Histoire*, I, 41-2) reads: "Les Négocians avoient pourvu à l'avenir, en demandant à leurs correspondans des marchandises pour deux ou trois ans avant que cette résolution fût adoptée. Si le Ministère Anglais avoit eu la patience d'attendre que ces marchandises fussent consommées, il est probable que la nécessité auroit naturellement forcé les Colons à se départir

[373]

de leur dessein, et que fort peu d'entre eux auroient eu la constance de renoncer aux aisances de la vie, pour la procurer à une postérité incertaine. L'interêt de la patrie auroit insensiblement cédé à l'intérêt particulier, le *Moi* n'auroit pas manqué de prévaloir, et cette association seroit tombée d'elle-même. L'enthousiasme n'a jamais pu être détruit que par lui-même. Les persécutions n'ont fait que lui donner de nouvelle forces, et un martyr a toujours produit vingt prosélytes." However, owing to TJ's opinion (and evidently also to that of another person, who may have been Crèvecœur), Soulés added the following: "Il y a néamoins des gens fort instruits de la façon de penser des Américains, et entr'autres, deux hommes du premier mérite, et pour l'opinion desquels nous avons les plus grands égards, qui sont persuadés que les Colons auroient eu assez de constance pour persévérer dans leurs résolutions, et que les privations de toute espèce, la misere et la mort même, n'auroient pas été capables de les ébranler. Cette opinion est, sans doute, fondée sur les preuves qu'ils donnèrent ensuite de leur attachement à la cause de la liberté, et sur la patience avec laquelle ils souffrirent toutes sortes de maux pour parvenir à leurs fins; mais les circonstances et les passions ont beaucoup d'influence sur les actions des hommes, et tel est timide, chancelant et incertain avant d'entreprendre une affaire sérieuse, ou de commencer une guerre ouverte avec son Gouvernement, qui devient ferme, intrépide et opiniâtre, lorsqu'il a une fois fait les premiers pas. Quoi qu'il en soit, les Anglais auroient dû essayer cette méthode, et ne point s'opposer directement aux résolutions des Colonies. Tout au contraire, aussitôt que le Ministère en fut informé, il prit des mesures qui paroissent réellement ridicules, et fit passer en Amérique des charges considérables de thé, comme s'il eût été possible de faire acheter aux Colons une marchandise dont ils avoient résolu de ne point se servir" (*Histoire*, I, 42-3). In Dft, TJ remarked, after referring to p. 43 and quoting the pertinent passage as above: "Experience proved this reasoning false. The goods were consumed, yet nobody relaxed in their opposition."

4 As finally published, the pertinent paragraph reads: "Le Ministère Anglais avoit changé le Gouverneur de la Province de Massachuset, M. Hutchinson, qui leur étoit si odieux, et avoit nommé à sa place M. Gage, qui, à la qualité de Gouverneur, joignoit celle de Généralissime de toutes les forces de Sa Majesté Britannique en Amérique." The sentence that TJ questioned was eliminated. Dft reads: "The substituting Gage for Hutchinson was not intended as a favor but as an addition of rigour." The reference to page 109 (*Histoire*, I, 102) is to the fact that the Articles of Association of 20 Oct. 1774 had included as a grievance the keeping of a standing army in the colonies in time of peace and particularly the fact that "le Général en chef de l'armée est, en tems de paix, nommé Gouverneur d'une Colonie."

5 Dft reads: "A grand jury cannot exceed 24." As finally published the passage reads: "Les grands Juries, suivant certains Auteurs, peuvent être composés de vingt-quatre personnes; mais ce nombre n'est pas absolument nécessaire, il suffit qu'il y en ait douze: d'autres soutiennent qu'il ne faut pas plus de vingt-trois, ni moins de treize personnes, pour former un grand *Jury*" (*Histoire*, I, 73).

6 The statement to which TJ objected was evidently the following: "Ce qui donna lieu à cette déclaration [that the colonists were entitled to the right of being tried by a jury of their peers], c'est que, lorsque les *Juries* refusèrent d'agir, on avoit menacé les Américains de les priver de ce privilège, et de les faire transporter en Angleterre, pour y être jugés par des *Juries* Anglais" (*Histoire*, I, 96); Soulés evidently altered this passage from its original reading by adding the phrase "on avoit menacé." Dft reads: "I think the English never carried a single criminal to England to be tried. They passed laws for it indeed."

7 In Dft there is the following which TJ did not include in his final comments: "105. de ne plus se servir des denrées des isles occidentales." The pertinent passage in Soulés' work reads as follows: "Le premier article de cette Convention contient une résolution de ne plus recevoir de marchandises des Isles Britanniques après le 1 Décembre, d'interdire toute entrée au thé des Indes Orientales de quelque partie du monde qu'on puisse le transporter, de ne plus se servir des denrées des Isles Occidentales appartenant à l'Angleterre, de ne plus tirer de vin de Madère, ni d'indigo de l'étranger" (*Histoire*, I, 98). The first Article of the Association of 1774 (see Vol. 1: 150) was in-

I. JEFFERSON'S COMMENTS

adequately summarized by Soulés, but TJ may have decided that it was a point not worth comment.

8 *Histoire*, I, 136. Soulés inserted the following passage in accordance with TJ's comment: "Il est néanmoins reconnu depuis, de manière à n'en pouvoir plus douter, que ce furent les Anglais qui attaquèrent les Américains, et que le Major Pitcairn donna le signal en tirant le premier coup de pistolet." Dft reads: "It ought to be said that the British fired first. See the journ. Congr. Pitcairn fired his pistol, and then followed a general discharge from his party."

9 *Histoire*, I, 140. The passage in question reads: "La vérité exige même que nous déclarions que les Anglais, dans le cours de ces querelles, furent coupables de bien des cruautés, et se départirent de cet esprit de tolérance et d'humanité, qui les avoit toujours distingués dans les guerres antérieures. Il ne faut cependant pas accuser la Nation entière de ces excès. Il y avoit en Angleterre une infinité de gens qui gémissoient des coups portés à leurs concitoyens de l'Amérique, et qui blâmoient ouvertement la conduite des partisans du Ministère." Soulés, in a context which declared that each party accused the other of great cruelties and that civil wars were more characterized by inhumanity than others, evidently altered the passage in accordance with TJ's suggestion, but not, perhaps, to his satisfaction. Dft reads: "l'humanité des Britons. Where are the proofs that this is their national character? Must not this history contradict it in a multitude of instances? History is no place for compliments."

10 *Histoire*, I, 141. Soulés adopted TJ's figures: "Le corps de milice qui étoit devant cette ville [Boston], montoit, à ce que l'on dit, à vingt-deux mille hommes, sous le commandement des Colonels Ward, Pribble, Heath, Prescot et Thomas, qui agissoient alors comme Généraux."

11 *Histoire*, I, 147. Soulés adopted TJ's suggestion: "Sur ces entrefaites quelques régimens du Connecticut arrivèrent dans le voisinage de la Capitale [New York], en apparence pour la protéger, et véritablement pour soutenir le parti du Congrès; car cette force n'étoit pas suffisante pour défendre la ville en cas qu'elle eût été attaquée par mer."

12 *Histoire*, I, 148. The pertinent passage reads: "Il fut même proposé de la réduire en cendres en cas que cela se trouvât nécessaire; mais heureusement pour *New-York*, les troupes que l'on y attendoit débarquèrent à Boston, où l'on en avoit alors plus de besoin." In Dft TJ merely wrote "Qu?" after the corresponding phrase from Soulés.

13 *Histoire*, I, 152. The passage, which may or may not have been altered, reads: "M. Franklin, connu sous le nom de Docteur Franklin." Dft reads: "Dr. Franklin had that appellation many years before the war. I remember it since the year 1760. His title in France was not Ambassador but Minister Plenipotentiary."

14 *Histoire*, I, 155. Soulés evidently altered the passage in accordance with TJ's suggestion and also on the basis of a comment supplied by someone else, perhaps Blackden: "le General Pigot ... fit mettre le feu à la ville [Charlestown, Mass.], et elle fut réduite en cendres. Cet action, suivant le rapport que m'a fait un Officier qui s'y est trouvé, représentoit une des scènes des plus terribles de la guerre." Dft reads: "The English set fire to Chas. T. unquestionably."

15 Dft reads: "169. 226 hommes de tués." Soulés evidently changed the passage in accordance with TJ's query; as printed it reads: "La perte de ces derniers [the Americans], suivant la relation qui fut ensuite publiée par le Congrès de la Province, étoit peu considérable, en comparaison de celle de leurs ennemis, ne montant qu'à quatre cens cinquante hommes, tant tués que blessés, et faits prisonniers. Leurs adversaires soutinrent que cette relation étoit fausse, et que, pour cacher le nombre de leurs morts, ils les enterroient durant l'action, chose qui paroît étrange, et qui n'est pas même probable" (*Histoire*, I, 158).

16 According to Dft, Soulés had first written: "Gates vivoit dans la N. York." This was altered in accordance with TJ's correction to read: "Lee et Gates étoient Anglais. ... Le dernier étoit un vieillard vénérable qui avoit depuis long-tems renoncé à la vie militaire, et qui vivoit tranquillement sur ses terres dans la province de Virginie avec son épouse, qui étoit Américaine" (*Histoire*, I, 168).

17 Dft reads: "Arnold planned the expedition up the Kennebec?" Soulés did not alter the passage, which reads: "M. Arnold avoit formé une entreprise, que sa nouveauté, le courage, et la

[375]

constance avec laquelle elle fut conduite, rendront à jamais digne de mémoire" (*Histoire*, I, 179). In August 1775 when Washington first unfolded his plan to Schuyler, he wrote that the Kennebec route to Canada had engaged his "Thought for several days"; such a plan had been specifically suggested in the spring of 1775 by Col. Jonathan Brewer and others may have advanced the idea (Washington to Schuyler, 20 Aug. 1775; *Writings*, ed. Fitzpatrick, III, 437; Freeman, *Washington*, III, 532).

[18] *Histoire*, I, 196. The passage in question reads: "Les Virginiens . . . avoient été des premiers à envoyer des Députés au Congrès Général, et à approuver ses mesures. Néamoins la plus grande tranquillité régnoit dans la province; et, quoique leur Assemblée eût été cassée, et qu'il ne leur fût plus permis de lever la milice, chose qui les mettoit dans le plus grand danger, puisque le nombre d'esclaves est dans ce pays-là fort considérable, ils avoient toujours eu toutes sortes d'égards pour le Comte de Dunmore leur Gouverneur." Soulés allowed this to stand, but he utilized TJ's comment in a footnote in the following manner: "Il y avoit une ancienne loi qui permettoit à la Virginie de lever la milice en cas d'invasion et de soulèvement parmi les Nègres. Comme cette loi étoit sujette à beaucoup d'inconvéniens, on en avoit donné une autre, qui permettoit de lever la milice pendant un certain nombre d'années, à l'expiration desquelles on pouvoit la renouveller, si on jugeoit à propos. Ce tems étant alors expiré, et Mylord Dunmore ne voulant pas permettre qu'on la renouvellât, les Virginiens agirent suivant l'ancienne loi" (*Histoire*, I, 196-7, note). On this, see Vol. 1: 160-2.

[19] *Histoire*, I, 202-3. In this passage Soulés gave an account of Dunmore's calling the Virginia General Assembly in order to lay before them Lord North's conciliatory propositions (see Vol. 1: 170-4; 225-30). Soulés utilized TJ's comment as follows: "L'Assemblée examina sur le champ le Bill du Ministère, et M. Jefferson, à présent Ministre Plénipotentiaire des Etats-Unis à la Cour de France, proposa la réponse qu'on devoit faire au Gouverneur. Il y eut de grands débats à ce sujet; mais il eut assez de crédit pour la faire approuver, malgré l'opposition de quelques Membres timides et chancelans, qui auroient souhaité qu'on tînt un langage différent." Dft reads: "After 'se plaignoient' insert 'My lord D. hoped the rather to prevail on assembly &c inasmuch as leading men were absent.'"

[20] Dft reads: "quelques centaines de blancs. They were Scotch &c. and again 233. les Americains &c." The passage in question (*Histoire*, I, 216-7) concerned Dunmore's proclamation of martial law and promise of freedom to such slaves as should join him: "Cet édit, et la présence de Mylord Dunmore, produisirent leur effet dans la ville de Norfolk, et dans les pays d'alentour, où plusieurs des habitans étoient attachés au Gouvernement. Quelques centaines de blancs et de noirs joignirent le Gouverneur, et d'autres qui refusèrent de prendre les armes, abjurèrent publiquement le Congrès, et tous ses actes."

[21] *Histoire*, I, 219. Soulés altered the phrase to read: "les gens du pays qui avoient joint Mylord Dunmore," which scarcely covered the objection made by TJ.

[22] *Histoire*, I, 230-1. Soulés made use of TJ's comment in the following manner: "Le Docteur proposa son plan au Congrès; mais il fut obligé d'agir avec beaucoup de circonspection, et de représenter cette mesure comme éloignée, quoiqu'il assurât qu'elle seroit absolument nécessaire si les Ministres de la Grande-Bretagne persistoient dans leur opiniâtreté à vouloir réduire les Colonies dans l'esclavage. Tous les Membres du Congrès n'étoient pas également clairvoyans. Il y en avoit beaucoup qui espéroient encore pouvoir se réconcilier avec Angleterre, et d'autres qui n'agissoient qu'avec timidité. On délibéra pour savoir si on recevroit le plan dans l'Assemblée, et il fut à la fin résolu qu'on le laisseroit sur la table pour l'examen de la Chambre, à condition cependant que cette résolution ne seroit point mise dans les Journaux."

[23] *Histoire*, I, 277. The passage concerned the communication sent to Washington from the Selectmen of Boston, 8 Mch. 1776, informing him that Sir William Howe had given them assurance he had no intention of destroying Boston unless his troops were molested by Washington's army upon their embarkation, but that if they were, the Bostonians could expect to be exposed to entire destruction (Freeman, *Washington*, IV, 42-3). Soulés altered the pertinent passage to read: "Il est à croire qu'il y avoit un accord secret entre les deux Généraux, et que M. Washington s'offrit de ne pas inquiéter

II. ANSWERS TO SOULES' QUERIES

les Anglais, à condition que ces derniers ne détruiroient point la ville." Dft reads: "It is a fact well known that there was such a convention. No secret was made of it on our part. I do not recollect precisely its terms, but I believe they were just what are stated here."

24 Dft reads: "This was sent among them by the English general." Soulés did not adopt TJ's suggestion. The passage reads: "Dans cet état de découragement, la petite vérole, ce fléau du Nouveau-Monde, et qui fait tant de dégât parmi ses habitants, parut dans le camp. Cette maladie, que les Américains regardent comme la peste, produisit les plus mauvais effets, et il fut presqu'impossible de maintenir discipline" (*Histoire*, I, 284).

II. Answers to Soulés' Queries
[13-18 Sep. 1786]

I am unable to say what was the number of Americans engaged in the affair of Bunker's hill. I am able however to set right a gross falsehood of Andrews. He says that the Americans who were engaged were constantly relieved by fresh hands. This is entirely untrue. Bunker's hill (or rather Brede's hill whereon the action was) is a peninsula, joined to the main land by a neck of land almost level with the water, a few paces wide, and between one and two hundred toises long. On one side of this neck lay a vessel of war, and on the other several gun-boats. The body of our army was on the main land; and only a detachment had been sent into the peninsula. When the enemy determined to make the attack, they sent the vessel of war and gun-boats to take the position before mentioned to cut off all reinforcements, which they effectually did. Not so much as a company could venture in to the relief of the men engaged, who therefore fought thro' the whole action and at length were obliged to retire across the neck thro' the cross fire of the vessels beforementioned. Single persons passed along the neck during the engagement, particularly General Putnam.

On the fall of Montgomery and his aids at Quebec, there were present Colo. Campbell and Major Dubois. Campbell, tho' having the rank of Colonel was only of the staff; Dubois was of the line. The usage of all nations therefore authorised the latter to take the command. But it was a case for which Congress had not yet provided. Campbell availed himself of this, and believing, on the sight of blood, that all was lost, ordered a retreat.

The speech to the Indians in Andrews page 357.[1] is a little altered and abridged. You will find the genuine one in the Journal of Congress of July 1775.

I do not distinctly enough recollect the anecdote of the Old man's company related by Andrews, to affirm it in all it's parts. I think I recollect in general that there was such a company.

COMMENTS ON SOULES' HISTOIRE 1786

The questions relative to General Thomas I could only have answered indistinctly from my own memory; but fortunately there came to Paris a few days ago, and will yet continue there a few days, a Colonel Blackden, an American officer of good understanding of truth, and who was at the latter part of the affair of Quebec. He was at the surprise of Ticonderoga by Allen, and continued with the army till 1781. I have spoken with him on this subject, and find he possesses treasures of details which will be precious to M. Soulés. Any day that Mr. Soulés will do me the honour to come and take a family soupe with me (after the 16th. inst.) if he will give me notice in the morning, I will ask Colo. Blackden to meet him here, and will make them acquainted. He is perfectly disposed to give all the information in his power to Mr. Soulés, and whatever he gives may be relied on. To him then I shall refer Mr. Soulés for answers to his military questions, and will wait his orders, recommending dispatch as Colo. Blackden has not long to stay.

The Stamp act was passed in Feb. 1765.

What powers the Parliament might rightfully exercise over us, and whether any, had never been declared either by them or us. They had very early taken the gigantic step of passing the navigation act. The colonies remonstrated violently against it, and one of them, Virginia, when she capitulated to the Commonwealth of England, expressly capitulated for a free trade. See the articles in the Notes on Virginia pa. 201. This capitulation however was as little regarded as the original right, restored by it, had been. The navigation act was re-enacted by Charles 2 and was enforced, and we had been so long in the habit of seeing them consider us merely as objects for the extension of their *commerce*, and of submitting to every duty or regulation imposed with that view, that we had ceased to complain of them. But when they proposed to consider us as objects of *taxation*, all the states took the alarm. Yet so little had we attended to this subject, that our advocates did not at first know on what ground to take their stand. Mr. Dickinson, a lawyer of more ingenuity than sound judgment, and still more timid than ingenious, not daring to question the authority to regulate commerce so as best to answer their own purposes, to which we had so long submitted, admitted that authority in it's utmost extent. He acknoleged in his Farmer's [Let]ters th[at th]ey could put down [rolling or sli]tt[ing mil]l[s] and other [in]st[rumen]t[s][2] of manufacture, that they could levy duties internal or external, paiable in Great Britain or in the States. He only required that these duties should be bonâ fide for the *regulation* of commerce, and not to raise

[378]

II. ANSWERS TO SOULES' QUERIES

a solid *revenue*. He admitted therefore that they might controul our commerce, but not tax us. This mysterious system took for a moment in America as well as in Europe. But sounder heads saw in the first moment that he who could put down the loom, could stop the spinning wheel, and he who could stop the spinning wheel could tie the hands which turned it. They saw that this flimsy fabric could not be supported. Who were to be judges whether duties were imposed with a view to burthen and suppress a branch of manufacture, or to raise a revenue? If either party, exclusively of the other, it was plain where that would end. If both parties, it was plain where that would end also. They saw therefore no sure clue to lead them out of their difficulties but reason and right. They dared to follow them, assured that they alone could lead them to defensible ground. The first elements of reason shewed that the members of parliament could have no power which the people of the several counties had not. That these had naturally a power over their own farms, and collectively over all England. That if they had any power over countries out of England it must be founded on compact or force. No compact could be shewn, and neither party chose to bottom their pretensions on force. It was objected that this annihilated the navigation act. True, it does. The navigation act therefore becomes a proper subject of treaty between the two nations. Or if Gr. Britain does not chuse to have it's basis questioned, let us go on as we have done. Let no new shackles be imposed and we will continue to submit to the old. We will consider the restrictions on our commerce now actually existing as compensations yielded by us for the protection and privileges we actually enjoy, only trusting[3] that if Great Britain, on a revisal of these restrictions, is sensible that some of them are useless to her and oppressive to us, she will repeal them. But on this she shall be free. Place us in the condition we were when the King came to the throne, let us rest so, and we will be satisfied. This was the ground on which all the states very soon found themselves rallied, and that there was no other which could be defended.

I will now proceed with remarks on the history.

I do not find that M. Soules mentions the affair of the Cedars which happened in April 1776. This was an affair of considerable[4] importance. A committee was appointed by Congress to institute enquiries concerning it, as may be seen by the journals of June 15 1776. The report of that committee is inserted in the journals of July 10. and I can assure Mr. Soulés that the facts therein stated

COMMENTS ON SOULES' HISTOIRE 1786

were proved incontestably to the committee by witnesses present at the transaction, and who were on watch. I have the originals of that enquiry in my possession in America. The Captn. Foster therein mentioned was afterwards taken with Burgoyne's army; tho permitted to go at large on his parole, he was not received into any American company, nor did the British officers, his fellow prisoners, chuse to be seen in company with him, so notorious and so detestable had been this transaction.[5]

Vol. 1. pa. 324.[6] I have been very well informed that during all the latter part of this defence, the garrison were obliged to return the canon balls of the enemy, with which indeed the ground was covered, having none of their own left.

pa. 325.[7] 'Il y eut un Serjent &c. This particular truly related in Andrews.

Vol. 2. pa. 5.[8] 'Ils en vinrent le 10. de Juin à cette resolution que ces Colonies &c. See the Journ. of Congr. that it was on that day put off to the 1st. of July. This was done at the instance of the members opposed to it. The friends of the resolution objected that if it were not agreed to till the 1st. of July they would after that have to frame a Declaration of Independence and that more time would thus be lost. It was therefore agreed between the two that the resolution should be put off till the 1st of July, and that a committee should be immediately appointed to draw a declaration of Independence conformable to the resolution, should it be adopted. A committee was accordingly appointed the next day. On the 1st of July the resolution was proposed, and when ready for a vote, a state required it to be put off till the next day. It was done, and was passed the next day, 2d. of July. The declaration of Independance was debated during the 2d. 3d. and 4th. days of July and on the last of these was passed and signed.

Pa. 6. a.[9] 'Se retirerent ensuite du Congrés.' I do not remember that the delegates of Maryland retired from Congress, and I think I could not have forgotten such a fact. On the contrary I find by the Journals of Congress that they were present and acting on the 11th. 12th. 17th. 18th. and 24th. of June.

Pa. 7. a.[10] 'La plus *grande* partie.' It should rather be 'the most *important* parts.'

Pa. 7. b.[11] 'Les etats unis feroient encore aujourdhui partie de l'empire Britannique.' M. Soulés may be assured that the submission of the states could not have been effected but by a long series of disasters, and such too as were irreparable in their nature. Their

II. ANSWERS TO SOULES' QUERIES

resources were great, and their determination so rooted, that they would have tried the last of them. I am as satisfied, as I can be of any thing, that the conjectures here stated would not have been verified by the event.

Pa. 14.[12] 'provinces unis.' Should not this always be 'etats-unis.'

Pa. 15.[13] 'Mais qu'on pouvoit aussi les interpreter &c.' His exact answer was that 'it was true the &c. might include *any thing*, but that they might also include *nothing*.'

Pa. 16.[14] 'Tant de confiance &c. Their main confidence was in their own resources. They considered foreign aid as probable and desireable, but not essential. I believe myself, from the whole of what I have seen of our resources and perseverance 1. that had we never received any foreign aid, we should not have obtained our independance, but that we should have made a peace with Great Britain on any terms we pleased, short of that, which would have been a subjection to the same king, an union of force in war &c. 2. that had France supplied us plentifully with money, suppose about 4. millions of guineas a year, without entering into the war herself at all, we should have established our Independance, but it would have cost more time, and blood, but less money. 3. that France, aiding us as she did, with money and forces, shortened much the time, lessened the expence of blood, but at a greater expence of money to her than would otherwise have been requisite.

Pa. 18.[15] 'l'*extremité* septentrionale &c. I think the word 'cote' would be better adapted than 'extremité' to the form of the island.

Pa. 21.[16] '3000 hommes'. Enquire of Colo. Blackden.

Perhaps the propositions of Congress to the Hessians may be worth mentioning. See their Journals 1776. Aug. 14.

I will make a general observation here on the events of Long island, New York &c. at this time. The maxim laid down by Congress to their Generals was that not a foot of territory was to be ceded to their enemies where there was a possibility of defending it. In consequence of these views, and against his own judgment, Genl. Washington was obliged to fortify and attempt to defend the city of New York. But that could not be defended without occupying the heights in Long island which commanded the city of New York. He was therefore obliged to establish a strong detachment in Long island [to] defend those heights. The moment that detachment was routed, which he had much expected, his first object was to withdraw them, and his 2d. to evacuate New York. He did this therefore immediately, and without waiting any movement of the enemy. He brought off his whole baggage, stores, and

COMMENTS ON SOULES' HISTOIRE 1786

other implements, without leaving a single article except the very heaviest of his cannon and things of little value. I well remember his letter to Congress wherein he expresses his wonder that the enemy had given him this leisure, as, from the heights they had got possession of, they might have compelled him to a very precipitate retreat. This was one of the instances where our commanding officers were obliged to conform to popular views tho' they foresaw certain loss from it. Had he proposed at first to abandon New York, he might have been abandoned himself. An obedience to popular will cost us an army in Charlestown in the year 1779.

Pa. 30.[17] 'Une fuite precipitée.' It was a leisurely retreat as I have before observed.

Pa. 41.[18] 'Que je n'ai pu obtenir que d'un Anglois.' Colo. Blackden can probably give M. Soulés good intelligence on this affair. I think I recollect the slaughter on Kniphausen's side to have been very great.

PrC (DLC); in TJ's hand at head of text TJ wrote: "Answers to the queries of M. Soulés"; PrC is faded and has been overwritten in places by someone at a later date, partly in pencil and partly in ink, in an effort to restore the text, with the result that at least one error was committed (see note, TJ to Carmichael, 22 Aug. 1822).

THE AFFAIR OF THE CEDARS concerning which TJ asserted that he had ORIGINALS IN MY POSSESSION IN AMERICA was one on which TJ had, in fact, drawn the report which Congress authorized to be published (see Vol. 1: 396-9; 400-4). Soulés adopted the suggestion (*Histoire*, I, 286-9); his account appears to have been based upon the published report, but certain observations in it may have been supplied by TJ in conversation.

[1] An error for "341"; TJ here cited the page reference for Soulés next query.

[2] Most of the last line of the third page of MS is illegible. The reading has been supplied conjecturally in part with the aid of a footnote citation in "Farmer's Letters," iv, Dickinson's *Political Writings*, Wilmington, 1801, I, 182, referring to 23rd Geo. II, c. 29, sect. 9.

[3] This word interlined by TJ in substitution for another word that appears to be "providing."

[4] As overwritten by someone at a later date, this phrase reads: "of no small importance." This is an error, for TJ wrote the phrase as given above.

[5] Below the word "detestable" in this sentence there appear the letters "ckden." It is possible that TJ had written something like the following: "[Enquire about this of Col. Bla]ckden," for approximately this number of words is missing and TJ employed the same words elsewhere.

[6] *Histoire*, I, 308. This passage concerned the attack on Fort Moultrie on 28 June 1776; Soulés stated that the Americans claimed that the silence of their batteries was due to the fact that "ils n'avoient plus de poudre, et qu'ils furent obligés d'attendre qu'il leur en vînt du continent. Cette relation paroît véritable, et le feu des navires retarda encore davantage l'arrivée de cette poudre."

The reference to pages "6.a." of the 1785 edition of Soulés' work is explained by the fact that there was an error in the pagination of the second volume, each of pages 6, 7, and 8 being repeated.

[7] *Histoire*, I, 309. Dft reads: "325. The colours of the fort were cut down by a canon ball, and fell outside of the fort. The serjeant (a gentleman of fortune) jumped over the wall in the hottest of the fire, took up the colours, climbed up again, and planted them. See Andrews."

[8] Dft reads: "Vol. 2. pa. 5. ils en vinrent le 10. de Juin à cette resolution. On the contrary they put it off to

[382]

II. ANSWERS TO SOULES' QUERIES

the 1st. of July and agreed to it on the 2d. But on the 10th they made a provisional order to draw declaration conformable to this resolution in case it should be agreed to." Soulés followed TJ's account of the immediate background of the Declaration of Independence, except that he added the names of the Committee of Five (which he must have obtained from TJ); he still confused the resolution of independence and the Declaration itself; and, instead of stating that the latter was passed and signed on 4 July 1776 as TJ had, he wrote: "mais les Membres étant à la fin réunis, le Congrès déclara, le 4, l'indépendance des Colonies, et les nomma, *les Etats-Unis de l'Amerique*" (*Histoire*, I, 315-7).

9 Dft reads: "se retirerent du Congrès. I do not remember their retiring. On the contrary I see by the journ. Congr. they were present and named on committees June 11. 12. 17. 18. 24." Dft ends at this point. Soulés did not delete the phrase about the withdrawal of the Maryland delegates (*Histoire*, I, 316).

10 *Histoire*, I, 318. The phrase suggested was adopted. Soulés wrote: "Les places les plus importantes de la Nouvelle-York étant sur des isles longues et étroites, se trouvoient exposées à l'artillerie de la flotte et aux descentes des troupes Anglaises."

11 *Histoire*, I, 319. Soulés' statement about the ministry's plan for the subjugation of the colonies in 1776 was: "Ce plan étoit certainement des mieux formés; et si les Généraux employés pour l'exécuter avoient montré autant d'habileté que ceux qui l'avoient tracé, les Etats-Unis feroient encore aujourd'hui partie de l'Empire Britannique; mais ils commirent des fautes impardonnables, et firent même croire à toute l'Europe qu'ils agissoient de concert avec l'ennemi." This statement remained unchanged despite TJ's disagreement.

12 *Histoire*, I, 326. The phrase was altered as suggested. This occurred in the passage concerning Sir William Howe's letter addressed "*To George Washington Esquire &ca. &ca. &ca.*" without mentioning the rank he held "dans le service des Etats-Unis" (see Washington, *Writings*, ed. Fitzpatrick, v, 297, 321-3, note).

13 *Histoire*, I, 326-7. Soulés wrote: "M. Washington repliqua . . . qu'il etoit vrai que les & *cætera* renfermoient tout, mais qu'on pouvoit aussi les interpreter de la manière qu'on vouloit, et qu'il ne recevroit pas une lettre qui lui étoit adressée comme à un particulier, touchant les affaires de l'Etat." He evidently did not accept TJ's suggestion. According to the memorandum of Lt. Col. James Patterson that Congress authorized to be published on 20 July 1776, Washington's remark was "that it was true the *&c.&c.&c.* implied everything, and they also implied anything" (Washington, *Writings*, ed. Fitzpatrick, v, 322, note).

14 *Histoire*, I, 327-8. Soulés did not accept TJ's suggestion. Discussing the treatment of the Loyalists by the Americans, he remarked: "Tant de confiance à la veille d'une invasion, marquoit, ou beaucoup de présomption, ou une connoissance parfaite des ressources du pays, ou une certitude de recevoir du secours des Puissances étrangères."

15 *Histoire*, I, 329. Soulés adopted TJ's suggestion in the following sentence: "Le Général Putnam étoit alors campé à une place appellée *Brook-Lyn*, sur la côte septentrionale, ayant à gauche ce qu'ils appellent la Rivière de l'Est, qui sépare *Long-Island* de la Nouvelle-York."

16 *Histoire*, I, 332. The phrase occurred in the following sentence concerning the Battle of Long Island: "On fait monter leur perte dans cette action à trois mille hommes, y compris mille prisoniers. Presque tout un régiment de jeunes gens de famille de la province de Maryland y fut taillé en pièces."

17 *Histoire*, I, 340. The passage referred to was probably revised by Soulés. It reads: "Les Américains quittèrent aussi-tôt la ville capitale et leurs postes de ce côté-là, et se retirèrent vers la partie septentrionale, où étoit leur principale force. Ils abandonnèrent quelques pièces d'artillerie, un peu de provisions et de bagage."

18 *Histoire*, I, 349-50. The passage, involving an account of the attack on Kings Bridge, N.Y., was evidently revised by Soulés, perhaps after consultation with Col. Blackden.

To John Stockdale

Sir Paris Sep. 13. 1786.

Your letter of Aug. 8. with the books accompanying it came safely to hand, as did the reviews for August, and Priestly's pamphlet lately sent. I now trouble you for the books written below. I write by this post to Colo. Smith for a number of books from Lackington's catalogue for 1787. I wish those, with yours, could come in one parcel, as, coming separately, they occasion double trouble with the Custom houses. They will come best and speediest by the Diligence from the White bear Picadilly. Have you had an opportunity of sending the books I desired to Virginia? I am Sir Your very humble servant, Th: Jefferson

Linnaeus on the sexes of plants. Eng. by Smith 8vo. Nicol.
Hutton's mathematical tables. 8vo.
Schomberg on the maritime laws of Rhodes. 8vo.
An account of the present state of Nova Scotia. 8vo. Longman.
Samwell's narrative of the death of Cook. 4to. Robinson.
Brook Taylor's treatise on Perspective.
to be sent in boards.

PrC (DLC); endorsed.

To Mary Barclay

[*Paris, 14 Sep. 1786.* Entry in SJL under this date reads: "Mrs. Barclay. No copy kept." Not found; TJ had received Barclay's letter of 11 Aug. on 13 Sep. 1786, and the missing letter must have reported this fact to her and may also have conveyed a letter from her husband.]

To Biron

[*Paris, 14 Sep. 1786.* Entry in SJL under this date reads: "Marechal de Biron. [No cop. ⟨pris⟩ kept]." Not found, but see Biron to TJ, 12 Sep. 1786.]

From Etienne Clavière

rue Coqhéron hôtel DeLessert
Monsieur Paris le 14e. 7bre 1786.

Je crois que l'on peut poser en principe qu'en Europe le Cultiva-

[384]

teur est dans une condition trop misérable pour tenir volontairement au travail de la terre. Doù il suit que la Culture de toute production étrangére à la Classe des comestibles, comme le tabac et la garence ne convient pas à l'Europe: une Charue conduite à regrêt ne fertilise guères, et l'Europe doit cependant songer avant tout à se nourrir.

Je crois de plus avoir entendu dire que le tabac et la garence épuisaient le sol: or l'Europe n'ayant qu'un sol généralement épuisé, on ne doit à plus forte raison lui demander que le nécessaire.

Si cet effet du tabac est Certain, il arrive sans doute qu'en Virginie et dans le Maryland, qui produisent la plus grande partie du tabac Américain, on n'attend pas qu'il ait épuisé le sol et qu'on en porte sans cesse la culture sur une terre nouvelle. Les Européens n'ont pas cette ressource, tandis que les Américains auront encore longtems des terres vierges à leur disposition.

Mais ce n'est de ma part qu'une conjecture. L'intérêt que vous prenez, Monsieur, à l'ouvrage, entrepris par Monsieur Brissot de Warville, me persuade que vous voudrés bien nous donner, sur ce que je viens de vous exposer, les lumières qui nous manquent.

Les rapports entre L'Amérique et l'Europe doivent être fondés non sur des Systêmes fantastiques, mais sur des Convenances solidement établies.

Tout ce que vous voudrez bien ajouter d'important sur les tabacs Américains, leur quantité, celle de l'exportation, et ce que vous prévoyez de l'avenir, rélativement à Cette plante, considérée comme production de L'Amérique, ne pourra que nous être très utile.

Agréez, Monsieur, les assurances de ma vénération, et que je me félicite à vos yeux d'avoir vû un de ces hommes à jamais célèbres qui ont le plus contribué à la seule révolution tout à la fois utile et glorieuse, dont les hommes puissent se vanter, du moins entre Celles qui nous sont Connuës.

J'ai l'honneur d'être, Monsieur Votre très humble & très Obeissant serviteur,   E Claviere

RC (MoSHi); endorsed.

L'OUVRAGE, ENTREPRIS PAR MONSIEUR BRISSOT DE WARVILLE: Clavière was joint author with Brissot of the book *De la France et des Etats-Unis*. See TJ to Brissot, 16 Aug. 1786.

From Ezra Stiles

Sir   Yale College Sept 14 1786

I take the Liberty to inform you that, yesterday at the public anniversary Commencement in this University, the Senatus Aca-

14 SEPTEMBER 1786

demicus did themselves the Honor to confer upon you the Degree of Doctor in Laws. We ask your Acceptance of it as a Token of the high Estimation and Respect we have for your literary Character, as well as for your Patriotism and Fidelity to the united [States.]

Our Enemies are fomenting Discord among us and have succeeded to excite some Tumults and popular Insurrections. But there will be great Wisdom in Exercise both in Congress, the Legislatures and the executive Administrations, which will controll, rectify and regulate all Things. All will conspire to prepare the People at large to see the necessity both of Paying the Interest of the foreign Debt, and of Enlarging the Powers of Congress. Congress ought to and will grow up into a very powerful Senate; but it is impossible it should with all the Cessions of the People acquire a Power dangerous to LIBERTY so long as Property in the United States is so minutely partitioned and transfused among the Inhabitants. I pray God to give Success to your Negotiations. Sorry I am that yourself and Dr. Adams must have the Mortification of seeing the National Faith of the United States in Reproach among the European Powers. Our Ingratitude to France and Holld. particularly is great and unpardonable. However national Patience and Forbearance on their side, will give us opportunity to feel the Possibility of being disagreeably coerced and at length to learn the Wisdom and Necessity of exerting ourselves. We know France can declare Naval Reprisal upon us—this will br[ing] us to ourselves. But France will wisely procrastin[ate] such a Measure—for she will surely obtain her Repayment without it. The Western Territory will so diminish our Debt that we shall in a few years recover our justly lost national Credit. Must we also Subsidize Algiers? Why do the European Nations suffer the prædatory Wars of the Barb[ary] States? Delenda est Carthago. Algiers must be subu[ed.] In the mean Time we must expend £200,000 and subsi[dize] that piratical State. Peace with that and Morocco, may open a Mediterranian Commerce to us of £200,000 ⅌ annum. Excuse my free Remarks. I have the Honor to be, Sir, Yr. most obedt. very hble servt.,

EZRA STILES

I have graduated this Commencement 83. Of these 51 Bachelors of Arts, 29 Masters of Arts; we conferred three Doctorates in Law on yourself, Dr. Mackennen, and Professor Williams of the University of Cambridge.

RC (DLC); addressed: "His Excellency Thomas Jefferson, Esq. LL.D. Ambassador from the United States to the Court of France, Paris"; postmarked;

slightly mutilated where the seal was broken, with loss of some parts of words. Noted in SJL as received 6 Dec. 1786.

From John Banister, Jr.

DEAR SIR   Nantes Septr. 16th. 1786

I received yours of the 7th. inst. yesterday inclosing me some very satisfactory letters from America. Since I last wrote you I have felt the effects of this months unhealthiness which has been ever formidable to me; at present I am better, but fear I shall not be able to arrive in Paris before you leave it. Nevertheless on your return hope to be there. I mean to take l'Orient, Brest, Cherbourg, Havre and Rouen in my rout and should be much obliged to you for any letters you may think proper to favor me with for these places. A passport also would I think be serviceable. After seeing what is curious in Paris I shall set out for Italy immediately my Father seeming as desirous as myself that I should visit that country. Traveling leisurely is rather serviceable to me than otherwise. I am with the sincerest acknowlegement for your friendly offers Dear Sir your obliged friend and Servt.,

JNO. BANISTER Junr.

RC (MHi); endorsed. Noted in SJL as received 19 Sep. 1786, but erroneously dated 14 Sep.

From James Maury

DR SIR   Liverpool 17 Sepre. 1786

I am lately arrived here and settling in the Virginia Business. In July I left Fredericksburg, not long before when I had been in Albemarle at the Election, where I saw many of your Friends. They made a good Choice, and indeed I am happy to inform you the people have generally chosen more judiciously this year than last. At least I think so, several of Mr. Madison's most powerful opponents having been left out and made way for as powerful Auxiliaries.

It must be pleasing to you to be informed the Internal Navigations of Virginia are in a promising way. A Boat laden with eight Hhds. Tobaccoe was navigated last Spring from Rockbridge to Westham without stopping except where the River passes the Blue ridge. There they took out one half the Cargo, which, after having passed and landed the other on the Eastern side of the Mountain,

[387]

17 SEPTEMBER 1786

they returned for. This successful Essay has given the Transalpines a proper Idea of the advantages to be derived from the Undertaking. At Alexandria they say the Potomack Navigation will not prove so tedious nor so expensive as the Company reckoned on.

The Crop of Tobaccoe of the growth of last year was nearly come to Market when I left Virginia and I believe has proved the greatest ever made, and unless the excessive rains in May and June have prevented, the present year's will be at least equal. As I passed thro' your Territories last Spring, I observed your people making preparations accordingly. Should they succeed and you be disposed to order any to an English Market I take the Liberty to offer you my services. The prices here have generally been equal to any in Europe, and now are especially for stemed and good Mountain Leaf Tobaccoe, and if you should wish any part of the Returns in the necessary Goods for your Estate, there is no port in England whence they can be furnished you on better terms.

I had the Honor of a Line from you last year by Monsr. Doradour and forwarded him to the Mountains, where he staid some Time, but, as I learn from Col. Lewis and Dr. Gilmer, much disappointed and disgusted, especially because the people could not speak French, altho' *featured and organized like French people*. I suspect he will represent us as a parcel of Hottentots.

Almost ever since you left America have I been waiting for the Consular arrangement to take place, til at length I became quite tired of remaining in Suspense and came out. My friends in Congress, however, stil assure me I am continued on the list of Candidates and that if the Business should come on the Tapis during their being in office, they will attend as much to my Interest as if present. If in the Course of your Correspondence it occur, you'll much oblige me by putting our friends in Mind of me. London is my first object, and if this cannot be had, it would be a secondary one to be appointed for this place in the Sub class. This is now become the second port in Britain for Trade in General or with America in particular. I beg the favor of you to inform me if Mr. Adams has power to make any temporary appointments in this Line. I wish to be made known to him and, if it be perfectly agreeable and convenient, I will be very much obliged to you for a Line to him, as I expect to be in Town this fall.

An extraordinary (and I fear, improper) Rigor has taken place this spring in the Custom House department of Virginia. At least six or seven capital Vessels, British and American, have been siezed condemned and sold by the last of July and some of them for mere trifles. It would be but fair in our Consuls on the Continent to give Notice of it, that any Foreigners going thither might take all necessary precautions.

Mrs. Maury joins me in best Respects to you and Miss Jefferson. My good Mother some how or other has heard of Miss Patsy's having been in a Convent which has made her very uneasy and I am afraid she will not easily forgive you. I have the Honor to be with much respect and Esteem, Dr Sir Yr obliged & very hble servt, JAMES MAURY

RC (DLC); addressed only: "His Excellency Thomas Jefferson Esqire"; endorsed. Noted in SJL as received 23 Sep. 1786.

Thomas Barclay to the American Commissioners

GENTLEMEN Ceuta 18th. Septr. 1786

As you will probably wish to know the particulars of the Negotiations of the Treaty with the Emperor, and as the perusal will not take up a great deal of time, I shall lay them before you.

After the first Audience was over Mr. Taher Fennish, in whose Hands the Negotiation was placed, came from the Emperor and informed me that His Majesty had read the Translation of the Letters, That he had made a Treaty with Spain very favorable for that Country, that he would write to His Most Catholic Majesty to give a Copy of that Treaty, from which, one with the United States might be formed and that he would either request the King of Spain to order it to be signed at Madrid, or it might be sent to Morocco for Signature by Express. I replied that "I had taken a long Journey in order to make this Treaty and that I would be very sorry to return untill it was finished. If Mr. Fennish would give a Copy of the Spanish Articles I would point out such as would be necessary for us, and I doubted not but we would soon agree upon them."

Mr. Fennish said that some of the Papers were at Mequinez and some at Fez, and that it would be impossible to collect them so as to make them useful on this Occasion. I answered that If permission was given to me I would lay before the Emperor through him the Heads of such a Treaty as I imagined would be perfectly agreeable to both Countries, that if any objections should appear, we would talk them over, and after due Consideration, do what would seem right. To this Mr. Fennish agreed, promising his best Offices to

18 SEPTEMBER 1786

forward and settle every thing on good and reasonable Terms. The next day but one, the Heads of the Treaty in Arabic, were put into the Hands of Mr. Fennish, who shew'd them to the Effendi, by whom Seven of the Articles were objected to as highly unreasonable; They were however read before His Majesty and some of the principal Officers of the Court, when all the Articles except four were admitted without hesitation; and the next Morning I received a Message from one of the Persons who was present at the reading, with Compliments upon the Progress I had made, and taking to himself entirely, the Merit of removing three of the Objections.

When the proposition for an Exchange of Prisoners was read The King said "This is not right, why are the Christians Powers so averse to go to war with me? It is the Fear of their Subjects falling into Slavery." To which the Kings Preacher replyed, These People deserve more indulgence from you than many others with whom you are in Alliance. They are nearer our Religion, and our Prophet mentions those who profess their manner of Worship, with Respect. Upon which the Emperor said, Let this Article be admitted. The next day I put the Treaty at full length into the Hands of the Interpreter to get it translated into Arabic and in a few days a rough draught in Arabic formed from my draught but much curtailed was delivered to me by the Talbe who had drawn it up by His Majesty's Instructions, and who though he had altered it in the Form, preserved the Substance; I caused this draught to be translated into English by one Person, and into French by another and agreed to receive the Treaty as it then stood, as I was the more anxious not to differ upon points of Form merely, because I knew the Effendi, who is the chief Officer at Court wanted to embarrass me and to draw the Affair into a length of time, and to get it into his own Hands, and this disposition had appeared on various Occasions, indeed on all that offered.

In the opening of the Affair I was asked by the Interpreter what I had to offer on the side of the United States by way of Presents in future, or by way of Tribute, to which I replyed (supposing the Question might come from Mr. Fennish on the Part of the Emperor) that I had to Offer to His Majesty the Friendship of the United States and to receive his in Return, to form a Treaty with him, on liberal and equal Terms. But if any engagements for future presents or Tributes were necessary, I must return without any Treaty; I took Care that these Sentiments should be conveyed to Mr. Fennish, and nothing was afterwards said about it, nor a hint droped that any thing was expected. While the last draught of the

18 SEPTEMBER 1786

Treaty was making, I was told it would be proper that the Delivery to me in behalf of the United States should be inserted, to which I very readily acquiesced, and wrote on a piece of Paper what I wished should be added; when the Treaty was finally put into my hands, seald by the Ring, and not 'till then, did I see or suspect in what Manner that Insertion is made, and which I wish with all my Heart was extinguished, at least one of the two.

Mr. Fennish being confined to his Chamber our Papers fell into the Hands of the Effendi, who notwithstanding the Emperor had ordered them to be delivered, detained them under various pretences. But at length (without our coming to an open quarrel) He sent them, when on examination we found the Talbe had omitted a Matter of some Consequence in one of the Articles, the rectifying of which and the getting a Declaration made by Mr. Fennish by order of the King, took up a Day or two. I was asked to sign an Acceptation of the Articles on the Part of the United States but as the Treaty was not drawn up in the Form I expected, I excused myself without however giving any Offence, referring Mr. Fennish to Congress and the Ministers. It is a Friendly well intended Treaty given by the Emperor without much being demanded on his Part; If it proves satisfactory it will be proper for you Gentlemen to give your Sentiments of it to Mr. Fennish and that Congress ratifies it. —And here perhaps it may not be unnecessary to say, that Mr. Fennish throughout the whole as far as I can judge, has acted with the Utmost Candor and veracity, and I thought myself very happy in having been put into his hands. When the Business was over, the Emperor sent a Message to me by Mr. Fennish, desiring to know whether I had anything to ask and (to repeat the Words in which it was delivered) if I had, not to be ashamed or backwards in doing it. I was prepared for this Compliment before I left Spain and was advised to request a Permission to export twenty thousand Fanegas of Wheat without Duty by which I should probably gain as many Dollars, and with great Truth I assure you that I am persuaded it would have immediately been granted. But I did not chuse to end an Embassy, begun avowedly on disinterested Principles, by making such a Request, especially as I was informed he would look on the United States as under some Obligations for such an Indulgence shewn their Servant. And as the Professions of an Inclination to give a mark of his Approbation of the transaction were repeated, I accepted them and pointed out a Manner in which he might shew the friendly disposition he had expressed; This was by his giving Letters to Constantinople, Tunis, Tripoli and Algiers

18 SEPTEMBER 1786

recommending to these several States to enter into an Alliance with the United States and by advising them to receive in the most friendly manner such Agents and propositions as should be sent them from America. The Emperor immediately came into these Views and Mr. Fennish desired that I would draw up the Form of a Letter such as I wished should be written, which I did and the indisposition of this Gentleman, was the Reason given why I did not get them at Morocco. I wrote twice to the Emperor and waited in Tangiers for an Answer, which I received from Mr. Fennish saying the Letters were not prepared, and at present I shall add no more than that the Emperor is perfectly well informed that I had no orders to ask such Letters and that if there is any thing wrong in having done it, it is entirely an act of my own. The Treaty having been compleated His Majesty gave a written Paper not only discribing our Rout but the time we should remain at the principal Towns. We came to this place to avoid a Quarenteen in Spain, and have been detained by some tempestuous weather. The Commandant of the Marine at St. Roque hearing we were at Tangiers and at a Loss how to reach Spain without performing a Quarenteen sent a Vessel for us, directing the Commander to attend us wherever we should choose.

I think it probable that you will not judge it necessary for me to go up the Mediterranean as Mr. Lamb I hear has returned to Algiers, a Circumstance that will make me very happy, for though I was not backward in offering my Services, I was influenced only by the necessity I thought there was of doing something.

Therefore if I do not receive your decided Orders at Cadiz to pursue these African Objects, I will embrace the first Opportunity of embarking from Spain for America.

I beg leave to assure you of my being with every Sentiment of Esteem and Respect Gentlemen Your most obt. humble Servant,

THOS. BARCLAY

RC (DNA: PCC, No. 91, I); in a clerk's hand, signed by Barclay; on verso, in Barclay's hand: "No.10" (i.e., enclosure No. 10 in Barclay to Commissioners, 2 Oct. 1786). PrC of a Tr (DLC); in Short's hand, faded and partly illegible. Not recorded in SJL.

I WISH WITH ALL MY HEART [THAT INSERTION] WAS EXTINGUISHED: The insertion to which Barclay objected so strenuously was the following: "We have delivered this Book into the Hands of the before-mentioned Thomas Barclay on the first day of the blessed Month of Ramadan, in the Year One thousand two hundred." A similar date was affixed to the ships' signals agreement. Barclay did the best he could by writing underneath his signature to the translation of the additional Article: "Note, The Ramadan of the Year of the Hegira 1200 Commenced on the 28th. June in the Year of our Lord 1786." See Miller, ed., *Treaties and other International Acts of the United States*, II, 217-9.

[392]

From William Stephens Smith

Dr. Sir   London Septr. 18th. 1786.

I have only time to enclose your Excellency a Copy of a Letter received yesterday from Mr. Barclay, and to acknowledge the receipt of your favour of the 9th. Ulto. by Mr. Bullfinch. The maps, occasioned by Mr. B's excursion in the country after his arrival, did not reach me untill the 6th. inst. Mr. Neele took them in hand on the 7th. and will finish the plate within the period mentioned and for the sum agreed upon with you. The printing press was shiped before the receipt of yours, therefore it was not in my power to detain it for the harpsicord. I find Dr. Burney is not in town therefore must wait his arrival before any thing can be done in the musical Line. The Harness for Chariot and Cabriolet shall be forwarded, after they are compleat according to your *taste*. The form of the ornaments and the spring swivels, together with the breastplates shall also be attended to. And as much economy used in scathring the amount of your Bill, as possible, which I am already possessed of.—If you will send the other map of 12 sheets which you speak of, I can get them done as you wish. I would now send you the Copy of the joint letters you request, but Mr. Adams has the Books in Grosr. square.—Mrs. Smith is much obliged by the articles you sent her and desires her Compliments. Your letters for America I have dispatched, and find my time pass so agreably when engaged in executing your orders, that I must beg a continuance of them.   W. S. Smith

RC (MHi). Noted in sjl as received 23 Sep. 1786. Enclosure (DLC): Tr in Smith's hand of Barclay's letters to Jay, 30 July, and to Adams, 31 July 1786.

From Maria Cosway

Parigi Mercoledì Sera [20 Sep. 1786]

[I hope?] you dont always judge by appearances [or it wo]uld be Much to My disadvantage this day, without [my] deserving it; it has been the day of contradiction, I meant to have had the pleasure of seing you *Twice*, and I have appeard a Monster for not having sent to know how you was, the *whole day*. I have been More uneasy, Than I can express. This Morning My Husband kill'd My project, I had proposed to him, by burying himself among Pictures and forgeting the hours, though we were Near your House coming to see you, we were obliged to turn back, the time being much past that we were to be at St. Cloud to dine with the Duchess of Kingston; Nothing was to hinder us from Coming in the Evening, but Alas! My good intention prov'd only a disturbance to your Neighbours, and just late enough to break the rest of all your servants and perhaps yourself. I came home with the disapointment of not having been able to Make My appologies in *propria Persona*. I hope you feel my distress, instead of accusing me, the One I deserve, the other not. [We will] come to see you tomorrow Morning, [if nothing?] hapen to prevent it! Oh I wish you was well enough to come to us tomorrow to dinner and stay the Evening. I wont tell you what I shall have, Temptations now are too Cruel for your Situation. I only Mention my wish, if the executing them shou'd be possible, your Merit will be grater or my satisfaction the More flatter'd. I would Serve you and help you at dinner, and divert your pain after dinner by good Musik.—Non[1] so perche ho scritto tanto in una lingua che non m'appartiene, Mentre posso scriver nella Mia, che lei intende tanto bene, non ò pensato all'Amor proprio altrimenti non l'avrei fatto, in qualunque Modo Mi creda sempre sua obligatissima serva, e vera Amica,

MARIA COSWAY

RC (MHi); top of Ms torn, cutting into a few words of the text at the beginning and end of the first two lines at the top of each page; without date and not recorded in SJL; but undoubtedly written the first Wednesday after TJ's injury to his wrist, which occurred on 18 Sep. 1786.

[1] *Translation*: I don't know why I have written so much in a language which does not belong to me, while I can write in my own, which you understand so well. I did not think of myself otherwise I would not have done so. Anyway, believe me always your most obliged servant and true Friend.

From Fantin Latour

MONSIEUR Grenoble ce 20. 7bre. 1786.

Un jeune homme à qui ses parents ont Laissé une Légitime De 8000 Livres, Desireroit se transporter avec Sa petite fortune dans Les états confédérés De L'Amérique pour y acquérir une propriété et y respirer L'air De La Liberté. Auriés la Bonté, monsieur, De lui Donner Les Renseignemens et Les instructions nécessaires pour cela?

Cette Légitime ne Doit lui être payée qu'en Deux termes, quatre mille livres Dans trois ans, et Les quatre autres mille trois encore aprés, c'est à Dire, Dans Six ans. Il voudroit cependant effectuer Son projet à présent, et son frere ne seroit peut-être pas D'humeur De Se Liquider envers lui avant L'échéance. Seroit il possible, monsieur, De prendre Des arrangemens convenables à cet égard? Je vous Demande mille pardons, monsieur, si ma lettre vous Dérange un seul instant De vos importantes occupations; je vous aurai une obligation infinie si vous Daignés m'éclairer De vos avis.

J'ai L'honneur D'être avec un profond Respect, Monsieur Votre très humble et très obeissant Serviteur,

FANTIN LATOUR
demeurant cour De [Chaulne]
grande rüe à g[renoble][1]

RC (MHi); endorsed by TJ with his left hand: "Fantin." Noted in SJL as received 23 Sep. 1786.

[1] MS torn; text in brackets supplied from Latour's letter of 4 Oct. 1787.

To Charles Thomson

SIR   Paris the 20 Septemr 1786

This will be handed you by a Gentleman of the Family of Lecoutoux who is going with his wife to Settle himself as a farmer in Someone of the middle States of America. As his Establishment will not be great, it is the more important that it be judiciously made. Being acquainted with his family, they have asked of me lettres of recommendations for him. Knowing no person better acquainted than yourself with the middlestates and with all the Circumstances and difficulties with[1] Surround a new Settler, nor any one more disposed to perform those duties of humanity which we all owe the one to the other, I take the Libertey of introducing him to you, and praying that you will aid him with your information and Counsel, which I Shall Consider as an obligation Conferred on me. A dishability of my right hand which I hope will not be of Long Continuance obliges me to avail myself of the pen of another to assure you of the Sincere esteem and Friendship with which I have the honour to be dear Sir Your Most Obedient Most humble Servant,

TH: JEFFERSON

RC (DLC: Thomson Papers); in an unidentified hand, probably that of a Frenchman and possibly that of the person in whose behalf the letter was written (see note 1). PrC (DLC: TJ Papers); endorsed by TJ with his right hand.

LECOUTOUX: On 8 Sep. 1786 Le Veillard wrote to William Temple Franklin: "One M. Le Coulteux is to settle in Pennsylvania. He is bringing out a young woman whom he has just married. She is the daughter of M. Clouet, custodian of the powder magazine, collector of taxes of Paris, and very intimate with M. Dailley" (Franklin Papers, PPAP).

[1] Thus in MS; TJ plainly intended "which."

From Nathaniel Tracy

[*Before 20 Sep. 1786.* A letter, without indication of place or date, recorded in SJL as received on this date. Not found.]

To Thomas Barclay

SIR Paris Septr. 22d. 1786

I was honored a few days ago with the reciept of your letter of Aug. 11th. In my last to you I informed you that I had proposed to Mr. Adams to avail ourselves of your service at Algiers. I acknowlege that I had no expectation that with our small means you could effect a treaty there; but I thought that their ultimatum might be discovered and other intelligence obtained which might repay us the trouble and expence of the journey. I wished also to know what might be the effect of the interposition of the Court of Madrid now that it is at liberty to interpose. A letter recently recieved from Mr. Carmichael informs me that it is the opinion of the Counts de Florida Blanca and D'Espilly that nothing can be effected at Algiers till there be a previous treaty with the Ottoman Porte: independently of that information Mr. Adams is of opinion that no good can result at present from a further attempt at Algiers. The Porte, Algiers, Tunis and Tripoli must remain for the further deliberations of Congress. Of course we have not occasion to trouble you with any further visits to those powers, and leave you at liberty to return here, to London, or to America as you shall think proper. We are happy that your successful efforts with the Emperor of Morocco have left the Atlantic open to our commerce and little dangerous.

I have the pleasure to inform you that Mrs. Barclay and Family are well and am with sentiments of the most perfect esteem & respect Your very humble servant,

WSHORT FOR TH JEFFERSON

PrC (DLC); in Short's hand, including signature. There is a letter to Mrs. Barclay recorded in SJL under 22 Sep., but none to Barclay. TJ probably had received a reply (missing) to his to Mrs. Barclay of 14 Sep. and thus confused the entry.

To William Carmichael

Paris 22d. Septr. 1786

Mr. Jefferson's Compliments to Mr. Carmichael and begs the

favor of him to convey the inclosed letters. He has recieved his letter of the 4th. of Septr. and is in hopes that one which he had written to Mr. Carmichael on the 22d. of August will have answered some of his enquiries. An indisposition likely to continue some time will necessarily retard his answer to the rest. He begs Mr. Carmichael to be assured of his esteem & respect.

PrC (DLC); in Short's hand. The enclosed letters have not been precisely identified, but they were addressed to Barclay and Lamb (see Carmichael to TJ, 3 Oct. 1786) and they must have included TJ to Barclay of this date.

To C. W. F. Dumas

SIR Paris Septr. 22d. 1786

I am honored with your letter of the 12th. of Septr. and condole with you very sincerely on the domestic loss you have sustained. The affairs of your Republic seem at present under a cloud which threatens great events. If the powers of the Stadtholder should be thereby reduced to such only as are salutary and the happiness of the people placed on a basis more within the command of their own will, it will be worth a great deal of blood. These struggles are a great sacrifice to the present race of men but valuable to their posterity. I sincerely wish the issue of this contest may give to the mass of the people that increase of happiness which alone can justify its being attempted.

I thank you for the copy of Turgot's life, and will forward those directed to Mr. Jay, Dr. Franklin and Mr. Morris. I inclose you a copy of the Article *Etas Unis* of the new Encyclopedie lately published here. You will find in it some few errors of little consequence but many details new, exact and authentic.

The bill for six hundred and fifty dollars which you mention that you shall draw soon shall be duely honored.

Our intelligence from America is very flattering. The price of produce and of labor is very high and that of foreign goods low. Of course those of the people may be happy who will confine themselves to such enjoyments as are proportioned to their condition of life. Our Governments are tranquil and proceeding with a steady pace in their improvements, particularly a [di]sposition to center in the hands of Congress all powers re[spec]ting our connection with foreign nations is becoming universal. It is better that improvements should be late when thereby all voices can be united in making them. I have the[1]

22 SEPTEMBER 1786

PrC (DLC); in Short's hand; endorsed by TJ with his right hand. Enclosure: Démeunier's *Essai sur Les Etats-Unis* (see under 22 June 1786).

¹ PrC ends at this point; see Vol. 9: 217, note 1.

From William Stephens Smith

Dr. Sir London Septr. 22d. 1786.

I had the honor of addressing you on the 18th. inst. in answer to your favor of the 9th. of August, since which I have received yours of the 13th. inst. Mr. A. returned here on the 7th. or 8th. He took up the subject on which you impatiently wait an answer on his arrival, a short letter on which, you must have received before this. However he is still thinking on it, and you will hear more from him soon. I wish you much satisfaction on your tour to the south, and shall make the communication to Mr. P. which you wish.

I have delivered the Letter to Stockdale, visited Lackington, and having got all the books agreable to your list, which he had, sent them to Stockdale to be packed by him, with others which he was to procure, and forward by the Dilligence to your address. The list of the Books, I will send by some private hand, *as the funds are low* the expence of postage will be saved.

A few sett of Ramsay's History will be sent by the Dilligence and orders forwarded to Ostend to have the others put in such a channel that they may reach you. As yet there are no very striking symptoms that your order from Mr. Grand, on M. Tessier will fall short of its object. If it should, I have a little Credit here yet, thank God, which shall always be at your service.

The Taylor is very busy, already, and your breeches and waistcoats shall be forwarded in the manner you point out. The engraver shall be hurried three times a week, and nothing left undone, that is in my power to forward your wishes. Apropos, I have spoke to Faden about the 12 sheet map, and made arrangements for its being engraved, reserving the number of Copies for you which you requested. The sooner you forward it the better.

You mention Trumbull having left you 3 day's before the date of yours. Where is he? He has not yet made his appearance here. I hope he is not lost in the storm which raged the last week. In your Letter of the ninth of August you request me to send three ream of copying paper and a proportionable supply of ink-powder. Do you mean, in addition to the 3 ream sent with the Press? I observe by Woodmason's account the paper sent is folio paper. Is this such

[398]

as you wish? Mr. Lackington sent a Catalogue to me addressed to Mr. Madison of Virginia, and I forwarded it by the last Ship.—I have no letters from America lately, and the newspapers are scarcely worth perusing.—Mrs. Smith desires her compliments. As the King of P. is dead, the affairs of Holland undecided, and So. A. very distant from us, and the falls of the Missisipi do not interrupt our slumbers, and our scalps are, pro tem., perfectly safe, I won't bore you on any of these Subjects. But I shall embrace every opportunity of assuring you with what respect I am Dr. Sir. Your most Obedient Humble Servt., W. S. SMITH

RC (MHi). Noted in SJL as received 26 Sep. 1786. MR. P.: John Paradise.

From John Bondfield

DR SIR Bordeaux 23 Sept. 1786

Since mine of the 5. August I am honor'd with your favor of the 8th. I receiv'd yesterday eighteen Cases Arms from the Manufactory Royal de Tulle No. 69 a 86 which with the other eighteen Cases are lodged in a dry Store waiting permission for their Exportation, which so soon as obtain'd please to transmit to me.

Vessels with Tobacco for the Contract arrive frequently. They are the only ships we see from America. It is with concern I am obliged to unite in the General Cry against America for the Cruel retard in the remittances. Where inability is the cause necessity pleads the excuse. But debts due by men who are in great affluence and detain considerable Capitals Years without making the least return makes the load less supportable and deprives us from continueing or renewing any Commercial Operations, a Suspention to certain Branches of Trade is not prejudicial to America. The American States may be regarded on a very different footing than any of the European Powers. An introduction of Riches in few hands can only serve to give influence to a particular order of Cityzens without increasing her Husbandry and new Settlements and preserves thereby in Towns bordering on the Coast numbers of hands, that neither encrease population nor promotes the Establishment of Morals. The less influence the Commercial Spirit has on the Community for the first Century may possibly tend to its advantage.

By arrivals from New Orleans the Inhabitants of Louisianna appear apprehensive of troubles taking place in that neighbourhood

23 SEPTEMBER 1786

from the great increase of the Settlement at Kentucey and the inflexible opposition in the Spaniards to the free Navigation of the Mississipi.

I have the honor to be with due Respects, Sir, your most Obedient Humble Servant, JOHN BONDFIELD

RC (DLC); endorsed. Noted in SJL as received 26 Sep. 1786.

There is in Vi a letter from Bondfield to St. Victour & Bettinger, 23 Sep. 1786, acknowledging the receipt of cases No. 69 to 86, together with a certificate from the Royal Manufactory at Tulle, signed by Dubois Descordal, dated 30 Aug. 1786, with an endorsement by St. Victour, for the company, dated 11 July 1787, acknowledging payment by TJ of 14,850₶ for 540 muskets contained in the 18 cases.

To William Stephens Smith

DEAR SIR   Paris Septr. 23. 1786.

Being desired by a friend to procure him a copying press I take the liberty of putting the inclosed under cover to you and of requesting you to pay for it and have it sent as therein desired. I wish it may be in time to come with the other articles that it may not multiply my applications for passports. Be so good as to let me know whether Mr. Tessier has any hesitations about going beyond the extent of Mr. Grand's letter. If he has, though I do not know the exact sum that will be necessary I will send another letter of Credit at random. My dislocated wrist prevents my writing to you in my own hand. Present me affectionately to Mrs. Smith, to Mr. and Mrs. Adams and be assured of the sincere esteem with which I have the honor to be, dear Sir, your most obedient humble Servant,   W SHORT FOR TH. JEFFERSON

RC (MHi: Washburn Collection); in Short's hand, including signature; postmarked; addressed; and endorsed. PrC (DLC); endorsed by TJ with his left hand. Enclosure (missing): Letter to Woodmason concerning a copying press; there is an entry in SJL for a letter to Woodmason under this date which has not been found, but which Smith mentioned as having been enclosed in this letter in his to TJ of 1 Oct. 1786.

From La Rouerie

SIR   La Rouerie 25 7bre. 1786.

When your letter of June last came at la Rouerie, I was at the waters of Cautrét where Mde. de la Rouerie died; it was sent to me a month after but my mind was far from being so tranquille as to take any interest whatever in things strangers to the loss I had

[400]

made. Now that the care of my fortune call on my immediate attention, I will have the honor to answer your letter.

The gentlemen of the board of treasury might without falling down a single line from the dignity in which they are elevated by their high station, have answered a letter from a gentleman of the army and besides a creditor of their sovereign.

When Mr. Morris was minister of finances we have been well payed; he held his office from the honorable the Congress as the board of treasury hold it now; allso it is not on Congress that must fall the blame of the Bankruptcy, for there is no other word, proper to the circumstance, which we experience from the united states.

I wishes more for your country, sir, than for my own interest, america had been more faithfull in her engagements; they were controuled in the infancy of her sovereignty, when she was much in trouble, when she was weak and wanted assistants; now that she has a sort of consistants, she is honest and grateful agreeable to her own ease. For my part I have too many private attachements in that country and too great an affection for her form of government, not to suffer a great deal by the diminishing of her first repute and you must know, sir, how much the several parts on which that repute was established, are faln in discredit.

This, sir, is the last letter I shall have the honor to write to you on the subject of our arrearages; I acknowlege that I am much indebted to you for the activity with which you have acted in that affaire. We are all persuaded of your sincerity and good will and we shall express with much pleasure these sentiments in all the proceedings which the conduct of the board of treasury does and will suggest to us.

I have the honor to be with great respect your excellency's sir the most obdt. hble. servant, ARMAND M. DE LA ROUERIE

RC (ViWC); endorsed by TJ with his left hand. Noted in SJL as received 2 Oct. 1786.

From James Smith

L'hotel Warsovie, Rue neuve des
bons enfans, Monday night
[25 Sep. 1786]

I beg pardon of your Excellency for giving you but short notice of my departure. The fact is that the letter which I waited to determine me to go or stay arrived but to day. I shall therefore quit

Paris certainly Wednesday morning and if you have anythings to send shall esteem myself honored with the conveyance of them. At the same time I must thank your excellency for the civilities I have received from your hands. I am sorry that pressing circumstances prevent me from going by the way of Rouen. I shall be retarded upon enquiry two if not three days and much more fatigued than by the way of Calais. I had fixed upon chusing the former road and am obliged to cede to necessity and the zeal I had to serve my country by that means must change into regret. Perhaps we shall be made acquainted with the advantage of sending our rice to Havre when you yourself shall be better informed of its utility; and then the propositions coming from the best authority will have greater weight and be sooner followed. In some conversation your Excellency did me the honor of mentioning to me an Abbé who was going to set up a boarding house. I took the liberty then of disapproving of the plan from the authority of Monsr. Mercier because I did not know the person nor his intentions in detail. Since, I have found that it is Monsr. L'Abbé André, formerly my preceptor who with the meekness of the lamb in his exterior, I believe has not more guile. He was recommended to me by the president de Salaberri, at whose chateau I passed so much agreable time last winter, for a man of litterature and of worth. He has been French master to two or three of my American friends who have always spoke highly of him, so that if your Excellency should find any persons willing to adopt his plan under his direction you may safely say what I have written on his account.

Knowing that your Excellency has received a dislocation I shall not require an answer in writing with out it is as well as I wish. If what is to be sent can be made up and delivered Tuesday night your Excellency will confer an additional favor upon those already bestowed upon your very humble and obed. sevt.,

JAMES SMITH

RC (DLC); addressed; endorsed by TJ with his left hand. The date has been supplied from internal evidence and the reference to "Mr. Smith" in TJ to John Adams, 26 Sep. 1786 (Monday was on 25 Sep.).

To John Adams

DEAR SIR   Paris Septr. 26th. 1786.

My last letter to you was dated the 27th. of August since which I have recieved yours of Sep. 11th. The letter to Mr. Lamb therein

26 SEPTEMBER 1786

inclosed I immediately signed and forwarded. In mine wherein I had the honor of proposing to you the mission of Mr. Barclay to Algiers, I mentioned that my expectations from it were of a subordinate nature only. I very readily therefore recede from it in compliance with your judgment that this mission might do more harm than good. I accordingly wrote to Mr. Barclay that he was at liberty to return to this place, to London or to America, as he should think best. I now inclose you copies of such letters from him, Mr. Lamb and Mr. Carmichael as have come to hand since my last to you. I have had opportunities of making further enquiry as to the premium of insurance at L'Orient for Vessels bound to or from America, and I find that no additional premium is there required on account of the risque of capture by the Barbary States. This fact may be worth mentioning to American merchants in London.

We have been continually endeavoring to obtain a reduction of the duties on American whale oil; the prospect was not flattering. I shall avail myself of the information contained in your letter to press this matter further. Mr. Barrett is arrived here, and the first object for his relief is to obtain a dissolution of his former contract.

I will thank you for some copies of the Prussian treaty by the first opportunity and take the liberty of troubling you to forward the packets of letters which Mr. Smith the bearer of this will have the honor of delivering to you. I beg the favor of you to present my most respectful compliments to Mrs. Adams, and to be assured yourself of the sentiments of sincere esteem & respect with which I have the honor to be dear Sir, Your most obedient & humble Servant, WSHORT FOR TH. JEFFERSON

RC (MHi: AMT); in Short's hand, including signature; endorsed. PrC (DLC). Enclosures: (1) Barclay to Commissioners, printed at end of July 1786. (2) Same to same, 11 Aug. 1786. (3) Lamb to TJ, 10 Aug. 1786. (4) Carmichael to TJ, 4 Sep. 1786. MR. SMITH THE BEARER: See James Smith to TJ, preceding. THE LETTER TO MR. LAMB: See Commissioners to Lamb, this date.

From Thomas Barclay

DEAR SIR Cadiz 26 Sepr. 1786.

On my arrival here yesterday I had the pleasure of Receiving your letter of the 31st. of last month. My being a little indisposed I shall only say at present that on Sunday Next I propose setting out for Madrid where I will wait untill I hear from you and Mr. Adams. Mr. Franks will Immediately proceed with some letters which I wrote to you from Tangiers and Ceuta, and with several other Papers which will Close all the Matters that were put under my Care. In the mean time I am very much Dear Sir Your very obedt. Thos. Barclay

RC (DLC). Noted in SJL as received 14 Oct. 1786.

From C. W. F. Dumas

Monsieur La Haie 26e. 7br. 1786

Je reçois la faveur dont Votre Excellence m'a honoré en date du 25 Août dernier par les mains de M.M. Morris et de Mr. De Basseville leur Mentor. Le grand respect que j'ai pour Monsieur leur digne Pere, et la recommandation de Votre Excellence, feroient aller mon Zele, consacré à tout ce qui tient aux Etats-Unis, à des choses bien au-delà des légers services qu'ils me demandent. J'aurai l'honneur de les présenter demain matin à Mr. l'Ambassadeur de France. Ils paroissent déterminés à partir demain au soir pour Amsterdam.

J'avois remis le 23 un paquet pour le Congrès sous l'adresse de Votre Excellence à l'hôtel de France. Ce paquet, par une inadvertance qui m'a fait beaucoup de peine, dont je suis néanmoins prudent de dissimuler une grande partie, n'a point été emporté par le Courier qu'on a expédié. On cherche à m'en consoler, en me promettant qu'on l'enverra cette semaine encore par une autre occasion. En attendant, je joins ici la Gazette et Note incluse, que Votre Excellence voudra bien avoir la bonté d'insérer dans le dit paquet, lorsqu'Elle l'aura reçu.

Un précédent Courier de France doit avoir fait remettre à Votre Excellence un autre paquet, contenant 4 Exemplaires de la Vie de Mr. Turgot, dont Votre Excellence voudra bien agréer un Exemplaire, et acheminer les 3 autres à Leurs Excellences MM. Franklin, R. Morris, et Jn. Jay, selon l'indication écrite en marge des frontispices.

C'est avec un très vrai et grand respect que je suis De Votre Exc. Le très-humble & très-obéissant serviteur,

CWF Dumas

RC (DLC). FC (Rijksarchief, The Hague, Dumas Papers; photostats in DLC). Noted in SJL as received 30 Sep. 1786.

To John Jay

Sir   Paris Sep. 26. 1786

The last letters I had the honor of writing you were of the 11th. and 13th. of August. Since that I have been favored with yours of July 14th and Aug. 18th.—I now inclose you such letters on the Barbary negociations as have come to hand since my last. With these is the copy of a joint letter from Mr. Adams and myself to Mr. Lamb. In mine of Augst. 13th. I mentioned that I had proposed it as a subject of consideration to Mr. Adams whether the mission of Mr. Barclay to Algiers might answer any good purposes. He is of opinion that it could not. I have therefore informed Mr. Barclay, who by this time is probably in Spain, that he is at liberty to return to this place, to London or America as he shall think proper. You will perceive by the letter from Mr. Carmichael that it is the opinion of the Counts de Florida Blanca and D'Expilly that a previous treaty with the Ottoman Porte is necessary before one can be made with Algiers: such a treaty will require presents, not indeed as the price of their peace but such as are usually made in compliment to their ministers. But as it would be ineffectual towards opening to us the Mediterranean until a peace with Algiers can be obtained, there seems to be no reason for pressing it till there is a prospect of settlement with the Algerines.

Since the death of the King of Prussia the Symptoms of war between the Porte and The Russians and Venetians have become stronger. I think it is the opinion of this court however that there will be no war shortly on the Continent. I judge this as well from other information as from the circumstance of a late reduction of their land force. All their military preparations seem to be against a naval war. Nevertheless their treaty with England has lately taken a sudden start: declarations have been exchanged between the Negociators in the nature of preliminaries to a definitive treaty. The particulars of these declarations are not yet certainly known.

I was lately asked by the Imperial Ambassador whether I had received an answer on the subject of his proposition to renew our powers to treat with his Sovereign. A discrimination which they understand to have been made in America between the subjects of powers having treaties with us and those having none, seems to be the motive of their pressing this matter.

It being known that M. de Calonne the Minister of Finance for this country is at his wit's end how to raise supplies for the ensuing year a proposition has been made him by a dutch company to pur-

26 SEPTEMBER 1786

chase the debt of the United States to this country for twenty million of livres in hand. His necessities dispose him to accede to the proposition, but a hesitation is produced by the apprehension that it might lessen our credit in Europe and perhaps be disagreeable to Congress. I have been consulted hereon by the Agent for that company. I informed him that I could not judge what effect it might have on our credit and was not authorized either to approve or disapprove of the transaction. I have since reflected on this subject: If there be a danger that our payments may not be punctual, it might be better that the discontents which would thence arise should be transferred from a court of whose good will we have so much need to the breasts of a private company. But it has occurred to me that we might find occasion to do what would be grateful to this court and establish with them a confidence in our honor. I am informed that our credit in Holland is sound. Might it not be possible then to borrow there the four and twenty millions due to this country and thus pay them their whole debt at once. This would save them from any loss on our account; nor is it liable to the objection of impropriety in creating new debts before we have more certain means of paying them: it is only transferring a debt from one creditor to another, and removing the causes of discontent to persons with whom they would do us less injury. Thinking that this matter is worthy the attention of Congress I will endeavour that the negociation shall be retarded till it may be possible for me to know their decision, which therefore I will take the liberty of praying immediately.

You will have heard before this comes to hand that the parties in the United Netherlands have come to an open rupture. How far it will proceed cannot now be foreseen. I send you herewith the Gazettes of France and Leyden to this date, and have the honor of being with Sentiments of the most perfect esteem & respect, Sir, your most obedient & most Humble Servt., TH. JEFFERSON
Test. W Short

RC (DNA: PCC, No. 87, I); in Short's hand, including signature. PrC (DLC). Tr (DNA: PCC, No. 107). Enclosures: (1) Barclay's letters to Commissioners of 16 July, July (printed at end of July), and 11 Aug. 1786. (2) Lamb to TJ, 10 Aug. 1786. (3) Extracts of Carmichael's letters to TJ, 17 Aug. and 4 Sep. 1786. (4) Commissioners to Lamb, 26 Sep. 1786.

For a brief summary of the story of TJ's proposal concerning the French loan, of the disinclination by Jay and Congress to sanction the suggestion, and of Hamilton's political use of the present letter, see Malone, *Jefferson*, II, 188-9, and, especially, TJ to Jay, 12 Nov. 1786; TJ to Adams, 1 July 1787; Adams to TJ, 25 Aug. 1787; and Jay to TJ, 24 Oct. 1787.

[406]

American Commissioners to John Lamb

SIR [26 Sep. 1786]

We have recieved your two letters of the 15 and 18 July from Alicant and are sorry to learn that your indisposition discourages you from travelling by land or by sea.

We still think it most advisable both for your own interest and that of the United States, that you should return to Congress for their further instructions as soon as possible, and we again propose to you to embark from Spain by the first opportunity.

Congress have never informed us of any promise made or encouragement given you, that you should be settled with in Europe, and we think it best you should settle with their board of Treasury. Nevertheless if you transmit to us your account, we will adjust it, as far as lies in us, subject to the revision of Congress. Your letter of credit we wish you to return to one of us, by the first opportunity, as you will not have occasion to draw again by virtue of it.

Mr. Randal is gone to New-york and it is our wish that you might be there with him, that Congress might have an opportunity of recieving from both together as much Information as possible, that you might mutually aid each other in settling your accounts.

We have the Honor &c., JOHN ADAMS

Tr (DNA: PCC, No. 87, I); in Short's hand; at head of text: "Copy"; at foot of text: "John Lamb Esqr. Alicant." PrC of the preceding (DLC). Tr (DNA: PCC, No. 107). This letter, enclosed in Adams to TJ, 11 Sep. 1786, was evidently signed by TJ, or for him, and sent to Lamb on this date; there is the following entry in SJL under 26 Sep.: "no date. Lamb John."

To the Prévôt des Marchands et Echevins de Paris, with Enclosure

GENTLEMEN Paris Sep. 27. 1786.

The Commonwealth of Virginia in gratitude for the services of the Major General the Marquis de la fayette, have determined to erect his bust in their capitol. Desirous to place a like monument of his worth and of their sense of it in the Country to which they are indebted for his birth, they have hoped that the City of Paris will consent to become the depository of this second testimony of their gratitude. Being charged by them with the execution of their wishes, I have the honor to sollicit of Messieurs Le Prevot des

27 SEPTEMBER 1786

Marchands et Echevins on behalf of the City their acceptance of a Bust of this gallant officer, and that they will be pleased to place it where, doing most honor to him, it will most gratify the feelings of an allied nation.

It is with true pleasure that I obey the call of that Commonwealth to render just homage to a character so great in its first developements that they would honor the close of any other. Their Country covered by a small army against a great one, their exhausted means supplied by his talents, their enemies finally forced to that spot whither their allies and confederates were collecting to recieve them, and a war which had spread its miseries into the four quarters of the earth, thus reduced to a single point where one blow should terminate it, and through the whole an implicit respect paid to the laws of the land—these are facts which would illustrate any character and which fully justify the warmth of those feelings of which I have the honor, on this occasion, to be the organ.

It would have been more pleasing to me to have executed this office in person, to have mingled the tribute of private gratitude with that of my country, and at the same time to have had an opportunity of presenting to your honorable body the homage of that profound respect which I have the honor to bear them. But I am witheld from these grateful duties by the consequences of a fall which confine me to my room. Mr. Short therefore, a Citizen of the State of Virginia, and heretofore a Member of its Council of State, will have the honor of delivering you this letter together with the Resolution of the General Assembly of Virginia. He will have that also of presenting the Bust at such time and place as you will be so good as to signify your pleasure to recieve it. Through him I beg to be allowed the Honor of presenting those sentiments of profound respect and veneration with which I have the Honor to be, Gentlemen, your most obedient & most humble Servant,

TH: JEFFERSON

ENCLOSURE
In the House of Delegates. 1st. December 1784.

Whereas it was unanimously resolved on the 17th. Day of December 1781 that a bust of the Marquis de la Fayette be directed to be made in Paris of the best marble employed for such purposes with the following inscription

"This Bust was voted on the 17th Day of December 1781 by the General Assembly of the State of Virginia to the honorable the Marquis de la Fayette (Major General in the Service of the United States of America, and the late commander in chief of the Army of the United

27 SEPTEMBER 1786

States in Virginia) as a lasting monument of his merit, and their gratitude."

Resolved unanimously that the Governor with the advice of the Council be authorized and desired to defray the expence of carrying the said Vote into execution out of the Fund allotted for the contingences of Government, that he cause the said bust to be presented in the name of this Commonwealth to the City of Paris with a request that the same may be accepted and preserved in some public place of the said City.

Resolved unanimously that as a further mark of the lasting esteem of this Commonwealth for the illustrious qualities and services of the Marquis de la Fayette the Governor with the advice of the Council be authorized and directed to cause another Bust of him, with a similar inscription, to be procured by Draught on the said fund and that the same when procured be fixed in such public place at the Seat of Government as may be hereafter appointed for the erection of the Statue voted by the general assembly of General Washington.

Teste JNO BECKLEY C.H.D.

1784 Decr. 13th.
Agreed to by the Senate WILL DREW C.S.

RC (Archives Nationales, Paris); in Short's hand, including signature; at head of text in clerk's hand: "La traduction de cette lettre est à la 7me. page du procès verbal" and "Na. L'expedition de La deliberation des etats de Virginie du 1er Xbr. 1784. qui rappelle celle du 17 Xbr. 1781. est jointe a cette Lettre. Vû—De Corny." PrC (DLC); dated, as first written, "Paris Sep. 28. 1786"—the date on which the ceremonies took place —but corrected by TJ with his left hand to read as above; complimentary close omitted (see Vol. 9: 217, note 1). PrC of a Tr (DLC); in TJ's right hand, being made at a later date and evidently the PrC of the Tr enclosed in TJ to Hopkinson, 1 Aug. 1787; at head of text: "Copy of a letter to the Prevot des marchands et Echevins de Paris." Tr and translation (Vi); incorporated in *procès-verbal* of the ceremonies held at the acceptance of the bust of Lafayette, enclosed in LePelletier to TJ, 1 Feb. 1787. Enclosure (Archives Nationales, Paris); in hand of John Beckley; this resolution had been transmitted to TJ by Patrick Henry, 16 June 1785.

For good accounts of the negotiations leading up to this unprecedented event (from which TJ was obliged to be absent owing to his injured wrist), see Marie Kimball, *Jefferson: The Scene of Europe*, p. 63-6, and Gottschalk, *Lafayette, 1783-89*, p. 250-2. De Corny who shared Lafayette's advocacy of liberty and reason, had served as his aide-de-camp in the American army, was a fellow member of the Society of the Cincinnati, and at this grand ceremony accepted the bust as *procureur du roi*. Recalling that in 1774 he had administered to Lafayette as captain in the French army an oath never to serve a foreign power, De Corny thought it appropriate that the one who had administered the oath should have arrived at the same destination as the one receiving it; and in the course of this principal address of the occasion, he exclaimed: "A quel dégré de splendeur ne doit pas parvenir une Nation libre . . . qui compte en naissant des Washington, des Franklin, des Adams, des Jefferson dont l'ancienne Rome se seroit honorée. . . ." Thus, comments Gottschalk, "was disobedience to kings made into a virtue by the servant of a king—with Jefferson in the background" (MS copy of procès-verbal, Vi; Gottschalk, *Lafayette, 1783-89*, p. 251). An altered copy of part of the present letter was printed in *The Columbian Magazine*, Dec. 1786, p. 204. This was chiefly a rephrasing of the first paragraph. TJ had anticipated that a garbled account of the proceedings would be published in Europe, and had requested permission to publish an authorized narrative (TJ to Rayneval, 30 Sep. 1787). He was much displeased with the distorted paragraph in *The Columbian Magazine* and protested to Francis Hopkinson; the result was that a full and correct text of the letter was

[409]

published in the same magazine, Oct. 1787, p. 705-6 (see TJ to Hopkinson, 1 Aug. 1787). A translation of part of TJ's letter also appeared in the account of the proceedings as published in *Journal de Paris*, 8 Oct. 1786, and *Gazette de Leide*, 17 Oct. 1786.

From Jean Baptiste Le Roy

aux Galeries du Louvre ce 28 Septembre

Je me proposois Monsieur d'avoir L'honneur de vous voir pour vous demander quelques éclaircissemens sur un fait que M. Le Chevalier de Chatelux rapporte dans son voyage de L'amèrique Septentrionale et qu'il dit tenir de vous. Mais etant obligé d'aller à La Campagne J'ai espèré que vous me pardonneriez de vous en écrire, et que vous voudriez bien avoir la bonté de satisfaire à ce Sujet ma Curiosité. Voici de quoi il est question: M. Le Chevalier de Chastelux dit dans ce voyage que dans la belle maison que vous avez Scu vous construire sur les montagnes qui sont à l'ouest de la Virginie vous avez fait une Observation singulière, c'est que les vents venoient souvent de la partie de l'ouest ou de l'Ouest Nord Ouest tandis que dans la Virginie au dessous les vents qui regnoient en même tems étoient de la partie *Est*, ou *est Nord Est* ou à peu près. Or comme le vent d'Ouest ou tenant de la partie de L'Ouest est jusqu'à un certain point le vent alisée des zones tempèrées dans un certain tems de l'année il me paroit bien extraordinaire qu'on ait en même tems, dans la Virginie un Vent d'Est ou tenant de la partie de L'est. M. Le Chevalier de Chatelux semble annoncer que Si on continuoit à abattre les bois qui s'étendent en Virginie jusqu'au pied des Montagnes Le vent d'est s'y feroit sentir, cela pourroit être, mais je doute fort que si on abattoit ces Montagnes ce vent continua au delà. Je crois bien plutôt, au contraire, qu'alors le vent d'ouest se feroit sentir En Virginie Et Je suis fort porté à croire que si dans la chaine des Montagnes dont Je viens d'avoir L'honneur de vous parler il y avoit quelques vallées ou quelques gorges profondes à travers lesquelles le vent put s'échapper on y éprouveroit ce vent d'Ouest qu'on n'observe que sur le haut de ces Montagnes. Pardonnez Monsieur mon Indiscrétion, mais vos connoissances profondes dans toutes les Sciences, La maniere dont vous les communiquez m'ont fait esperer que vous excuseriez la liberté que prend un homme fort désireux de s'instruire de tous les phénomenes de cette partie Intéréssante de la physique du Glôbe dont il s'est fort occupé. J'ai été si occupé depuis le départ de M. Franklin, Les communications sont si difficiles dans cette ville immense que c'est bien malgré moi Monsieur, Je vous assure, que Je n'ai pas mieux profité de L'honneur que J'ai eu de vous connoître chez ce Nestor de L'Amérique; mais c'est avec grand plaisir que Je profite de cette Occasion de vous assurer des Sentimens distingués d'estime que vous m'avez Inspirés et avec Lesquels J'ai l'honneur d'être Monsieur Votre trés humble et trés obéïssant Serviteur,

LE ROY
de L'Académie des Sciences

RC (ViWC); endorsed by TJ with his left hand. Not recorded in SJL; see TJ's reply of 13 Nov. 1786.

Jean Baptiste Le Roy (1720-1800), a physicist, was a member of the Académie Royale des Sciences, of the Royal Society of London, and of the American Philosophical Society (*Almanach Royal*, 1786, p. 514).

From William Carmichael

DEAR SIR   Madrid 29th. Septr. 1786

I received on the 17th. Inst. your Letter of the 22d. Ulto. I shall take such measures in future that you will be advised at an early period of the bills which I may have occasion to draw for my appointments. My Banker here has been too negligent in that particular, for I have generally intrusted to his Care letters of advice at the Time I signed my bills of Exchange. I know and feel for the Low State of the Finances of the States in Europe and I do assure you that Nothing but my desire to keep myself as independant as possible here, would induce me ever to draw without a certainty that my bills could be conveniently honored. The map I sent you cannot be purchased here. It was executed by order of Government and some copies given in presents to Foreign Ambassadors, when suddenly from Political Motives the Distribution and the Sale was forbidden. The Chevalier Bourgoyng can give you an ample detail on this affair. I hope one Day or other to see it in your house in Virginia. I wish it was of more durable materials, that it might remain a lasting proof of my sentiments of respect for the present proprietor. I should be ashamed to exhibit you an account of the prices demanded for several of the books in your Catalogue. To exonerate Myself from any blame in not having executed your Orders, I intreat you to speak to the Above-mentioned Gentleman who is conversant in these affairs. Besides the desire of knowing the situation in which we stand in Europe, I had *particular* motives with respect to Naples and Denmark which I will on another occasion explain to you in the manner you desire. Since I had the

29 SEPTEMBER 1786

honor to receive your Letter, I have taken the Liberty of expressing a wish to Mr. Lamb of having the original of the paper in question to be sent me by a safe conveyance. That Gentleman thinks without a *peremptory* order, He ought not to send it. All his Money Affairs were arranged here, before I received your Letter. I have pressed him in the most friendly manner to settle his Accounts, that is to send a State of them to your Excellency and Mr. Adams, so that being accountable for the balance whatever it may be, you might appropriate it agreable to the orders you may have or that you may receive from Congress. I have done this without Authority. But I have been actuated by public considerations and at the same time by private so far as they respect Mr. Lamb to whom I wish well. The inclosed Letters from Algiers contain the Last Intelligence I have received from thence. I should not send them to you, if I did not know you would make large Allowance for the prejudices of persons in their deplorable situation. Mr. Lamb corresponds with a person of some weight in that Regency. In my last Letter to him, I advised him to send this Correspondence to you. I could, when I please, either put a stop to or continue myself this Correspondence. But I wish not to Intermeddle with the Affairs of Others. At the Same time I think that No person unauthorized should continue a similar correspondence without your knowledge of the Nature of it. [I] Inclose you a printed copy of the Spanish Treaty with Algiers which I received from the Secretary of States Office. It is not as yet made public here. I also send you a copy of the memorial presented by the Dutch Ambassador, to which no answer has yet been given.

The Popes Nuntio took from me the Italian Copy of the act for religious freedom of the Assembly of Virginia and has sent it to Rome. Mr. Mattzei however has sent another copy in the same Language to my good Friend Mr. Celesia, at whose house yesterday we drank his health in Chiante. You will please to tell Mr. Mattzei that if he can prevail on Congress to provide for my old Friend Dumas and send me to the Hague where I shall be contented with 500 Stg. pr. Anm. in case there is a civil war, that I shall be much obliged to him, for I am heartily tired of doing little or nothing here in comparison of what I should wish to do. The Article Etats Unis has given much pleasure and I shall endeavour to have it Translated here. The Death of Gl. Cadwallader and Gl. Tilgman affects me much. Our Acquaintance and I may say friendship had subsisted more than 15 years. I know Telfair and Collins if they are the same who served in Congress in 1779, intimately well. They are well meaning men. S. A. has something in view, or he experiences the fate of those who entirely trust to popularity for their support. At present it is confidently asserted that the Courts of Naples and Spain will be soon reconciled. I wish that these assertions may be well founded. In a little time I hope to have an opportunity of writing you more at my ease. In the mean time I intreat you not only to give me such intelligence as you may judge proper to communicate to me, but your Advice for what ought to be my conduct here as a Countryman and I would wish to flatter myself, as a friend. This you can do in the Manner you propose. It has been asserted to me by the British Consul General that after the Capture of the Algerine vessel under the guns of Gibraltar, Genl. Elliot informed the Portuguese Commodore that he would not permit him to sail, until he had received an Answer from his Court to the Dispatches he sent on this occasion. I can not vouch for the Truth of this Intelligence. But I know that the Abovementioned Governor has taken every precaution to give satisfaction to the Algerines. I know that Mr. Barclay was at Tangiers the 26th. Ulto. But I have no Letters from him since his Arrival there. I forwarded your enclosures regularly. You will excuse the haste and consequently the Innacuracy with which this is written. I avail myself of a courier of the Cabinet. You will return me by the Same occasion the papers inclosed. I have no Letters from America except from Mr. Gardoqui the 30th. June.

I have the honor to be With the greatest respect & Esteem Your Excys Obliged & Obedient Hble. Servt.,

WM. CARMICHAEL

RC (DLC). Noted in SJL as received 12 Oct. 1786. Enclosures (missing): These enclosures, which Carmichael asked to have returned to him, cannot be precisely identified; they probably included, however, a long letter on Algerine affairs and the condition of the American prisoners there from Richard O'Brien to William Carmichael, 13 Sep. 1786 (Tr, in the hand of William Short, in DNA: RG 59, Consular Dispatches; PrC of same, DLC; portions of the letter are printed in *Naval Documents related to the United States Wars with the Barbary Powers*, Washington, 1939, I, 13-14). See TJ to Jay, 31 Dec. 1786.

S.A.: Samuel Adams.

From Madame de Tessé

a Châville ce 29 septembre

La Reconnoissance présente mille hommages très sensibles à Monsieur Jefferson qui comble à la fois Me. de Tesse des dons les plus précieux. Le nouvel acte d'indépendance médité dans des

[413]

jardins embellis par les productions de l'heureuse Virginie eut rempli tous les voeux du sage epicure. La prose francoise de Mr. Short se perfectionne chaque jour. On le Remercie très sensiblement de celle qu'il a bien voulu adresser à Chaville. Me. de Tott et Me. de Tessé le supplient d'écarter une mauvaise honte qui nuiroit à ses progrès et de leur mander si le mauvais tems n'a point Rendu quelques souffrances à Monsieur Jefferson.

RC (DLC); endorsed by TJ with his left hand.

To Rayneval, with Enclosure

Sir   Paris Sept. 30th. 1786.

Desirous that the circumstances relative to the bust of the Major General the Marquis de la fayette may not be disfigured or misrepresented by the writers of newspapers I take the liberty of submitting to your inspection the inclosed narrative of them. May I presume to ask either the order or the permission for its publication, either in the present form, if there be nothing improper in that, or with such alterations as you may think expedient.

I have the honor to be with Sentiments of the most perfect esteem & respect, Sir

ENCLOSURE
Extrait d'une Lettre de Paris du 9 Octobre

"D'après les Résolutions de l'Etat de Virginie, le Célèbre Artiste Mr. Houdon a été chargé d'éxécuter deux Bustes du Marquis de la Fayette, l'un pour être placé à coté du Général Washington dans la Capitale de cet Etat, et l'autre pour être présenté, au nom de la République, à la Ville de Paris par le Ministre-Plénipotentiaire des Etats-Unis. Cette Cérémonie eut lieu le 28. Septembre dernier de la manière la plus solemnelle. Mrs. les Prévôt des Marchands et Echevins s'étant rendus dans la Grande-Salle de l'Hôtel-de-Ville, l'on y a introduit Mr. Short, Ancien-Membre du Conseil-d'Etat de Virginie; Mr. Jefferson, Ministre-Plénipotentiaire des Etats-Unis, étant retenu chez lui par les suites d'une chute, Mr. Short a présenté à l'Assemblée le Buste, ainsi que les Résolutions de l'Etat, et une Lettre de M. Jefferson dont voici la Copie."

Messieurs

La République de Virginie, en reconnaissance des services du Major-Général Marquis de la Fayette, a résolu d'élever son Buste dans la Capitale de l'Etat; et désirant placer un Monument pareil de son mérite, et de l'opinion de la République, dans le Pays, Auquel Elle a l'obligation de sa naissance, elle espère que la Ville de Paris voudra bien devenir dépositaire de ce second témoignage de sa gratitude.

30 SEPTEMBER 1786

Chargé par elle de l'exécution de ses intentions, j'ai l'honneur de prier Mrs. les Prévôt des Marchands et Echevins, représentant la Ville, d'accepter ce Buste, et de le placer à l'endroit le plus honorable pour le Marquis et le plus satisfaisant pour les sentimens d'une Nation Alliée.

C'est avec un vrai plaisir, que j'obéis à la Republique, en présentant son juste hommage pour un caractère, si grand dans les premiers développemens de sa vie, qu'ils auraient honoré la fin de telle vie que ce pût être. Notre Pays, couvert par une Armée peu nombreuse contre une beaucoup plus considérable, des talens qui ont feu suppléer à l'épaisement de nos moyens, des manoeuvres qui ont fini une longue Campagne par obliger nos Ennemis de s'enfermer dans un Point marqué pour rendez-vous aux Alliés et Confédérés, qui devoient se réunir contre eux, de manière qu'un seul coup ait décidé le sort d'une Guerre, qui s'étoit repanduë dans les quatre Parties du Monde, et pendant toute cette conduite l'attention la plus sontenuë pour les Loix Civiles et les Droits des Citoyens. Tels sont les faits, qui eussent ajouté à la gloire des plus grands caractères connus, et qui expliquent parfaitement la chaleur des sentimens, dont j'ai en cette occasion l'honneur d'être l'organe.

Il eut été plus agréable pour moi d'avoir exécuté cet Office en personne, d'avoir mêlé le tribut de ma reconnaissance particulière à celle de mon Pays, et de présenter moi-même à votre honorable corps l'hommage de mon respect: Mais, puisqu'un accident grave me prive de remplir un devoir si cher, Mr. Short, ancien Membre du Conseil-d'Etat de la Republique, aura l'honneur de vous remettre cette Lettre avec les Résolutions de l'Assemblée-Générale et de vous présenter le Buste: Il vous offrira aussi les sentimens de la vénération etc.

"M. le Pelletier de Morfontaine, Conseiller-d'État et Prévôt des Marchands, après un Discours, qui excita une vive sensation, fit faire la lecture des Résolutions de l'Etat, de la Lettre du Ministre Américain et de celle de M. le Baron de Bréteuil, Ministre d'Etat au Département de Paris, qui annonçoit l'approbation du Roi: Et Mr. Ethis de Corny, Avocat et Procureur du Roi, prononça un Discours très-intéressant, en requérant la transcription des Pièces ci-dessus sur les Régistres de la Ville, et l'acceptation du Buste, qui fut placé dans la grande Salle de l'Hôtel-de-Ville, au bruit des applaudissemens et d'une Musique militaire."

PrC (DLC); in Short's hand; unsigned. Enclosure (missing): An account of the proceedings of 28 Sep. 1786 in the Hôtel de Ville at which the Houdon bust of Lafayette, commissioned by the General Assembly of Virginia, was presented by Short, representing TJ and accepted by Ethis de Corny, *avocat et procureur du roi*. In the absence of the narrative enclosed by TJ to Rayneval it cannot be certainly established that the account published in the *Gazette de Leide* was the same, but the following facts indicate that it was. On 5 Oct. 1786 Short sent to C. W. F. Dumas at The Hague a copy of the proceedings; this was before any account had been published in Paris (see references, Gottschalk, *Lafayette, 1783-89*, p. 252, note; also *Journal de Paris*, 8 Oct. 1786—the earliest account, and similar to that in the *Gazette de Leide*). Dumas sent Short's letter and the article to Luzac, publisher of the *Gazette de Leide*: "Après avoir lu l'article ci-joint, et la Lettre dont j'ajoute la copie, vous ne serez pas surpris de l'empressement et du plaisir avec lequel j'ai l'honneur de postuler une place pour le dit article dans un papier aussi justement et universellement estimé que le vôtre. Qoique persuadé que vous trouverez que son agreable contenu la merite, je ne vous serai pas moins redevable de la promptitude avec laquelle vous voudrez bien l'accorder, pour nombre de bonnes raisons, dont la Lettre de Mr. Short en insinue une" (Rijksarchief, The Hague, Dumas Letter Book, 14 Oct. 1786). In consequence of this appeal, Dumas was able to write Short a few days later: "J'ai reçu en son temps la faveur de la vôtre du 5e court.; et vous aurez vu par le Supplément 83 de Leide que les desirs de votre ami ont été fidelement remplis" (Dumas to Short, 23 Oct. 1786; DLC: Short Papers). From the latter it can be safely concluded that the faithful execution of TJ's wishes meant a careful publication of the narrative prepared by him or by Short under his supervision. Accordingly, the text of the enclosure is that which appeared in Supplement No. 83 of the *Gazette de Leide*, 17 Oct. 1786.

"Few episodes in all his [Lafayette's] career," writes Gottschalk, "had yet received more attention from European journalists and aroused more general interest than this offering made by a thankful American commonwealth to Europe's greatest metropolis and approved by a magnanimous king" (*Lafayette, 1783-89*, p. 252). *The Journal de Paris* said that a man of letters who was present—perhaps Marmontel, who later wrote a poem commemorating the occasion—"a appliqué heureusement à M. *de la Fayette* ce que dit Tacite de Germanicus: FRUITUR FAMA SUI." Short wrote to his friend William Nelson: "The city of Paris has at length received the Marquis de la fayette's bust by the permission of the king and this was done in solemnity on the 28th of Septr. last. Mr. Jefferson being confined to his room I was obliged to represent him on the occasion. Our account of this ceremony has been inserted at large in several European papers. The sensation it made in Paris is inconceivable. I think the Marquis has never felt himself more flattered on any occasion whatever and Mde. de la Fayette was present at the ceremony and I am persuaded she did not receive more pleasure on the night of her marriage. Many tears were shed at the moment of the music commencing and the placing the bust" (Short to Nelson, 25 Oct. 1786; PrC in DLC: Short Papers). See also Trumbull to TJ, 3 Nov. 1786, for a comment on the garbled accounts in English newspapers.

From Richard Peters

DEAR SIR   Philada. Oct. 1. 1786

I hope your Friendship will induce you to excuse the Trouble I give you in negotiating a little Affair for me. I recieved 930 Dollars for a Captain Capitaine which has been lying in our Bank for a long Time as I could not pay it before I recieved a proper Power of Attorney from Mr. Capitaine to make a Settlement of his Accounts. Having now recieved it and got thro' the necessary Forms I have troubled you to find him out and pay him the Sum mentioned in the enclosed Bill taking his Reciept therefor of which I beg you will be pleased to inform me. Be assured of the most respectful and sincere Esteem with which I am Your obed hble Servt.,
RICHARD PETERS

He was Aid to the Marquis de la Fayette who will inform you of the Place of his Residence.

RC (MHi); endorsed by TJ with his right hand. Noted in SJL as received 25 Feb. 1787. Dupl (MHi); noted in SJL as received 3 May 1787. Enclosures not found, but see Capitaine to TJ, 6 Dec. 1786; TJ to Peters, 26 Feb. 1787; TJ to Capitaine, 25 Feb. 1787; Short to TJ, 23 Mch. 1787.

Michel Capitaine du Chesnoy (1746-1804) was one of Lafayette's aides-de-camp, an *ingénieur-geographe*, a founder of the Society of the Cincinnati, and an officer attached to the regiment of Aquitaine. He was promoted to the rank of major in the American army in 1778 and was honorably discharged in Nov. 1783 (Lasseray, *Les Français sous les Treize Etoiles*, p. 141-4).

From William Stephens Smith

Dr. Sir   London Octr. 1st. 1786.

I have received yours of the 23d. ulto. The first printing press has been forwarded some time. Mr. Woodmason is disposed to consider himself free'd from every obligation respecting the safe conveyance of his machine to Paris. He looks upon himself acquitted on presenting the Bill of lading, and receipt of the Captain. Upon this principle, the one is forwarded and payed for. I hope no inconvenience will arise to you, from the mode. I will endeavour to alter it hereafter.—I suppose Mr. Stockdale has forwarded your Books. Homers Odesey and Iliad not being ready at the time, I have got them bound, and shall forward them, with your waist coats and breeches, by the diligence, if you think best, for I find Dr. Bancroft will not visit Paris for some time, and as the period of your excursion approaches fast, I shall expect further directions by the return of Post.—The Harness is lodged with the master of the diligence and will proceed in the morning. I have got them made so that the Chariot and Cabriolet match, and I hope they may please you. I am apprehensive I execute your orders too rapidly. You wish the press, which your Letter to Mr. Woodmason demands, should be in time to come with the other articles. Every thing else is on the way to you already, except the harpsicord, which must remain in check, untill Dr. Burney returns from the Country. However I will now order everything from this period to my house, and when a Collection is great enough, they shall go together.—You must not be so uneasy about money and Bills. Your Credit stands high, and I dare trust you if necessary. I should not be fond of putting Mr. Tessier's complisance to the test on money matters—he is a merchant. Will you permit me, Sir, to beg you will send me a map of the United States, published at Paris in 1783. addressed to Dr. Franklin by Lattré No. 20 Rue St. Jacques. Mrs. Smith desires her Compliments and I have the honor to be with great respect Your Excellency most obedt. and obliged servt.,

W. S. Smith

N.B. We pray for your speedy recovery. Mr. A. is very anxious to know how you hurt yourself. Will you enable me to answer him? Be pleased to send me the Chevalier Chastelux's Journal.

RC (MHi). Noted in SJL as received 3 Oct. 1786.

Thomas Barclay to the American Commissioners

GENTLEMEN Cadiz 2d. Octr. 1786

By the Bearer Colonel Franks I do myself the honor to send you in a small Box the following Articles.

1. A Book containing the original Treaty in Arabic between the Emperor of Morocco and the United States.
2. Three translations of the Treaty in English to each of which is added a Translation of a Declaration made by Tahar Fennish by order of His Majesty in addition and explanation of the 10th. Article.
3. A letter from the Emperor to the President of Congress.
4. Translation of this Letter in English.
5. Translation of the Emperor's Letter to the King of Spain.
6. A Letter from Tahar Fennish to the Ministers at Paris and London and Translation.
7. Signals agreed on by which the Moorish and American Vessels may distinguish each other at Sea.
8. The answer to Queries which you put to me, dated Tangier 10th. September.
9. An Account of some other particulars relative to this Country dated Tangier 13th. September.
10. An Account of the proceedings relative to the Treaty dated Ceuta 18th September.
11. Copy of a Commission given to Francis Chiappi of the City of Morocco until the pleasure of Congress shall be known and the Names of the Agents at Mogadore and Tangier.

These matters have been detained a considerable time from you by various Accidents, among which contrary Winds and stormy Weather were a Part. But I hope as all such impediments are removed you will receive them with the utmost Expedition.

The Original of the Declaration made by Mr. Fennish could not be placed in the same Book with the Treaty sealed by the Emperor, the Moorish Forms not permitting it, therefore Mr. Fennish wrote it in another Book which I had placed in his hands with a

TREATY WITH MOROCCO 1786

Copy of the Treaty for examination in order that he might certify the verity of it, lest any accident should happen to the original, which Book with authenticated Copies of the other Papers remain in my hands. I am with great Respect, Gentn. your most obt. humb. Servt.,

THOS. BARCLAY

RC (MHi: AMT); in clerk's hand, marked "Copy" by Barclay and signed by him. Dupl (DLC); in clerk's hand, signed by Barclay; at foot of text, in Barclay's hand: "(Copy) original by Col. Franks"; endorsed by TJ with his right hand. Tr (DNA: PCC, No. 91, I); in another clerk's hand, signed by Barclay and marked by him "Copy." PrC of a Tr (DLC); in Short's hand; at head of text: "(Copy of a duplicate)." Enclosures: For notes to (1) and (2), see Treaty with Morocco, following. (3) Letter from the Emperor of Morocco; dated 1 Ramadan, A.H. 1200 (28 June 1786), from translation (4) made by the interpreter Isaac Cardoza Nuñez and certified by Barclay, stating that the treaty had been completed "on the terms desired of us, and the articles are inserted in a book, confirmed by our royal seal being affixed thereto" (PrC of a Tr [DLC] in Short's hand; printed in *Dipl. Corr., 1783-89*, II, 698-9). (5) Translation by Nuñez of letter from Emperor of Morocco to King of Spain, acknowledging a letter from the latter on Barclay's behalf and announcing that a treaty of peace with the United States had been executed—the source whence news of the treaty first reached America (PrC of a Tr [DLC] in Short's hand; printed in *Dipl. Corr., 1783-89*, II, 699-700, also certified by Barclay. (6) Taher Fennish to Commissioners, 28 June 1786. (7) Ships' signals agreement (Tr in clerk's hand [MHi: AMT] with two lines in Arabic badly written and with serious errors, consisting of an authorization on behalf of the Emperor of Morocco; signed by Barclay; PrC [DLC], in Short's hand; printed in Miller, ed., *Treaties of the United States*, II, with the Arabic in facsimile and with a commentary on it by Dr. C. Snouck Hurgronje). (8), (9), and (10) Barclay to Commissioners, 10, 13, and 18 Sep. 1786, respectively. (11) Copy of commission issued by Barclay to Francis Chiappe, a resident at Morocco, to act as temporary consul for the United States, together with notation that like commissions had been issued to Joseph Chiappe for Mogadore, and to Girolamo Chiappe for Tangiers (Tr in MHi: AMT; PrC of same in DLC in Short's hand; printed in *Dipl. Corr., 1783-89*, II, 725).

Treaty with Morocco

To all Persons to whom these Presents shall come or be made known.

Whereas the United States of America in Congress assembled by their Commission bearing date the twelvth day of May One thousand Seven hundred and Eighty four thought proper to constitute John Adams, Benjamin Franklin and Thomas Jefferson their Ministers Plenipotentiary, giving to them or a Majority of them full Powers to confer, treat and negotiate with the Ambassador, Minister or Commissioner of His Majesty, the Emperor of Morocco concerning a Treaty of Amity and Commerce, to make and receive propositions for such Treaty and to conclude and sign the same, transmitting it to the United States in Congress assembled for their final Ratification, And by one other Commission bearing date the Eleventh day of March One thousand Seven hundred and Eighty five did further empower the said Ministers Plenipotentiary or a Majority of them, by writing under their hands and Seals to appoint such Agent in the said Business as they might think proper with Authority under the directions and Instructions of the said Ministers to commence and prosecute the said Negotiations and Conferences for the said Treaty provided that the said Treaty should be signed by the said Ministers: And Whereas, We the said John Adams and Thomas Jefferson two of the said Ministers Plenipotentiary (the said Benjamin Franklin being absent) by writing under the Hand and Seal of the said John Adams at London October the fifth, One thousand Seven hundred and Eighty five, and of the said Thomas Jefferson at Paris October the Eleventh of the same Year, did appoint Thomas Barclay, Agent in the Business aforesaid, giving him the Powers therein, which by the said second Commission we were authorized to give, and the said Thomas Barclay in pursuance thereof, hath arranged Articles for a Treaty of Amity and Commerce between the United States of America and His Majesty the Emperor of Morocco, which Articles written in the Arabic Language, confirmed by His said Majesty the Emperor of Morocco and seal'd with His Royal Seal, being translated into the Language of the said United States of America, together with the Attestations thereto annexed are in the following Words, To Wit:[1]

In the Name of Almighty God,
This is a Treaty of Peace and Friendship established between us and the United States of America, which is confirmed, and which we have ordered to be written in this Book and sealed with our Royal Seal at our Court of Morocco on the twenty fifth day of the blessed Month of Shaban, in the Year One thousand two hundred, trusting in God it will remain permanent.

.1.

We declare that both Parties have agreed that this Treaty consisting of twenty five Articles shall be inserted in this Book and delivered to the Honorable Thomas Barclay, the Agent of the United States now at our Court, with whose Approbation it has been made and who is duly authorized on their Part to treat with us concerning all the Matters contained therein.

.2.

If either of the Parties shall be at War with any Nation what-

TREATY WITH MOROCCO 1786

ever, the other Party shall not take a Commission from the Enemy nor fight under their Colors.

.3.

If either of the Parties shall be at War with any Nation whatever and take a Prize belonging to that Nation, and there shall be found on board Subjects or Effects belonging to either of the Parties, the Subjects shall be set at Liberty and the Effects returned to the Owners. And if any Goods belonging to any Nation, with whom either of the Parties shall be at War, shall be loaded on Vessels belonging to the other Party, they shall pass free and unmolested without any attempt being made to take or detain them.

.4.

A signal or Pass shall be given to all Vessels belonging to both Parties, by which they are to be known when they meet at Sea, and if the Commander of a Ship of War of either Party shall have other Ships under his Convoy, the Declaration of the Commander shall alone be sufficient to exempt any of them from examination.

.5.

If either of the Parties shall be at War, and shall meet a Vessel at Sea, belonging to the other, it is agreed that if an examination is to be made, it shall be done by sending a Boat, with two or three Men only, and if any Gun shall be fired and injury done without Reason, the offending Party shall make good all damages.

.6.

If any Moor shall bring Citizens of the United States or their Effects to His Majesty, the Citizens shall immediately be set at Liberty and the Effects[2] restored, and in like Manner, if any Moor not a Subject of these Dominions shall make Prize of any of the Citizens of America or their Effects and bring them into any of the Ports of His Majesty, they shall be immediately released, as they will then be considered as under His Majesty's Protection.

.7.

If any Vessel of either Party shall put into a Port of the other and have occasion for Provisions or other Supplies, they shall be furnished without any interruption or molestation.

.8.

If any Vessel of the United States shall meet with a Disaster at Sea and put into one of our Ports to repair, she shall be at Liberty to land and reload her Cargo, without paying any Duty whatever.

.9.

If any Vessel of the United States shall be cast on Shore on any

TREATY WITH MOROCCO 1786

Part of our Coasts, she shall remain at the disposition of the Owners and no one shall attempt going near her without their Approbation, as she is then considered particularly under our Protection; and if any Vessel of the United States shall be forced to put into our Ports, by Stress of weather or otherwise, she shall not be compelled to land her Cargo, but shall remain in tranquillity untill the Commander shall think proper to proceed on his Voyage.

.10.

If any Vessel of either of the Parties shall have an engagement with a Vessel belonging to any of the Christian Powers within Gunshot of the Forts of the other, the Vessel so engaged shall be defended and protected as much as possible untill she is in safety; And if any American Vessel shall be cast on shore on the Coast of Wadnoon or any Coast thereabout, the People belonging to her shall be protected, and assisted untill by the help of God, they shall be sent to their Country.

.11.

If we shall be at War with any Christian Power and any of our Vessels sail from the Ports of the United States, no Vessel belonging to the Enemy shall follow within twenty four hours after the Departure of our Vessels, and the same Regulation shall be observed towards the American Vessels sailing from our Ports—be their Enemies Moors or Christians.[3]

.12.

If any Ship of War belonging to the United States shall put into any of our Ports she shall not be examined on any Pretence whatever, even though she should have fugitive Slaves on Board, nor shall the Governor or Commander of the Place compel them to be brought on Shore on any pretext, nor require any payment for them.

.13.

If a Ship of War of either Party shall put into a Port of the other and salute, it shall be returned from the Fort, with an equal Number of Guns, not with more or less.

.14.

The Commerce with the United States shall be on the same footing as is the Commerce with Spain or as that with the most favored Nation for the time being and their Citizens shall be respected and esteemed and have full Liberty to pass and repass our Country and Sea Ports whenever they please without interruption.

TREATY WITH MOROCCO 1786

.15.

Merchants of both Countries shall employ only such interpreters, and such other Persons to assist them in their Business, as they shall think proper. No Commander of a Vessel shall transport his Cargo on board another Vessel, he shall not be detained in Port, longer than he may think proper, and all persons employed in loading or unloading Goods or in any other Labor whatever, shall be paid at the Customary rates, not more and not less.

.16.

In case a War between the Parties, the Prisoners are not to be made Slaves, but to be exchanged one for another, Captain for Captain, Officer for Officer and one private Man for another; and if there shall prove a difficiency on either side, it shall be made up by the payment of one hundred Mexican Dollars for each Person wanting; And it is agreed that all Prisoners shall be exchanged in twelve Months from the Time of their being taken, and that this exchange may be effected by a Merchant or any other Person authorized by either of the Parties.

.17.

Merchants shall not be compelled to buy or Sell any kind of Goods but such as they shall think proper; and may buy and sell all sorts of Merchandise but such as are prohibeted to the other Christian Nations.

.18.

All goods shall be weighed and examined before they are sent on board, and to avoid all detention of Vessels, no examination shall afterwards be made, unless it shall first be proved that contraband Goods have been sent on board, in which Case the Persons who took the contraband Goods on board shall be punished according to the Usage and Custom of the Country and no other Person whatever shall be injured, nor shall the Ship or Cargo incur any Penalty or damage whatever.

.19.

No Vessel shall be detained in Port on any pretence whatever, nor be obliged to take on board any Article without the consent of the Commander who shall be at full Liberty to agree for the Freight of any Goods he takes on board.

.20.

If any of the Citizens of the United States, or any Persons under their Protection, shall have any disputes with each other, the Consul shall decide between the Parties and whenever the Consul

TREATY WITH MOROCCO 1786

shall require any Aid or Assistance from our Government to enforce his decisions it shall be immediately granted to him.

.21.

If a Citizen of the United States should kill or wound a Moor, or on the contrary if a Moor shall kill or wound a Citizen of the United States, the Law of the Country shall take place and equal Justice shall be rendered, the Consul assisting at the Tryal, and if any Delinquent shall make his escape, the Consul shall not be answerable for him in any manner whatever.

.22d.

If an American Citizen shall die in our Country and no Will shall appear, the Consul shall take possession of his Effects, and if there shall be no Consul, the Effects shall be deposited in the hands of some Person worthy of Trust, untill the Party shall appear who has a Right to demand them, but if the Heir to the Person deceased be present, the Property shall be delivered to him without interruption; and if a Will shall appear, the Property shall descend agreeable to that Will, as soon as the Consul shall declare the Validity thereof.

.23.

The Consuls of the United States of America shall reside in any Sea Port of our Dominions that they shall think proper, And they shall be respected and enjoy all the Privileges which the Consuls of any other Nation enjoy, and if any of the Citizens of the United States shall contract any Debts or engagements, the Consul shall not be in any Manner accountable for them, unless he shall have given a Promise in writing for the payment or fulfilling thereof, without which promise in Writing no Application to him for any redress shall be made.

.24.

If any differences shall arise by either Party infringing on any of the Articles of this Treaty, Peace and Harmony shall remain notwithstanding in the fullest force, untill a friendly Application shall be made for an Arrangement, and untill that Application shall be rejected, no appeal shall be made to Arms. And if a War shall break out between the Parties, Nine Months shall be granted to all the Subjects of both Parties, to dispose of their Effects and retire with their Property. And it is further declared that whatever indulgences in Trade or otherwise shall be granted to any of the Christian Powers, the Citizens of the United States shall be equally entitled to them.

.25.

This Treaty shall continue in full Force, with the help of God for Fifty Years.

We have delivered this Book into the Hands of the before-mentioned Thomas Barclay on the first day of the blessed Month of Ramadan, in the Year One thousand two hundred.

I Certify that the annex'd is a true Copy of the Translation made by Isaac Cardoza Nuñez, Interpreter at Morocco, of the treaty between the Emperor of Morocco and the United States of America.[4]

THOS BARCLAY

Translation of the additional Article

Grace to the only God

I the underwritten the Servant of God, Taher Ben Abtelhack[5] Fennish do certify that His Imperial Majesty my Master (whom God preserve) having concluded a Treaty of Peace and Commerce with the United States of America has ordered me the better to compleat it and in addition of the tenth Article of the Treaty to declare "That, if any Vessel belonging to the United States shall be in any of the Ports of His Majesty's Dominions, or within Gunshot of his Forts, she shall be protected as much as possible and no Vessel whatever belonging either to Moorish or Christian Powers with whom the United States may be at War, shall be permitted to follow or engage her, as we now deem the Citizens of America our good Friends."

And in obedience to His Majesty's Commands I certify this Declaration by putting my hand and Seal to it, on the Eighteenth day of Ramadan in the Year One thousand two hundred.

(signed)

The Servant of the King my Master whom God preserve.

TAHER BEN ABDELHACK FENNISH[6]

I Do Certify that the above is a True Copy of the Translation made at Morocco by Isaac Cardoza Nunes, Interpreter, of a Declaration made and Signed by Sidi Hage Tahar Fennish in addition to the Treaty between the Emperor of Morocco and the United States of America which Declaration the said Tahar Fennish made by the Express Directions of His Majesty.

THOS BARCLAY

Note, The Ramadan of the Year of the Hegira 1200 Commenced on the 28th. June in the Year of our Lord 1786.[7]

TREATY WITH MOROCCO 1786

Now know Ye that We the said John Adams and Thomas Jefferson Ministers Plenipotentiary aforesaid do approve and conclude the said Treaty and every Article and Clause therein contained, reserving the same nevertheless to the United States in Congress assembled for their final Ratification.

In testimony whereof we have signed the same with our Names and Seals, at the Places of our respective residence and at the dates expressed under our signatures respectively.[8]

JOHN ADAMS
London January 25. 1787.
THOMAS JEFFERSON
Paris January 1. 1787.

Tr (DNA: PCC, No. 91, I, 215-29); in Franks' hand; certification signed by Barclay; translation of the additional article in another clerk's hand, followed by the certification and note explaining the date in Barclay's hand; first, second, and final pages executed in Paris and in Franks' hand; signed and dated by TJ in Paris on 1 Jan. 1787 and by Adams in London on 25 Jan. 1787. Another Tr (MHi: AMT); similar in all respects to the foregoing except as indicated below. PrC of Tr (DLC); in Short's hand; includes preamble and text of concluding page (see note 1 below). Tr (MHi: AMT); in Short's hand, consisting of the declaration as to the additional Article, certified by Barclay and dated "Madrid 4 Dec. 1786." PrC (DLC); consisting of only that part of the foregoing embraced by Barclay's certification. Tr (DNA: PCC, No. 107, I); clerk's copy of the declaration as certified by Barclay on 4 Dec. 1786. (The declaration as to the additional Article was enclosed in Barclay to TJ, 4 Dec. 1786.)

The original Arabic text of the treaty as enclosed in the "book" sent by Barclay to the Commissioners, 2 Oct. 1786, is reproduced in facsimile in Miller, ed., *Treaties of the United States*, II, 186-211, with a commentary by Dr. C. Snouck Hurgronje on the translation by the interpreter Isaac Cardoza Nuñez as printed above. Barclay had been authorized by the Commissioners to negotiate a preliminary treaty with such person or persons as the Emperor of Morocco might appoint for the purpose, to sign the Articles agreed upon in preliminary form, and to transmit the result to the Commissioners for "definitive execution" (see Vol. 8: 611-4). Actually, as Barclay's letters and the documents transmitted with his communication of 2 Oct. 1786 show, the Arabic text of the treaty was, as Miller points out, somewhat similar to the idea of a unilaterally executed grant, bearing only the seal of the Emperor of Morocco and not signed or sealed on behalf of the Commissioners or by them. The "book" embracing this original Arabic text is "literally a book, in leather covers, with the text running from the back leaf on alternate pages and the front pages blank" (Miller, ed., *Treaties of the United States*, II, 225). The signing of the above text by the Commissioners is therefore not to be considered as one of the original texts of a treaty in the usual sense; in view of the fact that the treaty was already completed on the part of Morocco and awaiting only ratification and promulgation by Congress, the above text is to be considered primarily as a part of the Commissioners' report to Congress of the mission with which they were charged and which, in this instance, they had delegated to Barclay. See TJ to Adams, 23 Oct. 1786. On the ratification and promulgation, see Miller, same, II, 225-7; the instrument of ratification by the United States was published in the *Daily Advertiser* (N.Y.), 21 July 1787.

[1] This preamble is lacking in Tr of text in MHi: AMT; it and the concluding paragraphs (see note 8, below) were drawn up by TJ in Paris in December 1786. Both are embraced in the first two leaves of the PrC of Short's Tr (DLC: TJ Papers, 22: 3847-8), where, after the words "To Wit," is the following: "(here insert the treaty)." The text of the treaty in PrC of Short's Tr is to be found in DLC: TJ Papers, 22: 3849-57 (final page missing).

[426]

² This word interlined in substitution for "property," deleted. Tr (MHi: AMT) reads "Effects," with no deletion; so does PrC of Short's Tr.
³ Preceding six words evidently inserted later, being in a different hand; they are in Franks' hand in Tr (MHi: AMT).
⁴ This certification in an unidentified clerk's hand; signature in Barclay's hand—both being the same in Tr (MHi: AMT).
⁵ This name interlined in substitution for "Abdelmelick," deleted.
⁶ Translation of the additional Article in an unidentified clerk's hand in above text and in Tr (MHi: AMT).
⁷ Certification, signature, and note in Barclay's hand. Tr (MHi: AMT) ends at this point.
⁸ This paragraph was added in Paris and is in Franks' hand; signatures and date-lines in hands of Adams and TJ respectively; see note 1, above.

From José da Maia

Monsegneur   Montpellier 2 d'Octobre de 1786

J'ai une chose de tres grande consequence à Vous communiquer; mais comme l'etat de ma santé ne me permet pas de pouvoir avoir l'honeur d'aller Vous trouver à Paris, je Vous prie de vouloir bien avoir la bonté de me dire, si je puis avec sureté Vous la communiquer par lettre; puisque je suis etranger, et par consequent peu instruit des usages du pays. Je Vous demande bien pardon de la liberté, que prends, et je Vous prie aussi d'en adresser la reponse à Mr. Vigarons Conseiller du Roy, et Professeur en medicine a l'Université de Montpellier.

Je suis avec tout le respect, Monsegneur, Votre tres humble, et obeissant serviteur,   Vendek

RC (DLC); endorsed by TJ with his left hand.

VENDEK: A young Brazilian revolutionary whose real name was José da Maia and who, along with other Brazilian students, had been taking courses at the University of Montpellier (Percy A. Marvin, trans. and ed., Calogeras, *History of Brazil*, Chapel Hill, 1939, p. 45). See Da Maia to TJ, 21 Nov. 1786; TJ to Jay, 4 May 1787.

From William Carmichael

My Dear Sir   Madrid 3d. Octr. 1786.

On the 29th Ulto. I had the honor to address you by a courier which this Court dispatched to the Marquis del Campo at London. This courier hath not set off at the time expected, so that you will receive this with the one of the date Abovementioned. [This day yours of the 22d Septr. inclosing Letters for Messrs. Lamb and Barclay reached me. The former is still at Alicant and this Night I forward your Letter for him. The Latter arrived at Cadiz the 25th Ulto and as he informs me, is now on his way to this Capital;

[427]

3 OCTOBER 1786

So that I shall keep your Letter until his arrival. Mr. Lamb continues to write me. I have pressed him to send the Account of his disbursements to yourself and Mr. Adams, in order that you may know what Money remains in his hands and that whatever its amount may be, it should remain at your disposition. I know that he continues to Correspond with the Minister of the Marine at Algiers and I think that whatever may be the resolution of Congress, the Algerines ought to think we wish to have peace with them, at the same time that we do not fear their hostilities. This is a correspondence that requires some address and if Mr. Barclay should remain here, I am persuaded he would execute your orders with precision. I believe Mr. Lamb extremely zealous for the Interests of his Country, But I cannot permit myself to say that He has the qualifications necessary for a Negotiator. He has displeased and is displeased with the French and Spanish Consul and Agent at Algiers and you can scarcely conceive the pain that these little minute circumstances have occasioned me. I beg you to Beleive that it is with pain I enter into the smallest details which if known can injure any one of my country men.][1] I write to you with Confidence, because I have long been taught to consider you as a disinterested True Republican. I return you once more my thanks for the Letter you had the goodness to write me the 22d. Augt. The temerity with which I tresspassed on your patience can only be excused by the extreme desire that I feel not to appear ignorant on points which ought to be known to all who have the honor to serve their Country, which ought indeed to be known by every Citizen of America. During the seven years that I have been employed *here* It would surprise and astonish you to see the contents of my official Information. In the Gazette of the Court, that is of Madrid, there has lately appeared an article of the flourishing State of their Marine. In All parts of this Peninsula, There are complaints of the ruinous situation of their Commerce, Altho' I know it is the Intention of the Minister to revive and extend it. The Affair of Naples appears once more attended with difficulties which originate from the King. G.B. is doing every thing in its power to alienate this Court from its Attachment to France. The Ct. D'Expilly returns once more to Algiers. I have seen the work of the Marquis de Chastellux. I believe I was one of the first who gave a discription of the Natural Bridge which excited so strongly his Admiration. In the course of a Voyage which I undertook for my health to the Springs of Augusta County, I was induced to visit that as well as several other Natural Curiosities of the Country.

[428]

3 OCTOBER 1786

On my return to Maryland I endeavoured to engage Mr. Peale a painter, to make the same tour, with the view of taking views of many remarkable situations which struck me, then in the full enjoyment of a Romantic enthusiasm. I spoke to him so feelingly of this wonderful Bridge that he was induced to ask me a copy of my notes containing the Impression it made on me, assuring me that these only would enable him to sketch the Object. I gave him a very hasty and incorrect copy and I soon after saw it printed in a Philadelphia newspaper. I have still my journal of this voyage. The impressions it made on me are so strong, that if ever I return to America, It is my Intention to sell my little property and to establish myself beyond the Allegany Mountains, where by all forgot I may pass the rest of my days Inoffensively for others, doing all the good in my power and vegetating and decaying like the Trees which surround me, Affording shade in their prime and in their decay manure to the Soil they cover. I think I had the honor to mention this Natural Bridge to the Marquis de Chastellux, then Chevalier, during my residence in Paris in 1776-7. If the Notes on Virginia are really in circulation, you will permit me to ask a copy for myself, another for the Ct. de Campomanes, which I wish should be presented to him in your name. You are not uninformed of his Literary Abilities nor of his patriotic sentiments. He has been ever and is my warmest friend here, On whose advise I can rely and on whose inclination to serve me I can depend. You will perceive that I write you with the freedom of an acquaintance; In Republics of a Democratical Nature like ours, The Talents the Lumieres of every citizen is an appenage of the Society at large. "Their Light is not to be hid under a Bushel." On this principle I demand at the same time your Indulgence and pardon. I enclose you a Letter from Mr. Celesia the Genoese Minister here to Mr. Matzei. I Do not know whether the Latter might not make a useful Voyage to Spain and whether his knowledge of the Cultivation of vines, might not enable him to make discoveries useful to America, The Latitude being nearly similar. At All Events He will be perfectly well received here. With real esteem & Respect I have the honor to be Your Excellencys Obliged & Most Obed. Sert.,

WM. CARMICHAEL

RC (DLC); endorsed by TJ with his left hand. Tr of an extract (MHi: AMT); in Short's hand; see note 1, below. Noted in SJL as received 12 Oct. 1786. Enclosure not further identified.

[1] Text in brackets (supplied) represents the whole of the extract in MHi: AMT, which was enclosed in TJ to Adams, 23 Oct. 1786.

From John Jay

Sir   Office of foreign Affairs 3d. October 1786

I have the Honor of transmitting you herewith enclosed the following Papers, Viz.

No. 1. a Copy of the Consular Convention signed by the french and american Plenipotentiaries.

No. 2. a Copy of the Act of Congress under which the american Plenipotentiary signed the same.

No. 3 a Copy of a Scheme of a Convention mentioned and referred to in said Act.

No. 4 a Copy of a Report on the said Convention.

No. 5 a Copy of an Act of Congress containing Instructions and giving Authorities to you on the Subject of the said Convention.

These Papers will possess you fully of the whole Business. I am persuaded that it will appear to you as it does to Congress, to be a delicate one, and to require delicate Management.

The original Scheme of the Convention is far from being unexceptionable, but a former Congress having agreed to it, it would be improper now to recede; and therefore Congress are content to ratify a Convention made conformable to that Scheme, to their Act of the 25th. Day of January 1782, provided a Clause limiting its Duration be added. It will be proper therefore to press on the Court, *only* such Objections to the Convention, as arise from its Departure from the Scheme. On making an accurate Comparison, such Departure will appear manifest to his Majesty; and there is Reason to expect from his Candor, that he will readily consent to remove the Objections occasioned by it.

As it certainly is wise to try the Merits of Institutions entirely new, by actual Experience, before Nations adopt them forever, the Propriety of rendering this Convention probationary in the first Instance, is unquestionable. Congress cannot therefore presume that his most Christian Majesty will object to a Clause for limiting its Duration. The Design of this Convention being for mutual and reciprocal Benefit and Convenience, it would be doing Injustice to his Majesty to suppose, that he would wish to provide for its existing longer than it should prove useful and satisfactory.

If after the Experience of a few Years, it should be found to answer the Purposes intended by it, both Parties will have sufficient Inducements to renew it, either in its present Form, or with such

Alterations and Amendments as Time, Experience and other Circumstances may indicate.

With great Respect and Esteem, I have the Honor to be &c.,

JOHN JAY

FC (DNA: RG 59, PCC, No. 121). Noted in SJL as received 20 Dec. 1786. Enclosures (all in DLC except No. 5): (1) Clerk's copy of French text of Consular Convention as signed by Vergennes and Franklin, 29 July 1784 (translation printed in JCC, XXXI, 725-35). (2) Copy in Thomson's hand, signed by him, of resolution of Congress, 25 Jan. 1782 authorizing Franklin to negotiate such a convention (JCC, XXII, 46-7); there is also in DLC: TJ Papers, 7: 1209, a copy of this resolution in Short's hand, endorsed by TJ: "Consular convention Duplicate." (3) Copy of the scheme of a convention referred to in the preceding resolution (printed in JCC, XXII, 47-54; also, XXXI, 715-25). In DLC: TJ Papers, 11: 1780-5, there is a copy of the 11-page printed pamphlet embracing the first and third items of the enclosures, with notation "No. 3" and "Translation of No. 1" on pages [1] and 6 respectively, and bearing a few minor corrections, one or two in TJ's hand (see JCC, XXVII, 723, No. 442). (4) Copy of Jay's report to Congress of 4 July 1785 in which he analyzed the differences between the scheme as approved by Congress and the convention as negotiated by Franklin; printed in JCC, XXIX, 500-15 (a copy of the 9-page printed pamphlet embodying this report is in DLC: 13: 2215-9 and this was evidently the copy enclosed by Jay). (5) Copy of the resolution of Congress instructing TJ to reopen negotiations on the basis of this report as approved by Congress (JCC, XXXI, 712-3).

For the protracted and delicate negotiations on this matter, see S. F. Bemis, "John Jay," in Bemis, ed., *American Secretaries of State*, I, 253-9; Burnett, *Letters of Members*, VIII, No. 379, note 5.

From William Stephens Smith

DR. SIR London octr. 4th. 1786.

Mr. Adams wrote you on the 11th. ulto. by post, accompanied with an Answer to Mr. Lamb signed, the receipt of which is not yet acknowledged. I immagine he is waiting for your answer to that before he decides on the subject.—The business of the Secretary has been long done, but whether it will be made use of I cannot yet discover. I am Sir your Excellency's most obedt Humble servt.,

W. S. SMITH

RC (MHi); endorsed by TJ with his left hand. Erroneously recorded by TJ in SJL as received, with Smith's letter of 1 Oct., on 3 Oct. 1786.

To Maria Cosway

TH: JEFFERSON TO MRS. COSWAY Thursday [5 Oct. 1786]

I have passed the night in so much pain that I have not closed my eyes. It is with infinite regret therefore that I must relinquish your charming company for that of the Surgeon whom I have sent

[431]

5 OCTOBER 1786

for to examine into the cause of this change. I am in hopes it is only the having rattled a little too freely over the pavement yesterday. If you do not go to day I shall still have the pleasure of seeing you again. If you do, god bless you wherever you go. Present me in the most friendly terms to Mr. Cosway, and let me hear of your safe arrival in England. Addio Addio.

Let me know if you do not go to day.

RC (Charles Geigy-Hagenbach, Basel, Switzerland, 1947); addressed: "A Madame Madame Cosway rue Coqueron"; on verso, in Mrs. Cosway's hand: "This letter was writing when Mr. Jefferson was Envoy from America at Paris in 1785 with his left hand having sprained his wright by a fall. Maria Cosway." Not recorded in SJL. Not dated, but there can be no question that it was written in the early morning of the day that the Cosways left Paris; see below and also illustration in this volume.

This is the earliest surviving letter written by TJ to Mrs. Cosway and, aside from endorsements and signatures, the earliest manuscript written with his left hand after the injury to his right wrist. For the background, dating, and other facts pertaining to this letter, see L. H. Butterfield and Howard C. Rice, Jr., "Jefferson's Earliest Note to Maria Cosway with Some New Facts and Conjectures on his Broken Wrist," WMQ, 3rd ser., V (1948), 26-33. Randall, Life, I, 456, gave 4 Sep. 1786 as the date of injury to TJ's wrist, basing his conclusion on the entries in TJ's Account Book, and all subsequent narratives down to the publication of the article by Messrs. Butterfield and Rice followed Randall's conclusion. That article placed the date at some time between 13 and 22 Sep. and evidently after 16 Sep., when an entry appeared in TJ's Account Book for "seeing Desert"—the last entry before that on 18 Sep. when TJ paid "two Surgeons 12f." (Another important contribution in this article was the identification of the Désert de Retz as the "Desert" in question, an estate on the northwestern corner of the Forest of Marly, about four miles from St. Germain-en-Laye, whose vast, romanticized gardens were in the Anglo-Chinese manner; Thiéry, Guide des Amateurs, II, 348; Marie Kimball, Jefferson: The Scene of Europe, p. 166-7.) A letter from Le Veillard to William Temple Franklin, Passy, 8 Sep.-15 Oct. 1786, discovered subsequently by Mr. Butterfield in PPAP: Franklin Papers, confirmed these findings and definitely fixed the date of injury as being 18 Sep. 1786. Under date of 20 Sep. Le Veillard wrote: "Mr. Jefferson s'est demis avant hier le poignet de la main droite en voulant sauter par dessus une barriere du petit cours, le poignet est bien remis mais il a beaucoup souffert et je ne vois pas qu'il puisse ecrire d'ici a un mois" —"Day before yesterday Mr. Jefferson dislocated his right wrist when attempting to jump over a fence in the 'Petit Cours.' The wrist is in place all right but he has suffered a great deal and I do not see how he can write for another month." Mr. Rice identifies the "petit cours" as the Cours la Reine, the concourse or promenade which extends along the Seine westward from the Place de la Concorde; in the 18th century it was referred to either as the "Cours la Reine" or the "Petit Cours" to distinguish it from the "Grand Cours" which was another name for the Champs Elysées (see WMQ, 3rd ser., V [1948], 620-1; Thiéry, Guide des Amateurs, I, 51 ff.). TJ himself never referred to the date of his accident more precisely than in the letter to Carmichael of 26 Dec. 1786, when he said that it had occurred "three or four days" before he wrote Carmichael on 22 Sep. The nearest he ever came to explaining it was in his letter to Smith, 22 Oct. 1786, in response to a direct inquiry: "How the right hand became disabled would be a long story for the left to tell. It was by one of those follies from which good cannot come, but ill may." There can be no question, however, but that he injured the wrist as a result of a fall (see TJ to the Prévôt des Marchands, 27 Sep. 1786; article in Gazette de Leide, prepared by or under TJ's direction, printed above as enclosure to TJ to Rayneval, 30 Sep. 1786, referring to an "accident grave" and to "une chute"; Mazzei, Memoirs, p. 296, note, refers to a fall while TJ was walking in the Champs Elysées). Nor can there be any doubt that, as Madame de Doradour

[432]

said, the fall must have been "bien violente." It is not known whether he was with Maria Cosway at the time this accident occurred, but, in view of the cryptic remark in the letter to Smith and the suggestion of a "long story," it is highly probable that TJ and Mrs. Cosway were together on this September day as they had been more or less constantly in their perlustrations about Paris for the preceding two or three weeks.

In consequence of Mrs. Cosway's reply to the present letter (following), TJ dismissed the surgeon whom he had sent for and, despite pain and sleepless exhaustion, took what was for him the remarkably impulsive step of going with the Cosways as far as St. Denis (see TJ to Maria Cosway, 12 Oct. 1786).

From Maria Cosway

[5 Oct. 1786]

I am very, very sorry indeed, and [. . .][1] for having been the Cause of your pains in the [Night];[2] Why would you go? And why was I not more friendly to you and less to Myself by preventing your giving me the pleasure of your Company? You repeatedly said it wou'd do you no harm, I felt interested and did not insist. We shall go I believe this Morning, Nothing seems redy, but Mr. Cosway seems More dispos'd then I have seen him all this time. I shall write to you from England, it is impossible to be wanting to a person who has been so excesvely obliging. I dont attempt to make Compliments, they can be None for you, but I beg you will think us sensible to your kindness, and that it will be with infinite pleasure I shall remember the charming days we have past together, and shall long for next spring.

You will make me very happy, if you would send a line to the *post restante* at Antwerp, that I may know how you are.

Believe me dr: Sir your Most obliged affectionate servant,

MARIA COSWAY

RC (MHi); MS mutilated at the top, as are all of the early letters from Maria Cosway. This mutilation, which evidently is the work of a rodent, suggests that all of Maria Cosway's letters were at one time bundled together, since, on being placed in juxtaposition, the serrated edges of the tops of her early letters coincide; there is no particular significance in this fact, for the alphabetical grouping of in-letters was no doubt a normal procedure with TJ. Date supplied from internal evidence; see TJ to Maria Cosway, 29 Nov. 1786.

[1] Five or six words missing. Randolph, *Domestic Life*, p. 86, reads: ". . . very sorry indeed, and [blame myself] for having been the Cause," &c.; this reading for the two words in brackets (supplied) is conjectural, though there is no statement that the MS was mutilated (as it was) at the time Randolph published it. This reading may be correct in substance, but it is erroneous in phraseology, for fully half a line is missing and the remnant shows the descender of a letter at the end of the first word, indicating that it could not have been "blame."

[2] One word missing. Randolph, same, p. 86, reads "wrist," which is obviously an error since there is the remnant of a descender showing.

[433]

From C. W. F. Dumas

Monsieur La Haie 6e. Octob. *1786*

J'ai reçu avec bien de la reconnoissance l'estimable cadeau de l'*Essai sur les Etats unis,* que Votre Excellence a eu la bonté de m'envoyer en date du 22 7br. Le témoignage qu'en rend Votre Excellence me le rend très-précieux. Je vois d'ailleurs de combien son Auteur est redevable à vos excellentes notes sur la Virginie. Je n'ai pu encore que le parcourir superficiellement moi-même, parce que des personnages à qui je n'ai rien à refuser me l'arrachent et se l'arrachent: mais mon tour viendra le plutôt que je pourrai.

Votre Excellence aura la bonté de lire l'incluse pour le Congrès, et puis la garder avec les papiers annexés, ainsi que ceux que j'ai eu l'honneur de Lui envoyer dans une précédente, pour les joindre au paquet annoncé, qui a été oublié ici par le dernier Exprès, mais qu'un autre, qu'on m'assure devoir dépecher Lundi ou Mardi prochain, Lui apportera, pour expédier ensuite ce tout le plutôt le mieux ensemble, comme aussi les ci-jointes pour LL. EE. MM. Franklin et Morris. Votre Excellence verra par cette Lettre, sur le contenu de laquelle Elle peut faire fond, que rien n'y est hazardé, ni exagéré, que la Noble et interessante Cause de la Liberté civile se plaide ici avec un succès toujours augmentant;—And although the Struggle as Your Excellency very well says, would be *worth a great deal of blood*, yet happily there will be no occasion for it. Tyranny will be subdued without more than that of about 200 of their mercenary regulars, which has been really shed by their conquering the little defenceless City of Hattem althò they endeavour to disguise the loss by sparging the poor fellows having deserted.

Je suis avec le plus respectueux dévouement, De Votre Excellence le très-humble et très-obéissant serviteur,

C W F Dumas

RC (DLC); endorsed by TJ with his left hand. FC (Rijksarchief, The Hague: Dumas Papers; photostats in DLC); varies slightly from RC. Noted in SJL as received 10 Oct. 1786. Enclosures (FC of each in Rijksarchief; photostats in DLC): (1) Dumas to Benjamin Franklin, 27 Sep. 1786, requesting aid in procuring a treasury order for his arrearage of pay and interest thereon; stating that he has asked Congress for credentials accrediting him to the Netherlands as resident, or at least as chargé d'affaires with a salary of three to four thousand dollars, thereby enabling Congress to save the expense of a minister who would cost three times as much—in support of which Congress could not be ignorant of his useful and agreeable services, as proved by the pension of 1500 livres given him by the King of France; and informing him that he has sent the *Vie de M. Turgot* through TJ, of which the authorship could be attributed to Condorcet. (2) Dumas to Robert Morris, 27 Sep. 1786, saying that he has sent a copy of the *Vie de M. Turgot* through TJ, that he has seen

The Halle aux Bleds, Paris, by Maréchal, 1786. (See p. xxix.)

Th: Jefferson to mrs Cosway

I have passed the night in so much pain that I have not closed my eyes. it is with infinite regret therefore that I must relinquish your charming company for that of the Surgeon whom I have sent for to examine into the cause of this change. I am in hopes it is only the having rattled a little too freely over the pavement yesterday. if you do not go to day I shall still have the pleasure of seeing you again. if you do, god bless you wherever you go. present me in the most friendly terms to mr Cosway, & let me hear of your safe arrival in England. Addio Addio.

Thursday

let me know if you don't go to day.

Jefferson's first letter to Maria Cosway written with his left hand. (See p. xxix.)

Morris' sons and has given them letters for friends in Leiden, Harlem, and Amsterdam; repeating his wishes (as in the letter to Franklin) about payment and preferment; and soliciting Morris' influence. (3) Dumas to Jay, 3 Oct. 1786, reporting on affairs in the Netherlands, predicting that in spite of all appearances of a civil war the events will terminate to the satisfaction of the republican party, that there will be no anarchy, and that "certaines Puissances qui voudroient s'en mêler ne le pourront, et que tout rentrera dans l'ordre Constitutionnel"; and adding: "Je m'étois proposé d'entrer dans quelque détail sur ce qui me regarde, en recapitulant à Votre Excellence ce que j'ai eu l'honneur de lui écrire après avoir reçu l'Acte à mon égard du Congrès du 14 Octobre 1785. Mais je suis malade et par dessus le marché toujours affligé d'embarras domestiques toujours renaissants, que je dois m'efforcer constamment de cacher à tout ce qui est autour de moi, tant amis qu'ennemis, pour l'amour des Etats Unis comme pour ma propre tranquillité et paix. . . . P.S. du 6 Octobre. Nous attendons à tout moment la nouvelle que les Etats tronqués d'Utrecht, qui siègent depuis quelque tems schismatiquement à Amersfort, se mettent à la raison, et acceptent la médiation des autres Provinces entre eux et la Ville, qui en est le 3e. Membre. En attendant, celle-ci vient de déposer son Grand-Officier, Athlone, de race angloise; lui, avec un Perponcher, de race Polonoise, et deux ou 3 Pesters sont les plus violents boutefeux du Parti oligarchique.—J'ai la satisfaction de pouvoir assurer Votre Exc. que le Cabinet de France et le Parti vraiment républicain et national ici, heureusement dominant, qui est de sa nature le sien, sont parfaitement d'accord, et que la plus grande confiance, candeur et cordialité, dont je suis à toute heure le fidèle témoin et confident, règne entre eux,—que le Ministre d'Angleterre ici, en s'efforçant d'exciter quelques Provinces contre la Hollande, n'aboutira qu'à faire toujours plus haïr sa nation; —et que probablement le nouveau Plénipotentiaire de Prusse, pour s'y être mal pris et n'avoir fait que compromettre le Roi son Maître, finira par devoir demander son rappel *rebus infectis*.—*Les associations bourgeoises armées en Hollande, à Utrecht*, et jusqu'en *Zélande, Groningue, en Overyssel*, triomphent et par leur masse et légalement. On veut les comprimer en *Gueldre* et en *Frise*, leur ressort forcera aussi le doigt oligarchique qui presse encore sur lui. Ceci me conduit à une remarque importante: Toutes les fois que ce pays a été ou administré ou influé par des Etrangers, faute d'en bien connoître le Peuple, ils ont fini par le forcer à se soulever pour secouer ce joug odieux. Témoins Granville, et sa sequelle, Leicester, la feue Princesse mère du présent Stadhouder, le Chevalier York, le Duc L. de Brunswick . . ." (RC of this letter is among those recorded as missing in *Dipl. Corr., 1783-89*, III, 540).

From Thevenard

MONSIEUR Lorient le 6. Octobre 1786.

J'ai reçû le Portrait du Général Washington par Detems aprés La Lettre dont votre Excéllence m'a honoré pour me l'annoncer. Je ne doute pas qu'il ne Soit aussi ressemblant à ce grand homme, que L'exécution de la Peinture en est parfaitte. Votre Excéllence ayant bien Voulüe prendre des précautions, Soit pour le choix de L'Artiste, qui à fait cette Copie d'aprés Wright, Soit en priant M. Hudon d'en inspecter le Travail. Ma Joye est extrême de posseder la ressemblance d'un homme Immortel, de la devoir à Vos bontés et de pouvoir la Joindre à celle que je posséde, du Docteur Francklin, si célebre aussi à tant d'égards et dont le Nom ne s'effacera Jamais.

7 OCTOBER 1786

Ma reconnoissance est infinie des bontés que vôtre Excéllence m'a accordé dans cette Occasion. Il ne me reste plus qu'à vous prier, Monsieur, de vouloir bien me faire connoître les frais en Argent qui ont été faits pour ce Portrait, afin que J'en fasse aussitôt le remboursement.

Je suis avec un attachement infini et bien du Respect De Vôtre Excéllence Le très humble et très obéïssant Serviteur,

A. THEVENARD

RC (DLC); endorsed by TJ with his left hand. An entry in SJL of the receipt on 10 Oct. 1786 of a letter from Thevenard dated 8 Oct. probably refers to this letter; no letter of 8 Oct. has been found.

TJ's letter to Thevenard, announcing that the portrait of Washington is being sent, has not been found and is not recorded in SJL.

From Abbé André

SIR paris 7. 8br. 1786.

You have been so good as to favour me with your Recommandation. I Hope I shall be happy enough to not disgrace it; and to deserve it, I will make my utmost Endeavours. I have no other way to return you my dutiful thanks but to attend the most as possible the young Gentlemen you will send to my boarding. Mr. Barett and Mr. St. John de Crevecour Called upon me yesterday for their sons; I hope I may be Entrusted with them; I desire this favour very Earnestly, in order to be able of answering to the Character Mr. Smith invested in me, when he recommended me to your Excellency. I beg his leave I may wait on you, and present my thanks and respects with which I am Sir of your Excellency the most obedient and Dutiful Servant

L'ABBÉ ANDRÉ

RC (MHi); endorsed by TJ with his left hand.
TJ's RECOMMANDATION, perhaps in the form of a letter in Short's hand, has not been found; but see James Smith to TJ, 25 Sep. 1786.

To William Macarty

SIR Paris Octr. 7th. 1786

I took the liberty of troubling you when you were here with a pattern of my table-china. I now take that of sending you a list of the articles which I should be glad to have bought as nearly like the pattern as they can be found. Should you be able to find none but what is very different, preserving only the same colours

[436]

I would wish to receive only half the quantity written for; but the whole if it can be found to match tolerably. I would wish to recieve it by the roulier as I am in immediate want of it. Your bill on me for the amount shall be duely honored and many thanks for your kindness from Sir, your very humble servant,

Th: Jefferson

16. plats d'entrée portant 11. pouce de diametre.
16. autres plats d'entrée portant 10. pouces et demi de diametre.
18. plats d'entremets portant 9 pouces et demi de diametre.
 4. plats de rôt portant un pied deux pouces de longueur et 10. pouces et demi de largeur.
 4. plats de rôt portant un pied de longueur et 9. pouces de largeur.
12. compôtiers.
36. petits pots.
 4. saladiers.

PrC (DLC); endorsed by TJ with his left hand; in Short's hand, including signature; at foot of text: "(Test W. Short Secy.)."

From Benjamin Franklin

Dear Sir   Philada. Oct. 8. 1786

I obey with Pleasure the Order of the Philosophical Society, in transmitting to you the enclos'd Proof of their Respect for you, and of the honour they have done themselves, in chusing you one of their Members.

With this you will receive several Diplomas for foreign Gentlemen in different Parts of Europe, which I imagine you may convey to them thro' the Ministers of different Courts residing at Paris; and hope you will excuse my giving you the Trouble. There are some also for Gentlemen in France.

I have the honour to be with the highest Esteem, Sir, Your Excellency's most obedt. humble Servant,   B. Franklin

I send herewith the 2d Vol. of our Transactions, which please to accept.

RC (DLC: TJ Papers). FC (DLC: Franklin Papers). Noted in SJL as received 6 Dec. 1786. The various diplomas of membership in The American Philosophical Society were not enclosures, but were sent under separate cover (see TJ to Franklin, 23 Dec. 1786). For a note on TJ's mixed-up certificate of membership in the Society, see Vol. 4: 544-6. For the list of other diplomas for "foreign Gentlemen," see TJ's letter to new members of the Society, 4 Feb. 1787.

From John Trumbull, with a Note from Maria Cosway

Dr. Sir   Antwerp Monday 9th. Octr. 1786.

The only proper apology, for not having written you since I left Paris, is this which I now offer, a long letter, and I trust your goodness to pardon my negligence.

Mr. and Mrs. Cosway arriv'd this morning at 3 o Clock having rode all night in the rain, not much I fear to the benefit of his Health. I am very sorry to learn from them the unfortunate accident which has happen'd to you; much pain it must have cost you; and it will require great attention lest the consequences should be still more disagreeable than the present suffering. Your intended tour I hope you will not undertake untill your Arm is perfectly able to bear the motion of the Carriage.

My little tour has been infinitely more pleasant than I expected. I quitted Paris with regret, and the Idea of travelling alone in a Country whose Language I did not understand was very unpleasant. But I have been disappointed, in happily finding always some Companion who spoke French, and frequently those who spoke English. I have found the distances more considerable, and the roads worse in some parts than they were represented, by which means I arriv'd here only the 6th. at night, several days later than I intended.—From Paris to Metz my road was thro' a part of the wine country of Champagne, very beautiful, rough, and finely cultivated; at *Epernay*, I saw one of the great wine Cellars and tasted the finest wine I ever saw: The Country soon after sinks to a level sandy plain, cover'd with corn, but the soil very poor. Entering Lorrain at Clermont, you have again a rough broken Country, but fertile; Corn, Vines, Orchards, Meadows and Woods are intermix'd with the most beautiful variety, and the people appear to live plentifully and rich:—From this to Metz the same style of Country and Cultivation continues, but with much more poverty, both of Soil and Inhabitants:—The Situation of Metz is beautiful in a delightful Valley, upon the banks of the Moselle, which is navigable for small boats. The Town is very strongly fortified and the Garrison numerous. But there is no appearance of Commerce, Manufactures or Industry among the Inhabitants. From Metz to Frankfort, the distance is 55 Lea. thro' the territory of Deuxponts and part of the Palatinate of the Rhine, the Country generally mountainous, poor and thinly inhabited, and the roads a

9 OCTOBER 1786

deep heavy sand. At the distance of 6 or 8 Lea. from the Banks of the Rhine, we leave the mountains and enter one of the most beautiful and fertile Valleys of the World. The Vines which we had scarcely seen after leaving Metz recommence, and the country is cover'd with every variety of production, and enrich'd with Villages. The Villages and Inhabitants do not however bear those marks of Ease and competency which one would expect even in an arbitrary Country, from so opulent a Soil. The City of Worms is the first on the Banks of the River, Old, illbuilt, and ruinous.— I should have suppos'd it had suffer'd a seige but a few weeks before I pass'd. To Openheim where we cross'd the River, and for 2 Lea. on the other side the Road is fine, and the Country a perfect Garden, to Gerau. From this to very near Frankfort a dead barren Soil, with no trace of Cultivation and no production but starved white Birch and pine, the roads a deep sand, so heavy, that Truck Waggons coming from the fair drawn by 20 horses, and scarce able to proceed even with such a number.

The Situation of Frankfort is again delightful. The Town well built, full of Inhabitants and Opulent. The Fair is rich in the productions of every part of the World. The business which is done during the four weeks which it continues is very considerable, and the number of Strangers who are brought together by their affairs or by Curiosity very great. The business of all the interior part of Germany for the year is transacted at this time. From Frankfort to Mayence, I went by water, down the Maine, in a barge in which were 2 or 300 animals of all Ages, Ranks, Sexes and Religions, Jew pedlars, Catholic priests, Ladies, Market Women, Beggars, blind fiddlers and German Counts; at first entering the boat I was a little disconcerted, without a Companion in such a Chaos. I look'd round however, for some one with a good Coat, and addressed myself to an elderly decent man, in *my best* French, which Grace a Dieu, he understood. I found afterwards a Lady of Mayence with her daughter, who spoke French also, and pass'd the day pleasantly. At Mayence (the Maguntium of Caesar) are several remains of Roman power. A town in the Citadel call'd the monument of Drusus, and ruins of a Bridge across the Rhine visible only when the River is very low. The Town is large, well fortified, pretty well built, but little commerce, an University &c.—From Mayence I embarkd for Cologne, but the Weather became bad, the Wind contrary, and I was oblig'd to leave the water at Andernach 20 Lea. above Cologne. The Country through which the River takes its course, is for 8 Lea. level, fertile, and rich. It then meets

9 OCTOBER 1786

a Chain of Mountains similar to those on the North River, becomes contracted, the current broken by Rocks and small rapids which render the Navigation somewhat dangerous. The Shores are picturesque in the highest degree; precipices of Rock, Mountains, sometimes barren, again covered with Vines, and the Summits of those which are least accessible cover'd with the Ruins of ancient Gothic Chateaux, Ruins of Barbarism which one contemplates with pleasure, as they are so many monuments of the advances of Civilization and Happiness.—The River was really dangerous before we quitted it, and even then we left it with reluctance, so great were its beauties. I rode post all night thro Bonne and Cologne, and therefore know little of the Country or towns, except that the latter is large and very ill built. The Country from this to Dusseldorp is flat, beautiful, highly cultivated. Dusseldorp is a pleasant little town, remarkable for nothing but the Electoral palaces and Gallery. But such a Gallery as would well repay the trouble of a much longer and less pleasant Journey. The works of Rubens which are the finest part of the Collection are wonderfull, much beyond all that I had imagin'd, but an attempt at Description would be ridiculous. I stay'd here three days, and then took the German Post Waggon for Aix la Chapelle (willing to try all the varieties of travelling). So execrable a Machine is not in use in any civilized part of the World I believe, as this—A common Jersey Waggon is elegant and easy in comparison. We were fourteen, squeez'd, jolted, Bruised most insufferably;—arriv'd in the Evening at Aix, which has little to boast but its Baths and Gambling houses, of which the Prince Bishop of Liege is principal Banker. The Town is large, dirty, illbuilt.—From Aix to Liege, thro' a beautiful country and bad road.—Liege is delightfully situated on the Meuse, which is navigable for large boats. The Town is rich in manufactures of Iron, Mines of Coal, large, ill built, and the inhabitants the dirtiest people I ever saw. I stay'd the Sunday there and was in several Churches. Am therefore safe in pronouncing them superlatively dirty and ugly.—From Liege to Louvain, famous for Theology, Stupidity and Strong beer—to Brussels, elegant, well built, clean, the inhabitants genteel, very hospitable to strangers. Stay'd with great pleasure there and, the sixth, came on by the Canal to this place. The new palace and park of the Archduke near Brussels is the most elegant that I have seen since I left England, the grounds laid out with great Taste and Simplicity in the English style, and the house neat, and a good Style of Architecture. In this town I find an immense quantity of the finest works of Rubens, Van

Dyke &c. Some of them I have seen; shall stay yet a few days, and I believe shall return to London by Helvoetsluys, taking the Hague in my way. I am Dr. Sir very gratefully and affectionately yours,

JNO. TRUMBULL

Aggiungo due versi per domandarle come sta, Spero il viaggio a St. Dennys non fu cagione che si ricordò di Noi con pena, riceverò presto notizia del suo perfetto ristabilimento, qual cosa darà infinito piacere alla sua sempre obligata ed affta. Amica.

MARIA COSWAY

Mr. Cosway unisce i suoi ai miei Complimenti. Arrivammo qui domenica, tre ore doppo Mezza Notte.

RC (DLC); endorsed, in TJ's left hand: "Trumbull John." Recorded in SJL as received 13 Oct. 1786. The note from Mrs. Cosway is written just below Trumbull's signature.

Translation: I am adding a couple of lines to ask you how you are. I hope the trip to St. Dennys did not cause you to remember us painfully, [and that] I shall soon receive news of your complete recovery, which will give infinite pleasure to your always obliged and affectionate Friend, Maria Cosway.— Mr. Cosway adds his compliments to mine. We arrived here Sunday, three hours past midnight.

MR. AND MRS. COSWAY ARRIV'D THIS MORNING: As Mrs. Cosway's note shows, they arrived on Sunday morning, 8 Oct.; Trumbull probably finished the letter on Monday. See Theodore Sizer, ed., *Autobiography of Colonel John Trumbull*, p. 121-46, for an account of Trumbull's journey that is similar in many respects to that in the present letter, even in the identity of some of its phrases. LOUVAIN, for example, is described in the journal as "famous at present for its university, general stupidity and strong beer" (p. 142).

From John Lamb

SIR Alicante Octr. 10th 1786

I have received your Excellency letter. I am not able to take passage by Sea nor land. I have been confined this three months.

I am Exceeding Sorry that I cannot have a full Settlement in Europe. What I have wrote concerning it is real.

The letter of Credite I will return by the first safe hand. By post all my letters are broke. Therefore I think it will be unsafe by that method of Conveyance, but in the mean time Shall Draw no more. Your Excellencys Obedient Hmbl Servt.,   J: LAMB

RC (DLC); endorsed by TJ with his right hand. Tr (DNA: PCC, No. 87, I); in Short's hand, and with various corrections of grammar and spelling; see *Dipl. Corr., 1783-89*, II, 15. Tr (DNA: PCC, No. 107). Noted in SJL as received 19 Nov. 1786.

To Lewis Littlepage

Sir Paris Octob. 10. 1786

Your favor of July 12 did not come [to hand until the 3]d of Sep., a very few days after which I incurred the accident of a dislocated wrist which for some time interrupted my attention to affairs. I now receive that of Sep. 12 and am still able to write with the left hand only. In my first letter to the Governor of Virginia after your arrival in Paris I informed him of the circumstances which had prevented your execution of his wishes relative to the money. I communicated to him your information that your [. . . .] in a settlement with you, and were therefore [. . . .] fore a settlement of it [. . . .] never, and will write again. The result was recommunicated to [. . .] known to me. The Marquis de la Fayette offered me the bill you were so kind as to remit, but I declined receiving it till I should know that it would not be a double paiment. In the meantime I suffer no inconvenience, the state having a fund here. I beg you therefore to feel no uneasiness on that account, and to accept assurances of the respect with which I have the honour to be Sir Your most obedient and most humble servant,

Th: Jefferson

PrC (DLC); in TJ's left hand; MS mutilated: a hole, measuring approximately one and one-quarter by two and three-quarters inches, appears in the center of the page, so that parts of four lines are missing. For the background of the present letter, see TJ to the Governor of Virginia, 24 Jan. 1786; Littlepage to TJ, 21 Jan., 12 July, and 12 Sep. 1786; Lafayette to TJ, 2 Aug. 1786; and Randolph to TJ, 28 Jan. 1787.

From Jean Chas

rue st. thomas du Louvre no. 22.
Monsieur paris ce 11 8bre. 1786.

Je vais donner au public par Souscription L'histoire politique et philosophique des révolutions d'angleterre depuis la descente de jules cesar jusqu'a La paix de 1783. Mon ouvrage contient La révolution de L'amérique qui est le phénomene le plus extraordinaire, et Le plus interessant que nous offrent les annales du monde. J'ai épuisé toute La force de mon genre pour prouver que les colonies americaines avoient le droit de rompre les neuds qui les unissoient a La metropole, j'ai examiné leur origine, et leur anciene constitution. Je les ai suivies dans leurs travaux et leurs progrès, j'ai rendu compte des services qu'elles ont rendues a

L'angleterre, des injustices et de La tyranie par le gouvernement britanique, j'ai developè les erreurs, la fausse politique, et les passions des ministres de georges, et j'ai rendu un hommage sincère à ces braves deffenseurs de La Liberté americaine qui ont fondé, et consolidé un empire nouveau qui va briller par sa sagesse, ses Loix et ses meurs. Je ne suis ni enthousiaste, ni flateur, ni courtisan, mais j'aime La justice et La verité.

La nation francoise connoit, monsieur, vos vertus et vos vastes coinéssances: vous representés un etat que je respecte, que j'admire, et que j'honore. Je dois, monsieur, vous faire coinetre mon ouvrage avant qu'il soit publie pour suprimer, retrancher, ou augmenter ce que vous trouverés a propos. En remplissant un devoir si cher a mon coeur, je jouirai de cet avantage précieux d'obtenir votre suffrage, et votre estime. Daignés donc, monsieur, me fixer le jour ou je pourois me rendre chez vous.

Je suis avec respect, monsieur, votre tres humble et tres obeissant serviteur,   CHAS
                                                                     Avocat

RC (MoSHi); endorsed. MON OUVRAGE: *Histoire Politique et Philosophique de la Revolution de l'Amérique septentrionale, par les citoyens J. Chas et Lebrun,* Paris, 1801, for which Chas claimed sole authorship; Sowerby, No. 485. See TJ to Chas, 7 Dec. 1786; 3 Sep. 1801; Chas to TJ, 1 Apr. and 12 Dec. 1801.

From De Langeac

[*11 Oct. 1786*. Entered in SJL as received 11 Oct. 1786. Not found; but see TJ to De Langeac, 12 Oct. 1786.]

To Maria Cosway

[MY DEAR] MADAM[1]   Paris Octob. 12. 1786.

Having performed the last sad office of handing you into your carriage at the Pavillon de St. Denis, and seen the wheels get actually into motion, I turned on my heel and walked, more dead than alive, to the opposite door, where my own was awaiting me. Mr. Danquerville was missing. He was sought for, found, and dragged down stairs. [We] were crammed into the carriage, like recruits for the Bastille, and not having [sou]l enough to give orders to the coachman, he presumed Paris our destination, [and] drove off. After a considerable interval, silence was broke with a

12 OCTOBER 1786

'je suis vraiment affligé du depart de ces bons gens.' This was the signal for a mutual confession [of dist]ress. We began immediately to talk of Mr. and Mrs. Cosway, of their goodness, their [talents], their amability, and tho we spoke of nothing else, we seemed hardly to have entered into matter when the coachman announced the rue St. Denis, and that we were opposite Mr. Danquerville's. He insisted on descending there and traversing a short passage to his lodgings. I was carried home. Seated by my fire side, solitary and sad, the following dialogue took place between my Head and my Heart.

Head. Well, friend, you seem to be in a pretty trim.

Heart. I am indeed the most wretched of all earthly beings. Overwhelmed with grief, every fibre of my frame distended beyond it's natural powers to bear, I would willingly meet whatever catastrophe should leave me no more to feel or to fear.

Head. These are the eternal consequences of your warmth and precipitation. This is one of the scrapes into which you are ever leading us. You confess your follies indeed: but still you hug and cherish them, and no reformation can be hoped, where there is no repentance.

Heart. Oh my friend! This is no moment to upbraid my foibles. I am rent into fragments by the force of my grief! If you have any balm, pour it into my wounds: if none, do not harrow them by new torments. Spare me in this awful moment! At any other I will attend with patience to your admonitions.

Head. On the contrary I never found that the moment of triumph with you was the moment of attention to my admonitions. While suffering under your follies you may perhaps be made sensible of them, but, the paroxysm over, you fancy it can never return. Harsh therefore as the medicine may be, it is my office to administer it. You will be pleased to remember that when our friend Trumbull used to be telling us of the merits and talents of these good people, I never ceased whispering to you that we had no occasion for new acquaintance; that the greater their merit and talents, the more dangerous their friendship to our tranquillity, because the regret at parting would be greater.

Heart. Accordingly, Sir, this acquaintance was not the consequence of my doings. It was one of your projects which threw us in the way of it. It was you, remember, and not I, who desired the meeting, at Legrand & Molinos. I never trouble myself with domes[2] nor arches. The Halle aux bleds might have rotted down before I should have gone to see it. But you, forsooth, who are

[444]

eternally getting us to sleep with your diagrams and crotchets, must go and examine this wonderful piece of architecture. And when you had seen it, oh! it was the most superb thing on earth! What you had seen there was worth all you had yet seen in Paris! I thought so too. But I meant it of the lady and gentleman to whom we had been presented, and not of a parcel of sticks and chips put together in pens. You then, Sir, and not I, have been the cause of the present distress.

Head. It would have been happy for you if my diagrams and crotchets had gotten you to sleep on that day, as you are pleased to say they eternally do. My visit to Legrand & Molinos had publick utility for it's object. A market is to be built in Richmond. What a commodious plan is that of Legrand & Molinos: especially if we put on it the noble dome of the Halle aux bleds. If such a bridge as they shewed us can be thrown across the Schuylkill at Philadelphia, the floating bridges taken up, and the navigation of that river opened, what a copious resource will be added, of wood and provisions, to warm and feed the poor of that city. While I was occupied with these objects, you were dilating with your new acquaintances, and contriving how to prevent a separation from them. Every soul of you had an engagement for the day. Yet all these were to be sacrificed, that you might dine together. Lying messengers were to be dispatched into every quarter of the city with apologies for your breach of engagement. You particularly had the effrontery [to] send word to the Dutchess Danville that, in the moment we were setting out to d[ine] with her, dispatches came to hand which required immediate attention. You [wanted] me to invent a more ingenious excuse; but I knew you were getting into a scrape, and I would have nothing to do with it. Well, after dinner to St. Cloud, from St. Cloud to Ruggieri's, from Ruggieri to Krumfoltz, and if the day had been as long as a Lapland summer day, you would still have contrived means, among you, to have filled it.

Heart. Oh! my dear friend, how you have revived me by recalling to my mind the transactions of that day! How well I remember them all, and that when I came home at night and looked back to the morning, it seemed to have been a month agone. Go on then, like a kind comforter,[3] and paint to me the day we went to St. Germains. How beautiful was every object! the Port de Neuilly, the hills along the Seine, the rainbows of the machine of Marly, the terras of St. Germains, the chateaux, the gardens, the [statues] of Marly, the pavillon of Lucienne. Recollect too Madrid,

12 OCTOBER 1786

Bagatelle, the King's garden, the Dessert. How grand the idea excited by the remains of such a column! The spiral staircase too was beautiful. Every moment was filled with something agreeable. The wheels of time moved on with a rapidity of which those of our carriage gave but a faint idea, and yet in the evening, when one took a retrospect of the day, what a mass of happiness had we travelled over! Retrace all those scenes to me, my good companion, and I will forgive the unkindness with which you were chiding me. The day we went to St. Germains was a little too warm, I think, was not it?

Head. Thou art the most incorrigible of all the beings that ever sinned! I reminded you of the follies of the first day, intending to deduce from thence some useful lessons for you, but instead of listening to these, you kindle at the recollection, you retrace the whole series with a fondness which shews you want nothing but the opportunity to act it over again. I often told you during it's course that you were imprudently engaging your affections under circumstances that must cost you a great deal of pain: that the persons indeed were of the greatest merit, possessing good sense, good humour, honest hearts, honest manners, and eminence in a lovely art: that the lady had moreover qualities and accomplishments, belonging to her sex, which might form a chapter apart for her: such as music, modesty, beauty, and that softness of disposition which is the ornament of her sex and charm of ours. But that all these considerations would increase the pang of separation: that their stay here was to be short: that you rack our whole system when you are parted from those you love, complaining that such a separation is worse than death, inasmuch as this ends our sufferings, whereas that only begins them: and that the separation would in this instance be the more severe as you would probably never see them again.

Heart. But they told me they would come back again the next year.

Head. But in the mean time see what you suffer: and their return too depends on so many circumstances that if you had a grain of prudence you would not count upon it. Upon the whole it is improbable and therefore you should abandon the idea of ever seeing them again.

Heart. May heaven abandon me if I do!

Head. Very well. Suppose then they come back. They are to stay here two months, and when these are expired, what is to follow? Perhaps you flatter yourself they may come to America?

12 OCTOBER 1786

Heart. God only knows what is to happen. I see nothing impossible in that supposition, and I see things wonderfully contrived sometimes to make us happy. Where could they find such objects as in America for the exercise of their enchanting art? especially the lady, who paints landscape so inimitably. She wants only subjects worthy of immortality to render her pencil immortal. The Falling spring, the Cascade of Niagara, the Passage of the Potowmac thro the Blue mountains, the Natural bridge. It is worth a voiage across the Atlantic to see these objects; much more to paint, and make them, and thereby ourselves, known to all ages. And our own dear Monticello, where has nature spread so rich a mantle under the eye? mountains, forests, rocks, rivers. With what majesty do we there ride above the storms! How sublime to look down into the workhouse of nature, to see her clouds, hail, snow, rain, thunder, all fabricated at our feet! And the glorious Sun, when rising as if out of a distant water, just gilding the tops of the mountains, and giving life to all nature!——I hope in god no circumstance may ever make either seek an asylum from grief! With what sincere sympathy I would open every cell of my composition to receive the effusion of their woes! I would pour my tears into their wounds: and if a drop of balm could be found at the top of the Cordilleras, or at the remotest sources of the Missouri, I would go thither myself to seek and to bring it. Deeply practised in the school of affliction, the human heart knows no joy which I have not lost, no sorrow of which I have not drank! Fortune can present no grief of unknown form to me! Who then can so softly bind up the wound of another as he who has felt the same wound himself? But Heaven forbid they should ever know a sorrow!—Let us turn over another leaf, for this has distracted me.[4]

Head. Well. Let us put this possibility to trial then on another point. When you consider the character which is given of our country by the lying newspapers of London, and their credulous copyers in other countries; when you reflect that all Europe is made to believe we are a lawless banditti, in a state of absolute anarchy, cutting one another's throats, and plundering without distinction, how can you expect that any reasonable creature would venture among us?

Heart. But you and I know that all this is false: that there is not a country on earth where there is greater tranquillity, where the laws are milder, or better obeyed: where every one is more attentive to his own business, or meddles less with that of others: where

[447]

12 OCTOBER 1786

strangers are better received, more hospitably treated, and with a more sacred respect.

Head. True, you and I know this, but your friends do not know it.

Heart. But they are sensible people who think for themselves. They will ask of impartial foreigners who have been among us, whether they saw or heard on the spot any instances of anarchy. They will judge too that a people occupied as we are in opening rivers, digging navigable canals, making roads, building public schools, establishing academies, erecting busts and statues to our great men, protecting religious freedom, abolishing sanguinary punishments, reforming and improving our laws in general, they will judge I say for themselves whether these are not the occupations of a people at their ease, whether this is not better evidence of our true state than a London newspaper, hired to lie, and from which no truth can ever be extracted but by reversing everything it says.

Head. I did not begin this lecture my friend with a view to learn from you what America is doing. Let us return then to our point. I wished to make you sensible how imprudent it is to place your affections, without reserve, on objects you must so soon lose, and whose loss when it comes must cost you such severe pangs. Remember the last night. You knew your friends were to leave Paris to-day. This was enough to throw you into agonies. All night you tossed us from one side of the bed to the other. No sleep, no rest. The poor crippled wrist too, never left one moment in the same position, now up, now down, now here, now there; was it to be wondered at if all it's pains returned? The Surgeon then was to be called, and to be rated as an ignoramus because he could not devine the cause of this extraordinary change.—In fine, my friend, you must mend your manners. This is not a world to live at random in as you do. To avoid these eternal distresses, to which you are for ever exposing us, you must learn to look forward before you take a step which may interest our peace. Everything in this world is matter of calculation. Advance then with caution, the balance in your hand. Put into one scale the pleasures which any object may offer; but put fairly into the other the pains which are to follow, and see which preponderates. The making an acquaintance is not a matter of indifference. When a new one is proposed to you, view it all round. Consider what advantages it presents, and to what inconveniencies it may expose you. Do not bite at the bait of pleasure till you know there is no hook beneath it. The art of life is the art of avoiding pain: and he is the best pilot who steers clearest of the

12 OCTOBER 1786

rocks and shoals with which it is beset. Pleasure is always before us; but misfortune is at our side: while running after that, this arrests us. The most effectual means of being secure against pain is to retire within ourselves, and to suffice for our own happiness. Those, which depend on ourselves, are the only pleasures a wise man will count on: for nothing is ours which another may deprive us of. Hence the inestimable value of intellectual pleasures. Ever in our power, always leading us to something new, never cloying, we ride, serene and sublime, above the concerns of this mortal world, contemplating truth and nature, matter and motion, the laws which bind up their existence, and that eternal being who made and bound them up by these laws. Let this be our employ. Leave the bustle and tumult of society to those who have not talents to occupy themselves without them. Friendship is but another name for an alliance with the follies and the misfortunes of others. Our own share of miseries is sufficient: why enter then as volunteers into those of another? Is there so little gall poured into our own cup that we must needs help to drink that of our neighbor? A friend dies or leaves us: we feel as if a limb was cut off. He is sick: we must watch over him, and participate of his pains. His fortune is shipwrecked: ours must be laid under contribution. He loses a child, a parent or a partner: we must mourn the loss as if it was our own.

Heart. And what more sublime delight than to mingle tears with one whom the hand of heaven hath smitten! To watch over the bed of sickness, and to beguile it's tedious and it's painful moments! To share our bread with one to whom misfortune has left none! This world abounds indeed with misery: to lighten it's burthen we must divide it with one another. But let us now try the virtues of your mathematical balance, and as you have put into one scale the burthens of friendship, let me put it's comforts into the other. When languishing then under disease, how grateful is the solace of our friends! How are we penetrated with their assiduities and attentions! How much are we supported by their encouragements and kind offices! When Heaven has taken from us some object of our love, how sweet is it to have a bosom whereon to recline our heads, and into which we may pour the torrent of our tears! Grief, with such a comfort, is almost a luxury! In a life where we are perpetually exposed to want and accident, yours is a wonderful proposition, to insulate ourselves, to retire from all aid, and to wrap ourselves in the mantle of self-sufficiency! For assuredly nobody will care for him who cares for nobody. But friendship is

12 OCTOBER 1786

precious not only in the shade but in the sunshine of life: and thanks to a benevolent arrangement of things, the greater part of life is sunshine. I will recur for proof to the days we have lately passed. On these indeed the sun shone brightly! How gay did the face of nature appear! Hills, vallies, chateaux, gardens, rivers, every object wore it's liveliest hue! Whence did they borrow it? From the presence of our charming companion. They were pleasing, because she seemed pleased. Alone, the scene would have been dull and insipid: the participation of it with her gave it relish. Let the gloomy Monk, sequestered from the world, seek unsocial pleasures in the bottom of his cell! Let the sublimated philosopher grasp visionary happiness while pursuing phantoms dressed in the garb of truth! Their supreme wisdom is supreme folly: and they mistake for happiness the mere absence of pain. Had they ever felt the solid pleasure of one generous spasm of the heart, they would exchange for it all the frigid speculations of their lives, which you have been vaunting in such elevated terms. Believe me then, my friend, that that is a miserable arithmetic which would estimate friendship at nothing, or at less than nothing. Respect for you has induced me to enter into this discussion, and to hear principles uttered which I detest and abjure. Respect for myself now obliges me to recall you into the proper limits of your office. When nature assigned us the same habitation, she gave us over it a divided empire. To you she allotted the field of science, to me that of morals. When the circle is to be squared, or the orbit of a comet to be traced; when the arch of greatest strength, or the solid of least resistance is to be investigated, take you the problem: it is yours: nature has given me no cognisance of it. In like manner in denying to you the feelings of sympathy, of benevolence, of gratitude, of justice, of love, of friendship, she has excluded you from their controul. To these she has adapted the mechanism of the heart. Morals were too essential to the happiness of man to be risked on the incertain combinations of the head. She laid their foundation therefore in sentiment, not in science. That she gave to all, as necessary to all: this to a few only, as sufficing with a few. I know indeed that you pretend authority to the sovereign controul of our conduct in all it's parts: and a respect for your grave saws and maxims, a desire to do what is right, has sometimes induced me to conform to your counsels. A few facts however which I can readily recall to your memory, will suffice to prove to you that nature has not organised you for our moral direction. When the poor wearied souldier, whom we overtook at Chickahominy with his pack on his back, begged us to let him get up behind our chariot, you began to calculate that the road was full of souldiers, and that if all should be taken up our horses would fail in their journey. We drove on therefore. But soon becoming sensible you had made me do wrong, that tho we cannot relieve all the distressed we should relieve as many as we can, I turned about to take up the souldier; but he had entered a bye path, and was no more to be found: and from that moment to this I could never find him out to ask his forgiveness. Again, when the poor woman came to ask a charity in Philadelphia, you whispered that she looked like a drunkard, and that half a dollar was enough to give her for the ale-house. Those who want the dispositions to give, easily find reasons why they ought not to give. When I sought her out afterwards, and did what I should have done at first, you know that she employed the money immediately towards placing her child at school. If our country, when pressed with wrongs at the point of the bayonet, had been governed by it's heads instead of it's hearts, where should we have been now? hanging on a gallows as high as Haman's. You began to calculate and to compare wealth and numbers: we threw up a few pulsations of our warmest blood: we supplied enthusiasm against wealth and numbers: we put our existence to the hazard, when the hazard seemed against us, and we saved our country: justifying at the same time the ways of Providence, whose precept is to do always what is right, and leave the issue to him. In short, my friend, as far as my recollection serves me, I do not know that I ever did a good thing on your suggestion, or a dirty one without it. I do for ever then disclaim your interference in my province. Fill paper as you please with triangles and squares: try how many ways you can hang and combine them together. I shall never envy nor controul your sublime delights. But leave me to decide when and where friendships are to be contracted. You say I contract them at random, so you said the woman at Philadelphia was a drunkard. I receive no one into my esteem till I know they are worthy of it. Wealth, title, office, are no recommendations to my friendship. On the contrary great good qualities are requisite to make amends for their having wealth, title and office. You confess that in the present case I could not have made a worthier choice. You only object that I was so soon to lose them. We are not immortal ourselves, my friend; how can we expect our enjoiments to be so? We have no rose without it's thorn; no pleasure without alloy. It is the law of our existence; and we must acquiesce. It is the condition annexed to all our pleasures, not by us who re-

12 OCTOBER 1786

ceive, but by him who gives them. True, this condition is pressing cruelly on me at this moment. I feel more fit for death than life. But when I look back on the pleasures of which it is the consequence, I am conscious they were worth the price I am paying. Notwithstanding your endeavors too to damp my hopes, I comfort myself with expectations of their promised return. Hope is sweeter than despair, and they were too good to mean to deceive me. In the summer, said the gentleman; but in the spring, said the lady: and I should love her forever, were it only for that! Know then, my friend, that I have taken these good people into my bosom: that I have lodged them in the warmest cell I could find: that I love them, and will continue to love them thro life: that if fortune should dispose them on one side the globe, and me on the other, my affections shall pervade it's whole mass to reach them. Knowing then my determination, attempt not to disturb it. If you can at any time furnish matter for their amusement, it will be the office of a good neighbor to do it. I will in like manner seize any occasion which may offer to do the like good turn for you with Condorcet, Rittenhouse, Madison, La Cretelle, or any other of those worthy sons of science whom you so justly prize.'

I thought this a favorable proposition whereon to rest the issue of the dialogue. So I put an end to it by calling for my nightcap. Methinks I hear you wish to heaven I had called a little sooner, and so spared you the ennui of such a tedious sermon. I did not interrupt them sooner because I was in a mood for hearing sermons. You too were the subject; and on such a thesis I never think the theme long; not even if I am to write it, and that slowly and awkwardly, as now, with the left hand. But that you may not be discoraged from a correspondence which begins so formidably, I will promise you on my honour that my future letters shall be of a reasonable length. I will even agree to express but half my esteem for you, for fear of cloying you with too full a dose. But, on your part, no curtailing. If your letters are as long as the bible, they will appear short to me. Only let them be brim full of affection. I shall read them with the dispositions with which Arlequin in les deux billets spelt the words 'je t'aime' and wished that the whole alphabet had entered into their composition.

We have had incessant rains since your departure. These make me fear for your health, as well as that you have had an uncomfortable journey. The same cause has prevented me from being able to give you any account of your friends here. This voiage to Fontain-

12 OCTOBER 1786

bleau will probably send the Count de Moutier and the Marquise de Brehan to America. Danquerville promised to visit me, but has not done it as yet. De latude comes sometimes to take family soupe with me, and entertains me with anecdotes of his five and thirty years imprisonment. How fertile is the mind of man which can make the Bastille and Dungeon of Vincennes yeild interesting anecdotes. You know this was for making four verses on Mme. de Pompadour. But I think you told me you did not know the verses. They were these. 'Sans esprit, sans sentiment, Sans etre belle, ni neuve, En France on peut avoir le premier amant: Pompadour en est l'epreuve.' I have read the memoir of his three escapes. As to myself my health is good, except my wrist which mends slowly, and my mind which mends not at all, but broods constantly over your departure. The lateness of the season obliges me to decline my journey into the South of France. Present me in the most friendly terms to Mr. Cosway, and receive me into your own recollection with a partiality and a warmth, proportioned, not to my own poor merit, but to the sentiments of sincere affection and esteem with which I have the honour to be, my dear Madam, your most obedient humble servant,   TH: JEFFERSON

PrC (DLC); written entirely with TJ's left hand; enclosed in his to Mrs. Cosway of 13 Oct. and that in turn was enclosed in TJ to Trumbull, 13 Oct. 1786.

This remarkable letter—one of the most revealing in the entire body of TJ's correspondence, and one of the notable love letters in the English language—owes much of its distinction to the fact that its recipient, who unquestionably had captivated TJ momentarily, could not be quite certain whether the Head or the Heart had won the argument, nor avoid the feeling that even the lines given to the Heart to utter were coolly and skilfully contrived by the Head. Her baffled and ineffectual response of 30 Oct. showed an awareness of what the Heart had to say, but little understanding of the essential nature of the man to whom reason was not only enthroned as the chief disciplinarian of his life but also, as revealed in the nature of his response to its commands, was itself a sovereign to whom the Heart yielded a ready and full allegiance, proud of its monarch and happy in his rule.

The letter must have been preceded by a composition draft. The literary device of the dialogue—familiar enough in French and English letters of the 18th century, and employed, for example, by TJ's friends DuPont and Franklin as well as by his beloved Sterne; the painstaking regularity of the disciplined lines and letters, with even the ligatures being formed as carefully as when he drafted the Bill for Proportioning Crimes and Punishments; the fiction of sitting before his fire on the evening of the Cosways' departure, reminiscing about the delightful events of preceding weeks (he had, by his own confession, slept none at all the night before, owing to the excruciating pain in his wrist); the retaining a press copy—without which the text would have been lost to the world; the skilfully-wrought texture of the whole integrated composition—all presuppose the existence of a composition draft. But no such draft, nor any fragment of it, is known to be in existence. The recipient's copy, despite extensive efforts on the part of Editors and others, has not been found; it is possible, however, that it has escaped the ravages of time and may be found in some private autograph collection (as, for example, was TJ's letter to Mrs. Cosway of 5 Oct. 1786); or it may yet be found among the Cosway papers in the Col-

[453]

12 OCTOBER 1786

legio delle Grazie di Maria SS Bambina at Lodi, Italy, where the miniature of TJ, painted by Trumbull for Mrs. Cosway, has recently been found (Elizabeth Cometti, "Maria Cosway's Rediscovered Miniature of Jefferson," WMQ, 3rd ser., IX [1952], 152-5); or—what is far less likely in view of the great destruction of property occurring in Ireland in the past century—it may possibly be found among the letters that Maria Cosway entrusted to her sister, Charlotte Combe, sometime before the death of the latter's husband, William Combe, author of the *Tour of Dr. Syntax*, to whom she had written about "publishing a Correspondence" that she had had with eminent persons (George C. Williamson, *Richard Cosway, R.A.*, London, 1905, p. 92; Williamson stated that "Information in other family letters leads me strongly to believe that papers and letters relating to Cosway and his wife still exist, and are probably in Ireland, but, like others who have searched before me, I also have to lament my inability to find the missing treasures," p. 94; the Editors wish to acknowledge the able assistance of Dr. R. J. Hayes, Director of the National Library of Ireland, Dublin, in a further effort in 1953 to find these papers).

The letter consists of twelve pages—"three mortal sheets of paper" as TJ described it in his letter of the 13th—and each of these contains not less than 22 nor more than 25 lines, all regularly spaced, the words that were so laboriously formed by the left hand amounting in all to something over four thousand. As he stated later, TJ found writing with his left hand "too slow and awkward to be employed but in cases of necessity" (TJ to Thomson, 17 Dec. 1786), and the present letter accounted for more of the words written with his left hand in this period than all others combined. Such a remarkable feat must have required more than one day, and it is quite likely that the composition draft (assuming there was one) and the fair copy required much of the time between 5 and 12 Oct., despite the words YOUR FRIENDS WERE TO LEAVE PARIS TO-DAY. The letter has been published many times, its first appearance being in the *Virginia Advocate*, 23 Aug. 1828; it was also published in *Atkinson's Casket* (Dec. 1828), No. 12, p. 554-8; it has appeared in all previous editions—TJR, II, 46-55; HAW, II, 31-43; Ford, IV, 311-23; and L & B, V, 43-48—and it provided the title and one of the central features of Helen Duprey Bullock's *My Head and My Heart: A Little History of Thomas Jefferson and Maria Cosway*, New York, 1945.

The exact date when TJ and Trumbull met the Cosways at the HALLE AUX BLEDS has not been determined, but it was after 2 Aug. when Trumbull arrived and presumably not too long after that date. The first mention of the Cosways in Trumbull's journal is that for Thursday, 10 Aug. when he (and others, perhaps including TJ) went "to the Luxembourg palace with Mr. and Mrs. Cosway" (Sizer, ed., *Autobiography*, p. 107). Trumbull mentions MADRID on 7 Aug., but does not name his companions on that day (TJ visited Madrid on 5 Sep.; Account Book). Concerning the period from 20 Aug. to 10 Sep. for which the pages of his original journal are missing, Trumbull remarked many years later: "I regret very much the loss of these twenty days; for after fifty years, memory unaided, can do little to restore the chasm. I distinctly recollect, however, that this time was occupied with the same industry in examining whatever relates to the arts, and that Mr. Jefferson joined our party almost daily; and here commenced his acquaintance with Mrs. Cosway" (Sizer, ed., same, p. 120). This would seem to indicate that TJ did not meet the Cosways until after 20 Aug., but Trumbull's memory may have misled him. The letter or note that TJ WROTE TO THE DUTCHESS DANVILLE has not been found, but the excuse which it contained—DISPATCHES ... WHICH REQUIRED IMMEDIATE ATTENTION—points toward an earlier meeting with the Cosways than has generally been assumed. On 1 Aug. TJ received a large packet of letters from America—from the Governor of Virginia, from Madison, Monroe, Jay, and Humphreys; and on the next day letters from John and Abigail Adams, Smith, and Paradise arrived with Trumbull. But from 28 July to 7 Aug. 1786 no letter by TJ is recorded in SJL. It seems quite possible, therefore, that TJ met the Cosways almost immediately after Trumbull arrived.

[1] PrC mutilated; reading of salutatation taken from TJR, II, 46; see also TJ to Mrs. Cosway, 13 Oct. 1786.
[2] This word appears to have been written over "vaults."

³ This word written originally as "companion," and then altered to read as above.

⁴ This occurs at the bottom of the fifth page.

From John Jay

Dr. Sir   Office for for. Affairs 12 Octr. 1786

Since my last to you of the 18 Augt.———I have received and laid before Congress the Letters you did me the Honor to write on the 18. July last.

I have some Dispatches of Importance ready for you, but I prefer sending them by a Conveyance that will offer about ten Days hence.

I enclose a certified copy of an Act of Congress for recalling Mr. Lamb, another Copy has been sent to Mr. Adams.

As the Dispatches above alluded to are particular, I shall at present only add an Assurance which I always make with Pleasure, Vizt. that I am with very sincere Esteem and Regard Dr Sr Your most ob. & hble servt.

Dft (NK-Iselin). FC (DNA: PCC, No. 121). Noted in SJL as received 6 Dec. 1786. Enclosure: Resolution of Congress of 26 Sep. 1786: "That the commission and instructions issued to Mr. John Lamb, for the purpose of negotiating with the Barbary powers, be and they are hereby vacated and annulled; and that the Secretary for foreign Affairs take the necessary measures for directing Mr. Lamb immediately to repair to New York" (JCC, XXXI, 692).

THE LETTERS . . . ON THE 18TH: An error for TJ's letter of 8 July, at which time he wrote only one letter with numerous enclosures, transmitted by Jay to Congress on 26 Sep. (DNA: PCC, No. 87). SOME DISPATCHES: Jay to TJ, 3 Oct. 1786, sent with Jay to TJ, 27 Oct. 1786.

To De Langeac

Sir   Paris Octr. 12th. 1786

An officer having some time ago left an opposition here against the payment of the rent due and to become due for the house, I asked information of some gentlemen of the diplomatic corps as well as at Versailles, of the manner in which I should conduct myself on such occasions. The result was that when an opposition should be made by an officer I was at liberty either to disregard it or to have the parties punished: but that when it should be asked by the party himself without the intervention of an officer, it would be expected that I should comply with it; or that it might become the subject of a complaint to my sovereign. Two persons having

12 OCTOBER 1786

applied without observing the proper form I took no notice of them, but continued to pay you the rents; but a third, of the name of Jacques De Veaux Meunier Platrier au dessus de la rue de Clichy, having asked me by letter to retain in my hands a sum for which he has brought suit against you, I consider myself as bound to comply with his request. I took the liberty therefore of expressing to you my wish that you could make such arrangement with him as would leave me at liberty to make my payments to yourself as usual. I would greatly prefer the paying these monies as they become due to yourself and unacquainted as I am with the laws of the country, it would be a great perplexity to me to be placed between opposing demands. As a proof of my wish to conform myself to your desire, I now enclose you an order on Mr. Grand for the quarter's rent which will become due the middle of this month, and I shall be happy if either a public order or private arrangement may relieve me from the obligation of complying with De Veaux's request at some future time.

The persons whom you shall send to examine the works of Carpentry in the basse-cour shall be recieved and I shall be happy in every occasion of satisfying you of the respect with which I have the honor to be Sir your most obedient humble Servant,

Th: Jefferson

PrC (DLC); in Short's hand, including signature, with one correction and endorsement by TJ with his left hand; at foot of text: "(Test: W. Short Secry.)."

From James Monroe

Dear Sir   New York Octr. 12. 1786.

Since my last I have receiv'd yours of the 9. of July. I advis'd you therein of the progress that had been made by *Mister*[1] *Jay* in the *Spanish negociation*, that he had brought *a project before Congress for shutting the Mississippi* and *not* for *opening it* for the term of *twenty five* or *thirty years* combin'd with some *commercial stipulations*, the latter to be the price of the former, although admitted they *opened* no new *port* nor admitted us *into* those now *open upon better terms than* those we *now enjoyed*. Since this *project* was presented, the *negociation* has been more *with Congress* to *repeal the ultimata* than *with Spain* to carry *the instructions* into effect. I inform'd you of the proposition from *Massachusetts* for the repeal in Committee of the Whole. This was carried by *Pennsylvania* inclusive *eastward, Maryland* inclusive *southward* being

[456]

12 OCTOBER 1786

against it. *Delaware* was *absent*. In the house we mov'd to postpone the report of the Committee in order to take up propositions to the following effect. *That the negotiation* as to the *Mississippi* and *the boundaries* be taken out of the hands of the *Secretary and committed* to *Carmichael*. The following points to be agreed on there and afterwards concluded here. 1st that *New Orleans* be made *an entrepot* for *exports*, that they be shipp'd thence *in the bottoms of America, Spain* and *France* under the regulations of each party. 2d. That they pay at said port a duty of 2½ pr. centm. ad valorem to *the crown* of *Spain* as a compensation for port duties. 3d. That *imports* be *prohibited*. 4th. That the instructions of Annapolis be reviv'd as *the basis of a treaty* of *commerce*. 5th. That two additional *commissioners* be *appointed* with equal *powers* with *the secretary* to conclude the same. Upon this there was precisely the same division. The question was then taken on the report and carried by 7. states. Upon this the following proposition was mov'd, "is the repeal constitutionally carried by 7. states so as to give a new instruction materially different from the former" and set aside by the previous question. We are told he will proceed, but of this have no certain information. It is extraordinary he *should have taken* up *the* subject of *trade*, as powers upon principles that applied to all *nations alike* had already been given under a commission which had at the time his were, near one year to run to *form a treaty with Spain*, which were not repeal'd by these nor the subject mention'd except by a distant implication. I do suspect the business rests for the present untill the new *Delegates* take their seats, in which case *he* will be govern'd by circumstances. I suspect the point will ultimately be carried, but this is yet doubtful. I forgot above to mention the *negotiation was* to have been carried on in our propositions under *the mediation* of *France*. I sit out tomorrow for Virginia with Mrs. Monroe by land. My residence will be for the present in Fredericksburg. My attention is turn'd to Albemarle for my ultimate abode. The sooner I fix there the more agreeable it will be to me. I should be happy to keep clear of the bar if possible and at present I am wearied with the business in which I have been engag'd. It has been a year of excessive labor and fatigue and unprofitably so. What you find in the journals, especially the regulation of the coin, pass'd upon the report of the Board of treasury without examination, or with very little. Our minds were generally at the time otherwise engag'd. Mr. Madison and myself have been desirous if possible of forming an engagment for land in this State *which would hereafter put us at ease*. He promis'd me *to advise you* of it, *and to* tell you of our little plan. If *it were an object with you to*[2] *your property* in my estimation a better opportunity cannot present itself. I shall write you more fully on my arrival home on many publick affairs, which at present I have not leasure for. Tell Short he has the friendship of the delegation and always will have it. No appointment of secretary of legation will take place to that court and if one did he would have the good wishes of our State. I am affectionately your friend and servt.,

JAS. MONROE

RC (DLC); partly in code. Noted in SJL as received 6 Dec. 1786.

[1] This and subsequent words in italics are written in code and were decoded interlineally by TJ, with his right hand; his decoding has been verified by the Editors, employing Code No. 9.

[2] The code symbol for "increase" or "augment" or some similar word was omitted here.

To Maria Cosway

MY DEAR MADAM   Paris Octob. 13. 1786

Just as I had sealed the inclosed I received a letter of a good length, dated Antwerp, with your name at the bottom. I prepared myself for a feast. I read two or three sentences: looked again at the signature to see if I had not mistaken it. It was visibly yours. Read a sentence or two more. Diable! Spelt your name distinctly. There was not a letter of it omitted. Began to read again. In fine after reading a little and examining the signature, alternately, half a dozen times, I found that your name was to four lines only instead of four pages. I thank you for the four lines however because they prove you think of me. Little indeed, but better a little than none. To shew how much I think of you I send you the inclosed letter of three sheets of paper, being a history of the evening I parted with you. But how expect you should read a letter of three mortal sheets of paper? I will tell you. Divide it into six doses of half a sheet each, and every day, when the toilette begins, take a dose, that is to say, read half a sheet. By this means it will have the only merit it's length and dulness can aspire to, that of assisting your coëffeuse to procure you six good naps of sleep. I will even allow you twelve days to get through it, holding you rigorously to one condition only, that is, that at whatever hour you receive this, you do not break the seal of the inclosed till the next toilette. Of this injunction I require a sacred execution. I rest it on your friendship, and that in your first letter you tell me honestly whether you have honestly performed it.—I send you the song I promised. Bring me in return it's subject, *Jours heureux!* Were I a songster I should sing it all to these words 'Dans ces lieux qu'elle tarde à se rendre'! Learn it I pray you, and sing it with feeling.—My right hand presents it's devoirs to you, and sees with great indignation the left supplanting it in a correspondence so much valued. You will know the first moment it can resume it's rights. The first exercise of them shall be addressed to you, as you had the first essay of it's rival. It will yet, however, be many a day. Present my esteem to Mr. Cosway, and believe me to be yours very affectionately,

TH: JEFFERSON

PrC (DLC); written with TJ's left hand. Enclosures: (1) TJ to Mrs. Cosway, 12 Oct. 1786, which was 12 pages in length, or "three mortal sheets of paper." (2) Song from *Dardanus* (see below; also Helen Duprey Bullock, *My Head and My Heart: A Little History of Thomas Jefferson and Maria Cosway*, New York, 1945, p. 27-8).

THE SONG I PROMISED: *Dardanus*, a tragedy based on a poem by Le Bruère, adapted by Guillard and set to music by Sacchini, included in Act II, Sc. 4 the lines mentioned by TJ:

"Jour heureux, espoir enchanteur!
Prix charmant d'un amour si tendre!
Je vais la voir, je vais l'entendre,
Je vais retrouver le bonheur!

Dans ces lieux écartés qu'elle tarde à se rendre!
De quel trouble nouveau je me sens agité!
Moment que j'ai tant souhaité
Ah! ne vous faites plus attendre!"

Dardanus was produced at the Académie Royale de Musique on 3 Oct. 1786 (*Journal de Paris*, same date). There is no indication in TJ's Account Book, but it is quite possible that a party including the Cosways, TJ, and perhaps others saw the play two days before the former left Paris and that—perhaps on the route to St. Denis the morning of the 5th—TJ made the promise that he fulfilled in the present letter.

From Madame de Marmontel

ce vendredi matin [13 Oct. 1786?]

Md. de Marmontel a l'honneur de faire mille compliments à Monsieur De Gefferson et de le prevenir qu'on donne aujourdhui aux variettés amusantes Ruse contre Ruse; quelle y a une Loge et une place a lui offrir. Md. de Marmontel seroit ravie que cela put amuser Monsieur de Gefferson et lui procurer le plaisir de passer quelques moments avec lui. Si Monsieur Gefferson accepte la proposition de Md de Marmontel il demandera la loge de Mr. le Baron de Breteuil.

RC (ViWC); endorsed by TJ with his right hand. This letter has been placed under 13 Oct. 1786 because the play *Guerre ouverte, ou Ruse contre Ruse* had its first performance on 4 Oct. 1786, but the first Friday on which a performance was given was 13 Oct. (*Journal de Paris*, 1786, p. 1148, 1184).

To John Trumbull

DEAR SIR   Paris Oct. 13. 1786.

Not knowing Mrs. Cosway's address, I take the liberty of putting the inclosed under your cover, and of begging you to deliver it personally. Your reward will be the visit it will occasion you. She promised to write to me. Be so good as to take charge of her letters, and to find private conveiances for them, or to put them under cover to Mr. Grand banker rue neuve des Capucins à Paris. Or she will do the last herself. All letters directed to me are read in the post offices both of London and Paris.

I duly received your favor dated Antwerp, and notwithstanding the little disappointment occasioned by a circumstance which Mrs. Cosway will explain to you, I was much entertained with it. It revived my inclination to travel, an inclination which always lies uppermost. My first wish was to see the places you described; my second to see in preference Italy, Greece &c. But god knows when I may be able to see either, or if ever. I intended to have visited the South of France this fall, but am prevented by this unlucky accident to my wrist which I cannot in the least use yet. We are now however satisfied that it is set, and that time alone is necessary for it's reestablishment. In the mean time the left hand is learning to perform the functions of the right. This however it does awkwardly and slowly. It is with pleasure it executes that of assuring you of the sincere esteem with which I have the honour to be Dear Sir your friend & servant,   TH: JEFFERSON

PrC (DLC); written by TJ with his left hand, endorsed by him with right. Enclosures: TJ to Mrs. Cosway, 12 and 13 Oct. 1786.

NOT KNOWING MRS. COSWAY'S ADDRESS: This could not have been the actual reason for TJ's sending letters to Mrs. Cosway through Trumbull, for the fact is that he did know her address. On an undetermined date in 1786 TJ wrote on a fragment of paper (part of an address-cover to some unidentified letter he had received):
"What is Mrs. Cosway's address?
Mr. Trumbull   Th:J."
Beneath this, and on the same fragment, Trumbull wrote:
"Mrs. C— Pall Mall   London"

(MHi; the fragment also contains on verso a number of calculations of uncertain meaning, including "Grand 2613.₶"). This note may have been sent to Trumbull by a servant, but this seems unlikely in view of its character—and especially in view of the fact that Trumbull stayed with TJ at the Hôtel de Langeac. So informal a scrap would certainly not have been sent to Trumbull in London; hence the conclusion that it was written between 2 Aug. and 9 Sep. 1786 when Trumbull was in Paris. Possibly, too, it was written while TJ and Trumbull, with the Cosways and others, were on one of their numerous excursions around Paris.

[460]

From John Bondfield

Bordeaux, 14 Oct. 1786. Expects the "Intendant General" to arrive in a few days; will immediately procure clearance for the 34 cases now ready and any others which may arrive; will ship on the *Commerce* if she is still in port. Asks TJ to honor two drafts: one for 498 livres for articles shipped for his personal account; the other for 1,502 livres for his advances for shipping the arms for Virginia; will send a general account and draw for the balance when the transaction is completed. "The Contract Ships arrive but none others tho we have given every encouragement and have considerable funds on the other side that are greatly in retard." This discourages new speculation.

RC (DLC); 2 p.; endorsed by TJ with left hand. Noted in SJL as received 18 Oct. 1786.

The draft for 498ᵗᵗ for TJ's personal account, drawn in favor of Dumez, payable 19 Oct. 1786, is in DLC: TJ Papers, 25:4316. THE CONTRACT SHIPS: Ships carrying tobacco under Robert Morris' contract with the farmers-general.

From the Rhode Island Delegates in Congress

SIR   New York 14th: of October 1786.

In compliance with the request of the Honourable the Corporation of the College at Providence in the State of Rhode Island, transmitted in their vote of the 7th. of September last. we take the liberty to inform your Excellency that the College under their direction was founded in the year 1764, and received the small endowments of which it is now possessed, solely, from the beneficence and contributions of individuals, the Government not being sufficiently impressed with an idea of the importance of Literature to afford its Patronage, or lend it any further assistance than that of granting it a Charter. With these small beginnings, however, at the commencement of the late war, the Corporation had the pleasure to see that beautiful Edifice, erected on the hill at Providence, and upwards of forty students matriculated, together with a large Latin School, as a necessary to supply it with Scholars.

The whole of the College endowments consisted of one Thousand Pounds Lawful money as a fund, with six Acres of Land adjoining it. At that period the young Institution was rapidly growing in reputation, as well as in number of Scholars, but on the arrival of the enemy in that State, in the year 1776 it was seized by the public for the use of Barracks and an Hospital for the American Army, and continued to be so occupied until a little before the arrival of

14 OCTOBER 1786

the Armaments of his Most Christian Majesty at Rhode Island when it was again taken out of the hands of the Corporation by an order of government, and delivered up to our Allies for the same uses to which it had been applied by the American Army; and they held it till their Army marched for the Chesepeak. To accommodate the Building to their wishes they made great alterations, highly injurious to the designs of its founders. This with the damages done to it by the Armies of both nations, while so occupied, subjected the Corporation to great expence to repair it; and that when the deranged state of our finances prevented us from making scarcely any advantage of the Interest of our little fund, in the State Treasury. Having, at their own expence made these repairs they applied first to the Legislature of the State, and afterwards repeatedly to Congress for some compensation, but have not been able to obtain the least. Thus circumstanced they think it their duty to solicit the patronage of his Most Christian Majesty, in the manner they have done in the memorial which accompanies this letter.

We have the pleasure to inform your Excellency that there are now upwards of fifty students belonging to the College, with flattering prospects of an increase. The aforegoing is a brief account of the origin and present state of the College at Providence. We only beg leave to add, that this Institution embraces in its bosom, and holds out equal priviledges to all denominations of Protestants. And its Corporation, agreeably to Charter, is, and must forever be composed of some of all Denominations of Christians.

We have the Honour to be Sir Your very Humble and most obedient Servants,
              JAMES MANNING
              NATHAN MILLER

RC (DLC); endorsed by TJ: "Rhode island Delegates Rhode island college." Noted in SJL as received 24 Jan. 1787. Enclosures (DLC): (1) Extract of the minutes of a meeting "of the Corporation of Rhode Island College, in Providence, Sept. 6, 1786," directing that "the Subject of an address to His Most Christian Majesty, ordered in the year 1784, be resumed"; that TJ be requested to present the address and "support the same with his interest at that Court"; and that a committee, consisting of Benjamin Waterhouse, Solomon Drown, and David Howell, prepare the memorial and forward it to the delegates in Congress with the request that they transmit it "with such remarks as, in their opinion, may prove advantageous: Noting the rise, progress and actual Circumstances of the College." (2) Letter from the committee, named in the preceding extract, to the Rhode Island delegates in Congress, 9 Sep. 1786, stating that a memorial to the King of France, "soliciting his royal patronage," had been sent to Benjamin Franklin in 1784, but the College was never informed that the memorial reached him; requesting that the renewed address be sent to TJ, "in whose abilities, candor and readiness to promote the Interest of Learning in General and of this Seminary in particular, the Corporation repose perfect confidence. . . . It is with peculiar satisfaction that this Negotiation is now committed to a Character not only Dear to the Citizens of America in general but particularly so to some of the Friends of this College, to a Gentleman who has honour'd this Town and College with a personal Visit and left impressions on the minds of many here highly favorable to his Character as a Philosopher and Gentleman as well as a Politician." (3) Tr of a memorial to the King of France, dated 9 Jan. 1784, signed by Stephen Hopkins, Chancellor, and James Manning, President; certified and signed, 8 Sep. 1786, by Jabez Bowen, Chancellor, James Manning, President, and David Howell, Secretary; soliciting the King's aid in establishing a collection of French books and a professorship of the French language in the college (printed in R. A. Guild, *Early History of Brown University*, Providence, 1897, p. 350-1). See TJ to Rhode Island Delegates, 22 July 1787.

From Edward Rutledge

DEAR SIR   New York October 14th: 1786.

On my arrival in this City a few Weeks ago, I was told that you had made some Communications to Congress on the Subject of the Staple Commodity of Carolina; and on application to our mutual Friend Mr. Jay I obtained an Extract of your Dispatch, of the 27th of May last. I think you my dear Sir, for the Interest which you have taken in this Business, and I am persuaded my Countrymen will be truly sensible of your attention. But you must suffer me to add a little, to the trouble which you have already imposed on yourself; and I assume this Liberty the more readily, as I am conscious that your Regard for every part of America, as well as your particular Friendship for the writer of this Letter, will exceedingly lighten the Burden.

You say that, "the Rice of Carolina on its arrival in France, is fouler and cheaper than the Mediterranean Rice; but if the Makers of it were to adapt their preparation of it to the Taste of that Country so as to give it the Advantage over the Mediterannian, of which it seems susceptible, it would very much increase the Consumption." This is exactly what I wish to have done; and to accomplish it, I must request the Favor of you, to obtain for me, an accurate Account of the Process by which the Mediterranian Rice is prepared for Market; and, if any particular Practices are used in Thrashing, grinding, beating, or winnowing, other than those which are mentioned in the Post-script I shall be obliged to you, to send me a Model of them, either directly to Charleston, or by the way of New York, to the care of Mr. Jay. I will very thankfully repay whatever Expences may be incur'd in the Execution of this Business. If you could send at the same time, a small sample of the Mediterranian Rice with an account of the relative Price which it bears to the Carolina, on its first Importation, and on the Sale to

[463]

14 OCTOBER 1786

the Consumer, after that from America has been cleansed; and also what has been the average Price since the Peace, it would be of advantage. We are now in the Season for reaping, but a considerable Quantity of Rice will remain unthrashed until January and some even until February; if I could therefore receive a Satisfactory Answer to this Letter, by the End of January; I would have a parcel prepared according to the Mediterranian Plan; and ship'd to any House of Credit in France, concerned in the Commerce of Rice. The February Packet will be the first that will sail from L'Orient; but Mr: Adams will transmit thro' the Hand of Mr. Jay any Letters, with which you may favour me by an English Packet and an opportunity you know will offer in every Month.

You are so great a Friend to the Dignity of Man and so thoroughly convinced of its being nearly connected with an agricultural Life, that you must be pleased to hear how extensively your Countrymen have turned their Minds to rural Affairs. Societies, for their promotion, are forming in various parts of America; and one Society has been already established in Carolina, under the Auspices of our most enlighten'd Characters. This is an happy Application of Abilities, as all the Necessaries, and most of the Conveniences of Life, are to be obtained, within the Limits of our own Territories. Before I conclude I must acknowledge the Pleasure which I have received in reading your Notes on Virginia. They do credit to your Understanding and your Heart. They have not found their way as far South as Carolina; and from the injunction which you impose on those, whom you have favoured with a Copy there is no probability of their getting there. But there are some things which to know, would provoke a Voyage to New York. Adieu my dear Sir and believe me to be with much Esteem your very sincere Friend, EDWARD RUTLEDGE

P.S. Our Mode of manufactoring Rice is to thrash it with a Flail, as other small Grains usually are; then the Chaff, and broken Straw, are winnowed from the Rough Rice, either by a Fan upon the Dutch Construction, or by the Wind, from a Scaffold, erected in the open Air. The Rough Rice is then ground between two large Pieces of Wood, imitating Mill Stones; which operation takes off the entire Husk, or rough Coat. It is then winnowed, which is always thro' a Fan; then, it is put into large wooden Mortars, beat by Means of a Machine worked by Water, Horses, or Oxen, until a part of the inner Husk is taken off; it is then winnowed again; again beat, and then sifted thro' wire Sieves, to separate the Flour and broken, or what we call the Small Rice, from the whole, which is packed in Barrels, and exported.

RC (DLC); endorsed by TJ with his right hand. Noted in SJL as received 6 Dec. 1786.
The copy of *Notes on Virginia* that Rutledge read in New York may have been that of Charles Thomson; Jay did not receive a copy until 1787 (see TJ to Rutledge, 14 July 1787; Rutledge to TJ, 23 Oct. 1787).

To Achard Frères

GENTLEMEN Paris Octr. 15th. 1786

I am honored with your letter of the 9th. inst. informing me of the arrival of two cases of wine from Lisbon addressed to me. I now inclose a passport for it. I will beg the favor of you to send it to this place by water, and shall be ready to answer your draught for any expenses you have incurred, with many thanks for your kindness. I have the honor to be with the most perfect respect Gentlemen your most obedient humble servant,   TH: JEFFERSON

PrC (MHi); in the hand of William Short, including signature; endorsed by TJ with his right hand; at foot of text: "Test. W Short S."
The letter of Achard Frères of THE 9TH. INST. is recorded in SJL as received 10 Oct. 1786, but has not been found.

From Louis Guillaume Otto

MONSIEUR Newyork le 15. 8bre. 1786.

Le Congrès ayant pris une resolution concernant notre convention Consulaire, il dependra desormais en grande partie de Votre Excellence que cette affaire soit terminée à la satisfaction des deux nations. J'ai lieu de croire que Vous recevrés par le paquebot qui Vous portera cette lettre des instructions qui y sont relatives et sans entrer dans aucun detail sur les vues du Congrès je me borne à Vous expliquer les raisons qui rendent la conclusion de cette affaire infiniment interessante pour les deux puissances.

Le Commerce reciproque entre la France et les Etats unis commence à reprendre quelqu'activité, et il augmentera à mesure que le Contrat des fermiers generaux tirera vers sa fin. Les liaisons des Antilles Françoises avec la Nouvelle Angleterre sont deja très considerables et l'on a conté dans le Connecticut seulement plus de 400. Batimens expédiés dans une année pour nos Colonies. Mais ce Commerce naissant se trouve sans cesse gêné par les difficultés que nos Armateurs eprouvent dans les ports Americains. La dispersion des equipages leur est surtout infiniment desavantageuse. Nos matelots connoissant le peu de pouvoirs des Consuls s'adressent très souvent à des Juges Americains pour faire annuller les engagemens pris en France et nos Capitaines sont obligés de les remplacer à très grands frais par des matelots etrangers qui profitent de l'occasion pour demander des salaires exorbitans. Les Contrats faits dans les Chancelleries des Consuls se trouvent sans vigueur et sans execution et les Armateurs ne sont jamais surs de leurs proprietés puisque les Consignataires, mal intentionnés, tirant parti de la difference des loix et des formes ont soin de faire annuller par un Juge Americain les conventions faites en France conformement à nos loix et à nos usages. D'ailleurs les delais et les longs detours de la Jurisprudence civile ne conviennent pas à des Capitaines dont le sejour est limité et très dispendieux. Tous ces inconveniens, Monsieur, ont singulierement decouragé nos Negocians et l'on peut être certain que le Commerce entre les deux nations languira autant que les Consuls n'auront pas les pouvoirs qui leur sont attribués par la convention. Vous avés donné tant de preuves de Votre desir de faciliter les liaisons commerciales avec les Etats unis, que je vous parle de cet objet avec la confiance la plus entiere.

Tous les bons patriotes, Monsieur, voyent avec peine que le Congrès n'ait pas encore pu etablir le droit de 5. pour o/o. Quoique tous les Etats ayent actuellement fait des actes qui le lui accordent, ces actes se trouvent si différens entre eux mêmes qu'ils ne sauroient servir de base à un reglement general.

La *Convention* Commerciale s'est assemblée à Annapolis dans le Courant du mois dernier, mais ne se trouvant pas assés nombreuse pour entrer en matière elle s'est bornée à adresser aux differentes Legislatures un raport par lequel elle demande des pouvoirs plus etendus pour prendre en consideration tout ce qui peut interesser l'harmonie et la consistance nationale des Etats unis. Il n'est pas bien certain que ces pouvoirs soient accordés.

Vous trouverés dans les gazettes, Monsieur, de longs details sur la revolte de plusieurs districts de la Nouvelle Angleterre. On y demande à hauts cris la cessation des Cours de justice. Tout le monde croit que les seditieux n'obtiendront rien et que ces commotions ne serviront qu'à fortiffier le Gouvernement et la Constitution.

M. Monroe est sur le point de s'en retourner en Virginie. Le Congrès perd en lui un Membre très assidu. Il sera probablement remplacé par M. Madison.

J'ai l'honneur d'être avec le plus respectueux attachement Mon-

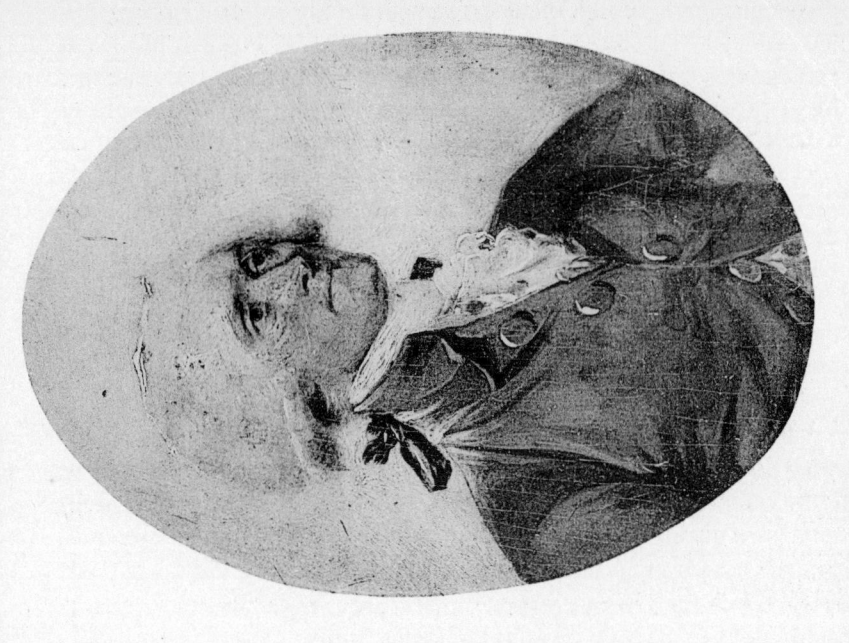

Trumbull's miniatures of Jefferson painted for Maria Cosway and Angelica Schuyler Church. (See p. xxix.)

Richard Cosway's miniature of Maria Cosway. (See p. xxx.)

John Trumbull's portrait of Angelica Schuyler Church. (See p. xxx.)

sieur, De Votre Excellence, le très humble et très obeissant serviteur,
                                                          OTTO

RC (DLC); endorsed by TJ with his right hand. Noted in SJL as received 6 Dec. 1786.

UNE RESOLUTION: See Jay to TJ, 3 Oct. 1786.

To Vergennes, with Enclosure

SIR   Paris Octr. 15th. 1786

I had the honor some time ago of asking from your Excellency by letter a permission to export from the Ports of Bourdeaux and Havre certain arms and accoutrements which I had had made for the State of Virginia, which request I now take the liberty to repeat. I beg leave to sollicit at the same time a passeport for the entrance of certain articles for my own private use, some of which are arrived and the others expected. A list of them I herein enclose.

The accident of a dislocated wrist has for some time past prevented me the honor of paying my respects to the King and to yourself at Versailles. The slowness of the cure seems likely to delay that honor for some time to come. I hope that this circumstance will apologize for my not attending on a court to which it is my duty and my desire to render at all times the homage of my most perfect respect.

I have the honor to be with sentiments of the most profound esteem and respect, Your Excellency's most obedient and most humble Servant,
                                                TH: JEFFERSON

ENCLOSURE

A List of articles for the private use and [. . .] of M. Jefferson, Minister Plenipotentiary of the United States of America, for which a passeport is desired.

From Marseilles.	72 bottles of Frontignac wine
From Leghorn.	36 bottles of Cyprus wine
From Lisbon.	212 bottles of Malvoisie de Madeire
From London.	Harness for three horses
	Two copying-presses, with paper and appendages
	A Harpsichord

                          TH: JEFFERSON
                          (Test: W Short sec.)

RC (Arch. Aff. Etr., Corr. Pol., E.-U., XXXII); in Short's hand, including signature; at foot of text: "(Test: W Short sec.)" PrC (MoSHi); lacks date and complimentary close (see Vol. 9: 217, note 1); endorsed by TJ with his left hand: "Paris Oct. 15. 1786."

On the subject of this appeal, see TJ to Lafayette, 3 Nov.; Vergennes to TJ, 4 Nov.; Brissot de Warville to TJ, 10 Nov.; and TJ to Colonia, 22 Nov. 1786.

From Circello

Fontainebleau, 17 Oct. 1786. Informing TJ that, the day before, he had had his first audience with the king, queen, and royal family as ambassador of the king of the Sicilies.

RC (DLC); 2 p.; in French; addressed.

From C. W. F. Dumas

MONSIEUR La haie 17 Oct. 1786

La Dépeche ci-jointe,[1] que Votre Excellence comme toujours lira avant de l'acheminer avec mes précédentes déjà reçues et le paquet annoncé, qui partira enfin demain, me dispense de Lui répéter ce à quoi je n'ai rien à ajouter.

Mr. le Ms. De la Fayette m'ayant fait l'honneur de m'écrire, pour me proposer de le mettre au fait des affaires de la République, je crois ne pouvoir mieux remplir son desir qu'en priant Votre Excellence de lui faire voir toutes mes Dépeches susdites avec les Pieces annexées. Je n'oserois prendre cette Liberté, si je ne savois combien il fait de nos affaires les siennes, et son assiduité et intimité personnelle auprès de votre Excellence. [J'aurai l'honneur de lui écrire en conséquence l'ordinaire prochain.][2] Je dois pareillement réponse à Mr. Short. Il voudra bien me faire crédit jusqu'à ce que j'apprenne que la Commission dont il m'a chargé est remplie.

Votre Excellence, en m'apprenant que dans l'Essai des Etats unis dont Elle m'a régalé, il n'y a que quelques erreurs de peu de conséquence, m'a laissé l'appétit ouvert pour avoir une petite note de ces erreurs. Puis-je, sans trop exiger, l'espérer de la bonté de Votre Excellence.

Je suis avec grand respect, De Votre Excellence, Le très-humble et très-obéissant serviteur, C W F DUMAS

RC (DLC). FC (Rijksarchief, The Hague, Dumas Papers; photostats in DLC); with several variations in the text, two of which are noted below. Noted in SJL as received 27 Oct. 1786. Enclosure (FC in Dumas Papers): Dumas to John Jay, 15 Oct. 1786, continuing his account of affairs in the Netherlands.

REPONSE À MR. SHORT: See note to TJ to Rayneval, 30 Sep. 1786 for Short's COMMISSION and Dumas' reply to it.

[1] FC reads: "L'incluse pour le Congres."

[2] Text in brackets (supplied) is not in FC.

From Charles Boromée LeBrun

A Monsieur prevote à Coutances le 17 8bre 1786
Monsieur de jefferson ministre plenipotentiaire des etats unis de L'amerique Septentrionale

Supplie humblement Charles Boromée leBrun procureur du Roi au Bailliage de coutances

Et a L'honneur de vous Exposer que jerome michel leBrun de Bellecour, son frere, auroit occupé différens postes dans les troupes des etats unis de l'Amerique, que lors du decompte qui eut lieu en mil sept cent quatre vingt[. . .] il auroit obtenu du congrès six certificats montant à cinq mille six cent quatre vingt huit piastres portant intérêt à six pour cent. Le sieur lebrun de Bellecour après que le traité de paix fut signé, se disposoit à repasser en france pour y revoir sa famille et satisfaire à des obligations [que] son départ avoit nécessités. Il n'a pu Executer ce projet [ayant] eté assassiné en janvier mil sept cent quatre vingt cinq dans les deserts qui séparent le duché de Kentuke de la virginie. Le suppliant, informé que les certificats cydessus mentionnés avoient eté confiés à un sieur de coutures laM[. . .] qui avoit repassé en france, s'est empressé de les recouvrer a[ux] fins de faire honneur aux engagemens qui son frere avoit contractés et que son etat l'obligeoit de remplir.

En consequence un mandataire du suppliant est allé le mois d'aoust mil sept cent quatre vingt cinq chès M. g[rand] Banquier des états unis et y a représenté lesdits certif[icats.] Examen fait d'iceux on luy a payé la somme de [*dix*]*huit cent quarante trois livres un sou*. Le premier janvier de cette année etant echu un arrérage, [le] mandataire s'est présenté au Bureau et même y a [fait] jusqu'à ce jour differens voiages. La seule reponse [qu'on] luy ait faite a toujours été qu'on attendoit des ordres pour payer. Ce retardement que le suppliant ne p[ouvoit] prévoir, fait qu'il est poursuivi par nombre de créanciers auxquels il avoit promis de commencer à [. . .] en payment vers la fin du mois de janvier. Obligé de manquer à sa parole le suppliant a été personnellement inquiété; pour faire cesser les poursuites il ne luy [reste] d'autre ressource que dans le placet qu'il à [l'honneur] de présenter à Votre Excellence.

À ce qu'il vous plaise, Monsieur, Envoyer [. . .] un ordre aux fins de recevoir de M. grand [la somme] de dix huit cent quarante trois livres un sol echue en janvier dernier. Le suppliant ne cessera de [. . .] ses voeux, pour la prosperité des etats unis de l'A[merique]

et la prolongation des jours d'un ministre aussi [. . .] et aussi eclairé.

LeBrun

RC (ViWC); MS mutilated. Noted in SJL as received 20 Oct. 1786.

On 29 Apr. 1785 Arthur Campbell reported to Gov. Henry that JEROME MICHEL LEBRUN had been murdered by William Baker and Peter Taffe, inhabitants of Hampshire County. Both men were apprehended, but early in June Campbell stated that the saddle bags of Major LeBrun, containing "near five hundred pounds in gold, some Bonds, and several Bills of Exchange, together with many letters and other papers, with some cloaths," had been found about two miles below the point where "the Major was lost, lodged among some drift-wood, on the point of an island," a circumstance which caused doubt as to whether LeBrun had been murdered or had met with an accident. Later Campbell reported that it was thought LeBrun had been murdered "as much on account of his tory principles as for his money" and that the "Tory party had exhibited unwarrantable partiality" toward one of the suspects (Campbell to Henry, 29 Apr., 3 and 15 June, and 23 Sep. 1785; William Robison to Henry, 20 July 1786; CVSP, IV, 27, 32, 37, 43, 57).

From C. W. F. Dumas

Monsieur La haie 19 Oct. 1786

J'espere que Votre Excellence a reçu les miennes du 6 et 17 de ce mois.

Je laisse l'incluse pour Mr. De La Fayette ouverte, afin que Votre Excellence la lise, et la remette. L'Extrait de la même est copié pour le Congrès afin de lui completer aussi l'idée qu'il faut avoir des affaires d'ici, qui sont vraiment interessantes. Comme cela change à chaque instant comme un verre à facettes, il faudroit des voulumes s'il falloit entrer dans les détails. Par exemple, je viens d'apprendre de source qu'à Harlem 900 notables Bourgeois, le Secrétaire de la ville à leur tête, viennent de présenter à leur Régence où ils supplient que l'*insensé* Str. soit à jamais exclus et éloigné de l'administration d'un Etat qu'il rend si malheureux.

Je suis avec grand respect de V.E. le très humble et très obéissant serviteur,

C W F Dumas

RC (DLC). Noted in SJL as received 24 Oct. 1786. Enclosures: Dumas to Lafayette, 19 Oct. 1786 (FC in Rijksarchief, The Hague, Dumas Papers; photostats in DLC), a detailed account of the political situation in the Netherlands; extract of Dumas' letter to Lafayette to be forwarded to Congress.

To De Corny

Sir Paris Oct. 20. 1786.

By the first conveyance which shall offer I propose to report to the Governor of Virginia the manner in which the wish of the state relative to the bust of the Marquis de La Fayette has been carried into execution, and of the friendly and flattering attentions paid by Messieurs le Prevot des Marchands et Echevins de Paris to them and to the character to which they desired to shew their gratitude. It would enable me to do this with more exactness could I obtain copies of the proceedings which attended the inauguration of the bust. Your goodness, already so often manifested in this business, encourages me to endeavor to obtain these thro' your intervention. I do it the rather as it furnishes me an occasion very grateful to my feelings, of returning to you at the same time my sincere thanks for the zeal with which you have seconded the views of the state, the readiness with which you have condescended to give me information in the course of the proceedings, and to secure by your influence the success of those proceedings. This friendly assistance in the discharge of a public duty has added to the many motives of private esteem and attachment with which I have the honour to be Sir Your most obedient & most humble servant, TH: JEFFERSON

PrC (DLC); written with TJ's left hand.

From Plowden W. Garvey

SIR Rouen the 20 october 1786

We have the honor to advise your Excellency that we retired from on board the Adventure, Capn. Daman, arrived here from London one Case directed to you shipped by Mr. Woodmason ⅌ order of Coll. Smith, one ditto containing Printed Books by Mr. Chs. Dilly. We got them Corded and Plumbed and sent them off yesterday to your address by Millard's Cart to deliver them in five days. He has got an Acquit a Caution No. 113 that prouves these effects were not opened here, you'll please to have it discharged at your Custom house and returned us.

Our Common Worthy friend Mr. Barclay addressed us by a Ship now at Havre a Case of Books for your Excellency. We have given our friend there orders to retire and send it us, when here shall forward it to Paris, and advising the departure let you know what expences we have been at for that expedition.

We are with very great respect Sir Your Excellency's most huml. & very obedt. Servants, by procn. of R. & A. Garvey,

PLOWDEN W. GARVEY

20 OCTOBER 1786

The bad weather and scarcity of Cart men retarded much the above Expedition.

RC (MHi). Noted in SJL as received 22 Oct. 1786.

From Zachariah Loreilhe

SIR   Bergerac October 20th. 1786

I have the honour of acquainting you that I have received a letter from Mr. Thos. Barclay dated the 3d. of October where in he Desires me to engage 200 Barrels of the best gun Powder, 100 thousand Flints, and 100 Reams of Cartrige Paper, and to look out for a Good stout Vessel to proceed with them to Richmond in Virginia. Mr. Barclay informs me also that if any difficulty shall arise either in procuring a Vessel for Richmond or in executing any other part of the order to acquaint your Excellency therewith; at present I See but one difficulty which is how I am to Pay for those articles. Therefore I must beg your Excellency will be so obliging as to Inform me if there is any Particular funds appropriated for this Purpose, and how I am to procure it. If this Difficulty is remouved, I make no Doubt but I will be able to Execute the order to the advantage and Satisffaction of the State of Virginia; however if any unforeseen difficultys should arise, depending on your Excellency's goodness I shall acquaint you with it to the End that they might be remouved.

I have the honour to be with very great respect your Excellency most humble & most obedient Servant,   Z. LOREILHE

RC (DLC); endorsed by TJ with his left hand. Noted in SJL as received 29 Oct. 1786.

To Stael de Holstein

Paris, 20 Oct. 1786. This letter is almost identical with TJ's letter of this date to Vergennes, q.v. for note on enclosure and variations in the text.

PrC (DLC); 1 p.; in the hand of William Short; at foot of text, written by TJ with his left hand: "Stael Baron de."

To Vergennes

SIR   Paris Octr. the 20th. 1786

I have the honor of communicating to your Excellency the copy

[472]

of a treaty of amity and commerce concluded between the United States of America and his late Majesty the King of Prussia, in the two languages in which it was written, each of which was agreed to be equally original. The exchange of ratifications was made but a little before the death of the King. This circumstance with the delays which have attended the printing and transmitting the copies of the treaty to me have prevented my making an earlier communication of it to your Excellency as a confidence and respect [due to the friendly dispositions which His Majesty the King has been always graciously pleased to shew towards us.][1]

I have the honor to be with sentiments of the most perfect respect and esteem, your Excellency's most obedient & most humble servant,
TH JEFFERSON

RC (Arch. Aff. Etr., Corr. Pol., E.-U., XXXII); in Short's hand, including signature; at foot of text: "(Test: W. Short sec.)." PrC (DLC); lacks complimentary close. Enclosure: Copy of the printed text of the Treaty with Prussia—not the broadside described in JCC, XXXI, 962, No. 533; nor, evidently, was it one of the texts printed by Adams, which was "only in French" (Adams to TJ, 11 Sep. 1786).

[1] For the text in brackets (supplied), the letter of this date to Stael de Holstein reads: "we bear to the nation whom you so worthily represent here and with which we have the honor of being allie[d]."

From Achard Frères

SIR   Rouen 21 8ber. 1786.

We have received the Passeport your Excellence has been so good as to send us. Your two Cases are on Board of the Diligence L'Adelaide and we hope they will Come Safe in the hands of your Excellence.

Here inclosed is a note of our Expences which have been paid to us by the Master of the Diligence to whom we beg of your Excellence to reimburse them.

We are most respectfully Your Most obedient Humble Servants,
ACHARD BROTHERS & Co.

P.S. Your Excellence will be pleased to give orders that the aquit à Caution No. 115 be Sent back to us, which is made on purpose to avoid any duties to your Excellence.

RC (MHi). Noted in SJL as received 22 Oct. 1786. Enclosure (MHi): Account of expenditures on TJ's behalf (freight, commission, &c.), for wine imported from Lisbon, amounting to 32.₶2.

From Calonne

à Fontainebleau le 22 8bre. 1786

L'intention du Roi etant, [Monsieur,][1] de favoriser autant qu'il est possible le commerce des Etats unis, j'ai l'honneur de vous faire part de quelques dispositions prises a cet egard.

Par ma[2] Lettre du 9 Janvier 1784 a M. Le Marquis de la Fayette, je lui annonçois qu'au lieu de deux ports francs promis par le traité aux Etats unis, le Roi s'etoit determiné a leur en accorder quatre, [ce qui s'est effectué,][3] et je lui promettois de m'occuper des douannes, des droits de traites qui gênent le Commerce, en lui observant que cet objet demandoit un travail considerable; il[4] n'est pas encore complette. Par une autre Lettre je l'informois que Sa Majesté avoit supprimé les droits sur la Sortie des[5] Eaux de vie, et esperois que cette Suppression seroit utile au Commerce Americain; je lui promettois aussi que les droits du Roi et de l'amirauté payables par un Navire Americain à son arrivée[6] dans les Ports de France[7] seroient diminués, et que ce qui en resteroit seroit reduit a un seul droit qui seroit reglé d'après le nombre de mâts ou le tirant d'eau, et non d'après l'estimation trop incertaine du Jaugeage. Cette reduction exige une connoissance exacte de tous les droits qui se perçoivent dans les ports, et comme il y en a d'un grand nombre d'especes, les Etats que j'en fais faire ne sont pas encore achevés.[8]

Vous savés, Monsieur, que le Roi a chargé un Comité particulier d'examiner nos rapports de Commerce avec les Etats unis, et que M. Le Marquis de la Fayette y a porté un projet analogue aux idées que presente[9] votre Lettre a M. Le Comte de Vergennes: mais vous sentés combien il seroit imprudent[10] de hazarder par un changement de Sistème, le produit d'une[11] branche de revenus qui s'eleve a[12] 28. millions sans porter sur un objet de premiere necessité. Aprés une ample discussion de tout ce qu'on pourroit faire en ce moment pour favoriser l'Importation en France des tabacs de l'Amerique, il a été arreté,[13] non que le marché fait avec[14] M. Morriss seroit rompu;[15] mais qu'après l'expiration de ce Contrat, il n'en seroit plus fait de pareil, et qu'en attendant les fermiers généraux se soumettroient a acheter annuellement environ quinze mille boucauds de tabacs d'amerique venant directement des Etats unis sur des batimens françois et Americains aux mêmes prix et conditions qui sont stipulés par le contrat fait avec M. Morriss.[16]

Vous vous rappellerés, Monsieur, qu'en attendant qu'il fut statué sur les demandes qui avoient été faites[17] en faveur des huilles

22 OCTOBER 1786

de Baleine, M. Le Marquis de la Fayette avoit fait un arrangement particulier avec M. Sangrain pour qu'il reçût des envois de cette denrée jusqu'a la concurrence de 800 mille Livres, et que je lui avois accordé[18] des passeports pour exempter ce premier envoi de tous droits quelconques. Le même M. Sangrain a fait ensuite un marché avec les Negocians de Boston pour 400 mille Livres par an, pendant six années, pour lequel Sa Majesté a promis les mêmes faveurs dont jouissent les villes anséatiques.

Cette matiere ayant été dernierement examinée sous un point de vûe plus général, l'administration a qui le Comité a rendu Compte de son voeu conforme a la demande de M. Le Marquis de la Fayette, et a votre opinion pour l'entierre abolition de tous droits sur ces huiles, a reconnu qu'elle ne pouvoit y consentir quant a present, a cause des engagemens pris avec d'autres puissances. Tout ce qu'on a pû faire a été d'assurer pour dix ans a l'huile de Baleine, au Spermaceti, et a tout ce qui est compris sous ces denominations, venant des Etats unis sur batimens françois ou Americains, les mêmes faveurs, la même moderation de droits dont jouissent les villes anséatiques.[19]

Sa Majesté espere que les Liaisons de commerce entre les Etats unis et la France, deviendront assés etendues pour l'engager a continuer l'effet de cette decision provisoire;[20] et comme il a été observé dans le Comité qu'on percevoit un droit de fabrication considerable sur les huiles de Baleine les plus favorisées, et même sur les huiles nationales,[21] Sa Majesté consent a abolir ce droit de fabrication a l'egard des huiles de Baleine et Spermaceti venant directement des Etats unis, a bord des batimens françois ou Americains, de maniere que ces huiles et Spermaceti n'auront a payer pour tous droits quelconques pendant dix[22] ans qu'un droit de 7.ᵗ10s. et les dix sols pour livre, cette derniere augmentation de 10. sols pour livre devant finir en 1790.

Il a été reglé qu'on prendroit des informations particulieres sur la consommation du Ris de Caroline en france, et qu'on chercheroit a en encourager l'Importation.

Sur les representations qui ont été faites touchant les droits considerables perçus à l'entrée des Potasses connues en Amerique sous le nom de *Potach et Pearl-ach*, ainsi que sur les droits perçus pour les peaux et poil de Castor et pour les Cuirs verds, Sa Majesté a supprimé tous les droits perçus sur la potasse, sur les poils et peaux de Castor et Cuirs verds venant du crû des Etats unis, a bord des batimens françois ou Americains. Elle s'occupera aussi des en-

22 OCTOBER 1786

couragemens a donner a tous les articles du Commerce de Pelleterie.

Sa Majesté a egalement consenti a decharger de tous droits les mâtures, vergues, courbes de toute espece, le cedre rouge, le chene verd, en un mot tous les bois propres a la construction des navires venant des Etats unis sur les batimens françois ou Americains.

Le Comité ayant aussi representé qu'il y avoit un droit de 5. ℔ o/o sur l'achat des Navires construits chés l'Etranger, et que ce droit nuisoit a la vente des Navires Americains, Sa Majesté a bien voulu y avoir egard et exempter de tous droits, l'achât des Navires qu'on prouvera avoir été construits dans les Etats unis.[23]

Il se perçoit aussi des droits très forts sur les arbres, arbustes, et graines d'arbres, dont Sa Majesté a accordé l'abolition pour tous les envois qui seront faits des Etats unis et portés sur batimens françois ou Americains.

Comme il a été representé que l'Etat de Virginie faisait faire en France une fourniture d'armes pour sa Milice, il a été reglé que les prohibitions qui jusqu'a present ont empeché[24] l'exportation des armes et poudre a tirer, ainsi que les droits exigés dans les cas ou on en accorde des permissions particulieres, seroient abolis, et que toutes les fois que les Etats unis voudroient tirer de France des armes, des fusils, de la poudre a tirer, ils en auroient la Liberté[25] pourvu que ce fut sur batimens françois ou Americains, et que ces objets ne seroient soumis qu'a un droit très modique, destiné seulement a calculer les exportations.

Enfin Sa Majesté a reçû avec la même faveur la demande faite au Comité de supprimer les Droits considerables[26] qui s'exigent a present sur les livres et papiers de toute espece. Sa Majesté supprime tous[27] droits sur les objets de ce genre destinés aux Etats unis et embarqués sur batimens françois ou Americains.

C'est avec plaisir, Monsieur, que je vous annonce ces dispositions de Sa Majesté, qui vous Sont un nouveau temoignage du desir qu'elle a[28] d'unir intimement le Commerce des deux nations, et de l'attention favorable qu'elle donnera toujours, aux propositions qui lui seront faites au nom des Etats unis de l'Amerique.[29]

J'ai l'honneur d'etre[30] avec un sincere attachement, Monsieur, votre très humble et très obeissant serviteur, DE CALONNE

Votre nation, Monsieur, verra sans doute avec plaisir, Les facilités que Le Roi vient d'accorder pour La sortie des vins de Bordeaux, de Guyenne et de Touraine, et Les suppressions des Droits accordees a cet effet par differens arrets du Conseil dont M. Le Mis de la Fayette pourra vous donner connoissance.

RC (DNA: PCC, No. 87, I); in a clerk's hand, with signature and postscript in Calonne's hand; with English translation by John Pintard. Noted in SJL as received 24 Oct. 1786, which is obviously an error—TJ enclosed it in his to Jay of 23 Oct. 1786; he evidently received it from the hands of Lafayette on the evening of 22 Oct. (see Lafayette to TJ, under 23 Oct. 1786; also Gottschalk, *Lafayette, 1783-89*, p. 256). Printed text in French (copies in DLC: TJ Papers: Arch. Aff. Etr., Corr. Pol., E.-U., XXXII; DNA: PCC, No. 87, I; and DLC: Rare Book Room [see Sowerby, No. 2303 for a description of the second printed text that belonged to TJ]); pages [1]-7; at head of text: "Lettre Adressée à M. Jefferson, Ministre Plénipotentiaire des Etats-Unis d'Amérique." The text was also printed in E. Clavière and J.-P. Brissot de Warville, *De la France et des Etats-Unis*, p. 330-6; Brissot de Warville, *Travels in the United States of America*, II, 178-85; and *American Museum*, I, 200. PrC of Tr (DLC); in Short's hand, in French, the Tr of which was probably employed between 23 and 27 Oct. as the text for the printed copy. Tr of translation (DNA: PCC, No. 107). Another Tr of translation (DNA: RG 59, State Department Records); see under 1 Feb. 1791. Tr of Dft prepared by the American Committee and submitted to Calonne (DNA: PCC, No. 87, I); in French, in Short's hand; at head of text: "Projet de la lettre de Mr. le Controlleur-general à Mr. Jefferson" (referred to in the notes below as Dft). PrC of preceding (DLC). Translation of projet by Pintard (DNA: PCC, No. 87, I). Tr (DNA: PCC, No. 107).

For a brief account of the immediate background of this general code of regulations affecting trade between the United States and France, see Gottschalk, *Lafayette, 1783-89*, p. 238-40, 249-50, 255-6. TJ had furnished Lafayette statistics and general information on American trade in order to support the latter's efforts in the American Committee (TJ to Lafayette, 17 July 1786). Under Lafayette's guidance, the Committee recommended the general regulations contained in the present letter and submitted the draft of a letter to be signed by Calonne. Whether TJ himself had any hand in the drafting of this letter cannot be ascertained, but there can be little doubt that he and Lafayette were in close touch with each other while it was being prepared and that Lafayette's sponsorship in the American Committee was indispensable. TJ reported to Jay that the letter as signed by Calonne was "almost a verbal copy" of the draft submitted by the Committee (TJ to Jay, 23 Oct. 1786); but see the variations indicated below. The letter was evidently handed to TJ by Lafayette on the evening of 22 Oct. and the speed with which TJ informed Jay, Adams, and merchants interested in Franco-American trade about this new regulation suggests the importance that he attached to it. Lafayette, in reporting these developments to Washington, paid a gracious tribute to TJ: "Mr. Jefferson is a most able and respected representative, and such a man as makes me happy to be his aid de camp. Congress have made a choice very favorable to their affairs" (Lafayette to Washington, 26 Oct. 1786; Gottschalk, ed., *Letters of Lafayette to Washington, 1777-1779*, p. 314). And to McHenry he wrote: "Mr. Jefferson . . . is one of the most amiable, learned, upright and able men who ever existed, and is much beloved in France for his amiable disposition and much respected for his abilities" (Gottschalk, *Lafayette, 1783-89*, p. 258). For TJ's later observations on Calonne's regulations, see under 3 July 1787.

[1] Text in brackets (supplied) is not in Dft.
[2] Dft and printed text read: "une."
[3] Text in brackets (supplied) not in Dft.
[4] Dft reads: "qui."
[5] Dft reads: "les."
[6] Dft reads: "qu'un navire Americain paye en arrivant."
[7] These two words not in Dft.
[8] Instead of "qui seroit reglé . . . encore achevés," Dft reads: "payable d'aprés le nombre de mâts ou le tirant d'eau et non d'aprés la maniere plus incertaine du Jaugeage: cet objet demande un relevé trés considerable à cause de la différence de ces droits dans les ports qui n'est pas encore terminé."
[9] Dft reads: ". . . un projet pour la destruction de la Ferme generale du tabac qui avait votre approbation et se rapportait aux principes de."
[10] Dft reads: "mais lors même que les calculs justifieraient cette Ideé, vous conviendrez, Monsieur, qu'il est difficile de proposer au Roi."
[11] Dft reads: ". . . de Sistême une branche."

22 OCTOBER 1786

[12] Dft reads: "de" instead of "qui s'eleve a."
[13] Dft reads: ". . . de premiere necessité, et qui par conséquent est moins onereuse au peuple que quelques autres, mais il a éte decidé."
[14] Dft reads: "du" instead of "fait avec."
[15] Dft adds at this point: "malgré les plaintes recuës de toutes les parties d'Amerique, parce que tout engagement de Commerce doit être respecté."
[16] Instead of "se soumettroient . . . avec M. Morriss," Dft reads: "prendroient annuellement de 12. à 15. mille boucauts de tabacs d'Amérique venant directement des Etats unis sur des Batiments Francais ou Americains au même prix et conditions que celles du central fait avec Mr. Morris."
[17] Dft reads: "la decision solliciteé du Gouvernement."
[18] Instead of "que je lui . . . accordé," Dft reads: "qu'il avoit obtenu."
[19] In Dft this paragraph reads: "Mais cette matiere ayant été dernierement examinée au Comité sur un point de vue général le Gouvernement en regrettant de ne pouvoir adopter le projet de M. le Mis. de la Fayette egalement consacré par votre opinion pour l'entiere abolition de tous droits sur ces huiles, à cause de ses engagements avec d'autres puissances, s'est determiné cependant d'assurer pour 6. ans à l'huile de baleine, l'huile de spermæceti et ce qui est compris en general sous le nom de spermæceti, venant directement des Etats-unis sur Batiments Francais ou Americains la même faveur dont jouissent les Villes Anséatiques."
[20] Dft reads: "cette faveur" instead of "l'effet de."
[21] Instead of "de fabrication considerable," Dft reads: "très considérable sur les huiles de baleine les plus favorisées, qui porte même sur les huiles d'olives et des noix nationales."
[22] Dft reads: "6."
[23] Instead of this paragraph, Dft reads: "Sur la representation qui a eté egalement faite par le comité qu'il y avoit un droit de 5. p. $\frac{0}{0}$ sur l'achat des navires Americains; sa Majesté exempte de tous droits l'achat des navires qu'on prouvera avoir eté construits dans les Etats-unis."
[24] Instead of "il a été . . ." Dft reads: "et qu'il seroit utile aux Etats-unis de detruire la prohibition qui existe sur."
[25] Instead of "les droits exigés . . ." Dft reads: "tres forts qui sont perçus dans le cas ou cette prohibition etoit leveé, Sa Majesté permet l'exportation des armes fusils et poudre à tirer pour les Etats-unis."
[26] Instead of "Enfin sa Majesté . . ." Dft reads: "Sur la demande également faite dans le comité de supprimer des droits très forts."
[27] Dft reads: "les droits."
[28] Instead of "qui vous Sont . . ." Dft reads: "et le desir qu'elle a."
[29] Instead of "et de l'attention . . ." Dft reads: "ainsi que la consideration personelle de Gouvernement pour vous me feront toujours recevoir avec les plus grands égards toutes les propositions que vous croirez devoir nous faire."
[30] Dft ends at this point.

To William Stephens Smith

Dear Sir   Paris Oct. 22. 1786.

How the right hand became disabled would be a long story for the left to tell. It was by one of those follies from which good cannot come, but ill may. As yet I have no use of that hand, and as the other is an awkward scribe, I must be sententious and not waste words. Yours of Sep. 18 and 22. and Oct. 1. and 4. have been duly received, as have been also the books from Lackington and Stockdale, and the second parcel from Dilly. The harness is at the Douane of Paris, not yet delivered to me. Dilly's first parcel of books, and the first copying press are arrived at Rouen. You see how much reason I have to say 'well done thou good and faithful

[478]

servant.' With Chastellux' voiages and Latré's map I took a great deal more trouble than was necessary, such as going myself to the book shop when a servant might as well have gone &c. merely from a desire to do something in return for you, and that I might feel as if I had done something. You desire to know whether the 2d. order for copying paper and ink was meant to be additional to the former? It was, but I had now rather not receive the paper because I have found a better kind here. The ink I shall be glad of. The twelve sheet map I shall send by the first good opportunity: and hope ere long to receive the plate of mine from Mr. Neele. I will trouble you to have the inclosed note to Jones delivered. Will you undertake to prevail on Mr. Adams to set for his picture and on Mr. Brown to draw it for me? I wish to add it to those of other principal American characters which I have or shall have: and I had rather it should be original than a copy. We saw a picture of Sr. W. Raleigh at Birmingham, and I do not know whether it was of Mr. Adams or yourself I asked the favor to get it for me. I must pray your taylor to send me a buff Casimir waistcoat and breeches with those of cotton, and of my shoemaker to send me two pr. of thin waxed leather slippers. Things of this kind come better by private hands if any such should be coming within any reasonable time. The accident to my wrist has defeated by views of visiting the South of France this fall. Present me very affectionately to Mrs. Adams and Mrs. Smith. I hope the former is very well, and that the latter is, or has been very sick, otherwise I would observe to you that it is high time. Adieu. Yours affectionately,

TH: JEFFERSON

PrC (DLC); written and endorsed with TJ's left hand. The enclosed note to Jones has not been found and is not recorded in SJL, but see William Jones to TJ, 10 Nov. 1786.

MR. BROWN: Mather Brown (1761-1831), a native of Massachusetts who, like other Americans, had gone to London to study under Benjamin West, and who painted the portrait of Adams for TJ.

To John Adams

DEAR SIR   Paris Octr. 23d. 1786

Your favor of Sept. the 11th. came to hand in due time and since that I have recieved the copies of the Prussian treaty you were so kind as to send me. I have recieved a short letter from Mr. Barclay dated Cadiz Septr. 25th. only announcing his arrival there and that he should proceed immediately to Madrid. At this latter place he would meet my letter informing him that we did not propose any thing further with the Piratical states at this time. The inclosed extract of a letter from Mr. Carmichael also mentions Mr. Barclay's arrival at Cadiz. A letter from Mr. Carmichael some time ago informed me that a bill had been drawn on him by Mrs. Lamb in America, by order as she said of Mr. Lamb; This gentleman not proposing to proceed either to New-York, London, or Paris to settle his accounts, I desired Mr. Carmichael, if any money remained yet in the hands of Mr. Lamb's banker at Madrid, to obstruct it's going out until he could give us information. His answer was that it was all withdrawn by Mr. Lamb. By some means or other I omitted to mention these circumstances to you at the time. I mention them now to explain the reasons of Mr. Carmichael's touching on that subject in the inclosed. We may now hourly expect from Mr. Barclay a copy of the preliminary treaty with Morocco. Is it your opinion that the definitive one should be executed through his agency, or that of Colo. Franks or of any other person? I beg you to present my most friendly respects to Mrs. Adams and to be assured yourself of the esteem and attachment with which I have the honor to be Sir, your most obedient humble Servant,

                 Th: Jefferson

RC (MHi: AMT); in Short's hand, including signature; at foot of text: "(Test W Short Sec)"; addressed and endorsed. PrC (DLC). Enclosure (MHi: AMT): Extract of Carmichael to TJ, 3 Oct. 1786, q.v., note 1.

LETTER FROM MR. BARCLAY . . . SEPTR. 25TH: An error for 26 Sep., under which date the letter is printed above. THE DEFINITIVE ONE: The definitive treaty, at least so far as Morocco was concerned, had already been concluded; see notes to Treaty with Morocco, printed immediately following Barclay to the Commissioners, 2 Oct. 1786. When TJ found that no addition could be made to the "book" to which the Emperor of Morocco had set his seal, and that Barclay had transmitted three copies of the English translation of the treaty, he attached a preamble and conclusion to one copy, which he and Adams then signed and transmitted to Congress even though it could not be regarded as an original in the usual sense.

From C. W. F. Dumas, with Enclosures

Monsieur   La haie 23e. Octobre 1786

Je profite d'un Courier que M. l'Ambassadeur se propose d'expédier demain ou après-demain à sa Cour, pour faire parvenir à Votre Excellence et par Elle au Congrès les deux Pieces ci-jointes, que j'ai traduites pour Lui et pour Mr. l'Ambassadeur, qui les fait pareillement passer à sa Cour. Vous verrez, et s'il vous plait Mr. le Ms. De la Fayette aussi, par l'une de ces Pièces, que les Etats d'Hollande persistent avec vigueur dans l'assertion de leur Souve-

[480]

raineté, et dans l'autre le début de la sentence d'un *insensé* prononcée par toute la nation: car l'électricité de cette vive étincelle va se communiquer à la ronde de ville en ville, et consigner son objet flétri à l'univers et la postérité. En attendant, une Commission secrete ici s'occupe des moyens de procurer du soulagement aux parties souffrantes dans les Provinces de Gueldre et d'Utrecht, jusqu'à ce qu'ils puissent avoir la satisfaction et le dédommagement qui leur sont dûs.

Votre Excellence aura déjà vu par le Supplément No. 84 de Leide, qu'on a fait des intelligences agréables qu'Elle m'a fait parvenir dans deux de ses Lettres un usage discret approprié aux circonstances de ce pays, où si l'on laissoit faire des têtes trop chaudes, tout seroit en combustion et gâté.

Je suis avec grand respect De Votre Excellence le très-humble et très obéissant serviteur, C W F Dumas

ENCLOSURE I

(Extract of a letter from New York, July 6)

Une des preuves, que ce Pays-ci jouit actuellement d'un des plus grands bonheurs dont une République soit susceptible, sçavoir d'une tranquilité parfaite, c'est qu'il n'y a pas de Nouvelles éclatantes à mander ici. Le Commerce est sur un pié fort avantageux pour l'Amerique. Le Prix des Productions de la Terre, ainsi que celui de la main d'oeuvre, est fort haut. Les Marchandises, importées de l'Etranger, sont au contraire à un taux fort bas. Ainsi ceux d'entre le Peuple, qui sçavent se contenter de leur situation, en se bornant aux jouissances proportionées à leur manìere d'être, ne peuvent que vivre heureux sous un Gouvernement doux et juste. La tranquilité regne dans tous les Etats; et les différentes Assemblées font des progrès, lents à la vérité, mais sûrs et non interrompus, pour se perfectionner de plus en plus. Les dispositions y augmentent particulièrement pour concentrer dans les mains du Congrés tous les pouvoirs, qui ont rapport à nos liaisons avec les Puissances Etrangères; et la conviction devient tous les jours plus universelle, qu'une République Fédérative ne sçaurait subsister longtems sans un lieu commun, qui ne portant point de préjudice à l'indépendence individuelle de chacun de ses Membres, en forme néanmoins une Puissance unique à l'égard de l'Etranger. La Jalousie, si naturelle dans cette espèce de Gouvernement, a d'abord empêché, qu'on n'écoutât cette vérité, quoique généralement sentie: Mais, à mesure que le tems et l'expérience font mûrir la réflexion, (ce qui d'ailleurs est l'avantage d'un tel Gouvernement) on revient de ces préjugés; et l'on y porte remède. Ce remède n'est pas promt; mais c'est un petit sacrifice, si, par la lenteur de l'amélioration, celle-ci en devient plus unanime: Et dans toute Republique l'on ne peut que regarder comme Ennemis du bien-être commun ceux, qui veulent redresser les abus ou corriger les erreurs avec précipitation et par violence.—Quant au Traité, qui se négocie depuis si longtems avec l'Angleterre, l'on ne prévoit point, qu'il soit porté bientôt à conclusion. Les Anglais ne peuvent (à ce qu'il parôit) oublier, qu'ils ont été nos maîtres: Ils prétendent nous dicter les conditions d'un commerce réciproque sur un pié, qui leur convient à eux seuls; et ils persistent dans ce dessein avec une assurance que bien des gens ici regardent comme une insulte. Ainsi, malgré la conformité de Langue et de Moeurs, l'antipathie Nationale, bien loin de diminuer, s'enracine toujours plus profondément; et un jour l'on pourra voir renouveller l'example, qu'on trouve assez souvent dans l'Histoire ancienne, de Colonies devenues ennemies irréconciliables de leur Mère-Patrie: Les animosités entre Souverains sont temporaires; elles s'adoucissent, elles changent selon les circonstances: Celles entre Peuples ne meurent jamais; et l'on a tout à craindre d'une Nation aigue, qui influe directement sur les mesures de l'Administration. Heureusement, la Guerre n'est pas de notre intérêt. La Paix et l'Amitié du Monde entier est la plus sage Politique que nous puissions suivre; et dès-à-présent nous nous réjouissons de posséder l'affection des Puissances les plus respectables de l'Europe.

ENCLOSURE II

C. W. F. Dumas to John Jay

Monsieur   Lahaie 23e. Oct. 1786

Je me hâte de faire parvenir à Votre Excellence la suite des transactions vraiment intéressantes qui ont lieu autour de moi. Monsieur l'Ambassadeur de France les trouvé si bien telles qu'il m'a prié de lui prêter tout ce que j'en ai de ma traduction, depuis Janvier 1785 où commença son Ministere ici, afin de les faire toutes copier pour son propre usage. Votre Excellence trouvera ci-joint:

La Résolution de L.N. et G.P. pour casser le serment clandestin que prêtoient les Gardes du Corps au Prince d'Orange.

L'Adresse de 923 les plus notables Citoyens de Harlem, qui va être suivie de celles de la plupart des villes à la ronde, pour donner le démenti le plus eclattant à une Assertion inconsidérée.

Une Résolution notable de Ziriczée opposée à une Résolution provinciale.

3 Gazettes de Leide où sont une Lettre excellente et touchante des Etats de Groningue aux Etats de Gueldre, Le commencement d'une longue lettre du Prince d'Orange aux Etats Generaux remplie de ses griefs et principes ordinaires repétés. J'y ajoute un article de N.York inséré sur de bonnes intelligences, espérant que Votre Excellence l'approuvera. Je la prie de conserver ces Gazettes pour les ranger avec celles dont les paquets lui parviennent par vaisseaux d'Amsterdam.

Je suis avec grand respect

FC (Rijksarchief, The Hague, Dumas Papers; photostats in DLC). Noted in SJL as received 29 Oct. 1786. Enclosure I: Supplement No. 84, *Gazette de Leide*, 23 Oct. 1786. One of the letters from TJ to Dumas that the latter used in fabricating this "letter from New York" was that of 6-10 May 1786; some of its expressions were discreetly omitted. Enclosure II (FC in Rijksarchief, The Hague, Dumas Papers; photostats in DLC) had among its enclosures a copy of Supplement No. 84, *Gazette de Leide*.

From Francis Eppes

Dr. Sir   Eppington October 23d. 1786

Your favours of 22d. of April and 22d. of July were handed me on the twentieth inst. The agent of Farell & Jones has long since been with me on the subject of their demand against Mr. Wayles's Estate. I have been pretty plain with the gentleman and cant help acknowledging I have been rather bitter in some of my expresions on the sales of our tobacco but really their conduct on that occasion has been so iniquitous I lose all patience whenever I think of it. As to Carys demand I know its just and ought to be immediately paid. Mrs. Nicks's demand I know nothing of however its extraordinary as long as I lived in Charles City that no application shou'd ever been made to me.

I have had several applications from the agent of Kippen & Co. but have declined giving any answer but shall now inform them of good intentions towards them. You must not expect that this debt and your proportion of Mr. Wayles's can be paid out of your crops. When ever the time arrives for their being paid a sale must take place. When I informd you that what was already sold wou'd pay all your debts except your proportion of Mr. Wayles's I knew nothing of the amount of Kippen & Co. debt. I am sorry you appear disappointed at Polly's not being sent but your letters in which you positively direct she shou'd be sent arriv'd too late in the Summer to comply with your directions respecting the ship and the time she was to leave Virginia. You may assure yourself of seeing [her] next summer. She and all of us are well and unite in our best wishes for yourself and Patsey. Betsy is much oblig'd for present of Anchovies oil &c. I have just received Mr. Bondfields letter informing me of those articles and 4 boxes of claret which he sent in April 1785 to the care of Mr. Beal in Wmsburg. However if he has received them he has not been polite enough to give information of them. I shall immediately send to Wmsburg. and to Portsmouth. I must return you my thank for the Claret and hope soon to drink your health in a bottle of it. I am with much esteem Dr. Sir Your Most Obdt.,   Frans. Eppes

RC (ViU); addressed and endorsed. Noted in SJL as received 31 May 1787.

To John Jay

SIR Paris Oct. 23. 1786.

In a letter of Jan. 2. I had the honor of communicating to you the measures which had been pursued here for the improvement of the commerce between the U.S. and France, the general view of that commerce which I had presented to the C. de Vergennes, the circumstance of the renewal of the farms which had obliged me to press separately and in the first place, the article of tobacco, and that which had also brought forward that of whale oil: and in my letters of May 27. and 31. I informed you of the result on the first of these articles. During the course of these proceedings a Committee had been established for considering the means of promoting the general commerce with America, and the M. de la Fayette was named of that committee. His influence in obtaining that establishment was valuable, but his labors and his perseverance as a member of it became infinitely more so. Immediately after the committee of Berni, of which my letter of May 27. gave an account, we thought it expedient to bring the general subject of the American commerce before the Committee; and as the members were much unacquainted with the nature and value of our Commercial productions, the Marquis proposed that in a letter to him as a member I should give as particular details of them as I could, as a ground for the committee to proceed on. I did so in the letter, a copy of which I have now the honour to inclose. The committee were well disposed, and agreed to report not only the general measures which they thought expedient to be adopted, but the form of the letter to be written by the Minister of finance to me, for the communication of those measures. I have received his letter this morning and have now the honour to inclose it. I accompany it with the one proposed by the committee, of which you will perceive that it is almost a verbal copy: it furnishes a proof of the disposition of the king and his ministers to produce a more intimate intercourse between the two nations. Indeed I must say that, as far as I am able to see, the friendship of the people of this country towards us is cordial and general, and that it is a kind of security for the friendship of ministers who cannot in any country be uninfluenced by the voice of the people. To this we may add that it is their interest as well as ours to multiply the bands of friendship between us. As the regulations stated in the minister's letter are immediately interesting to those concerned in our commerce, I send printed copies of it to the seaport towns of

France. We may consider them as an ultimate settlement of the conditions of our commerce with this country: for tho the consolidation of ship duties and the encouragements for the importation of rice are not finally decided, yet the letter contains a promise of them so soon as necessary facts shall be known. With a view to come at the facts relative to the two last objects, I had proposed whenever I should receive the final decision now inclosed, to avail myself of the pause which that would produce, in order to visit the seaport towns with which we trade chiefly and to collect that kind of knowlege of our commerce, and of what may be further useful to it which can only be gathered on the spot, and suggested by one's own inspection. But the delay which has attended the obtaining the final determination has brought us to the entrance of winter, and will oblige me to postpone my journey to the spring. Besides the objects of public utility which induce me to make a tour of this kind, that of health will oblige me to pay more attention to exercise and change of air than I have hitherto done since my residence in Europe: and I am willing to hope that I may be permitted at times to absent myself from this place, taking occasions when there is nothing important on hand nor likely to arise.

The assistance of the M. de la Fayette in the whole of this business has been so earnest and so efficacious that I am in duty bound to place it under the eye of Congress, as worthy their notice on this occasion. Their thanks, or such other notice as they should think proper, would be grateful to him without doubt. He has richly deserved and will continue to deserve it whenever occasions shall arise of rendering service to the U.S. These occasions will continually occur. Tho the abolition of the monopoly of our tobaccoes can not be hoped under the present circumstances, changes are possible which may open that hope again. However jealous too this country is of foreign intercourse with their colonies, that intercourse is too essential to us to be abandoned as desperate. At this moment indeed it cannot be proposed: but by watching circumstances, occasion may arise hereafter, and I hope will arise. I know from experience what would in that case be the value of such an auxiliary.

I have the honour to be with sentiments of the most perfect esteem & respect Sir your most obedient & most humble servant,

Tʜ: Jᴇꜰꜰᴇʀꜱᴏɴ

RC (DNA: PCC, No. 87, i); written with TJ's left hand; endorsed by Charles Thomson on p. 761 of enclosures: "Read 8 March 1787. March 13 Referred to the Secy for foreign Affairs to report particularly on Mr Jefferson's request to be permitted to travel on Account of his health and on what respects the

23 OCTOBER 1786

Marqs de la Fayette." PrC (DLC). Tr (DNA: PCC, No. 107). Enclosures: (1) TJ to Lafayette, 17 July 1786 and its enclosures. (2) Calonne to TJ, 22 Oct. 1786 (draft by the American Committee). (3) Same to same, 22 Oct. 1786 (both the draft prepared by the American Committee and the RC). (4) Printed texts of the Arrets mentioned in the postscript of Calonne's letter: those of 11 Nov. 1785, 27 May 1786, and 10 Sep. 1786 (these, with English translations by John Pintard, are to be found in DNA: PCC, No. 87, p. 734-60).

From Lafayette

[23 October 1786]

Inclosed, my dear sir, I Send You the arrêts du Conseil about Wines. While you are printing Mr. de Calonne's letter, Could you not Have it on two Columns, the one in English. It will be better translated By Mr. Short than By our News paper printers, and prove Convenient to such of our friends who Cannot well Read french. Let me have twenty Copies.

Our last Evening's Conversation, together with the Neopolitain ideas Have Raised into my Head a plan of which I will speak to You to Morrow. It is to propose myself as a Chief to the Antipiratical Confederacy. I will ask of Sum of Monney from Naples, Portugal, Rome, Venice, and some German towns, Naval stores, and Sea Men from America, a treaty with Maltha, a Harbour in Sicily, and keep up two or three fifties, six large Frigats, and a Number of smaller Vessels filled with Marines to Board the privateers. There will be alwais two thirds of the squadron out, and one third Refitting, and should a land opportunity offer the King of Naples will lend some Regiments.

The devil of it will Be to make it Agreable to this ministry that I should meddle with the War.

RC (DLC); without signature, name of addressee, or date; endorsed by TJ with his left hand: "Fayette. On confederation against Pyratical states" (see under 1 Dec. 1786). Date supplied from internal evidence and from statement in postscript of Calonne to TJ, 22 Oct. 1786. Enclosures: Arrets of 11 Nov. 1785, 27 May 1786, and 10 Sep. 1786, granting exemptions from or reductions of duties on the exportation of wines (printed copies, with English translations by Pintard, in DNA: PCC, No. 87, I, p. 734-60).

TJ had evidently sent MR. DE CALONNE's letter to the printer immediately on receiving it and therefore Lafayette's suggestion of printing it in English and French came too late to be adopted; printed texts in French were ready for inclusion in TJ to Jay, 27 Oct. 1786. On the ANTIPIRATICAL CONFEDERACY, see under 1 Dec. 1786 and Gottschalk, *Lafayette, 1783-89*, p. 265-6.

[486]

To John Adams

Dear Sir   Paris Oct. 27. 1786.

I formerly had the honour of mentioning to you the measures I had taken to have our commerce with this country put on a better footing; and you know the circumstances which had occasioned the articles of whale oil and tobacco to be first brought forward. Latterly we got the committee, which had been established for this purpose, to take up the other articles, and on their report the King and council have come to the decisions explained in the inclosed letter from M. de Calonnes to me. The abandonment of revenues raised on articles of *importation* shews a friendly disposition. I have had thro this business a most zealous, and powerful auxiliary in the M. de La fayette, by whose activity it has been sooner and better done than I could otherwise possibly have expected. Tho you are free to shew the inclosed letter as you please, I would wish it to be kept out of the public papers two or three months. I am Dear Sir your affectionate friend & servant,

                                                    Th: Jefferson

RC (MHi: AMT); written with TJ's left hand; endorsed. PrC (DLC). Enclosure: Printed text of Calonne to TJ, 22 Oct. 1786. See Adams to TJ, 11 July 1786.

To John Jay

Sir   Paris Oct. 27. 1786.

By a confidential opportunity to London I had the honour of writing to you on the 23d. instant, and of inclosing you the original letter of Monsieur de Calonnes to me on the subject of our commerce. As it is probable however that the French packet which is to sail from Lorient the 1st. of the next month will sooner reach you, I inclose some printed copies of the same letter by that conveiance, and have the honour to be with sentiments of the most perfect esteem and respect, Sir Your most obedient & most humble servant,   Th: Jefferson

RC (DNA: PCC, No. 87, I); written with TJ's left hand. PrC (DLC). Tr (DNA: PCC, No. 107). Enclosure: Printed copies of Calonne to TJ, 22 Oct. 1786. Letter and enclosures were transmitted to Congress by Jay on 3 May 1787 (JCC, XXXII, 257).

From John Jay

Dr. Sir   New York 27th. October 1786

I wrote you a few Lines by the last french Packet mentioning the Letters I had received from you, and that by another Conveyance you would receive particular and important Dispatches from me.

Those Dispatches relate to the Consular Convention; they begin with a Letter from me of the 3d. Inst. which, among other Matters, enumerates the Number of Papers annexed to it.

After those Dispatches were completed it was accidentally and seasonably discovered, that the Entry of the *Scheme* of the Convention in the Books of this Office was erroneous. As in forming my Report I considered this Scheme as really being what it appeared to be from that Entry, correspondent Errors naturally took place in the Report.

On making that Discovery I wrote a Letter to the President of Congress dated the 9th. Instant, a Copy of which you will find to be the last Paper which forms the Packet herewith enclosed. On that Letter Congress were pleased to direct me to take Order, which is in other Words saying, that they approve of the Opinion given in the last Paragraph of the Letter.

We learn from the Chargé des Affaires of France that a Treaty is concluded for us with Morocco.[1] We are anxious to be ascertained of the Fact, and to receive a Copy of it, that positive and accurate Information on the subject may be published. It is long since we heard that a Treaty with Portugal was likewise concluded, but it has not yet arrived, nor are we advised of the Reasons which retard its Conveyance.

In my Opinion you and Mr. Adams should have Commissions to treat with the Emperor and some other Powers, but it so happens that more domestic Objects divert the Attention of Congress in a considerable Degree, from their Affairs abroad.

The inefficacy of our Government becomes daily more and more apparent. Our Credit and our Treasury are in a sad Situation, and it is probable that either the Wisdom or the Passions of the People will produce Changes.

A Spirit of Licentiousness has infected Massachusetts, which appears more formidable than some at first apprehended; whether similar Symptoms will soon mark a like Disease in several other States, is very problematical.

The public Papers herewith sent contain everything generally

27 OCTOBER 1786

known about these Matters. A Reluctance to Taxes, an Impatience of Government, a Rage for Property, and little Regard to the Means of acquiring it, together with a Desire of Equality in all Things, seem to actuate the Mass of those who are uneasy in their Circumstances; to these may be added the Influence of ambitious Adventurers, and the Speculations of the many Characters who prefer private to public good, and of others who expect to gain more from Wrecks made by Tempests, than from the Produce of patient and honest Industry. As the Knaves and Fools of this World are forever in Alliance, it is easy to perceive how much Vigour and Wisdom a Government from its Construction and Administration should possess, in Order to repress the Evils which naturally flow from such copious Sources of Injustice and Evil.

Much I think is to be feared from the Sentiment which such a State of Things is calculated to infuse into the Minds of the rational and well intentioned. In their Eyes the Charms of Liberty will daily fade, and in seeking for Peace and Security, they will too naturally turn towards Systems in direct Opposition to those which oppress and disquiet them.

If Faction should long bear down Law and Government, Tyranny may raise its Head, or the more sober part of the People may even think of a King.

In short, my Dr. Sir; we are in a very unpleasant Situation. Changes are Necessary, but what they ought to be, what they will be, and how and when to be produced, are arduous Questions. I feel for the Cause of Liberty and for the Honor of my Countrymen who have so nobly asserted it, and who at present so abuse its Blessings. If it should not take Root in this Soil little Pains will be taken to cultivate it in any other.

This Letter will be carried to London by the Revd. Mr. Provost, who will with his own Hands deliver it to Mr. Adams[2] with one from me, requesting him to convey to you by some trusty Hand.

I have the Honor to be with great Respect & Esteem &c.,

JOHN JAY

P.S. I also enclose Copies of three Acts of Congress Vizt. of 16. 20. and 21. Inst.

FC (DNA: PCC, No. 121). Dft (NK-Iselin). Recorded in SJL as received 20 Dec. 1786. Enclosures: (1) Jay to TJ, 3 Oct. 1786 and its enclosures. (2) Jay to the president of Congress, 9 Oct. 1786, and its enclosure, reporting that Remsen had found, on comparing the printed "Scheme of a consular Convention" with the copy in the files of the Office for Foreign Affairs, additional discrepancies, and concluding: "I confess that the Scheme now appears to me more ineligible than I before thought it, though I am still of the Opinion that the only prudent way of getting over this unpleasant Business, is to conclude a Convention similar even to the Scheme as it *now* appears to be, and render its Inconveniences temporary by an Article limiting its Duration"; this letter was accompanied by a Note showing "the Difference between the 12th. Article of the Scheme of the Convention, entered in the Year 1782 on the Journal belonging to the Office for foreign Affairs, and the said Article in the original Scheme, recorded in the secret Journal in the Secretary's Office: " 'They' (Consuls and Vice Consuls) 'may cause to be arrested and sequestered, every Vessel carrying the Flag of their respective Nations, *and even send them back to France or the United States as the case may be, as well as arrest any Captain, Master, Seaman or Passenger of their respective Nations.* They may cause to be arrested and detained in the Country, Sailors and Deserters of their respective Nations, or cause them to be transported therefrom.'—The *scored* lines shew where the Copy which Mr. Jay used when he made his Report on the consular Convention deviates from the Original"; there were some twenty other deviations discovered and corrections entered, but none materially affected Jay's report, hence no other was quoted in Jay's enclosed Note (RC in DNA: PCC, No. 80, III; endorsed by Thomson: "Read 10 Oct. Referred back to Secy for foreign Affairs to take Order"). (3) Copy of a resolution of Congress of 16 Oct. 1786, authorizing TJ to "cause the claims of the representatives of the late Daniel Schweighhouser, of Nantes, against the United States of America, to be adjusted in such manner as he shall judge most for the interest and honor of the said states" (JCC, XXXI, 878-80; see also Jay to TJ, 14 Dec. 1786). Although there is nothing in Jay's postscript to identify the "three Acts of Congress," the other two were doubtless the following: (4) A resolution of Congress of 20 Oct. 1786 providing for raising troops for the defense of the western country, and authorizing the board of the treasury "to devise ways and means for the pay and support of the troops of the United States" (JCC, XXXI, 891-3). (5) A resolution of Congress of 21 Oct. 1786 authorizing the board of treasury to "open a loan immediately to the amount of five hundred thousand dollars" (same, p. 893-6).

A FEW LINES BY THE LAST FRENCH PACKET: See Jay to TJ, 12 Oct. 1786.

[1] The following is deleted in Dft: "but not having received other."
[2] The following is deleted in Dft: "or Col. Smith."

To David Ramsay

DEAR SIR   Paris Oct. 27. 1786.

I mentioned to you in a former letter that as the booksellers in London were afraid to sell your book there, I would have some copies brought here, advertising in the London papers that they could be furnished weekly from hence by the Diligence. 50 copies are just arrived, and 50 more are on the way. The translation will come from the press in a few days.[1]

Having observed the immense consumption of rice in this country, it became matter of wonder to me why so few ships come here with that article from S. Carolina and Georgia. The information I received on my first enquiries was that little Carolina rice came here because it was less clean and less good than what is brought them from the Levant. Further enquiry however has satisfied me of the inexactitude of this information. The case is as follows. About one half the rice consumed in France is from Carolina. The other half is chiefly from Piedmont. The Piedmont rice is thought by connoisseurs to be best *au gras*, the Carolina rice best *au lait*. Yet the superior whiteness of the latter is so much more pleasing to the eye as to compensate with many purchasers it's deficiency in quality. Carolina rice sells at Havre by wholesale at 22, 23, and 24 livres the French quintal, the livre being 10d sterling and the French quintal 109 ℔. the English. At the approach of Lent it rises to 27 livres. It is retailed in Paris at from 6 to 10 sous the French pound according to it's quality, being sorted. Piedmont rice sells always at 10 sous (5d sterling) the pound. In the wholesale it is 3 or 4 livres the quintal dearer than Carolina rice. This would supplant that of Piedmont if brought in sufficient quantity, and to France directly. But it is first carried and deposited in England, and it is the merchant of that country who sends it here, [drawing] a great profit himself, while the commodity is moreover subjected to the expences of a double voiage. You will perceive by the inclosed letter that the government here is disposed to encourage it's importation. I think they will receive it duty free, or under a very light duty, barely sufficing to indicate the quantity imported. When I compare the price of this article here with what it is in London or Charlestown, I cannot help hoping the difference will be sufficient to draw to this country immediately what it's consumption would call for. It must come to Havre or Rouen and must arrive there in time to reach Paris by the 1st of February, that is to say a month before the Careme, as most persons lay in their provision of rice during that period. This condition is so indispensible that it certainly loses it's sale if it arrives later. I send you some specimens of the different kinds of rice as sold here. If by making known these details, you think the intercourse between our country and this may be improved, I am sure you will take on yourself the trouble of doing it, nobody being more sensible than you are of the motives both moral and political which should induce us to bind the two countries together by as many ties as possible of interest and affection. [I cannot pretend to affirm that this country will stand by us on every just occasion. But I am sure, if this will not, there is no other on earth that will. I am with very great esteem Dear Sir your most obedient & most humble servant, TH: JEFFERSON][2]

PrC (DLC); written with TJ's left hand. Enclosure: Printed text of Calonne to TJ, 22 Oct. 1786.

With the exception of the beginning and close of this letter, as indicated in notes 1 and 2, the full text was printed by Ramsay in the *South Carolina Gazette* on the suggestion of some members of the legislature to whom it had been shown and who thought it would be "beneficial to the public and not indelicate" to be printed (Ramsay to TJ, 7 Apr. 1787). Thus it came to be reprinted in other papers and in *The American Museum*, July 1787, II, 83. Otto in New York came upon this public version of the letter and transmitted it to Vergennes on 30 Mch. 1787 with the following comment: "Vous verrés par la lettre ci jointe de M. Jefferson que ce ministre desire infiniment d'attirer les Caroliniens en france. Le dernier paragraphe de cette Lettre contient un temoignage si evident de ses bonnes dispositions envers nous qu'il sert de preuve à ce que j'ai eu l'honneur de Vous mander précédemment à son egard" (Arch. Aff. Etr., Corr. Pol., E.-U., XXXII; the text of TJ's letter in French is in same, with the following caption: "Traduction d'une Lettre de M. Jefferson, Ministre Plenipre. des Etats unis près de Sa Majesté, à un Delegué de la Caroline Meridionale"—a translation of the caption with which TJ's letter appeared in print). The "dernier paragraphe" to which Otto referred was not, of course, the final paragraph of the letter as written. This partial publication was timely and perhaps helped to counterbalance the effect of the unauthorized publication of TJ's letter to Jay of 27 May 1786, q.v. At the time Otto transmitted the printed version, Van Berckel, the Dutch minister, had just protested to Congress against the Virginia Act granting exemption of duties to French brandies as being in violation of the most-favored-nation clause of the Treaty with the Netherlands of 1782, a protest which, on Jay's report, Congress in Oct. 1787 conceded to be valid (Van Berckel to Jay, 20 Feb. 1787, DNA: PCC, No. 99; JCC, XXXII, 116; XXXIII, 453, 676). The Virginia delegates in Congress met with Otto on this matter in Mch. 1787 —having already been in consultation with him on the Mississippi question (Madison to TJ, 19 Mch. 1787)—and agreed to argue that the Virginia Act was not in the nature of a special favor to France but "une compensation des avantages mentionnés dans la lettre de M. Calonne à M. Jefferson." Otto thought that this explanation, though a bit strained, would be useful, and added: "Les Virginiens . . . ne se bornent pas aux faveurs qu'ils ont accordées à nos eaux de vie et à nos vins, ils se proposent de les etendre à nos soiries et à nos draps. M. Grayson un de leurs Delegués qui nous est le plus devoué vient de me dire qu'il regarde cette mesure comme indispensable afin d'emanciper son Etat des entraves du Commerce Anglois. Il veut lui même en faire la motion dans la prochaine Assemblée et il m'a demandé si un droit de 100. sous par aune sur les etoffes Angloises n'equivaudroit pas à une prohibition. Je lui ai fait observer qu'il seroit dangereux de porter cette mesure aussi loin de peur de la faire annuller par une assemblée subsequente, mais qu'un droit modique suffiroit pour mettre le commerçant françois au dessus de la concurrence, ce qui auroit d'ailleurs l'avantage de ne pas exciter les clameurs et les intrigues du parti Anglois'—Il a gouté ce raisonnement et il va s'occuper des moyens de faire passer sa motion. J'entre dans ces details . . . puisque la Virginie ainsi que la Caroline offre sans aucune comparaison le plus grand debouché à notre commerce" (Otto to Vergennes, 30 Mch. 1787; Arch. Aff. Etr., Corr. Pol., E.-U., XXXII; transcripts in DLC). But this affair, as the ardent Francophile Grayson later pointed out in a "perfectly confidential" letter to William Short, had opened the eyes of Congress so that they were beginning to "recover from their *treaty madness*" (Grayson to Short, 16 Apr. 1787; Burnett, *Letters of Members*, VIII, No. 639).

[1] This paragraph is not included in the text as printed in *The American Museum* and newspapers, and is not in the translation as sent by Otto to Vergennes.

[2] The passage in brackets (supplied) is not in the text as published and is not in the Otto translation.

From John Bondfield

SIR Bordeaux 28. 8bre. 1786

By mine of the 14 Instant I advised of my having given two

drafts on you, favor Monsieur Dumez, together amounting to two Thousand Livres. If they have not been presented for payment I pray you to refuse payment of them having cause to suspect the due application for which they were intended. I have the honor to be respectfully Sir your most obedient Humble Servant,

JOHN BONDFIELD

RC (DLC); addressed; endorsed by TJ with his left hand. Noted in SJL as received 4 Nov. 1786.

Circular Letter to United States Consular Agents

SIR   Paris Oct. 29th. 1786

I inclose to you the copy of a letter which I have had the honor of receiving from his Excellency M. de Calonne, one of his Majesty's ministers, wherein he is pleased to communicate to me sundry regulations lately made for the encouragement of the commerce between France and the United States of America. The favorable footing on which American productions will now be received in the ports of this country, will, I hope, occasion a more general introduction of them; and when brought hither, I equally hope that motives both of interest and gratitude will combine to induce the importers to take in exchange the productions of this country. A commerce carried on by exchange of productions is the most likely to be lasting and to meet mutual encouragement. You will be pleased to communicate the contents of the inclosed letter to the persons at your port concerned in the American trade, but so that it may not get into the public papers. You will observe that the articles of rice and ship-duties are still to be provided for. I shall be obliged to you if you will inform me what duties are paid on American rice on it's importation into your port, and to give me a distinct detail of the several port duties and ship-duties paid by American vessels coming thither, noting on what or by what name they are payable, their amount, for whose profit they are, by what title they are received, and the laws which authorize them, in order that we may be enabled to get these articles settled also. I have the honor to be with great respect, Sir, your most obedient & most humble servant,   TH: JEFFERSON

PrC and 2d PrC (DLC); in Short's hand, including signature; at foot of text: "(Test: W Short Sec)." Enclosure: Printed copy of Calonne to TJ, 22 Oct. 1786.

From Maria Cosway

[London, 30 Oct. 1786]

[How I wish I?] could answer the Dialogue! But I hon[estly think my hear?]t is invisable, and Mute, at this moment more than usual[l it is?] full or ready to burst with all the variety of Sentiments, wh[ich] a very feeling one is Capable of; sensible of My loss a[t] separating from the friends I left at Paris, I have hardly time to indulge a shamisly[1] tribute; but My thoughts Must be contrasted by the joy of Meeting my friends in London. It is an excess which Must tear to peices a human Mind, when felt. You seem to be Such a Master on this subject, that whatever I may say will appear trifelling, not well express'd, faintly represented * * * but felt. Your letter could employ me for some time, an hour to Consider every word, to every sentence I could write a volume, but I could wish that my selfishness was not reproching to Me, for with difficulty do I find a line but after having admired it, I recolect some part concerns Me. Why do you say so Many kind things? Why present so many opportunities for my feeling undeserving of them, why not leave me a free consolation in admiring a friend, without the temptation [....] to my Vanity? I wish your heart [....] for it is too good. It expands to the Objects he [....] too Much of his own, and blinds the reality of its demerit.[2] Ma cosa fo! Che scrivo tanto Inglese, Mentre posso scrivere nella Mia lingua, e rendermi un poco Meno imbrogliata, non sapevo cosa facevo, la vorrei riscrivere. Ma non gli voglio Mandare il primo foglio, le prime righe scritte al mio arrivo a Londra, siano le consequenze qual si voglia, Oh Sir se la Mia Corrispondenza valesse la sua quanto sarebbe perfetta! Non posso che esprimere la mia riconoscenza nella sua Amicizia. Mi perdoni se i suoi Comandi non furono ubbiditi, riguardo il tempo limitatomi per leggere la sua lettera Fu uno dei Miei primi piaceri il trovarla e non potei resistere all desiderio di leggerla subito, anche a costo di cometter un Atto di disabidienza. Mi perdoni, il delitto lo Merita. Il nostro viaggio è stato felice, la Mia salute perfettamente ristabilita, il tempo buono eccettuato quei giorni precedenti alla nostra partenza da Parigi, la Compagnia di Mr. Trumbull [simpatica?] e piacevole. Ma Londra, l'ing[rata città?...] tra la nebbia e il fummo, la tristezza par [...]gra in ogni cuore, se si deve giudicare dalle fisonomie che s'incontrano; bisogna che ritorni il piu presto possibile alle mie Occupazioni per non sentire il rigore della Malinconia che inspira questo ingrato Clima, il ni Compagnia di amici che piacciono, esercitando un poco

30 OCTOBER 1786

le belle arti, si può spesso evitar la tristezza, se qualcosa Manca alla perfetta felicità. Tutto è tranquillo, quieto, e tristo, non ci son Campane che suonano per annunziarci qualche festa, uffizzio, o gala, anche quando richiamano un *Deprofundis* s'accompagna con la speranza che quel anima passata a Miglior Vita gode quelle quiete beata, che il Mondo non accorda Mai a pieno: qui si sente la notte una voce ad ogni Ora che c'annunzia che è passata, ci soviene che non torna piu, e ci lascia spesso con la Mortificazione che l'abbiamo *persa*. Non ci son Monasteri ore son rinchiusi religiosi i quali a tutte le ore pregano per noi, e per chi non prega, quanti son persi, o nelle strade, o all gioco, nel vizzio, e l'Ozzio. [. . . .] come a Cominciato, a scriv[ere; le sue lettere] non saranno Mai abbastanza lunghe, quando [. . .] nelle sere lunghe del'inverno che li rimane qualche Momento non Occupato, lo Sacrifichi a Me, a Mandarmi Sue Nuove. Mi par Mill'Anni di ricevere una lettera dalla Man dritta, gli deve esser Molto scomodo scrivere con la Manca. Questo Sacrifizio Sarà ricevuto con tanta gratitudine, che dando fede alle promesse fatteci per le buone azzioni, invocherò per la sua ricompensa.

Mio Marito gli fa Mille Complimenti, la prego presentar i Nostri a Mr. Short, a Monr. D'ancherville quando lo vede. Non Mi scorderò Mai della sua attenzione per nai. Qualche volta Mentoveremo il Meditato giro l'anno venturo, se a Parigi, se in Italia. Molte cose ponno impedirne l'esecuzione, Ma anche Maggior impossibilità Son State esercitate. Accetti i Miei auguri per la sua salute e felicità e Mi creda la Sua Molto obligata ed affma. Amica.

MARIA COSWAY

[*On verso of address cover:*] pray half of me with Madme D[e Corny . . .] always when you are with her. I [. . .] very Much, and shall be happy to be [. . .] remembered to her by you.

RC (MHi); MS mutilated, the top edges of the pages having been eaten away evidently by rodents; a few words or parts of words have been supplied conjecturally at the beginnings or ends of lines where at most three or four words have been lost from the text; the missing date has been supplied from internal evidence and from an entry in SJL of the receipt of a letter of this date on 8 Nov. 1786; at foot of text: "Mrs. Cosway Pall Mall London—questo indirizzo basta" (this address is sufficient).

Translation of that part of the text in Italian: But what am I doing, that I write so much English when I can write in my own language, and become a little less involved. I did not know what I was doing, I should like to write it over again. But do I not wish to send you the first sheet, the first lines written upon my arrival in London, let the consequences be what they may? Oh, Sir, if my correspondence equalled yours how perfect it would be! I can only express my gratitude in your friendship. Forgive me if your orders were not obeyed regarding the time allotted me to read your letter. It was one of my first pleasures to find it and I could not resist the desire to read it at once, even at the cost of committing an act of disobedience. Forgive me, the crime merits it. Our voyage was a happy one, my health perfectly restored, the weather good except for those days preceding our departure from Paris, the Company of Mr. Trumbull [congenial] and pleasant. But London, the [unpleasant city . . .] amid the fog and smoke, sadness seems [to reign] in every heart, if one is to judge from the physiognomies one meets; I must return as soon as possible to my occupations in order not to feel the rigor of the Melancholy which is inspired by this unpleasant climate. In the company of agreeable friends, practising the fine arts a little, one can often avoid sadness, even if something is lacking for perfect happiness. Everything is tranquil, quiet and gloomy, there are no Bells ringing to announce to us some festival, service or celebration; even when they call for a *Deprofundis* it is accompanied by the hope that that soul passed to a Better Life, is enjoying that blessed quiet which the World never grants in full: here at night you hear a voice at every hour which announces to us the fact that it has passed, which reminds us that it will never more return and often leaves us with the Mortifying sense that we have *lost* it. There are no Monasteries which contain men of God who at all hours pray for us and for all those who do not pray, all who are lost, either in the streets or gambling, in vice and Idleness. [. . .] you have begun to [write . . . your letters] will never be long enough, when [. . .] in the long winter evenings there is left some idle moment, sacrifice it to me, to sending me news of yourself. I can hardly wait to receive a letter from your right Hand, it must be very inconvenient for you to write with your Left. This sacrifice will be received with so much gratitude as, putting faith in the promises made us for good actions, I shall invoke for your reward.

My Husband sends you a thousand Compliments, I beg you to present ours to Mr. Short, to Monr. D'ancherville when you see him. I shall never forget your attentions to us. Some times we shall mention our contemplated tour next year, either to Paris or to Italy. Many things can prevent its execution, but even greater impossibilities have been carried out. Accept my best wishes for your health and happiness and believe me your much obliged and affectionate Friend.

[1] This word is as doubtful to the Editors as the spelling evidently was to Mrs. Cosway, part of the word being deleted and another version of that part interlined. She may have intended it to read "shameless."

[2] This word doubtful, but the meaning is evident.

To Charles Boromée LeBrun

SIR   Paris Oct. 30th. 1786

I have been honored with the memorial which you were pleased to address to me on the arrearages of interest due to you from the United States. It belongs to the Commissioners of the treasury of the United States to furnish monies to M. Grand who is their banker, so that it is a matter not at all within the limits of my office. However I have joined my representations to those of Mr. Grand in order to induce the Commissioners to enable him to comply with these demands, and I am persuaded they will do it the first moment it shall be in their power. As soon as Mr. Grand shall have received supplies, he will give notice to the Gentleman to whom monies are due, so that you may rely on hearing from him as soon as he shall be enabled to pay the interest due to you.

I have the honor to be Sir, your most obedient humble servant,

TH: JEFFERSON

PrC (DLC); in Short's hand, including signature; at foot of text: "(Test W Short Sec.)."

To Zachariah Loreilhe

Sir   Paris Octr. 30th. 1786

The order which you have received from Mr. Barclay for the purchase of gun-powder and other military items for the State of Virginia, was proper, and I believe the funds here would suffice to pay for them, though I have not lately enquired into their amount. But there is a circumstance of which Mr. Barclay is not apprized which will render it proper to defer the purchase till the spring of the year. At that time I shall take the liberty of writing to you and of availing the State of your willingness to execute the order.

I have the honor to be Sir, your most obedient humble servant,

Th: Jefferson

PrC (DLC); in Short's hand, including signature; at foot of text: "(Test: W Short Sec.)."

From William Macarty

Sir   Lorient 30th Octr. 1786.

I have procured some Dishes, petits Pots and Compotiers exactly like the patren and they will be sent off imediately. I cannot find any others that will answer. Should you want any larger Dishes, Soup Turiens, Sauce Boats or plates in plenty they can be had.

I am very Respectfully Your most obedt. Sert.,

Wm. Macarty

RC (DLC); endorsed by TJ with his left hand. Noted in SJL as received 3 Nov. 1786, but dated 31 Oct. in that entry.

From Vergennes

A fontau. le 31 8bre. 1786

Jai l'honneur Monsieur de vous envoyer les deux passeports que vous avez demandés pour la libre exportation des Ports de Bordeaux et du havre d'une certaine quantité de munitions de guerre que vous avez achetés par ordre de l'Etat de Virginie où vous vous proposez de les faire passer.

FC (Arch. Aff. Etr., Corr. Pol., E.-U.; XXXII; Tr in DLC). Noted in SJL as received 1 Nov. 1786.

To Chastellux

Th: J. to M. de Chastellux [Oct. 1786]

Among the topics of conversation which stole off like so many minutes the few hours I had the happiness of possessing you at Monticello, the Measure of English verse was one. I thought it depended, like Greek and Latin verse, on long and short syllables arranged into regular feet. You were of a different opinion. I did not pursue this subject after your departure, because it always presented itself with the painful recollection of a pleasure which, in all human probability, I was never to enjoy again. This probability like other human calculations, has been set aside by events: and we have again discussed, on this side the Atlantic, a subject which had occupied us during some pleasing moments on the other. A daily habit of walking in the Bois de Boulogne gave me an opportunity of turning this subject in my mind and I determined to present you my thoughts on it in the form of a letter. I for some time parried the difficulties which assailed me in attempting to prove my proposition: but at length I found they were not to be opposed, and their triumph was complete. Error is the stuff of which the web of life is woven: and he who lives longest and wisest is only able to wear out the more of it. I began with the design of converting you to my opinion that the arrangement of long and short syllables into regular feet constituted the harmony of English verse: I ended by discovering that you were right in denying that proposition. The next object was to find out the real circumstance which gives harmony to English poetry and laws to those who make it. I present you with the result. It is a tribute due to your friendship. It is due to you also as having recalled me from an error in my native tongue, and that too in a point the most difficult of all others to a foreigner, the law of it's poetical numbers.

MS (DLC); written with TJ's left hand. Not dated and not recorded in SJL, this letter may never have been sent, for the Editors are assured by M. le Duc de Duras, Chateau Chastellux, Yonne, France, that neither the essay, "Thoughts on English Prosody," nor the letter is among the Archives de Chastellux, though other letters from TJ to Chastellux are (see Vol. 7:581). The letter, being in TJ's left hand, was certainly written after 18 Sep. and probably before mid-November 1786. The rough draft of "Thoughts on English Prosody," which occupies 27 pages and is in DLC: TJ Papers, 234:41823-37 —though seriously disordered—has been printed without correction of the disorder in L & B, xviii, 413-51, and elsewhere; it will be published in the Literary Miscellany, Second Series. This draft is in TJ's right hand, and has numerous corrections and deletions, some of which are in his left hand. It could, therefore, have been written at any time between Aug. 1784 and 18 Sep. 1786. The Editors think that in all likelihood it was composed during the summer of 1786 and that TJ had about completed the rough draft when the accident to his wrist befell him. This accident threw an additional burden of work upon his secretary, William Short, and TJ, evidently not wishing to lose the value of a work on which he had clearly expended so great an amount of time and thought, composed the present letter, making also a few corrections on the manuscript itself preparatory to having a fair copy made. He may even have thought of transcribing it himself with his left hand or have laid it aside to copy when he recovered the use of his right hand. But that recovery was exceedingly slow, public business continued to press upon him, and in the spring of 1787 his long absence in the South of France added both to his own labors and to those of Short. The transcribing of so lengthy a document, which because of its very nature and the state of the rough draft would have been an arduous undertaking, may have been deferred from time to time until 24 Oct. 1788 when the death of Chastellux rendered it futile so far as its original purpose was concerned. This is conjectural, but it is a conjecture supported by the fact that the extant text of the letter is *not* a press copy but the original MS, a fact which it is difficult to explain on any other ground. If he had needed a retained copy, TJ surely would not have failed to use his copying press in this instance when, as he stated to Thomson, writing with his left hand was so slow and awkward as to be done but in "cases of necessity" (TJ to Thomson, 17 Dec. 1787); the "cases of necessity" may have included a four-thousand-word letter to Maria Cosway, but it is doubtful if they would have included the making of two copies of the present letter, one to be sent to Chastellux and the other to be retained. The absence of any acknowledgement from Chastellux of the letter or the essay on English versification points to the same conclusion. It is, of course, possible that Short transcribed copies of both the letter and the essay, but the Editors do not believe this likely; in view of all the circumstances, they are convinced that Chastellux never saw either the letter or the essay.

To Martha Jefferson

[Oct. 1786]

I will call for you today, my dear between twelve and one. You must be dressed, because we drink tea with Mrs. Montgomery. Bring your music and drawings. Adieu my dear Patsy.

MS not found; text printed from a photostat in NcD; unsigned, undated, and unaddressed. This note was written with TJ's left hand, and therefore belongs to some date after 18 Sep., when TJ injured his wrist, and before mid-November, when he began to resume use of his right hand (also Mrs. Montgomery left Paris soon after this; see TJ to Mrs. Montgomery, 19 Nov. 1786). It is certain that TJ saw Martha on 5, 10, and 19 Oct., and 9 Nov. 1786, for the Account Book for the first three of these dates reads: "gave Patsy 3f"; and for the last, "gave Patsy 6f." The first date is improbable, for that was the date when TJ had returned from St. Denis "more dead than alive" and in considerable distress from his wrist and his sleepless night; the last is also improbable, since TJ began soon after that date to use his right hand (see TJ to Jay, 12 Nov, 1786). It seems reasonable to conclude, then, that the note must have been written during Oct. and perhaps about mid-month. See also TJ to Martha Jefferson, 4 Nov. 1786.

From Jean Durival, with Enclosure

A fontainebleau le per. Novembre 1786.

Un écrivain, Monsieur, occupé d'un ouvrage monnétaire, m'a adressé le Mémoire cy-joint, et m'a engagé à avoir l'honneur de vous le communiquer en vous priant de vouloir bien lui procurer quelques lumieres sur les monnoyes fabriquées ou en circulation dans les Provinces Unies de l'Amérique Septentrionale. Si vous pouvez, Monsieur, concourir aux vuës louables de l'auteur monnétaire dont il s'agit, je vous serai très obligé de vouloir bien ajouter vos appostilles à côté du petit nombre d'articles de son Mémoire et de me le renvoyer pour le lui rendre.

Je profite avec empressement de cette occasion pour vous assurer du très parfait attachement avec lequel J'ai l'honneur d'être, Monsieur, Votre très humble et très obéissant serviteur,

DURIVAL

ENCLOSURE

Extrait du Courier de L'Europe du 14 mars 1786. No. 21. vol. 19 page 167.

Etats unis de L'Amerique 30. Xbre. 1785

Le Congrès vient de faire frapper des Espeçes de cuivre, qui sont actuellement en circulation; D'un coté on lit çes mots *Libertas et justitia*, qui entourent les lettres U.S. plaçées en Chifre dans le centre, les quelles signifient *united States*, (Etats unis), Sur le Revers on voit un soleïl levant Environné de treize etoiles, avec cette inscription autour, *constellatio nova*.

On desireroit Savoir Si, Comme l'annonçe le Courier de L'Europe dans le paragraphe cy-dessus Coppié, le Congrès a Reellement fait fabriquer Des Espeçes De cuivre a son coin?

Si ces Espeçes, sont comme celles de françe, Divisées en Sols, demi sols et quart de Sols; quelle est enfin leur Division, leur dénomination, et la valeur pour la quelle elles ont cours? quel peut estre le diametre de la principale de ces Espeçes, et de chacune de ses Subdivisions?

Si l'on avoit un Exemplaire de l'ordonnance qui en a autorisé la fabrication, et la circulation, on Desireroit d'En avoir une Coppie, ou la communication, on auroit soin de la rendre avec la plus grande Exactitude.

Le Congrès n'ayant jusques a present fait frapper aucunes Espeçes d'or et d'argent, on desireroit savoir pour quelle valeur, a peu près, les Espeçes d'or, et d'argent, d'angleterre, de françe, d'Espagne, du portugal et de la hollande sont admises communement dans la çirculation.

RC (DLC); in a clerk's hand, signed by Durival. Enclosure (DLC); in a clerk's hand; at head of text in Durival's hand: "à communiquer à M. Jefferson 1er. novembre 1786."

From Antoine-Félix Wuibert

Monsieur   Philadelphie 1r. 9bre. 1786.

Six Semaines après mon arrivée chez moi, J'ay Reçu, avec bien du plaisir, Vos deux Lettres de Mai et Juin derniers, dont il a plut à Votre Excellence m'honnorer. Dans la derniere etaient incluses quelqu'autres Lettres de ma famille de tout quoy Je Vous fais mes très Sincères remerciments.

Par Votre derniere Comme dans la prémiere, Je Reconnais que Vous avez bien Voulu avoir la Complaisance d'Intervenir; en mon nom, en Ce qui me Concerne en parts-de-prises, montant à la Somme de 2044.^{tt} argent de france, que Je ne peux, en Honneur! Considérer que Comme un acompte d'une plus forte part ou Somme et à raison du poste que J'occupais à bord du B. H. Richard pendant toute la Campagne de 1779, Sous Les yeux du Commodore P. Jones.

Depuis ma Lettre du Cap français à Votre Excellence, J'ai eté Instruit par mon Pere d'une Supercherie aussi malhonnête qu'injuste de la part d'un nommé Chamillard qui a touché la plus grande partie de mes parts-de-prises en Se donnant le titre de premier Commandant de Volontaires; Ce que J'avance ici, Monsieur, est un fait, découvert et reconnû par un des plus Honnetes Hommes de l'Univers, C'est Notre Digne Commodore. Il a Eu la Complaisance de protéger mes interets Vis-à-Vis du Commissaire, mais, le Sr. Clouët, ne Jugeant pas à propos de redresser l'Erreur à mon préjudice, l'a Laissé toujours Subsister: peu après Notre Commodore avertit Charitablement ma famille d'un procedé aussi detestable de la part de Ce Chamillard, qu'injuste de Celle du Sr. Clouët: de Sorte que Je regarde cette affaire Jusqu'aujourd'huy Comme très-imparfaite.

Sur L'avis du Commodore par la Lettre de mon pere, J'Eus l'Honneur d'Envoyer ma plainte en 2ta. [duplicata] à Mr. Le Maal. De Castries Les 4. et 8. mai dernier; jusqu'à présent J'ignore Si Ce ministre les a reçûes, Car Il y a plus d'Infidèles dans les Cours que dans Les provinces. Ma plainte est Sous deux Couverts, le premier J'ai Ecris "Pour Vous Seul Monseigneur" Le Second est directé Comme de Coutume. Je me Suis Servi de cette methode, parceque Les Commis ne Sont pas aussi Honnêtes que de raison et que Chamillard, pour Couvrir Son Escroquerie, peut S'Etre procuré quelque protecteur ou Protectrice dans les Bureaux. Si Cette plainte a Eu le bonheur de tomber entre Les mains du Marêchal, Je Compte Sur Sa Justice, Car Il a la reputation d'Etre très délicat

Sur le point d'Honneur: quoiqu'il en Soit, J'aimerais beaucoup mieux debattre pareille Cause ici, en Amérique! qu'en France, où Il faut un front-d'airain et une Langue-Dorée pour reussir dans tout Ce qu'on Entreprend généralement.

Permettez, Je Vous prie, Monsieur, de me reclamer de la Continuation de Vos bontées à mon Egard, au Cas que le Ministre de la Marine Daigne me rendre Justice. En Conséquence de quoy et reçevant ma Légitime part-de-prise, Je Serais au Comble de la Joye que Vous Voulussiez me l'Envoyer Comme Vous l'avez deja fait en partie. Puisse Votre Excellence mettre le Comble à Ses bontées, en prélevant et abandonnant à mon pere une Somme de 600.ᵗᵗ Je Dis *Six Cent Livres* argent de france au dessus et en outre de Celle de 400.ᵗᵗ qu'il a deja reçû; C'est tout Ceque Je peux faire actuellement, Je Verrai a mieux faire par la Suite. L'argent dur est très rare ici et J'en ai grand besoin pour faire [face aux] Circonstances imprévuës et fréquentes dans un pays où Il n'y a qu'un papier Courrant. Mon Pere injustement me fait des Reproches, Je ne puis qu'y faire, Je ne suis pas le maitre des Evenemens et des affaires: Je Serais au Comble de la Joye de pouvoir Vivre chez Lui, mais l'Expérience que J'ay aujourdhuy de la Morgue française et le Dégout que J'ay pour son Gouvernement, me faira Vivre pour toujours en Amérique: C'est un parti pris et dont Je m'applaudis tous Les Jours.

Depuis que le Comptrolleur-général de la Pennsylvanie a accepté mon Certifficat de paye de la guerre derniere, l'Interet annuel me mêt à meme de Vivre avec Satisfaction, et tel qu'un Homme Sage doit Vivre, Je Sçais me passer de beaucoup de choses depuis dix Ans. Actuellement Je me porte bien, à l'Exception de ma Jambe gauche qui est encore un peu Enflée, mais Cet Hiver y mettra bon ordre et J'Espere que Je reverray encore une fois les pays-indiens qui ont pour moi plus de Charmes que les grandes Villes du monde.

Daignez, Monsieur, Agréer Les Voeux les plus fervents que J'adresse au Ciel pour L'accomplissement général de Vos desirs et l'Heureuse Conservation de Votre Personne.

J'ay L'Honneur d'Etre avec un profound Respect Monsieur De Votre Excellence Le plus Humble & plus Obeissant Serviteur,

    Colonel Wuibert, Cincinnatus

RC (DLC); endorsed. Noted in sjl as received 25 Feb. 1787.

vos deux lettres: TJ to Wuibert, 22 May 1786 and TJ to Wuibert, 3 June 1786; the latter has not been found, but is recorded in sjl under that date with the following notation: "inclosing papers from M. Troye."

From John Banister, Jr.

Dear Sir   Nantes Novr. 2d. 1786

Since I had the pleasure to address you last a severe fit of illness seized me which together with the idea I had of your having left Paris was the cause of my long silence. Mr. Short in a letter he wrote me gave me the disagreeable intelligence of your having been prevented undertaking your intended journey by the ill effects of a fall the consequences of which I hope are not very serious. Long before this I expected to be in Paris, and waite now, only for strength to set out, so that the time is not far distant as I recover with great rapidity. The latest accounts I have from America are dated in June but they contain nothing of consequence, except infinite murmurs in some of the Northern states on account of the emission of a paper currency.

In the idea of being informed of your perfect recovery I have the plesure to be with the greatest respect Dear Sir your friend and Servt.,   Jno. Banister Junr.

RC (MHi). Noted in SJL as received 5 Nov. 1786.

To John Bondfield

Sir   Paris Novr. 2d. 1786

I have now the honor to inclose you the passeport for two thousand five hundred stand of arms, powder and other articles purchased and to be purchased for the State of Virginia. This passeport is to serve as well for what you have received as for what you will receive hereafter till its amount is satisfied. You will observe they are to pass free of all duty, but whether this will entitle us to have the duties already paid, remitted to us, you will have the goodness to see. Notwithstanding constant sollicitation I have not been able to obtain the passeport sooner, owing I suppose to the delay of the bureaux. Considering that the winter is now set in, I refer it to your better judgment, whether it might not be more advisable to defer the shipment of these articles till the spring of the ensuing year.

I have the honor to be Sir, your most obedient humble servant,
                                                Th: Jefferson

PrC (DLC); in Short's hand, including signature; at foot of text: "(Test W Short Sec)." Enclosure not found.

To Calonne

Sir   Paris Novr. 2. 1786

I have been honored with your Excellency's letter of October the 22d. wherein you communicate to me the regulations which His Majesty the King has been pleased lately to establish in favor of the commerce between his subjects and the Citizens of the United States. I availed myself of the first occasion of conveying this information to Congress, who will recieve with singular satisfaction this new proof of His Majesty's friendship, and of his willingness to multiply the ties of interest and of intercourse between the two nations. Favors are doubly precious which, promoting the present purposes of interest and of friendship, enlarge the foundations for their continuance and increase. The part which your Excellency has been pleased to take in the establishment of these regulations merits and meets my sincere thanks, and add a title the more to those sentiments of profound esteem and respect with which I have the honor to be your Excellency's most obedient and most humble servant,   Th: Jefferson

PrC (DLC); in Short's hand, signed by TJ with his left hand.

To André Limozin

Paris, 2 Nov. 1786. This letter is almost identical with TJ's letter to John Bondfield of this date, q.v., with the exception that it encloses passports for "two thousand four hundred cartouch boxes and accoutrements which will be the amount of the whole purchase when it shall be completed."

PrC (DLC); 1 p.; in Short's hand, including signature; at foot of text: "(Test W Short Sec)."

From C. W. F. Dumas

Monsieur   La haie 3e. Nov. 1786

Vos précieuses Notes sont actuellement entre les mains d'un Lecteur qui sait vraiment lire, qui me remercie toutes les fois que nous nous voyons de l'avoir ragouté par ce morceau, parce qu'il ne paroissoit depuis longtemps que de la crême fouettée. Il me fait des excuses de ce qu'il lit lentement, parce que cette Lecture mérite de n'être pas faite en courant: Que maintes lignes y ont couté autant d'années de travail et de recherches, et qu'il lui faut autant de jours pour les savourer.

Permettez que je présente à Mr. le Ms. de la Fayette les assurances de mon respect. Je suis avec tout celui qui vous est si justement dû, De Votre Excellence, le très-humble et très obeissant serviteur, C W F Dumas

RC (DLC). FC (Rijksarchief, The Hague, Dumas Papers; photostats in DLC). Noted in SJL as received 8 Nov. 1786.

Although no enclosure is mentioned in this letter, it is probable that Dumas transmitted with it his letter to Jay of 4 Nov. 1786 (FC, same), giving further news of political developments in Holland and urging relief for himself in respect to arrearages due from Congress. Dumas may also have written TJ on 7 Nov. 1786, for on that date he wrote Lafayette: "J'envoie aujourd'hui à Mr. Jefferson une Lettre . . . qui contient une Piece très-remarquable: c'est le Contre-Protest de la Majorité des Villes de Hollande opposé au Protest du Corps des Nobles. Cette Piece pourroit parôitre longue et tédieuse à certain vulgaire qui voudroit que tout fût Epigramme et Vaudeville. Mais il n'en est pas ainsi de vous, M. le Marquis, de Mr. Jefferson et du Congrès, près desquels la matiere me rassure, sur la forme et sur la peine que j'ai prise de la rendre fidelement.—Je serai bien aise, Mr. le Marquis, que vous voyiez aussi ma Lettre qui y est jointe à Mr. Jay. Vous jugerez avec Mr. Jefferson que l'insouciance continue de me faire mourir à petit feu, en me faisant mâcher à vide pour environ 30 m. Liv. t. d'arrerages qui me sont dus independamment des interets et que je ne puis toucher faute d'un ordre de la trésorerie, sur quoi au moins je croyois pouvoir compter, puisque c'est la volonté du Congrès, et que les Banquiers ici ne demanderaient pas mieux que de satisfaire à un tel ordre" (FC, same).

To Lafayette

Dear Sir   Paris Novr. 3d. 1786

I have recieved your favor of the second instant. The reason for my importing harness from England is a very obvious one. They are plated, and plated harness is not made at all in France as far as I have learnt. It is not from a love of the English but a love of myself that I sometimes find myself obliged to buy their manufactures. I must make one observation with respect to the use I make of my privilege. The minister of France in America has an unlimited privilege as to things *prohibited* as well as *dutied*. One third at least of the articles of consumption in his family must be foreign; not a twentieth part of those consumed in my family here are foreign; of course the loss of duties on that side the Atlantic is the triple of what it is on this. I have been moderate in my applications for passeports hitherto and I shall certainly continue to be so.

I shall be happy to know of your arrival in town and am with sincerity your affectionate friend & servant,

Th: Jefferson

3 NOVEMBER 1786

PrC (DLC); in Short's hand, including signature; at foot of text: "(Test W Short Sec)"; endorsed.

YOUR FAVOR OF THE SECOND INSTANT: Lafayette's letter of 2 Nov.
has not been found and is not recorded in SJL, but its import is as clear as TJ's resentment of the implications; see TJ to Vergennes, 15 Oct. 1786.

From John Trumbull

Dr. Sir   London 3d. Novr. 1786.

On my arrival I had the pleasure to find your letter of the 13th. Octr. enclosing one to Mrs. Cosway. You may conceive with what alacrity I executed the commission of delivering it with my own hand; you, who have so justly estimated the value of her acquaintance. I now have the pleasure of enclosing to you her return.

Thanks to her kind dissuasion, I did not go to Holland:—The Season of the Year, and the disturbd state of the country were arguments against the tour, but I should not have been deterrd by Dangers or Inconveniencies:—Her Voice was a more powerful Charm, and I could not resist the pleasure of accompanying her thro' Flanders:—We pass'd a fortnight in Antwerp and searchd the Town from the Cellar to the Garret—not a public or private collection, not a picture or print merchant escap'd us. We saw a multitude of fine things. Mr. Cosway bought several; and who would beleive it, I caught at last the mania, and bought for the first time two pictures:—From Antwerp we visited Ghent, stay'd 4 or 5 Days, and saw whatever was worth notice. Mr. Cosway again found some good bargains—One honest man among others we found, who sells pictures by weight. He had just dispos'd of 2 or 300 ℔, he told us, at seven sous the pound:—When you wish for bargains therefore, let me recommend this worthy man of Ghent. From Ghent we passed thro Menin, Ypres, Dunkirk &c. to Calais, where His Grace of Kingston had arriv'd the day before us. [It] was impossible to pass and not pay our Devoirs:—this stoppd us two days:—We cross'd in fine weather, with a fair wind, but not without many a sigh as the happy shore lessend behind us.

We reachd London the last of the Month and are at this moment buried in the melancholy obscurity of Smoke and Fog,—and surrounded by Faces, in whose gloomy length of feature the Month is sadly legible.

I am very sorry to learn that the hurt of your Arm is of such tedious consequence. Yet your philosophy draws good from the evil, and the accomplishment of writing with the left hand, which you have already, *à merveille*, is some consolation.—I wish you speedi-

[506]

est recovery and the enjoyment of a happier winter than I anticipate in this dirty Town.

I am Dr Sir with the warmest Esteem & Gratitude Your Obligd Friend & Servant,   JNO. TRUMBULL

P.S. I have also Mr. Short's of the 9th. enclosing an account of the placing of the Marquiss's Bust. As some account had already appear'd in the English papers, I was at a loss 'till I enquir'd of Colo. Smith and shew'd him WS's enclosure. As it is very different from what had appear'd Colo. S. has charg'd himself with the publication.

RC (DLC); addressed "Mr Jefferson"; endorsed by TJ with his left hand. Noted in SJL as received 8 Nov. 1786. Enclosure: Mrs. Cosway to TJ, 30 Oct. 1786.

From Cavalier, Fils

[*Dieppe, 4 Nov. 1786.* Recorded in SJL as received 7 Nov. 1786. Not found.]

To Martha Jefferson

MY DEAR PATSY   Saturday Nov. 4. [1786]

Two of your country-women, Mrs. Barrett and Mrs. Montgomery, will dine with me tomorrow. I wish you could come and dine with them. If you can obtain leave let me know in the morning and I will come for you between one and two o'clock. You must come dressed. Adieu my dear Patsy your's affectionately,

TH: J.

MS not found. Text printed from a photostat of RC in NcU; the following note appears on the verso of the second leaf: "Given to M. J. T. Burke by M. J. Randolph—July 22d. 1874." The year 1786 has been supplied in the date because the letter is written with TJ's left hand, and Saturday fell on 4 Nov. in that year. Not recorded in SJL.

From Vergennes

fontainebleau le 4 Novembre 1786

J'ai fait expédier, Monsieur, comme vous l'avez demandé, un Passeport de franchise pour quelques parties de vins étrangers qui doivent vous arriver des Ports de Marseille, Livourne et Lisbonne, pour votre usage et la consommation de votre maison à Paris. J'y ai fait comprendre le Clavecin qui vous vient de Londres, quoique cet objet de pur agrément, ne puisse pas être rangé dans la classe des articles usuels et de consommation. J'aurois desiré, Monsieur, pouvoir y faire employer aussi les harnois de fabrication angloise venant de Londres. Mais cet article est réputé Marchandise de contrebande, dont l'introduction dans le Royaume, au cas présent, ne peut pas être admise.

Quant aux presses à copier que vous attendez pareillement d'Angleterre, je vaïs en écrire à M. le Garde des Sceaux qui a la direction Générale de la Librairie, pour juger, si l'entrée de ces machines peut être autorisée sans inconvénient.

Dès que le passeport contenant les quatre autres articles cydessus, sera revêtu des formalités de règle en finance, j'aurai l'honneur de vous l'adresser.

J'ai celui d'être très parfaitement, Monsieur, Votre très humble et très obeissant Serviteur, DE VERGENNES

RC (DLC); endorsed by TJ with his left hand. Noted in SJL as received 6 Nov. 1786.

To John Bondfield

SIR   Paris Novr. 6th. 1786.

Your favor of the 28th. of October came to hand the day before yesterday. In the mean time your two bills had been presented; the smaller one drawn on my private account I had paid on sight; under the larger one I had written an acceptance and I think an order to Mr. Grand to pay it. I went immediately to Mr. Grand's; the bill had not been presented for payment and they assured me that by the usage of merchants in this country, the acceptor of a bill of exchange is bound to pay it; that it is no longer a debt of the drawer but of the acceptor, and that it would be personally dishonorable to me, were I to countermand the payment. Under this information I could not undertake to stop the payment. I have therefore only to lament that your letter did not arrive before I had paid the one bill of exchange and accepted the other, as I should have been happy to have done any thing I could to have guarded against a payment of the money, likely to be injurious to you.

I have the honor to be Sir your most obedient humble Servant,

TH: JEFFERSON

PrC (DLC); in Short's hand, including signature; at foot of text: "(Test W Short Sec)."

To St. John de Crèvecoeur

SIR   Paris Novr. 6th. 1786.

Congress have as yet come to no resolution as to the general redemption of paper money. That it is to be redeemed is a principle of which there is no doubt in the mind of any member of Congress, nor of any citizen of the United States. A Resolution of Congress taken in a particular case, which stood on the same ground on which the general one will stand, founds a presumption amounting nearly to certainty that they will pay to the holder of every bill what it cost him, or the persons whom he represents, at the time of recieving it, with an interest from that time of 6. ℞ Cent. They have of course established no rules of evidence as to the time of recieving the money. I think however that it would be advisable for M. de Lisle, or the representatives of Pelcerf to establish the time at which the money was recieved by the affidavits of such persons as know it. Those of disinterested persons would be best; but if there is no disinterested person acquainted with the fact, they will do well to take the affidavits of persons interested. It is probable that this kind of testimony will be admitted. At any rate it can do no harm. No particular form nor no terms of art are requisite for these affidavits. It will suffice if they state facts substantially and that the oath be administered by some person who by the laws of the country in which it is administered, is authorized to administer an oath.

I have the honor to be Sir your most obedient humble Servant,

TH: JEFFERSON

PrC (DLC); in Short's hand, including signature; at foot of text: "(Test W Short Sec)."

Thomas Barclay to the American Commissioners

GENTLEMEN   Madrid 7th. Nov. 1786.

I wrote to you from Cadiz the 2d. of last Month a Copy of which goes under the Cover of this and the Original with the Papers mentioned therein will I hope be very soon delivered to you by Colonel Franks.

On my arrival here I had the pleasure of receiving Mr. Jefferson's Letter of the 26th. of Septr. informing me that for the present any further attempts to arrange Matters with the Barbary States are

[509]

7 NOVEMBER 1786

suspended. I had determined as soon as I should know this to be the Case, to embark for America; but the Season being so far Advanced I shall put off the Voyage untill Spring, and hope to have the satisfaction of taking your Commands personally before I go. Mr. Carmichael communicated the whole of the Letters which Mr. Lamb has written to him from the time of his first leaving Madrid, and on the perusal it struck me that an interview with him might be attended with some desirable Consequences, especially as he had on Account of his Health declined Mr. Carmichael's request of coming to meet me at this place. If I had any doubts of the propriety of this Measure, they would have been removed by Mr. Carmichael's Opinion, and by the paragraph of a Letter written by Mr. Jefferson to Mr. Carmichael the 22d. of August. I need not add that the Objects which I have in View are to obtain as distinct an Account as possible of what has been done and of what may be done and to give Mr. Lamb an Opportunity of Settling his Accounts. Tho' I have a Commission from Congress to settle all their Accounts in Europe, perhaps Mr. Lamb may not think that his Engagements are included in this general Power, or he may not chuse to communicate freely with me without the Permission of the Ministers, And therefore if Mr. Jefferson approves of it, I wish he would write a Letter to Mr. Lamb, mentioning me to him as a confidential Servant of the public, to whom he may safely trust the particulars of our Situation and give me such information as he will be sure to have faithfully delivered to Congress if I arrive safe in America.

Mr. Jefferson will also if he pleases point out to Mr. Lamb how convenient the Opportunity will be for an Adjustment of the Accounts, and if there is any Ballance to be remitted by Mr. Lamb to Mr. Adams, I will give my best advice as to the mode in which it may be done with the greatest advantage and security to the public.

If Mr. Jefferson writes to Mr. Lamb on this Subject he will be so good as to inclose it to me with such hints and instructions as he shall judge proper under Cover to Mr. Carmichael. It will be some time before I can set out on this Journey as I am charged with a Letter to the King from the Emperor of Morocco, which by an Appointment I am to deliver at the Escurial the 13th. The Count D'Espilly came to Town yesterday and tomorrow I expect to see him as it is certainly in his Power to give a good deal of information respecting the Barbary States; whatever I can collect shall be communicated to you, and I only add that I am clearly of opinion that this Journey is not only proper but necessary. I am with great Respect Gentlemen Your most obt humble Servt.,

THOS BARCLAY

RC (DLC); in David Franks' hand, signed and addressed to TJ by Barclay. PrC of a Tr (DLC); in Short's hand. Enclosure: Dupl of Barclay to TJ, 2 Oct. 1786. MR. JEFFERSON'S LETTER OF THE 26TH: An error for TJ's letter to Barclay of 22 Sep. 1786.

To Jean Durival

SIR Paris Novr. 7th. 1786

I am honored with your letter of the 1st. inst. inclosing enquiries on the subject of the coins of the United States. Some time during the last year Congress decided that the Spanish milled Dollar should be their money unit, and that their coins should be in a decimal progression above and below that. Some intermediate coins will also be doubtless made for convenience and indeed they determined that their smallest copper coin should be the two hundredth part of a dollar. They did not determine how much pure silver their money unit should contain, nor establish the proportion between their silver and gold coins. No other resolutions were entered into, nor has any thing been done to effectuate these. What is said therefore on this subject in the Courier de l'Europe is entirely fable, unless the compiler of that paper has recieved information of a later date than the middle of August, which is the date of my last letters. I do expect that Congress will some time soon complete their system and resolutions on this subject, and carry them into effect.

I have the honor to be with sentiments of the highest respect, Sir, your most obedient & most humble Servant,

TH: JEFFERSON

P.S. I omitted to observe that most of the gold and silver coins of Europe pass in the several States of America according to the quantity of precious metal they contain.

PrC (DLC); in Short's hand, including signature; at foot of text: "(W Short Sec)."

From Francis Hopkinson

MY DEAR SIR Philada. Novr. 8th. 1786

I do not know how long it is since I wrote to you, but am sure

8 NOVEMBER 1786

it is much longer since I heard from you. I am in daily expectations of a Letter in answer to some of mine.

I send you another Packet of News Papers and enclose the Leg of a strange Bird which has nothing curious in it but a fine small toothed Comb annexed to one of its Toes, and three very beautiful Feathers (of which I send two) growing out of the Top of the Head. I have not yet heard from the Gentleman going to Pittsburg who promised to send me some of the Nuts you required. It is not yet Time to expect them. Pheasants are now beginning to make their appearance in our market but are not yet Plenty. The weather being warm for the Season, I shall find great Difficulty in preparing so large and fleshy a Bird, but will take Advise and do my best Endeavours.

I enclose two numbers of a monthly Magazine just set up. I have subscribed for you and myself. I also enclose for your Amusement a News Paper, containing one of my off hand Performances. It had the full Effect I intended, which was to put an End to a foolish Quarrel in which many began to interest themselves, and which in all Probability must have ended in one or more Duels. The Laugh of the Town was turned upon the Combatants and they could not support, with any Degree of Dignity, a Quarrel which they found turned into Ridicule and every one disposed to join in the Laugh.

Pennslvania, Delaware and Maryland have appointed Commissioners for carrying into Effect a Scheme which has been long in Contemplation, that of running a Canal between Chesapeak and Delaware and improving the Navigation of the Susquehannah. I am one of the Commissioners for this State, Mr. Rittenhouse another. There are five Commissioners from each State and we are all to meet at Wilmington on the 27th. of this Month to hold a Conference on this Important Affair.

Dr. Franklin is well—Mr. Rittenhouse [is] in a poor State of Health.

My mother desires to be kindly remember'd to Miss Jefferson. Adieu Yours Sincerely,   Fs HOPKINSON

I had the Misfortune to be robbed last Tuesday Night of all the little Plate I had, Cloathing &c. to the Amount of 70 or £80. A very unlucky Circumstance for me at this Time.

I do not send the Gazette, because it is good for Nothing. The Independent Gazetteer is become a daily Paper and good for nothing also.

RC (DLC); addressed and endorsed. Noted in SJL as received 28 Mch. 1787. Enclosures (aside from the claw and crest feathers of the Night Heron): (1) Two issues of *The Columbian Magazine* (see TJ to Hopkinson, 1 Aug. 1787). (2) Evidently a copy of the *Penna. Packet* for 2 Aug. 1786, containing Hopkinson's satire, "A Plan for the Improvement of the Art of Paper War" (see Hastings, *Hopkinson*, p. 422).

From David Ramsay

DEAR SIR   Charleston Novr. 8th 1786

Your favor of the tenth of July was a few days ago received by the way of New-York. Your friendly interposition in respect of my work lays me under great obligations. I have long since thought that the mode you have adopted was the best the nature of the case admitted of to introduce it to the people of England.

I wish that some copies might in some way or other be introduced to Ireland. The sales in America have fallen many hundred dollars short of my actual expences. I am nevertheless not discouraged but going on with a larger work on the continental system. I have now the first volume nearly ready for the press which will bring the history down to the close of 1776. When I shall print I know not as I mean to take time and to publish the volumes seperately and in different years. I wish I had an opportunity of submitting the sheets to your perusal. I have sent the first part to New-York to the care of Charles Thomson who is authorised and request'd to put it into the hands of well informed gentlemen for their remarks.

By this conveyance I send you the Magnolias and Dionea Muscipulea. Watson objects to move them before fall and as no direct conveyance to France now offered I shall send them to Mr. Otto to go by the packets.

Our State has much more Tranquillity than the eastern ones. What they have attempted to do by mobs as far as the recovery of debts was concerned we have done by law. When the courts are opened I fear there will be some difficulty in enforcing regular justice. Every crop since the peace has failed and it is calculated that nothing less than two or three good crops would pay our debts. We are at present very tranquil. The creditors grumble and the debtors are unmolested. Our enemies hope that our confusions will dispose us to reunite with Great Britain; but I never hear a word in favor of any such plan. Independence though hitherto unproductive of the blessings expected from it is yet the idol of the people. With the most exalted sentiments of respect & esteem I have the honor to be your most obedient & very humble servt.,

DAVID RAMSAY

RC (DLC); endorsed. Noted in SJL as received 26 Jan. 1787.

The MAGNOLIAS AND DIONEA MUSCIPULEA were intended for Madame de Tessé (see TJ to Ramsay, 27 Jan. 1786; also Madame de Tessé to TJ, 30 Mch. 1787). On 7 Nov. 1786 William Short wrote to Col. Eveleigh on this same subject: "my letter of May the 9th. of May last . . . was to interest you in behalf of a Lady here of very great merit, and who does me the honor of an intimate friendship. Don't suspect this friendship of any thing improper, since she is at least fifty years of age. She is very desirous to naturalise a great number of the American trees shrubs &c. at her beautiful country seat near Versailles. By the advice of Mr. McQuinn, who was here we addressed this matter to a Mr. Watson seedsman near Charleston. I wrote to beg you would press the greatest punctuality on Watson (supposing you sometimes at Charleston) and even to advance him the money if necessary. I begged you at the same time to draw for the amount of it on Mr. Thomson the Secretary of Congress to whom Mr. Jefferson had written to desire he would pay your order for that sum, or the order of Mr. Watson if he should draw for it. I sent this letter by Mr. McQuinn together with the list of the articles given me by the Countess de Tesse. Mr. McQuinn left this place for L'Orient from whence he was to embark with a General Duplessis (to whom he had sold lands in Georgia) for America. I have since learnt by accident that at Lorient he changed his project, and went to Amsterdam. As Genl. Duplessis continued his Voyage, I hope that Mr. McQuinn forwarded my letters by him, and that they may have arrived before this. Not knowing his address at Amsterdam I cannot write to him on the Subject . . ." (DLC: Short Papers).

From Brissot de Warville

MONSIEUR Paris 10 9bre. 1786.

Craignant que vous n'aiés besoin de vos Lois de la Virginie pendant mon sejour à Orléans, et ne pouvant m'occuper de L'extrait que je veux en faire, et en publier dans mon ouvrage, Je prens le parti de vous le renvoier, en me reservant de Vous le redemander à mon retour.

Je me suis trouvé à diner aujourdhui avec Messrs. Desaint et Brack directeurs des traites foraines à La douane, dont le dernier est mon ami particulier. Je leur ai parlé, de vos harnois anglois, qui etoient arretés et des demarches inutiles que vous aviés faites pour Les ravoir. Ils m'ont dit que si vous vouliés leur faire L'honneur de les voir à leur bureau à la douane, rue du Bouloy, ou leur envoier M. Short, ils termineroient l'affaire à votre satisfaction, car cela depend d'eux; je vous conseille donc de les voir. M. Brack surtout est un jeune homme de merite et obligeant au delà de toute expression.

Je vous remercie bien sincerement de vos souhaits pour mon voiage, et Je vous prie d'etre bien persuadé que je n'ai rien tant à coeur que de meriter votre estime et L'amitié des americains dont Je me regarde deja comme Le frere. Je suis avec un veritable atachement Monsieur Votre trés humble et Obt. serviteur,

BRISSOT DE WARVILLE

P.S. Me permettrés vous d'assurer ici Monsr. Short de mes civilités amicales.

J'oubliois, Monsieur, de vous parler d'une persone et d'un ouvrage que je me suis chargé de vous recomander; Voici ce dont il s'agit:

M. Lardizabal, Espagnol celebre par plusieurs ouvrages sur la Jurisprudence et la Legislation, a entrepris un code criminel, et pour le bien faire, Il rassemble des Materiaux et des ouvrages de tous Les cotés. Il m'a adressé M. son frere tant pour Les ecrits que J'ai faits sur cette matiere, que pour se procurer des renseignemens sur tout ce qui avoit eté publié. Je Lui ai parlé de vos Lois sur la Virginie, et des notions Interessantes qui se trouvent à cet egard dans vos *Notes on Virginia*. Ces faits Lui ont fait naitre Le desir de vous entretenir, si vous Lui acordiés cette faveur, sur ce point important. Je Lui ai assuré, que vous ne Le refuseriés pas, Connoissant combien Vous desiriés etendre partout Le bien qui se faisoit en Amerique. Je Lui ai donc fait esperer une audience de vous, s'il se presentoit. Une autre raison qui pouroit Vous engager à L'accueillir est que cet Espagnol est Chargé d'une Mission particulière de la Cour d'Espagne près de la cour de france. Il doit etre reexpedié pour Madrid sous 8 ou 10 Jours. M. Lardizabal demeure hotel de Bayonne rue traversiere. Il aura surement L'honneur de Vous ecrire.

Je vous demande Mille pardons de la Liberté de cette Recomandation. Votre amour pour L'humanité me fera sans doute excuser.

RC (DLC); not recorded in SJL. Enclosure: TJ's copy of the *Report of the Committee of Revisors*, 1784.

From William Jones

Sir London Novr 10th. 1786

This day Col. Smith did me the honour to leave your note ordering a Ferguson's Perspective Machine which I shall immediately put in hand and have it finished agreeable to the Description, and your amendments.—I am sorry Sir that the hurry of business has prevented me from closing investigating the principle, and action of the Air Pump; but I recollect some time back, that myself and two or three ingenious Mechanics, had agreed that the Friction, unavoidably attending the acting parts, would totally destroy the feasibility of the effect of the Machine. I have once since almost experienced it in the construction of a Condensing Syringe made

10 NOVEMBER 1786

for a Gentleman, something, or rather greatly similar to the plan of that Pump. I am extremely happy, nay I always thirst to hear of Inventions, or Improvements in Speculative, and Practical Philosophy. And as you are now Sir seated in a Nation whose emulation, and ingenuity rivals ourselves, I shall consider it as the greatest honour to be informed even in the least degree of any essential philosophical Invention or publication, made in the parisian world. —I beg pardon for scrolling out this philosophical rhapsody and recollect myself to be only Sr Your Much Obliged Humble Servt.,

WM. JONES

RC (DLC); addressed; endorsed: "Jones Wm. (London)," to distinguish the present writer from William Jones of Bristol, England, one of TJ's creditors. Noted in SJL as received 28 Nov. 1786.

YOUR NOTE: TJ's note to Jones has not been found; it was enclosed in TJ to Smith, 22 Oct. 1786.

From John Paradise

DEAR SIR London Novr. 10th. 1786.

Doctor Burney has just this moment been with me to acquaint me that the harpsicord that was bespoken for you has been finished by Kirkman a considerable time, and is now in the hands of Mr. Walker, who is affixing to it his Celestini stop, upon a new construction, according to your Excellency's wish and idea. The Doctor has been in daily expectation ever since his arrival in town, of hearing from Mr. Walker that the instrument was ready for trial, with his new machine for the celestini stop. He has postponed writing to you till he could speak to all the particulars belonging to this harpsicord, which he is ambitious should be as complete as possible. He intends calling again to-morrow upon Mr. Walker in order to see what forwardness it is in, and if finished, will give you an account of it by the next post. I hope soon to have the happiness of seeing you. Mrs. Paradise and my daughters join with me in every good wish to you and your amiable family, and I have the honour to be with the greatest respect Yr. most faithful and obligd. hble. servt., JOHN PARADISE

RC (DLC). Noted in SJL as received 15 Nov. 1786.

From John Bondfield

[Bordeaux, 11 Nov. 1786. Recorded in SJL as received 15 Nov. 1786. Not found.]

To Famin

Sir   Paris Novr. 11th. 1786

This will be handed you by Colo. Blackden heretofore an officer in the American army, at present engaged in trade. He goes to Honfleur with a view to examine the commercial relations which may be established between that port and the United States. He wishes particularly to see the nature of its harbour, the conveniences already established for commerce and to know something of the productions which can be taken and given there in exchange. Knowing your desire to assist in drawing the American commerce to that port I take the liberty of recommending this gentleman to your acquaintance and of praying you to procure him the information he wishes.

Some late regulations of the King and Council in favor of the commerce of the U. States having given us reason to hope that our endeavours may be successful to remove a good part of it from G. Britain to France, Honfleur presents itself as a more important instrument for this purpose than it had heretofore appeared. We are therefore now pressing more earnestly its establishment as a free port, and such other regulations in its favor as may invite the commerce to it. I have the honor to be Sir, your most obedient & most humble Servant,   Th: Jefferson

PrC (DLC); in Short's hand, including signature; at foot of text: "(Test: W Short Sec)."

Honfleur: On the effort to establish it as a free port, see TJ to Lafayette, 15 and 17 June 1786; Crèvecoeur to TJ, 16 Dec. 1786; Gottschalk, *Lafayette, 1783-89*, p. 238-9.

To Anthony Garvey

Sir   Paris Novr. 11th. 1786

This will be handed you by Colo. Blackden, heretofore an officer in the American army and at present engaged in trade. He passes by the way of Rouen with a view to collect some information relative to the commerce which may be carried on between the United States and that part of France. He is a man of merit and as such I take the liberty of introducing him to your acquaintance. If you can be useful to him in procuring the information he desires, I shall be obliged to you. I have the honor to be Sir, your most obedient & most humble servant,   Th: Jefferson

PrC (DLC); in Short's hand, including signature, and attested by Short.

From William Stephens Smith

Dear Sir   London Novr. 11th. 1786.

Inclosed is Mr. Jones's answer to your Question. I have given to Mr. Stockdale 4 Vols. of Pope's Iliad and Odysey, which were not ready in time for the last parcel. They will accompany those last ordered from *Stocke*. The Compendio del Vocabolerio degli Accademici della Crusca for Mr. Short at 13/6 and Cicero on old age, I think for you, price 1/6.—I forward Lackingtons list of the books sent you. Those omitted in your original list were not to be had.

Chastellux's Voyages and Latre's map I have received, and shall take the earliest oppertunity to request Mr. Woodmason to separate the paper from his package, but I am rather apprehensive, you will have to take it for the present. I should have waited on Mr. Neele this morning to have seen whether your plate is finished, that I might have embraced this oppertunity by Mr. Derby to have sent it, but I have been tormented with politicans and their long winded story's and they have scarcely left me time to answer yours of the 22d. ulto.—I will endeavour to surprize Mr. Adams, soon, and forward your wishes about his picture, but at present he is so much engaged in writing to *me* that it is impossible for him to spare a morning.—Your buff Casimir waistcoat and breeches must also remain in check, for during a general mourning such as at present overshadow's the Kingdom, in consequence of the departure of the Princes Amelia, Taylors are allowed by some act or other double price for their work. As I send the Cotton pairs, by this conveyance, it is pretty clear you cannot want, therefore shall wait untill the Lads will work cheaper. As you was not particular in the discription of your Buff, I have ordered them of the same kind you had made when here. I still possess the memorandum about the picture at Birmingham, and shall endeavour to obtain it for you.

The Slippers shall be made agreable to your directions and forwarded by a private hand as Mr. Shorts note by the last post requests. As I go to leave this Letter I will call at Mr. Neel's, and if the plate is finish'd endeavour to forward it. Mrs. Adams is very well, and Mrs. Smith has been a little indisposed but is now much better. *I thank you*. I have answered Mr. Mazzei's Questions about Anderson and the Fœdera. You will find the latter spoken of, by Monsieur LeClerc in his 16th. Volume of his Bibliotheque Choisie. —I have now only to assure you of the respect with which I am dr. Sir Your obliged Humble Servt.,   W. S. Smith

RC (MHi); endorsed by TJ with his left hand. Noted in SJL as received 28 Nov. 1786. Enclosures: (1) Jones to TJ, 10 Nov. 1786. (2) Lackington's list of books (missing, but see TJ to Smith, 13 Sep. 1786).

To John Banister

Dear Sir   Paris Novr. 12th. 86.

Your favor of July the 18th came duly to hand. Monsr. De Vernon, thinking it necessary that an immediate stop should be put to the reciept of monies by Mr. Mark on account of their house, has given me the inclosed power of attorney which is left blank in hopes that you will be so good as to fill it up with the name of some proper person on whose integrity and punctuality confidence can be placed. It is accompanied by a letter from Mr. Mark containing a state of the company's affairs. They desire that the attorney whom you shall appoint may press an immediate recovery of their monies so far as they are in the hands of Mr. Mark and secure to them those lodged in the public funds.

I have a letter from your son about a week ago. He has been for some time past at Nantz; he has had a small attack of his disorder lately but when he wrote me he was so far recovered as to be about setting out for this place; where I hope to see him within a few days. I am with very sincere esteem, dear Sir, your friend & servant,   Th: Jefferson

Jan. 2. 1787.
P.S. The want of an opportunity of sending this letter till now, gives me the pleasure of informing you that your son arrived in Paris about a fortnight ago in as good health as he ever was and that appearances are very flattering that he will continue so.

Th: Jefferson

PrC (DLC); endorsed; the letter of 12 Nov. 1786 is in Short's hand, including signature, and attested by him; the postscript of 2 Jan. 1787 is written by TJ with his right hand, and signed by him. Enclosures: (1) Power of attorney of Dangirard & De Vernon, the form for which was drawn up by TJ and enclosed in TJ to Dangirard & De Vernon, 17 Aug. 1786, q.v.; see also the latter to TJ, following TJ's letter of 17 Aug., and references there. (2) The letter from Mark has not been found.

To John Jay, with Enclosure

Sir   Paris Nov. 12. 1786.

In a letter which I had the honor of writing you on the 26th. of

[519]

12 NOVEMBER 1786

Sep. I informed you that a Dutch company were making propositions to the Minister of finance here to purchase at a discount the debt due from the U.S. to this country. I have lately procured a copy of their memoir, which I now inclose. Should Congress think this subject worthy their attention, they have no time to lose, as the necessities of the minister, which alone has made him listen to this proposition, may force him to a speedy conclusion. The effect which a paiment of the whole sum would have here, would be very valuable. The only question is whether we can borrow in Holland, a question which cannot be resolved but in Holland. The trouble of the trial, and expence of the transaction would be well repaid by the dispositions which would be excited in our favor in the king and his ministers. I have the honor to be with sentiments of most perfect esteem and respect Sir Your most obedient & most humble servant, TH. JEFFERSON

ENCLOSURE

Memorial

The United States have borrowed a large sum of money from France for which they pay an interest untill they reimburse it at the rate of Six per cent per annum. It is not known whether the periods of this reimbursement are fixed or whether they are left to the convenience of the Ud. States; the quota of this sum is also unknown. It is supposed that it cannot be less than Twenty four Millions and that the period of reimbursement is not near. It is thought that the two nations consider their mutual benefit and upon this supposition an arrangement of the debt of the Ud. States is proposed, which appears to suit the interest of both these powers.

On the part of France, the want of money to facilitate its reimbursements and improvements should induce her to fix a certain price for the actual return of so large a sum.

On the part of the Ud. States the scarcity of money which they experience and the want of it which the natural extension of their situation occasions must render every measure precious that will bring into circulation the sum they have borrowed; and under such a form that this circulation will take place as well in the Ud. States as elsewhere.

This mode offers of itself. It consists in converting the American debt in Bills payable to the bearer in sums from Five Hundred to a Thousand French Livres and annexing dividends to these Bills for receiving the interest in such places as shall be agreed and fixed on. It is by no means to be doubted but that Commerce and the Europeans who would settle in the Ud. States would carry there great number of these Bills which would probably be reimbursed there. The Ud. States would find two great advantages from this operation. The first by acquiring in their circulation at home, a paper which by the full credit it would have, would answer all the purposes of cash. Secondly, being able to pay at home a part of the debt and the interest, and to reduce it by degrees, by means of the purchase of lands with these Bills payable to the bearer; for the speculators in land could pay for them in this way with advantage, both on account of their being able to procure these Bills in Europe on better terms than specie, and that it would particularly suit the Ud. States to encourage the exchange of uncultivated lands which they have to sell for Bills which they must reimburse and which in the mean time cost them an annual interest.

These instances will serve to prove the great benefit which France would procure for the Ud. States by converting the credit she has given them into Bills payable to the Bearer which might be brought into circulation.

With respect to the benefit France would reap, it is very probable that she might dispose of all these bills at once, to a company who would take them up in consideration of some sacrifice and facilities that are customary in transactions of such magnitude. It must be observed here that this arrangement is determined upon the presumption as far as the nature of the case will admit, that this debt is recoverable.

It will therefore follow that France will obtain for the purposes of government a speedy return of a sum of money which will proportionably lessen the loan that may be otherwise necessary.

On the first reflection it might appear that France ought not to sell her debt with the Ud. States especially on terms favorable to the purchasers but on condition of not being obliged to guaranty the same against accidents which may render it doubtful, as this might occasion a distrust against the credit of the Ud. States which might be prejudicial to them, and which would be impolitic on the part of France and inconsistent with the reciprocal friendship between her and the Ud. States. This objection will be removed by France continuing to be guaranty for the payment of the Bills with interest. This guaranty therefore is not only necessary to the success of the proposed arrangement, but the dignity of France also requires it; less hazard will attend this, than the risk that attended the losing the sum lent to aid a revolution which she judged important; the solvability of the Ud. States depending upon their independance, France ought not to expect any premium for guarantying the solvability, the basis of which it is her interest to support. Should the removal of this objection be opposed by observing that the speedy benefit of Twenty Millions is not of sufficient consideration to determine France to make a change when she would not thereby free herself at least from risk with the Ud. States, We answer that the Advantage of restoring these Twenty Millions into circulation and thereby preventing the borrowing of this sum, is not the only one.

The Ud. states are not yet free from all apprehension of danger: there appear some difficulties between them and England with regard to fulfilling the treaty of peace. The policy as well as the inclinations of the Ud. States require their firmness in every thing they have to transact with that power. They may therefore be under the necessity of demanding further pecuniary aid. The circumstances that may render this necessary may likewise render it difficult to obtain, especially

12 NOVEMBER 1786

should they defer asking them untill these circumstances are made public. This arrangement then may facilitate this aid; should it require promptness and should it be impolitic or too hazardous to seek it elsewhere than in France, she may then grant it without being obliged to increase her taxes, by means of the actual product of her debt. If this consideration has any weight, it follows that the proposed arrangement should be delayed as short as possible. The English funds fall, which can only be attributed to the apprehensions that a dangerous contest may be occasioned by the refusal of the Court of London to evacuate the Forts.

The proposed arrangement requiring His Majesty's Arret, the following sketch of one is offered.

Sketch of an Arret. Lewis &c.—Upon representation made unto us that the sum we have lent to the Ud. States our dear Allies, will not be reduced untill a distant period; and that by turning our debt into negociable bills they will enter immediately into circulation and will afford the said States advantageous opportunity of discharging the same, both by means of removing the necessity of remitting to Europe the necessary funds for the payment of the interest and capital of part of their debt represented by the bills which their circulation shall have brought among them, as also by the opportunities that this circulation may offer of exchanging lands for these bills which will thereby give a new spring to the cultivation which the Ud. States desire to extend and accelerate, and upon being assured that such an operation would really produce those advantages to the Ud. States without the least inconveniency which suggested the measure, especially by guarantying the payment of said bills to the possessors, we have therefore &c. &c.

Another preamble. Lewis &c.—Ever considering what may be advantageous to the Ud. States and facilitate to them the means of extracting themselves from a debt which they have been obliged to contract as well with us, as with other powers and particularly their liberation from the loan of the year ——— the period of reimbursement being near at hand, we have conceived that it will be a fresh proof of our good will, by giving a form to this loan which will bring it into circulation by making it negotiable. It appears to us that by converting this sum of ——— into bills payable to the bearer to the amount of ——— Livres each with terms of interest payable at fixed places, we should furnish the Ud. States with a simple mode of reimbursing successively within themselves and without any distress these bills which will be thrown into commerce. In operating this conversion, we have thought it incumbent on our justice, the dignity of our crown and our affection for our dear allies, to guaranty the Security and the payment of these bills with their interest. This guaranty will moreover afford a fresh proof of the value we fix on preserving our alliance with the Ud. States. We have been the more inclined to adopt this advantageous method for the Ud. States as it is perfectly reconcileable with the interests of our subjects with the circumstances and disposition we are in to free our State by degrees of all its debts and charges. For these reasons &c. &c.

The Articles of the Arret will have in view. (1st) To create Bills payable to the bearer to the amount of the sum lent to the Ud. States in the year ——— the first period of whose reimbursement falls in ——— which Bills shall each be of ——— and Amounting to ——— Numbers from No. 1 to No. ——— agreable to the model annexed to the Arret. (2dly) To fix the periods of reimbursement and the number of Bills which shall be reimbursed at each period, this must be determined by lot. The reimbursements to be made in Paris, Amsterdam, Philadelphia, Boston, New York, Charleston, with Bankers who shall be appointed. (3dly.) The Numbers of Bills which by lot are to be reimbursed shall be published four months before the date of the reimbursement by means of the public prints most generally known in Europe and America. (4th) To determine where the Lots shall be drawn. This would appear to be most proper in one of the cities of the Ud. States. (5th) Untill the reimbursements, the bills shall draw an annual interest of 6 percent which shall be paid every year commencing from ——— in the cities marked out in the ——— article and by the Bankers to be appointed. This payment shall have effect on presentation of the original bill to which shall be annexed the dividends of interest agreable to the model &c. (6th) The reimbursed Bills shall be withdrawn as being extinguished as also the interest not due. The Bankers who shall have paid them shall account for the same with the Ud. States by representing them, and these shall successively forward the list to His Majestys Ambassador to serve as a discharge for His Majesty guaranty, in proportion as the Ud. States shall reimburse them.

N.B. It appears indispensable to prevent counterfeits and remove all obstacles in the way of the circulation of the bills that they be stamped by the Ambassador of the Ud. States, an operation which as well as the others mentioned in the arret, only to be announced in concert with the Ud. States.

Faithfully translated from the Original by   John Pintard.

RC (DNA: PCC, No. 87, 1); written with TJ's right hand, and—despite the use of literary license in his letter to Mrs. Cosway of 19 Nov. 1789—evidently the first to be so written after his injury. PrC (DLC). Tr (DNA: PCC, No. 107). Enclosure: Translation by John Pintard (DNA: PCC, No. 87, 1, from a Tr in French in the hand of William Short; PrC of Short's Tr in DLC and Tr of Pintard's translation in DNA: PCC, No. 107).

It is not certain how TJ PROCURED A COPY of the memoir of the Dutch company, but it was possibly through the intermediation of Clavière, who was known to TJ and who was negotiating for the purchase of the French loan (see TJ to Osgood, 5 Jan. 1787).

From Zachariah Loreilhe

Bergerac, 12 Nov. 1786. Informing TJ that he had written a letter on 20 Oct. asking information about the purchase of powder, flints, and cartridge paper for the state of Virginia, but that he has had no reply thereto.

RC (DLC); 2 p. Noted in SJL as received 18 Nov. 1786.
See Loreilhe to TJ, 20 Oct. 1786 and TJ to Loreilhe, 29 Oct. and 19 Nov. 1786.

From James Smith

Sir   London Novr. 12. 86.

I quitted Paris in great haste to arrive here time enough to embark for Charleston but have been detained three weeks longer than I expected. I have now the honor of adressing your Excellency in behalf of my nephew Mr. Thomas Smith, for whom I beg the favor of your countenance and protection. He is young, and I believe prudent, but let him be ever so much so, he will find your Excellency more capable of garding him than himself. Besides that being at Paris he cannot dispense with the duty of paying his respects to a dignified character who has conferred many favors on his uncle and who represents his country there with much credit and applause.

My nephew is at Paris to inquire of some physicians the best situation in France for his [1] complaint. Wherever he goes, he will probably want the assistance of your excellency in procuring him such acquaintances of his own rank as may contribute to the restoration of that health he seeks after, by causing him to pass his time agreably and advantageously; which will be conferring a singular favor upon him and increase the obligations of Sir your Excellency's most obedt. humble sevt.,   James Smith

P.S. If it be not too much trouble, I would request that my particular compliments may be presented to Mr. Shaw.[2]

RC (DLC).
[1] Blank in MS; perhaps Smith intended to fill in the nature of his nephew's complaint later.
[2] I.e., Short.

To Jean Baptiste Le Roy

Sir   Paris Nov. 13. 1786.

I received the honour of yours of Sep. 18.[1] a day or two after the accident of a dislocated wrist had disabled me from writing. I have waited thus long in constant hope of recovering it's use. But finding that this hope walks before me like my shadow, I can no longer oppose the desire and duty of answering your polite and learned letter. I therefore employ my left hand in the office of scribe, which it performs indeed slowly, awkwardly and badly.

The information given by me to the Marquis de Chastellux, and alluded to in his book and in your letter, was that the sea breezes which prevail in the lower parts of Virginia during the summer months, and in the warm parts of the day, had made a sensible progress into the interior country: that formerly, within the memory of persons living, they extended but little above Williamsburg; that afterwards they became sensible as high as Richmond, and at present they penetrate sometimes as far as the first mountains, which are above an hundred miles farther from the sea coast than Williamsburg is. It is very rare indeed that they reach those mountains and not till the afternoon is considerably advanced. A light North-Westerly breeze is for the most part felt there, while an Easterly, or North Easterly wind is blowing strongly in the lower country. How far Northward and Southward of Virginia this Easterly breeze takes place, I am not informed. I must therefore be understood as speaking of that state only, which extends on the sea coast from $36\frac{1}{2}$ to $38°$ of latitude.

This is the fact. We know too little of the operations of Nature in the physical world to assign causes with any degree of confidence. Willing always however to guess at what we do not know, I have sometimes indulged myself with conjectures on the causes of the phænomena above stated. I will hazard them on paper for your amusement, premising for their foundation some principles believed to be true.

Air, resting on a heated and reflecting surface, becomes warmer, rarer and lighter: it ascends therefore, and the circumjacent air, which is colder and heavier, flows into it's place, becomes warmed and lightened in it's turn, ascends and is succeeded as that which went before. [2] If the heated surface be circular, the air flows to it from every quarter, like the rays of a circle to it's center. If it be a zone of determinate breadth and indefinite length, the air will flow from each side perpendicularly on it.   If the currents of air flowing from opposite sides be of equal force, they will meet in equilibrio at a line drawn longitudinally thro the middle of the zone. If one current be stronger than the other, the stronger one will force back the line of equilibrium towards the further edge of the zone, or even beyond it: the motion it has acquired causing it to overshoot the zone, as the motion acquired by a pendulum in it's descent causes it to vibrate beyond the point of it's lowest descent.

Earth, exposed naked to the sun's rays, absorbs a good portion of them; but being an opaque body, those rays penetrate to a small depth only. It's surface, by this accumulation of absorbed rays, becomes considerably heated. The residue of the rays are reflected into the air resting on that surface. This air then is warmed 1. by the direct rays of the sun. 2. by it's reflected rays. 3. by contact with the heated surface.   A Forest receiving the sun's rays, a part of them enter the intervals between the trees, and their reflection upwards is intercepted by the leaves and boughs. The rest fall on the trees, the leaves of which being generally inclined towards the horizon, reflect the rays downwards. The atmosphere here then receives little or no heat by reflection. Again, these leaves having a power of keeping themselves cool by their own transpiration, they impart no heat to the air by contact. Reflection and contact then, two of the three modes beforementioned of communicating heat, are wanting here, and of course the air over a country covered by forest must be colder than that over cultivated grounds.

The sea being pellucid, the sun's rays penetrate it to a considerable depth. Being also fluid, and in perpetual agitation, it's parts are constantly mixed together; so that instead of it's heat being all accumulated in it's surface, as in the case of a solid opaque body, it is diffused thro' its whole mass. It's surface therefore is comparatively cool, for these reasons, to which may be added that of evaporation.[3] The small degree of reflection, which might otherways take place is generally prevented by the rippled state of it's surface. The air resting on the sea then, like that resting on a forest, receives little or no heat by reflection or contact; and is therefore colder than that which lies over a cultivated country.

To apply these observations to the phænomena under construction.

The first settlements of Virginia were made along the sea coast, bearing from South towards the North, a little Eastwardly. These settlements formed a zone in which, tho every point was not cleared of it's forest, yet a good proportion was cleared and cultivated. This cultivated earth, as the sun advances above the horizon in the morning, acquires from it an intense heat, which is retained and increased through the warm parts of the day. The air resting on it becomes warm in proportion and rises. On one side is a country still covered with forest: on the other is the ocean. The colder air from both of these then rushes towards the heated zone to supply the place left vacant there by the ascent of it's warm air. The breeze from the West is light and feeble; because it traverses a country covered with mountains and forests, which retard it's current. That from the East is strong; as passing over the ocean wherein there is no obstacle to it's motion. It is probable therefore that this Easterly breeze forces itself far into, or perhaps beyond the zone which produces it. This zone is, by the increase of population, continually widening into the interior country. The line of equilibrium between the Easterly and Westerly breezes is therefore progressive.

Did no foreign causes intervene, the sea breezes would be a little Southwardly of the East, that direction being perpendicular to our coast. But within the tropics there are winds which blow continually and strongly from the East. This current affects the courses of the air even without the tropics. The same cause too which produces a strong motion of the air from East to West between the tropics, to wit, the Sun, exercises it's influence without these limits, but more feebly in proportion as the surface of the globe is there more obliquely presented to it's rays. This effect, tho' not great, is not to be neglected when the sun is in, or near, our summer solstice, which is the season of these Easterly breezes.

The Northern air too, flowing towards the equatorial parts to supply the vacuum made there by the ascent of their heated air, has only the small rotatory motion of the polar latitudes from which it comes. Nor does it suddenly acquire the swifter rotation of the parts into which it enters. This gives it the effect of a motion opposed to that of the earth, that is to say of an Easterly one. And all these causes together are known to produce currents of air in the Atlantic, varying from East to North East as far as the 40th. degree of Latitude. It is this current which presses our sea breeze out of it's natural South Easterly direction to an Easterly and sometimes almost a North Easterly one.[4]

We are led naturally to ask where the progress of our sea breezes will ultimately be stopped? No confidence can be placed in any answer to this question. If they should ever pass the Mountainous country which separates the waters of the Ocean from those of the Missisipi, there may be circumstances which might aid their further progress as far as the Missisipi. That Mountainous country commences about 200 miles from the sea coast, and consists of successive ranges, passing from North East to South West, and rising the one above the other to the Alleghaney ridge, which is the highest of all. From that, lower and lower ridges succeed one another again till, having covered in the whole a breadth of 200 miles from South East to North West, they subside into plain, fertile country, extending 400 miles to the Missisipi, and probably much further on the other side towards the heads of it's Western waters. When this country shall become cultivated, it will, for the reasons before explained, draw to it winds from the East

13 NOVEMBER 1786

and West. In this case, should the sea breezes pass the intermediate mountains, they will rather be aided than opposed in their further progress to the Missisipi. There are circumstances however which render it possible that they may not be able to pass those intermediate mountains. 1. These mountains constitute the highest lands within the United States. The air on them must consequently be very cold and heavy, and have a tendency to flow both to the East and West. 2. Ranging across the current of the sea breezes, they are in themselves so many successive barriers opposed to their progress. 3. The country they occupy is covered with trees, which assist to weaken and spend the force of the breezes. 4. It will remain so covered; a very small proportion of it being capable of culture. 5. The temperature of it's air then will never be softened by culture.

At present I suppose the currents of air between the Atlantic and the Western heads of the Missisipi may be represented as in the following diagram of a horizontal section of that country.

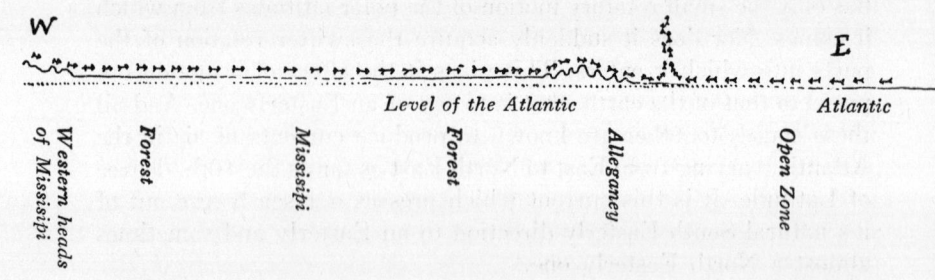

W   E

Level of the Atlantic   *Atlantic*

Western heads of Missisipi   *Forest*   *Missisipi*   *Forest*   *Alleganey*   *Open Zone*

But that when the plane country on both sides of the Missisipi shall be cleared of it's trees and cultivated, the currents of air will be in the following directions.

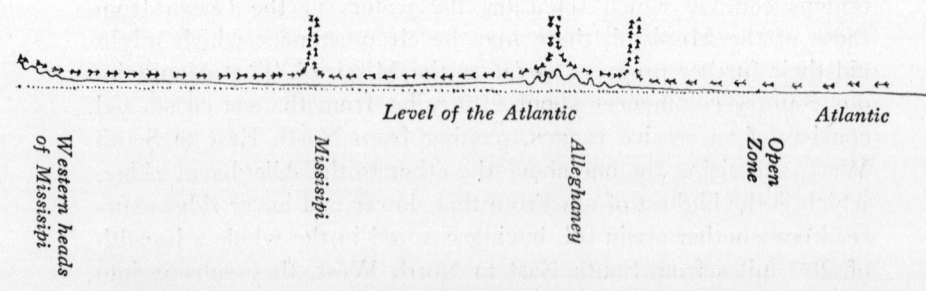

Level of the Atlantic   *Atlantic*

Western heads of Missisipi   *Missisipi*   *Alleghaney*   *Open Zone*

Whether, in the plane country between the Mississipi and Alleganey mountains Easterly or Westerly winds prevail at present, I am not informed. I conjecture however that they must be Westerly, as represented in the first diagram: and I think, with

[528]

13 NOVEMBER 1786

you Sir, that if those mountains were to subside into plane country as their opposition to the Westerly winds would then be removed, they would repress more powerfully those from the East, and of course would remove the line of equilibrium nearer to the sea-coast for the present.

Having had occasion to mention the course of the Tropical winds from East to West, I will add some observations connected with them. They are known to occasion a strong current in the ocean in the same direction. This current breaks on that wedge of land of which Saint Roque is the point; the Southern column of it *probably* turning off and washing the coast of Brazil. I say *probably* because I have never heard the fact and conjecture it from reason only. The Northern column, having it's Western motion diverted towards the North and reinforced by the currents of the great rivers Orinoko, Amazons and Tocantin, has probably been the agent which formed the gulph of Mexico, cutting the American continent nearly in two in that part. It re-crosses into the ocean at the Northern end of the gulph, and passes, by the name of the Gulph stream, all along the coast of the United States to it's Northern extremity. There it turns off Eastwardly, having formed, by it's eddy at this turn, the banks of New found land. Thro' the whole of it's course, from the gulph to the banks, it retains a very sensible warmth. The Spaniards are at this time desirous of trading to their Philippine islands by the way of the Cape of good hope: but opposed in it by the Dutch, under authority of the treaty of Munster, they are examining the practicability of a common passage thro' the Streights of Magellan, or round Cape Horn. Were they to make an opening thro the isthmus of Panama, a work much less difficult than some even of the inferior canals of France, however small this opening should be in the beginning, the tropical current, entering it with all it's force, would soon widen it sufficiently for it's own passage, and thus complete in a short time that work which otherwise will still employ it for ages. Less country too would be destroyed by it in this way. These consequences would follow. 1. Vessels from Europe, or the Western coast of Africa, by entering the tropics, would have a steady wind and tide to carry them thro' the Atlantic, thro America and the Pacific ocean to every part of the Asiatic coast, and of the Eastern coast of Africa: thus performing with speed and safety the tour of the whole globe, to within about 24°. of longitude, or 1/15 part of it's circumference, the African continent, under the line, occupying about that space. 2. The gulph of Mexico, now the most dangerous navigation in

13 NOVEMBER 1786

the world, on account of it's currents and moveable sands, would become stagnant and safe. 3. The gulph stream on the coast of the United States would cease, and with that those derangements of course and reckoning which now impede and endanger the intercourse with those states. 4. The fogs on the banks of Newfoundland,* supposed to be the vapours of the gulph stream rendered turbid by cold air, would disappear. 5. Those banks, ceasing to receive supplies of sand, weeds and warm water by the gulph stream, it might become problematical what effect changes of pasture and temperature would have on the fisheries.   However it is time to relieve you from this lengthy lecture. I wish it's subject may have been sufficiently interesting to make amends for it's details. These are submitted with entire deference to your better judgment. I will only add to them by assuring you of the sentiments of perfect esteem and respect with which I have the honor to be Sir your most obedient and most humble servant,

TH: JEFFERSON

* This ingenious and probable conjecture I find in a letter from Dr. Franklin to yourself published in the late volume of the American Philosophical Transactions.

PrC (DLC); written partly with TJ's left hand, and partly with his right (see note 4 below); at foot of text: "M Le Roy de l'Academie des Sciences."

[1] An error: Le Roy's letter was dated 28 Sep. 1786; it was on the 18th that TJ suffered the accident to his wrist and he may, therefore, have subconsciously transposed the dates in this context.

[2] Here and elsewhere in his letters TJ employed a space to indicate a break approximately equal in value to the break signified by a new paragraph. This custom was not unique with him, but since his handwriting was regular and disciplined, it is clear that the space was intended and it will therefore be observed in the printing of his letters, as well as in those written to him when (as in the case of William Short) it appears to be an intended usage.

[3] The following is deleted at this point: "In proportion as it falls short of perfect [. . .]."

[4] The letter up to this point was written with TJ's left hand; the remainder with his right.

From [Madame de La Rochefoucauld?]

Ce 13 9bre [1786?]

Md. La Dsse. d'Enville a toussé depuis quatre heures jusqu'a cinq Et demie sans discontinuer, En suite Elle a dormi par intervalle Et Elle avoit un peu de fievre ce matin.

Mde. de chabot a eu hier un accés qui a duré jusqu'a deux heures du matin, malgré cela elle a eu assez de calme Et meme des moments de Sommeil, Elle a toussé Et craché moderement. Elle Est tranquille dans ce moment cy.

Mr. le Duc de La Rochefoucauld a bien dormi, a peu toussé. Son pied va bien.

RC (ViWC); without signature or name of addressee; the year has been supplied from internal evidence.

This note was possibly written by the wife of LE DUC DE LA ROCHEFOU-CAULD, in reply to a (missing) inquiry from TJ. MD. LA DSSE. D'ENVILLE, the "old Duchesse" was the mother of the duke. MDE. DE CHABOT was the duke's sister. The latter died on 12 Dec. 1786 (see TJ to Benjamin Franklin, 23 Dec. 1786).

From Vergennes

[*Ca. 14 Nov. 1786.* Entry in SJL under this date reads: "Vergennes. Ct. de (passport)." Not found, but it must have enclosed the passport promised by Vergennes in his letter of 4 Nov. 1786.]

To George Washington

SIR   Paris Nov. 14. 1786.

The house of Le Coulteux, which for some centuries has been the wealthiest of this place, has it in contemplation to establish a great company for the fur trade. They propose that partners interested one half in the establishment should be American citizens, born and residing in the U.S. Yet if I understood them rightly they expect that that half of the company which resides here should make the greatest part, or perhaps the whole of the advances, while those on our side the water should superintend the details. They had at first thought of Baltimore as the center of their American transactions. I have pointed out to them the advantages of Alexandria for this purpose. They have concluded to take information as to Baltimore, Philadelphia and N. York for a principal deposit, and having no correspondent at Alexandria, have asked me to procure a state of the advantages of that place, as also to get a recommendation of the best merchant there to be adopted as partner and head of the business there. Skill, punctuality, and integrity are the requisites in such a character. They will decide on their whole information as to the place for their principal factory. Being unwilling that Alexandria should lose it's pretensions, I have undertaken to procure them information as to that place. If they undertake this trade at all, it will be on so great a scale as to decide the current of the Indian trade to the place they adopt. I have no

14 NOVEMBER 1786

acquaintance at Alexandria or in it's neighborhood. But believing you would feel an interest in it from the same motives which I do, I venture to ask the favor of you to recommend to me a proper merchant for their purpose, and to engage some well informed person to send me a representation of the advantages of Alexandria as the principal deposit for the fur trade.

The author of the Political part of the Encyclopedie methodique desired me to examine his article 'Etats unis.' I did so. I found it a tissue of errors. For in truth they know nothing about us here. Particularly however the article 'Cincinnati' was a mere Philippic against that institution: in which it appeared that there was an utter ignorance of facts and motives. I gave him notes on it. He reformed it as he supposed and sent it again to me to revise. In this reformed state Colo. Humphreys saw it. I found it necessary to write that article for him. Before I gave it to him I shewed it to the Marq. de la fayette who made a correction or two. I then sent it to the author. He used the materials, mixing a great deal of his own with them. In a work which is sure of going down to the latest posterity I thought it material to set facts to rights as much as possible. The author was well disposed: but could not entirely get the better of his original bias. I send you the Article as ultimately published. If you find any material errors in it and will be so good as to inform me of them, I shall probably have opportunities of setting this author to rights. What has heretofore passed between us on this institution, makes it my duty to mention to you that I have never heard[1] a person in Europe, learned or unlearned, express his thoughts on this institution, who did not consider it as dishonourable and destructive to our governments, and that every writing which has come out since my arrival here, in which it is mentioned, considers it, even as now reformed, as the germ whose developement is one day to destroy the fabric we have reared. I did not apprehend this while I had American ideas only. But I confess that what I have seen in Europe has brought me over to that opinion: and that tho' the day may be at some distance, beyond the reach of our lives perhaps, yet it will certainly come, when, a single fibre left of this institution, will produce an hereditary aristocracy which will change the form of our governments from the best to the worst in the world. To know the mass of evil which flows from this fatal source, a person must be in France, he must see the finest soil, the finest climate, the most compact state, the most benevolent character of people, and every earthly advantage combined, insufficient to prevent this scourge from rendering exist-

14 NOVEMBER 1786

ence a curse to 24 out of 25 parts of the inhabitants of this country. With us the branches of this institution cover all the states. The Southern ones at this time are aristocratical in their disposition: and that that spirit should grow and extend itself is within the natural order of things. I do not flatter myself with the immortality of our governments: but I shall think little also of their longevity unless this germ of destruction be taken out. When the society themselves shall weigh the possibility of evil against the impossibility of any good to proceed from this institution, I cannot help hoping they will eradicate it. I know they wish the permanence of our governments as much as any individuals composing them.[2]— An interruption here and the departure of the gentleman by whom I send this obliges me to conclude it, with assurances of the sincere respect and esteem with which I have the honor to be Dear Sir Your most obedt. & most humble servt.,   TH: JEFFERSON

RC (DLC: Washington Papers); written with TJ's right hand; endorsed by Washington. PrC (DLC: TJ Papers). Tr of an extract (MHi: Knox Papers); in an unidentified hand; endorsed by Knox, to whom it was forwarded by Washington on 27 Apr. 1787. Enclosures: (1) Démeunier's *Essai sur les Etats-Unis* (see under 22 June 1786). (2) The "Article [on the Cincinnati] as ultimately published," referred to by Washington as a "translation" but by Hume as TJ's notes on the Cincinnati; the actual enclosure is missing, but it was presumably a translation by Short of that part of the "Article as ultimately published" that pertained to the Cincinnati (Washington to Knox, 27 Apr. 1787, *Writings*, ed. Fitzpatrick, XXIX, 208; E. E. Hume, ed., *General Washington's Correspondence Concerning the Society of the Cincinnati*, p. 270).

TJ's letter evidently arrived at Mount Vernon on 25 Apr. 1787, adding to the acute embarrassment Washington was experiencing over the question of attendance at the forthcoming general meeting of the Cincinnati scheduled for the first Monday in May (7 May 1787). On 31 Oct. 1786—no doubt recalling his experience of 1784—he had dispatched a circular letter to the various state societies saying that he could not attend the forthcoming meeting and expressing his desire not to be elected to the presidency since he would be "under the necessity of declining the acceptance of it" (Fitzpatrick, same,

XXIX, 31-3; Hume, same, 264-5). No sooner had this been written than Washington received Madison's letter of 8 Nov. 1786 advising him that he had been designated at the head of the Virginia delegation to the Federal Convention, scheduled for the second Monday in May 1787. To this Washington replied on 18 Nov. 1786 that, despite his determination to retire from "the public walks of life," he would have obeyed the wish of the General Assembly if it were not "now out of my power to do this with any degree of consistency"; informing Madison of his recent letter to the Society, he added: "Under these circumstances it will readily be perceived that I could not appear at the same time and place on any other occasion, without giving offence to a very respectable and deserving part of the Community, the late officers of the American Army" (Fitzpatrick, same, XXIX, 71-2; he wrote similarly to Theodorick Bland the same day, p. 73). However, Madison's insistence, Gov. Randolph's formal notification, and other circumstances by mid-December brought Washington to a state of acute distress; sending to David Humphreys extracts of his correspondence with Madison and Randolph, he asked: "Should this matter be further pressed . . . what had I best do?" (Fitzpatrick, same, XXIX, 76, 115, 119, 120, 127-9). By March Washington could write Jay: "My name is in the delegation . . . but it was put there contrary to my desire, and remains contrary to my request. Several reasons

[533]

at the time of this appointment and which yet exist, conspired to make an attendance inconvenient, perhaps improper, tho' a good deal urged to it." At last, on 28 Mch. 1787, he informed Gov. Randolph that he would yield to the unusual "degree of sollicitude" of his friends and attend the convention provided the late afflictions of a "rheumatic complaint" did not interfere, but that if he did go, he would set off for Philadelphia "the first, or second day of May, that I may be there in time to account, personally, for my conduct to the General Meeting of the Cincinnati which is to convene on the first Monday of that month" (Fitzpatrick, same, XXIX, 177, 187). It was in this context that TJ's letter arrived with its disturbing implications. On Thursday, 26 Apr., Washington received "an Express between 4 and 5 Oclock this afternoon informing me of the extreme illness of my Mother and Sister Lewis" and "resolved to set out for Fredericksburgh by daylight in the Morning, and spent the evening in writing some letters on business respecting the Meeting of the Cincinnati, to the Secretary General of the Society, Genl. Knox" (Fitzpatrick, ed., *Diaries of George Washington*, III, 205). There were two letters to Knox, both dated the 27th but evidently written the evening of the 26th. The first explained how he had yielded to the "wishes of many . . . friends" that he attend the Federal Convention, but that "(within this hour) I am called by an express, who assures me not a moment is to be lost, to see a mother and *only sister* (who are supposed to be in the agonies of Death) expire; and I am hastening to obey this Melancholy call after having just buried a brother who was the intimate companion of my youth, and the friend of my ripened age. This journey of mine then, 100 miles in the disordered frame of my body, will, I am persuaded, unfit me for the intended trip to Philadelphia, and assuredly prevent my offering that tribute of respect to my compatriots in Arms which results from affection and gratitude for their attachment to, and support of me, upon so many trying occasions." He then explained that he had determined to "shew . . . respect to the General Meeting of the Society by coming there the week before" the meeting of the Convention, but that, since this was not possible, he was forwarding such papers as he had that required the attention of the Cincinnati. The letter, evidently intended to be read to the Society, closed thus: "I make a tender of my affectionate regard to the members who may Constitute the General Meeting of the Society" (*Writings*, ed. Fitzpatrick, XXIX, 208-10; Hume, ed., *General Washington's Correspondence Concerning the Society of the Cincinnati*, p. 305, includes this letter to Knox with the heading: "General Washington notifies the Secretary General of the Cincinnati that he will attend the General Meeting after all"; but, despite the fact that Hume's volume appeared two years after Fitzpatrick's volume XXIX, it does not include the other letter to Knox of the same date). Washington then—perhaps on the evening of the 26th, but giving "April 27, 1787" as the date—wrote Knox a second letter: "Hurried as I am I cannot (not expecting to see you in Philadelphia) withhold the copy of a Paragraph in a letter which came to my hands yesterday from Mr. Jefferson. . . . In my present state of mind I can hardly form an opinion whether it will be best to lay the matter before the Society as coming from Mr. Jefferson or as from a person of as good information as any in France. I must therefore leave it wholly with you to do as you may think most proper. You know my sentiments from the proceedings of the last General meeting and from my Circular" (*Writings*, ed. Fitzpatrick, XXIX, 208). Washington's sentiments as expressed at the "last General meeting" had been profoundly affected by another timely interposition on the part of TJ (see Vol. 7: 105-10).

On the 27th Washington began his journey "About sun rise . . . as intended." He arrived at Fredericksburg early that same afternoon, finding his sister out of danger and his mother better than he had expected. He remained at Fredericksburg over the week-end, returning to Mount Vernon late in the afternoon of Monday the 30th. He was worn with fatigue, but "rid to all the Plantations on Tuesday," 1 May, and all of the remainder of that week he was actively engaged in supervising his plantations. By 5 May his "rheumatic complaint" had improved, and he still intended to leave for Philadelphia (as originally planned) on Monday or early Tuesday. But on Sunday "Company, and several other matters" pressed upon him and obliged him to postpone his journey a day longer; the company

[534]

included Dr. Craik to whom he had intrusted the Cincinnati documents to be carried to Philadelphia, and Col. John Fitzgerald and Dr. David Stuart who doubtless discussed the important matter of the fur trade opened up by TJ in the present letter (see Washington to TJ, 30 May 1787). Monday, 7 May, Washington spent at "home preparing for my journey." Tuesday the 8th being "squally with showers," he decided to postpone the start again. On Wednesday the 9th, a little after sunrise he crossed the Potomac and pursued the "rout by way of Baltimore." On the fifth day, Sunday the 13th, he arrived in Philadelphia in the afternoon, alighted at Mrs. Mary House's boarding-house at Fifth and Market streets, but was "pressed by Mr. and Mrs. Robert Morris to lodge with them," which he did (Fitzpatrick, ed., *Diaries of George Washington*, III, 205-16; *Writings*, XXIX, 210-3). From this chronology it is evident that Washington was at no special pains to get to Philadelphia in time to participate in the General Meeting. But the delegates to the Federal Convention arrived slowly and tardily, the members of the Society were still in session, and, on the very day that Washington arrived in Philadelphia, Arthur Lee wrote from New York that he had received private information that the General Meeting intended to "re-elect you as their President, notwithstanding your letter. They think you are so plegd to them, by some of your letters that you cannot refuse the Presidency" (Hume, ed., *General Washington's Correspondence Concerning the Society of the Cincinnati*, p. 307). Washington replied on the 20th, but made no allusion to Lee's remark: on the 18th he had in fact been elected president-general. To TJ he wrote—stating that the present letter did not "come to my hands till the first of the present month"—that he had not been at Liberty to decline the presidency "without placing myself in an extremely disagreeable situation with relation to that brave and faithful class of men, whose persevering patriotism and friendship I had experienced on so many trying occasions" (Washington to TJ, 30 May 1787). The letter was signed by Washington, but that part of it pertaining to the Cincinnati was drafted by Humphreys, to whom he had turned for advice as on many other occasions. Thus in silence Washington accepted the embarrassing advantage that his former comrades in arms had taken of his reluctant presence in Philadelphia—a presence resulting from his conviction that it was "a public duty to which every private consideration should give way" (Washington to Jabez Bowen, 9 Jan. 1787, *Writings*, ed. Fitzpatrick, XXIX, 138).

[1] This word interlined in substitution for "seen," deleted.

[2] Tr of extract that Washington sent to Knox includes the text from the beginning of the paragraph to this point.

Thomas Barclay to the American Commissioners

GENTLEMEN Escurial 15th. Novr. 1786

I came here a few days ago to deliver a letter from the Emperor of Morocco to the King, which I put into the hands of the Count de Florida Blanca, acknowleging the Sense I had of his Attentions and thanking him with great sincerity on the Part he had taken in our business at Morocco. He seemed very much pleased with our success and smiling replied "Now that we have happily finished this Treaty, we will see what we can do with others for you." I am persuaded that this Minister is extremely well disposed to serve our Country, and I doubt not but this Court will greatly strengthen our endeavours with the Barbary Powers. It is the decided opinion

of the Count D'Espilly that nothing ought to be attempted with Algiers at present and that you should begin with the Porte. He proposes setting out for Africa some time hence and promises a continuation of his good offices. He remarked that if we could capture one Algerine Cruizer it would greatly facilitate a Treaty. But this mode of negociating would I think prove more expensive than any other and it ought to be our last Resort. I am informed by a letter from Mr. Chiappi of Mogadore that a vessel is arrived there, the master of which Reports, that on his Passage from Lisbon he saw an Algerine Frigate of 40 guns and four Xebecks, and that the people who were on board one of them informed him they were going to cruise on the Coast of America. But I cannot give entire Credit to the Account as the Season of the year is far advanced, and we have not heard that any of the Algerine Cruisers have passed the Streights of Gibraltar, within which I hope the Portuguese Squadron will keep them, this being all that may be expected from them. To-morrow I shall return to Madrid and from thence to Alicant from whence I shall give you as clear an Account of Mr. Lamb's situation as Circumstances will admit of. I believe there are some Effects belonging to the United States at Corunna worth looking after, it is some Years since in Consequence of a Letter from Mr. Morris, I endeavoured to recover them. I shall take all the information I can of their Value and if it appears clearly that they are worth so much Attention, I will return to France by that place, if not I shall go as soon as possible home by the shortest Rout. I am with great Respect Gentlemen, your most obt. humble servt,
THOS. BARCLAY

RC (MHi: AMT); in a clerk's hand, signed by Barclay; addressed; endorsed. Tr (DNA: PCC, No. 91, I); in the hand of William Short. PrC of Tr (DLC). Noted in SJL as received 6 Dec. 1786.

From William Carmichael

DEAR SIR Escurial 15th. Nov. 1786

Colonel Franks whom various circumstances have detained longer than Mr. Barclay or himself expected will have the honor to deliver you this with that Gentlemans dispatches. As these contain every thing material relative to his Mission, I will only remark on this Subject that his Conduct in this Country has been such, as hath acquired him the Esteem of all those who have known him here as well Natives as Foreigners and by all Accounts hath made the most favorable impression of those he represented in

Africa. His Reception by the King and the Prince was very gracious. I have introduced him to the Count D'Expilly. Colonel Franks who was interpreter on that Occasion will have the honor to give you the Detail of what passed, the Mission of Mr. Lamb to Algiers made the principal Subject; Mr. Barclay to whom I had communicated my Correspondence with Mr. Lamb, had resolved to go to Alicante previous to our departure from Madrid. This Conversation and a Letter which I received here of the bad State of Health of the latter confirmed him in his resolution entirely grounded on his desire to promote the public Service. In case of Mr. Lamb's Death, his papers, the funds with which he has been entrusted may fall into improper hands, from which consideration I presume Your Excellency will not find it improper to give the necessary Powers to Mr. Barclay to prevent any ill Consequences which may happen from a similar Event. Mr. Barclay will report to you the Conversation we had with the Count de Florida Blanca. His Language has ever been the same to me Viz: that the instant this Court had adjusted its Affairs with Algiers, it would employ its best Offices to promote ours. In refering your Excellency to Colonel Franks for more particular information, permit me to observe that the Ministry appears hurt at the little Notice Congress takes of this favorable disposition on their Part. I have no intelligence from that Body for several Months except what you have given me. Here there are many Projects but few effectually pursued. This Country suffers by epidemical disorders, the Treasury is at expedients. On monday last the French Ambassador had a private Audience of the King and a long conference with the Minister on the subject of a Letter written by the Queen of France to His Catholic Majesty on the family difference between this Court and that of Naples. In a few days I shall know the Effects of this Letter. I have the honor to inclose you two articles lately published here. The one to diminish the Cavalry the other to augment the Infantry. You will perceive the avowed motive by the preamble to each. The fact is the Cavalry will be reduced immediately and it will be a long time before the new additional Batallions to the infantry will be raised, those on the antient establishment being far from efficient. In the mean time the Sale of the Horses will put some funds into the Treasury. The Sale of the Officers Commissions for the Batallions to be raised will add to that Sum, and this small Capital will cost at least eight per cent to Government. I have reason to think that additional Battallions will be raised in their Possessions in America on the same Plan. It is unecessary perhaps for me to recommend Colonel Franks to your Excellencys notice. I have long been acquainted with this Gentleman and his activity and zeal for a number of years in our Countrys service will I am persuaded induce you to further his views as they be consistent with your own Ideas of Propriety. With very great Respect & Esteem I have the honor to be Your Excellencys Most Obedt. & very Hble. Sert.,

WM. CARMICHAEL

RC (DLC); endorsed. Noted in SJL as received 6 Dec. 1786. Enclosures missing.

From Maria Cosway

[17 Nov. 1786]

Cosa vuol dir questo silenzio? O aspettata la posta con tanta Ansietà, ed ecco che ogni volta arriva senza apportarmi alcuna lettera da Parigi, veramente sono inquieta, temo che sia indisposizione o che il braccio stà peggio, penso a Mille cose alla volta fuor che i miei amici si sieno già scordati di me; se medita di farmi un altro gran regalo di una lunga lettera, la supplicherò di mandarmele piu corte, ma piu spesse. Non o piu pazzienza di aspettare e mi rischio di prender la penna senza esser sicura se devo lagnarmi, se devo rimproverare, se devo implorar la pazienza, raccontar la mia mortificazione, e inquietudini di questo disapuntamento, forse una lettera e per istrada, intanto mi lagnerò perche tanto ritarda ad arrivare. [. . . .]ndo[1] false, non senza [. . . .][2] non apportano che delle consequenze che spesso ci fanno dispiacere, si suol pensare con sodisfazione alle eccelenti qualita delle persone per le quali si à della stima, della nostra felicità in poterne gustare il valore, e provare il piacere che un anima sensibile sente nell'Amicizia, e cos'è la vita, privata di questo sentimento? Ma quando ci allontaniamo, passata la pena della separazione, si vive in continua inquietudine, non si riceve lettere si immagina mille disgrazzie, se qualche accidente accade, non si può accorrere con soccorso o consolazione, ne riceverne informazioni.

Il tempo qui e molto cattivo, malinconico, tristo. Molti de miei Amici, sono in campagna, sicche passo il mio tempo con quei pochi che ci sono, in dipingere, suonare l'arpa, il cimbalo e cantare, in questo modo lei mi dirà non si può che esser contenti, l'approvo anch'io, ma non so c'e qualcosa di tanto pesante in quest'aria, che tutto quel che fo mi par [. . .] dissipar la [noia . . . .][3] ancora che per

17 NOVEMBER 1786

[. . . .]³ che c'impone questo clima si starebbe [. . . .]² Night Thoughts, avanti al fuoco, e quando l'immaginazione e ben riscaldata, si potrebbe andar a raffreddarsi in un fieume. Non credo che neppur gli Dei sarebbero testimonij di questa stravaganza, tanto l'aria e cupa dalla nebbia e fummo, che impedisce i celesti abitatori di penetrar i loro sguardi fino alle debolezze umane di quest'isola.

Avrà inteso parlare dell sussurro che a fatto in questi giorni Lord G. Gordon. La Morte della Principessa Amelia, per novità non e tempo di mandargliene, ne empierò un altra lettera. Quando cominciai questa pensai di [non] dir che tre parole, ma insensibilmente sono arrivata fin qui senza neppur sapere cosa o detto, ma quando le donne cominciano a parlare e difficile il trattenerle, ancorche abbino l'avvertenza che dicono degli spropositi. O veduto piu volte Mr. & Mrs. Paradise ed o il piacere di parlar di lei spesso con loro. Sarà sempre un infinita sodisfazione il mentovar il nome d'una persona che stimo, e questa la prova la sua vera amica,   MARIA COSWAY

Ricevo in questo momento due lettere da Parigi, ma non da lei.

RC (MHi); MS mutilated, the top of the leaves being eaten away; salutation and date line are missing on the first page and all or part of three lines of text on the second and third pages are missing or illegible; addressed. The date has been supplied from internal evidence and an entry in SJL for the receipt of a letter of this date on 24 Nov. 1786.

Translation: But what does this silence mean? I have awaited the post with so much anxiety and lo each time it arrives without bringing me any letters from Paris, I am really worried, I fear lest it be illness or that your arm is worse, I think of a thousand things at once except that my friends should so soon have forgotten me; If you are contemplating making me another big gift of a long letter, I shall beg you to send them to me shorter but more frequent. I no longer have the patience to wait and I am venturing to take up the pen without being sure whether I am to complain, whether I am to reprove, or whether I am to implore patience, to express my mortification and anxieties of this disappointment, perhaps a letter is en route, in the meantime I shall complain because it delays so long in arriving. [. . . .] not without [. . . .] bring only consequences which often displease us, one is wont to think with satisfaction about the excellent qualities of the persons for whom one has esteem, of our happiness in being able to savour of their value, and to experience the pleasure which a sensitive soul feels in friendship, and what is life, deprived of this sentiment! But when we separate, after the pain of separation is past, one lives in continual anxiety, one does not receive letters, one imagines a thousand misfortunes, if some mishap occurs one cannot run with succour or comfort, nor receive news of it.

The weather here is very bad, melancholy, sad. Many of my friends are in the country, so that I spend my time with those few who are here, in painting, playing the harp, the harpsichord, singing, in this way you will tell me one can only be content, I too approve it, but I don't know there is something so heavy in this air, that all that I do seems to me [. . . .] to dissipate my [. . . .] although for [. . . .] which this climate imposes upon us [. . . .] Night Thoughts, before the fire, and when the imagination is well warmed up, one could go cool off in a river. I do not believe that even the gods would be witnesses to this fantastic performance, so much is the air darkened by the fog and smoke that it prevents the celestial inhabitants from penetrating with their gaze the human foibles of this island.

You will probably have heard of the sensation that Lord G. Gordon has occasioned recently [and of] the death of Princess Amelia. As far as news goes there is no time to send you any, I shall fill another letter with it. When I began this I intended to say only three words but unconsciously I have arrived this far without even knowing what I have said, but when women begin talking it is difficult to hold them back, even if they are aware of their saying foolish things.

I have seen Mr. and Mrs. Paradise several times and I often have the pleasure of talking with them of you. It will always be an infinite satisfaction to mention the name of a person whom I esteem, and this is felt by your true friend . . . I receive in this moment two letters from Paris, but not from you.

[1] Top of page missing, affecting at least three lines of text; the 1st line which is apparent is entirely illegible and only the words "ndo false, non sensa" are legible in the next line.
[2] Three or four words missing.
[3] Half a line missing.

From C. W. F. Dumas

Monsieur   Lahaie 17e. Nov. 1786

La présente parviendra à Votre Excellence par Mr. le Cte. Coëtloury, Ami de Mr. l'Ambassadeur, du Ms. De la Coste, du Rhingrave de Salm, et qui m'honore aussi de son amitié. Il reviendra ici vers Noël.

Nous attendons d'un moment à l'autre Mr. De Raineval, qui trouve que cette Republique, dans ces circonstances surtout, mérite qu'on l'étudie de près.

Permettez que je place mes respects pour Mr. le Ms. De la Fayette, auprès de tout celui que je vous dois et avec lequel je suis, De Votre Excellence Le très-humble et très-obéissant serviteur,
                                        C W F Dumas

RC (DLC). FC (Rijksarchief, The Hague, Dumas Papers; photostats in DLC); dated only "1786" and with names deleted. Noted in SJL as received 28 Nov. 1786.

Though no mention is made of the fact, the present letter was undoubtedly accompanied by Dumas' letter to Jay of 17 Nov. 1786, transmitting various marked copies of the gazettes containing addresses of various cities and towns to the States General; recurring to the old theme of his personal needs; and urging that an order be issued authorizing the repair, payment of taxes, and sale of the "hôtel des Etats-Unis" (FC, same).

To Ralph Izard

Sir   Paris Nov. 18. 1786.

I have received your favor of the 1st. July and congratulate you Sincerely on the marriage of your second daughter. Besides the happiness which will be felt by Mrs. Izard and yourself in the establishment of your daughters so much to your mind, I am in

[540]

18 NOVEMBER 1786

hopes the public will derive advantage also from it as it leaves an obstacle the less to your devoting your services to them. I have been in constant hope of your being fixed at the Hague which (with the convenience of the European post) would make us neighbors.

Soon after my arrival here the minister passed the arrets allowing certain articles of provision to be carried from the U.S. to the French islands. Such was the humour of the merchants against it that it required all the firmness of the minister not to retire from the measure, and it was even thought at times that it might endanger his place. The circumstances convinced me that it was not the moment for attempting the regulation of our trade with their West Indies. This must lie by till the clamour against the first indulgence has subsided and their benefit to France become manifest from experience. In the mean time I have been endeavoring to get our commerce with France put on a proper footing. The inclosed letter will inform you of the progress made in that. [. . .][1] the duties on most of our productions imported here [. . .][2] are still unfinished. I have in vain tried [. . .][3] to find out the duties paid on these articles in the several ports. In hopes of accomplishing this, as well as for the sake of my health I shall set out soon to make the tour of the seaports. With respect to rice however I am persuaded it is already received on very favorable terms. The consumption of that article in this country is immense, and the whiteness of the Carolina rice makes it gain ground daily. I think the whole of that article which you make could find vent here. Hitherto they have received it from the London merchants who pocket the difference between what you receive and 30. livres the French hundred, the common price here. We are endeavoring to get Honfleur made a free port in hopes it may become the deposit for rice, instead of Cowes. Supposing the want of correspondents here might be one reason why the rice of S. Carolina is not sent here immediately, I have advised a Mr. Barrett to turn his attention to this article. He is connected with the Le Coulteux, which for centuries has been the richest house in France. He has shewed me a circular letter he has written on the subject, one of which I think he addresses to you. The sum allowed to be drawn in the moment of shipping is certainly not very tempting. However he is an honest man, will do you justice, and if it becomes an object, the house will see their interest in admitting larger draughts. I much wish to see this branch of commerce opened between this country and us directly. It will be a strong link of connection the more with the only nation on earth on whom we can solidly rely for assistance till we can stand on our own legs. Morocco has made peace with us. Algiers will not. I am with sincere esteem Dr. Sir your affectionate humble servt., TH: JEFFERSON

PrC (DLC); written with TJ's right hand. MS faded. Enclosure: Printed copy of Calonne to TJ, 22 Oct. 1786.

[1] Four or five words illegible.
[2] Two or three words illegible.
[3] Two words illegible.

From Presolle

Paris, 18 Nov. 1786. Transmits receipt for payment for cartridge boxes, fittings, and arms purchased for the state of Virginia and shipped on 16 July, 8 and 13 Sep. 1786; the order has received careful attention and should be satisfactory; if further supplies are needed, requests that he be honored with the order.

RC (Vi); 2 p.; endorsed by TJ, in part: "Presolle." Enclosure (Vi); 2 p.; endorsed by TJ:
"2000 sets @ 7ᵗᵗ.16 [15773]
 1406   @ 7 .16 11098-10
 3406   26871-10";

certified, 9 Dec. 1789, by J. Latil, in part: "I do Certify that the above receipt acknowledges payment made by Mr. Jefferson."

To Maria Cosway

Paris Nov. 19. 1786

I begin, my dear Madam, to write a little with the right hand, and you are by promise, as well as by inclination entitled to it's first homage. But I write with pain and must be short. This is good news for you; for were the hand able to follow the effusions of the heart, that would cease to write only when this shall cease to beat. My first letter warned you of this danger. I became sensible myself of my transgression and promised to offend no more. Your goodness seems to have induced you to forgive, and even to flatter me. That was a great error. When sins are dear to us we are but too prone to slide into them again. The act of repentance itself is often sweetened with the thought that it clears our account for a repetition of the same sin. The friendly letter I have received from you might have been taken as a release from my promise: but you are saved by a cruel cramp in my hand which admonishes me in every line to condense my thoughts and words.

I made your excuses to Madame de Corny. She was as uneasy, as you had been, under the appearance of a failure in point of civility and respect. I knew the key to the riddle, and asked her on what day she had returned to town. She said on the 6th. of October. I told her you had left it on the 5th. Thus each stands excused in the eye of the other, and she will have the pleasure of seeing you in London. Nothing more will be necessary, for good people naturally grow together. I wish she could put me into her pocket, when she goes, or you, when she comes back.—Mercy, cramp! that twitch was too much. I am done, I am done.—Adieu ma chere madame: je ne suis plus à moi. Faites mes compliments à Monsieur Cosway, assurez le de mon amitié, et daignez d'agreer vous meme l'hommage d'un sincere & tendre attachement. Encore adieu.

PrC (ViU); unsigned; endorsed.
YOU ARE . . . ENTITLED TO IT'S FIRST HOMAGE: TJ's letters to Jay, 12 Nov., to Le Roy, 13 Nov. (in part), to Washington, 14 Nov., and to Izard, 18 Nov., had been written with his right hand.

To Zachariah Loreilhe

Sir   Paris Nov. 19. 1786.

I had the honour of receiving your letter of Octob. 20. on the 29th. of the same month, and wrote an answer the day following directed to you at Lorient. This went by post. Your favor of the 12th. instant which came to hand last night, informs me that mine had not been received. I therefore have the honor of now inclosing a copy of it.   A dislocated wrist has for two months passed disabled me from writing myself. I begin to write a little, but with pain. I am strongly advised to go to the waters of Aix, for the reestablishment of my arm, and am inclined to do it, if business permits. In this event I shall have the honor of writing to you before my departure. I have the honor to be Sir Your most obedient & most humble servt.,   Th: Jefferson

PrC (DLC). Enclosure: Copy of TJ to Loreilhe, 30 Oct. 1786.

To Dorcas Montgomery

Madam   Paris Nov. 19. 1786.

Your friendly offer on the subject of my daughter, which I this moment receive, merits and meets my warmest thanks. I have unfortunately but a choice among difficulties and disagreeable things for her. Of the plans practicable in my situation I have been obliged to adopt that which presented the fewest objectionable circumstances. She is at present engaged in courses of French drawing &c. in which she has yet made a progress by no means sufficient. I am unwilling therefore to interrupt these and the rather as neither her nor my return to America are ever considered as very distant, tho' I fix no time. These considerations induce me to think it best for her to continue her present pursuits. Otherwise I should have been happy in confiding her to so good hands for shewing her those countries which of all others I have ever thought most worthy of being seen. I have therefore to repeat my thanks to you for your goodness, and according to your desire I inclose your letter, which, while you prohibit me from mentioning it to others, shall ever be remembered by him who has the honour to be with sentiments of the most perfect esteem & respect, Madam, your most obedient & most humble servant, Th: Jefferson

P.S. I am in hopes your departure will not be so sudden but that I may have the honour of your company to dinner on Thursday next.

PrC (ViWC); added at foot of text, evidently written much later by TJ: "Mrs. ⟨Cosway⟩ ⟨Church⟩ Montgomery"; endorsed similarly. Mrs. Montgomery's letter to which this is an answer has not been found, but see Mrs. Montgomery to TJ, 21 Aug. 1786 and TJ to Martha Jefferson, 4 Nov. 1786. Enclosure missing.

To Martin Oster

Sir   Paris Nov. 19. 1786

I have lately recieved the inclosed letter from a Mr. Warneck who stiles himself the brother of an officer of that name who died in Virginia. Not doubting Sir that you will be better acquainted than I am with the nature of what he requires and what may best suit his purpose, I have taken the liberty of inclosing you his letter and begging the favor of you to do in this case what your acquaintance with the laws of the two countries may make you suppose necessary. I hope you will be so good as [to] excuse this freedom on my part and be assured Sir of [those] sentiments with which I have the honor to be your most obedient humble Servant,

Th: Jefferson

PrC (DLC); in the hand of William Short, including signature; at foot of text: "(Test W Short Sec)"; and, in TJ's hand, "M. Oster Consul of France in Virga." Enclosure: ——— Wernecke to TJ, 9 Nov. 1786 (see TJ to Wernecke, following).

To —— Wernecke

Sir   Paris Nov. 19. 1786.

I have received the favor which you did me the honor to address me on the subject of your brother deceased in Virginia. As the French Consul who resides there will [. . .][1] in his power [. . .] to do what may be necessary for in This instance, I have inclosed him your letter and noted my request to him to interest himself in it. As soon as [I am able to give you] any information on the subject I will communicate it to you with very great pleasure. In the mean [time] I have the honor to be Sir Your most obedient humble Servant,
                                        Th: Jefferson

PrC (DLC); in Short's hand, including signature; at foot of text: "(Test. W Short Sec)."

THE FAVOR . . . TO ADDRESS ME: The following entry is recorded in SJL under 18 Nov. 1786: "Warneck. Lt. Col. de cavalerie à Phaltzbourg à Bonquenon Lorraine Allemand. Nov. 9."; Wernecke's letter of 9 Nov. was enclosed in TJ to Martin Oster, 19 Nov., q.v., and has not been found. See Vol. 4: 474; Vol. 6: 644.

[1] Four words illegible.

From John Stockdale

Sir   Picadilly London 20th. Novr. 1786.

I received your Order ℔ favor of Coll. Smith, which is nearly ready and will be sent of from London in about three days. I shall esteem it as a great favor if you'll be so kind as to send me the History of Sandford and Merton, in French, which I am this Instant Inform'd is Just Translated by Mr. Berquin, the Author of the Childrens Friend. I beg pardon for the Liberty taken, as I am very anxious for a Copy (the Original being my own Publication), having no friend in Paris beside the Duke of Dorset, Mr. Stone his Secretary, and yourself. Should there be any difficulty, I think Mr. Stone will willingly convey it to me. Some time past two French Gentlemen call'd upon me, with a Copy of your Minutes of Virginia, with a View to have it Printed, but I inform'd them that I had some reason to believe that a New Edition was coming out with corrections by the Author, and Coll. Smith Inform'd me that a large Map was engraving for the Work. I have some doubts wether it would pay the expences, at same time have a Wish to Publish it, with your Name, as I am convinced it is a Work of great Merit. I have spoken to Mr. Adams and Coll. Smith on the Subject who wish much to see the Work Published in England.

I have the honor to be with great Respect, sir, Your much oblig'd & very hble. Servt.,   JOHN STOCKDALE

RC (MHi). Not recorded in SJL.

To John Trumbull

DEAR SIR   Paris Nov. 20. 1786.

I begin to write a little with my right hand but with much pain. I can therefore only acknolege the receipt of your letter from London, and pray you to deliver the inclosed. My hand mends so slowly that I am advised by the faculty to go to the waters of Aix in Provence. If I do you will hear from me. I am with sincere esteem Dr. Sir Your friend & servant,   TH: JEFFERSON

PrC (DLC); endorsed. Enclosure: TJ to Maria Cosway, 19 Nov. 1786.

From José da Maia

MONSEGNEUR   à Monpellier 21 de 9bre. de 1786

Je viens de recevoir l'honeur de Votre lettre de 16 d'Octobre, et je suis extremément faché de ne l'avoir pas reçu plutot; mais il m'a fallu rester en campanhe jusqu'à present par raport à ma santé: et puisque je vois, que mes informations Vous parviendront assurément, je vais avoir l'honeur de Vous les communiquer.

Je suis Bresilien, et Vous savez, que ma malheureuse patrie gemit dans un affreux esclavage, qui devient chaque [jour] plus insupportable depuis l'epoque de Votre glorieuse independence, puisque les barbares Portugais n'epargnent rien pour nous rendre malheureux decrainte que nous suivions Vos pas; et comme nous connoîçons, que ces usurpateurs contre la loi de la nature, et de l'humanité ne songent, que à nous accabler, nous nous sommes decidés à suivre le frappant exemple, que Vous venez de nous donner, et par consequence à briser nos chaines, et à faire revivre notre liberté, qui est toutàfait morte, et accablée par la force, qui est le seul droit, qu'ont les Européens sur l'Amerique. Mais il s'agit d'avoir une puissance, qui donne la main aux Bresiliens, attenduque l'Hispanle ne manquera pas de se joindre à Portugal; et malgré les avantages, que nous avons pour nous defendre, nous ne pourrons pas le faire, ou du moins il ne seroit pas prudent de nous hazarder sans etre surs d'y reussir. Cela posé, Monsegneur,

[546]

c'et Votre nation, que nous croyons plus propre pour donner du secours non seulement parceque c'est elle, qui nous a donné l'exemple, mais aussi parceque la nature nous a fait habitants du meme continent, et par consequence en quelque façon compatriotes; de notre part nous sommes pre[ts] à donner tout l'argent, qui sera necessaire, et à temoigner en tout temps notre reconnoissence envers nos bienfaisants.

Monsegneur, voila à peu près le precis de mes intentions, et c'et pour m'acquiter de cette commition, que je suis venu en France; puisque je ne pouvois pas en Amerique sans donner des soupçons à ceux qui en sçussent, c'est à Vous maintenant à juger s'elles peuvent avoir lieu, et dans le cas, que Voulussiez en consulter Votre nation, je suis en etat de Vous donner toutes les informations, que Vous trouverez necessaires.

Je l'honeur d'etre avec la consideration la plus parfaite Monsegneur Votre tres humble, et tres obeissant serviteur,

VENDEK

RC (DLC). Noted in SJL as received 30 Nov. 1786.
VOTRE LETTRE DE 16 D'OCTOBRE: TJ's letter of this date has not been found and is not recorded in SJL; see Da Maia to TJ, 2 Oct. 1786.

To Achard Frères

GENTLEMEN   Paris Nov. 22. 1786.

I have now the honor to inclose you the acquit à caution for the two cases of wine. They arrived only two days ago which has occasioned the delay of returning you this paper. I return you many thanks for your services and have the honor to be gentlemen your most obedient & most humble servant,   TH: JEFFERSON

PrC (MHi); endorsed. Enclosures not located.

From Stephen Cathalan, Jr.

[*Marseilles*, 22 Nov. 1786. Recorded in SJL as received 30 Nov. 1786. Not found.]

To Colonia

Mercredi 22me Novembre. 1786.

Il est arrivé à la Douane de Paris pour Monsieur Jefferson ministre plenipotentiaire de l'Amerique un harnois à trois chevaux

[547]

23 NOVEMBER 1786

qu'il a fait venir d'Angleterre pour son usage particulier. Pour le retirer de la Douane il faut un ordre de Monsieur le Controleur General. Si Monsieur de Colonia voudroit bien l'obtenir et le lui faire passer Monsieur Jefferson lui en auroit beaucoup d'obligation. Il ne demande pas un exemption des droits. Ce pourroit occasionner des délais, qui seroient incommodes, entant qu'il est sur le point de faire une voiage.

PrC (MHi); endorsed.

TJ did in fact pay duties on the harness: an entry in Account Book shows that on 1 Dec. 1786 he paid Petit "duty on harness 111^{tt}-0-6." See TJ to Lafayette, 3 Nov. 1786.

From Tarbé

[*Rouen, 23 Nov. 1786.* Recorded in SJL as received 24 Nov. 1786. Not found.]

From Brissot de Warville

[*Orléans, 23 Nov. 1786.* Recorded in SJL as received 24 Nov. 1786. Not found.]

From John Ledyard

London Novr. 25th. 1786

My friend, my brother, my Father—I know not by what title to address you—you are very very dear to me. Embrace the dear Marquis La Fayette for me: he has all the virtues of his country without any of its little foibles. I am indeed a very plain man, but do not think that mountains or oceans shall oppose my passage to glory while I have such friends in remembrance—I have pledged myself—difficulties have intervened—my heart is on fire—ye stimulate, and I shall gain the victory. Thus I think of you—thus I have thought of you daily—and thus I shall think of you *(untill it ceases to be a virtue to think—with regard to myself this cannot be the case while either of you exist)*.[1] After all the fair prospects that attended me when I last wrote—I still am persecuted—still the slave of accident and the son of care. The Ship I embarked in was seized by the Custom house and is this day exchequered. If a small subscription now begun in London by Sr. Joseph Banks and Doctr. Hunter will enable me to proceed you will probably hear from me

[548]

25 NOVEMBER 1786

at Hamburgh: if I arrive at Petersbourg you most certainly will. You see the course I was purs[u]ing to fame reversed and I am now going across Siberia as I had once before intended from Paris this time twelve month—what a Twelve months! I do defy fortune to be more malicious during another. I fear my subscription will be small: it adds to my anxiety to reach those dominions where I shall not want money—I do not mean the dominions that may be beyond death: I shall never wish to die while you the Marquis and Mr. Barclay are alive:—Pray Sir if that dear and genuine friend of mine is any where near you, do Me the honour to present me sur mes genoux devant lui—J'adore son coeur genereux. May I beg to be presented to Mr. Short, to Commodore Jones and to Colo. Franks if with you: ⟨a present je pense comme lui de la gouvernement de cet pays ici—tout est un cabal meme dans leur [. . .]us—heureusment pour moi j'entend bien a don[ner] des coups du poins, and have litteraly been obliged to thrash 5 or 6 of these haughty turbulent and very insolent people: one of them at the theatre where I assure you one is still more liable to insult than in the streets even⟩.[1] I have just parted with Colonel Smith: he is well and is trying also to do something for me. I hear you have not been very well lately, tho now better—take care of your health for the sake of our Country and for his sake who begs the honor to subscribe himself with all possible respect & esteem Sr. your most humble & most obedt. servant, JNO LEDYARD

RC (NHi: Ledyard Papers); endorsed. Tr (Mrs. Jane Ledyard Remington, Cazenovia, N.Y., 1951); with several minor errors in transcription. Noted in SJL as received 20 Dec. 1786.

[1] The deleted passage is not in Tr.

From James Madison

DEAR SIR Richmond Novr. 25th. 1786.

The inclosed letter did not get to my hands till very lately though it was covered by one from Mrs. Carr dated Aug: 21. I conferred a few days ago with Mr. Wythe on the subject of your Nephew in Williamsburg, and had the pleasure of receiving the most favorable account of his capacity, his diligence and his disposition. He is now in the College and enjoys the advantage of Mr. Wythe's valuable patronage and instructions. Mr. Wythe assures me that he is an excellent Latin Scholar, and from the Greek classics which he has read and is reading, he must shortly merit the same character in the latter language. I have communicated to

[549]

26 NOVEMBER 1786

Mr. Wythe the plan of education which you wished t[o b]e pursued, and can count with perfect assurance on every attention on his part which the most zealous friendship to you and a particular affection to your Nephew can inspire. The evidence in favor of your younger Nephew is of the negative kind only, no late information having been received concerning him. Mr. D. Fitzhugh is here a member of the Assembly. He has not yet put into my hands the small sum which I was authorized to receive. He intimated to me a few days ago that he regretted the delay, and that he had a prospect of shortly putting an end to it. This letter goes by Mr. Chevalier who sets out tomorrow morning for N.Y. where he takes the packet on the 15th. prox. I do not include any public matters, because I expect to bring them down to a later period in a letter which will reach N.Y. in time for the same conveyance. Ad[ie]u.

Js. Madison Jr.

RC (DLC: Madison Papers); address leaf mutilated, but portions of the address and TJ's endorsement remain. Noted in SJL as received 24 Jan. 1787, together with Madison's letter of 4 Dec. Enclosure (missing): Martha Jefferson Carr to TJ, 5 May 1786, recorded in SJL as received with the above letter.

ONE FROM MRS. CARR: On 21 Aug. 1786 Mrs. Carr had written to Madison: "Your kind attention to my sons excites in me an anxiety to acquaint you with every change in their situations. They have both been placed agreeable to your appointments but by a letter which I have just receiv'd from my Eldest son I find he now only boards with Mr. Maury, and at the particular request of Mr. Wythe is going through a course of reading with him, laid down by his Uncle Jefferson. From the exalted Character of that Gentleman I think my son highly honoured by his notice. But your approbation of every step of this kind that he takes, is necessary to my happyness. I must therefore Sir trouble you with a request that should you see any Impropriety in this change you will be so Obliging as to point it out, and rest assured that any plan you shall think proper to propose shall be punctually Observed" (DLC: Madison Papers).

From Chenier de St. André

Rue Culture St Gervais. Dimanche 26 9bre. 1786.

Mr. Chenier de St. André a l'honneur de présenter ses complimens à monsieur jefferson. Il le prie d'etre persuadé que ce n'est ni par négligence ni par oubli qu'il a passé si long-Tems sans aller le voir, et le remercier de ses politesses. Il a été un mois à la campagne; il n'en est pas revenu bien portant; et il loge dans le quartier de Paris le plus éloigné de Monsieur jefferson. Il compte partir pour Nice dans huit jours. Il espere avant ce Tems-la aller savoir des nouvelles de la Santé de Monsieur jefferson, et si son bras est entierement rétabli.

Il le prie d'agréer les assurances de sa parfaite considération.

RC (ViWC); endorsed.

From Vergennes

A Versailles le 26. Novembre 1786.

J'ai déjà eû l'honneur, Monsieur, de vous addresser les deux passeports que vous aviez demandés pour la libre exportation des munitions de guerre que vous avez achetées pour l'Etat de Virginie. Je m'empresse, Monsieur, de vous faire part que M. le Contrôleur-Général vient de m'informer que les ordres ont été donnés pour que ces munitions passent à leur destination sans païer aucun droit.

J'ai l'honneur d'être très sincèrement, Monsieur, votre très-humble et très-obéissant Serviteur,   De Vergennes

RC (DLC); in clerk's hand, signed by Vergennes. FC (Arch. Aff. Etr., Corr. Pol., E.-U., XXXII; Tr in DLC). Noted in SJL as received 27 Nov. 1786.

From Abraham Walton

Sir   Orleans. 26 No. 1786

I sit down with the greatest pleasure to enquire after your health. I have made Enquiry about the College here; and am sorry to inform you that there are no Professors either of Chemistry or Botany. Of the other Branches I beleive the Professors are very good. I will be glad of your advice whether you think I should attend the Philosophical Classes or not. By the Letters that I received from Gentlemen that I was acquainted with in Paris, I am very well recommended, but at the same time I will be much obliged to you if you will take the trouble of asking the Letter from the Marquis de la Fayette, which he was so good as promise me, presenting my best Respects to him and the Marchioness. I divert myself here with Fencing and Dancing and have also a French Master. Every Evening I am either invited to some Gentleman's house or I go to the Opera, so that on the whole I shall spend an agreeable Winter. There are about 12 English here amongst whom is a Lad who has shewn me great Civility. I will be much obliged to you for the honor of an answer and in the mean time I will remain with the sincerest Regard and Esteem Sir Your most obdt. humble Sert.,   Abm: Walton

NB. Present my Compliments to the Gentleman whom I had the honor of seeing always at your house and whose name I have

27 NOVEMBER 1786

forgot. Please direct to me chez Mr. Oliviè le Maître, Place Matrois a Orleans.

RC (DLC); endorsed. Noted in SJL as received 27 Nov. 1786.

From Henry Champion, for Zachariah Loreilhe

[*L'Orient*, 27 Nov. 1786. Recorded in SJL as received 30 Nov. 1786. Not found.]

From Maria Cosway

[27 Nov. 1786]

Ho scritto due volte senza aver ricevuta una lettera da lei doppo la prima quale trovai all mio arrivo qui, e quale mi prometteva il piacere d'una piu frequente corrispondenza: Ogni giorno di posta o aspettato con inquietudine. Temo che il suo braccio sia peggio, ma anche questo non l'impedirebbe scrivermi. Prendo questa occasione di mandarli due linee per domandarli se a ricevute le mie lettere, per pregarla di mandarmi sue Nuove, e per ricordarli che sono piena di stima. Sua sincera ed affma. Amica,

MARIA COSWAY

RC (MHi); MS mutilated, the upper part of the leaf being eaten away; salutation and date entirely missing; the latter has been assigned from internal evidence and an entry in SJL for the receipt of a letter of this date on 20 Dec. 1786.

Translation: I have twice written without having received a letter from you after the first which I found on my arrival here and which promised me the pleasure of a more frequent correspondence: Every post-day I have waited anxiously. I fear lest your arm be worse, but even that would not prevent your writing me. I take this occasion to send you a couple of lines to ask if you have received my letters, to beg you to send me news of yourself, and to remind you that I am full of esteem Your sincere and affectionate friend.

From Duler

Reville, Normandy, 27 Nov. 1786. Has considered for two months the possibility of appealing for aid; was introduced to TJ, in Charlottesville, by John Walker about three years before; but, Congress having sent TJ to Europe shortly thereafter, was deprived of strengthening the acquaintance. Sailed from France in 1778 with a cargo for America; was cast away on the eastern shore of Virginia; salvaged most of the cargo, selling part of it to the natives and part to the army

[552]

stationed near Philadelphia; lost three small vessels and cargo, purchased for the return trip, to the enemy and was left with a parcel of paper money and $7,200 in loan office certificates "which remain still in nature, and intirely useless." Unable to recoup his fortunes in America, he returned to Bordeaux, then proceeded to "this Province of Normandy Expecting to find some means of getting my life by the mutual trade that is going to take place between France and England"; again had the bad fortune to be cast away and "oblig'd to throw my Self in the Sea, and Swim a Shore to Save my life." Asks TJ to assist him in getting employment which will provide subsistence for himself, his wife, and two daughters; does not ask pecuniary aid, "but only for work in some offices house or Bureau"; had he been "brought up in any handy Craft trade," would not trouble TJ with this petition.

RC (DLC); 4 p.; endorsed. Noted in SJL as received 4 Dec. 1786.

From William Stephens Smith

London, 28 Nov. 1786. Requests that TJ obtain letters of introduction from his friends in Paris for James and Nathaniel Hayward, of Charleston, S.C., who expect to reside for some time in Dijon in order to acquire a knowledge of the language; has made the same request of Lafayette. They are "young Gentlemen of Character and Fortune" who will "do honour to your Introduction"; if they go to Paris they will present themselves to TJ.

RC (MHi); 1 p.

To Madame de Tott

Paris Nov. 28. 1786

I profit, Madam, of the permission which your goodness has induced you to give me, and commence the pleasing office of studying with you the rythm of Homer. For this purpose I have committed to writing the few rules of Greek prosody which must be indispensably known. Those in the first page should be fixed in the memory: what follows need only be read once. If you do not find them sufficiently intelligible, I will have the honor of explaining them to you when I shall do myself that of waiting on you in Paris.

If from the nature of my office I may assume to myself just so much merit as to claim your acceptance of the best edition extant of your divine countryman Homer, which is sent me from London, I shall be extremely gratified. Permit me then, Madam, to ask this favour in his name as well as my own. Besides the beauty of the

28 NOVEMBER 1786

type, it has the particular merit of being without a single typographical error. To so perfect an edition then of so charming a poet, allow me to add so charming a reader, and oblige by this further proof of your goodness him who has the honour to be with sentiments of the most perfect esteem and respect, Madam, your most obedient & most humble servant, TH: JEFFERSON

PrC (MoSHi). Enclosure: "A Short Greek Prosody," to be printed in the Literary Miscellany, Second Series. See TJ to Chastellux, Oct. 1786.

From Madame de Tott

A Paris ce 28—9bre [1786]

Rien n'est si beau, si magnifique Monsieur que L'edition d'homere que [vous] Voulez bien me Sacrifier et que J'accépte avec Reconnoissance et Confusion. Qu'il me seroit doux de pouvoir Vous exprimer Combien Je suis touchée, pénétrée, de L'extrême bonté que Vous avez de Vous occuper de moi, Combien Je suis honorée de L'interêt que Vous me témoignez, Combien Je serois fière si Je pouvois croire que J'ai merité Un moment cet interêt d'un homme tel que Vous! Ajoutez Je Vous Supplie A toutes Les marques de bonté dont Vous m'avez Comblée, celle de me procurer Le plutôt possible Le plaisir de Vous en Remercier moi même chez maman, et de Vous prier d'agréer Les Sentiments de Reconnoissance et d'admiration avec lesquels J'ai L'honneur d'être Votre très humble et très Obeïssante Servante,

LA CTESSE. DE TOTT

RC (MoSHi). Not recorded in SJL; the year has been supplied in the date from TJ's letter to Madame de Tott, preceding. MAMAN: That is, Madame de Tessé; see note, Madame de Tessé to TJ, 20 July 1786.

To John Bondfield

SIR   Paris Novr. 29. 1786

I have the honor of inclosing you a copy of a letter from the Count de Vergennes. It will shew you that such orders have been given by the Controller general as leave a free exportation to the articles for which I lately forwarded you the passeports. I am Sir, with the most perfect consideration your very humble Servant,

TH: JEFFERSON

PrC (DLC); in Short's hand, including signature; at foot of text: "(Test W Short Sec)." Enclosure: Vergennes to TJ, 26 Nov. 1786.

[554]

To Maria Cosway

Paris Nov. 29. 1786.

My letters which pass thro' the post office either of this country or of England being all opened, I send thro' that channel only such as are very indifferent in their nature. This is not the character, my dear madam of those I write to you. The breathings of a pure affection would be profaned by the eye of a Commis of the poste. I am obliged then to wait for private conveiances. I wrote to you so long ago as the 19th. of this month by a gentleman who was to go to London immediately. But he is not yet gone. Hence the delay of which you express yourself kindly sensible in yours of the 17th. instant. Could I write by the post, I should trouble you too often: for I am never happier than when I commit myself into dialogue with you, tho' it be but in imagination. Heaven has submitted our being to some unkind laws. When those charming moments were present which I passed with you, they were clouded with the prospect that I was soon to lose you: and now, when I pass the same moments in review, I recollect nothing but the agreeable passages, and they fill me with regret. Thus, present joys are damped by a consciousness that they are passing from us; and past ones are only the subjects of sorrow and regret. I am determined when you come next not to admit the idea that we are ever to part again. But are you to come again? I dread the answer to this question, and that my poor heart has been duped by the fondness of it's wishes. What a triumph for the head! God bless you! May your days be many and filled with sunshine! May your heart glow with warm affections, and all of them be gratified! Write to me often. Write affectionately, and freely, as I do to you. Say many kind things, and say them without reserve. They will be food for my soul. Adieu my dear friend!

P.S. No private conveiance occurring I must trust this thro' the post-office, disguising my seal and superscription.

PrC (ViU); unsigned; endorsed.
In the absence of the RC it cannot be determined in what manner TJ disguised his SEAL AND SUPERSCRIPTION, but one wonders whether the disguise was intended to mislead the COMMIS OF THE POSTE or Mr. Cosway, or both.

From Guiraud & Portas

[*Cette,* 29 *Nov. 1786.* Recorded in SJL as received 9 Dec. 1786. Not found.]

From John Trumbull

Dr. Sir   London November 29th. 1786.

I have the pleasure of committing to Colo. Smith's care for you, a letter of Mrs. Cosway, and a book of songs of her composition. She has written twice to you before, since receiving your first and only one thru my hands; and having no answer, is anxious least they should have missd their way tho I addressed them in the manner you directed.

I am sorry to learn from Colo. S. that his last letters from you were still written with the left hand. I hope however that ere this time you begin to recover the use of the right.

We have late accounts from America but they contain nothing which can give you pleasure. I am not only unwilling to be the messenger of ill news, but asham'd to relate the follies of my neighboring countrymen.—We have been reproach'd with dishonesty. I am sorry to see such a Character confirmed by an open opposition to the course of Law, and the rights of Creditors.

I am Sir With the highest Esteem Your oblig'd friend & servant,

Jno. Trumbull

RC (DLC); endorsed. Noted in SJL as received 20 Dec. 1786.

The letter sent through Smith was that from Mrs. Cosway of 27 Nov. 1786. The BOOK OF SONGS OF HER COMPOSITION was *Songs and Duets Composed by Mrs. Cosway* (1786); see Helen Duprey Bullock, *My Head and My Heart: A Little History of Thomas Jefferson and Maria Cosway*, p. 50-1; TJ's copy of *Songs and Duets* is at Monticello and is owned by The Thomas Jefferson Memorial Foundation. SHE HAS WRITTEN TWICE: See Mrs. Cosway's letters under 30 Oct. and 17 Nov. 1786.

From John Adams

Dear Sir   Grosvenor Square Nov. 30th. 1786

By Dr. Gibbon a young Gentleman of Philadelphia whom I beg Leave to introduce to you, I have the Honour to send you a few more Copies of the Prussian Treaty; and to inclose in this, a Resolution of Congress of September 26. annulling Mr. Lambs Commission and Instructions. Mr. Jay desires me to transmit it to him, and although I hope Mr. Lamb is on his Passage to New York or already arrived there, it is proper to send it along to Mr. Carmichael who will be so good as to convey it, if Mr. Lamb should not be departed. The favour of transmitting it to him let me ask of you.

You ask me in your last Letter my opinion who should be sent

[556]

to exchange the Treaty with Morocco? I am content that either Mr. Barclay or Mr. Franks should go, or to leave it to Mr. Barclay to go in Person or send Mr. Franks as you shall judge best. But I wonder the Treaty has not arrived, to you.

Dont be allarmed at the late Turbulence in New England. The Massachusetts Assembly had, in its Zeal to get the better of their Debt, laid on a Tax, rather heavier than the People could bear; but all will be well, and this Commotion will terminate in additional Strength to Government.

With great and Sincere Esteem, I have the Honour to be, Sir your most obedient and humble Servant, JOHN ADAMS

RC (DLC); endorsed. FC (MHi: AMT); in Smith's hand. Noted in SJL as received 20 Dec. 1786. Enclosures: (1) Copies of the printed treaty with Prussia (see Adams to TJ, 11 Sep. 1786). (2) Resolution of Congress recalling Lamb (see Jay to TJ, 12 Oct. 1786).

To Abigail Adams

DEAR MADAM   Paris [Nov. 1786]

I am never happier than when I am performing good offices for good people; and the most friendly office one can perform is to make worthy characters acquainted with one another. The good things of this life are scattered so sparingly in our way that we must glean them up as we go. Yourself and Madame de Corny then must avail yourselves of the short time she will remain in London to make each other happy. A good heart and a good head will ensure her a place in your esteem. I have promised it to her: and she has yet a better title, a high respect for your character. I asked her to carry me in her pocket, that I might have the pleasure of bringing you together in person; but on examining the treaty of commerce, she found I should be contraband; that there might be a search—and seizure—and that the case would admit very specially of embarras. So instead of my having the honour of presenting her to you, she will have that of putting this into your hands, and of giving you assurances of her esteem and respect, with which permit me to mingle those of, dear Madam, your most obedient and most humble servant, TH: JEFFERSON

PrC (DLC); without date, which has been conjectured from internal evidence (see TJ to Maria Cosway, 19 Nov. 1786, for a similar request of Madame de Corny to CARRY ME IN HER POCKET). Not recorded in SJL.

From C. W. F. Dumas

Monsieur Lahaie 1er. Dec. 1786

Nayant pas en ce moment le pouvoir de consulter la date d'où Votre Excellence m'a accusé pour la derniere fois la réception des miennes, parce que je n'étois pas chez moi, je la supplie de vouloir bien par un mot m'instruire du sort de toutes celles que je lui ai adressées pendant les 3 derniers mois, afin que je sache si elle les a bien reçues, pour ma tranquillité.

L'incluse, y compris ce qui parviendra à Votre Excellence de ma part par un Courier de Mr. l'Ambassadeur est de très-grande importance. Je n'ai aucune objection à ce que Votre Excellence les fasse voir chez Elle en confiance à Mr. le Ms. de la Fayette seul; mais il ne faut pas que personne en prenne copie, ni en parle.

Je suis avec le plus respectueux dévouement, De Votre Excellence, le très humble et très obéissant serv.,   C W F Dumas

Je joins ici 2 Lettres arrivées ici pour MM. Wm. Livingston et Jn. Rutledge. Le nom de Beaune, d'où elles viennent, me fait conjecturer qu'elles sont de quelque Marchand de Vin de ladite Ville, qui a vu leurs noms sur la Gazette et qui sollicite leur chalandise. Quoiqu'il en soit, j'ai cru ne pouvoir mieux faire que de mettre leur sort entre les mains de Votre Excellence.

RC (DLC). FC (Rijksarchief, The Hague, Dumas Papers; photostats in DLC). Noted in SJL as received 10 Dec. 1786. Enclosures (FC in same): (1) Dumas to Jay, 29 Nov. 1786, transmitting three extracts and stating that in order to understand them it is necessary to know that on 21 Nov. Dumas had been asked by Messrs. de G[oertz] and "P—" to assist in translating letters from Lestevenon and Swan; that these translations were taken to the French ambassador who, with Rayneval, agreed that a letter should be sent to Lestevenon at once; that the following evening their Royal Highnesses sent off similar messages, including one to Swan ordering him to keep the mouth of the Swin closed, which should have been done two years ago. (2) Another letter to Jay, same date, reporting that Rayneval arrived on the 18th and had a conference at the French ambassador's which included Goertz. The King wishes peace and a secret meeting was arranged to further this end, but Dumas believes that a French alliance will be difficult to arrange. Rayneval believes he was sent to sound out the opinion of the Prussian court secretly but when Prussia starts negotiating, the question of the status of the Stadtholder and his constitutional rights will arise; the Stadtholder has no constitutional rights but his position is based on the esteem and affection of the regency and the people. Dumas believes no deliberations on government can be effective—especially for Gelderland, as long as the oppressive laws of 1674 are in effect there. He will report on future conferences. Hopes he may receive the money due him from Congress. (3) Two letters from unidentified persons to Livingston and Rutledge.

From John Jay

Dr Sir   Office for foreign Affairs 1st. Decemr. 1786

The Frigate called the South Carolina, belonging to that State, assisted Spain at the Reduction of Providence and the Bahama Islands. To obtain Compensation for which Congress, at the Instance of the State, have directed Application to be made to the Court of Madrid. The Prince of Luxemburgh is it seems interested in the Frigate, and in the expected Compensation. The Delegates of South Carolina think his Influence if exerted would conduce much to the Success of the Application. Your Endeavors to obtain his Aid and Support are requested, and I have the Honor of transmitting to you herewith the Papers relative to that Transaction under an unsealed Cover, directed to Mr. Carmichael, to whom be pleased to forward them, and from Time to Time to give him such Advice and Intelligence, as may facilitate the Execution of his Instructions on this Subject.

With great Esteem & Regard I have the Honor to be &c.,

JOHN JAY

FC (DNA: RG 59, PCC, No. 121). Noted in SJL as received 24 Jan. 1787. Enclosures: Jay to Carmichael, 1 Dec. 1786, enclosing a duplicate copy of an act of Congress of 3 May 1784; copy of a letter on the subject of the *South Carolina* from John Kean to Jay, 4 Nov. 1786, enclosing the papers concerning the case; copies of Jay to Kean, 7 and 8 Nov. 1786; copy of Kean to Jay, 11 Nov. 1786 (Jay's letter to Carmichael and all of the above enclosures are printed in full in *Dipl. Corr., 1786-89*, III, 323-47).

To the Ambassadors of Portugal and Russia

[*Paris, 1 Dec. 1786.* An entry in SJPL under this date reads: "Russie & Portugal. Ambassadors. A combined operation against the Barbary powers." Neither letter has been found, but see TJ's plan of operation against the Barbary states, following.]

Jefferson's Proposed Concert of Powers against the Barbary States

[July-Dec. 1786]

I. PROPOSED CONVENTION AGAINST THE BARBARY STATES
II. PROPOSED CONFEDERATION AGAINST THE BARBARY STATES

EDITORIAL NOTE

This remarkable proposal, which ran counter to the realities of 18th century political and commercial rivalries, was foredoomed to failure, but for a time it seemed promising. Jefferson's account of it in his Autobiography, together with the methods he employed in urging it upon the attention of Congress, has caused some confusion about the plan, its evolution, and its background.

"Our commerce in the Mediterranean," the account in the Autobiography states, "was placed under early alarm by the capture of two of our vessels and crews by the Barbary cruisers. I was very unwilling that we should acquiesce in the European humiliation of paying a tribute to those lawless pirates, and endeavored to form an association of the powers subject to habitual depredations from them. I accordingly prepared and proposed to their ministers at Paris, for consultation with their governments, articles of a special confederation." At this point, Jefferson inserted in his Autobiography the text of the "articles of a special confederation." But the text of the proposal that he thus inserted was not one by which the contracting powers agreed to "form a confederation," but one stating that they merely would "enter into a Convention" for the purpose. The distinction is an important one in itself and in showing the development of the idea. The texts here presented as Documents I and II represent the earlier and later states of the proposal, though by inserting the former in his Autobiography Jefferson conveyed the impression that that text reflected the fully evolved plan. That this was a mistaken impression is proved not only by a textual comparison but also by the chronology of the proposals and by the background of discussions that the American Commissioners had carried on for some time.

The evolution of Jefferson's ideas of a policy concerning the depredations of the Barbary pirates may easily be traced in his letters of 1785 and 1786 (see especially TJ to Adams, 27 Nov. 1785; to Monroe, 6 Feb. 1786; to Jay, 23 May 1786; and to Adams, 11 July 1786). From the beginning he was strongly opposed to the idea of ransom or tribute, and preferred an American naval force as being less costly, more effective, and best calculated to support the national dignity. The conversations in London in the spring of 1786 concerning the price of peace tentatively set by the Tripolitan minister at 30,000 guineas—a price Jefferson later stated to be "beyond the limits of Congress, and of reason" (TJ's Report to Congress, 28 Dec. 1790)—

EDITORIAL NOTE

deepened the already apparent difference of opinion between him and John Adams as to the policy to be pursued. Jefferson had been impressed by an expedient for maintaining a blockade at small cost as reported to him by D'Estaing, and he transmitted the idea to Congress and urged Lafayette to associate himself with it (see Lafayette to TJ, 6 Mch. 1786; D'Estaing to TJ, 17 May 1786; TJ to Jay, 23 May 1786). On his return from London, and perhaps soon after he received D'Estaing's communication, Jefferson evidently drew up the plan for a proposed convention for a jointly sponsored naval force to cruise in the Mediterranean, to be managed at some European court by a council of the diplomatic representatives of the powers engaged in the enterprise. No rough draft of this proposal is known to exist, but the text as submitted to the minister of the court of Naples, Del Pio, very probably was substantially if not precisely in the form here presented as Document I (or a translation of it). No covering letter to Del Pio has been found, and none is recorded in SJL. Jefferson was on friendly terms with the Neapolitan minister and it is likely that he handed the text of the proposal to him in a personal interview. This must have been late in May or early in June, for the court of Naples informed Del Pio on 4 July 1786 of its views. Del Pio transmitted this communication to Jefferson. The date of his doing so appears neither in Jefferson's endorsement nor in SJL, but it must have been in July. Jefferson explicitly opened the subject in a letter to Monroe of 11 Aug. 1786, but he did not state then or in any other contemporaneous letter that he had advanced such proposals or had discussed them with any foreign diplomatic agent. On Lafayette's return from Auvergne early in October, Jefferson resumed discussions with him concerning the propositions of the Committee relative to American trade, and on 22 Oct. when that matter received Calonne's formal approval and Lafayette handed to Jefferson Calonne's letter on the subject, they discussed the plan against the Barbary pirates. The next day Lafayette wrote to Jefferson enthusiastically about the "Antipiratical Confederacy" (Lafayette to TJ, [23 Oct.] 1786). Lafayette's reference to "Neapolitain ideas" in this letter suggests that the advice from Naples to Del Pio had been received and probably was discussed with Lafayette at this time. In proposing himself as a chief to the "Antipiratical Confederacy" Lafayette outlined his plans of operation and stated the force that he would require. He also correctly defined one of the chief obstacles: "The devil of it will Be to Make it Agreable to this Ministry that I should meddle with the War."

It is significant that there seems to exist no copy of the later text of the proposal in TJ's hand, but only French and Italian translations (Document II). The consultations with Lafayette in late October occurred during the time that Jefferson was unable to use his right hand for writing. Possibly translations were prepared on the basis of corrections of the earlier text. These corrections consisted primarily in the dropping of one article and in changing the character of the proposal from a convention to a confederation. No covering letters of transmittal from Jefferson to any ministers or ambassadors have been found, but the entry in SJL for 1 Dec. 1786 shows that he sent copies to the Portuguese ambassador and to the Russian minister.

The account given by Jefferson in the Autobiography states that "Portugal, Naples, the two Sicilies, Venice, Malta, Denmark and Sweden were favorably disposed to such an association; but their representatives at Paris expressed apprehensions that France would interfere, and either openly or secretly support the Barbary powers; and they required that I should ascertain the dispositions of the Count de Vergennes on the subject. I had before taken occasion to inform him of what we were proposing, and therefore did not think it proper to insinuate any doubt of the fair conduct of his government; but stating our propositions, I mentioned the apprehensions entertained by us that England would interfere in behalf of those pyratical governments. 'She dares not do it' said he. I pressed it no further. The other Agents were satisfied with this indication of his sentiments, and nothing was now wanting to bring it into direct and formal consideration, but the assent of our government, and their authority to make the formal proposition. I communicated to them the favorable prospect of protecting our commerce from the Barbary depredations, and for such a continuance of time as, by an exclusion of them from the sea, to change their habits and characters from a predatory to an agricultural people: towards which however it was expected they would contribute a frigate, and it's expences to be in constant cruize. But they were in no condition to make any such engagement. Their recommendatory powers for obtaining contributions were so openly neglected by the several states that they declined an engagement which they were conscious they could not fulfill with punctuality; and so it fell through."

This statement conveys the erroneous impression that Jefferson himself made a formal communication of the plan to Congress. There is no evidence that he did send it to Jay or even that he discussed its outlines in any communications to the secretary for foreign affairs. Jefferson's summary of the proposal in his private letter to Monroe of 11 Aug. 1786 appears to be the nearest approach that he made to a communication of the subject to Congress. Nor is there any evidence that he discussed the idea with his fellow Commissioner, John Adams, or even raised with him the question of submitting it to Congress. On the contrary, the evidence available suggests that his and Adams' difference of opinion on policy led to his use of Lafayette to obtain action in America as well as in Europe.

A few days after his conversation with Jefferson on 22 Oct., Lafayette wrote to George Washington: "There is betwen Mr. Jefferson and Mr. Adams a diversity of opinion respecting the Algerines. Adams thinks a peace should be purchased from them, Mr. Jefferson finds it as cheap and more honourable to cruize against them. I incline to the later opinion, and think it possible to form an alliance betwen the United States, Naples, Rome, Venice, Portugal and some other powers, each giving a sum of monney not very large, whereby a common armement may distress the Algerines into any terms. Congress ought to give Mr. Jefferson and Adams ample powers to stipulate in their names for such a confederacy" (Gottschalk, ed., *Letters of Lafayette*

EDITORIAL NOTE

to Washington, 1777-1799, p. 315). It is to be observed that Lafayette failed to mention that Jefferson had drafted a plan "to form an alliance," giving it only as his opinion that such could be done. He also failed to mention the idea that he had advanced so enthusiastically in his letter to Jefferson a few days earlier—that he would be ready to act as a "Chief to the Antipiratical Confederacy." Also, while emphasizing the difference of opinion between Adams and Jefferson, Lafayette flatly urged that Congress ought to give the Commissioners "powers to stipulate in their names for such a confederacy"—that is, to grant what Jefferson called in his Autobiography "their authority to make the formal proposition." On the same day that Lafayette wrote to Washington, he similarly wrote James McHenry (Gottschalk, *Lafayette, 1783-89*, p. 255). Two days later he wrote to John Jay: "Altho there May be a Diversity of Opinions, wether a peace Must Be purchaced at Any Rate from the Barbary Powers, or a War must Be Carried Against them Until they Come to proper terms, there can in ⟨*My Opinion*⟩ No Mind Be Any doubt about the Advantages of a third Measure—Viz a Confederacy of six or seven powers, Each of them giving a small quota, the Reunion of which would insure a Constant and Sufficient Cruise against those Pirats, and after they are Brought to terms, would guard Against the Breaking of a peace which the Powers would Mutually Guarantee to each other.—Portugal, Toscany, Naples, Venice, and Genoa are Now at war with those Regencies, and I would like at the same time to Manage the Armament so as to Use American flour, fish, and naval stores. This plan is not as yet very well diggested in My Head, But Beg leave to submit to Congress the propriety to Empower their Ministers to stipulate for such an Arrangement. . . . Should Any thing turn out, that May Employ The Servants of the United States, I Hope they know my zeal" (Lafayette to Jay, 28 Oct. 1786; DNA: PCC, No. 156, in Lafayette's hand entirely; endorsed by Charles Thomson in part: "Read 19 Feby 1787"). This letter, it may be noted parenthetically, has been printed in *Dipl. Corr., 1783-89*, I, 319-20, from a copy prepared in Jay's office. For example, the words "I would like at the same time to Manage the Armament so as to Use American flour, fish, and naval stores"—an argument that was evidently intended to obtain support in Congress by appealing to those interested in the welfare of New England fisheries, the grain and flour trade of the middle states, and production of naval stores in the southern states—was altered to read: "I would like at the same time *to have the armament so managed* as to use American flour, fish, and naval stores." Again, the concluding remark "Any thing . . . that May Employ the Servants of the United States" was altered to read "any thing . . . that may employ *me as a servant* of the United States" (italics supplied). The first of these variations had the effect of minimizing Lafayette's role in the proposed enterprise, and the second of placing him almost in the position of an applicant for employment. When or by whose authority these variations were made is not clear; they and others in the passage could scarcely have been the result of clerical errors. Nevertheless, as proved by Thomson's endorsement, Lafayette's original letter was read in Congress.

[563]

THE BARBARY STATES 1786

Jay acknowledged Lafayette's letter the day after he had forwarded it to Congress, and remarked: "What plan or system Congress will adopt relative to the hostile Barbary States is not yet decided. The one you suggest has advantages. The great question, I think, is whether we shall wage war or pay tribute? I, for my part, prefer war, and consequently am ready for every proper plan of uniting and multiplying their enemies" (Jay to Lafayette, 16 Feb. 1787; *Dipl. Corr., 1783-89*, I, 321). The opinion here given was somewhat different from that presented by Jay to Congress a few months later.

In view of these communications, it is clear that Jefferson and Lafayette were working in close collaboration. It is equally clear that it was Lafayette and not Jefferson who formally requested Jay to submit to Congress the idea of a policy of concerted action. The obvious and most plausible inference to be drawn from these facts is that Jefferson himself did not wish to be the channel of communicating what could only have accentuated the difference of opinion existing between himself and Adams. To have done so would not merely have made it more difficult to reconcile differences of opinion with one who was both a friend and a fellow Commissioner, but would also have weakened the presentation of the plan to Congress. By letting it appear that the idea was Lafayette's, Jefferson doubtless felt, with reason, that the chances of Congressional support for the requested authority would be greatly augmented. Thus it was that both Adams and Congress were intentionally kept in the dark as to the true origin of the proposed policy. Even so careful a scholar as Gottschalk was misled by these behind-the-scenes maneuvers (and by Adams' letter to Jefferson of 11 July 1786 in which he suggested that "our noble Friend the Marquis" be consulted) to attribute authorship of the plan itself to Lafayette (Gottschalk, *Lafayette, 1783-89*, p. 264-6). Lafayette does deserve full credit for interceding with Washington, Jay, and McHenry in America; for planning some of the details of operation; and doubtless for assistance in the discussions with European diplomatic agents. But there can be no doubt that Jefferson was the author of the "articles of a special confederation."

Washington was non-committal in his reply to Lafayette, and Jay equally so in transmitting Lafayette's formal request to Congress (Washington to Lafayette, 25 Mch. 1787; *Writings*, ed. Fitzpatrick, XXIX, 185; Jay to Congress, 15 Feb. 1787; JCC, XXXII, 65). The matter languished in Congress for some months. On 27 July 1787 William Grayson, a Virginia delegate, an ardent friend of France, and a political enemy of John Jay, moved that the "Minister plenipotentiary of the United States at the Court of France be directed to form a Confederacy with the powers of Europe who are now at War with the piratical states . . . or may be disposed to go to War with them." The resolution also stipulated that "it be an Article in the said Confederation" that none of the contracting powers could make peace with any of the Barbary states unless the "whole Confederacy" were included, and that in case of a general peace between the belligerent powers, the "whole Confederacy" should guarantee that peace and, in case of aggression by the Barbary states, hostilities would commence

[564]

EDITORIAL NOTE

again and continue until the object had been achieved. Grayson's resolution also stipulated that the quotas of the different powers in men and shipping, the ascertaining of the stations at different periods, and the fixing of the general command should form another Article. A proviso that the quota of the United States should be limited to "one frigate and two sloops of war" was struck out. The following list of powers on Grayson's motion was also crossed off: "The Pope, The Venetians, Genoese, Emperor, Milan, Turin, Sweden, Denmark, Hanse Towns, two Sicilies, Sardinia, Portugal, Russia, Tuscany, Malta." It was also moved that this motion be referred to the secretary for foreign affairs to report. Only the two New Jersey delegates and Yates of New York voted against the motion (JCC, XXXIII, 419-20). Despite this overwhelming vote, Jay reported on 2 Aug. 1787, that the motion was "rendered unseasonable by the present State of our Affairs"; that if such a confederation should be achieved, it was highly probable that the quota expected from the United States would be much greater than would be in their power to supply; and that it would "not become their Dignity to take the Lead in forming such a Confederation, unless they were prepared to support such spirited Propositions by spirited and important Operations." He concluded by expressing doubt that Congress could build and keep manned even three frigates, and for this reason it would "be most prudent for Congress to delay entering into the proposed, or indeed any other Engagements, until the Means of executing them appear clearly to be within their Reach" (JCC, XXXIII, 451-2).

Jefferson, in his Autobiography, placed the blame for failure solely upon the inability of Congress to meet its responsibilities under such a plan. But there are two facts which modify this view. The first is that Vergennes, on learning of Lafayette's participation in the proposed enterprise, invited him to dinner and "bluntly advised him to desist" in his promotion of a scheme foredoomed to failure because of the opposition of France and England (Gottschalk, *Lafayette, 1783-89*, p. 266). The second is that Jefferson, in 1790 and after the impotence of the federal government had been effectively removed by the grant of power to tax, returned to a variation of the idea that he had advanced four years earlier. In his Report to Congress on 28 Dec. 1790 he still felt that it was "reasonable to presume that a concert of operation might be arranged among the powers at war with the Barbary states, so as that each performing a tour of a given duration, and in a given order, a constant cruise, during the eight temperate months of every year may be kept up before the harbour of Algiers 'till the object of such operations be completely obtained." Stating that it was up to Congress to decide upon ransom, tribute, or war, he concluded: "If [Congress decide upon] war, they will consider how far they will enable the Executive to engage, in the forms of the Constitution, the co-operation of other powers."

The failure of Congress to explore the possibilities either on his indirect urging in 1786 or on his official recommendation as secretary of state in 1790 suggests that another possible explanation ought to be considered: that is, whether in this as in so many other issues in

[565]

Congress in the 1780's and 1790's the matter was decided by becoming enmeshed in the struggles of the pro-French and the pro-British elements in Congress. American policy in respect to the Barbary states was a subject on which neither France nor England was impartial or indifferent, as the documents of the period abundantly prove. Jefferson's private communication to Monroe on 11 Aug. 1786 in behalf of such a concert of power—he referred to it both as a "convention" and as a "confederacy"—anticipated all of the obstacles that would be encountered by the plan both at home and abroad, especially that on which Jay rested his report: "It will be said there is no money in the treasury. There never will be money in the treasury till the confederacy shews it's teeth." Jefferson looked upon the plan as an opportunity whereby the United States might have "the honour and advantage of establishing such a confederacy" as that proposed against the Barbary states. He argued that if this opportunity were seized and allowed to stand as the ostensible cause for establishing a naval force, an element of compulsion necessary to the strength of the union would be happily achieved. But the weakness of the union that Jefferson saw as the ultimate object to be remedied, Jay used as an argument to defeat the plan. It was not the first nor the last time that Jefferson's imagination and daring collided with Jay's caution. It is difficult to believe that the attitude of either was uninfluenced by the manner in which he regarded the question whether the future of the United States lay most within the orbit of Great Britain or within that of France.

When Lafayette and Jefferson held their conversation on the evening of October 22d, they had just completed with brilliant success a long collaboration in behalf of Franco-American trade. They immediately launched another collaboration that promised to achieve what both so greatly desired—promotion of American trade, the strengthening of the Confederation, and an opportunity for further military glory for the marquis. But this time Lafayette's whole-hearted efforts to drive Jefferson's nail ended in failure when the nail came in contact with John Jay's inflexible opposition.

I. Proposed Convention against the Barbary States

[Before 4 July 1786]

Proposals for concerted operation among the powers at war with the Pyratical states of Barbary.

1. It is proposed that the several powers at war with the Pyratical states of Barbary (or any two or more of them who shall be willing) shall enter into a Convention[1] to carry on their operations against those states in concert, beginning with the Algerines.

2. This convention shall remain open to any other power who shall at any future time wish to accede to it: the parties reserving

I. CONVENTION AGAINST THE STATES

a right[2] to prescribe the conditions of such accession according to the circumstances existing at the time it shall be proposed.

3. The object of the convention[3] shall be to compel the pyratical states to perpetual peace, without price, and to guarantee that peace to each other.

4. The operations for obtaining this peace shall be constant cruizes on their coast, with a naval force now to be agreed on. It is not proposed that this force shall be so considerable as to be inconvenient to any party.[4] It is believed that half a dozen frigates with as many Tenders, or Xebecks, one half of which shall be in cruize while the other half is at rest, will suffice.

5. The force agreed to be necessary shall be furnished by the parties in certain quotas now to be fixed: it being expected that each will be willing to contribute in such proportion[5] as circumstances may render reasonable.

6. As miscarriages often proceed from the want of harmony among officers of different nations, the parties shall now consider and decide whether it will not be better to contribute their quotas in money to be employed in fitting out and keeping on duty a single fleet of the force agreed on.

7. The difficulties and delays too which will attend the management of these operations if conducted by the parties themselves separately, distant as their courts may be from one another and incapable of meeting in consultation suggest a question whether it will not be better for them to give full powers for that purpose to their Ambassador or other minister resident at some one court of Europe, who shall form a Committee or Council for carrying this Convention[6] into effect; wherein the vote of each member shall be computed in proportion to the quota of his sovereign, and the majority, so computed, shall prevail in all questions within the view of this Convention. The court of Versailles is proposed on account of it's neighborhood to the Mediterranean and because all those powers are represented there who are likely to become parties to this convention.[3]

8. To save to that Council the embarassment of personal sollicitations for office, and to assure the parties that their contributions will be applied solely to the object for which they are destined, there shall be no establishment of officers for the said council, such as Commis, Secretaries or of any other kind, with either salaries or perquisites, nor any other lucrative appointments but such whose functions are to be exercised on board the said vessels.

9. Should war arise between any two of the parties to this

Convention,[7] it shall not extend to this enterprize, nor interrupt it: but as to this they shall be reputed at peace.[8]

10. When Algiers shall be reduced to peace, the other Pyratical states, if they refuse to discontinue their pyracies, shall become the objects of this Convention,[3] either successively or together as shall seem best.

11. Where this Convention[9] would interfere with treaties actually existing between any of the parties and of the said states of Barbary, the treaty shall prevail, and such party shall be allowed to withdraw from the operations against that state.

MS (DLC: TJ Papers, 232: 41539, 41539a); entirely in TJ's hand. PrC of preceding (ViWC); at foot of text (written by TJ and missing from MS): "Ambassador of Portugal & Minister of Russia"; this has a line through it, obviously drawn at a later date and presumably by Henry A. Washington, who also in an effort to restore the faded PrC overwrote some of the words and put at the foot of the text: "Nov. 1786"; Washington also added at the foot of the text a note drawn substantially from information in TJ's Autobiography and printed in HAW, IX, 307-8. Tr in TJ's hand as inserted in his Autobiography (DLC), which varies only slightly in capitalization, punctuation, and spelling of a few words. PrC of a Tr (DLC: TJ Papers, 26: 4472-4); in the hand of William Short. Tr (DLC: TJ Papers, 155: 27166-7); in French, in the hand of an unidentified French clerk, with one interlineation in TJ's hand (see note 5, below). Tr of the preceding translation (MHi, in a bound MS volume incorrectly labelled "Law Treaties"); in the hand of William Short. PrC of the preceding Tr (DLC: TJ Papers, 36: 6241-2).

[1] French text reads "une Coopération."
[2] French text reads: "le droit des conféderes."
[3] French text reads: "la confederation."
[4] French text reads: "aucun des Confederés."
[5] TJ first wrote: ". . . in proportion to their abilities," and then altered the phrase to read as above. The French text originally read: "On réglera en même tems que la force de L'Escadre le Contingent de chaque confederé et l'on se flatte qu'ils voudront bien le proportionner à leurs moyens." TJ deleted the clause "qu'ils voudront bien le proportionner à leurs moyens" and began to revise it interlineally, writing "que chaque puissance"; he then restored the text as originally written, substituting only "leur situation" for "leurs moyens." It is this alteration which proves that the French text is prior in time to that of Document II, though it will be noted that this French text (while including Article 9 as the text of Document II does not), uses the word "Confederation," &c., indicating that it belongs to an intermediate stage of translation between Document I and Document II.
[6] French text reads: "cette Cooperation."
[7] French text reads: "deux des Conféderés."
[8] This Article was dropped and Articles 10 and 11 re-numbered before the text as shown in Document II was prepared.
[9] French text reads: "cette confederation."

II. Proposed Confederation against the Barbary States

[ca. Oct. 1786]

Propositions pour une operation combinée entre les puissances en guerre avec les Etats Barbaresques.

1o. Que les differentes puissances en guerre avec les Etats Barbaresques (ou deux ou plusieurs d'elles) forment une confederation, pour diriger leurs operations contre ces Etats, commencant par les Algeriens.

2o. Que par la suite toute puissance qui desireroit d'entrer dans cette confederation y soit admise, les puissances contractantes se reservant le droit de prescrire les conditions de cette admission, suivant les circonstances qui existeront alors.

3o. Que l'objet de cette confederation soit d'obliger les Etats Barbaresques (et sans presens ou prix quelquonque) à une paix perpetuelle avec les puissances confederées, lesquelles se garantiront mutuellement la dite paix.

4o. Que les operations pour obtenir cette paix de la part des Etats Barbaresques soient une croisiere etablie constament sur leurs cotes, avec des forces navales dont on conviendra en formant la confederation. L'on propose qu'elles ne soient pas assez considerables pour etre une veritable géne pour une des parties contractantes. L'on croit que six fregates avec autant de corvettes ou chebecs, dont une moitie seroit en croisiere tandis que l'autre seroit en relache, rempliroient l'objet que l'on se propose.

5o. Que les forces navales que l'on Jugera necessaires soient fournies par les parties contractantes, suivant la quote-part qui doit etre determinée lors de la confederation. L'on espere que chaque puissance contribuera en telle proportion que les circonstances peuvent Justifier.[1]

6o. Comme le manque d'harmonie et d'accord entre des officiers de differentes nations entraine souvent le mauvais succès des operations, les parties contractantes doivent considerer, et déterminer s'il n'est pas à propos que chaque puissance fournisse sa quote-part en argent, pour etre emploié à armer et à entretenir une flote de la force dont on sera convenue.

7o. Les difficultés et longueurs qui se rencontreroient dans la conduite de ces operations, si elles etoient dirigées par les puissances separement, eloignées comme elles sont les unes des autres, font naître une question, s'il ne seroit pas plus avantageux pour elles de donner des pleins pouvoirs à ce sujet à leur Ambassadeur ou Ministre à une même cour, et qui formeroient un conseil pour mettre ce plan à execution, et où la voix de chaque membre seroit comptée en proportion de la quote-part fournie par son souverain; la majorité des voix estimées de cette maniere determineroit toutes les questions. L'on propose la Cour de Versailles pour le lieu d'assemblée de ce conseil, à cause de sa proximité de la Méditerranée, et parceque toutes les puissances qui entreront probablement dans cette confederation y sont representées.

8o. Afin d'eviter à ce conseil la fatigue de sollicitations pour des places, et en meme tems assurer aux parties que leurs contributions seront uniquement emploiées à l'objet auquel elles sont destinées, l'on n'etablira pour ledit conseil aucune place de commis, secretaire, &c. avec appointemens ou emolumens, et il n'y aura d'emploi lucratif que pour les personnes à bord des batimens.

9o. Lorsque la Regence d'Alger aura eté reduite à faire la paix avec les Puissances contractantes, si les autres Etats Barbaresques refusent de discontinuer leurs pirateries, la confederation dirigera ses operations contre eux, ou successivement ou contre tous à la fois, suivant qu'il paroitra plus avantageux.

10o. Si cette conféderation etoit contraire à des traités actuellement existans entre une ou plusieurs des parties contractantes et quelquesuns des Etats Barbaresques, ces puissances auroient la liberté de se retirer de la conféderation lorsqu'elle dirigeroit ses operations contre lesdits Etats.

MS (DLC: TJ Papers, 36: 6240); in an unidentified hand. Tr (DLC: TJ Papers, 36: 6239); in Italian, in the hand of Philip Mazzei; at head of text: "Proposizione per le Potenze che sono in guerra cogli Stati di Barberia." Mazzei's translation corresponds in all respects to the French text; it employs the word "Unione" for "Confederation."

[1] This French text, here and elsewhere, varies considerably in phraseology from that described in the notes to Document I. See especially note 5, Document I.

To Philippe-Denis Pierres

Paris 1er. Decembre [1786]

Dans les changemens que je propose de faire, Monsieur, dans mon livre, il y a deux conditions qui me genent. 1.º de deranger les pages aussi peu que possible. 2.º que les feuilles changeés peuvent etre substituées commodement dans les livres reliés au lieu des feuilles qu'il y trouvent. Voyant donc l'impossibilité de mettre dans les quatres pages tout ce que j'ai desiré et du meme caractere,

2 DECEMBER 1786

j'aimerais mieux de le faire d'un caractere plus petit, ainsi que le tout peut etre compris dans les quatres pages, et c'est ce Monsieur que je vous prierai de vouloir bien me faire faire. J'ai l'honneur d'etre avec le plus grand respect Monsieur votre tres humble et tres-obéissant serviteur,
TH: JEFFERSON

PrC (MHi); endorsed; the year has been supplied from an entry for a letter to Pierres under this date in SJL, and from internal evidence.

LES CHANGEMENS QUE JE PROPOSE: For a bibliographical description of the cancellations in *Notes on Virginia*, see Coolie Verner, *A Further Checklist of the Separate Editions of Jefferson's Notes on the State of Virginia*, Charlottesville, 1950, p. 5; see also Alice H. Lerch, "Who Was the Printer of Jefferson's *Notes*?" *Bookmen's Holiday, Notes and Studies Written in Tribute to Harry Miller Lydenberg*, N.Y., 1943, p. 54 ff.

From Jean Chas

rue St. thomas du Louvre N. 22.
paris ce 2. xbre. 1786.

MONSIEUR

Je soumets a votre examen, et a votre censure L'histoire de La revolution de L'amerique qui fait partie de mon histoire philosophique, et politique des revolutions d'angleterre; je vous observe que le manuscrit que je vous envoye est un original dont je n'ai point conservé de copie, ainssi je viendrai Le retirer. Lorsque vous en aurés fait La lecture, vous aurés La bonté de me fixer le jour ou je pourai avoir L'honneur de vous voir.

Je m'estime fort heureux, monsieur, de pouvoir rendre un hommage public au courage et aux vertus d'un peuple que j'admire, et que je respecte. Vous honorés La nation americaine par votre patriotisme, et vos talens; jugés de mon empressement a entretenir une relation aussi interessante, et aussi précieuse.

Vous trouverés quelques fautes dans mon manuscrit, elles seront corrigées. Je vous envoye aussi le prospectus de mon ouvrage. Il ne faut point oublier que je traite L'histoire en philosophe.

Je suis avec respect, monsieur, votre très humble et très obeissant serviteur,
CHAS
avocat

RC (MoSHi); endorsed. Enclosures: Chas' MS, and presumably the prospectus also, was returned to him in TJ to Chas, 7 Dec. 1786. See Chas to TJ, 11 Oct. 1786.

From C. W. F. Dumas

[*The Hague, 2 Dec. 1786.* Immediately after the entry in SJL recording the receipt of Dumas' letter to TJ of 1 Dec. 1786, q.v., there

[571]

is the following (also under 10 Dec.): "do. cover of letter to Mr. Jay of Dec. 2." This probably referred not to a covering letter to TJ—none is recorded in Dumas' Letter Book and none has been found—but merely to an address cover. The letter of Dumas to Jay of 2 Dec., with a postscript of 6 Dec., thus enclosed informed him that "Mr. De R[ayneval] me paroît toujours sympathiser assez bien avec nos amis sur les principes généraux du système adopté"; that a second conference was held and Dumas' "Esprit familier" tells him that the duties of the Captain-General and the prefect Captain-General were worked out, the question of military duties was raised and the baleful effect of these last successfully brought to Rayneval's attention; on the 24th of November a memoir had been drawn up dealing with the duties of Stadtholder. Dumas translated this and gave it to Rayneval on the 25th. He encloses a copy. Rayneval was to make a résumé of the memoir, with additional observations of his own, finally discussing it with its authors and showing his fundamental agreement with them. All these dispatches he was to send on the 29th to Versailles. "Le zele éclairé" with which Rayneval went about this makes one hope for the best. Dumas assumes that the Prussian Court will urge the Stadtholder to cooperate as much as possible, or it will abandon him. More particularly he should try to make the majority of the people in Gelderland accept mediation, but he should work at this "non en apparence, mais de bonne foi." Neither G[oertz] nor Th[ulemeier] seem suited to this. The latter has lost his hold on the republicans here, and the former is completely discredited not only here but in the King's eyes as well. In the meantime mediation proceedings in regard to Utrecht should be undertaken soon.—Will the planning of military duties be turned over to the Captain-General? Before William III ("dont les Hollandais n'aiment pas la Mémoire") the Captain-General had no such power, but nevertheless misused whatever power he did have. Some people say *"Rien de cela* ne seroit arrivé sans la Révolution Américaine." (6 Dec.). Today the Deputies of the Council of war of the Bourgeoisie of Amsterdam are arriving with their speech of approval: on Saturday there were 12,000 arrivals with many more to follow. The speeches of other towns and cities continue to come in showing that only a little clique was against their Royal Highnesses. The ambassador waits only for this speech and Dumas' translation in order to hurry a messenger off with it to the King. The messenger will also take the present dispatch which is enclosed (FC in Rijksarchief, The Hague, Dumas Papers; photostats in DLC; this letter is among those from Dumas to Jay listed as missing in *Dipl. Corr. 1783-89*, III, 541).]

From Abigail Adams Smith

London December 2d 1786.

Mrs. Smith presents her Compliments to Mr. Jefferson and is very sorry to trouble him again upon the Subject of the Corsetts, but not having received them, She fears Mademoisell Sanson has not been so punctual as she promised. If Mr. Jefferson will permit Petit to inquire after, and forward them by an early opportunity, Mrs. S. will be much obliged.

RC (MHi); endorsed. Enclosed in William Stephens Smith to TJ, 5 Dec. 1786.

From Thomas Barclay

DEAR SIR   Madrid 4th. Decr. 1786

Having written to you very fully by Col. Franks, who set forward from the Escurial the 16th. of last Month, I shall not at present take up much of your Time. I Now Inclose you a Copy of the Declaration made by Tahar Fennish in addition to the 10th. Article of the Treaty with the Emperor of Morocco. It is in Arabic and signed by Himself. The Necessity of a second Copy of that Declaration Did Not Appear obvious to me, untill I got to Tangier, and within this hour is Now reach'd me. You have Also the Translation annex'd to it. I have Just Received letters from Sale and Tangier, without News. I am made to Expect more from the Emperor shortly.

In an Hour or two I shall be on my way to Alicante, and in the Mean time Conclude with great Sincerity Dear Sir Your Very obed servt.,
                                                              THOS BARCLAY

RC (DLC); endorsed. Tr (DNA: PCC, No. 91, I); in a clerk's hand, signed and marked "Copy" by Barclay. Noted in SJL as received 21 Jan. 1787. Enclosure: Arabic text and translation of the declaration concerning the addition to Article X of the Treaty with Morocco; the Arabic text has not been found (see Miller, *Treaties of the United States*, II, 224), but the translation is printed above with the treaty, immediately following Barclay's letter to the Commissioners of 2 Oct. 1786. On this same date Barclay wrote Adams: "I wrote you this Day by a Courier going to Paris Inclosing you Copys of some letters written to you and Mr. Jefferson" (MHi: AMT); from this it appears that Barclay may have enclosed in the letter to TJ copies of the LETTERS FROM SALE AND TANGIER or some others for the Commissioners.

From Madame de Doradour

au chateau de Sarlant par Issoir En
auvergnne ce 4 Xbre 1786

Je répond Monsieur sur le champ à votre lettre. Je suis dezollée de l'accident que vous avés eprouvé. Il faut que la chute que vous avés faite aye été bien viollente. Que j'aurois desirois etre a paris pour pouvoir vous tenir quelque fois compagnie. Ma qualité de votre compatriote m'aures donnés des droits Monsieur a vous servir

[573]

de garde malade et j'aurois jouie avec delices de cette avantage. Je ferrai l'impossible pour m'y rendre cette hivers. Sy vous recevés ma lettre avant votre depart pour aix je vous demande en grace Monsieur de me donner de vos nouvelles. Je suis fort inquiete d'imaginer que vous alles voyager dans une mauvaise saison. Je vous suplie donc, sy vous ne pouvés pas ecrire, de me faire dire un mot par celui de vos gens qui sauras e[crire]. Cela m'est indifferent pourveu que je sois instruite de votre etat. Le tems n'y l'elloignnement ne dim[inueront] jamais Monsieur le sincere attachement que je vous est vouë. Mon Mari ne mas point laissée ignorée l'interest que vous lui avés marques. Je trouve un avantage considerable dans l'acquisition qu'il a fait qui est celle Monsieur d'avoir toujours le droit de reclamer vos bontees; ayant des proprietes en amerique je veut esperer que vous me traiteres comme votre compatriote que vous ne m'oublires pas et que vous daignneres vous resouvenir que je vous demande avec instances de vos nouvelles ainsi que d'être persuadé Monsieur de l'attachement avec lequel j'ai l'honneur d'être votre tres humble et tres obeissante servante,

Mille chose je vous prie de ma part a Melle votre fille.

DUBOURG DORADOUR

RC (DLC); endorsed. Not recorded in SJL.

VOTRE LETTRE: From the context it is plain that TJ's letter to Madame de Doradour (not found) was written some time after 18 Sep. It may have been written because of the unfavorable impressions of Virginia received by De Doradour (see, for example, the account of Maury, 17 Sep. which TJ received on 23 Sep. 1786).

From James Madison

DEAR SIR Richmd. Decr. 4. 1786.

Your last favor which was of the 25th. of April has already been acknowledged. My last inclosing a letter from Mrs. Carr, was dated a few days ago only. It was put into the hands of Monr. Chevalier who has gone on to N. York, whither I shall forward this to his care. He is to embark in the packet which will sail on the 15th. inst:

The recommendation from the Meeting at Annapolis of a plenipotentiary Convention in Philada. in May next has been well received by the Assembly here. Indeed the evidence of dangerous defects in the Confederation has at length proselyted the most obstinate adversaries to a reform. The unanimous sanction given by the Assembly to the inclosed compliance with the Recommendation marks sufficiently the revolution of sentiment which the experience

[574]

4 DECEMBER 1786

of one year has effected in this country. The deputies are not yet appointed. It is expected that Genl. Washington, the present Govr. E. Randolph Esqr. and the late one Mr. Henry will be of the number.

The project for bartering the Mississipi to Spain was brought before the Assembly after the preceding measure had been adopted. The report of it having reached the ears of the Western Representatives, as many of them as were on the spot, backed by a number of the late officers, presented a Memorial, full of consternation and complaint, in consequence of which some very pointed resolutions by way of instruction to the Delegates in Congress were *unanimously* entered into by the House of Delegates. They are now before the Senate who will no doubt be also unanimous in their Concurrence.

The question of paper money was among the first with which the Session opened. It was introduced by petitions from two Counties. The discussion was faintly supported by a few obscure patrons of the measure, and on the vote it was thrown out by 85. vs.17. A petition for paying off the public securities according to a scale of their current prices, was *unanimously* rejected.

The Consideration of the Revised Code has been resumed and prosecuted pretty far towards its conclusion. I find however that it will be impossible as well as unsafe to give an ultimate fiat to the System at this Session. The expedient I have in view is to provide for a supplemental revision by a Committee who shall accomodate the bills skipped over, and the subsequent laws, to such part of the Code as has been adopted, suspending the operation of the latter for one year longer. Such a work is rendered indispensible by the al[te]rations made in some of the bills in their passage, by the change of circumstances which call for corresponding changes in sundry bills which have been laid by, and by the incoherence between the whole code and the laws in force of posterior date to the Code. This business has consumed a great deal of the time of two Sessions, and has given infinite trouble to some of us. We have never been without opponents who contest at least every innovation inch by inch. The bill proportioning crimes and punishments, on which we were wrecked last year, has after undergoing a number of alterations got thro' a Committee of the Whole; but it has not yet been reported to the House, where it will meet with the most vigorous attack. I think the chance is rather against its final passage in that branch of the Assembly, and if it should not miscarry there, it will have another guantlet to run through the Senate. The

4 DECEMBER 1786

bill on the subject of Education, which could not safely be brought into discussion at all last year, has undergone a pretty indulgent consideration this. In order to obviate the objection from the inability of the County to bear the expence, it was proposed that it should be passed into a law, but its operation suspended for three or four years. Even in this form however there would be hazard in pushing it to a final question, and I begin to think it will be best to let it lie over for the supplemental Revisors, who may perhaps be able to put it into some shape that will lessen the objection of expence. I should have no hesitation at this policy if I saw a chance of getting a Committee equal to the work of compleating the Revision. Mr. Pendleton is too far gone to take any part in it. Mr. Wythe I suppose will not decline any duty which may be imposed on him, but it seems almost cruel to tax his patriotic zeal any farther. Mr. Blair is the only remaining character in which full confidence could be placed.

The delay in the administration of Justice from the accumulation of business in the General Court and despair of obtaining a reform according to the Assize plan have led me to give up this plan in favor of district Courts; which differ from the former in being cloathed with all the powers of the General Court within their respective districts. The bill on the latter plan will be reported in a few days and will probably tho' not certainly be adopted.

The fruits of the impolitic measures taken at the last Session with regard to taxes are bitterly tasted now. Our Treasury is empty, no supplies have gone to the federal treasury, and our internal embarrassments torment us exceedingly. The present Assembly have good dispositions on the subject, but some time will elapse before any of their arrangements can be productive. In one instance only the general principles of finance have been departed from. The specie part of the tax under collection is made payable in Tobacco. This indulgence to the people as it is called and considered, was so warmly wished for out of doors, and so strenuously pressed within that it could not be rejected, without danger of exciting some worse project of a popular cast. As Tobacco alone is made commutable, there is reason to hope the public treasury will suffer little if at all. It may possibly gain.

The Repeal of the port bill has not yet been attempted. Col. Mason has been waited for as the hero of the Attack. As it is become uncertain whether he will be down at all, the question will probably be brought forward in a few days. The repeal were he present would be morally certain. Under the disadvantage of his

4 DECEMBER 1786

absence it is more than probable. The question of British debts has also awaited his patronage. I am unable to say what the present temper is on that subject, nothing having passed that could make trial of it. The repeated disappointments I have susteined in efforts in favor of the Treaty make me extremely averse to take the lead in the business again.

The public appointments have been disposed of as follows: The contest for the Chair lay between Col. Bland and Mr. Prentis. The latter prevailed by a majority of near 20 votes. Mr. Harrison the late Speaker lost his election in Surry which he represented last year; and since has been equally unsuccessful in his pristine County Charles City where he made a second experiment. In the choice of a Governor Mr. E. Randolph had a considerable majority of the whole in the first ballot. His competitors were Col. Bland and R. H. Lee, each of whom had between 20 and 30 votes. The delegation to Congress contained under the first choice Grayson, Carrington, R. H. Lee, Mr. Jones and myself. Col. H. Lee of the last delegation was dropt. The causes were different I believe and not very accurately known to me. One of them is said to have been his supposed heterodoxy touching the Mississipi. Mr. Jones has since declined his appointment and Col. Lee has been re-instated by an almost unanimous vote. A vacancy in the Council produced by the Resignation of Mr. Roane is filled by Mr. Bolling Starke. Cyrus Griffin was a candidate but was left considerably in the rear. The Attorney Generalship has been conferred on Col. Innis. Mr. Marshal had a handsome vote.

Our summer and fall have been wet, beyond all imagination in some places, and much so every where. The crops of corn are in general plentiful. The price up. The country will not exceed 8/ or 10/. In this district it is scarcest and dearest, being already [as] high as 12/ or 15/. The crop of Tobacco will fall short considerably it is calculated of the last year's. The highest and lowest prices in the Country of the new Crop are 25/ and 20/. A rise is confidently expected.—My next will be from N.Y. whither I shall set out as soon as the principal business of the Session is over. Till my arrival there I postpone communications relative to our national affairs, which I shall then be able to make on better grounds, as well as some circumstances relative to the affairs of this State, which the hurry of the present opportunity restrains me from entering into. Adieu. J. M. Jr.

RC (DLC: Madison Papers); endorsed by Madison late in life when his letters were returned to him after TJ's death. Noted in SJL as received 24 Jan.

1787. Enclosure (DLC: Madison Papers): Clipping from a Richmond newspaper giving several resolutions of the House of Delegates, including that quoted below.

THE INCLOSED COMPLIANCE: Resolution of the House of Delegates, 3 Nov. 1786: "*Resolved unanimously*, That an act ought to pass, in conformity to the report of the Commissioners assembled at Annapolis on the 14th of September last, for appointing Commissioners on the part of this State, to meet Commissioners on the part of the other States, in Convention at Philadelphia, on the second Monday in May next, with powers to devise such further provision as shall appear to them necessary to render the constitution of the fædral government adequate to the exigencies of the Union; and to report such an act for that purpose to the United States in Congress assembled, as when agreed to by them, and afterwards confirmed by the Legislatures of every State, will effectually provide for the same."

From William Macarty

SIR   L'orient 5th. Decemr. 1786.

I have the honour to inclose you a note of the Chinia, which was omitted. I hope it is safe arrived, and am very Respectfully Sir Your most obedt Sevt.,   WM. MACARTY

RC (DLC); endorsed; at foot of text in TJ's hand: "Amounting to 202^{lt}-4s." Noted in SJL as received 9 Dec. 1786. Enclosure not found. See Macarty to TJ, 30 Oct. 1786.

From William Stephens Smith

DR. SIR   London Decr. 5th. 1786.

Inclosed are the Copies of the Letters which you requested in one of *yours*. I have no tolerable excuse to offer for not sending them before and I cannot yet tell a —— without a qualm of conscience. Mrs. Smith I suppose is disposed to open a Corespondence, as she requests me to forward a note addressed to you. I am too Gallant a H———d to enquire of the contents, as it is sealed. I also send those parts of newspapers which will explain to you the Commotion in the Eastern Continent, and the rising of the Commercial Convention, without entering on business. The papers sent by Mr. Jay I suppose will inform you of the expectation of a *General Indian War* and that Congress are raising troops on that ostensible Ground and for that ostensible reason. How they mean to employ 2 Companies of Dragoons of 120 Rank and File in this service I am not yet informed. Be pleased to put the question to our freind the Marquis and ask him if he was going against *Indians* in what manner he would employ this Horse, or whether he would not exchange them for 60 Virginia rifle men.—I am apprehensive you are out of

[578]

all patience with Mr. Neele. I was with him the day before yesterday, and desired that when it was finished (which will be in the course of the week) that he would send it to me, with a Letter containing the reasons why so much more time has been expended than (at first) he supposed necessary, which I proposed forwarding to you. I send you one pr. of Slippers, the other will appear by the next conveyance. Your Buff-cotton Vest and Breeches, I sent by a young Bostonian some time past. The Bearer Dr. Gibbons conveys the Casemier. Not having any Letters on my file unanswered, I shall not trouble you further. I am with my usual respect & esteem Your Excellency's most. obedt. Humble Servt.,

W. S. SMITH

RC (DLC); endorsed. Noted in SJL as received 20 Dec. 1786. Enclosures: (1) Tr of American Commissioners to Jay, 28 Mch. and 25 Apr. 1786, requested in TJ to Smith, 9 Aug. 1786. (2) Abigail Adams Smith to TJ, 2 Dec. 1786. (3) Unidentified newspaper clippings.

From Wilt, Delmestre & Co.

MONSIEUR L'Orient le 6. Decbre. 1786.

Votre Silence à la Lettre que nous eumes l'honneur de vous addresser le 8. du Mois dernier relativement au refus que nous font les Bureaux des fermes de nous faire jouir de la reduction des Droits sur les huiles de Poisson que vous a annoncé Mr. le Controleur Général par sa Lettre en date du 22. Octobre, nous fait craindre, Monsieur, que des interêts plus importants vous ont fait perdre de vue l'objet de notre Lettre. Cependant, chargés d'une partie considerable d'huile de Baleine, de Spermacety et de Morue, nous nous voyons à la veille d'etre obligé de céder aux prétentions des Agents de la ferme génerale, affin de pouvoir vendre pour faire face aux Traites que nos amis de l'Amerique ont fait sur nous pour le montant de ces mêmes huiles. Ainsi, Monsieur, nous venons vous suplier de nouveau de daigner avoir egard à notre exposé et nous honorer d'une reponse.

Nous sommes avec respect Monsieur Vos tres humbles Serviteurs, WILT DELMESTRE & CO.

RC (DLC); endorsed. Noted in SJL as received 11 Dec. 1786.
LA LETTRE QUE . . . VOUS ADDRESSER: Wilt, Delmestre & Co's. letter of 8 Nov. 1786 has not been found; it was recorded in SJL as received 14 Nov.

To Jean Chas

Sir   Paris Dec. 7. 1786.

I should with great pleasure have perused your manuscript of the history of the American revolution, but that it comes to me in the moment of my setting out on a journey into the South of France where I am to pass the winter. In the few moments of leisure which my preparations for that journey admitted, I have read some detached parts, and find that it would have been very interesting to me. In one of these, page 60. I have taken the liberty of noting a circumstance which is not true, and to which I beleive M. D'Auberteuil first gave a place in history. In page 75. again I observed it said that Congress removed to Hartford. But this is a misinformation: they never sat there. In general I would observe to you that where there is no other authority for a fact than the history of M. D'Auberteuil, and the Histoire impartielle, it will not be safe to hazard it. These authors have been led into an infinitude of errors, probably by trusting to the English papers, or to the European ones copied from them. It is impossible to resort to a more impure source. I am much pleased to find that you concur in the justice of the principles which produced our revolution, and have only to wish that I could have been able to go through the whole work. I have the honour to be with much respect Sir your most obedient & most humble servant,   Th: Jefferson

PrC (DLC). Although TJ does not mention an enclosure, he doubtless returned Chas' MS (see Chas to TJ, 2 Dec. 1786).

Histoire Impartielle: The Abbé Longchamps' *Histoire Impartiale des Evénemens militaires et politiques de la dernière guerre, dans les quatre parties du monde* (Amsterdam and Paris, 1785); TJ possessed a copy of this as well as two copies of Hilliard d'Auberteuil's *Essais Historiques et Politiques sur les Anglo-Américains* (Sowerby, Nos. 477, 450).

To Gelhais

A Paris ce 7. Xbre[1] 1786.

J'ai reçu la lettre, Monsieur, que vous m'avez fait l'honneur de m'écrire au sujét de la demande de Monsr. Friguet directeur de la regie generale à Meaux contre M. le Comte de Langeac.

Pour la forme, je ne puis pas recevoir ici un Huissier ou autre Officier quelconque de la Justice; mais quand il aura eté constaté à la justice du pays et decidé par elle que la demande de M. Friguet est juste et doit être payée, si vous aurez de la complaisance de m'envoyer sous enveloppe une copie duement legalisée de cette decision je me ferai un devoir de m'y prêter en payant a M. Friguet les loyers de la maison que je tiens de M. de Langeac quand ils seront echus jusqu'à la concurrence de la somme decretée. J'ai l'honneur d'etre, Monsieur votre très humble et très obeissant Serviteur, TH: JEFFERSON

PrC (DLC); endorsed; in Short's hand, with signature, substitution in date (see note 1, below) and the following, at foot of text, in TJ's hand: "M. Gelhais procureur au Chatelet. rue du four prés St. Eustache."

J'AI REÇU LA LETTRE: The letter from Gelhais to TJ has not been found and is not recorded in SJL, but see TJ to De Langeac, 12 Oct. 1786, to which, evidently, there had been no reply.

[1] Short wrote "10bre."; TJ substituted "Xbre."

To Abraham Walton

SIR   Paris Dec. 7. 1786

The Marquis de la Fayette happened to be out of town when I received the honor of your letter. This circumstance has occasioned the delay of my answer. I now inclose you his letter to the Bishop of Orleans. He desires me also to inform you that he had recommended you to the Marquis du Crest, Chancellor to the D. d'Orleans, now at Orleans, who is therefore prepared to receive you, should you think proper to wait on him. As you are pleased to ask my opinion as to the courses of lectures worthy your attention, I take the liberty of giving it, that there being no professors of botany or chemistry, it will be more advantageous to you to apply your whole time to the French language than to lectures in any other branch of science; if you could have an opportunity there of learning Italian or Spanish, either of these would well merit to divide your time with the French. I expect within about a fortnight to go to the South of France to try whether the mineral waters there can restore to me the use of my hand. I shall probably be absent two or three months. If I can render you any service before my departure, I beg you to command it, as I shall be happy in finding an occasion of being useful to you. I have the honor to be Sir your most obedient & most humble servant,   TH: JEFFERSON

PrC (DLC); endorsed. The enclosed letter from Lafayette to the Bishop of Orleans has not been found.

From Hilliard d'Auberteuil, with Enclosure

Rue des fossés Mr. Le prince No. 35.

Monsieur Ce 8e. decembre 1786

Des circonstances qui me reduisent à contracter diverses obligations envers Mr. Le marquis de La fayette, ne me permettent pas de me livrer à tout le plaisir que j'aurais à lui donner des éloges publics; je craindrais qu'ils ne fussent attribués à des motifs qui ne sont pas dans mon coeur. Je suivais mon penchant en louant son courage en 1781, et ayant besoin de lui en 1786, je me reduis au silence.

Cependant je desirerais repandre en Amerique et en france quelques vers qui me semblent exprimer la reconnaissance qu'on lui doit, et je ne crois pas pouvoir mettre mon secret en de meilleures mains que celles de votre excellence.

Que mes vers soient connus si vous les trouvez convenables au Sujet, mais que l'auteur demeure ignoré de Mr. de la Fayette lui même.

Je travaille toujours à achever l'histoire de la revolution de l'amerique Septentrionale, elle remplira quatre volumes, et Mr. de la fayette m'a fait esperer que vous voudriez bien ajouter les materiaux que vous avez à ceux que j'ai rassemblés depuis douze ans.

Je serai toujours très flatté de rendre mes devoirs à votre excellence et je suis avec un profond respect Monsieur Votre très humble et très obeissant serviteur, Hilliard d'Auberteuil
auteur des Essais historiques et politiques sur la revolution de l'amerique.

ENCLOSURE

Inscription

pour être Gravée sur l'airain aux murs de l'hotel de ville de Paris.

Hommage rendu par les états de l'Amerique au Marquis de la Fayette dans le sein de sa patrie.

"L'Amerique Brisait le joug de l'Angleterre,
et preferait aux fers le fleau de la guerre,
alors que La Fayette apui des malheureux
lui porta le premier un secours genereux;
suivant à dix sept ans le char de la victoire,
bravant l'amour, les pleurs, heros né pour la gloire,
il partit de la france et traversa les mers,
pour remplir de son nom Boston et l'univers.

8 DECEMBER 1786

L'amitié, la sagesse à Washington le lient,
vainqueurs et vertueux, leurs triomphes s'allient,
et pour les consacrer, Mars et la liberté,
ont dedié ce marbre à l'immortalité."

RC (DLC). Enclosure in author's hand is in DLC: TJ Papers, 26:4491; a copy in TJ's hand is in same, 53:9036. See TJ to D'Aubertueil, 27 Jan. 1787.

From Michel Capitaine

Mézieres en Champagne, 8 Dec. 1786. Inquires about a power of attorney forwarded to Peters in June, about which he has had no news; gives his address and asks to have anything received for him forwarded.

RC (MHi); 2 p.; in French; endorsed. Noted in SJL as received 11 Dec. 1786. See Richard Peters to TJ, 1 Oct. 1786.

To St. John de Crèvecoeur

DEAR SIR   Friday Dec. 8.

Having this moment finished reading the New York papers, I send them to you. As soon as you are done with them I shall be glad to receive them again, as Mr. Short has not read them. Mr. and Mrs. Marmontel come to take a dinner with me the day after tomorrow. (Sunday.) I wish the good Countess D'Houdetot may be disengaged for that day and would be so friendly as to come also. We dine at three o'clock. I do not ask you, because a person (Mr. P. M.) will come with Monsr. Marmontel, who is I believe disagreeable to you. Nevertheless of this you are the best judge; you know I shall be happy to see you if the party will be agreeable to you. Will you be so good as to make the proposition to the Countess and to send me her answer? Bon soir, your's affectionately,

TH: JEFFERSON

RC (Louis Saint-John de Crèvecoeur, Montesquieu-sur-Losse, France, 1947); in margin in an unidentified hand: "traduit." No year appears in the date, but 1786 is the only year in which 8 Dec. fell on Friday while TJ was in France.

MR. P.M. was evidently Philip Mazzei, who was in Paris at this time and who was a friend of Marmontel; he and Crèvecoeur were not friendly to each other (see Howard C. Rice, Jr., *Le Cultivateur Américain*, Paris, 1933, p. 200-1; Mazzei, *Memoirs*, p. 297-9).

To Duler

SIR   Paris Dec. 8. 1786.

The circumstance had escaped me of my having had the honor

[583]

8 DECEMBER 1786

of being made known to you by Mr. Walker at Charlottesville. However I should not have been the less ready, had it been in my power, to have aided you in procuring emploiment in some bureau here. But a stranger as I am, unconnected and unacquainted, my sollicitations on your behalf would be as ineffectual as improper. I should have been happy to have been able to render you this service, as I am sincerely concerned at the circumstance which has placed you in need of it.

As to the paper money in your hands, the states have not yet been able to take final arrangements for it's redemption. But as soon as they shall have got their finances into some order, they will surely pay for it what it was worth in silver at the time you received it, with an interest. The interest on Loan office certificates is I think paid annually in all the states; and in some of them they have begun to make paiments of the principal. These matters are managed for foreigners by the Consul of their nation in America, where they have not a private friend to attend for them. I have the honour to be with much respect Sir your most obedt. humble servt.,

TH: JEFFERSON

PrC (DLC); at foot of text in TJ's hand: "Monsr. Duler, negociant par Vallogne & La Hogue chez M. Louis Gosselin à Reville, Normandie." See Duler to TJ, 27 Nov. 1786.

From Ezra Stiles

SIR   Yale College Decr. 8. 1786.

At our public Commencement 13th. Septr. last, the Reverend the Corporation of this College conferred upon yourself the Degree of *Doctor in Laws*. Immediately after, I journeyed to Albany, Ft. Edward, and Lake George, and was absent from home about six Weeks. Before my Departure I wrot a Letter to you advising this Transaction, and left it with my Family to forward by the first Opportunity. But it has been neglected. You will be pleased to accept this as a Token of our Respect and Honor for one of the first Literary Character in the Republic of Letters. We esteem ourselves highly honored in enrolling your Name in the Catalogue of this University. Hereafter I will do myself the Honor of transmitting to you the Diploma of your Doctorate.

I sent you last Spring the Drawing of some curious antique Fortifications at the Confluence of Muskinghum River with the Ohio. I expected that Dr. Wales would have delivered it to you in

8 DECEMBER 1786

person at Paris. But when he left Port l'Orient without proceeding to Paris, he forwarded it to you from thence.

In my Journey I visited the medical Springs near Balltown 12 or 14 m. North of Schenectady, at Saratoga 12 m. beyond, and that at New Lebanon about 25 m. SE from Albany on the Line between the States of Massachts. and N York and 6 m. W. from Pittsfield. The Latter was not in Taste different from common spring water. The Tastes of the two former were alike, saline, very acidulous and astringent, and as disagreeable as a solution of Epsom Salts. I immersed a Fahr: Pocket Thermometer about 12 or 15 minutes in each and found the Mercury to stand at 53 and 54, when the Temperature of the external Air was 76. Immersed in Hudsons River the ☿ stood at 54. I immersed it in Lebanon Springs and it stood at 71 when in the external Air it was 65. So the last was warmer than the external Air. All three springs were very ebullient or incessantly boiling—a boiling caused, not by Heat, but by Protrusion from the subterraneas fountain. There are about a dozen of these saline Springs (from which Salt has been procured) on the Banks of a Ravine at Saratoga, within about 100 Rods. The upper Saratoga Spring is in a Rock or incrusted Concretion in a conica[l] form 8 feet in the horizontal Diameter of the Base and 4 f. high, with a hollow Perforation in the manner of a Millstone thus

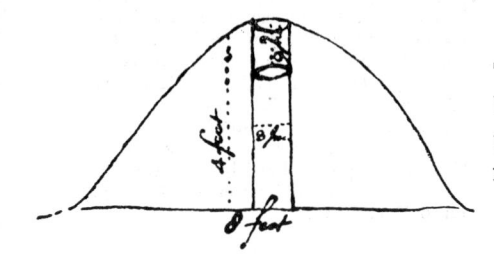

This Protuberance seems to have been formed or grown in a Tractofages from a muriatick Despusmation of the mineral Waters.

Very seldom does the Water overflow the Top. Ordinarily the Water is stationary within nine Inches of the Top. Neither is there any Hole on the side of this Rock, nor any Discharge at or near the Bottom from whence there is any apparent Evacuation or Discharge of the internal water. And altho' Gallons are daily drawn out from the Hole in the summit, there is no Diminution of the Altitude of the Water. A fine attenuated volatile and pungent Vapor incessantly, but invisibly exhales from the Perforation. In this probably the essential Efficacy consists, For where the Water is transported in well closed glass or wooden Vessels to any distance, it ever

8 DECEMBER 1786

looses its Virtue or Efficacy entirely. These Waters have been tried chemically, but I have not the Experiments.

Col. Humphreys, who was a Member of our Assembly the last Session, and by the Assembly appointed Colonel to command the Connectt. Quota of about 180 or 200 Troops for the Defence of the Frontiers against Indian Incursions, has obliged me with the two Volumes of the American Travels of the Marquiss de Chattelux. I have just finished Reading them with great Pleasure and Entertainment. They have afforded me a most delicious and exquisite satisfaction. The Observations on our Country political, physical or natural, military, historical, literary and characteristics made by so ingenious, sagacious learned and patriotic a Foreigner, are highly informative. I am surprized that a Stranger should enter so deeply and judiciously into the genius, Manners, Laws, and political Institutions of our Country. Will you be pleased to make my most Respectful Compliments to that illustrious Nobleman and General, and beg him to accept my Thanks for the Honor he has done us by his Pen and his Arms; even tho' I might not in every Thing concur with some of his critical and learned Remarks, particularly on the wonderful Pont-naturel. Wishing you every Blessing, I am, Dear Sir, with the greatest Esteem & Respect, Yr obedt very hble servt.,   EZRA STILES

RC (DLC); addressed and endorsed; postmarked: "New York." Noted in SJL as received 25 Jan. 1787.

TRACTOFAGES: The word seems to read thus, though it appears to be unknown to geologists as a description of calcareous tufa. Stiles, in developing his rather ponderous academic jargon, may have invented a compound word from *travio*, meaning to penetrate or go through, plus *faex*, meaning sediment, resulting in *trautofæges*. This is conjectural; but compare Stiles' scientific style with that of TJ in, for example, his letter on air currents to Le Roy, 13 Nov. 1786—or with any of Benjamin Franklin's scientific writings. BALLTOWN: Ballston Spa. A LETTER TO YOU . . . HAS BEEN NEGLECTED: The neglect must have been slight, for TJ received Stiles' letter of 14 Sep. on 6 Dec. 1786.

To John Stockdale

SIR   Paris Dec. 8. 1786.

I have sent by the Diligence the three first numbers of Sandford et Merton, being all which has yet appeared. A number comes out every month, and it will be nine months before the whole will be out. You shall receive them as they appear, and always by the Diligence unless you would prefer any other channel of conveyance. I am Sir your very humble servt.,   TH: JEFFERSON

[586]

PrC (DLC); endorsed. It will be noted that TJ did not respond to that part of Stockdale's letter of 20 Nov. 1786 concerning the publication of an English edition of *Notes on Virginia*. This may have been because TJ was at this time thinking of bringing out an English edition to be printed by Hoffman's Imprimerie Polytype (see the series of documents under 1 Sep. 1786, Document II).

From Lewis Alexander

[*Bayonne, 9 Dec. 1786*. Recorded in SJL as received 17 Dec. 1786. Not found.]

From Francis Hopkinson

Dear Sir   Philada. Decr. 9th. 1786

Your Letter of the 14h. Augt. did not get to Hand till the 29th. of Novr. so that I fear my Endeavours to comply with your Request will be too late to answer your Purpose. However, I will take the Chance and accordingly I enclose satisfactory Answers to your Queries, hoping, rather than expecting, that they may reach you in Time.

I have not Time to examine your Epistolary Account but am sure the Ballance is considerably in my favour, only observing that your Letter of July 8th. 1785 was never received.

The Lunarium is still in Contemplation, and will I believe, be executed some Time or other. The particular Æra may be within the Ken of inspired Prophecy, but is certainly not within the Reach of Astronomical Calculation. I have just look'd at my File of Letters and find that you have not credited me for a Letter of May 27h. 1786, and another dated June 28h. 1786. Since which I have wrote by a Vessel to Bordeaux and sent a Package of Papers, Magazines &c.

Doctor Franklin is well. Mr. Rittenhouse not in a good State of Health.

I have only Time to add that I am ever Your truly affectionate

Fs. Hopkinson

I must put you to the Expence of Packet Postage for this, which I would not do but for Sake of the Enclosure.

RC (DLC); addressed and endorsed. Noted in SJL as received 24 Jan. 1787. Enclosures missing.

Your letter of July 8th. 1785: That is, the postscript in TJ's letter of 6 July 1785.

From James Maury

Sir   Liverpoole 10 Decr. 1786

I had the honor to write to you the 17th Septr. informing you of my arrival and fixing here in the Mercantile Line; to which having had no answer and imputing it to miscarriage, the Contents were to inform you of the State of Things in Virginia.

I have late letters thence advising of the Crop of Corn being so uncommonly abundant that the price was expected to be a dollar the Barrel, of Tobacco a middling Crop, but much injured by great rains.

I have two vessels to sail for Virginia in January to accomodate my friends there with freight for their Tobaccoes, one for James River, the other for Rappahannock. Should you be disposed to make Trial of this market with any part of your SoW. Mountain Crop, you may relie on my best endeavors for the Interest in the sales. The present prices in France are good for ordinary quality; but they do not make that distinction between fine and Common that we do at this place. There is not above one Guinea ℔ hhd. between the eastern Shore Trash and Superfine James River. Here the difference in favor of the latter would be from six to eight and even ten Guineas ℔ hhd.

I intend shortly to London and have a letter of Introduction to Mr. Adams from the president of Congress. In the Course of your Correspondence I will be much obliged by your strengthening it with one of your own. May I take the Liberty to refer Mess. De Neufville & Co. of Amsterdam, Messrs. Wilfelshieme & Co. of Nantes and Mess. Schweighauser & Dobreé of the same place to you for a Character of me? I have the Honor to be with the highest Respect Dr Sir yr most obt Svt,   James Maury

RC (MHi). Noted in sjl as received 19 Dec. 1786.

To R. & A. Garvey

Sir   Paris Dec. 11. 1786.

I have now the satisfaction to return you the Acquit a caution No. 113 you were so kind as to enter into for me. The copying press being a prohibited article, has occasioned a considerable delay in obtaining it from the Douane. It was not till yesterday I was able to withdraw your acquit a caution. I thank you for the trouble you

[588]

have taken herein and am Sir your most obedt. & most humble servt., TH: JEFFERSON

PrC (MHi); endorsed: "Garvey Mr." The missing RC may actually have been addressed to Plowden Garvey of the firm of R. & A. Garvey of Rouen.

To Wilt, Delmestre & Co.

GENTLEMEN   Paris Dec. 11. 1786.

Your favor of the 6th. inst. is duly come to hand, as had done that also of the 8th. of Nov. I was much obliged to you for your observations and information on the late regulations. I have received and am still receiving, from other quarters, other hints for it's improvement. I cannot propose these to the minister as they arrive, because, besides the perpetual fatigue to him, the business would not be so well done in the end. As soon as all the defects of the new arrangements shall be discovered by a little experience as well as by their being submitted to the gentlemen concerned in the commerce, I shall be able, by bringing all the amendments necessary, into a single proposition, to submit them at once to the consideration of the minister. It will probably be yet some months before this can be done. In the mean time we must be contented to submit a little longer to those remnants of burthen which still rest on our commerce. In this view I will still thank you for any new hints of amendment which may occur to you in experience, assuring you they shall be put to good use when the occasion shall serve. I have the honor to be with much respect, Gentlemen, your most obedient & most humble servant, TH: JEFFERSON

PrC (DLC). The letter of 8 Nov. 1786 has not been found; see Wilt, Delmestre & Co. to TJ, 6 Dec. 1786.

From John Bondfield

SIR   Bordeaux 12 Xbre. 1786

Having sent to take out the clearances at the Custom house for the arms that I proposed to ship to Day on board the Ship Marquis de lafayette bound to Norfolk, The Receiver with whom lays the duty to expedidite the proper papers refused to grant the clearance alledging that the signature of the Controleur General on the face of the Passport was indispensable to enjoy the privaledges granted. I waited on the Director and presented the Letter you forwarded to me of Monsr. De Vergennes. He inform'd me that they could not diviate from the forms prescribed to them by the Direction at Paris. I therefore transmit you the Passport to which you will please to obtain the signature of the Controleur General and on your returning it to me shall forward the arms that are all ready by the first Vessel. The Alliance arrived here a few Days past with 900 hhds. Tobacco, two ships are lost on the Coast coming in with Tobacco two others are arrived, many are expected on private Accounts so soon as this Crop will be fit for Shiping. The advices receivd in America of the result of your applications and the resolution of the Committee at Berni has caused great sensation to the article of Tobacco in Virginia but Specie is very scarce. The other resolutions you transmitted me will also change the channel of them productions.

On concluding the Treaty with france I informd the Commissioners it was necessary that a ministerial Copy of such parts of the Treaty as related to privaledges and advantages granted to America in their Trade with france should be transmitted to the Farmers General who in consequence would transmit them to the different Burreaux de la Douanne. The Commissioners from multiplicity of affairs omitted, I wrote to the Doctor on the same subject. He intimated to me that it was an affair of internal Police and lay with the french Ministry to attend too. The matter has consequently laid Dormant and in all our Exports and Imports we have paid Alien Duties say double the Duties which by Treaty we are entitled. As I observed your attention to all Commercial matters I take the liberty to represent to you the state of this affair for your consideration. We pay on all Imports 6 ⅌ % and on Exports 5 ⅌ % which are the double of them paid by the favord Nations in Treaty with this Kingdom.

A further regulation is necessary, by the indulgence Granted in the Controleurs Letter to you of the 22 October for the perticular encouragement of the Navigation of the two Nations is stipulated a diminution of the Admiralty fees on all American Ships bringing American Produce to france. The non Establishment of Consular regulations lays this article open to Impossions by English Ships Arriving from America with American Produce enjoying all the advantages granted to Americans which thereby perverts and entirely counter Acts the favor'd intentions of the two Nations, to prevent which were all Masters of American Ships arriving in france before admitted to an Entry obliged to produce in the Consular office the Ships Registers which is the proof of National property and receive a Certificate from the Consul or Vice Consul that the National Papers are in Due form, without which the Ship to be refused an Entry. This as is practiced by the other Nations would establish the due observance of the Articles. Excuse the liberty I take in pointing out these subjects but being in some measure sole in this part of the Kingdom and having from the begining of our conections with th[is] Kingdom had an attentif Eye to what could promote the Interets of the United States, honord from the time of my Arrival in france with the Correspondence of the Ministers, I presume my remarks may not be thought out of place.

With due respect I have the Honor to be Sir Your most Obedient Humble Servant, JOHN BONDFIELD

RC (DLC); endorsed. Noted in sJL as received 17 Dec. 1786. The enclosed passport was transmitted for Colonia's signature in TJ to Colonia, 20 Dec. 1786.

From St. John de Crèvecoeur

SIR　　　　　　　　　　Wednesday Morn. [13 Dec. 1786]

I dined Yesterday with M. le Couteulx and asked him the question you desired I shou'd, concerning the fate of such letters as might arrive at the House the day preceding that of the Packet's Sailing. His answer was, that after the Mail shou'd be closed and carried on board, a Private Box wou'd [be] kept by the Captn. for the reception of such late Letters, and that There was not the least danger of their being opened.—I saw Yesterday the good duke of Harcourt, who Told me that as soon as he has received the final answer from the Farmers General, he will open the Matter of Honfleur To the Ministers and pursue this Important objet untill it is accomplish'd. He thinks that he cannot possibly meet with any Very great difficulties and depends much on his Influence.—In 3 or 4 days Mr. Le Couteulx is to make the Report of our Committee to Mr. de Villedeuille. Wou'd you be so Kind as To Send me by the bearer your Notes on Virginia and your Map, which I will Carefully return.

I am Your Very Humble Servant,
　　　　　　　　　　ST. JOHN DE CRÈVECOEUR

RC (DLC); addressed and endorsed. The date has been supplied from internal evidence (see Crèvecoeur to TJ, 16 Dec. 1786).

From John Jay

Dr Sir   Office for foreign Affairs 13th. Decemr. 1786

Since closing my Dispatches to you of the 1st. Inst. I learn from the Consul of France, that the Prince of Luxemburgh was only the ostensible owner of the South Carolina Frigate, and that she in reality belonged to the King of France, who was entitled to a fourth of her Prizes and Profits. This Information induces me to think, that it would be adviseable to converse on the Subject with the Count de Vergennes previous to any Application to the Prince. Those Dispatches will explain this Letter.

With great Respect and Esteem I have the Honor to be &c.,

JOHN JAY

FC (DNA: PCC, No. 121). Noted in SJL as received 24 Jan. 1787.

From André Limozin

Le Havre, 13 Dec. 1786. The small box which was to have gone with Mr. De la Croix arrived after he left; asks permission to send the box by a vessel about to sail for Norfolk and asks to whom it should be consigned there; will appreciate learning whether the observations in his letter of 1 Dec. met with TJ's approbation.

RC (MHi); 2 p.; endorsed.
Limozin's letter of 1 Dec. 1786 has not been found; see TJ to Limozin, 16 Dec. 1786.

From George Wythe

GW TO TJ   Williamsburgh 13 decemb. 1786.

By the letter, which i lately received from you, i find myself indebted further for that kind attention to me, to prove which you never suffer an opportunity to pass unheeded. I am endeavouring to satisfy the inquiry of the Tagliaferris, near Florence, about their emigrant kinsman, according to Mr. Fabbroni's desire. At present i incline to think that this person was he whom Buchanan, rerum scoticarum lib. xiii. c. 41, mentions calling him 'Laurentium Taliferreo, virum probum et doctum, e puerii regiis,' and that one of his posterity, rather than himself, was founder of the virginian family, for the year 1500, or between it and 1515, was the time when this Laurence was in Scotland. Peter Carr attends the professors of natural and moral philosophy and mathematicks, is learning the french and spanish languages, and with me reads Aeschylus and

[592]

Horace, one day, and Herodotus and Cicero's orations the next; and moreover applies to arithmetic. The pleasure, which he gives me, will be greater, if you approve of the courses, or will recommend another. I think him sensible and discreet, and in a fair way of being learned, to which one great encouragement, both of him and many others of our youth, is the specimen of its ability which they admire in one of their countrymen in another quarter of the globe. His notes on Virginia, whatever he writes, says, or thinks, is eagerly sought after; and this not by youth alone. His sentiments are most earnestly desired on the grand subject of the inclosed act by the oldest (except one) of the commissioners appointed by it, who supposes that he cannot be directed so well by any other luminary. You must have advanced money for me. Let me know the amount; and whether by a draught on a merchant in London, or in what other manner i shall discharge it. On these terms (but not else) i wish you to send to me Polybius and Vitruvius. Adieu.

RC (DLC); endorsed. Noted in SJL as received 6 Apr. 1787. Enclosure (missing): "An act for appointing deputies from this commonwealth to a convention proposed to be held in the city of Philadelphia in May next, for the purpose of revising the federal constitution" (Hening, XII, 256-7).

From John Bartram

SIR   At My Garden Near Philad. December 14th 1786

I recievd Your favour of January 27 with Lennaeus Systema vegetabilium ⚕ favour Mr. Bingham which I acknowledg as a perticular favour—pleas to Excep of My harty thanks. I have Made frequent enquirey after vessels Bound to the Ports Mentionen in Your Letter without Success. I Conclude its Not Prudent to Send a Large quantity as I dont know of any Convenient opertunity at this time. I have pact up a small Box of Seeds pleas to Except of as a present. From Your Asured. Friend to Serve,

JOHN BARTRAM

N.B. Catalogue of Seeds is Naild up in the box as I thought it the Safest way. Dear Sir if You should have any orders for American Seeds or plants for the future I shall Chearfully Comply, if opertunity will permit.

RC (MHi); endorsed. Noted in SJL as received 26 Aug. 1787; it was enclosed in Hopkinson to TJ, 8 July 1786.
There is in MHi a two-page MS endorsed by TJ "Bartram" and listing over two hundred plants, entitled: "Catalogue Seeds of American Forest Trees, Shrubs and Herbacious Plants." This may have been the catalogue of seeds that Bartram NAILD UP IN THE BOX.

To Elizabeth Wayles Eppes

Dear Madam   Paris Dec. 14. 1786.

I perceive indeed that our friends are kinder than we have sometimes supposed them, and that their letters do not come to hand. I am happy that yours of July 30. has not shared the common fate. I received it about a week ago, together with one from Mr. Eppes announcing to me that my dear Polly will come to us the ensuing summer. Tho' I am distressed when I think of this voiage, yet I know it is necessary for her happiness. She is better with you, my dear Madam, than she could be any where else in this world, except with those whom nature has allied still more closely to her. It would be unfortunate thro' life both to her and us, were those affections to be loosened which ought to bind us together, and which should be the principal source of our future happiness. Yet this would be too probably the effect of absence at her age. This is the only circumstance which has induced me to press her joining us.— I am sorry the garden seeds were so little attended to by the Mr. Fitzhughs. I fear that several other little parcels sent at different times from London, from Bourdeaux, &c. may have never reached you. I am obliged to cease writing. An unfortunate dislocation of my right wrist has disabled me from writing three months. I have as yet no use of it, except that I can write a little, but slowly and in great pain. I shall set out in a few days to the South of France to try the effect of some mineral waters there. Assure Mr. and Mrs. Skipwith of my warm affections. Kiss the little ones for me. I suppose Polly not to be with you. Be assured yourself of my sincere love and esteem, Your's affectionately,   TH: JEFFERSON

PrC (CSmH). YOURS OF JULY 30: Not found but recorded in SJL as received 28 Nov. 1786.

To Francis Eppes

Dear Sir   Paris Dec. 14. 1786.

I am favored with yours of Aug. 31. and am happy to hear that my dear Polly will come the next summer and by a good opportunity. If she comes to London, address her to Mrs. Adams who will receive her and advise me of her arrival. If to any port of France, the Agent of the United States at the port will do the same.—A dislocated wrist, not yet at all reestablished, obliges me to be very short. By a state of my affairs received from Mr. Lewis I may hope there

14 DECEMBER 1786

remains no debt on my estate except those to Farrell & Jones and to Kippon & Co. I wish therefore to apply to the paiment of these the whole profits of my estate. I am desirous of proposing to them the annual paiment of a fixed sum of money till I shall be cleared of them. The question is what annual sum I may undertake to pay one year with another, and when can the paiments begin. To this question I must beg your's and Mr. Lewis's answer. In the mean time I shall be arranging with them the conditions I shall insist on. 1. No interest during the war. 2. That their accounts shall remain open to every just rectification. I will intreat your answer to this as soon as possible.—I am glad to hear my bill of scantling is nearly got through. I hope they will secure the stuff from depredation. It is a great object with me. The excessive pain in which I write permits me only to add assurances of the sincere affection with which I am Dr. Sir your friend & servt.,

Th: Jefferson

Since writing the within I have reflected on the article of tobacco and think it material to mention to you what I have done to Mr. Lewis. He writes me the price was 22/6. I can always receive for it at Havre 36/ Virginia money for the Virginia hundred weight. From this is to be deducted freight, commission, insurance and post charges. You can judge what these will be, and whenever you find it will still leave more than the Virginia price, it will be worth while to ship it to me by some vessel coming to Havre, and to no other port. If the proceeds are wanting in Virginia, draw on me, only taking care that the bill shall not be presented before the tobacco arrives, and that there be such an usance in it as will give me time to sell the tobacco and receive the paiment before the bill becomes due. If the proceeds are for Jones and McCaul, no draught need be made on me, as I can remit the money from hence. Should this plan as to your own tobacco appear advantageous to you, if you think proper to ship it to me in like manner, I will dispose of it for you as my own. But in that case it must come under my mark. Your favor of Octob. 30. is just come to hand. I have written to London to enquire after the Magnolia seed which should have come with it. I thank you for them, and in advance also for the others you are about to send. Adieu!

PrC (CSmH); endorsed. YOURS OF AUG. 31 (missing) is recorded in SJL as received 28 Nov. 1786. YOUR FAVOR OF OCTOB. 30 (missing) is recorded as received 4 Jan. 1787. The postscript to this letter was probably written about 4 or 5 Jan. 1787. Throughout the latter part of December TJ wrote a number of letters to America in anticipation of David S. Franks' return to Congress which would provide a safe conveyance for them; consequently, this letter and probably others were begun on the dates indicated and so recorded in SJL but held until Franks actually departed (see TJ to Edward Carrington, 16 Jan. 1787).

From John Jay

DR. SIR Office for for: Affairs 14 Decr. 1786

My last to you was dated the 27 October by the Way of London, since which I have been honored with yours of the 11 and 13 August.—They both arrived the 23 Novemr. last but Congress not having made a house since the 7th. of that Month, they have not yet been officially communicated.

The Information relative to Sr Guy Carlton's Instructions is in direct Opposition to Intelligence I have received on the same Subject from Persons in London who have Opportunities of knowing the Truth, and whose Credit is unquestionable. It is possible however that they may have been either accidentally or designedly decieved. A Variety of Considerations and some Facts afford Room for Suspicions, that there is an understanding between the Insurgents in Massachusetts and some leading Persons in Canada, but whether with or without the Consent or Connivance of the british Government, is still[1] to be ascertained. There is so much Evidence of their having sent Emissaries to Quebec, and of Propositions made to and received by them from a Character of Distinction there, that I am induced to think there is at least some Truth in it. A Report has also circulated that the Insurgents have Money, and pay not only for supplies and ammunition, but also for personal services. This Fact is as yet supported by slender Proof, so much so that my Judgment remains undecided and in suspence about it. Intimations have been given that the People of Vermont are less and less anxious to be admitted into the Confederacy, and that they rather incline to a Connection of some kind or other with Britain than with us. This also remains to be proved. Two Circumstances however give it some Appearance of Probability, Vizt. It is said and believed that they talked with Sr Guy Carlton during the War, and they know that by remaining separate from the States, they will also remain uncharged with our Debts.

An Idea that may do[2] Mischief has been very incautiously dropped where it should never have entered, that the Interests of the Atlantic and Western Parts of the United States are distinct, and that the growth of the latter tending to diminish that of the former, the western People have Reason to be jealous of the northern. If Britain really means to do us Harm she will adopt and impress this Idea.

You will perceive from the public Papers, that the Government of Massachusetts has behaved with great Moderation and Condescension towards the Insurgents, more so than in my Opinion was wise. Obsta Principiis always appeared to me to be a Maxim very applicable to such Cases. Those Malcontents undoubtedly mean more than the Redress of the Grievances which their Leaders complain of, and there is little Doubt but that those Leaders have more extensive Views than their Followers suspect. During the Winter they may perhaps continue quiet, but if during the[3] Course of it they should be able to bring their Affairs into system and either obtain or be promised foreign Countenance and aid, they will probably give us Trouble in the Spring. These People bear no Resemblance to an English Mob—they are more temperate, cool and regular in their Conduct—they have hitherto abstained from Plunder, nor have they that I know of committed any outrages but such as the accomplishment of their Purpose made necessary. I hear to Day that some of their Leaders in one of the Counties have certainly been taken by a Party of Horse from Boston.

In my Letter of the 27. October I enclosed a Copy of an Act of Congress, authorizing you to settle the Affairs of ——— Schweighauser, and directing the Board of Treasury to furnish you with the necessary Information. I presume therefore that such part of your Letter of the 11th. Augt as relates to that Matter, will be referred to the Board, and that the Commissioners according to Order will collect and transmit to you the Intelligence in Question. My sentiments respecting the Discussion of this Matter with the Court, perfectly correspond with yours.

The Situation of our captive Countrymen at Algiers is much to be lamented, and the more so as their Deliverance is difficult to effect. Congress cannot command Money for that nor indeed for other very important Purposes. Their Requisitions produce little, and Government (if it may be called a Government) is so inadequate to its objects that essential alterations or essential Evils must take place. I hope you have received the order of Congress for Mr. Lambs Recall—another Copy of it is herewith enclosed.

It seems probable that the Delays of Portugal proceed from the Cause you suggest. We hear the Treaty between France and Britain will be concluded. If so, many Consequences will doubtless result from it to us as well as to Portugal. Some suspect that France and England will pursue similar Systems of colonial Commerce with us. Of this however some Doubts remain on my Mind. This Country

14 DECEMBER 1786

is still exceedingly out of Humour with Britain, and Every commercial Privilege we have from France, beyond what Britain admits, encreases it and strengthens our Predilection for[4] France.[5] It appears to me, that the Court is not sufficiently apprized of the Expediency of having a discreet, liberal minded Minister here. It is important to both Countries that France should have none but exact and candid Representatives from hence—and altho that may possibly be the Case in general at present, yet there is some Evidence of one of their Consuls having written, that we suspect their sincerity in promoting our Peace with Barbary. Such Communications may tend to illustrate the Penetration and Intelligence of the writer, but I have no Reason to think them warranted by Facts, nor conducive to mutual Confidence. We know that european commercial Nations never rejoice to see a Rival at peace with those Pirates, but we nevertheless think that France has more Inducements to do us good than Evil, especially on that and such occasions. If our Government could draw forth the Resources of the Country which, notwithstanding all appearances to the contrary, are abundant, I should prefer War to Tribute, and carry on our Mediterranean Trade in Vessels armed and manned at the public Expence. I daily become more and more confirmed in the Opinion, that Government should be divided into executive, legislative and judicial Departments. Congress is unequal to the first, very fit for the second, and but ill calculated for the third. So much Time is spent in Deliberation, that the Season for action often passes by before they decide on what should be done, nor is there much more Secrecy than Expedition in their Measures.—These Inconveniences arise not from personal Disqualifications, but from the Nature and Construction of the Government.

If Congress had Money to purchase Peace of Algiers or redeem the Captives there, it certainly would according to their present Ideas be well to lose no Time in doing both.[6] Neither Pains nor Expence, if within any tolerable Limits, should be spared to ransom our fellow Citizens, but the Truth is that no Money is to be expected at present from hence, nor do I think it would be right to make new Loans, until we have at least some Prospect of paying the Interest due on former ones. Our Country is fertile, abounding in useful Productions, and those Productions in Demand and bearing a good Price, yet Relaxation in Government and Extravagance in Individuals, create much public and private Distress, and much public and private Want of good Faith.

The public Papers will tell you how much Reason we have to

apprehend an Indian War, and to suspect that Britain instigates it. In my Opinion our Indian Affairs have been ill managed. Details would be tedious. Indians have been murdered by our People in cold Blood and no satisfaction given,[7] nor are they pleased with the avidity with which we seek to acquire their Lands. Would it not be wiser gradually to extend our Settlements, as want of Room should make it necessary, than to pitch our Tents through the Wilderness in a great Variety of Places, far distant from each other, and from those Advantages of Education, Civilization, Law, and Government which compact Settlements and Neighbourhood afford? Shall we not fill the Wilderness with white Savages,[8] and will they not become more formidable to us than the tawny ones who now inhabit it?

As to the Sums of Money expected from the Sale of those Lands, I suspect we shall be deceived, for at whatever price they may be sold, the collection and payment of it will not be easily accomplished. I have the Honor to be &c.,

FC (DNA: RG 59, PCC, No. 121). Dft (NK-Iselin). Noted in SJL as received 24 Jan. 1787. Enclosure: Dupl of resolution of Congress recalling John Lamb, first transmitted in Jay to TJ, 12 Oct. 1786.

[1] In Dft "doubtful" is deleted.
[2] In Dft "much" is deleted.
[3] In Dft preceding three words interlined in substitution for "there is Reason to apprehend," deleted.
[4] In Dft this passage originally read: ". . . strengthens the Interest of France throughout the States," and was then changed to read as above.
[5] Jay found unusual difficulty in composing this passage, a fact evidently reflecting his concern lest Otto's dispatches resulting from conversations with Virginia delegates in Congress over the Mississippi question and the consular Convention should add strength to the growing Franco-American ties manifested, for example, by the decision at Berni of 24 May and by Virginia's exemption of duties on French brandies. At this point in Dft there were several successive deletions, of which one, as first phrased, read: "I am aware that some of the French ⟨Consuls⟩ Correspondents display their [. . .] Penetration by ⟨Conveying⟩ [. . .] Communications ⟨of great⟩ which to the Court," &c.
[6] In Dft this sentence was first phrased to read: "If we had money to purchase Peace of Algiers or to redeem the Captives there, it would certainly in my opinion be well to lose no time in doing the latter, and at the same time obtain every necessary Information respecting the former." This was deleted in Dft and then phrased as above.
[7] In Dft the following was deleted at this point: "We are taking their Lands from them before we want them."
[8] In Dft the words "instead of Law" are deleted.

To Eliza House Trist

DEAR MADAM Paris Dec. 15. 1786.

I have duly received your friendly letter of July 24. and received it with great pleasure as I do all those you do me the favor to write me. If I have been long in acknowleging the receipt, the last cause

[599]

15 DECEMBER 1786

to which it should be ascribed would be want of inclination. Unable to converse with my friends in person, I am happy when I do it in black and white. The true cause of the delay has been an unlucky dislocation of my wrist which has disabled me from writing three months. I only begin to write a little now, but with pain. I wish, while in Virginia, your curiosity had led you on to James river. At Richmond you would have seen your old friends Mr. and Mrs. Randolph, and a little further you would have become acquainted with my friend Mrs. Eppes whom you would have found among the most amiable women on earth. I doubt whether you would ever have got away from her. This trip would have made you better acquainted too with my lazy and hospitable countrymen, and you would have have found that their character has some good traits mixed with some feeble ones. I often wish myself among them, as I am burning the candle of life without present pleasure, or future object. A dozen or twenty years ago this scene would have amused me. But I am past the age for changing habits. I take all the fault on myself, as it is impossible to be among a people who wish more to make one happy, a people of the very best character it is possible for one to have. We have no idea in America of the real French character. With some true samples, we have had many false ones. —I am very, very sorry I did not receive your letter three or four months sooner. It would have been absolutely convenient for me while in England to have seen Browse's relations, and I should have done it with infinite pleasure. At present I have no particular expectation of returning there. Yet it is among possible events, and the desire of being useful to him would render it a pleasing one. The former journey thither was made at a week's warning without the least previous expectation. Living from day to day, without a plan for four and twenty hours to come, I form no catalogue of impossible events. Laid up in port, for life, as I thought myself at one time, I am thrown out to sea, and an unknown one to me. By so slender a thread do all our plans of life hang!—My hand denies itself further, every letter admonishing me, by a pain, that it is time to finish, but my heart would go on in expressing to you all it's friendship. The happiest moments it knows are those in which it is pouring forth it's affections to a few esteemed characters. I will pray you to write to me often. I wish to know that you enjoy health and that you are happy. Present me in the most friendly terms to your mother and brother, and be assured of the sincerity of the esteem with which I am, Dear Madam, your affectionate friend & humble servant, TH: JEFFERSON

PrC (MHi); endorsed. Tr (DLC); in the hand of Nicholas P. Trist; at foot of text: "The original of the foregoing sent to Eugene A. Vail, at Paris, by N. P. Trist, October 1840."

TJ had received Mrs. Trist's LETTER OF JULY 24. on 22 Sep. 1786, only four days after the injury to his wrist, but it was not literally accurate to state that he had been DISABLED ... FROM WRITING THREE MONTHS.

From St. John de Crèvecoeur

SIR   Paris 16th. Xre. 1786

Agreable to what I Told you last Wednesday I Saw Yesterday morning the Duke of Harcourt, To whom I most particularly Explained the Motives which had hitherto obliged you to decline Solliciting from the Government the Freedom of Honfleur. Here follows his answer.

"I am Conscious that on many accounts that Freedom will be at least as usefull to us as to The americans; but as the nature of our Government does not admit of Publick debates on such national Subjects as might Tend to Enlighten our Rulers, the only ressource left in that Case is to *ask*. From what Mr. de Villedeuil Intendant of Rouen and the Marèchal de Castries have [told me][1] They desire that it may be done, but they can't well bring the Matter in Council untill the First demand has been made on the part of the Americans by their ambassadeur.—As soon as Mr. Jefferson has Taken that Step I will Cheerfully follow it, and make use of all my Influence."

I beg you to believe that what few Steps I have Taken in this Matter have been urged by the desire of doing what I Thought might be usefull, and not in consequence of any Presumptuous Motives; I was Encouraged beside by the Friendship the duke honord me with, and by the Knowledge I had of his being Extremely desirouse To unite some part of the american Trade with the Province he Governs, of which he is a Native. I am with great Respect Sir Your very Humble Servt,

ST. JOHN DE CREVECOEUR

RC (DLC); in a clerk's hand, signed by Crèvecoeur; endorsed. Noted in SJL as received 16 Dec. 1786. See TJ to Harcourt, 14 Jan. 1787.

[1] MS appears to read "talme"; but "told me" was evidently intended.

To André Limozin

SIR   Paris Dec. 16. 1786.

Your favor of Dec. 13. is this moment put into my hands. I will be obliged to you to send the box (which was to have gone by La

16 DECEMBER 1786

Croix) by the Le Couteulx to Norfolk. I have no correspondent in Norfolk, and will therefore beg the favor of you to address it to yours at that place, with a request that he will forward it to a Colo. Richard Cary near Hampton (to whom, if I recollect rightly, it is addressed). Hampton is only across the river from Norfolk.

I will take this opportunity of acknowleging the receipt of yours of Dec. 1. inclosing your observations on M. de Calonne's letters. Those observations are judicious and exact, and shall be put to good use whenever opportunity will permit. I beg you to accept my thanks for the attention you paid to these subjects, and for the information conveyed to me by your remarks, and have the honor to be with much respect, Sir, your most obedient & most humble servant, TH: JEFFERSON

PrC (DLC).

THOSE OBSERVATIONS . . . SHALL BE PUT TO GOOD USE: TJ evidently accumulated the letters that he had received from various merchants with comments on Calonne's trade regulations as announced in his letter of 22 Oct. 1786, and used them in the formulation of his observations on Calonne's letter (see under 25 July 1787). Lewis' letter OF DEC. 1 has not been found.

To James Madison

DEAR SIR Paris Dec. 16. 1786.

After a very long silence, I am at length able to write to you. An unlucky dislocation of my right wrist has disabled me from using my pen for three months. I now begin to use it a little, but with great pain; so that this letter must be taken up at such intervals as the state of my hand will permit, and will probably be the work of some days. Tho' the joint seems to be well set, the swelling does not abate, nor the use of it return. I am now therefore on the point of setting out to the South of France to try the use of some mineral waters there, by immersion. This journey will be of 2. or 3. months. —My last letters to you were of Apr. 25. and May 29. the latter only a letter of recommendation. Yours of Jan. 22. Mar. 18. May. 12. June 19. and Aug. 12. remain unacknowleged.

I inclose you herein a copy of the letter from the Minister of finance to me, making several advantageous regulations for our commerce. The obtaining this has occupied us a twelvemonth.[1] I say us, because I find the M. de la Fayette so useful an auxiliary that acknowlegements for his cooperation are always due. There remains still something to do for the articles of rice, turpentine and shipduties. What can be done for tobacco when the late regulation

[602]

expires, is very incertain. The commerce between the U.S. and this country being put on a good footing, we may afterwards proceed to try if any thing can be done to favour our intercourse with their colonies. Admission into them for our fish and flour is very desireable. But unfortunately both these articles would raise a competition against their own.

I find by the public papers that your Commercial Convention failed in point of representation. If it should produce a full meeting in May, and a broader reformation, it will still be well. To make us one nation as to foreign concerns, and keep us distinct in Domestic ones, gives the outline of the proper division of powers between the general and particular governments. But to enable the Federal head to exercise the powers given it, to best advantage, it should be organised, as the particular ones are, into Legislative, Executive and Judiciary. The 1st. and last are already separated. The 2d should also be. When last with Congress, I often proposed to members to do this by making of the Committee of the states, an Executive committee during the recess of Congress, and during it's sessions to appoint a Committee to receive and dispatch all executive business, so that Congress itself should meddle only with what should be legislative. But I question if any Congress (much less all successively) can have self-denial enough to go through with this distribution. The distribution should be imposed on them then. I find Congress have reversed their division of the Western states, and proposed to make them fewer and larger. This is reversing the natural order of things. A tractable people may be governed in large bodies; but in proportion as they depart from this character, the extent of their government must be less. We see into what small divisions the Indians are obliged to reduce their societies. This measure, with the disposition to shut up the Missisipi give me serious apprehensions of the severance of the Eastern and Western parts of our confederacy. It might have been made the interests of the Western states to remain united with us, by managing their interests honestly and for their own good. But the moment we sacrifice their interests to our own, they will see it better to govern themselves. The moment they resolve to do this, the point is settled. A forced connection is neither our interest nor within our power.—The Virginia act for religious freedom has been received with infinite approbation in Europe and propagated with enthusiasm. I do not mean by the governments, but by the individuals which compose them. It has been translated into French and Italian, has been sent to most of the courts of Europe, and has been the best evidence of the falshood of those reports which stated us to be in anarchy. It is inserted in the new Encyclopedie, and is appearing in most of the publications respecting America. In fact it is comfortable to see the standard of reason at length erected, after so many ages during which the human mind has been held in vassalage by kings, priests and nobles; and it is honorable for us to have produced the first legislature who has had the courage to declare that the reason of man may be trusted with the formation of his own opinions. I shall be glad when the revisal shall be got thro'. In the criminal law, the principle of retaliation is much criticised here, particularly in the case of Rape. They think the punishment indecent and unjustifiable. I should be for altering it, but for a different reason: that is on account of the temptation women would be under to make it the instrument of vengeance against an inconstant lover, and of disappointment to a rival.—Are our courts of justice open for the recovery of British debts according to the Septennial act? The principles of that act can be justified; but the total stoppage of justice cannot. The removal of the negroes from New York would only give cause for stopping some of the last paiments, if the British government should refuse satisfaction, which however I think they will not do.

I thank you for your communications in Natural history. The several instances of trees &c. found far below the surface of the earth, as in the case of Mr. Hay's well, seem to set the reason of man at defiance. Another Theory of the earth has been contrived by one Whitford, not absolutely reasonable, but somewhat more so than any that has yet appeared. It is full of interesting facts; which however being inadequate to his theory, he is obliged to supply them from time to time by begging questions. It is worth your getting from London. If I can be useful to you in ordering books from London you know you may command me. You had better send me the duplicate volume of the Encyclopedie. I will take care to send you the proper one. I have many more livraisons for you and have made some other inconsiderable purchases for you in this way. But I shall not send them till the spring, as a winter passage is bad for books. I reserve myself till that time therefore to give you an account of the execution of your several commissions, only observing that the watch will not be finished till the spring and that it will be necessary for me to detain her some time on trial, because it often happens that a watch, looking well to the eye, and faithfully made, goes badly at first on account of some little circumstance which escapes the eye of the workman when he puts

16 DECEMBER 1786

her together and which he could easily rectify.—With respect to the proposition about the purchase of lands, I had just before made the experiment desired. It was to borrow money for aiding the opening of the Patowmac, which was proposed to me by Genl. Washington. I had the benefit of his name, and the foundation of a special act of assembly. I lodged the papers in the hands of Mr. Grand to try to obtain money on loan at 6. per cent. assuring him that the securities should be made compleatly satisfactory to the lenders. After long trial he told me it could not be done; that this government has always occasion to borrow more money than can be lent in this country; that they pay 6. percent per annum in quarterly paiments, and with a religious punctuality; that besides this they give very considerable douceurs to the lenders; that every one therefore would prefer having his money here rather than on the other side the Atlantic, where distance, want of punctuality, and a habitual protection of the debtor would be against them. There is therefore but one way in which I see any chance of executing your views. Monied men sometimes talk of investing money in American lands. Some such might be willing to ensure an advantageous investiture by interesting trust-worthy characters in the purchase, and to do this might be willing to advance the whole money, being properly secured. On this head no satisfaction should be wanting, which I could give them; and as persons with these views sometimes advise with me, I shall be attentive to propose to them this plan. I consider it's success however as only possible, not probable.

When I wrote you by the Fitzhughs I informed you I had lent them 600 livres; but after this I received notice of their bill on me in favor of Limozin for 480 livres which I paid in December 1785. so that the sum I would wish you to receive from them is 1080 livres.—The bickerings between Russia and the Porte are again patched up by this court. Those between Spain and Naples never looked towards war. The only danger was that Naples might throw itself into the arms of the house of Austria. This court is labouring at a reconciliation. It will probably end in a settled coolness between the two kings, father and son, and the former withdrawing from all interference with the affairs of Naples: while the latter will keep himself clear of new connections. There have been serious fears of a rupture of the equilibrium by a shifting of Prussia into the Austrian scale. This country will certainly support the patriotic party in Holland, even at the expence of a war. It is rather beleived the new king of Prussia will not go so far in favor of the Stadholder, tho much interested for him. This is the only germ at present, the development of which can produce war. I am Dear Sir with sincere esteem your friend & servant,

TH: JEFFERSON

P.S. Since writing the above I have received the deficient volume of the encyclopedie for you. The price of Buffon's plates coloured are
   Oiseaux. 1008. Plates in 42 quires 630 livres
   Quadrupedes 27. quires   194 - 8
They cannot be bought uncoloured separate from the text.

RC (DLC: Madison Papers); endorsed. PrC (DLC: TJ Papers); faded and in part overwritten by someone at a later date. Enclosure: Printed copy of Calonne to TJ, 22 Oct. 1786.

ANOTHER THEORY OF THE EARTH . . . BY ONE WHITFORD: TJ confused the name of the author, who was John Whitehurst (1713-1788), and his work was *An Inquiry into the Original State and Formation of the Earth; deduced from Facts and the Laws of Nature* (2d ed., London, 1786; see Sowerby, No. 641). TJ correctly referred to Whitehurst in his letter to Thomson of 17 Dec. 1786.

[1] The words "us a twelvemonth" are written over the words "the M. Fayette [. . .]."

From William Carmichael

DEAR SIR   Madrid 17 Decr. 1786

I have the honor to inclose your Excellency two Letters which Mr. Barclay requested me to forward by the 1st. safe opportunity. None having offered until the present, the Return of the Duke of Vauguyon to Paris, you will find them of an old date.

Mr. Barclay wrote me the 20th. from Alicant. Before his arrival Mr. Lamb had gone to Minorca. He is therefore much at a loss with respect to his future proceedings, and I think it is probable he will soon return to France; unless he should receive Letters from you, that may direct his conduct. The Cte. D'Expilly is now at Carthagena on his way to Algiers, to which place he will be accompanied by the Envoys of Naples and Portugal. The Ambassador from the Latter to this court assures me that he has no expectation of concluding a peace with the Regency. The Cte. D'Expilly has promised me to continue his Attention to our Prisoners during his Stay at Algiers and I have also engaged the Consul of Spain who remains there on his return to take care of them. Advances have been made for their support, which ought to be refunded. I have no Letters from Congress, the Cte. de Florida Blanca tells me that he hopes the Treaty will soon be concluded. Mr. Gardoqui writes me to the same purpose. I am told the English Commercial Treaty with this Country goes on Slowly. The difference between this court and that of Naples still subsists,

17 DECEMBER 1786

altho many efforts have been made to reconcile the Father and Son.

The Abrupt departure of the French Ambassador occasions various conjectures. All that I know with certainty on the Subject is, that he presented a Letter from his Sovereign to this, advising that his Ambassador having asked a Congé for six weeks for his private affairs he had granted it to him. The Cte. de Florida Blanca, on being questioned, answered to the purport just mentioned. The situation of our Affairs having taken another turn during the residence of this Ambassador, than what they were in the time of his Predecessor the Ct. de Montmorin, it has not been in my power without forwardness on my part to see him so often as I had occasion to see the Latter. He has always treated me politely and I have endeavoured as far as circumstances would permit to show Him those proofs of attachment which are particularly due from me to his Nation. He has ever expressed a great desire of cultivating your acquaintance and I suppose he will now have an opportunity. His Son the Prince of Carency engages to send this to your Excellency. He is a promising young Nobleman. Indeed the Family attachment of this great house does honor to the Individuals which compose it, and I fear there are very few similar Examples in high Life. An Article which I saw in the Gazette of Paris some time ago, gives me some uneasiness for your health. I have forwarded to Congress the answer of this Court to the Memorial of the Dutch Ambassador, of which I sent you Copy. I think the reflections, which accompanied this answer, convincing. I continue to receive from the Ct. de F.B. every proof that I can wish in my little sphere, of his desire to promote a good Understanding between our respective Countries. He is no Stranger to the difficulties which Congress encounter, and I seize every occasion of removing any impressions which such Information might make on him. With Sincere Wishes for your health and happiness I have the honor to be Your Excys. Obliged & Obedt. Hble. Servt.,

Wm. Carmichael

25 Decr. 1786.

P.S. Since writing the preceeding, the Portuguese Ambassador has pressed me to hint, that the present moment is favorable to push our Treaty with his Court. I answered generally that I was not well informed on what it *now* stood to give my opinion. I therefore merely repeat this for your Information. He also insinuated that we might make mutual arrangements for repressing the piracies of the Barbaresque Powers. I am &c. W.C.

RC (DLC); endorsed. Noted in SJL as received 21 Jan. 1787. Enclosures: Only one letter from Barclay (that of 4 Dec. 1786) is recorded in SJL as being received with this letter; the other was probably a Dupl of an earlier letter by another conveyance.

To Charles Thomson

DEAR SIR   Paris Dec. 17. 1786

A dislocation of my right wrist has for three months past disabled me from writing except with my left hand, which was too slow and awkward to be employed but in cases of necessity. I begin to have so much use of my wrist as to be able to write, but it is slowly and in pain. I take the first moment I can however to acknowlege the receipt of your letters of Apr. 6. July 8. and 30. In one of these you say you have not been able to learn whether, in the new mills in London, steam is the immediate mover of the machinery, or raises water to move it? It is the immediate mover. The power of this agent, tho' long known, is but now beginning to be applied to the various purposes of which it is susceptible. You observe that Whitehurst supposes it to have been the agent which, bursting the earth, threw it up into mountains and vallies. You ask me what I think of his book? I find in it many interesting facts brought together, and many ingenious commentaries on them. But there are great chasms in his facts, and consequently in his reasoning. These he fills up by suppositions which may be as reasonably denied as granted. A sceptical reader therefore, like myself, is left in the lurch. I acknolege however he makes more use of fact than any other writer of a theory of the earth. But I give one answer to all these theorists. That is as follows: they all suppose the earth a created existence. They must suppose a creator then; and that he possesed power and wisdom to a great degree. As he intended the earth for the habitation of animals and vegetables is it reasonable to suppose he made two jobs of his creation? That he first made a chaotic lump and set it into rotatory motion, and then waiting the millions of ages necessary to form itself, that when it had done this he stepped in a second time to create the animals and plants which were to inhabit it? As the hand of a creator is to be called in, it may as well be called in at one stage of the process as another. We may as well suppose he created the earth at once nearly in the state in which we see it, fit for the preservation of the beings he placed on it. But it is said we have a proof that he did not create it in it's present solid form, but in a state of fluidity,

[608]

because it's present shape of an oblate spheroid is precisely that which a fluid mass revolving on it's axis would assume. But I suppose that the same equilibrium between gravity and centrifugal force which would determine a fluid mass into the form of an oblate spheroid, would determine the wise creator of that mass, if he made it in a solid state, to give it the same spheroidical form. A revolving fluid will continue to change it's shape till it attains that in which it's principles of contrary motion are balanced; for if you suppose them not balanced, it will change it's form. Now the same balanced form is necessary for the preservation of a revolving solid. The creator therefore of a revolving solid would make it an oblate spheroid, that figure alone admitting a perfect equilibrium. He would make it in that form for another reason, that is, to prevent a shifting of the axis of rotation. Had he created the earth perfectly spherical, it's axis might have been perpetually shifting by the influence of other bodies of the system, and by placing the inhabitants of the earth successively under it's poles, it might have been depopulated: whereas being Spheroidical it has but one axis on which it can revolve in equilibrio. Suppose the axis of the earth to shift 45.° Then cut it into 180 slices, making every section in the plane of a circle of latitude, perpendicular to the axis. Every one of these slices, except the equatorial one would be unbalanced, as there would be more matter on one side of it's axis than on the other. There could be but one diameter drawn through such a slice which would divide it into two equal parts. On every other possible diameter the parts would hang unequal. This would produce an irregularity in the diurnal rotation. We may therefore conclude it impossible for the poles of the earth to shift, if it was made spheroidically, and that it would be made spheroidal, tho' solid, to obtain this end. I use this reasoning only on the supposition that the earth has had a beginning. I am sure I shall read your conjectures on this subject with great pleasure, tho' I bespeak before hand a right to indulge my natural incredulity and scepticism. The pain in which I write awakens me here from my reverie and obliges me to conclude with compliments to Mrs. Thomson, and assurances to yourself of the esteem and affection with which I am sincerely Dear Sir your friend & servt.,

TH: JEFFERSON

P.S. Since writing the preceding, I have had conversation on the subject of the steam mills with the famous Boulton, to whom those of London belong, and who is here at this time. He compares the effect of steam with that of horses in the following manner. 6 horses, aided with the most advantageous combination of the mechanical powers hitherto tried, will grind six bushels of flour in an hour; at the end of which time they are all in a foam, and must rest. They can work thus 6. hours in the 24, grinding 36. bushels of flour, which is 6. to each horse for the 24 hours. His steam mill in London consumes 120 bushels of coal in 24 hours, turns 10. pr. of stones, which grind 8 bushels of flour an hour each, which is 1920 bushels for the 24. hours. This makes a peck and a half of coal perform exactly as much as a horse in one day can perform.

RC (DLC: Thomson Papers). PrC (DLC: TJ Papers).
WHITEHURST: See note to TJ to Madison, 16 Dec. 1786.

To John Trumbull

DEAR SIR   Paris. Dec. 17. 1786.

I wrote you a letter above a month ago, which should have been delivered by Colo. Blackden, who was to have left Paris for London the next day. But he is still at Paris, and that letter, with this, will be delivered by another hand. It covers one to Mrs. Cosway. I am now to trouble you for the widow and the orphan, and I appeal to your charity for pardon. As a further plea for it, I will assure you you cannot serve two more deserving objects. Nicholas Trist, a British officer, married the daughter of Mrs. House in Philadelphia, and had by her an only son. He died in the year 1783, at his settlement near the Natchez on the Missisipi, leaving his wife guardian to his son. His mother, in England, died the year following either not knowing of his death, or not altering her will, in which she had bequeathed 1000£, the interest to him annually during his life for the education of his children, and at his death the principal to be divided equally among his children. Of course this belongs wholly to his son. My petition to you is that you will procure for me the copy of this clause of the will, and find out who and where are the executors. For the expences I will beg you to apply to Colo. Smith. But you must have some indications to begin your enquiries. I can give you only the following. 1. I conjecture the mother to have lived near Totness in Devonshire, because it is said almost all the family lived in that neighborhood. 2. For the same reason I conjecture that a Mrs. Champernoune resides there, a sister of Mr. Trist, who has written very friendly letters to his widow, and who gave her notice of this legacy. 3. Mr. Hore Browse

18 DECEMBER 1786

Trist, uncle to the deceased Mr. Trist, after whom he named his son, lives at his seat a mile from Totness. He has an estate of 3000£ a year. So if you should be obliged to resort to him for information, he will be easily found. 4. There was a Mr. Richard Trist of Arundel street, Strand, London, a distant relation of the deceased, and whose house he made his home when in London. If he be living, he can probably give all the necessary information. Should your enquiries bring you into the presence of any of the family, be so good as to inform them that the widow of Mr. Trist is a rare pattern of goodness, prudence and good sense; that the son is a beautiful boy of 10 or 11 years of age, of the sweetest dispositions possible, and of the most promising talents. As yet the mother has been able to supply the calls of his education, which she has conducted judiciously and carefully: but as he advances, the expences will increase, while her means will be diminishing, for she is left in very straightened circumstances. The family is rich. Should any of them be disposed to know any further of Mrs. Trist or her son, if they will be so kind as to write to me, I will give them all the information they may desire. I am enabled to do this from a very intimate acquaintance with them, and their situation, and from letters from Mrs. Trist, with whom I correspond constantly, and for whom I have a great friendship. After repeating my prayers that you will forgive this trouble, I conclude with assurances of the esteem with which I am Dear Sir your friend & servant, TH: JEFFERSON

P.S. After writing the above I received yours of Novr. 29. in time to inclose one herein for Mrs. Cosway.

PrC (DLC); the paper on which this copy was made evidently slipped while in the press and portions of the text are badly blurred by a double impression. Enclosures: TJ to Trumbull, 20 Nov. 1786, with its enclosure, TJ to Mrs. Cosway, 19 Nov. 1786. Although this letter is dated 17 Dec. and is entered in SJL under that date, it was probably not sent until 24 Dec., for it evidently enclosed TJ to Maria Cosway of that date, q.v. Trumbull's of 29 Nov. was received on 20 Dec. 1786.

To James Monroe

DEAR SIR   Paris Dec. 18. 1786.

Your letters of Aug. 19. and Oct. 12. have come duly to hand. My last to you was of the 11th. of August. Soon after that date I got my right wrist dislocated, which has till now deprived me of the use of my pen: and even now I can use it but slowly and with

[611]

18 DECEMBER 1786

pain. The revisal of the Congressional intelligence contained in your letters makes me regret the loss of it on your departure. I feel too the want of a person there to whose discretion I can trust confidential communications, and on whose friendship I can rely against the unjust designs of malevolence. I have no reason to suppose I have enemies in Congress: yet it is too possible to be without that fear. Some symptoms make me suspect that my proceedings to redress the abusive administration of tobacco by the Farmers general have indisposed towards me a powerful person in Philadelphia, who was profiting from that abuse. An expression in the inclosed letter of M. de Calonnes 'il a eté arreté, non que le marche fait avec M. Morris seroit rompu, mais qu'aprés l'expiration de ce contrat il n'en seroit plus fait de pareil.' This expression, I say, would seem to imply that I had asked the abolition of Mr. Morris's contract. I never did; on the contrary I always observed to them that it would be unjust to annul that contract. I was led to this by principles both of justice and interest. Of interest, because that contract would keep up the price of tobacco here to 34. 36. and 38. livres from which it will fall when it shall no longer have that support. However I have done what was right, and I will not so far wound my privilege of doing that, without regard to any man's interest, as to enter into any explanations of this paragraph with him. Yet I esteem him highly, and suppose that hitherto he had esteemed me.—You will see by Calonne's letter that we are doing what we can to get the trade of the U.S. put on a good footing. I am now about setting out on a journey to the South of France, one object of which is to try the mineral waters there for the restoration of my hand, but another is to visit all the seaports where we have trade, and to hunt up all the inconveniencies under which it labours, in order to get them rectified. I shall visit and carefully examine too the Canal of Languedoc. On my return, which will be early in the spring I shall send you several livraisons of the Encyclopedie, and the plan of your house. I wish to heaven you may continue in the disposition to fix it in Albemarle. Short will establish himself there, and perhaps Madison may be tempted to do so. This will be society enough, and it will be the great sweetener of our lives. Without society, and a society to our taste, humans are never contented. The one here supposed we can regulate to our minds, and we may extend our regulations to the sumptuary department, so as to set a good example to a country which needs it, and to preserve our own happiness clear of embarrasment. You wish not to engage in the drudgery of the bar. You have two asylums from that. Either to accept a seat in the council, or in the judiciary department. The latter however would require a little previous drudgery at the bar, to qualify you to discharge your duty with satisfaction to yourself. Neither of these would be inconsistent with a continued residence in Albemarle. It is but 12. hours drive in a sulky from Charlottesville to Richmond, keeping a fresh horse always at the half way, which would be a small annual expence. I am in hopes that Mrs. Munroe will soon have on her hands domestic cares of the dearest kind, sufficient to fill her time and ensure her against the tedium vitae; that she will find that the distractions of a town, and waste of life under these, can bear no comparison with the tranquil happiness of domestic life. If her own experience has not yet taught her this truth, she has in it's favor the testimony of one who has gone through the various scenes of business, of bustle, of office, of rambling, and of quiet retirement, and who can assure her that the latter is the only point upon which the mind can settle at rest. Tho not clear of inquietudes, because no earthly situation is so, they are fewer in number, and mixed with more objects of contentment than in any other mode of life. But I must not philosophize too much with her lest I give her too serious apprehensions of a friendship I shall impose on her.—On the subject of the lands in New York, I have written fully to Mr. Madison who will communicate to you. The prospect is very slender not to say desperate. The bickerings between Russia and the Porte are patched up by this court for the present. Those between Spain and Naples never had a tendency towards war. How the affairs of Holland will be settled is not very certain. The new king of Prussia is much more disposed to support the Stadholder than the old one was, and this court will support the patriotic party even at the expence of war. It is thought the K. of Prussia will relax. There has been some fear that this circumstance might shift him into the scale of Austria, Russia and England which would very soon engender a war much to the disadvantage of this country.—I shall hope a continuance of your correspondence. State politics and small news, of infinite value at this distance, will furnish you more copious materials than I shall be able to repay. I am with very real esteem Dear Sir your sincere friend and servt.,

Th: Jefferson

RC (NN); endorsed. PrC (DLC). Enclosure: Printed copy of Calonne to TJ, 22 Oct. 1786.

A powerful person in Philadelphia: That is, Robert Morris.

To Nicholas Lewis

Dear Sir   Paris Dec. 19. 1786.

I have duly received your favors of March 14. and July 16. My last to you was of Apr. 22. from London. I am obliged to you for the particular account you give me of my affairs, and the state of the cash account made out by the steward. His articles however were generally so shortly expressed as to be quite unintelligible to me. Of this kind are the following.

To James Foster and Benjamin Harris pr. Carter Braxton.	£131.10
To Richard James and Wm. Clark for cash.	20.
To Joseph Ashlin and C. Stone for cash at different times.	74.10.2
To Vincent Markham and Richd. James pr. Doctr. Gilmer.	385.0
To Tandy Rice and Charles Rice for cash.	69.18.8½
To David Mullings and Henry Mullings for cash.	31.15
To Carter Braxton pr. settlement by Colo. Lewis.	119.12.8
To do. for cash.	11.17.4

The steward intended this account for my information but mentioning only names and sums without saying in some general way why those sums were paid to those names, leaves me uninformed. However the account having passed under your eye leaves me also without a doubt that the articles are right. I suppose, in the 1st. article for instance, that Carter Braxton (to whom I was indebted for a doz. bottles of oil only) stands in the place of some person to whom I owed £131.10, &c. and so of the rest. As you give me reason to hope that all other debts will now be paid off, I am in hopes the shoulder can be laid solidly to those of Farrell & Jones, and Kippen & Co. To these objects, I would wish to apply the whole profits of the estate, except the maintenance and education of my sister Carr's two sons, and the interest of my sister Nancy's debt. I shall propose therefore to Jones & Mc.Caul the paying them an annual sum till their debts shall be discharged, and I have asked the favor of Mr. Eppes to consult with you and let me know what sum you think I may engage to pay them on an average of one year with another? And that you will be so good as to let me know this as soon as possible that I may arrange the matter by agreement with them. You mention that the price of tobacco is at 22/6. I can always be sure of receiving for it delivered at Havre 36/

Virginia money for the Virginia hundred weight. Whenever therefore the price with you is less than this after deducting freight, insurance, commission and port charges, if a conveiance can be obtained for it to Havre, it would be better to ship it to me. You may at the same time draw bills on me for the whole amount taking care that they shall not be presented till the tobacco is arrived at Havre, and that there be such an usance in them as will give me time to sell it and receive the money. Or, for so much of the tobacco as can be destined to Jones & Mc.Caul, no bills need be drawn, as I can remit them the proceeds. In all this however you will act according to your own good judgment which is much better than mine. I cannot help thinking however that it might be worth the experiment to ship me at any rate a small adventure to see how it will turn out, but Havre is the only port at which I could manage it.

I observe in your letter of March 14. after stating the amount of the crop, and deducting Overseer's and steward's parts, transportation, negroes clothes, tools, medicine, and taxes, the profits of the whole estate would be no more than the hire of the few negroes hired out would amount to. Would it be better to hire more where good masters could be got? Would it be better to hire plantations and all, if proper assurance can be provided for the good usage of every thing? I am miserable till I shall owe not a shilling: the moment that shall be the case I shall feel myself at liberty to do something for the comfort of my slaves.   Mr. Eppes writes me that my bill of scantling was nearly finished. I think it will be absolutely necessary to have it under lock and key, or it will certainly be stolen. It should be laid up open to the air. I am much obliged to your for your attention to my trees and grass. The latter is one of the principal pillars on which I shall rely for subsistance when I shall be at liberty to try projects without injury to any body. The negro girl which I sent to Nancy Bolling was not sent as a gift from me. I understood she was claimed under a supposed gift from my mother, which tho' I thought ill founded I did not chuse to enter into disagreeable discussions about. I meant therefore to abandon my right to her, and I have no further pretentions to her.   With my letter from London, I sent under care of Mr. Fulwar Skipwith a trunk containing some little matters for Mrs. Lewis and my sister Nancy. I hope it got safe to hand. I have long had (as I once wrote you) a pretty little peice of furniture, a clock, which I meant for Mrs. Lewis. Tho it is so small that it might almost be put into a pocket, I have as yet

19 DECEMBER 1786

found it impossible to get a safe conveiance for it. The case being of marble, and very slender, it cannot bear transportation but by water. I am obliged therefore to wait till some person shall be going from Havre to Richmond. Monsr. Doradour was to have carried it, but he was not able. He is safely returned to his family, and in good humor with our country. He made a considerable tramontane purchase. His trip upon the whole turned out better than I had expected. I am glad on account of Madame de Doradour who is a lady of great merit. I have never seen her since the departure of her husband: but I suppose she will decline further views on America. I shall endeavor to send with this a packet of the seeds of trees which I would wish Anthony to sow in a large nursery noting well their names. There will be a little Spanish St. foin, represented to me as a very precious grass in a hot country. I would have it sowed in one of the vacant lots of my grass ground. I have but just room to render you a thousand thanks for your goodness, to make as many apologies for the details I trouble you with, to recommend myself to the friendly remembrance of Mrs. Lewis, and to assure you of the sincere esteem with which I am, Dr. Sir your friend & servt.,   TH: JEFFERSON

Sent. Sulla. Span. St. foin
       Spanish broom
       Yellow flowering locust
       Bladder Senna
       Thuya

PrC (DLC); endorsed.
YOUR FAVORS OF MARCH 14. AND JULY 16.: Not found; Lewis' letter of 14 Mch. 1786 is recorded in SJL as received 29 June, and that of 16 July (recorded in SJL as 16 June) as received 19 Sep. 1786.

From André Limozin

MOST HONORED SIR   [19 Dec. 1786]

Agreable to the directions your Excellency hath favord me with the 16th of this Month, I have Shipp'd on board Le Couteulx, John Lymburn Master, not only the Small Box but that containing the model in Plaister for the Capitol of Virginia; in consequence whereof I have the Honor to inclose your Excellency the two Bills of Lading for the two Boxes; I have consignd them to M. Le Bailly in Norfolk to whom I gave hint of your directions how these two Boxes were to be forwarded at Richmond. My disbursments for the Box containing the model in plaister amount to 22 Lvres.

[616]

4d. as ℔ annexed noted, for which I have charged your Excellencys Account Debtor.

I am Surely very happy to hear that the observations I took the Freedom to address to your Excellency meet with his approbation. I shall at times do all what lays in my power to deserve your Friendship and to convince you that I am with as much attachement as with the highest regard, Your Excellency's Most obedient & very Humble Servant, ANDRE LIMOZIN

RC (ViWC); addressed; postmarked; without date which has been supplied from Limozin's enclosed statement. An entry in SJL for the receipt of a letter on 26 Dec. 1786 reads: "Limozin. Havre. (no date) announces departure of model of Capitol." Enclosures: Two bills of lading (missing); statement of disbursements for the shipment of the box containing the model of the capitol (Vi), dated 19 Dec. 1786, in the amount of 22.₶4s; endorsed, 9 Dec. 1789, by J. Latil: "I do certify that the above account amounted to 22 Livres 4 Sols."

From John Stockdale

KIND SIR　　　　　Piccadilly London 19th. Decr. 1786.

I have this Instant your's of the 8th. Inst., and Yesterday Sandford and Merton, for which I return you my very sincere thanks, for the great favor that you have done me, as the immediate procuring of this Work was of great consequence to me. I am afraid it will be deem'd an encroachment on good Nature, to request the favor of having sent by the first dilligence the friend of Youth by Mr. Berquin, a Work now publishing. I believe the conveyance by the dilligence will be the most certain. As I do not intend to take this liberty in future, I beg you will excuse it. I received your former Letter with an Order for the Beauties of Shakespeare after the Box was packt up and was of course stopt untill I got them bound, which owing to a combination among the Journeyman Bookbinders I could not get done as soon as I could wish. But it was Yesterday sent by the Dilligence, which I hope you'll receive, before you go on your long Journey. I shall be happy to hear from you and to execute any Commands I may be favour'd with, from whatever point of the World you may be in. I am sir with great Respect Your much oblig'd & very humble Servant,

JOHN STOCKDALE

P.S. Mr. S. will thankfully receive the remainder of the Volumes of Sandford and Merton as they come out by the Dilligence. The Post going out I am not able to send the list of the Books, but they are all sent that you have Order'd.　　　　　JS

20 DECEMBER 1786

RC (MHi); endorsed. Noted in SJL as received 26 Dec. 1786.
TJ's FORMER LETTER WITH AN ORDER FOR THE BEAUTIES OF SHAKESPEARE has not been found; it may have been the letter from TJ to Stockdale of 27 July or 13 Aug. 1786, neither of which has been found.

To John Adams

DEAR SIR Paris Dec. 20. 1786.

Colo. Franks will have the honor of delivering you the treaty with the emperor of Marocco, and all it's appendages. You will perceive by Mr. Barclay's letters that it is not necessary that any body should go back to Marocco to exchange ratifications. He sais however that it will be necessary that Fennish receive some testimony that we approve the treaty: and as, by the acts of Congress, our signature is necessary to give validity to it, I have had duplicates of ratification prepared, which I have signed, and now send you. If you approve and sign them send one back to me to be forwarded to Fennish thro' Mr. Carmichael. Perhaps a joint letter should be written to Fennish; if you think so, be so good as to write and sign one and send it with the ratification and I will sign and forward it. The other ratification is to go to Congress. Colo. Franks wishes to proceed with the papers to that body. He should do it I think immediately, as Mr. Jay in a letter to me of Oct. 26.[1] says that Congress have heard thro' the French Chargé des affaires that the treaty was signed, and they wonder they have not heard it from us.

I inclose you a copy of a letter from Mr. Lamb, by which you will perceive he does not propose to quit Alicant. I will forward the resolution of Congress to Mr. Carmichael which was inclosed of yours of Nov. 30. to see if that will move him. As the turn of this resolution admits a construction that Congress may think our original appointment of him censurable, I have, as in justice I ought, in a letter to Mr. Jay,[2] taken on myself the blame of having proposed him to you, if any blame were due. I have inclosed him a copy of my letter to you of Sep. 24. 1785. Mr. Barclay has proposed to go to Alicant to settle Lamb's accounts, and has asked to be strengthened with our authority. If Lamb will obey the resolve of Congress it will be better to let him go and settle his account there. But if he will not go back, perhaps it might not be amiss for Mr. Barclay to have instructions from us to require a settlement, those instructions to be used in that case only. If you think so, be so good as to write a joint letter and send it to me. But this,

[618]

if done at all, should be done immediately. How much money has Lamb drawn?—I have suggested to Mr. Jay the expediency of putting the Barbary business into Carmichael's hands, or sending some body from America, in consideration of our separate residence and our distance from the scene of negociation.

I had seen, without alarm, accounts of the disturbances in the East. But Mr. Jay's letter on the subject had really affected me. However yours sets me to rights. I can never fear that things will go far wrong where common sense has fair play. I but just begin to use my pen a little with my right hand, but with pain. Recommending myself therefore to the friendship of Mrs. Adams I must conclude here with assurances of the sincere esteem of Dr. Sir your friend and servant, Th: Jefferson

Should a Mr. Maury of Virginia, but now a merchant of Liverpool, present himself to you, I recommend him to your notice as my old schoolfellow, and a man of the most solid integrity.

RC (MHi: AMT); endorsed, in part: "Ansd. Jan. 25. 1787." PrC (DLC). Enclosure: Tr of Lamb to TJ, 10 Oct. 1786.

The DUPLICATES OF RATIFICATION had not yet been signed by TJ and were not signed until 1 Jan. 1787 (see Morocco Treaty under 2 Oct. 1786).

[1] An error for Jay's letter of 27 Oct. 1786.

[2] TJ's letter to Jay on this matter was not written until 31 Dec. 1786.

To Colonia

ce 20me. Xbre. 1786.

Monsieur Jefferson a eu l'honneur de recevoir de Monsieur le comte de Vergennes un passeport pour des armes qu'il doit expedier pour l'etat de Virginie. Son agent l'ayant presenté au Receveur et Directeur à Bourdeaux d'ou cet envoi devoit etre fait, ils lui ont dit qu'on ne pouvoit pas en admettre l'expedition sans que le passeport soit signé de Monsieur le Controleur general. Monsieur Jefferson prend la liberté de prier Monsieur de Colonia de vouloir bien lui procurer la signature de Monsieur le Controleur general au passeport qu'il a l'honneur de lui envoyer. L'experience qu'il a eu de la complaisance et de la bonté de Monsieur de Colonia sur une autre occasion l'enhardit de s'adresser à lui encore pour cet objet. Il a l'honneur de lui presenter ses compliments.

PrC (DLC); TJ wrote at foot of text (not for inclusion in RC): "M. de Colonia. pap. Jos. ⟨. . .⟩ gr. press."; these cryptic notes evidently referred to one of the large copying presses. Enclosure: Passport for the Virginia arms, forwarded to TJ in Bondfield's letter of 12 Dec. 1786.

To William Stephens Smith

Paris Dec. 20. 1786.

'Not having any letters on my file unanswered, I shall not trouble you further.'—Is this you?—Did you count 10. distinctly between the origin of that thought, and the committing it to paper? How could you, my dear Sir, add reproach to misfortune with a poor cripple who but now begins to use his pen, a little, and that with so much pain that it is real martyrdom? However I believe I am even with you by the constant tangle in which I keep your head with my commissions. The harpsicord, Mr. Adams's and Sir. Walter Raleigh's pictures, the map and some other trifles are still on your files, if I mistake not. I must acknolege the receipt of the cotton and cloth waistcoats and breeches, a pr. of slippers, one of the copying presses and Dilly's second cargo of books. For these I must give you my thanks, and particularly for the copies of the joint letters which came in good time.—I had first viewed the Eastern disturbances as of little consequence. A letter afterwards received had represented them as serious. But Mr. Adams's puts me to rights again. Congress raising troops in the Eastern states alone, to make war against the *Shawanese* is a new idea. I suppose those governments asked it. I hope however the troops will not be necessary, and that the good sense of the people will be found the best army. I write to Mrs. Smith. You are too much a man of honour to pry into that secret. My wrist forbids my adding more than assurances of the sincere esteem with which I am Dr. Sir your friend and servt.,

TH: JEFFERSON[1]

P.S. I send the map of S. America for which I will pray you to take arrangements with Faden or any other. He is the best. For his gain he will wish to make the map large. For that of the public and for their convenience I wish to debarrass it of all useless margins.

RC (MHi: DeWindt Collection); endorsed in part: "ansr. 29th [Jan.] 1787"; signature cut away. PrC (DLC); endorsed.

I SEND THE MAP OF S. AMERICA: The twelve-sheet map of South America by Cruz Cano, printed in 1775, was evidently sent to London through David S. Franks (see TJ to Smith, 10 Aug. 1786 and TJ's suggestions for republishing the map, immediately following the letter to Smith). I WRITE TO MRS. SMITH: No letter to Abigail Adams Smith of this date has been found and none is recorded in SJL until that of 15 Jan. 1787, which seems to be a reply to Mrs. Smith's letter of 2 Dec. 1786. DID YOU COUNT 10: See Smith to TJ, 5 Dec. 1786; Adams to TJ, 6 June 1786, note 2.

[1] Signature has been clipped from RC, but is intact in PrC.

To Abigail Adams

Dear Madam   Paris Dec. 21. 1786.

An unfortunate dislocation of my right wrist has for three months deprived me of the honor of writing to you. I begin now to use my pen a little, but it is in great pain, and I have no other use of my hand. The swelling has remained obstinately the same for two months past, and the joint, tho I beleive well set, does not become more flexible. I am strongly advised to go to some mineral waters at Aix in Provence, and I have it in contemplation.—I was not alarmed at the humor shewn by your countrymen. On the contrary I like to see the people awake and alert. But I received a letter which represented it as more serious than I had thought. Mr. Adams however restores my spirits; I believe him and I thank him for it. The good sense of the people will soon lead them back, if they have erred in a moment of surprize.—My friends write me that they will send my little daughter to me by a Vessel which sails in May for England. I have taken the liberty to tell them that you will be so good as to take her under your wing till I can have notice to send for her, which I shall do express in the moment of my knowing she is arrived. She is about 8. years old, and will be in the care of her nurse, a black woman, to whom she is confided with safety. I knew your goodness too well to scruple the giving this direction before I had asked your permission. I beg you to accept assurances of the constant esteem with which I have the honor to be Dear Madam your most obedient & most humble servt.,

                                    Th: Jefferson

RC (MHi: AMT); endorsed. PrC (DLC); written at the foot of text by TJ, much later, "Mrs. Adams."

From S. J. Neele

Sir   London No. 352 Strand Decr. 21st. 1786

Agreeable to Col. Smith's Order I now send you the Plate of the Map of Virginia &c. with the Original Maps Drawing and a Proof. As there is in it a very great Number of Words you will, I naturally suppose upon inspecting it critically find some Corrections necessary; I could have wished to have inserted them myself, but as your Receipt of the Plate renders that impracticable, they must consequently be done by one of the Map Engravers at Paris.

[621]

21 DECEMBER 1786

The Drawing was unfortunately made on a Paper much too soft, so that, (after it was rubbed down on the Wax prepared on the Plate to receive its Impression previous to tracing), in taking it off, some Parts of its surface tore away, and remained on the Wax, and of course obliterated the Drawing in those Parts.

In consequence of this accident, you will find in the body of the Map two Names unfinished and a few on the Coast to the Eastward of Delaware Bay, all of which, as well as every other necessary Correction may be made in a few Hours. Col. Smith has expressed his Approbation of the Engraving, I therefore flatter myself it will likewise meet with yours and be a means of securing your future Favors, which will add to the Obligation already confered on Sir Yours (with much respect), S. J. NEELE

RC (MHi); addressed and endorsed. Noted in SJL as received 4 Jan. 1787. THE PLATE OF THE MAP OF VIRGINIA and TJ's original drawing have evidently disappeared. The ORIGINAL MAPS that Neele returned were those that TJ had forwarded to Smith.

From Abraham Walton

Orléans, 21 Dec. 1786. Thanks TJ for his letter of 7 Dec. and asks him to thank Lafayette for his letters of introduction to the local bishop and the Marquis du Crest; has dined with the latter three or four times. There are no masters of Italian or Spanish at Orléans; continues to study French, and reads nothing but French; amuses himself as formerly with dancing and fencing; hopes "the Waters may have the desired Effect."

RC (DLC); 1 p. Noted in SJL as received 24 Dec. 1786.

From De Blome

[*Paris*] 22 Dec. 1786. Sends TJ a package of books to be forwarded to Benjamin Franklin.

RC (PPAP); 2 p.; in French; addressed. See TJ to Franklin, 23 Dec. 1786.

From George Wythe

GW TO TJ   Williamsburgh 22 Decemb 1786

Lest a letter, which, a few days ago, i wrote to you, should not come to your hands, i now write this, to entreat, that you will let us have your thoughts on the confederation of the american states, which is proposed to be revised in the summer following. I men-

[622]

tioned in that letter, that Peter Carr was attending the professors of natural and moral philosophy, and mathematics, learning the french and spanish languages, and with me reading Herodotus, Aeschylus, Cicero, and Horace; and that i wished to know if you approved of the course, or would recommend any other. Farewell.

RC (DLC); endorsed. Noted in SJL as received 6 Feb. 1787.

To Brissot de Warville

Paris Dec. 23. 1786.

I return you, Sir, the paper wherein is inserted the letter under my name, with many thanks for the perusal of it. If the two columns whereon it is printed are not useful to you, I would venture to ask you for them: because the publication is not only without authority, but is surreptitious and mutilated to answer its purposes of a particular interest, and I would wish to make some observations on it to Congress in order to bring it under their notice.

The price of tobacco in Virginia at the public warehouses, that is to say in the port ready for shipping, was before the war on an average of one year with another about [18 livres?] the English hundred for the best quality and 15. for the worst. Since the war it has fluctuated from those prices up to the double of them. I believe we may fairly conjecture it will settle generally at the medium of the two, that is to say, about 27. livres for the best and 22 l. for the worst. I have the honor to be with sentiments of great respect & esteem Sir, your most obedient & most humble servant,

TH: JEFFERSON

PrC (DLC). Recorded in SJL as sent 22 Dec. 1786. Enclosure: The American newspaper returned with this letter has not been identified; for the extracts of TJ's letter printed in various newspapers see TJ to Jay, 27 May 1786, and notes there.

The PARTICULAR INTEREST that TJ had in mind was probably Robert Morris and his associates in the tobacco trade; the publication of his letter was without authority and it was evidently surreptitious, but the omissions or "mutilations" that were made were not those calculated to advance the interests of any particular individual or group: they were comments by TJ on Calonne and their elimination was an act on the part of Jay that spared TJ an even greater embarrassment than he experienced. French officials may have suspected this and have prompted Brissot to solicit the full text of TJ's letter "avec Les Corrections" (Brissot to TJ, 25 Dec. 1786). There is no evidence that TJ replied to this solicitation or that he furnished the "unmutilated" text.

To Benjamin Franklin

Dear Sir   Paris Dec. 23. 1786.

I have received your favor of Oct. 8. but the volume of the transactions mentioned to come with it, did not; but I have received one from Mr. Hopkinson. You also mention the diplomas it covered for other persons, and some order of the society relative to myself, which I suppose were omitted by accident and will come by some other conveiance. So far as relates to myself, whatever the order were, I beg leave to express to you my sense of their favor and wish to merit it. I have several livraisons of the Encyclopedie for yourself and Mr. Hopkinson which shall be sent in the spring when they will be less liable to injury. Some books also which I received from Baron Blome must await that conveiance. I receive some discouraging accounts of the temper of the people in our new governments. Yet were I to judge only from the accounts given in the public papers I should not fear their passing over without injury. I wish you may have given your opinion of them to some of your friends here, as your experience and knowlege of men would give us more confidence in your opinion. Russia and the Porte have patched up an accomodation through the mediation of this court. The coolness between Spain and Naples will remain, and will occasion the former to cease intermedling with the affairs of the latter. The Dutch affairs are still to be settled. The new King of Prussia is more earnest in supporting the cause of the Stadholder than his uncle was, and in general an affectation begins to shew itself of differing from his uncle. There is some fear of his throwing himself into the Austrian scale in the European division of power. Our treaty with Marocco is favourably concluded thro' the influence of Spain. That with Algiers affords no expectation. We have been rendered anxious here about your health, by hearing you have had a severe attack of your gout. Your friends here are in general well. Remarkeable deaths are the Dutchess of Chabot of the house of Rochefoucault, Beaujon, and Peyronet, the architect who built the bridge of Neuilly and was to have begun one the next spring from the place Louis XV to the Palais Bourbon. A dislocated wrist, not yet re-established, obliges me to conclude here with assurances of the perfect esteem and respect with which I have the honour to be your Excellency's Most obedient & most humble servt.,

                                    Th: Jefferson

P.S. Will you permit my respects to your grandson Mr. Franklin to find their place here?

PrC (DLC).   DUTCHESS OF CHABOT: The Duchesse de Chabot, Elisabeth-Louise de La Rochefoucauld, died 12 Dec. 1786 (*Journal de Paris*, 15 Dec. 1786).

To Francis Hopkinson

DEAR SIR   Paris Dec. 23. 1786.

My last letter to you was dated Aug. 14. Yours of May 27. and June 28. were not then received, but have been since. I take the liberty of putting under your cover another letter to Mrs. Champés as also an enquiry after a Dr. Griffiths. A letter to M. le Vieillard from the person he had consulted about the essence d'Orient will convey to you the result of my researches into that article. Your spring block for assisting a vessel in sailing cannot be tried here, because the Seine, being not more than about 40 toises wide, and running swiftly, there is no such thing on it as a vessel with sails. I thank you for the volume of the Phil. trans. which came safely to hand, and is in my opinion a very valuable volume and contains many precious papers. The Paccan nut is, as you conjecture, the Illinois nut. The former is the vulgar name South of the Patowmac, as also with the Indians and Spaniards, and enters also into the Botanical name which is Juglans Paccan. I have many volumes of the Encyclopedie for yourself and Dr. Franklin: but as a winter passage is bad for books, and before the spring the packets will begin to sail from Havre to New York, I shall detain them till then. You must not presume too strongly that your comb-footed bird is known to M. de Buffon. He did not know our panther. I gave him the stuffed skin of one I bought in Philadelphia and it presents him a new species, which will appear in his next volumes. I have convinced him that our deer is not a Chevreuil: and would you believe that many letters to different acquaintances in Virginia, where this animal is so common, have never enabled me to present him with a large pair of their horns, a blue and a red skin stuffed, to shew him their colour at different seasons. He has never seen the horns of what we call the elk. This would decide whether it be an elk or a deer.   I am very much pleased with your project on the Harmonica and the prospect of your succeeding in the application of keys to it. It will be the greatest present which has been made to the musical world this century, not excepting the Piano forte. If it's tone approaches that given by the finger as nearly only as the harpsichord does that of the harp, it will be very valuable. I have lately examined a Foot-bass newly invented here, by the celebrated Krumfoltz. It is precisely a Piano forte about 10. feet long,

23 DECEMBER 1786

18 inches broad and 9. I. deep. It is of one octave only, from Fa to Fa. The part where the keys are, projects at the side in order to lengthen the levers of the keys, thus

It is placed on the floor, and the harpsichord or other piano forte is set over it, the foot acting in concert on that while the fingers play on this. There are three unison chords to every note, of strong brass wire, and the lowest have wire wrapped on them as the lowest in the piano-forte. The chords give a fine, clear, deep tone, almost like the pipe of an organ.—Have they connected you with our mint? My friend Monroe promised me he would take care for you in that. Or perhaps the establishment of that at New York may have been incompatible with your residence at Philadelphia. A person here has invented a method of coining the French ecu of 6. livres so as to strike both faces and the edge at one stroke, and makes a coin as beautiful as a medal. No country has ever yet produced such a coin. They are made cheaper too. As yet he has only made a few to shew the perfection of his manner. I am endeavoring to procure one to send to Congress as a model for their coinage. They will consider whether, in establishing a new mint, it will not be worth while to buy his machines, if he will furnish them. A dislocation of my right wrist, which happened to me about a month after the date of my last letter to you has disabled me from writing 3. months. I do it now in pain and only in cases of necessity or of strong inclination having as yet no other use of my hand. I put under your cover a letter from my daughter to her friend. She joins me in respects to your good mother, to Mrs. Hopkinson and yourself, to whom I proffer assurances of the esteem with which I am Dear Sir your sincere friend & servant,

TH: JEFFERSON

PrC (DLC). Enclosures not found; but see Hopkinson's comments on them in his letter to TJ, 14 Apr. 1787.

YOURS OF MAY 27: Hopkinson's letter of this date has not been found but is recorded in SJL as received 18 Aug. 1786. ANOTHER LETTER TO MRS.

CHAMPÉS: There is no mention in any of TJ's extant communications to Hopkinson of an enclosed letter to a Mrs. Champés, but possibly one was transmitted in his missing letter of 27 May 1786.

[626]

From Francis Coffyn

[*Dunkirk,* 24 Dec. 1786. Recorded in SJL as received 27 Dec. 1786. Not found, but it must have related to the report that Coffyn made to Crèvecoeur about the accessibility of the port of Honfleur to American trading vessels; see Brissot to TJ, 27 Dec. 1786; Ducrest to TJ, 27 Dec. 1786.]

To Maria Cosway

Paris Dec. 24. 1786.

Yes, my dear Madam, I have received your three letters, and I am sure you must have thought hardly of me, when at the date of the last, you had not yet received one from me. But I had written two. The second, by the post, I hope you got about the beginning of this month: the first has been detained by the gentleman who was to have carried it. I suppose you will receive it with this.

I wish they had formed us like the birds of the air, able to fly where we please. I would have exchanged for this many of the boasted preeminencies of man. I was so unlucky when very young, as to read the history of Fortunatus. He had a cap of such virtues that when he put it on his head, and wished himself anywhere, he was there. I have been all my life sighing for this cap. Yet if I had it, I question if I should use it but once. I should wish myself with you, and not wish myself away again. En attendant the cap, I am always thinking of you. If I cannot be with you in reality, I will in imagination. But you say not a word of coming to Paris. Yet you were to come in the spring, and here is winter. It is time therefore you should be making your arrangements, packing your baggage &c. unless you really mean to disappoint us. If you do, I am determined not to suppose I am never to see you again. I will believe you intend to go to America, to draw the Natural bridge, the Peaks of Otter &c., that I shall meet you there, and visit with you all those grand scenes. I had rather be deceived, than live without hope. It is so sweet! It makes us ride so smoothly over the roughnesses of life. When clambering a mountain, we always hope the hill we are on is the last. But it is the next, and the next, and still the next.   Think of me much, and warmly. Place me in your breast with those who you love most: and comfort me with your letters. Addio la mia cara ed amabile amica!

After finishing my letter, the gentleman who brought yours sent me a roll he had overlooked, which contained songs of your composition. I am sure they are charming, and I thank you for them. The first words which met my eye on opening them, are I fear, ominous. 'Qua l'attendo, e mai non viene.'

PrC (ViU); endorsed: "Cosway Mrs."; not signed.
This letter, together with THE FIRST mentioned above, i.e., that of 19 Nov., was probably sent with TJ to John Trumbull, 17 Dec. 1786.

To James Maury

DEAR SIR   Paris Dec. 24. 1786.

Your favor of the 17th. of Sep. came to hand a few days after a dislocation of my right wrist had disabled me from writing. I only begin to write a little now, and that with pain. Your second letter of Dec. 10. is now received. I should be happy if any arrangements as to my tobacco could produce advantage to you, but having entirely abandoned the management of my affairs to my friends in Virginia, I do not venture to give any orders from here relative to them. I doubt too whether English prices for tobacco would be such as are given here, say 14. or 15.£ sterl. a hhd. for such tobacco as mine.   Your good mother's interesting herself on the subject of my daughter is flattering to me, as it is a proof I still retain a share in her friendship. I still continue to esteem most those whom I knew earliest in life. Will you be so good as to take the trouble to inform her that my daughter is indeed in a convent, but in one where there are as many protestants as Catholics, where not a word is ever said to them on the subject of religion, and where they are as free in the profession and practice of their own religion as they would be in their own country. It is a house of education only, where the menial offices for the scholars are performed by nuns, who retire at certain hours to perform their own religious rites unseen by the scholars. With this information I will ask the further favor of you to tender to your mother my most friendly respects. I have written to Mr. Adams by the present conveyance, and taken the liberty of making you known to him. My compliments attend on Mrs. Maury and I have the honour to be with much esteem Dr. Sir your friend & servt.,

TH: JEFFERSON

PrC (ViWC); endorsed.

To Ezra Stiles

SIR Paris Dec. 24. 1786

I feel myself very much honored by the degree which has been conferred on me by the Senatus Academicus of Yale college, and I beg leave through you, Sir, to express to them how sensible I am of this honor, and that it is to their and your indulgence, and not to any merit of my own that I am indebted for it.

The commotions which have taken place in America, as far as they are yet known to me, offer nothing threatening. They are a proof that the people have liberty enough, and I would not wish them less than they have. If the happiness of the mass of the people can be secured at the expence of a little tempest now and then, or even of a little blood, it will be a precious purchase. Malo libertatum periculosam quam quietam servitutem. Let common sense and common honesty have fair play and they will soon set things to rights.

The bickerings between Russia and the Porte are quieted for the moment. The coolness between the Kings of Spain and Naples will remain, but will have no other consequence than that of the former withdrawing from interference with the affairs of the latter. The present King of Prussia pushes the interests of the Stadholder more zealously than his uncle did. There have been fears that he might throw himself into the Austrian scale, which would greatly derange the European balance. This country is firm in support of the patriotic party in the United Netherlands.

We have made an advantageous treaty with Marocco, but with Algiers nothing is done. From what I learn of the temper of my countrymen and their tenaciousness of their money, it will be more easy to raise ships and men to fight these pirates into reason, than money to bribe them. I wish that something could be done in some form or another to open the Mediterranean to us. You will have seen that France is endeavoring to relieve and encourage our commerce with her.

The arts and sciences offering nothing new at this moment worth communicating to you I shall only add assurances of the respect and esteem with which I have the honor to be Dear Sir your most obedt. & most humble servt., TH: JEFFERSON

RC (Lewis S. Gannett, New York, 1944); wax seal attached, with inscription: "Per Aspera ad Astra" (rubbings and drawings of the seal supplied to the Editors through the kindness of Mrs. Gannett; this and other seals utilized by TJ will be discussed in Second Series); endorsed. PrC (DLC).

From John Banister

[*25 Dec. 1786.* Recorded in SJL as received 3 May 1787. Not found.]

From Nathaniel Barrett

Rouen, 25 Dec. 1786. Has been informed by Mr. Garvey that he communicated a copy of Calonne's letter to TJ of 22 Oct. 1786 to the local "Bureau"; "they say they have received no Orders on the subject, and can pay no attention to the Copy which he shewed them"; Barrett asks TJ to "have the Direction of the Controller General forwarded as soon as possible"; is obliged to give security for duties until this is done.

RC (DLC); 2 p.; endorsed. Noted in SJL as received 5 Jan. 1787.

From Brissot de Warville

Monsieur   Paris ce 25 Xbr. 1786.

Je vous remercie bien sincerement des instructions que vous avès bien voulu me donner pour Le tabac, et Je vous fais passer ci inclus La gazette americaine que vous desirès. J'avois dessein de faire usage de la Lettre qu'on vous y prete; mais puisqu'elle n'est ni autentique ni exacte, Je vous aurois une grande obligation de m'en faire passer une copie avec Les Corrections. Je m'en servirois pour L'ouvrage que je continue de faire imprimer sur Les Etats unis, avec toutes Les restrictions que vous voudriès bien m'indiquer. Je suis avec respect Monsieur votre très humble et très obeissant serviteur,   Brissot de Warville

RC (DLC); endorsed. Not recorded in SJL. See TJ to Brissot de Warville, 23 Dec. 1786.

To C. W. F. Dumas

Sir   Paris Dec. 25. 1786.

A dislocation of my right wrist has for upwards of three months prevented me the honour of writing to you. I begin to use it a little for the pen, but it is with great pain. To this cause alone I hope you will ascribe that I have to acknolege at one time the receipt of so many of your letters. Their dates are Sep. 12. 26. Oct. 6. 17. 19. 23. Nov. 3. 17. Dec. 1. and there is one without

[630]

a date. They were communicated to the M. de la fayette according to your desire, and those to Mr. Jay have been forwarded from time to time as private conveiances occurred, except some of the last for which no such conveiance has occurred till now, a gentleman is setting out for London and from thence for N. York.

We receive news from America of collections of the people in three or four instances in the Eastern states, demanding delays in the proceedings of the courts of justice. Those states, as you know, depended before the war chiefly on their whale oil and fish. The former was consumed in London, but being now loaded there with heavy duties, cannot go there. Much of their fish went up the Mediterranean, now shut to us by the pyratical states. Their debts therefore press them, while the means of paiment have lessened. The mobs however separated, without a single injury having been offered to the person or property of any one, nor did they continue 24. hours in any one place. This country has opened a market for their whale oil, and we have made a good treaty of peace with Marocco, but with Algiers we can do nothing.—An American paper has published a letter as from me to the Count de Vergennes, on the subject of our productions of tobacco and rice. It is surreptitious and falsified, and both the true and untrue parts very improper for the public eye. How a newswriter of America got at it, is astonishing, and with what views it has been altered. I will be much obliged to you if you will endeavor to prevent it's publication in the Leyden gazette.

The following question I take the liberty of proposing to you confidentially. This country wants money in it's treasury. Some individuals have proposed to buy our debt of 24. millions at a considerable discount. I have informed Congress of it, and suggested to them the expediency of borrowing this sum in Holland if possible, as well to prevent loss to this country, as to draw all their money transactions to one point. But could they borrow the money in Holland? I would be obliged to you for your opinion on this question, as it would decide me in pressing this matter further on Congress, or letting it drop. It will readily occur to you that the answer should come through the hands of your Ambassador here alone. The pain in which I write, obliges me, after many thanks for the interesting details of transactions in your country, to assure you of the esteem and respect with which I have the honor to be, Sir, your most obedient and most humble servant,

TH: JEFFERSON

PrC (DLC).

A LETTER AS FROM ME TO THE COUNT DE VERGENNES: This must have been a slip of the pen, for TJ clearly meant the letter that he had written to Jay on 27 May 1786, the publication of which in various American newspapers was at this time causing him as acute an embarrassment, perhaps, as the famous Mazzei letter later produced; as indicated in the note to that letter, its text was FALSIFIED by Jay only to the extent of removing two passages that would have caused TJ even more embarrassment. THERE IS ONE WITHOUT A DATE: This may possibly have been one recorded as "cover" in SJL under 2 Dec. 1786, q.v.

To James Buchanan and William Hay

GENTLEMEN   Paris Dec. 26. 1786.

It is with no small degree of surprize and vexation that I have this moment received from M. Limozin of Havre, the inclosed bill of lading for the Model of the Capitol, by which it appears that it has been shipped a few days ago. This model went out of my hands about the last of May or first of June, and would get to Havre in about 10. days, where I suppose it has lain neglected in a warehouse 6 months while there were tobacco ships constantly returning to Virginia. I had not an idea but that you had been in possession of it ever since the month of August. I hope you will be sensible that this extraordinary delay has been in no manner owing to me; and I still flatter myself it will arrive before the workmen can recommence their labours in the spring.

I have the honour to be with much respect, Gentlemen, your most obedient & most humble servt.,   TH: JEFFERSON

PrC (DLC). The enclosed bill of lading has not been found; see Limozin to TJ [19 Dec. 1786], and TJ to Buchanan and Hay, 13 June 1786.

To William Carmichael

DEAR SIR   Paris Dec. 26. 1786.

A note from me of the 22d. of Sep. apprised you it would be some time before I should be able to answer your letters. I did not then expect it would have been so long. A dislocation of my right wrist three or four days before that has disabled me from writing till lately, and I now write in great pain and only in cases of necessity. I am to acknolege the receipt of yours of Sep. 29. Oct. 3. and Nov. 15. I shall herein inclose the papers you had been so kind as to send me for my reading, without having retained copies. I also inclose a resolution of Congress recalling Mr. Lambe which I will beg the favor of you to have delivered him. I have

[632]

26 DECEMBER 1786

written to Mr. Adams on the subject of di[recting] him to settle with Mr. Barclay, and attend his answer. In the mean time I am not without hopes Mr. Barclay has done the business. I send also a note desiring Mr. Lambe to deliver you his cyphers and a copy of a letter from the minister of finance here to me, announcing several regulations in favor of our commerce. My Notes on Virginia, having been hastily written, need abundance of corrections. Two or three of these are so material that I am reprinting a few leaves to substitute for the old. As soon as these shall be ready, I will beg your acceptance of a copy. I shall be proud to be permitted to send a copy also to the Count de Campomanes as a tribute to his science and his virtues. You will find in them that the Natural bridge had found an admirer in me also. I should be h[appy] to make with you the tour of the curiosities you will find therein me[ntioned.] That kind of pleasure surpasses much in my estimation whatever I [find on] this side the Atlantic. I sometimes think of building a little hermitage at the Natural bridge (for it is my property) and of passing there a [part] of the year at least.

I have received American papers to the 1[st.] November. Some tumultuous meetings of the people have taken [place] in the Eastern states, i.e. one in Massachusets, one in Connecticut and one N. Hampsh. Their principal demand was a respite in the judiciary proceedings. No injury was done however in a single instance to the person or property of any one, nor did the tumult continue 24. hours in any one instance. In Massachusets this was owing to the discretion which the malcontents still preserved, in Connecticut and N. Hampshire, the body of the people rose in support of government and obliged the malcontents to go to their homes. In the lastmentioned state they seized about 40. who were in jail for trial. It is believed this incident will strengthen our government. Those people are not entirely without excuses. Before the war those states depended on their whale oil and fish. The former was consumed in England, and much of the latter in the Mediterranean. The heavy duties on American whale oil now required in England exclude it from that market: and the Algerines exclude them from bringing their fish into the Mediterranean. France is opening her ports for their oil, but in the mean while their antient debts are pressing them and they have nothing to pay with. The Massachusets assembly too, in their zeal for paying their public debt had laid a tax too heavy to be paid in the circumstances of their state. The Indians seem disposed too to make war on us. These complicated causes determined Congress to increase their forces to 2000 men. The latter was the sole object avowed, yet the former entered for something into the measure. However I am satisfied the good sense of the people is the strongest army our governments can ever have, and that it will not fail them. The Commercial convention at Annapolis was not full enough to do business. They found too their appointments too narrow, being confined to the article of Commerce. They have proposed a meeting in Philadelphia in May, and that it may be authorized to propose amendments of whatever is defective in the federal constitution. Congress have at length determined on a coinage. Their money unit is a dollar and the peices above and below that are in decimal proportion. You will see their scheme in all the papers, except that the proportion they established between gold and silver is mistated at upwards of 20. to 1. instead of about $15\frac{1}{4}$ to 1.

It is believed that this court has patched up an accommodation for the moment between Russia and the Porte. In Holland they find greater difficulties. The present king of Prussia is zealous for the Stadtholder, and the fear is of driving him into the Austrian scale of the European balance. Such a weight as this, shifted, would destroy all equilibriums and the preponderance once in favor of the restless powers of the north, the peace would soon be disturbed.

When I was in England I formed a portable copying press on [the] principles of the large one they make there for copying letters. I had a model made there and it has answered perfectly. A workman here has made several from that model. The itinerant temper of your court will, I think, render one of these useful to you. You must therefore do me the favor to accept of one. I have it now in readiness, and shall send it by the way of Bayonne to the care of Mr. Alexander there, unless Don Miguel de Lardizabal can carry it with him.

My hand admonishes me it is time to stop, and that I must defer writing to Mr. Barclay till tomorrow. I have the honor to be with sentiments of the highest esteem and respect Dear Sir your most obedient & most humble servt., TH: JEFFERSON

PrC (DLC); slightly mutilated. Enclosures: (1) Various unidentified papers which Carmichael had sent to TJ and asked to have returned. (2) Copy of resolution of Congress recalling Lamb, enclosed in Jay to TJ, 12 Oct. 1786. (3) Note from TJ to Lamb concerning the codes in his possession (not found and not recorded in SJL; see Lamb to TJ, 20 May 1787). (4) Printed copy of Calonne to TJ, 22 Oct. 1786.

Pedro Rodriguez, Conde de CAMPOMANES (1723-1802) was a Spanish statesman and economist to whom TJ later presented a copy of *Notes on Virginia* (TJ to Carmichael, 15 Dec. 1787). The demand for copies of TJ's work was increasing, in America as well as in Europe. The present letter, together with others of a later date, prove that the original printing was not exhausted at this time. But in the face of mounting requests, TJ evidently was obliged to discriminate, and the answers given were not always the same. A few days earlier William Short had written to Fulwar Skipwith: "I am extremely sorry not to be able to furnish you with the Copy of Mr. Jefferson's notes. He has given away all those which he had printed. As it is probable however that there will be a new impression made, I will take the first opportunity of procuring you one. I am glad you were pleased with them, and wish they may be often read and studied by our countrymen. They contain many valuable truths that I should be happy to see disseminated: being persuaded that whatever is true is good to be known, and that the more truths, either in government or religion with which the world is enlightened, the better for mankind." The explanation for Skipwith's failure to obtain a copy of the *Notes* may rest in the fact that he was engaged in tobacco trade with England, a subject on which TJ had strong feelings (e.g., TJ to Maury, 24 Dec. 1786). If so, Short's next paragraph has some piquancy: "Although I cannot have the pleasure of sending you this copy which you asked, I send you one which you did not ask. It is a copy of a letter from the Controller general to our Minister here respecting the American commerce. Perhaps it may not yet have reached Virginia, although copies have been already sent to New York. It will give you a perfect idea of the terms on which American produce is at present received in the French ports. I hope it will increase the communication between the two countries. I know not whether you are engaged in the French commerce; but still it may be agreeable to you to have this succinct view of it" (Short to Skipwith, 14 Dec. 1786; DLC: Short Papers). As if to drive the point home, Short mentioned the treaty of commerce between England and France which "some politicians" regarded as prolonging the peace between the two nations. Others, he said, thought that the seeds of a general European war were springing up in Holland, "and that France and England must necessarily take opposite sides."

There are evidences in Short's correspondence that TJ occasionally influenced him to make suggestions or hints to others, much as he influenced Lafayette to do the same. The present instance may have been such an occasion.

To Richard Cary

Dear Sir Paris Dec. 26. 1786.

In a letter of May 4. I mentioned to you that I had sent you an edition of the English Linneaus by M. de la Croix. The box got to Havre after his departure, so that the not carrying it was not imputable to him. My correspondent at Havre never informed me of this, and I supposed you had received the book when the inclosed bill of lading came to my hands by which it appears to have been sent off only a few days ago. I have now forgot what was in the box, but I think there were some few books for other persons. Doubtless each was directed to the person for whom it was destined, and I will beg of you to have them delivered according to their address. In my letter of Aug. 12. I desired you to send plants for me either to Havre or Lorient. I must correct that and pray them to come to Lorient[1] only, to the care of Monsieur Limozin. The packets which have heretofore plied between Lorient and N. York, will after February ply between Havre and N. York. This I think will be my best means of sending you any thing, because I can address to the care of the Virga. delegates at N. York, from whence I presume there are weekly conveiances to Norfolk. I am with great esteem Dr. Sir your friend & servt., TH: JEFFERSON

PrC (DLC). Enclosed bill of lading not found; see Limozin to TJ, 19 Dec. 1786.

[1] An error for "Havre"; see TJ to Richard Cary, 13 Aug. 1787.

To Fantin Latour

MONSIEUR Paris 26me Xbre. 1786.

L'accident d'un poignet demis m'a empeché jusques ici l'honneur de repondre à votre lettre du 20me 7bre. La personne qui se propose de s'etablir en Amerique fera bien de vendre sa legitime, qui n'est payable qu'a 3. et 6. ans pour de l'argent comptant: de placer cet argent chez un banquier connu: de passer en Amerique et d'y rester au moins un ans avant de faire un acquisition. Quand il l'aura fait il peut recevoir la bas de l'argent comptant pour ses billets d'echange, et il y gagnera un peu. Peutetre qu'il feroit encore mieux d'y passer premierement, et de voir si le païs est á son gré avant de vendre sa legitime, et de charger un ami de cette operation s'il trouve que le païs lui convient. J'ai l'honneur d'etre avec bien de respect Monsieur votre tres humble et tres-obeissant serviteur, TH: JEFFERSON

PrC (MHi); endorsed: "Fantin M."

To José da Maia

MONSIEUR Paris Dec. 26me. 1786.

J'attends à tout moment de faire une voiage dans les provinces meridionelles de France. J'avois tardé de repondre a votre lettre du 21me 9bre. en attendant que je pourrois vous annoncer le moment de mon depart, et le jour et le lieu auquel je pourrois avoir l'honneur de vous rencontrer. Mais jusques ici ce moment n'est pas decidé. Mais j'aurai surement l'honneur de vous en faire part, et de demander un rendezvous ou à Montpelier ou en sa voisinage. En attendant j'ai l'honneur d'etre avec bien de respect Monsieur votre tres humble et tres obeissant serviteur, TH: JEFFERSON

27 DECEMBER 1786

PrC (DLC); endorsed: "Vendek." TJ must have added a postscript to the (missing) RC stating that he would visit Nîmes, for José da Maia's response of 5 Jan. 1787 and TJ's report to Jay of 4 May 1787 both indicate that Nîmes was mentioned.

From Brissot de Warville

Monsieur   Ce Mardi une heure [26 Dec. 1786]

M. Le Marquis du Crest etoit sur le point d'aller au rendès vous que vous aviés bien voulu lui indiquer, Lorsqu'une affaire pressante et Imprevue, L'a forcé de rester. Il me Charge de vous en faire ses excuses, et de Vous temoigner tous ses regrets. Il aura L'honneur de Vous demander un autre Jour.

Je profite de cette occasion pour Vous envoier Le Volume des transactions philosophiques de philadelphie, et la Bouteille de vin de provence que Je vous prie de Vouloir bien gouter. Il n'a que deux ans. S'il plait aux americains Les persones qui Le fabriquent pourront en envoier en Amerique et retirer en echange de merrein [merrain] &c.

Agrées, Monsieur, Les sentimens d'estime et d'atachement respectueux avec Lequel J'ai L'honneur d'etre, Monsieur Votre trés humble et obt. Serviteur,   Brissot de Warville

P.S. M. Claviere a reçu des Nouvelles de M. Le Marquis de la fayette relativement au memoire que Je vous ai remis hier. M. De la fayette doit vous en entretenir à son retour qui est prochain et se concerter avec vous.

Voulés Vous bien accepter L'exemplaire d'un ouvrage que J'ai fait en faveur des Genevois Il y a 3 ans et qui vous donnera quelqu'i[dée] de Leurs afaires.

RC (DLC); endorsed; without date (except the day of the week) which has been supplied from internal evidence together with the contents of Brissot de Warville to TJ, and Ducrest to TJ, both 27 Dec. 1786.

To Thomas Barclay

Dear Sir   Paris Dec. 27. 1786.

Colo. Franks arrived some days ago with the Marocco treaty, and with your dispatches. I am persuaded they will give great satisfaction to Congress, and do you honor in their eyes. Colo. Franks waits for his baggage which he hourly expects. He will then proceed to London and from thence to New York. He carries

[637]

27 DECEMBER 1786

duplicate ratifications of the treaty from me, which being also signed by Mr. Adams, one will be sent on to Congress, the other returned thro' Mr. Carmichael or yourself to Fennish.

I think your general authority from Congress to settle all their European accounts is sufficient to justify a settlement with Mr. Lambe, without any order from us; and I am in hopes you will have made the settlement without waiting authority from us. I write however to Mr. Adams to join me in adding the weight of our desires, if that will avail. Mr. Lamb has importuned us for a settlement of his accounts where he is. He must therefore be in readiness, and as far as it shall depend on me I shall confirm the settlement he shall make with you. Congress have annulled his powers and required him to repair immediately to them. He will be sensible from this that there is some dissatisfaction on their part at his proceedings, and doubtless will wish to go there, and justify himself in their opinion and in that of his country. I have received authority to settle the affair between the U.S. and Schweighauser. Being very much uninformed in it I shall await your return. For American news I must refer you to Mr. Carmichael, a dislocation of my right wrist making it still painful to me to write. It recovers so slowly that I am much disposed to take the advice of my Surgeon and try some mineral waters in Provence. In this case I shall return circuitously by Bourdeaux, Nantes and Lorient. I may perhaps have the pleasure of meeting with you on the way. My departure being incertain, the time of my return is equally so. I expect to be absent from hence two or three months. I have the pleasure to inform you that Mrs. Barclay and your family are well, and of assuring you of the sincere esteem and respect with which I have the honour to be Dear Sir your most obedient & most humble servt, TH: JEFFERSON

PrC (DLC). On 14 Dec. Short wrote to Fulwar Skipwith that "Colo. Franks arrived here a few days ago from Morocco" (DLC: Short Papers). It is probable, therefore, that Franks had been in Paris most of December.

From Brissot de Warville

MONSIEUR Paris 27 Xbre. 1786

On ne peut pas trop tot mettre les fers au feu, Vu la Lenteur avec Laquelle Les afaires s'expedient ici. D'après La conversation que J'ai eue L'honneur d'avoir avec Vous, et une autre que J'ai eue ensuite avec M. de Crevecoeur, J'ai determiné M. Le Marquis du

[638]

Crest à choisir pour Le Prince un Ingenieur qui allat à Honfleur. Mais Il faut que Les Americains aient un representant à cette visite qui aide L'Ingenieur de ses Lumieres, dans le raport que cette affaire aura avec les Americains. Il n'apartient qu'à vous, et à M. Le Marquis de la fayette Le protecteur du commerce americain de le choisir. Ce meme Capitaine Coffin dont J'ai vu La Lettre adressée à M. de crevecoeur ne pourait il pas convenir.

Croiés que dans mon particulier Je ferai tout ce qui dependra de moi pour accelerer L'execution du projet. Aussitot Le procès-verbal fait, Je dresserai Le Memoire pour Le Gouvernement.

Si vous desiriés encore quelque renseignement de moi Je suis à vos ordres, et Je vous prie de me croire avec estime et respect Monsieur Votre trés humble et trés obeissant serviteur,

Brissot de Warville

P.S. M. Le Mis. du crest ecrit à M. Le Marquis de la fayette La meme Lettre qu'à vous.

RC (DLC); endorsed. Noted in SJL as received 28 Dec. 1786.

From Ducrest

Paris 27 Xbre. 1786

Je vois avec plaisir, Monsieur, par une lettre du Capitaine Coffin Américain, en date du 21 Xbre. qu'après avoir examiné le port d'Honfleur, il le trouve très susceptible de devenir un port pour tous les Vaisseaux Marchands venant des Etats unis. Pour achéminer en conséquence le projet que Vous m'avez Communiqué à cet égard, le prémier pas qu'il y ait à faire est de constater par des hommes experts. 1º. L'état actuel du port d'Honfleur, de la quantité d'eau qu'il contient dans les différentes marées, de la navigation de la Seine aux environs. 2º. D'estimer ce qu'il faudroit faire pour l'aggrandir, le rendre encore plus sûr, et en faire le rendez-vous général de la navigation américaine. C'est sur le procès verbal qui offrira le résultat de ce travail que nous pourrons fonder les demandes à faire au Gouvernement; mais pour lui donner toute la Sanction Convenable, il me semble qu'il faut appeler à ce travail deux personnes dont l'une soit choisie Par S. A. P. et l'autre Par les Américains. Je Consens de tout mon Coeur à y envoyer aux Dépens du Prince, un de Ses ingenieurs, et je vous prie de Vouloir bien de Votre Côté m'indiquer la personne versée dans cette partie qui constatera les choses pour les Américains. Aussitôt que votre choix me sera connu, je m'empresserai de prendre les Moyens pour faire faire promptement cette visite.

J'ai l'honneur d'être, avec un très-sincère attachement, Monsieur, votre très humble et très obéïssant serviteur, Mis. Ducrest.

RC (DLC); endorsed. Noted in SJL as received 28 Dec. 1786.

S.A.P.: Son Altesse Puissance, Louis Philippe, Duc d'Orléans, to whom the Marquis Ducrest was attached as Chancelier-Garde des Sceaux, Chef du Conseil, et Surintendant des Maisons, Domaines, Finances, et Bâtimens (*Almanach Royal*, 1786). There is no evidence that TJ replied to this letter.

UNE LETTRE DU CAPITAINE COFFIN: This was probably a letter addressed to Crèvecoeur (see TJ to Coffyn, 24 Dec. 1786; Brissot to TJ, 27 Dec. 1786).

To the Georgia Delegates in Congress

Gentlemen   Paris Dec. 27. 1786.

I am now to acknolege the honour of your letter of Aug. 21. and to thank you for the attention you were so good as to shew to my application. I delivered a copy of your letter to the Count de Vergennes, who appeared satisfied. I had before been assured by a gentleman from Georgia that Genl. Oglethorpe had no possessions there. This however had only authorised me to suggest it as a [possibility.]

I have the honor to be with sentiments of the most perfect esteem and respect Gentlemen your most obedient & most humble servant,   Th: Jefferson

PrC (DLC). The GENTLEMAN FROM GEORGIA may have been John McQueen.

To Mézières

Paris 27me Xbre 1786.

Monsieur Jefferson a l'honneur de faire passer à Monsieur le Chevalier de Mezieres la reponse qu'il vient de recevoir de Messieurs les delegués de Georgie au Congrès à la lettre qu'il leur avoit ecrit, les priant de s'interresser auprès de l'Assemblée de Georgie pour M. le Chevalier de Mezieres. Il a l'honneur de lui presenter ses compliments.

PrC (ViWC); endorsed. Enclosure: Georgia Delegates in Congress to TJ, 21 Aug. 1786.

TJ had not just received the letter from the Georgia Delegates, as he states, but had had it since 6 Dec. 1786.

Moreover, thanks to the efficiency of the French intelligence service, Vergennes had obtained a copy of the letter and sent a translation of it to Mézières several days before TJ did. "J'aurois désiré, M[onsieur]," Vergen-

[640]

nes had written Mézières on 23 Dec. 1786, "qu'ils eussent été plus consonnes à votre attente et à vos espérances." Mézières replied to Vergennes on 30 Dec. 1786, enclosing a memorandum of his consultation with an advisor, that the Georgia Delegates were entirely mistaken and that there had never been any question of confiscation of the Oglethorpe estate in Georgia (Arch. Aff. Etr., Corr. Pol., E.-U., XXXII; Tr in DLC).

To Ferdinand Grand

SIR   Paris Dec. 28. 1786

It will be in good time if I receive the crowns to-day, tomorrow, or even the next day. I did not answer in the instant the letter you favoured me with yesterday, because I wished to reflect on the article of seeds for Dr. Franklin, on which you were pleased to ask my opinion. We import annually from England to every part of America garden seeds of all sorts. You may judge therefore that these and what we raise from them furnish garden vegetables in good perfection. The only garden vegetable I find here better than ours, is the turnep.

Of fruits, the pears, and apricots alone are better than ours, and we have not the Apricot-peche at all. Pears could only be sent in plants; which is troublesome and incertain. But the stones of good apricots and of the peach-apricot would answer well. The fruits of the peach-class do not degenerate from the stone so much as is imagined here. We have so much experience of this in America that tho' we graft all other kinds of fruit, we rarely graft the peach, the nectarine, the apricot or the almond. The tree proceeding from the stone yeilds a faithful copy of it's fruit, and the tree is always healthier.

I have the honour to be with much esteem & respect Sir your most obedient & most humble servant,   TH: JEFFERSON

P.S. I must add that tho' we have some grapes as good as in France, yet we have by no means such a variety, nor so perfect a succession of them.

PrC (DLC). THE LETTER YOU FAVOURED ME WITH YESTERDAY: Not found and not recorded in SJL. THE CROWNS: See TJ to Jay, 9 Jan. 1787.

From Jan Ingenhousz

SIR   Vienna Dec. 28. 1786

As I can make no doubt, but you will sometimes meet with a favourable oportunity of some traveller to forward this parcel,

28 DECEMBER 1786

directed to Dr. Franklin, containing three books, and six copies of a pamphlet, of which the author begs you the favour of accepting a copy which accompanies the parcel, and will be delivred to you by Mr. Barrois le jeun, I hope you will, in regard to our venerable old friend, excuse my taking this liberty, to which I am engaged not by choice but by necessity; as I do not know, by what other means I could possibly forward the parcel in a safe and expeditious way, so that the expenses of the freight should not exceed the value of the contents.

The parcel left to your care by Dr. Franklin, when setting out for America, came to hand, for which I beg you to accept my gratefull acknowledgment.

A few days ago I received from him a copy of the II volume of the American Philosophical transactions with two very affectionate letters, the one in writing, the other printed in that volume. It was conveyed to me by the chancery of state and was probably put in hands of the Imperial Ambassadour at Paris, who does me the pleasure of forwarding to me every parcel, which is not too big to be carryed by the court messenger who sets out once a month.

Dr. Franklin used to send me now and then some American newspapers, which I am fond of to read. If he should by a good opportunity send some of them recommended to your care, I beg you to send them to his excellency Count de Mercy, if the parcel does not exceed the bulk of a book in 8º of a moderate size.

I am very respectfully Sir Your most obedient humble Servant,

J. INGEN HOUSZ

P.S. Mr. Grand le Banquier pourroit peutetre avoir quelque bonne occasion d'envoyer le paquet a Mr. Franklin.

RC (DLC); endorsed by TJ: "Ingenhousz." Noted in SJL as received 3 May 1787.

From the Rev. James Madison

DEAR SIR   Williamsburg. Decr. 28th. 1786

Having just heard of Monsr. Quesnay's Departure for France I have requested the Favor of him to take Charge of the Shells mentioned in a former Letter. I thought they would probably be acceptable to you, especially whilst in Paris, where the Science of Natural History has so many able Votaries. Monsr. Buffon in his celebrated Epoques speaks of Shells found in the highest Parts of

28 DECEMBER 1786

this Country, and so do you in your Notes. I will not pretend to controvert the Method you suggest of accounting for their Existence —but I have designedly sent a small Collection of similar Shells, taken from that immense Bed which you know lies within the Vicinity of this Place, and indeed traverses the whole low Country. You will thus be enabled to compare them together and see whether their Similarity or other Properties do not point out an Identity of Cause in their Formation.—At all Events you will probably consider them as of some Importance in the History of the Earth. If so, I shall be happy in affording you the least Gratification by transmitting them to you.

We have nothing new here in the literary World. You have probably seen the 2d. Vol. of the American Phil. Transactions. Tho' they may not give the European World the highest Idea of our Progress I am well pleased that we have such a Repository of Facts.

In a Letter, received the other day from the President at Yale College Connecticut, there is the following Paragraph—"Near New Lebanon, 18 Miles East of Albany, now lives an Indian about 50, who for near two Years past, has been gradually whitening. It began on his Breast, and has transfused itself throughout the whole Body to the Extremities. Above half his Hands and Fingers and half his Feet and Toes are yet of the Indian Colour and his Face pied. The Skin on the other Parts is become a clear English White with *English Ruddiness*. The Complexion and Colour of his Skin is even clearer and fairer than most white Persons with whom he has been compared. He has had no Sickness but has continued all the while in good Health."—The Fact being so well authenticated, I thought it worth your Perusal. I know the Albinos are found among the Indians, especially the southern, as well as I recollect Buffon, but I doubt whether this gradual Conversion, together with the Ruddiness acquired, be mentioned by any one. It differs remarkably in the last particular from what the poor Black experiences.—It seems as if Nature had absolutely denied to him the Possibility of ever acquiring the Complexion of the Whites.

I have lately imported the Phil: Transactions of the London Society for 3 or 4 years past, in which I find a particular Account of some of the curious astronomical Discoveries you were so obliging as to communicate to me. Would the Transactions of the royal Academy at Paris be a valuable Acquisition to us? If so, we would import them annually.

I am happy to inform you that your nephew is studious, and promises to make a valuable Man. As far as my Assistance can be advantageous to him, it shall not be wanting. I hope the best supporters to our Republic will go forth from our University, and that with the Assistance of Science, Time will only serve to give her more and more Stability. Sure I am, and I believe you will rejoice to hear it, that the Spirit of Republicanism is infinitely more pure as well as more ardent in the rising Generation than among any other Class of Citizens.

You see from this how little we have here that is worth sending to you across the Atlantic. If however this letter be the Means of inducing you to continue a Correspondence so advantageous to me, and which I value so much, I shall think myself fortunate in sending it.

I am Dr. Sir with the sincerest Respect & Esteem Yr. Servt. & Friend, Js. MADISON

Your Book is read here, by every one who can get a View of it, with the greatest Avidity.—I flatter myself you would favour our University with some Copies, and I have not yet relinquished the Hope.

RC (DLC); endorsed: "Madison Jas. (Wmsbg)." Noted in SJL as received 21 Feb. 1787.

BUFFON IN HIS CELEBRATED EPOQUES: This was the *Supplément* (Volume 5) to Buffon's *Histoire naturelle, générale et particulière*, Paris, 1778, a copy of which he presented to TJ (Sowerby, No. 637). The arrival of Madison's packet of shells from tidewater Virginia just before TJ started on his Southern tour may account for the great interest he took in the study of shell formations on that occasion.

From C. W. F. Dumas

MONSIEUR   La Haie 29 Dec. 1786

Un Courier que Mr. l'Ambassadeur expédia hier à 4 heures après midi, porte à Votre Excellence une Dépeche No. 15 pour le Congrès, ainsi qu'une Lettre pour Mr. le Ms. De la Fayette, à laquelle je languis d'avoir réponse, comme aussi de Votre Excellence, pour être tranquille sur le sort de toutes mes précédentes. J'ai un No. 16 tout pret, mais je ne puis encore le lâcher, sur-tout par la Poste. En attendant, en voici une pour le Département militaire des Etats-Unis, laquelle je voudrois qui pût partir pour sa Destination, en même temps qu'une autre pour le même Département, laquelle j'ai eu l'honneur d'adresser en date du 9 de ce mois à Mr. le Ms. De la Fayette avec d'autres sous le même couvert, dont Mr. Le Chevr. De Muy a été le Porteur; parce que cette seconde sert de correctif à la premiere sur une matiere sur laquelle le Département m'avoit honoré de ses ordres, et que j'ai enfin trouvé moyen d'exécuter, après m'être longtemps donné des peines inutiles pour cela, faute des Directions que j'avois reçues lesquelles n'étoient rien moins qu'exactes. Je présente à Votre Excellence mes voeux pour sa prospérité, et pour tout ce qui Lui est cher, à l'occasion de la nouvelle année où nous allons entrer, en me recommandant à Sa bienveillance, que je tâcherai de mériter constamment par le respectueux dévouement avec lequel je suis, De votre Excellence, Le très-humble et très-obéissant serviteur,

C W F Dumas

RC (DLC). FC (Rijksarchief, The Hague, Dumas Papers; photostats in DLC). Noted in SJL as received 4 Jan. 1787. Enclosures (FC in same): (1) Dumas to Henry Knox, secretary at war, 29 Dec., supplementing one from Dumas to Knox of 9 Dec. 1786 (sent through Lafayette), and giving the address of "Mr. Wernecke" about whom Knox had inquired. (2) Dumas to Lafayette, 22 Dec. 1786, expressing anxiety about his previous letter of 8 Dec. and stating that he is sending today "à Mr. Jepherson" a letter for Congress, about the contents of which, until they are by degrees verified before the eyes of the public, "le moins qu'on en parle, le mieux." (3) Dumas to Jay, 22 Dec. 1786 ("Dépeche No. 15 pour le Congrès"), reporting that Rayneval, without compromising his court, is working in a manner which inspires the trust of the ministers of Holland and of the French ambassador (whose conduct has the complete approval of the King); that order is beginning to emerge and France continues to strengthen her position, which is to the real interest of both parties; that the affairs of the Republic seem to be moving toward a favorable conclusion: the statutes will be abolished in the Provinces, the authorities in The Hague will remain organized as previously arranged, the time-honored prerogatives of the Stadtholders will not be touched, but no special personal privileges will be granted since these could not be hereditary, but given or revoked according to the circumstances; that it is certain the Sovereign has not and will not entertain any proposal of mediation or conciliation and it is equally certain that France, the sole and powerful ally of this Republic, not becoming involved in internal affairs herself will not allow other foreign powers to do so; that the citizens of Utrecht at first took offense at the terms of mediation offered them by the Provinces and which had been accepted by the oligarchy of Amersfort, but after a conference held on the 16th with those members of the legislature who head the confederation of patriots, they will finally accede to it and thus enable Holland to join hands with the oligarchy as far as the use of military force is concerned, "for the people, now in full control, have only to vindicate their superior rights without conceding any of them"; that once this mediation has started the oligarchy in Guelderland must yield as well as another in Friesland; that meanwhile false rumors are started in order to frighten and divide the people; that this is known at ⟨. . .⟩ where Goertz went fifteen days ago, not to make offers as some people of ill will pretend, but to insist that the only thing to do is to stop stirring up trouble and to consent to the reforms as outlined in the memoir, a copy of which Dumas sent with his preceding letter—the only written account of this business done by "nos amis"; that Rayneval has consistently expressed himself to Goertz in person and in his correspondence as to the necessity of adhering firmly to the principles set down in this memoir; that meanwhile the people, more and more put out with ⟨the Stadtholder?⟩ and with the oligarchy, jealously watch everything that goes on, and it is difficult to stifle their resentment; that on the 16th seventeen eminent citizens came here demanding of "nos amis" an explanation of the rumor that things were to be settled without telling them; that they spoke directly to ⟨. . .⟩ before the conference, having a high opinion of his honesty and he tried to show them that, after the confederation of August, signed and sworn to mutually at Amsterdam, these friends could not be traitors; that the seventeen left satisfied, to allay the suspicion in their cities and towns; that he has another important "Divination" but cannot release it as yet; that "someone" will be ruined if that someone does not yield within six weeks; that the address of commendation delivered at Amsterdam on the 8th was signed by 16,257; and that since the above-mentioned conference 5 to 6,000 others regret that they did not sign it as well. (This letter—Dumas' "Divinatis Tertio"—is among those from Dumas listed as missing in *Dipl. Corr., 1783-89*, III, 541.)

To Benjamin Vaughan

Sir   Paris Dec. 29. 1786.

When I had the honour of seeing you in London, you were so kind as to permit me to trouble you sometimes with my letters and particularly on the subject of Mathematical or philosophical instruments. Such a correspondence will be too agreeable to me, and at the same time too useful, not to avail myself of your permission. It has been an opinion pretty generally received among philosophers that the atmosphere of America is more humid than that of Europe. Mr. de Buffon makes this hypothesis one of the two pillars whereon he builds his system of the degeneracy of animals in America. Having had occasion to controvert this opinion of his as to the degeneracy of animals there, I expressed a doubt of the fact assumed that our climates are moister. I did not then know of any experiments which might authorize a denial of it. Speaking afterwards on this subject with Dr. Franklin, he mentioned to me the observations he had made on a case of magnets made for him by Mr. Nairne in London. Of these you will see a detail in the 2d. vol. of the American Philosophical transactions, in a letter from Dr. Franklin to Mr. Nairne, wherein he recommends to him to take up the principle therein explained, and endeavor to make an Hygrometer, which, taking slowly the temperature of the Atmosphere, shall give it's mean degree of moisture, and enable us thus to make with more certainly a comparison between the humidities of different climates. May I presume to trouble you with an enquiry of Mr. Nairne whether he has executed the Doctor's idea? And if he has to get him to make for me a couple of the instruments he may have contrived. They should be made of the same peice, and under like circumstances, that sending one to America, I may rely on it's indications there compared with those of the one I shall retain here. Being in want of a set of magnets also, I would be glad if he would at the same time send me a set, the case of which should be made as Dr. Franklin describes his to have been, so that I may repeat his experiment. Colo. Smith will do me the favor to receive these things from Mr. Nairne and to pay him for them.

I think Mr. Rittenhouse never published an invention of his in this way, which was a very good one. It was of an hygrometer, which like the common ones was to give the actual moisture of the air. He has two slips of mahogany about 5 I. long, ¾ I. broad and $\frac{1}{10}$ I. thick, the one having the grain running lengthwise, and the other crosswise. These are glued together by their faces, so as to form a peice 5 I. long, ¾ I. broad and ⅕ I. thick, which is stuck, by it's lower end, into a little plinth of wood thus [*Fig. 1*] presenting their edge to the view. The fibres of wood you know are dilated but not lengthened by moisture. The slip therefore whose grain is lengthwise, becomes a standard, retaining always the same precise length. That which has it's grain crosswise, dilates with moisture and contracts with the want of it. If the right hand peice above represented be the cross grained one, when the air is very moist, it lengthens and forces it's companion to form a kind of interior annulus of a circle on the left thus [*Fig. 2*] When the air is dry, it contracts, draws it's companion to the right, and becomes itself the interior annulus, thus [*Fig. 3*] In order to shew this dilatation and contraction, an index is fixed on the upper end of the two slips: a plate of metal or wood is fastened to the front of the plinth so as to cover the two slips from the eye. A slit, being nearly the portion of a circle, is cut in this plate so that the shank of the index may play freely through it's whole range. On the edge of the slit is a graduation, so that the instrument shews somewhat thus [*Fig. 4*] The objection to this instrument is that it is not fit for comparative observations, because no two peices of wood being of the same texture exactly, no two will yeild exactly alike to the same agent. However it is less objectionable on this account than most of the substances used. Mr. Rittenhouse had a thought of trying ivory: but I do not know whether he executed it. All these substances not only vary from one another at the same time, but from themselves at different times. All of them however have some peculiar advantages, and I think this on the whole appeared preferable to any other I had ever seen. Not knowing whether you had heard of this instrument, and supposing it would amuse you I have taken the liberty of detailing it to you. I beg you to be assured of the sentiments of perfect esteem and respect with which I have the honor to be Sir your most obedient & most humble servant,

TH: JEFFERSON

From Peter Carr

Hon'd. Sir   Williamsburg Decembr. 30. 86.

A Ship being about to sail for Paris: I embrace the oppertunity of informing you (by Her) of my situation, and progress in Literature, since I wrote you last.—I left the grammar school in April last; In consequence of a polite and Friendly invitation given me by Mr. Wythe, to go through a course of reading with him; And as He thought it improper to begin in the middle of a course of Lectures, I defer'd it untill October last which was the commencement of a new course.—Here I attend the Professors of Moral and Natural philosophy, Mathematicks and Modern Languages and Mr. Wythe has invited me to attend His Lectures on Law.—With respect to Modern Languages I have read French mostly, the want of a Spanish dictionary has retarded my advancement in that language.

Mr. Bellini has prevailed on me to begin Italian as he thinks by the time you can send me a Spanish dictionary, I may be a tolerable Master of that language, also that it will greatly facilitate my progress in Spanish. I received from you last Spring a trunk of books, at same time a letter for both of which you receive my greatfull thanks.—I am now reading with Mr. Wythe the ancient history which you advised; am likewise reading the Tragedies of Aschylus, which as soon as I have finished I shall take up Aristophanes. You also advise me to read the works of Ossian, which I have done and should be more pleased with them if there were more variety. We have had very flattering accounts of my brother *Sam* lately. Dabney by the direction of Mr. Madison is at the Academy in prince Edward. My Mother and the family were well a few days ago; I also have the satisfaction to inform you Polly is well. Remember me Affectionately to my Cousin and believe me to be with due respect, Your affectionate Nephew,   Peter Carr

RC (ViU); endorsed. Noted in SJL as received 20 June 1787.

To John Jay

Sir Paris Dec. 31. 1786

I had the honor of addressing you on the 12th. of the last month, since which your favor of Oct. 12. has been recieved, inclosing a copy of the resolution of Congress for recalling Mr. Lamb. My letter by Mr. Randall informed you that we had put an end to his powers and required him to repair to Congress. I lately recieved a letter from him dated Alicant Oct. 10. of which I have the honour to inclose you a copy: by which you will percieve that the circumstance of ill health, either true or false, is urged for his not obeying our call. I shall immediately forward the order of Congress. I am not without fear that some misapplication of the public money may enter into the causes of his declining to return. The moment that I saw a symptom of this in his conduct, as it was a circumstance which did not admit the delay of consulting Mr. Adams, I wrote to Mr. Carmichael to stop any monies which he might have in the hands of his Banker. I am still unable to judge whether he is guilty of this or not, as by the arrangements with Mr. Adams, who alone had done business with the bankers of the U.S. in Holland, Mr. Lambe's draughts were to be made on him, and I know not what their amount has been. His draughts could not have been negociated if made on us both, at places so distant. Perhaps it may be thought that the appointment of Mr. Lambe was censurable in the moment in which it was made. It is a piece of justice therefore which I owe to Mr. Adams to declare that the proposition went first from me to him. I take the liberty of inclosing you a copy of my letter to Mr. Adams of Sep. 24. 1785. in which that proposition was made. It expresses the motives operating in my mind at that moment, as well as the cautions I thought it necessary to take. To these must be added the difficulty of finding an American in Europe fit for the business and willing to undertake it. I knew afterwards that Dr. Bancroft (who is named in the letter) could not, on account of his own affairs, have accepted even a primary appointment. I think it evident that no appointment could have succeeded without a much greater sum of money.

I am happy to find that Mr. Barclay's mission has been attended with complete success. For this we are indebted unquestionably to the influence and good offices of the court of Madrid. Colo. Franks the bearer of this will have the honor to put into your hands the original of the treaty with other papers accompanying it. It will

31 DECEMBER 1786

appear by these that Mr. Barclay has conducted himself with a degree of intelligence and good faith, which reflects the highest honor on him.

A copy of a letter from Capt. Obryan to Mr. Carmichael is also herewith inclosed. The information it contains will throw farther light on the affairs of Algiers. His observations on the difficulties which arise from the distance of Mr. Adams and myself from that place, and from one another, and the delays occasioned by this circumstance are certainly just. If Congress should propose to revive the negotiations, they will judge whether it will not be more expedient to send a person to Algiers who can be trusted with full powers: and also whether a mission to Constantinople may not be previously necessary. Before I quit this subject, I must correct an error in the letter of Capt. Obryan. Mr. Lambe was not limited, as he says, to one hundred, but to two hundred dollars a piece for our prisoners. This was the price which had been just paid for a large number of French prisoners, and this was our guide.

The difference between Russia and the Porte seems patched up for the present. That between Spain and Naples is not yet healed, and probably will not be cordially. But it does not lead to war. It will probably end in a settled coolness, and the King of Spain's ceasing to interfere with that government. The mediation of this court I suppose has been excited by the fear that Naples might throw itself into the other scale of the European balance. This has been much feared from the new king of Prussia. Such a weight as this shifted into the scale of the Emperor, Russia and England would spread a cloud over the prospects of this kingdom. Of the possibility of the event, you will be so much better informed by Mr. Dumas, that it would be going out of my province to take up more of your time with it. The Packets at Lorient have orders to go to Havre, from which place they will ply after the month of February. This will enable me to resume that channel of correspondence with you, as I can always send a confidential servant by the diligence in twenty-four hours to that place, to put my letters into the hands of our agent there, who will find a passenger or other trusty person to take charge of them, without their going into the post-mail. Through passengers and the same agent your letters to me may be safely conveyed, unopened. I inclose you the Leyden and French gazettes to this date. In the latter you will find an authentic copy of the treaty between France and England. I am also desired to send you the papers in the case of André Caron, praying that justice may be done him. I have the honour to be

DECEMBER 1786

with the most perfect esteem and respect, Sir, your most obedient and most humble servant, TH: JEFFERSON

RC (DNA: PCC, No. 87, 1); in the hand of William Short, signed by TJ. PrC (DLC). Tr (DNA: PCC, No. 107). Enclosures: (1) Tr of Lamb to TJ, 10 Oct. 1786. (2) Tr of an extract of TJ to Adams, 24 Sep. 1785 (1st letter under that date). (3) Tr of Richard O'Brien to Carmichael, 13 Sep. 1786, enclosed in Carmichael to TJ, 29 Sep. 1786, q.v. and note there. (4) Tr of André Caron to TJ, and John Paul Jones to TJ, both 16 Aug. 1786.

To La Valette

DEAR SIR   Paris Dec. 31. 1786.

I must beg your pardon for having been so long in answering your note, but it has not been in my power to do it sooner. I send you by the bearer five hundred and forty livres, which I think you said was the sum due you from M. La Fleury, and I will beg of you in return M. La Fleury's note to be assigned to me, constituting me his creditor instead of yourself, together with the letter of his hommes d'affaires engaging the paiment out of the interest due to La Fleury from the United states. I shall be happy to have news of your health and whether you have missed your fever yet. I am with very sincere esteem and respect Dr. Sir Your most Obedt. & most humble servt., TH: JEFFERSON

PrC (DLC); endorsed. YOUR NOTE: See Abbé Gibelin to TJ, 8 July 1786; TJ to Abbé Gibelin, 10 July 1786.

From David S. Franks

[*Paris*] *Dec. 1786.* Chateaumont, the gentleman Carmichael wished to be presented to TJ, could call this afternoon if convenient to TJ. Franks' trunks have not yet arrived but he will be ready to leave as soon as they are received; hopes it will be only two or three days.

RC (DLC); 3p.; addressed, in part: "Chaillot"; endorsed; without date and not recorded in SJL, but obviously written during December while Franks was in Paris.

From David S. Franks

[Dec. 1786]

I wished Your Excellency to have accepted of the Moorish Coins as a very small mark of the Attachment which I have allways had for you and when I presented them it was with that Intention.

[651]

DECEMBER 1786

Besides I owe you two hundred Livres which you kindly lent me at a time when I very much wanted it and for which tho' I can repay you I shall not think myself quit of the obligation. I shall have the pleasure of seeing you when we will Settle and at the same time I may have an opportunity of assuring you how much I am my dear Sir Your Excellency's most obt. & obliged Sert.,
DAVD. S. FRANKS

I have retaind the money having opend the packet sent. Mr. Chateaumont lives at the Hotel de Valois Rue Vantadour.

RC (DLC); endorsed; without date and not recorded in SJL, but, judging from the postscript, probably written shortly after the preceding letter.

From Madame de Tott

[Dec.? 1786]

Vous êtes Réellement d'une bonté et d'une Obligeance inéxprimable Monsieur. Les Livres que Vous Voulez bien me donner, sont d'un prix infini pour Une malheureuse grecque, qui Sans tous Les Soins que Vous Vous êtes donnés pour elle, Se Seroit Vue Réduite a L'affligeante extrêmité de Rennoncer au bonheur de Lire Le divin auteur qui a immortalisé Sa Langue.

Je suis bien heureuse, Monsieur, de l'esperance que Vous me donnez de Vous Voir encore demain, mais Si aulieu d'une simple Visite Vous Veniez diner avec nous, Vous feriez Le plus grand plaisir a maman et Vous me procureriez celui de Vous Voir plus Longtems, parceque Je Suis Obligée de monter a cheval demain a midi. Ma santé est infiniment meilleure et Je ne doute pas que je ne Vous doive encore des *Remerciments Sur cet Objet.* Agréez Les donc, Je Vous en Supplie, ainsi que tous ceux que je Vous dois pour tous Les Soins Obligeants dont Vous n'avez cessé de me combler.

RC (MoSHi); without date, but evidently written sometime after TJ's exchange of letters with Madame de Tott of 28 Nov. 1786.

From La Rochefoucauld

Mardi matin. [1786?]

Le Duc de la Rochefoucauld est bien fâché de ne pouvoir pas se rendre Vendredi à l'invitation de Monsieur Jefferson; il est

[652]

1786

engagé pour ce jour là à un diner de famille; il aura l'honneur d'aller chercher Monsieur Jefferson quelque matin, et delui demander même s'il le permet quelques éclaircissemens sur la Description de la Virginie.

RC (CtY); addressed in part: "Monsieur Jefferson . . . A la Grille des Champs Elysees"; undated, but, as the address shows, written at an indeterminate date after 17 Oct. 1785 when TJ moved into the Hotel de Langeac; at head of text in TJ's hand: "to decline an invitation."

Petition of an Impostor, with Jefferson's Comments

[1786?]

To his Excll the Honorable Minister of the Unaited State of America

The petition of Thos. Smith a Native of America, Humbly Sheweth

That whereas Your Excellencys Petitioner, is in this City of Paris Coming from a Slavery, where I being Tuoo years, and a half, taken under, the American colours bound from Lisbon, to America, and remain a Prisoner, a Board an Algerin Galeotta during the aforementioned space of time, Being afterward retaken bay the Fregate of Matra, I Landing in Carthagena, where I Coming in this Contry in order to Facilitate the return in to America.

And being entirely destitute, of money, and Likewise of Cloathing too in some measure, and being sensible, of Your Paternal affection, and Clemency towards, the Native of America, Presume to present this addres to Your Excellency to implore relief, which if your will Graciously be pleased to grant, Your bounty will be Receiv'd whith the deepest sencs, of gratitud, and your Petitioner as in duty bound shall forever Pray for Your Excellencys health, and happiness.   Thos. Smith

[*Memorandum by TJ on verso:*]

There was no such person in Obrian's roll.
He did not know the name of the brig calling her Polly.
He could not speak English but very broken.
He said at first he was an American from Chastown, then a French neutral born in Canada (because I objected to his dialect).

1786

I observed 'Smith' was no French name. He said he was of German extraction.

He had a pretended pass from a pretended John Lidderdale Consul of England at Carthagena. But the pass was in no form, broken English and in the same hand writing with this paper, which sets out by saying it is written in Paris.

MS (DLC); in the hand of "Thos. Smith"; TJ's observations, evidently set down shortly after an interview with the writer, are entered on verso of the petition; undated. This "Thos. Smith" is not to be confused with the Thomas Smith who wrote TJ on 9 July 1786, though his petition is catalogued under that date in DLC and the MS bears (in pencil and not contemporaneous) that mistaken date.

Preliminary indexes will be issued periodically for groups of volumes. An index covering Vols. 1-6 has been published. A comprehensive index of persons, places, subjects, etc., arranged in a single consolidated sequence, will be issued at the conclusion of the series.

The Papers of Thomas Jefferson is composed in Monticello, a type specially designed by the Mergenthaler Linotype Company for this series. Monticello is based on a type design originally developed by Binny & Ronaldson, the first successful typefounding company in America. It is considered historically appropriate here because it was used extensively in American printing during the last thirty years of Jefferson's life, 1796 to 1826; and because Jefferson himself expressed cordial approval of Binny & Ronaldson types.

✧

Composed and printed by Princeton University Press. Illustrations are reproduced in collotype by Meriden Gravure Company, Meriden, Connecticut. Paper for the series is made by W. C. Hamilton & Sons, at Miquon, Pennsylvania; cloth for the series is made by Holliston Mills, Inc., Norwood, Massachusetts. Bound by the J. C. Valentine Company, New York.

DESIGNED BY P. J. CONKWRIGHT

R0164166096 sscca   S
                     973
                     .46
                     J45

Jefferson, Thomas
The papers of Thomas
     Jefferson. Julian P. B

   VOL. 10

R0164166096 sscca   S
                     973
                     .46
                     J45

Houston Public Library
Social Sci